Work in the Digital Media and Entertainment Industries

This book is a first-of-its-kind critical interdisciplinary introduction to the economic, political, cultural, and technological dimensions of work in the rapidly growing digital media and entertainment industries (DMEI).

Tanner Mirrlees presents a comprehensive guide to understanding the key contexts, theories, methods, debates, and struggles surrounding work in the DMEI. Packed with current examples and accessible research findings, the book highlights the changing conditions and experiences of work in the DMEI. It surveys the DMEI's key sectors and occupations and considers the complex intersections between labor and social power relations of class, gender, and race, as well as tensions between creativity and commerce, freedom and control, meritocracy and hierarchy, and precarity and equity, diversity, and inclusivity. Chapters also explore how work in the DMEI is being reshaped by capitalism and corporations, government and policies, management, globalization, platforms, A.I., and worker collectives such as unions and cooperatives. This book is a critical introduction to this growing area of research, teaching, learning, life, labor, and organizing, with an eye to understanding work in the DMEI and changing it, for the better.

Offering a broad overview of the field, this textbook is an indispensable resource for instructors, undergraduates, postgraduates, and scholars.

Tanner Mirrlees is the current Director of the Communication and Digital Media Studies program in the Faculty of Social Science and Humanities at Ontario Tech University, where he has been teaching the Work in the Creative and Tech Industries course for over a decade. He is the author of numerous publications, including *Global Entertainment Media* (2013), *Hearts and Mines: The US Empire's Cultural Industry* (2016), and *EdTech Inc.: Selling, Automating and Globalizing Higher Education in the Digital Age* (2019).

Work in the Digital Media and Entertainment Industries
A Critical Introduction

Tanner Mirrlees

NEW YORK AND LONDON

Designed cover image: Jackyenjoyphotography/Getty Images

First published 2025
by Routledge
605 Third Avenue, New York, NY 10158

and by Routledge
4 Park Square, Milton Park, Abingdon, Oxon, OX14 4RN

Routledge is an imprint of the Taylor & Francis Group, an informa business

© 2025 Tanner Mirrlees

The right of Tanner Mirrlees to be identified as author of this work has been asserted in accordance with sections 77 and 78 of the Copyright, Designs and Patents Act 1988.

All rights reserved. No part of this book may be reprinted or reproduced or utilised in any form or by any electronic, mechanical, or other means, now known or hereafter invented, including photocopying and recording, or in any information storage or retrieval system, without permission in writing from the publishers.

Trademark notice: Product or corporate names may be trademarks or registered trademarks, and are used only for identification and explanation without intent to infringe.

Library of Congress Cataloging-in-Publication Data
Names: Mirrlees, Tanner, author.
Title: Work in the digital media and entertainment industries : a critical introduction/Tanner Mirrlees.
Description: New York, NY: Routledge, 2025. | Includes bibliographical references and index.
Identifiers: LCCN 2024000240 (print) | LCCN 2024000241 (ebook) | ISBN 9780367673758 (paperback) | ISBN 9780367673765 (hardback) | ISBN 9781003131076 (ebook)
Subjects: LCSH: Cultural industries--Technological innovations--Social aspects. | Cultural industries--Technological innovations--Economic aspects. | Digital media--Economic aspects. | Digital media--Social aspects. | Work. | Industrial sociology.
Classification: LCC HD9999.C9472 M56 2025 (print) | LCC HD9999.C9472 (ebook) | DDC 338.4/77--dc23/eng/20240328
LC record available at https://lccn.loc.gov/2024000240
LC ebook record available at https://lccn.loc.gov/2024000241

ISBN: 978-0-367-67376-5 (hbk)
ISBN: 978-0-367-67375-8 (pbk)
ISBN: 978-1-003-13107-6 (ebk)

DOI: 10.4324/9781003131076

Typeset in Sabon LT Pro
by KnowledgeWorks Global Ltd.

Contents

Acknowledgments   xv

Introduction: How I Learned to Stop Worrying about "Being Creative" and Love the "Labor Turn"   1

Introduction 1
"Being Creative" Without Distinction: My Path
  to Writing This Book 1
Going "Back to Work": Taking "the Labor Turn"
  in Communication and Media Studies 6
Why Does the Study of Work in the DMEI Matter
  and to Whom Does It Matter? 14

1   What Is Work? Meanings, Matters, Motivations   25

Introduction 25
Work's Meaning Is Constructed, Contextual
  and Contested 25
What Is Work? Labor, Leisure, Paid, Unpaid 28
  Work as Labor 28
  Work as Paid Labor 29
  Work as Unpaid Forced Labor 30
  Work as Unpaid Reproductive Labor 32
  Work as Unpaid Volunteer Labor 33
Why Does Work Matter? 34
  Work, Society and Environment 34
  Work and Identity: Self, Other, Status, Worldview, Health,
    and Wellness 36

How Is Work "Cultural"? 38
  Culture 38
  Organizational Ways of Work-Life 39
  Texts That Communicate Meaning 40
How Does Work Connect to Time and
  Space? 41
  Work and Time 41
  Work and Space 44
What Motivates People to Work? 46
  Subsistence: Work to Live 46
  Consumerism: Work to Shop 47
  Intrinsic-Extrinsic Rewards: Work for Meaning
    and Compensation 47
  Love: Work for Passion 48
  Hope and Aspiration: Work for Future
    Rewards 49
Toward Post-Work? Idleness, Refusals, and Great
  Resignations 50

2 What Are the Digital Media and Entertainment Industries (DMEI)? 15 Convergent Industry Groups, Central to Work in the Digital Society   53

Introduction 53
Culture, Inc.: A Very Brief History of Human Work and
  Labor in the Cultural Industries 53
A Digital Society, Made by Workers 56
Augmenting the "Cultural Industries": The Work of
  Classifying the Digital Media and Entertainment
  Industries (DMEI) 60
The DMEI's 15 Industry Groups/NAICS Codes 67
Why the "D" in the DMEI? Foregrounding the
  'Digital' 67
  Digitization 67
  From Analog to Digital 68
  Economic Convergence and Technological
    Convergence 69
How Is the DMEI Significant to Work in the Digital
  Society? 70

3 **What Is Research on Work in the DMEI? A Toolkit for Labor Theory and Method** 75

Introduction 75
To Research! 75
  From Curiosity to Question 75
  Scale: Micro, Meso, and Macro 76
  Conscience 76
  Theory and Method 77
Some Theories 78
  Organizational Sociology: Production of Culture/
    Circuit of Culture/Identity 78
  The Political Economy of Communication/Media
    Economics/Media Management 81
  Labor Process Theory (LPT)/Workerism/History
    from Below 85
Some Methods 90
For Normativity 94

4 **What Is Capitalism and How Do Corporations Shape Work in the DMEI?** 99

Introduction 99
The Making of the Industrial Working Class: A
  Revision 99
The Making of the DMEI's Working Class: Concepts
  and Figures 102
  Emotional Labor 103
  Knowledge Worker 104
  Immaterial Labor 104
  Artist 105
  Cultural/Creative Worker 106
  Cyber-Tariat/Tech Worker 107
  Digital Labor 108
  Platform Worker 108
Capitalism: A Class Society, Manifested in the Structure
  of the Corporation 110
  Mode of Production 110
  The Upper or Ruling Class: CEOs and
    Shareholders 111

viii Contents

      Middle Class/Professional Managerial Class
        (PMC) 113
      The Working Class 113
      Capitalism: Eight Logics at Work in the Corporations
        of the DMEI 114
        Corporate Ownership of Capital 114
        Waged Labor, Labor Markets, and a Division
          of Labor 115
        Production Driven by Profit, Rather than Human
          Need 117
        Market Competition and Market Control 118
      Media Concentration and Work in Canada: Findings from
        the Global Media & Internet Concentration Project
        (GMICP) and Canadian Media Concentration Research
        Project (CMCR) 120
        Exploitation: Profit Maximization, Labor Cost
          Minimization and IP Dispossession 121
        Crises, Cycles of Boom and Bust, and Creative
          Destruction 122
        Income, Wealth and Class Inequality 123
        Class Tension and Conflict 124

5 What Is the State and How Does It Govern Work in the DMEI? Explicit and Tacit Labor Laws, Policies, and Regulations   126

      Introduction 126
      The Return of the State 126
      The State as Neoliberal Superintendent for
        Capitalism 127
      The State's Explicit Labor Law: Maker, Investigator,
        and Enforcer ... Sometimes 129
      The Coogan Act and Kid Influencers 131
        The Wage and Hour Division (WHD): Fair Labor
          Standards Act (FLSA): Exempting "Crunch Time"
          in the Games Industries 132
        The National Labor Relations Board (NLRB):
          National Labor Relations Act (NLRA): Big Tech,
          Violating the Workers' Right to Unionize 134
        The Equal Employment Opportunity Commission
          (EEOC): Age Discrimination in Hollywood 135

The DOL's Office of Federal Contract Compliance
    Programs (OFCCP) and Civil Rights Center (CRC):
    Gendered Wage Discrimination in Silicon Valley 136
  The DOL's Occupational Safety and Health
    Administration (OSH) and the Occupational Safety
    and Health Act (OSHA): Labor Hazards and
    Whistleblowing 137
The State's Tacit Labor Law 138
  The Federal Communications Commission (FCC):
    Communication Policies and Regulations at
    Work 138
  The Copyright Office and Creators 140
  The US Department of Justice's Antitrust Division
    (DOJAD) and the Federal Trade Commission
    (FTC) 141
  The State as Subsidizer: The National Endowment for
    the Arts, The California Film Commission, DARPA,
    and More 142
  The State as Labor Force Trainer 143
  The State as Direct Employer 144
The Power and Politics of State Matter to Work in the
  DMEI 144

6 What Is the Management of Work in the DMEI?
  Putting Leadership Power, Decision-Making Power,
  Soft Power, Hard Power, and Market Power to Work
  on Workers   146

  Introduction 146
  Management: The Control and Organization of
    Something, Someone 147
  Management as Leader Power: "Great Leader Theory"
    (GLT) and Its Discontents 147
  Management as Decision-Making Power 151
  Management as Relational Power: Engineering Labor
    Processes and Human Relations 152
    Labor Process Engineering (Scientific Management):
      Fredrick Winslow Taylor 153
    Human Relations Engineering: Lillian Gilbreth 153
    Hard and Soft Power Tactics 154
    Corporate Governmentality: Michel Foucault 155

x   Contents

    Soft Power at Work: Managerial Control by Bureaucracy, Participation, Perks, Fun, and Games 155
        Management by Bureaucracy: Max Weber 155
        Management by Participation: Elton Mayo, Kurt Lewin, and Rensis Likert 156
        Management by Perks 157
        Management by Fun 158
        Management by Games 159
    The Humane Workplace of the DMEI 159
    Hard Power at Work: Managerial Control by Bullying, Surveillance, Silencing and Censoring, NCAAs, NCCs, NDAs, Union Busting, Firing, Blacklisting, and Canceling 160
        Management by Bullying 160
        Management by Surveillance 161
        Management by Silencing and Censoring: The Non-Disclosure Agreement (NDA) 161
        Management by "No Cold Call Agreements" (NCCAs) 162
        Management by "Non-Compete Clauses" (NCC) in Contracts 163
        Management by Union Busting 163
        Management by Firing and Unfair Termination 164
        Management by Blacklisting and Canceling 164
    Management by Markets: The Invisible Manager 165
    Beyond Management? Cooperatives and Unions 166

7 Is Meritocracy at Work in the DMEI? Intersectionality and Inequality, with Distinction   169

    Introduction 169
    "When You Wish Upon a Star": The Meritocratic Dream of the DMEI 169
    Meritocracy: Ideal and Reality 171
    The Meritocratic Ideal: Five Assumptions, Deconstructed 172
        The Just Allocation of Rewards Based on Individual Performance 172
        The Correlation Between Effort and Reward 173
        Equal Opportunities for All Irrespective of Background 174
        Society is a "Level Playing Field" 175
        The Attainability of Social Mobility 175

*Intersectionality: Class, Race, Gender, Age, and Ability at
   Work in the DMEI 176
   Class and Classism 177
   Race and Racism 178
   Sex, Gender and Sexism 179
   Age and Ageism 179
   Disability and Ableism 180
Do Black Lives Matter (BLM) to Hollywood's White
   Owners? 181
#SiliconValleySoWhite 182
Unequal Access to Work in the DMEI: Whose "Cultural
   Capital"? 183
   Economic Capital, Cultural Capital, Social Capital,
      and the Family 184
   Unequal Access to Education 187
   Unequal Access to Internships 187
   Unequal Access to Professional Networks 188
   Unequal Access to Time for Self-Branding 189
   Unequal Access to Equal Opportunity: Discrimination
      in Hiring 190
The Classism of the "Creative Class" 191
Meritocracy as Ideology 192*

8 What Is the Globalization of Work in the DMEI?
  Outsourced Hardware, Software, Content, and Service   193

  *Introduction 193
  Empire, Globalization, and the Nation-State 193
  The Globalization of Work in the DMEI: A World
     Labor Market, for Corporations 196
  AAMAM Goes to China: "Dying for an iPhone" 197
  Global Hollywood: Local Precarity 198
  Global Hollywood's Suicide Squad: Made
     in Canada, for Warner Bros 200
  The "McDonaldization" of Creativity? 201
  Global Games Making: Multinational Credit Roll 203
  Global Call Centers: "Englishization" and
     "Callcentrification" 204
  Global Remote Work: Down with Upwork 206
  Commercial Content Moderation (CCM): Facebook,
     Sama, and Neo-Colonialism 207*

xii *Contents*

> *The African Content Moderators Union 209*
> *Global Micro-Tasking and Ghost Work on Global Labor*
>   *Market Platforms 210*
> *Amazon Mechanical Turk (MTurk) 211*
> *Toward a New Labor Internationalism in the DMEI? 212*

9 What Is the Platformization of Work in the DMEI?
  Online Creators, Cultural Producers, and Influencers   216

> *Introduction 216*
> *Platforms and Society 216*
> *The Rise of the Creator Economy: Social Media*
>   *Entertainment and Platforms of Cultural Production 218*
> *Virtual Influencers: Automating Creators? 223*
> *What Is the Occupational Status of a Creator?:*
>   *Not Quite a Worker-Employee, Small Business*
>   *Owner-Entrepreneur, Self-Employed*
>   *Freelancer 224*
>   *Worker-Employee 224*
>   *Small Business Owner-Entrepreneur 225*
>   *Self-Employed Freelancer 226*
> *Creator Capitalism: Google-Meta-Amazon (GMA)*
>   *Rule: Structural and Relational Power 228*
>   *Corporate Ownership of Production, Distribution,*
>   *and Exhibition 228*
>   *Division between Owners and Workers 229*
>   *Waged Labor, Labor Market, Division of Labor 229*
>   *Production for Profit, Not for Human Need 230*
>   *Market Competition and Market Control 230*
>   *Exploitation 230*
>   *Crisis and Cycles of Boom and Bust 231*
>   *Class, Income, and Wealth Inequality 231*
>   *Class Tension and Conflict 232*
> *Labor Hazards of Creator Capitalism: Creator Collective*
>   *Action and Class Struggle 232*

10 What Is the Automation of Work in the DMEI?
   Generative AI and Labor-Saving Technologies (LSTs)   236

> *Introduction 236*
> *Generative AI and AI Art: The Death of the Artist*
>   *and Art, for AAMAM? 236*

Capitalism and LSTs 240
*LSTs and the Workers' Labor and Life Process: Five
    Stages* 241
    Deskilling 242
    Dependency 242
    Displacement 242
    Depression 242
    Development 243
*Self-Realization and Alienation
    at Work: Four Types of Estrangement in
    Capitalism* 245
Unemployment and "Technological Unemployment" 246
*Accelerating Technological Unemployment by Generative
    AI? Pumping the Breaks in Hollywood* 249
*Likeness Licensing, AI, and Celebrity Deepfakes: Scarlett
    Johansson vs. Open AI* 251
*Utopian Dreams and Dystopian Nightmares of Totally
    Automated AI Futures: What's Being Done About the
    Automation of Work in the DMEI? (AI Ethics,
    Neo-Luddism, Online Campaigns, Legal Action,
    Principled Regulation)* 253

11 **Is Work in the DMEI "Free?" Advertising, Audience
   Commodities, Social Media Users, Brand-Loyal
   Fans, Crowdsourced Task-Takers, Interns, and Athletes**   258

   Introduction 258
   *TV's Audience Commodity, Ratings' Commodity
       Audience, and Social Media's Prosumer
       Commodity* 258
   Capitalism, Advertising and the DMEI 258
   Advertising Corporations 259
   Advertising Business Models 259
   *The Advertising-Media Symbiosis: Valuing the
       Audience* 260
   *The Audience Commodity: Watching TV as
       Working* 261
   *The Commodity Audience: Ratings Workers Are
       Watching* 262
   *The Prosumer Commodity: Working While Posting,
       Liking, Sharing* 264

xiv   *Contents*

   Wages for Facebook 266
   Brand Equity: Brand Loyalty and Franchise Fandom as
      Unpaid Work 267
      Valuing Brand Equity 267
      The Work of Brand-Loyal Consumers 268
      Fandom for Franchises as Unpaid Work 269
   Entertainment News Platforms and Unpaid Fan
      Labor 270
   Crowdsourcing and 'Crowdsourced' Free Labor 270
   Apprenticeships, Internships, and Indentured Labor 272
   Freedom from Free Labor in the DMEI? Threats to
      Workers' Freedom of Expression 273

12 What Are Workers Doing to Make the DMEI's
    Future of Work Better for All? Collective Action!   277

   Introduction 277
   The Future of Work, from Below 277
   Barriers to Collective Action in the DMEI 279
   Openings to Collective Organization and Action in
      the DMEI 282
      Unions 282
      Fairness in Factual TV Campaign 284
      Cooperatives in the Arts and Tech 284
      Worker Social (Media) Movement Activism: "Make
         Amazon Pay," "#MeToo," "#OscarsSoWhite"
         and "No Tech for Apartheid" 287
      Workers' Law: Class Action 288
      Universal Basic Income (UBI) and Universal Public
         Goods (UPGs): Left and Right 289
      State and Power: Politics, Parties, Policies 291
      Blueprints and Real Utopias 293

13 Postscript: Not "Being Creative", For a Study of
    Work in the DMEI, Post-"Creative Exceptionalism"   294

   Bibliography   *300*
   Index   *378*

Acknowledgments

This book was made possible by the labors of many.

I extend my gratitude to Grace Kennedy and Sheni Kruger at Routledge for their patience and continuous support during the ups and downs of this project. Their accommodation of my needs, and their tireless encouragement, has been key to bringing this work to fruition.

Special thanks to Richard Maxwell, political economist of communication and media labor, and Kylie Jarrett, Marxist feminist digital labor researcher. Their generous and insightful feedback improved this book.

I am thankful to the Canadian Communication Association (CCA) for the chance to serve as its vice-president and president and collaborate with its dedicated members from 2018 to 2022. I'm also glad for the "Work, Labour and Class in Communication" research cluster, and the always high quality scholarship on work and labor in the creative and cultural industries presented at the CCA's annual conference. A special mention to my international colleagues in the Union for Democratic Communication and the IAMCR's political economy section—your sustaining of these critical traditions warms my heart. Also, kudos to all the wonderful co-organizers and participants I had the pleasure to meet at the ICA 2023 Creators4Change pre-conference (https://creators4change.com/), in Toronto, Canada. That was fun!

Thank you to my colleagues at Ontario Tech University, in the Faculty of Social Science and Humanities and Communication and Digital Media Studies Program. To the hundreds of students in my "COMM 3510— Work in the Creative and Tech Industries" course: your personal life stories of labor taught me. Your interest in "going to class" was fundamental to shaping this book's form and content. To Leo Panitch (1945–2020), Vincent Mosco (1948–2024), and Jane McAlevey (1964–2024), thank you for your labors of mentoring so many learners, activists, and workers, and dedicating so much of your lives to the struggle for a better and different society.

xvi *Acknowledgments*

To my friendlies in and around the GTA—Imre, Eva-Lynn, Joe, Mark, Andrew, Colin, Nicole, Matt, Alessandro, Dugan, Peter, Greg, Steven, Amir, James, Tyler, Chris, Brent, Alex, Andrea, Sibo, Vincent, Derek, Steph, and so many wonderful people, near and far—thank you for the walks, talks, pints, dinners, games, plays, texts, movies, and coffee stops.

To my family, thank you, always, and a shout out to my sweet nephews Ethan and Nolan for keeping it real. To my late cat Karl (2002–2020), thank you for carrying me through my broken ankle and surgery.

Finally, to Lauren Kirshner, my love and my best friend: your creativity inspires me, your sense of humor delights me, and your unique take on the world reminds me to take note of the finer details, from the molting wing pattern of Stringy the pigeon to our dear old cat Scarfie's finest tipped whisker, curling a Flehmen. I am so excited for our joint book launch and social event this fall in Toronto, and for our ongoing creative collaboration in life and love. Thank you for being you. I cherish you.

Introduction
How I Learned to Stop Worrying about "Being Creative" and Love the "Labor Turn"

Introduction

This chapter introduces the book's study of work in the Digital Media and Entertainment Industries (DMEI). It contextualizes the path toward the production of this book. It lays out the core questions the book seeks to answer, provides a broad overview of the scholars who went "back to work" and led the "labor turn" in communication and media studies, and details the key occupations researched and points of focus and concerns in this burgeoning field. It then elaborates the societal significance of studying work in the DMEI, presenting a multifaceted overview of this topic's relevance to researchers, teachers, learners, media literacy advocates, policy-makers, journalists, unions, activists, and workers. The chapter also makes a case for the importance of the study of work in the DMEI as a potent antidote to prevailing societal narratives of work dominated by technological determinism and far-Right disinformation and propaganda about the "mainstream media" (MSM). Overall, this introduction sets the stage for the book as a whole.

"Being Creative" Without Distinction: My Path to Writing This Book

This book holds immense personal significance for me, as it blends my longstanding interests in communication, creativity, and culture with my roles as a worker, teacher, researcher, writer, and lately, amateur YouTuber. From my earliest years, I was drawn to "being creative." I excelled in my art, drama, music, and literature courses, even singing in post-punk bands such as Dystopia and acting in plays, including some kitschy but enjoyable ones like the "high school musical" *Little Shop of Horrors*. After high school, I enrolled in a community college program in graphic design and worked as a shift manager at Blockbuster Video. Following a heart wrenching break-up, I left my small hometown for the University of

Guelph, where I pursued a double major in English and Theatre Studies. There, I learned to interpret texts, played in a band, and performed in theatrical productions each semester while also working for minimum wage and tips three nights each week at a Canadian wilderness-themed restaurant called "Caribou Creek." In my third year of study, my portrayal of "Sid" in Clifford Odets' iconic Depression-era production, *Waiting for Lefty*, and co-creation of an agitprop play about the Ontario "Days of Action" in protest of the conservative government's neoliberal assault on public service provision and labor rights, left a profound impact on me, demonstrating the political possibilities and limits of producing creative works, with the goal of making social change. Nonetheless, I was passionate. I thought of myself as a creative person. I felt most free when participating in creative projects, particularly during those fleeting moments absent from the pressures of making ends meet. My creativity was never motivated by an entrepreneurial spirit. It was joyful in itself. But as the millennium turned, my ethos seemed to be at odds with what the global creative industries, backed by many governments and educational institutions, wanted from youthful "creativity."

In *Be Creative* (2016), Angela McRobbie historicizes the rise of the "creativity dispositif." Spanning industry, state, and educational spheres and encompassing the discourses and practices that harness the ideal of creativity and put it to work for a changing economy, this form of neoliberal governmentality was driving a massive growth in Intellectual Property (IP) to support the bottom line of corporations at the helm of post-Fordist capitalism, trying to rejuvenate de-industrialized cities with a "creative class" and acculturating youth into a precarious way of life and work that was markedly different from what previous generations endured. Working-class students were being urged to eschew their proletarian past in favor of an aspirational future where all could become middle-class, some, their own boss, just by "being creativity." They were being taught to relinquish their parent's generation's expectation of standard employment, a legacy of history's labor union movements and social democratic states, and instead, to "get entrepreneurial," embrace risk, and hustle for gigs in pursuit of personal and professional growth. "The call to be creative" says McRobbie was a "new governmentality directed to the young in the educational environment, whose effect was to do away with the idea of welfare rights in work by means of eclipsing normal employment all together" (p. 14).

For me, the idea of trying to make a living from "being creative" had always seemed impractical. I was risk averse. My class background may have instilled in me the belief that while creativity is meaningful and fulfilling, it was unlikely to help me pay the rent or purchase creative goods made by others. Despite my love for creativity, I was never encouraged, whether as a child, teenager, or young adult, to view it as a viable career path or something I could make money at or subsist through. This sentiment persisted even in university, where my passions for music, art, and performance felt like just that—passions, rather than a means to "make a living." By my fourth year of university, I took on more bar tending shifts at the restaurant and also became more devoted to academic study. To keep up with high-achieving peers who seemed to always know more than me, I put many hours to the practice of reading and writing, often secluded in my room or the library. As a first-gen university student who discovered Pierre Bourdieu during my PhD, I now see my academic commitments as an unconscious but relentless quest for "cultural capital"—something I painfully realized I lacked, but strove to accumulate and display. My cultural distinction deficit brought a sense of shame but also a determination to learn more so I could one day contribute to the academic discourse happening around me. I gradually acquired academic knowledge and skills that were once obscure to me, recording new concepts I was being introduced to by academic books onto a cassette tape and frequently replaying these recordings through my headphones on my Sony Walkman while jogging or driving. My initial elation at receiving 72% on my first English essay—a grade often protested by today's students aiming for higher marks—underscored my anxiety and fear of complete failure. Despite doing exceptionally well in my final year of study, and being supported by brilliant and caring professors, I constantly wrestled with feelings of self-doubt at university and felt frustrated about the gap between theory and practice, particularly in discussions with socially conscious folk who lamented global problems but seemed not to know what should be done to solve them.

Nonetheless, I was thrilled to be invited by a professor to apply for a new MA program in English and Theatre Studies, especially upon realizing that I was eligible for a graduate scholarship and a paid teaching assistant (TA) position. Yearning for this chance to learn more, and get paid, I was overjoyed to be accepted into the MA program. Feeling like I was "moving up" in the world, I quit my job at Caribou Creek and sadly bid farewell to a newly formed band called Alight. The MA program's learning curve was mountain steep. I climbed and fumbled to the other side with a study of the FedEx-sponsored movie *Cast Away* (2000)—a case of global Hollywood's branded entertainment. I moved to Toronto in 2001 for a PhD in Communication and Culture at York University and Toronto Metropolitan University, working as a teaching assistant (TA) and research assistant (RA). There, I read as much as I could about the political economy of Empire and the media and cultural industries, with support from my advisors Colin Mooers, David McNally, and Scott Forsyth. After earning my PhD, I hustled for four years as a precariat instructor across three Toronto universities, teaching ten courses every year, being hired, fired, and rehired for the same courses every four months or so. The period of 2008–2012 was a tough time in my life, and I can't remember much of it. In 2012, I secured a tenure-track "dream job" at Ontario Tech University. Since then, my position as a salatariat has afforded me a great deal of privilege. Most of the time, I feel as though I am at one with myself through both my labor process (e.g., reading, researching, learning, teaching, writing and presenting) and its products (e.g., enriching student learning experiences, as well as articles, chapters, and books). Academia is no utopia, nor is it an Amazon warehouse, yet.

Over the past decade, creativity has remained a part of my life, though not as prominently as I'd like. At best, I'm a hobbyist. I've occasionally tinkered with new musical projects, found some time to sketch and paint pictures, tell myself that someday I'll write a coming of age novel, and every so often, I make digital posters for community events and create YouTube videos. However, much of my energy has been consumed by my academic commitments. One of these has been learning, reading, researching, thinking, writing, and teaching about capitalism—what this system is, how its logics get reproduced, and why they shape and reshape the conditions and experiences of work in the "knowledge," "information," "copyright," "creative," "media," "cultural," and "tech" industries. For the past ten years or so, I have taught about this topic in my course "COMM 3510 - Work in the Creative and Tech Industries." For a time, I also participated in the Democratic Socialist Project and the Centre for Social Justice, where I learned more about the political economy of capital and the state from Leo Panitch (1945–2020), Greg Albo, Sam Gindin, Stephen Maher and others, while co-organizing numerous community events on class and labor politics through initiatives like the Capitalism Workshop and RedTalks. This book represents a synthesis of my fourteen course lectures on the topic of work, written, revised, presented, and rewritten, and what I learned from participating in pro-worker and social justice communities, when doing public pedagogy.

Initially, I had intended to complete this book several years ago, but extensive service to my academic program and wider professional community significantly delayed my progress. My service roles ranged from eight years spent as the director of the Communication and Digital Media Studies (CDMS) program to vice-president and president of the Canadian Communication Association (CCA) (2018–2022). These commitments, alongside a serious injury just months before the onset of the COVID-19 pandemic and the death of my beloved 18-year-old cat Karl, necessitated a pause in the book writing process to allow time for recuperation and reflection. Despite the challenges that have marked the making of this book, writing it has been a deeply meaningful practice to me, a labor of love. I am thrilled to share this book with you, and I hope it will be useful to your teaching, research and learning.

In *Work in the Digital Media and Entertainment Industries: A Critical Introduction*, I present readers with key questions about work in modern society, particularly within the DMEI, a big and globalizing super-sector that includes media and tech giants like Walt Disney, Apple, and Google, mid-sized media contractors and studios, small teams, as well as millions of entrepreneurial creators—YouTubers, Instagram influencers, and Twitch streamers. The DMEI is fundamental to the financing, production, distribution, and exhibition of the proprietary hardware, software, and content that constitutes the digital society, and interfaces with everything billions of people do. Across the DMEI, a wide range of companies hire the labor of workers to create movies, TV series, and games, develop and sell digital services including platforms and apps, and design, produce, and promote devices from TV sets to smartphones to consoles and VR headsets. This book probes the power relations of work in this massively influential sector of the world economy. Chapters take up the following questions, which are central to researching, understanding, and changing the economics, politics, cultures, technologies, meanings, experiences, inequities and oppressions, and conflicts surrounding and shaping work in the DMEI (and wider society) today:

- What is work, why does it matter, and why do people do it?
- What is the DMEI and what's it got to do with work?
- What is research, and what theories and methods are used to study work?
- What is the working class, and how do capitalism and corporations shape work?
- What is the state, and how do state laws, policies, and regulations shape work?
- What is the "management" of work?
- What are "meritocracy" and "intersectional inequity"?
- What is the "globalization" of work?
- What is the "platformization" of work?
- What is the "automation" of work?
- Is work "free"?
- Is work "good"?
- What's being done by workers to make a better future of work?

By posing and offering tentative answers to these questions, this book is an introductory guide to studying the shifting material conditions of work in the DMEI and the possibilities and limits of worker agency to change these for the better. According to Raymond Williams (1981, pp. 30–31), to understand a culture, we must concern ourselves with "the social relations of its specific means of production" and "with the ways in which, within social life, 'culture' and 'cultural production' are socially identified and distinguished." An understanding of work in the DMEI is a way to understand a shifting culture. Through its overview of how capitalism, corporations, markets, states, laws, policies and regulations, parties and politics, repressive and persuasive management control techniques, new and emerging technologies, and workers themselves shape work in the DMEI, the book sheds light on the labor processes and often contentious social power relations behind the smartphones we use, the movies and TV shows we stream, the video games we play, and the platforms we log in to.

Designed as a "primer," the book explores continuity and change in the conditions and experiences of work in the DMEI. Throughout its pages, the structures, organizations, processes, practices, and social power relations that influence what workers do are explored, with attention to the social consequences that follow. Each chapter engages with key questions, topics, debates, concepts, cases, and themes and is packed with novel examples and relevant findings from the field. The book may hold particular relevance for researchers, teachers, and learners in media industries and labor studies, as well as workers, policy-makers, journalists, organizers, and activists. While the book is for anyone interested in the topic of work in the DMEI, it is written in solidarity with everyone fighting for labor rights and social justice within the world's most impactful super-sector. As such, this book is indebted to all the scholars who went "back to work," and led "the labor turn." The extensive Bibliography found at the end of this book lists the ground-breaking scholars and leading figures in the field who have significantly shaped its development, and who I am continuing to learn from.

Going "Back to Work": Taking "the Labor Turn" in Communication and Media Studies

Twenty-five years ago, the topic of work and labor within the field of communication and media studies was largely marginalized, with only a handful of scholars giving it the serious attention it deserved. As David Hesmondhalgh (2000, pp. 113–114) observed, "Many books exist on film, recording, broadcasting and publishing yet few make reference to the working conditions and financial recompense available to the people working in these industries." In *Culture Works: The Political Economy of Culture*, Richard Maxwell (2001, p. 2) concurred, emphasizing the need to balance attention paid to media CEOs and the images of celebrity movie stars with the "earthly reality of cultural production" experienced by low-waged workers in telecommunications, electronics, film and TV, and data and call-processing centers. In *Socialist Register 2001: Working Classes, Global Realities*, edited by Leo Panitch (1945–2020) and Colin Leys, Ursula Huws ("The Making of a Cybertariat? Virtual Work in a Real World") and Andrew Ross ("No-Collar Labour in America's 'New Economy'") probed the material underpinnings of labor processes in digital capitalism, establishing the backbone of their monumental books on the topic, published two years later: *The Making of a Cybertariat: Virtual Work in a Real World* (Huws, 2003) and *No-collar: The Humane Workplace and Its Hidden Costs* (Ross, 2003).

In *Cultural Work: Understanding the Cultural Industries*, Andrew Beck (2002) and contributors to this important volume considered the changing "character of work within the cultural and creative industries" (p. 1). In "Back to Work," the keynote for the volume, the eminent UK-based political economist of communication Graham Murdock (2002) noted how despite "the general dearth of work on cultural labor in media and cultural studies" (p. 17), there were "signs of a shift with researchers in media and cultural studies returning to work as a necessary focus of study" (p. 16). Murdock explained that the study of work is necessary because it is at the point of production "where creative agency rubs up against structural pressures, organizational strategies and occupational formations" and where "the cultural sites, experiences, and meanings offered to the public are shaped in decisive ways" (17). Over the next eight years or so, many scholars went "back to work."

Toby Miller and Richard Maxwell's (2005) special issue of *Social Semiotics* on the "labor of culture" and *Global Hollywood 2* (Miller et al., 2004), Mark Banks' (2007) *The Politics of Cultural Work*, Mark Deuze's (2007) *Media Work*, Deepa Kumar's (2007) *Outside the Box: Corporate Media, Globalization, and the UPS Strike*, Vincent Mosco and Catherine McKercher's (2007, 2008) *Knowledge Workers in the Information Society* and *The Laboring of Communication: Will Knowledge Workers of the World Unite?* and Vicki Mayer, Miranda J. Banks, and John T. Caldwell's (2008) *Production Studies: Cultural Studies of Media Industries* paved the way for more studies of work. From the UK, David Hesmondhalgh consistently showed the significance of studying work in the media and cultural industries, making numerous fresh contributions (Hesmondhalgh, 2006, 2008, 2009, 2010a, 2010b, 2010b; Hesmondhalgh & Baker, 2008, 2010). In the US, Jennifer Holt and Alisa Perren's (2009) *Media Industries: History, Theory, and Method* opened more space for studies of work, and established the excellent *Media Industries Journal*, now in its tenth year of publication (Herbert et al., 2020). As Holt and Perren (2019, p. 34) say, work has become one of the "sub-areas" of research in the media industries field: "scholarship on these industries has similarly proliferated and actively engaged with the evolving economic, social, and cultural conditions of media work."

From 2010 forward, numerous researchers followed in the footsteps of the aforementioned scholars' labor turn. Over the past fifteen years, the study of work in communication and media studies has not only seen substantial

8 Introduction

growth but has also become significant to many across a wide range of contexts. Simply put, a lot of researchers in the United States and around the world have gone "back to work." This is positively a "labor turn" in the field. For much of the fourth quarter of the 20th century, a great deal of communication and media studies scholarship concentrated on the interplay between media texts, audiences, and reception contexts, overlooking the lives and labor processes of ordinary workers within the industries. But by around 2010 or so, the "labor turn" was followed by many, marking an expansion in focus from the sphere of consumption, where we interpret the texts of media, to the sphere of production, where workers make the media products we consume. This labor turn represents a recognition and dignification of the essential and indispensable role that workers and their labor power always play in producing hardware, software, and content.

Nowadays, in communications and media studies, the study of work is well-established, and from a wide variety of sub-disciplines and fields, scholars have produced important research on the labors of:

- advertisers (Crain, 2021; McGuigan, 2023; Turow, 1997; Wu, 2014);
- Amazon warehouse workers (Delfanti, 2021a, 2021b);
- app and software developers (Bergvall-Kåreborn & Howcroft, 2013; Seaver, 2018a, 2018b);
- artists (Bain, 2005; Fine, 2003; Gandini et al., 2017; Menger, 1999; Mould, 2018; Stokes, 2021; Towse, 2006);
- aspiration, emotion, hope, passion and reputation (Bolton, 2005, 2009; Brook, 2009a, 2009b; Cech, 2021; Duffy, 2017; Gandini, 2016; Hochschild, 2000/1983; Jaffe, 2021; Kuehn & Corrigan, 2013; Taylor, 2001);
- audiences (Dolber, 2016a, 2016b; Joseph, 2022; Maxwell, 1991; McGuigan & Manzerolle, 2014; Meehan, 2002, 2005, 2018);
- authors and creative writers (Fisk, 2003a, 2003b, 2016; Kingston & Cole, 1986; Tuchman, 1989);
- branding and self-branding (Banet-Weiser, 2012; Gandini, 2016; Hearn, 2008a, 2008b, 2010b, 2014; Marwick, 2013; Scolere et al., 2018; Vallas & Hill, 2018);
- call center agents (Boussebaa et al., 2014; Brophy, 2017; Dillan, 2018; Woodcock, 2016);
- comedians (Trusolino, 2022a, 2022b);
- content moderators (Breslow, 2018; Chen, 2014; Jereza, 2022; Newton, 2019; Perrigo, 2022; Roberts, 2019);
- electronics assembly line workers (Bojczuk, 2019; Brophy & de Peuter, 2014; Chan et al., 2020; Huntemann, 2013; Maxwell & Miller, 2023; Pellow & Sun-Hee, 2002);

Introduction 9

- entrepreneurs (Bröckling, 2015; Campbell, 2021; DiMaggio, 2004; Irani, 2019; Kolb, 2015; Leadbeater & Oakley, 1999, 2005; Naudin, 2019; Neff, 2012; Szeman, 2015);
- fans of franchises (Andrejevic, 2008; Jenkins, 2006a, 2006b; Meehan, 2000; Milner, 2009);
- fashion designers and lifestyle bloggers (Arriagada & Ibáñez, 2019, 2020; McRobbie, 1998);
- freelance creators (Blaising et al., 2020; Nemkova et al., 2019; Popiel, 2017);
- freelance journalists (Cohen, 2011, 2012, 2016; Gynnild, 2005; McKercher, 2009, 2014; Salamon, 2016, 2018a, 2020);
- influencers on Instagram and other platforms (Abidin, 2018; Bishop, 2022; Carman, 2020; Cong & Li, 2023; Duffy, 2020; Glatt, 2022b, 2023; Hearn & Schoenhoff, 2015; Hudders & Lou, 2023; Hund, 2023; O'Meara, 2019; O'Neill, 2019; Psarras et al., 2023; Salamon, 2015; Stevens, 2023; Stoldt et al., 2019; Trujillo, 2016; Wellman, 2020, 2021);
- interns, paid and unpaid (Cohen & de Peuter, 2018; de Peuter et al., 2015; Mirrlees, 2015; Perlin, 2012);
- micro-taskers, crowdsourced and ghost workers (Aytes, 2012; Howcroft & Bergvall-Kåreborn, 2014; Brabham, 2012, 2017; Cushing, 2012; D'Cruz & Noronha, 2016; Dibbell, 2003; Dubal, 2020; Fish & Srinivasan, 2012; Gerber & Krzywdzinski, 2019; Gray & Suri, 2019; Grohmann & Araújo, 2021; Howe, 2008; Irani, 2015; Jones, 2021; Moreschi et al., 2020);
- Hollywood (Powdermaker, 1950; Regev, 2018; Rosten, 1941; Wasko, 1998, 2003), including animators (Stahl, 2010), motion picture casting directors (Hill, 2014), composers (Cannizzo & Strong, 2020), screenwriters (Bielby & Bielby, 1999, 2002; Conor, 2010, 2014; McCreadie, 2006), special effects technicians (Chung, 2018), star actors (Fortmueller, 2021; King, 1987; Rawlins, 2024), stunt workers (Gregory, 2015), talent agents (Kemper, 2009), and technical workers (Banks, 2008, 2009; Chanan, 1976, 1983; Caldwell, 2008; Mayer, 2017);
- musicians and recording artists (Arditi, 2020; Ayer, 2005; Barnett, 2014; Baym, 2018; Beech et al., 2016; Dowd & Blyler, 2002; Frith, 2007; Leonard, 2016; Peterson, 1997; Stahl, 2010, 2013, 2021);
- news workers and journalists (Becker et al., 1987; Carpenter & Lertpratchya, 2016; Cohen, 2012, 2015a, 2015b, 2016, 2018; Cottle, 2007; Cushion, 2007; Deuze, 2009; Gans, 2012; Hardt 1990; Hardt & Brennen, 1995; Im, 1997; Johnstone et al., 1976; Kaul, 1986; Lester & Fishman, 1981; McChesney, 2004, 2008; McChesney & Pickard, 2011; Örnebring, 2010; Pickard, 2019; Schudson, 2003, 2010; Smythe, 1980; Tuchman, 1973, 1978);

10 *Introduction*

- photographers (Battani, 1999; Coleman, James, and Sharma, 2018);
- platform, gig, and app workers (Alacovska et al., 2022; Azzellini et al., 2022; Chen, 2018; Delfanti & Sharma 2019; Graham & Woodcock, 2018; Grohmann, 2021; Huws et al., 2019; Jarrett, 2022; Srnicek, 2017a, 2017b; Posada & Shade, 2020; Rodino-Colocino et al., 2021; Scholz, 2017; Slee, 2015; Woodcock & Graham, 2019);
- online creators, social media entertainers, and platform cultural producers (Chayka 2021; Carpenter & Lertpratchya 2016; Cunningham & Craig, 2016, 2018, 2021; Duffy, 2017; Duffy et al., 2019; Duffy et al., 2021; Florida, 2022; Glatt, 2022b, 2023; Hund, 2023; Lin, 2023; Nieborg & Poell, 2018; Poell et al., 2021; Su, 2023; Yuan & Constine, 2020);
- public affairs and propaganda workers (Mirrlees, 2016, 2020, 2021);
- tech and ICT workers (Amrute, 2016; Bhatt, 2018; Dorschel, 2022; Fischer, 2018; Huws, 2003; Marks & Scholarios, 2007; Selling & Strimling, 2023; Yost, 2017);
- TV workers (Altheide, 1976; Altheide & Elliott, 1982; Alvarado & Stewart, 1985; Bielby & Bielby, 1994; Fisk and Szalay, 2017; Gitlin, 2005; Hesmondhalgh & Baker, 2008; Jamal & Lavie, 2020; Levine, 2001; Martin, 2018, 2021; Mayer, 2011, 2014; Ursell, 2000, 2006);
- reality-TV producers, casting agents, and contestants (Andrejevic, 2002, 2004, 2011; Arditi, 2023a; Blair, 2010; Cianci, 2009; Collins, 2008; Grindstaff, 2002; Hearn, 2010a, 2010b, 2014; Hendershot, 2009; Mirrlees, 2015, 2016; Murray & Ouellette, 2009; Raphael, 1997; Wells, 2015);
- sex workers on social media and porn platforms (Berg, 2021; Kirshner, 2024; MacDonald, 2023; Webber et al., 2023);
- sports athletes and skaters (Branch, 2011; Nichols, 2021, 2024; Nixon, 2014; Nocera & Strauss, 2016);
- social media users and Internet prosumers (Andrejevic, 2007; Arvidsson & Colleoni, 2012; Bruns, 2008; Bucher & Fieseler, 2015; Cohen, 2013; Comor, 2010; Fast et al., 2016; Fisher, 2015a, 2015b; Jung, 2014; Flisfeder & Fuchs, 2015; Fuchs, 2010, 2011, 2012a, 2012b, 2014, 2015; Gandini, 2020; Graham & Anwar, 2018; Hesmondhalgh, 2010; Lee, 2011; Ritzer & Jurgenson, 2010; Sandoval et al., 2014; Scholz, 2012; Terranova, 2000, 2004);
- video game coders, developers, modders, players, testers, and streamers (Briziarelli, 2014; Browne & Schram, 2021; Bulut, 2015, 2018, 2020; Chia, 2021; Cote & Harris, 2021, 2023a, 2023b; Deuze, Chase Bowen, and Allen, 2007; Dubois & Weststar, 2022; Dyer-Witheford & de Peuter, 2006, 2009; Hammar, 2020a; Harvey, 2019; Harvey

& Shepherd 2017; Heeks, 2009; Jia, 2021; Johnson & Woodcock, 2017, 2018, 2019; Keogh, 2019, 2021, 2023; Kline et al., 2003; Kücklich, 2005; Ter Minassian & Zabban, 2021; Nieborg & van der Graaf, 2008; O'Donnell, 2014; Schreier, 2021; Sotamaa, 2007; Sotamaa & Švelch, 2021; Tran, 2022; Thompson et al., 2016; Weststar & Dubois, 2022; Weststar, 2015; Weststar et al., 2018; Wu, 2020); and,
- YouTubers (Andrejevic, 2009; Bishop, 2018a, 2018b, 2019; Cunningham & Craig, 2017; Glatt & Banet-Weiser, 2022; Glatt, 2022a; Marwick, 2015; Postigo, 2016; Siciliano, 2021) and video editors (Delfanti & Phan, 2024)

Researchers have not only illuminated the conditions and experiences of various occupational positions and myriad forms of labor undergirding the production and circulation of hardware, software, and content but have also explored the dynamics of work in relation to topics such as:

- ableism and disability rights (Campbell, 2009; Cherney, 2011; Elber, 2018; Ellis, 2016; Galer, 2012; Goggin & Newell, 2002; Harpur, 2022; Goodley et al., 2019; Gulka et al., 2022; Kashani & Nocella, 2010; Lall, 2020; Nario-Redmond, 2019; Preston, 2016; Pullin, 2009; Shakespeare, 2013; Tucker, 2017);
- ageism (Rosales & Fernández-Ardèvol, 2020; Rosales & Svensson, 2021; Lincoln & Allen, 2004);
- algorithmic management (Ajunwa, 2023; Bishop, 2018a; Duffy & Meisner, 2022; Glatt, 2022a; Rauchberg, 2022);
- automation and artificial intelligence (Altenried, 2021; Bastani, 2019; Benanav, 2020; Chia, 2022; Duin & Pedersen, 2023; Dyer-Witheford et al., 2019; Filimowicz, 2023; Flew, 2023; Healy, 2020; Lewis, 2024; McChesney & Nichols, 2016; Napoli, 2014; Oppenheimer, 2019; Ovetz, 2023; Rhee, 2018; Srnicek & Williams, 2015; Steinhoff, 2021);
- class and classism (Amrute, 2016; Aronowitz, 2004; Artz, 2006; Bristol Creative Industries, 2021; Carey et al., 2021; Davis, 2020; Dworkin, 2007; Edgell, 1993; Grindstaff, 2002; Eidlin, 2016; Fantasia, 1989; Fraser, 2018; Grusky & Sørensen, 1998; Hesmondhalgh, 2017; Huws, 2014; Kendall, 2005; Lebowitz, 2003; Martin, 2019; Panitch, 2020; Pincus & Sokoloff, 2008; Polson et al., 2021; Reagan, 2021; Rosenfeld 2021; Skeggs & Wood, 2011; Standing, 2011; Wright, 1997);
- equity, diversity, and inclusivity (EDI) and forms of classist, racist, and sexist inequity, oppression and discrimination (Banks, 2017; Becker et al., 2003; Bielby, 2009; Bristol Creative Industries, 2021; Brook et al., 2023; Carey et al., 2021; Coles et al., 2022; Harrison, 2019;

Hesmondhalgh & Baker, 2015; O'Brien & Oakley, 2015; O'Brien et al., 2016; Brook et al., 2020, 2023; Stone, 1987, 1988; Swyngedouw, 2022; UCLA, 2020; van Doorn, 2017a; Williams & Bain, 2022);
- gender, sexism, and patriarchy (Consalvo, 2008; Cannizzo & Strong, 2020; de Castell & Skardzius 2019; Duffy, 2015a, 2015; Gregg & Andrijasevic, 2019; Handy & Rowlands, 2014; Harvey, 2019; Hill, 2014a, 2014b; Huws, 2015; Jarrett, 2016; Jones & Pringle, 2015; Kantor & Twohey, 2019; Liddy & O'Brien, 2021; Mayer, 2013; Milestone, 2015; O'Brien, 2019; Powell & Sang 2015; Ryan, 2023);
- good, bad, and just work (Banks, 2017; Hesmondhalgh, 2010, 2015; Muirhead, 2007);
- globalization, outsourcing, and the international division of labor (Huws, 2003, 2007a, 2014; Miller, 2016; Ross, 2008), for animation (Lent, 1998, 2010), devices and electronics (Chan et al., 2020; Lüthje & Butollo, 2017; McKay, 2007; Qiu, 2016a; Ross, 2007, 2008; Sandoval, 2013; Sussman & Lent, 1998), digital services (Casilli, 2017; Elliot, 2022; Freeman, 2000), motion pictures and TV series (Christopherson, 2006; Curtin & Sanson, 2016, 2017; Curtin, 2016; Collins & Power, 2019; Elmer & Gasher, 2005; Johnson-Yale, 2017; Kaur, 2020; Miller et al., 2004; Mirrlees, 2013, 2018; Pendakur, 1998; Wasko & Erikson, 2009), social media entertainment (Cunningham & Craig, 2016, 2019, 2021), and video games (Bratt, 2021; Dyer-Witheford, 2015; Dyer-Witheford & de Peuter, 2009, 2020; Kerr, 2017; Ozimek, 2019a, 2019b; Penix-Tadsen & Frasca, 2019);
- management (Albarran, 2006; Andrijasevic et al., 2021; Craig, 2019; Huws, 2010; Johnson et al., 2014; Küng, 2023; Liu, 2021; Mierzjewska & Hollifield, 2006; Ross, 2003; Williams, 2016);
- mental health and wellness (Bélair-Gagnon et al., 2024; Chan, 2020; Cullins et al., 2020; McRobbie, 2002; Mentortribes, 2022; Pollard, 1995; Ravindran, 2020; Salamon, 2023c);
- precarity (Beck, 1992; Christopherson, 2009; de Peuter, 2011; Deresiewicz, 2020; Duffy et al., 2021; Elefante & Deuze, 2012; Gill & Pratt, 2008; Gill, 2011; Glatt, 2022b; Miller, 2010; Morgan & Nelligan, 2018; Ross, 2009; Ruberg, 2019; Standing, 2011; Timburg, 2015);
- race, racialization, and racism (Amrute, 2016; Benjamin, 2019; Chan & Gray, 2020; Christin & Lu, 2023; Dowd & Blyler, 2002; Herman, 2020; Hunt, 2017; Jhally & Lewis, 2019; Martin, 2015, 2021; McIlwain, 2019; Nakamura, 2009; Noble & Tynes, 2016; Saha, 2018; Smith, 2013; Stevens, 2023); and,
- reproductive labor, care and housework (Baxter and Tai, 2016; Bhattacharya, 2017; Cowan, 1984; Duffy & Schwartz 2018; Federici, 2014; Jarrett, 2016; Kessler-Harris, 2003; Seccombe, 1974).

Introduction 13

Acknowledging that it's not enough to hold a mirror to capital's dominance over and attempts to control and exploit labor, researchers have also foregrounded workers' collective empowerment and capacity for refusal and resistance. In *The Laboring of Communication*, Vincent Mosco and Catherine McKercher (2008) asked, "Will the knowledge workers of the world unite?" Scholars have responded to this question with studies of worker-centered collective action, manifested in:

- communication and media activism (Brimeyer et al., 2004; Brophy et al., 2015; Carneiro & Costa, 2022; Cloud, 2005, 2017; Dencik & Wilkin, 2015; Hennebert et al., 2021; Lazar et al., 2020; Kumar, 2007; Maffie, 2020; Marszal, 2020; Mirrlees, 2020, 2023; Qiu, 2016b; Salamon, 2022a, 2023b, 2023d; Schradie, 2019);
- cooperatives (Boyle & Oakley, 2018; de Peuter et al., 2022; de Peuter et al., 2020; Grohmann, 2022, 2023; Muldoon, 2020, 2022; Nicoli & Paltrinieri, 2019; Papadimitropoulos, 2021; Sandoval, 2020; Scholz, 2016a) and solidaristic coworking (de Peuter et al., 2017; Gandini & Cossu, 2021);
- logging out, appropriating capital's tools for workers ends, and other forms of collective action, refusal, and resistance (Chen et al., 2023; de Peuter, 2014; Delfanti & Sharma, 2019; Grayer & Brophy, 2019; Percival & Lee, 2022);
- luddism and machine breaking (Jones, 2006; Merchant, 2023a; Mueller, 2021);
- platform organizing (Carneiro & Costa, 2022; Chen, 2018; Graham & Woodcock, 2018; Grohmann et al., 2023; Hennebert et al., 2021; Lazar et al., 2020; Maffie, 2020; O'Brien, 2010; Panagiotopoulos, 2021; Posada, 2019; Qiu, 2016b);
- union formation and campaigns in tech, motion picture and TV, news media, video game, and online creator industries (Banks, 2015; Brophy, 2006; Buhle & Wagner, 2002; Clark, 1995; Cohen & de Peuter, 2020; Coles, 2006, 2016, 2023; Craig & Cunningham, 2023; Fisk, 2016; Fortmueller and Marzola, 2024; Gray & Seeber, 1996; Hill, 2022; Horne, 2001; Hughes & Woodcock, 2023; Keogh & Abraham, 2022; Logic Magazine, 2019; Mari, 2018; McKercher, 2002; McKercher & Mosco, 2007; Mosco 2008, 2011; Nielsen & Mailes, 1995; Perry & Perry 1963; Press, 2019; Prindle 1988; Rodnitzky & Leab 1971; Ruffino 2021; Ruffino & Woodcock, 2021; Salamon, 2018b; Segrave, 2007, 2009; Stahl 2009; Tarnoff & Weigel, 2020; Weststar & Legault, 2017, 2019); and,
- strikes (Anguiano & Beckett, 2023; Banks, 2010; Banks & Fortmueller, 2023; Deneroff, 1987; Fleming, 2008; Fortmueller, 2023; Friedman, 2022; Handel, 2011; Harvey, 2023; Littleton, 2013).

- efforts to enforce and enhance labor rights with pro-worker laws, policies, and regulations, made in part by workers themselves (Bader Law, 2023; de Peuter, 2012; de Peuter & Cohen, 2015);
- intersectional working-class movement, organization, and party building that rejects the slogan that "there is no alternative" to capitalism and advances a pre-figurative politics, progressive reforms, including non-reformist reforms, resources of hope, new blueprints, and real utopias that aim to move society beyond capitalism (Fritsch et al., 2016; Gindin, 2018, 2019; Hahnel & Wright, 2016; Hughes & Woodcock, 2023; Milburn, 2019; Mirrlees, 2020, 2023; Panitch & Albo, 2016; Panitch et al., 2020; Reagan, 2021; Sears, 2014; Stanford, 2015; Sunkara, 2019; Thier, 2020).

Amid this abundant research on "cultural," "creative," "informational," "media," and "tech" labor in some of the most advanced sectors, industries and corporations of the first quarter of the 21st century, this book provides an interdisciplinary introduction to some of the biggest questions about the shifting terrain of work in society. This book brings together a wide range of topics and issues into one volume. It is a "big picture" overview of work in the DMEI that aims to balance a survey of key concepts with a material-empirical grounding built from popular examples, anecdotes, interpretations, and most importantly, research from scholars who have followed the "labor turn" in communication and media studies over the past few decades. This book recognizes that the study of work in the DMEI matters and matters to many.

Why Does the Study of Work in the DMEI Matter and to Whom Does It Matter?

The study of work in the DMEI matters to many people in multiple contexts: researchers; university teachers and learners; advocates of media labor literacy; proponents of media democracy; policy-makers who care about labor rights; labor journalists; and, workers and the labor movement. Furthermore, the study of work in the DMEI can provide a powerful counterpoint to unhelpful ways of thinking about society, those being, "technological determinism" and "mainstream media conspiracism" (MSMC).

The study of work in the DMEI matters to many research organizations, including the International Association for Media and Communication Research (IAMCR), International Communication Association (ICA), Union for Democratic Communications (UDC), National Communication Association (NCA), Canadian Communication Association (CCA), Canadian Association for Work and Labour Studies, International

Labor Organization (ILO), the Labor and Working-Class History Association (LAWCHA), and the Working-Class Studies Association (WCSA). Specialized research groups and interest groups, such as IAMCR's Media Production Analysis Working Group, ICA's Media Industry Studies Interest Group, the Society for Cinema and Media Studies' Media Industries Scholarly Interest Group, and CCA's Work and Labour research cluster, are also interested in matters of work. Additionally, organizations like the British Association of Film, Television and Screen Studies (BAFTSS), European Communication Research and Education Association (ECREA), and European Network for Cinema and Media Studies (NECS) are contributing to this field. Research collectives, including Cultural Workers Organize (https://culturalworkersorganize.org/), Notes from Below (https://notesfrombelow.org/), DigiLabour (https://digilabour.com.br/), Collective Action in Tech (https://collectiveaction.tech/), and the Labor Tech Research Network (http://labortechresearchnetwork.org/), advance research and support worker organizing. Scholarly journals such as *triple C: Communication, Capitalism & Critique*, *Media Industries*, *Social Media & Society*, *Communication and Critical/Cultural Studies*, *Journal of Labor and Society*, and *Work, Employment & Society* have published a variety of articles on work and labor in the DMEI, and an increasing number of journals across disciplines and fields are focusing on this area as well.

The study of work in the DMEI also matters to the many university and college faculties, departments, and programs that offer undergraduate and graduate courses on work and labor topics. In a context where higher education is expected to train the workforce of the future for the DMEI, courses about work in communications, cultural, creative, media, and tech industries have proliferated. Students who view a degree or a diploma as a stepping stone to a career in the DMEI, and pursue post-secondary education for this reason, are drawn to such courses because they appear "career-readying" and "labour-market facing." Many graduates go on to labor as communicators, storytellers, and social media managers for firms in sectors ranging from finance to retail to non-profit. Some even try to "break in" to the fast-growing Creator Economy as YouTubers or TikTok influencers. Beyond interlinking with higher education-for-capitalism's schooling exigencies and instrumentalization by neoliberal states, courses on work in the DMEI are valuable to students interested in understanding the real economic, political and technological conditions that shape their lives and labors. Courses on work in the DMEI can encourage students to think holistically about the structures of the economy and the state, and the operations of specific corporate organizations, that shape and reshape the real world of work. These courses can inspire and guide critical thinking about work in the DMEI. They can challenge the vocational and

16 *Introduction*

managerial mindset of the knowledge factory, which often reduces learners to mere human capital for corporate exploitation, and expects them to see themselves as such. Instead, these courses can empower learners to see themselves as workers with agency and labor rights. Furthermore, courses on work in the DMEI can encourage students to look beyond the grind of short-term gigs and show how cooperation and collective action can make a better world.

Furthermore, the study of work in the DMEI matters to those committed to the project of fostering media literacy within consumers and citizens. In society, media literacy—the ability to access, analyze, evaluate, use, and create media in a variety of forms—is widely encouraged and undeniably important. However, the study of work in the DMEI suggests a need for an equally strong emphasis on *media labor literacy*, or, an understanding of the conditions of work behind the hardware, software, and content we use and engage with daily, which tends to be shrouded in spectacle. The high-octane action of blockbusters like *Fast X* or the class-conscious narratives of dramas like *Nomadland* captivate us, drawing us into their fictional worlds, but how often do we consider the conditions under which these works are created? Fans may appreciate the "green messaging" of movies like *Avatar: The Way of Water*, but may not be aware of the environmental hazards faced by crews. Although behind-the-scenes reels on platforms like YouTube offer glimpses into the making of entertainment, they often serve as promotional material rather than knowledge about the complexity of the labor processes (and conflicts) involved. By teaching media labor literacy alongside traditional media literacy, educators can help to ensure that consumers, citizens, and future workers will not only be able to analyze media content and use new media tools but also contemplate the human labor that is core to the DMEI. Literacy about the labor behind the screen—from the electronics workers assembling smartphones and consoles to the warehouse workers boxing TV sets and books to the software developers coding apps and platforms to the online creators publishing videos—is vital. Labor media literacy encourages critical thinking about the broader system that shapes media production and consumption, fosters an ethical conscience about the conditions of all those laboring in the DMEI, and invites reasoned judgments about the quality of work, in support of workers' rights.

Additionally, the study of work in the DMEI is important to citizens who care about the quality of civic life and recognize how central media and digital technology are to the workings of democracy. The DMEI intertwines with the economies, polities and cultures of societies on a global scale: the hardware and software serve as the infrastructure of all mediated human communication and the content imparted and received are a powerful means of socializing the culture. The spread of misinformation and disinformation, the erosion of privacy by data-veillance, the rise of polarizing echo chambers, and the algorithmic manipulation of public opinion and behavior, harm democracy. However, these problems are not inherently "media" or "technological" problems, but stem from the system that incentivizes corporations to hire and compel workers to make means that serve ends that affront the public interest and undermine democratic principles and civic practices. Websites for companies relying on clickbait often compel workers to produce sensational or misleading headlines, spreading misinformation and disinformation that lure and deceive citizens. Platforms such as Elon Musk's rebranded X, aiming to increase user engagement and ad revenue when opening the floodgates to extremist content, overhaul the community guidelines and lay off the content moderators paid to enforce them, leading to the noxious and unchecked spread of anti-democratic content, like neo-Nazi hate speech. Overall, the conditions under which people are made or motivated to work in the DMEI intersect with and may significantly influence the overall quality of society's informational environment, and consequently, the health of democracy itself. The study of work in the DMEI matters to democratically minded citizens because it can shed light on how the production of hardware, software, and content—often dictated by corporate profit-motives—can either support or undermine democracy. Labor is an entry point for research that uncovers the structural incentives and organizational motives that drive workers to produce these goods and services. For citizens worried about the erosion of democracy in the digital society, the study of work in the DMEI provides an opportunity to open the "black box" of production and make transparent conditions and practices whose profitable outcomes threaten democratic values and practices.

Relatedly, the study of work in the DMEI is significant to the governments responsible for making, modifying, and enforcing the laws, policies, and regulations related to communications and media-culture, as well as those officially charged with establishing and upholding labor laws. Too often, the "public" laws, regulations, and policies that states use to govern the DMEI are made with the private interests of the companies that own the DMEI in mind, not the workers these companies employ. Big media and tech companies spend millions on lobbying to ensure it. Also, for too long, state efforts to protect and promote "national culture" have taken precedence over securing the health and wellness of workers against the corporations that exploit their labor. In the US, state policy frequently props up the growth and expansion of a US-centered DMEI oligopoly; outside, in countries around the world, state policy bolsters national DMEI monopolies. Infrequently do workers around the world factor into the policies multiple states develop in support of the national and transnational accumulation interests of the corporations that preside over the globalizing DMEI. Nonetheless, there are some progressive policy-makers in civil society, in political parties and in the state that care about workers' interests and strive to improve labor conditions in the DMEI. Relatedly, this book may be of interest to all those climbing the chasm between critical and administrative policy research. There's a need for "critical administrative researchers" who combine negative critique of the reigning policy framework for capital with the positive development of new policy formations in support of labor. The study of work in the DMEI enables ruthless criticism of what is and dreams of what could be.

The study of work in the DMEI is important to the journalists on the frontlines of the labor beat, and who play a key role in making the media agendas and frames that shape public opinion about work in our time. A century ago, labor reporting was a fundamental part of most major news organizations. Some news outlets were even affiliated with the union movement, like the Industrial Workers of the World's own publications, or the Federated Press labor news service and labor radio programs of the 1930s (Martin, 2019). Following a long decline in labor reporting from World War II forward through to the global financial crisis of 2007-2008, there's been a resurgence in labor journalism over the past fifteen years or so. More news workers, through their own experiences of the transformation of media industries and participation in unionization campaigns, forged a deeper understanding of capitalism and class politics, and started writing about it (Cohen & de Peuter, 2020; Nolan, 2024). The longstanding labor reporting about Hollywood and Silicon Valley by journalists such as Steven Greenhouse, Sarah Jaffe and Michelle Chen has been accompanied by an uptick in newer voices like Alex N. Press of *Jacobin*, and Sarah Kessler, who writes for *Bloomberg* and *Quartz*. Others, such as Noam Scheiber of *The New York Times* and Rebecca Greenfield of *Bloomberg*, cover labor issues in the tech industry. Emily Peck of *HuffPost*, *Teen Vogue*'s labor columnist Kim Kelly, and *Vice*'s Edward Ongweso Jr. also contribute to the media labor beat. Additionally, outlets like *The Hollywood Reporter*, *Variety*, *Los Angeles Times*, *Portside*, *The Nation*, and online platforms like LabourStart and Labor Notes provide extensive coverage of labor issues. Podcasts such as *The Belabored Podcast* (https://www.dissentmagazine.org/tag/belabored/), *Working Class History* (https://workingclasshistory.com/), and *Working People* (https://workingpeople.libsyn.com/) are shining examples of the production and circulation of digital media by, for, and about labor, in all its diversity.

The stories labor journalists are telling about workers who are joining and leading unions in the DMEI point to the significance of the study of work in the DMEI to the living labor movement of our time. Many workers in the DMEI are represented by unions, or, organized associations of workers formed to protect and advance their rights and interests through collective bargaining and action. For example, in the US, the Writers Guild of America (WGA) represents writers who write the scripts of our favorite TV series and motion pictures. The Screen Actors Guild-American Federation of Television and Radio Artists (SAG-AFTRA) covers actors to voiceover artists and broadcast journalists. The International Alliance of Theatrical Stage Employees (IATSE) includes technicians and craftspeople. The National Association of Broadcast Employees and Technicians (NABET-CWA), affiliated with the Communications Workers of America (CWA), represents broadcast technicians, camera operators, maintenance engineers and more. Internationally, some of the DMEI's workforce is represented by unions. In the UK, the Broadcasting, Entertainment, Cinematograph, and Theatre Union (BECTU) covers workers in broadcasting, film, and interactive media, while the Federation of Entertainment Unions (FEU) represents working professionals across the entire entertainment sector. In Canada, the Canadian Media Guild (CMG) covers workers in the Canadian Broadcasting Corporation (CBC) and other media outlets, with CWA Canada, a part of CWA, focusing on digital media workers (https://www.digitalmediaunion.ca/). The Media, Entertainment & Arts Alliance (MEAA) in Australia represents a range of workers, including journalists and actors.

These and many other unions are key to fighting for the rights and interests of workers in the DMEI, and securing workers' against the threats of poverty and precarity, a state partial to News Corp and Apple, and the vagaries of the online gig economy. Also, workers across various Big Tech companies, including Google, Apple, Amazon, Sega of America, and more, are driving new union campaigns. Many online creators—even some of the most popular and best paid—are trying to unionize (Craig & Cunningham, 2023; Stanley, 2024). Beyond traditional unions, a variety of organizations, associations, and networks also advocate for workers' labor rights in the DMEI. The Tech Workers Coalition (TWC) focuses on building communities among tech workers and designing ethical tech; Game Workers Unite fights for the rights of game workers; the Freelancers Union offers resources for independent workers facing precarity; the Internet Creators Guild provides education and support for online creators; the Digital Media Workers Association champions fair labor practices and equitable treatment.

For these and other union and non-union fronts of the contemporary labor movement, the study of work in the DMEI and its result—theoretical and applied knowledge about what's going on in this super-sector—is of strategic and tactical importance. The DMEI are the vanguard of capitalism and the production models their corporations innovate and new models of work they establish often become the models for other sectors, a prefigurative laboratory for everything else to follow. As the DMEI are at the forefront of new capital-labor trends, it is essential for the labor movement to understand what's going on in them, to be ahead them, in support of worker's rights. The production and circulation of research on work in the DMEI can foster a sense of solidarity within their labor forces by shining a light on common experiences of workers, identifying and challenging violations of labor rights, calling out alienating and immiserating working conditions and demanding better. It can furnish the labor movement with evidence in support of pro-worker consciousness raising, social media movement campaigns, and legal and policy reforms. The labor movement is a means of generating transformative ideas, and many of these depend on research. So, the study of how capitalism, and corporate and state practices, shape work in the DMEI, and how the agency of workers can reshape the world, is fundamental to labor movement advocacy and activism to make history.

Across the DMEI, many workers are uniting, and this contrasts with the oversimplified image of the "creative precariat" in post-Fordist management literature and some of the gloomiest socialist stories. This "figure of the self-reliant, risk-bearing, non-unionized, self-exploiting, always-on flexibly employed worker" tends to oscillate between idealizing workers in the creative industries as a "role model of contemporary capitalism" or pitying them as helpless victims needing rescue by others (de Peuter, 2014, p. 263). Such a binary outlook deflects attention away from the agency of these workers and their collective actions to contest precarity by forming mutual aid networks, unionizing, and launching campaigns to change state law and policy (de Peuter and Cohen, 2015). The study of work in the DMEI matters because it teaches us that workers are neither heroic role models nor pathetic dupes of the system. They are not passive reflections of capitalist structures nor are they necessarily the vanguard of a new world, understanding the world and changing it for the better. Workers have the potential to make history, but as Karl Marx famously observed, "they do not make it under self-selected circumstances, but under conditions directly encountered, given, and transmitted from the past." The study of work in the DMEI matters because it apprehends the system logics and corporate and state power relations that act upon workers, and it also recognizes how workers can actively challenge those logics and collectively organize against exploitative and oppressive conditions, sometimes even managing to transform them. The study of work in the DMEI can provide a dialectical view of the power of corporations to reconfigure labor for its ends, and the power of workers' self-activity to produce alternatives. The condition of work in the DMEI is very much a canary in the coal mine of global capitalism, but the canary may also escape, and take flight up toward a different horizon.

In sum, the study of work in the DMEI is important to researchers, teachers and learners, media literate consumers, citizens, policy-makers, journalists, the labor movement, and workers themselves. Beyond this, going back to work matters because it complicates some unhelpful yet pervasive ways of thinking about society: *technological determinism* and *mainstream media (MSM) conspiracism*.

The study of work in the DMEI is a rejoinder to the rhetoric of technological determinism that makes its ways into much business writing and political speeches about the transformation of work. All too often, new and emerging technologies—nowadays, Machine Learning, the Internet of Things, and Robots—get written and spoken of as the primary agents of history, "disruptive" and even "revolutionary" in their societal impacts, and dictator-like in making everything and everyone change, all at once. In the story of technological determinism, it is generative AI—not capital and certainly not class interests—that is putting millions out of work, and demanding skills retraining. It is the Internet of Things, not a decision made by CEOs for an Internet corporation, that is most responsible for fundamental changes to pre-existing ways of life and ways of work. It is the Robot holding a smartphone or operating the app or a combination of both, not the producers of such hardware and software, that have propelled human civilization as a whole forward, into some new historical period, epoch, era, or age. Technology undoubtedly matters and may even exercise a soft determinism in society, but foremostly, it is the power relations between people, often in significant organizations like DARPA or Google, that socially shapes technologies and then wields these as tools for reshaping the world. It is the national security prerogatives of states and the shareholder interests of capital that frequently design technology for political and economic ends, but no technology would ever exist without human labor. And technology's subordination to the powers of the state and capital is never a forgone conclusion. While military technocrats and CEOs frequently drive the labor force to research and develop new technological innovations in pursuit of security, efficiency, control, and profit, technologies made for one end can be redesigned for another, and sometimes, the workers' making and remaking of the hardware and software of the world is shaped by class struggle: "the clash between labor and capital must not be overlooked" (Chen et al., 2023, p. 3896). The study work in the DMEI can demystify the rhetoric of technological determinism by revealing the human design choices and labors behind all of the technologies mistakenly perceived as autonomous agents. It can also purposefully illuminate the interplay between the forces of production (technologies used in production) and the relations of production (power dynamics between bosses and workers). It can achieve this by emphasizing workers' contributions to all technological developments in the DMEI. After all, generations of workers are the sources of the infrastructure and superstructure of the DMEI: they not only create the "content" that informs and entertains and over which corporations assert copyright but also make the electronics and platforms essential for its production, circulation, and consumption. From computers, smartphones, apps, and social media sites to cloud services, telecommunications systems, and generative AI, the workers' labor is the source of the technologies that constitute the digital society.

Recognizing and researching work in the DMEI can be a salient way of dispelling the far-Right's ubiquitous conspiracism about the so-called "mainstream media" (MSM) (Phelan & Maeseele, 2023). The ascendance of far-Right social movements, parties, and politicians in the US and globally has been marked by the propagation of a ridiculous but widely believed conspiracy theory. This "alt" or white nationalist Right narrative posits that the MSM and Big Tech are dominated by "cultural Marxist" elites who, alongside "woke" and "politically correct" liberal states, parties, and political leaders, are conspiring to establish a totalitarian socialist "global government" (Mirrlees, 2018, 2019). Indoctrinated by this far-Right conspiracy theory of power (a pathetically unsubstantiated usage of "power elite theory"), more and more people may believe that all waged media and tech workers are "in on it." All too often, many of these workers are vilified, targeted with hate, harassed, and even attacked. The study of labor dynamics within the DMEI offers a reality check that effectively debunks right-wing delusions and distortions. Contrary to the specious conspiracy claim that everyone in the MSM and Big Tech industries are ideologically united in what they believe and produce (a Borg-like hive-mind), the DMEI are a contested terrain, a field of struggle. The labor force does not think and act with one mind; workers don't all feel the same about what they are paid to create, agree with their bosses and managers, let alone have a uniform political plan for what's to be done to solve local and global problems. Furthermore, whistleblowers within Hollywood and Big Tech frequently try to expose CEO corruption and misconduct, and some watchdog news workers often cover their revelations, informing the public while driving audience ratings and ad revenue. Workers can push back against owner-driven ideological agendas and frames, and challenge the conduct of the corporations that exploit their labor. The study of work in the DMEI, not far-Right conspiracy theory, yields insight into the real workings of capitalism, corporations, and the conflict unfolding between CEOs and workers, behind our screens. A useful counter-narrative to the far-Right's conspiracy theory of cultural Marxism, knowledge about work in the DMEI is the true "red pill" for those the far-Right's Matrix exploits, offering an escape from its engineered simulations, alluring distractions, and self-generated obfuscations.

The study of work can empower individuals to confront the truth of reality, however painful it may be, and to face with sober senses, the real conditions of life and relations with others in society. I hope the chapters contained in this book will be a useful guide to this world.

Chapter 1 examines the multifaceted meanings, significances, and motivations of work. Chapter 2 presents an overview of the DMEI and shows how this super-sector interlinks with and shapes modern work. Chapter 3 introduces the idea of research and opens up the toolkit to tinker with some theories and methods that can be used for research on work in the DMEI. Chapter 4 scans key conceptualizations of the "post-industrial" working class and shows how capitalism and its eight core system logics still fundamentally shape the conditions and power relations of work in the DMEI. Chapter 5 examines the significance of the state to work in the DMEI and provides a broad overview of how the state's explicit and tacit labor laws, policies, and regulations shape work. Chapter 6 probes the management of work in the DMEI, surveying ideas of management and scrutinizing the persuasive and repressive control techniques managers use to manage workers. Chapter 7 introduces the idea of meritocracy in the DMEI, interrogates its key assumptions with an intersectional labor lense attentive to historical and enduring inequities and oppressions, and shows how the interplay of "economic" and "cultural" capital limits people's access to good work in the DMEI. Chapter 8 focuses on the globalization of work in the DMEI, complicating the idea that any piece of media hardware, software, or content is exclusively "national" and highlighting the trans-nationality of their making by workers around the world. Chapter 9 explores the platformization of work in the DMEI, concentrating specifically on the conditions, characteristics, and experiences of online creators, cultural producers, and influencers and highlighting the dialectic of continuity and change in Creator Capitalism. Chapter 10 examines the accelerating automation of work in the DMEI, providing a broad overview of how labor-saving technologies (LSTs) are biased to capital and consequential to the workers' labor process, and also, considers the recent threat posed by generative AI to specific occupations in the DMEI. Chapter 11 examines so-called "free" labor within the DMEI, and the various forms it takes: audience work (audience commodity, commodity audience, prosumer commodity), brand and fan work, crowdsourced work, and interned and indentured work. It also considers the threats to workers' freedom of expression in the labor process and the product. Chapter 12 spotlights workers' collective action in the DMEI and the spectrum of strategies and tactics workers are using to contest capitalist exploitation and bring about a change to the DMEI, and the world, for the better. The postscript calls for a study of work in the DMEI that goes beyond "creative exceptionalism."

At the back of this book, you'll find a Bibliography packed with old and new key works in the field. Although it was not possible for me to directly cite, deeply engage with, or even summarize most of these texts within the framework of this particular book, their inclusion serves to acknowledge their role in establishing, catalyzing and contributing to important research on work and labor within communication, media and cultural studies. It's also a gesture of my deep appreciation for the authors' intellectual labors and production of a field from which I've learned so much and keep learning more. I hope you, too, will learn from and add to it in the future.

1 What Is Work?
Meanings, Matters, Motivations

Introduction

This chapter examines the major significations, significances, and motivations of "work." The chapter begins by establishing that the meaning of work is constructed, contextual, and contested. It then considers the many meanings of modern work, from work as labor to work as the opposite of leisure, to work as waged labor to unpaid labor encompassing forced labor or slavery, housework, volunteerism, and forms of free media labor. The chapter then addresses why work matters and examines how it does so. It considers work's relationship to the human species, its importance to society and environment, its intersection with identity, health, and wellness, its relation to "culture" (ways of work-life and works of intellectual activity), as well as to configurations of time and space, and importantly, its position as a site of contestation and struggle. Moving on to the varied *motivations* behind work, especially in the digital media and entertainment industries (DMEI), the chapter focuses on subsistence, consumerism, personal satisfaction, meaning and purpose, and love, hope, and aspiration. The chapter concludes by considering a world without work, or "post-work."

Work's Meaning Is Constructed, Contextual and Contested

In *Working: People Talk About What They Do All Day and How They Feel About What They Do*, Studs Terkel (1997) explored the relationship between work and the human experience in a landmark oral history. As Terkel found:

> Working is about the search for daily meaning as well as daily bread, for recognition as well as cash, for astonishment rather than torpor; in short, for a sort of life rather than a Monday through Friday sort of dying. Perhaps immortality, too, is part of the quest. To be remembered was the wish, spoken and unspoken, of the heroes and heroines of this book.
>
> (pp. xi–xii)

DOI: 10.4324/9781003131076-2

Terkel's words raise questions about the essence of why we work, suggesting that it is more than the mere act of earning a living, even though that is indeed significant, even necessary, to life in capitalism. He proposes that work is an intrinsic part of our search for meaning and self-fulfillment. It's not only about economic necessity ("daily bread") but also about seeking recognition and respect ("to be remembered"), as well as mental stimulation ("astonishment rather than torpor"). Terkel's quote challenges the idea of work as a mere instrumentality, a routine that serves as a means to an end, suggesting that without finding value or satisfaction in our work, life becomes a dull, degraded existence ("a Monday through Friday sort of dying"). Moreover, Terkel touches on a human desire for a meaningful life. He implies that through our labor process and its products, we aspire to leave an enduring positive impact, to be valorized for what we have contributed to the world. People express a deep-seated longing for significance and permanence in their work. Terkel's study of work elevates it from a mere subsistence activity to a key component of our identity, purpose, and legacy.

All in all, labor matters because it is inseparable from being human, even though it may make billions of people feel less than human when doing jobs they dislike, and sometimes more than human, if augmented by new tech. Work is essential to the happenings of society as a whole, as it is the labor of workers combined with machines and energy that produces the goods and services which meet subsistence needs such as food, water, and shelter, and cater to ubiquitous cultural wants, such as Marvel Universe movies, PS5 games, and tiktokcats. Yet, we may seldom think systematically about the conditions that shape the work we do and how work may shape us.

Work has always been part of the human condition, and it still is. But the specific form that work takes and the social definition given to work itself by those who preside over it and those who do it has varied greatly across historical periods and geographies. In ancient Confucian thought, work was seen as a moral duty and a means of contributing to societal harmony and stability, while in the 15th century, the Catholic Church taught that work was a means of fulfilling one's duty to God, apropos the concept of "laborare est orare" (to work is to pray). Nowadays, the meaning of work varies, from "doing what you gotta do" to pay the bills to "doing what you love" to achieve personal fulfillment. There is no single universally acceptable definition of work available, as most dictionaries will give "work" (as noun and verb) a wide range of meanings that are not all the same. As a noun, work tends to refer to an activity involving mental and physical effort done in order to achieve a purpose or result ("Rose and Rosie were wiped out after a day's work of scripting, performing in, shooting, editing and posting the YouTube video") or a task or tasks to be undertaken ("the indexing work agreed to by the author of this book has been proceeding too slowly"). As a verb, work means to be doing something for some outcome, being engaged in some kind of mental and physical activity aimed at a result ("all the men and women employed by Foxconn Technology Group have been working so hard for so little, 60 hours/week at a measly $3/hour to assemble Apple iPhones"). Or it can refer to a machine or algorithm that operates, ideally effectively, sometimes not ("the GPT-3 model DALL-E relies upon to generate images from text is not working—deploy the machine learning engineers, data scientists and quality assurance specialists!"). The meaning of work is therefore multifaceted.

Furthermore, work's meaning is most often constructed, contextually and contingently defined, not straightforward. What counts as "work" frequently depends on the social context in which it occurs and is apprehended, not by the essence of the activity or practice it entails. The very same activity—say, posting on Instagram, video gaming, or writing a story—can mean very different things depending on whether the activity is performed by someone who is doing it for pay in the context of an employment relation with another or by someone doing that activity in some other social context. From the nano-influencers with 1000–10,000 followers who get $10–$100 per post to the mega-influencers with 1,000,000+ followers who earn $10,000+ per post, all the influencers logged in to Instagram with the express function of shilling for brands and getting paid are technically "at work." But when I'm clumsily on Instagram, looking at my sister's family vacation photos or checking out Elden Ring reels, I'm not. Johan Sundstein has so far earned $7.18 million in winnings from eSports competitions, and for him, gaming is a lucrative career; but most of the more than 3 billion gamers in the world aren't working when playing. The student enrolled in a college creative writing course who is writing a short story that will be read and given a grade by a teacher is not conventionally perceived as a working author; the person who is contracted by the college to teach this course once a semester while chasing writing gigs on UpWork and collecting royalties off the sale of their last novel arguably is. While almost any activity in contemporary capitalism can be done for pay, there are also many examples of the very same activity being done for reasons that are irreducible to the cash nexus. What activity gets defined as "work" depends on social context, and the same set of practices that may be considered "work" in one context might be perceived as its opposite in another.

The line between what activity is and is not work can be blurry, and attending to how that line is drawn and who draws it requires a consideration of the power to define work in societies, past and present. Governments, corporations, non-governmental organizations, unions, media outlets, educational institutions, and various big thinkers contribute to shaping society's dominant notions of work, the value assigned to different types of work, and the standards and norms surrounding labor processes. Any society's authoritative and legitimized meaning of "work" is far from being value-neutral; rather, it is the result of decisions by governments and corporations, and sometimes even workers themselves that articulate and lock into the social imaginary, a dominant idea of work. The hegemonic idea of work in any society at a specific moment in history is far from fixed. It is the outcome of a continuously developing communicative practice of articulation, negotiation, and struggle. The influence of political and economic organizations, combined with the agency of workers themselves, frequently shapes prominent meanings about work in society and in the DMEI. What are some of the dominant meanings of work in society? How has the meaning of work changed over time, and how does work mean to us today? Why does work matter and who has made it matter so much? What motivates billions of people to do so much work? And might we begin to think and do without it?

What Is Work? Labor, Leisure, Paid, Unpaid

Work as Labor

Work has traditionally been equated with "labor," a term derived from the Latin "laborem," meaning "toil, exertion, hardship, pain." Activities that are relaxing, casual, easy, and pleasurable are frequently contrasted to labor and are not typically classified as work. Sir Dudley North (1641–1691) expressed this distinction succinctly: "If it was agreeable to do anything called work, it was not really so but pleasure.... It is incident to the true nature of work not to delight in it" (Thomas, 1999, p. xviii). During the rise of industrial capitalism, Enlightenment philosophers and political economists framed labor in utilitarian terms: a burdensome activity we do for necessity, a means to an end rather than an end in itself. In *Deontology*, Jeremy Bentham remarked: "[The] desire for labor for the sake of labor—of labor considered as an end, without any view to anything else, is a sort of desire that scarcely finds a place in the human breast" (Thomas, 1999, pp. 10–11). Alfred Marshall described labor in *Principles of Economics* (1890) as "any exertion of mind or body undertaken partly or wholly with a view to some good other than the pleasure derived from the work." By the early 20th century, the idea of work as "labor"—activities that were "hard, difficult, or painful" (Williams, 1976, p. 337) persisted. This notion of work as labor endures. In capitalism, it is frequently perceived and experienced as a necessary evil, and a mostly compulsory and deeply alienating activity that is antithetical to human freedom. As Thomas (1999, p. xiv) explains, work tends to be defined as something that "has an end beyond itself, being designed to produce or achieve something: it involves a degree of obligation or necessity, being a task that others set us or that we set ourselves; and it is arduous, involving effort and persistence beyond the point at which the task ceases to be wholly pleasurable."

When defined as labor, work is the antithesis of leisure. In medieval Europe, this distinction between work and play was often blurred; sporting activities like tournaments and archery served dual purposes as both pastime and preparation for war, rendering leisure a facet of labor for the state. While capitalism separated the space and time of leisure from labor, in the society of now, particularly within the DMEI, labor and leisure are frequently fused. The emergence of "playbour" illustrates this blend, where playing digital games productively contributes to money-making. For example, when "gold farming" in online games, players grind to produce and accumulate virtual goods and then sell these on the Internet for real-world money (Heeks, 2009). Augmented reality games like Pokémon Go prompt people to play for recreation, but this play aligns with the commercial aims of the developers and advertisers (Mirrlees, 2016). Game modders infrequently draw a hard line between their love of playing and the labor of making video games (Kücklich, 2005; Sotamaa, 2007). Video game testers undertake "productive play" (Bulut, 2015, p. 242) and game streamers live-play for fun and cash on YouTube and Twitch (Johnson & Woodcock, 2019a, 2019b). While labor is often seen as leisure's opposite, the two sometimes converge, online and off.

Work as Paid Labor

Most often, though, work is not pursued for pleasure, nor something that is experienced as a source of great fulfillment or happiness. Gallup's *State of the Global Workplace: 2022* report found that most workers polled were dissatisfied, detached, disengaged, and stressed out by their jobs on a daily basis, and some were worried, sad, and angry. For much of modern history, work meant paid labor—difficult, strenuous, compulsory, even painful activity—performed in service of others in return for payment. Thomas Hobbes noted as early as 1651 that labor could be exchanged for benefit, just like any commodity (Thomas, 1999). In *The Wealth of Nations*, Adam Smith (1776) observed that because most people favor leisure over "toil and trouble," the "sweets of labour" are primarily found in its compensation, or "recompense" ("recompense" means compensation given for harm suffered or damage incurred) (Thomas, 1999). As capitalism developed, selling one's labor to another for pay became a necessity for the many, the only way to prevent starvation, pay the rent, and purchase additional goods.

Unsurprisingly, very few people were in a rush to embrace waged labor. In *The Making of the English Working Class*, E. P. Thompson (1966, p. 599) noted how for 19th-century workers, the "gap in status between a 'servant', a hired wage-laborer subject to the orders and discipline of the master, and an artisan, who might 'come and go' as they pleased, was wide enough for men to shed blood rather than allow themselves to be pushed from one side to the other." In the transition to full-blown industrial capitalism, many workers resisted waged labor and fought to abolish what they called "wage slavery."

Today, though, work as waged labor is ubiquitous in society, in the DMEI as well. The physical and mental effort workers put into producing movies, conducting public opinion polls, or creating ads is often compulsory, not voluntary. It is done for pay, not for freedom. Often, work may be experienced or felt as freedom's opposite. When workers—from the Walt Disney "cast members" laboring in some sweaty Mickey costume at the theme park for $10/hour to the technical support representative for a telecommunications firm servicing angry customers for $15/hour—earn barely enough money to cover their basic living expenses and must work long hours every week to make ends meet without the possibility of improving their quality of life, work is experienced as forced, not freely chosen. All the talk about achieving a healthy "work-life" balance these days is thoughtful but somewhat cheap absent the demand for pay raises for the billions of people reportedly living paycheck to paycheck. Most people work not for self-actualization but for remuneration and typically work on behalf of another entity, like a company or client. For instance, a communications strategist may work for a PR firm whose biggest client is an oil company to pay off a mortgage, not out of enthusiasm for greenwashing. Similarly, an actor might work for a comic book franchise for quick cash rather than artistic fulfillment. Whether full-time, part-time, per gig, or salaried, the notion of work as paid labor is not the only form of work, yet it is the most dominant form in the 21st century. Yet, this often overshadows other important forms of work that are unrecognized and unpaid.

Work as Unpaid Forced Labor

Although "work" frequently refers to paid labor, much valuable work throughout history went unpaid, and even today, there are many forms of unpaid work, including forms of forced labor, reproductive, household and care labor, and voluntary labor. It is not enough to say that work is only what people do in a paid employment relation to someone else, some company or client. After all, many people are working without being paid: caregivers, volunteers, interns, college athletes, artists, coders, and writers.

Meanwhile, a fortunate few are getting paid without working: investors holding stocks and bonds, shareholders accumulating dividends, CEOs enjoying "golden parachutes," trust fund kids living large thanks to the inheritance passed down to them by parents, landlords collecting rent, and IP owners banking royalties. Although many are socialized to see paid employment as the only "real" form of work, a lot of value-adding work is undertaken outside of the formal labor market. Today, the DMEI harnesses unpaid labor to do what it does and, while uncompensated, this work contributes to profits.

One pervasive form of unpaid work is *forced labor*, defined as "all work or service which is exacted from any person under the menace of any penalty and for which the said person has not offered themselves voluntarily" (ILO, 2023). The history of money, and wealth accumulation itself, is intertwined with chattel slavery, serfdom, prison labor, bonded labor, and other forms of involuntary servitude (House & Rashid, 2022; McNally, 2020). Countless people were compelled to do indispensable labor for the building of ancient and modern empires, countries, and cities, yet they were never compensated for it. From antiquity to our time, individuals have been enslaved due to classist and racist ideologies, indebtedness, being captured in war, sold by their own families, penalized by authorities, or simply born the progeny of slaves. Ancient civilizations laid their foundations on the backs of slaves; similarly, the West's capitalist empires were built with forced slave labor. During World War II, the Nazi fascist regime infamously exploited slave labor, most notoriously in Auschwitz. Throughout history, millions have been subjected to slavery's violent and brutal conditions, and forced labor practices persist in various forms today. Yet, slavery in its traditional historical form, as a legalized or openly acknowledged system of forced labor, is generally abolished in most parts of the world. Unfortunately, forced labor still exists in many industries around the world (ILO, 2023), and in the DMEI.

In the Democratic Republic of Congo (DRC), forced labor is intertwined with the capitalist extraction of minerals essential for the production of digital devices such as cobalt (the key component in lithium-ion batteries that power smartphones and laptops) and coltan (integral to electricity storage in the tantalum capacitors in personal computers) (Kara, 2023). Content moderators in the Global South might be coerced by Silicon Valley sub-contractors to work for low to no pay while being exposed to harmful and hateful content with little to no psychological support, nor union protections (Perrigo, 2022, 2023). Freelancers might suffer debt bondage, compelled to service debts to banks and governments through continuous platform work with no hope of financial freedom. Online content creators bound to restrictive contracts that severely limit their autonomy and who are totally dependent on the platforms owned by big companies for a shot at of making a living might be "digital serfs" (Arditi, 2023b; Giblin & Doctorow, 2023). The billions of people logged on to social media platforms right now might be doing a compulsory form of unpaid work. We must use the Internet for communicating, socializing, working, playing, and more; the companies that own the sites we rely on, exploit our interactions for profit (Fuchs & Mosco, 2015a, 2015b; Srnicek, 2017a, 2017b; Zuboff, 2019, 2020).

Work as Unpaid Reproductive Labor

A second form of unpaid work is "reproductive labor," also known as "housework" or "care work" (Baxter & Tai, 2016; Bhattacharya, 2017; Bradley, 2016; Brenner & Ramas, 1984; Dalla Costa & James, 1975; Federici, 2014; Gardiner, 1975; Hartmann, 1976, 1981; Hester & Srnicek, 2023; Laslett & Brenner, 1989; Luxton, 2009; Milkman, 2016; Oakley, 2019). Daily tasks such as grocery shopping, meal preparation, cleaning, child-rearing, and providing emotional support—activities patriarchy traditionally gendered as "female" or "feminine" and expected women to do without pay—sustain the very foundation of capitalism, reproducing the conditions of support for wage-earning men. Mariarosa Dalla Costa and Selma James' (1975) *The Power of Women and the Subversion of the Community* brought to the forefront the paradox of this reproductive labor: vital for capitalism yet unacknowledged and unpaid. For example, in the post-war era, men enjoyed salaried positions as TV broadcasters, film directors, and newspaper editors while women were often expected to remain at home, doing the unpaid reproductive labor of caring for children, managing households, and supporting their husbands' career progress. The entertainment industries contributed to the ideological reproduction of this inequitable division of reproductive labor: TV shows often depicted women as homemakers supporting their breadwinning husbands, magazines targeted women with ads for household products, and movies frequently portrayed women as caregivers and nurturers. Reproductive labor's reinforcement in the household and in media representations perpetuated patriarchal capitalism and also sparked activism such as the International Feminist Collective's "Wages for Housework" campaign, which demanded women be compensated for their domestic labor (Federici, 2014; Toupin, 2018).

Despite some significant changes, the notion of housework as "nonwork" (at least not work deserving pay) lingers in society, as does a gendered and sexualized division of labor, where women are still assumed by sexists to be biologically or naturally inclined to toil in the household while men do otherwise. Men may be contributing to the unpaid tasks of housework and caregiving, but women globally still shoulder the bulk of this unpaid burden, typically performing nearly twice as much of this work—even as they engage in paid labor. In the DMEI, the "double shift" exemplifies the paid and unpaid labor many women do, a situation further intensified by the prevalence of remote work. Female journalists may work tirelessly to meet pressing deadlines, only to face a second round of demands in caregiving at home. Women in advertising may dedicate their day to developing brand campaigns for clients and feel obligated to devote the night to cooking, cleaning, and caring for their families. In the tech industry, the pattern repeats with women software developers switching from a day of programming for pay to evenings spent running their kid's coding camp for free. Despite strides toward gender equality, a patriarchal expectation persists: women who are laboring for wages and climbing the corporate ladder are still weighed down with a disproportionate amount of unwaged reproductive labor at home. This imbalance not only reproduces the cycle of capitalist production but also perpetuates a patriarchal society where men disproportionately benefit from the unpaid labor of women, contributing significantly less in return. Women's movements have changed some things, but the long history of patriarchy is still at work inside and outside the DMEI (Cannizzo & Strong, 2020; Conor et al., 2015; Gregg & Andrijasevic, 2019; Handy & Rowlands, 2014; Hill, 2014a, 2014b; Huws, 2015; Jarrett, 2016; Liddy & O'Brien, 2021; Mayer, 2013; Milestone, 2015; O'Brien, 2019).

Work as Unpaid Volunteer Labor

A third form of unpaid work is volunteerism. Organizations across the economy mobilize the labor of volunteers—individuals who willingly dedicate their time and labor to a good cause without the expectation of financial reward. The US Department of Labor defines a volunteer as "an individual who performs services for civic, charitable, or humanitarian reasons, without promise, expectation, or receipt of compensation for services rendered," also stipulating that a volunteer should not replace a paid employee or fill a role that would typically be remunerated. Despite not being compensated, the labor of volunteers is substantial across the economy. The 2021 *Volunteering in America Report* revealed that 60.7 million adults, constituting 23.2% of the population, volunteered a total of 4.1 billion hours in that year to various organizations and causes—the economic value of this unpaid labor was approximately $122.9 billion (United States Census, 2023).

In the DMEI, the labor of volunteerism is widespread. In the open-source software movement, developers volunteer their time and expertise to software projects without financial compensation. They do everything from making small fixes in code to designing entire software suites, all without pay. On platforms such as Wikipedia, volunteers dedicate countless hours to writing and editing articles. In the gaming industry, beta testers often volunteer to test games, providing valuable feedback to developers, which allows them to polish the final product before releasing it on the market. Also, independent online radio stations or podcasts, as well as film festivals and theatrical events, frequently rely on volunteers who do all kinds of tasks in support of the show. Supporters of certain social causes, charities, or non-profits often volunteer to manage online communities, forums, or pages, like a dedicated Facebook group or a Reddit community, relieving organizations of a paid social media coordinator. Everyone from Hollywood studios to Instagram influencers tap the voluntary labor of fans and online "community members" when encouraging them to promote franchises and brands on their own social media platforms, a free PR service and a cost savings to capital. While people volunteer for a host of reasons, from personal interest to pursuing some larger civic good to acquiring "experience" to put on the resume, the labor they provide adds value to the DMEI. The generous spirit of volunteerism is laudable, but too often, it can be exploited by some organizations that inappropriately use volunteer labor in lieu of hiring paid employees, circumventing labor costs and breaking some labor laws that try to prevent companies from misclassifying paid jobs as volunteer-based positions.

Why Does Work Matter?

Work, Society and Environment

Work matters, labor matters, to human survival. For hundreds of thousands of years, the survival of the human species has been indebted to a cooperative ability to forge new tools from nature and use these to act upon and transform nature. In *De Natura Deorum*, Cicero (1967, p. 271), the Roman philosopher and skeptic, described the human capacity to transform nature into what he called a "second nature": "We sow corn, we plant trees, we fertilize the soil by irrigation, we dam the rivers and direct them where we want. In short, by means of our hands we try to create as it were a second nature within the natural world." Cicero distinguishes between the natural world as it exists before human meddling and the "second nature" that humans produce within it. While chimps and birds use sticks and twigs, they do not fashion these tools to make new tools for drastically altering let alone destroying their habitats. Humans, however, can transform wood into books and minerals into microchips. They make a "second nature." When a dog encounters a rock, it may perceive it merely as an object to pee on or leap over before moving on; in contrast, humans, with their imagination, may see in a rock a multitude of possibilities: a club for war, a brick for building a home, or even a sculpted symbol of themselves. From temples and houses to skyscrapers, and from canals and railways to highways and telecommunications systems, to the satellites orbiting the planet to the videos streaming on YouTube, human labor makes things from nature, producing a "second nature" for living.

Yet, in the age of the Anthropocene or Capitalocene, nature and this "second nature" are interdependent. When human labor transforms the natural world, the resulting second nature, in turn, transforms the first. Capitalist production has long prioritized profit over environmental sustainability, and it has put human labor to work for its relentless drive for economic growth, ceaselessly exploiting people, finite energy systems and resources, leading to ecological degradation, global warming and class inequality (Huber, 2022; Malm, 2016). This is also true of work in the DMEI, which far from being "green and clean," is always immensely resource intensive and environmentally consequential (Maxwell and Miller, 2014, 2023). Just 1 hour of TV, whether it's a drama or a documentary, is estimated to generate 13 metric tons of carbon dioxide. In addition to emitting CO_2, Hollywood movie-making drives pollution (Vaughn, 2019). During the 2017 filming of *Pirates of the Caribbean: Dead Men Tell No Tales* in Queensland, Australia, the crew reportedly dumped chemical waste, contaminating local water sources. Telecommunication systems, essential for activities like calling in sick or working remotely, depend on underwater cables that can disrupt seabed habitats and marine life. The Internet's data centers and AI servers are powered by electricity whose carbon footprint is large and increasing. Far from being virtual, ethereal, or immaterial, all work in the DMEI is embodied, materially embedded, and environmentally consequential. The human species' making of a "second nature" from nature has led to many innovations, but also to many unwise and destructive outcomes. As the most influential species on Earth, it is incumbent upon humans to recognize and reign in the impact of their labors on the planet. With great power comes great responsibility.

In capitalism, this ideal often remains elusive for workers, who may support "degrowth" but lack the decision-making power to enact rapid decarbonization of production and a swift reduction in consumer outputs. Some workers in the DMEI may be environmentally conscious and eager to green their workplace by pressing their employers to divest from fossil capital and enact sustainability policies, but they often find that the CEOs and the shareholders they answer to are resistant to making the necessary changes. "Amazon Employees for Climate Justice" exemplify how workers can collectively organize to challenge their employers' ecological harms, yet also show how companies often ignore their green conscience

(Komenda, 2023). Furthermore, weighed down by the demands of wage labor and sweating the relentless pressure to make ends meet, some workers may not fully acknowledge the environmental consequences of their labor processes and products. Fearing employment deprivation, their immediate focus may be on doing what they've been paid to do, and what they must do to get paid. An Amazon warehouse worker racing against time to fulfill next-day delivery orders may not routinely contemplate this abode's high energy consumption, garbage piles, transport emissions, land usage, habitat disruption, and water pollution. Even when workers do reflect upon what the corporation they labor for *does* to the planet, and the adverse ecological impacts it has, they might find ways of repressing that awareness or rationalizing away the dissonance. After all, quitting a job carries heavy financial risks that most can't afford to take and challenging the CEO's decision will predictably be met with intensified discipline that most wish to avoid. Often, workers do what they feel they must do for the corporations that purchase their labor, not because they want to but for fear of not having enough money to get by if they don't. Freedom from the realm of necessity is a distant utopia for billions toiling right now. Nonetheless, some workers inside and outside the DMEI are organizing for climate justice, pushing companies to prioritize the planet over profit.

Work and Identity: Self, Other, Status, Worldview, Health, and Wellness

For many people, work means more than just the mere act of earning a living; it is entwined with the making and presentation of one's identity and sense of self. This has been a theme in sociological literature since E.C. Hughes (1958) wrote *Men* [sic] *and Their Work*. "What people do is, from their own point of view, the main thing about them," said Hughes, who argued that work was central to shaping how individuals perceive themselves and are perceived by others in society. The Hollywood star, the TikTok micro-celebrity, the PR expert see themselves and are seen as such. Despite the supposed proliferation of post-worker identities, where consumers ostensibly go shopping for the self in the marketplace and assemble a lifestyle from a bunch of branded products and services, the centrality of work to how individuals know themselves and get known by others remains profound, arguably now more than ever. Work's centrality to the making of identity is everywhere: parents guide their children on educational paths aligned with desired future careers ("when I grow up, I want to be…"), setting the stage for adulthood, with identities expressed through the labor process ("I am what I do"). In a society that places a premium on identity, people frequently seek careers that resonate with their ideal self-image, hoping for purpose and fulfillment, as well as recognition by others, in their labor.

In the DMEI, corporations have responded to this with training regimes and management practices aimed at forming workforce identities that conform with and give expression to their own brand identities. They construct ideal-type worker "subject-positions" or points of identification based on their respective "brand identities" and motivate full-time and part-time workers to identify with and perform these through their labor. Apple, Google, Walt Disney, Netflix, and the like, construct brands, inviting and cajoling the workers they employ to live and project the firm's values, mission statements, and products. Yet, the gig economy makes "living the brand" in a singular steady way impossible for the multitude of precariously employed workers competing for online contracts and flexibly adjusting themselves to the demands multiple clients in the DMEI make of them and their labor power. These enterprising workers' sense of self does not derive from one corporation's brand but, instead, is made through "personal branding" practices and performances of the "self-brand" for multiple firms (Burnside, 2014; Duffy & Hund, 2015; Gandini, 2016; Hearn, 2008a; Peters, 1997). Whether living a company's brand or selling one's own (Vallas & Hill, 2018), many still may derive a sense of self from what they do. This is why being without waged work, being unemployed, leaves so many people not only financially adrift but also socially and psychologically unmoored (Sennett, 1998). A YouTuber facing a decline in subscriptions, views, likes, and shares after years of trending might fear obsolescence not just for the loss of income it brings but for the erosion of her self-identity.

Work is also significant to identity by conferring and removing social status and prestige. We are taught to assess our self-worth and that of others based on the type of work performed for others, a topic uncomfortably broached in dinner party conversations through the question, "What do you do?" Although the "doing" typically refers to one's paid occupation, the underlying judgment is rooted in the perceived societal value of that work. Within every division of labor in every corporation, a hierarchy of roles exists, each valued disparately by capital and the wider society, impacting the worker's self-worth (Krauss & Orth, 2022). Historical shifts in the mode of production—from Fordism to post-Fordism—saw the prestige of blue-collar manufacturing work wane while increasing societal value was bestowed upon white-collar and no-collar service professions, resulting in a "hidden injury of class," the internal conflict in the heart and mind of the worker who judges themselves against those whose work and life society has given a special premium to (Sennett & Cobb, 2023). The hidden injuries of class likely persist in the DMEI. In Hollywood, A-list actors and directors often bask in the spotlight, enjoying fame and financial rewards, while sound engineers and grips receive less recognition and lower compensation. The publishing industry follows suit, where accolades for high-profile authors and editors eclipse copyeditors and typesetters. Big Tech CEOs—from Steve Jobs to Elon Musk—are mythologized as geniuses, overshadowing the talent of everyone else. Furthermore, a person's job can shape not just their status but their outlook. PR professionals, tasked with managing and shaping public perceptions, may extend these practices to their personal lives; advertisers who excel in storytelling might view life itself as a story to be told and sold (for whoever pays for it). Marketers, immersed in user data analytics, may approach personal decisions with the same emphasis on metrics and optimization.

Significantly, the conditions of work have serious implications for the workers' psychological and physical wellness. With so much of life lived laboring for an end decided by someone or something else, work is fundamentally intertwined with the workers' overall mental and physical health (or lack of it). The conditions of production can support or undermine the worker's overall wellness (Burgard & Lin, 2013; Prins et al., 2021; Theorell et al., 2015). Safe, fulfilling work conducted at a reasonable pace for decent pay under fair and respectful management can be a source of general wellness. In contrast, dangerous, unfulfilling work under precarious conditions and for low pay and mean management undergird mental and embodied harms. Unfortunately, the DMEI has long been afflicted by conditions that work against the overall wellness of workers. The conditions of work in the movie and TV movie industries are a case in point (Cullins et al., 2020). High performance expectations, public scrutiny, and insufficient support exacerbate isolation, and the troubles of anxiety and depression. *The Looking Glass* survey, conducted by the UK Film and TV Charity, found that nearly 90% of behind-the-scenes workers suffer from mental health issues (Ravindran, 2020). The tech sector faces similar problems (Mentortribes, 2022). A study by the British Interactive Media Association in the UK highlights how workers in this sector are five times more likely to experience depression compared to the general UK population (Johnson, 2019). OSMI (Open Sourcing Mental Illness) reports that a significant 51% of tech professionals have received a mental health diagnosis (Chan, 2020).

How Is Work "Cultural"?

Culture

Beyond these registers of work's significance, work matters because it is "cultural." Raymond Williams (1976, p. 87) described culture as "one of the two or three most complicated words in the English language."

Historically, culture pertained to the tending or cultivation of something, like crops or animals. By the 18th century, the definition of culture had evolved to encompass two key ideas: first, as "a particular way of life, whether of a people, a period, a group, or humanity in general" (Williams, 1976, p. 90); and second, as the "works and practices of intellectual and especially artistic activity" (Williams, 1976, p. 90). While cultures are not static, essential, or unchanging, they frequently exhibit certain residual, dominant, and emergent elements, passed down through various social structures and organizations over time and across space, shaping cultures and peoples. Work can be "cultural" in the two key senses of the term, as part of a whole way of organizational labor and life, and as mental and manual activities that produce and circulate symbolic artifacts and texts that communicate meanings about culture and society that are also consequential to shaping them.

Organizational Ways of Work-Life

In the first sense, an organizational culture of work-life includes norms, values, customs, ideas, and rituals that significantly shape the conditions and experiences of workers in a broad or narrow sense. While national work culture *norms* differ (e.g., Japan, China, and Sweden do not exhibit identical work cultures), those from countries like the US exert significant global influence, with American corporate governance structures and management practices exported and adopted worldwide. Yet, these norms can also vary by industry and firm. For example, the gaming industry often normalizes "crunch time," periods of intense work without overtime pay, while companies like Google, Apple, and Meta Platforms, despite their geographical proximity, maintain distinct organizational cultures based on their brands. Moreover, industries and companies may express *values* that guide their workforce's conduct. In Silicon Valley, the emphasis on laissez-faire capitalism and disruptive innovation drives companies and financialized startups to push boundaries. *Customs*, such as those in Hollywood where the Oscars and Emmys serve as both competitions and celebrations, reinforce the artistic and societal value of the entertainment industry. Additionally, work cultures embody specific *ideas* about a labor process and its product. Everyone from online creators to documentary movie-makers cherishes "storytelling" as a tool for societal change, perhaps believing that what they do and the narratives they script and tell will make world a better place. Ideas like individualism, freedom of expression, and meritocracy may contrast with realities of conformity, censorship, and entrenched hierarchies. Finally, work cultures entail *rituals* unique to each occupation. On a movie set, the crew prepares equipment before shooting; novelists adhere to dedicated writing routines; and, PR professionals begin their day with a "morning media monitor" to track client coverage. Studying the ways of work and life by sector, industry, firm, and occupation can illuminate the similarities and differences in the conditions and experiences of workers, both individually and collectively.

Texts That Communicate Meaning

Work is "cultural" in the second sense because it is essential to the production and circulation of texts that communicate meanings about culture and which represent, underrepresent, and misrepresent society (Hesmondhalgh, 2018; Kendall, 2005; Kirshner, 2024; Kumar, 2007; Martin, 2019; Murray & Ouellette, 2009; Ouellette & Hay, 2009; Polson et al., 2021; Puette, 1992; Skeggs & Wood, 2011; Wagner, 2014). Workers produce novels, plays, artworks, news stories, TV series, movies, podcasts, video games, ads, and online content that say something about the world. These texts are not mirrors that reflect reality. Instead, they represent reality in partial and selective ways and, when doing so, may construct and normalize certain perceptions, feelings, thoughts, and behaviors. These representations may intersect with and amplify regressive and progressive ideas about humanity and identity, about race, gender, class, religion, and lifestyle, about national self and other, about war and peace, about the environment, and more. They may reinforce or reject the dominant ideologies of a society, uphold or challenge specific discourses and practices of classism, racism, sexism, nationalism, militarism, and imperialism, affirm the status quo, or cheer dissent against it. Furthermore, they can even take sides in the "culture wars" of an age, register and respond to the hopes and fears of workers, and interrogate the changing conditions and experiences of work itself. For example, Amelia Horgan's novel, *Lost in Work: Escaping Capitalism*, decimates the ideology of meritocracy that normalizes so many bad jobs. TV series like *The Office* or *Silicon Valley* probe the absurdities of work. *Sorry to Bother You* (2018), directed by Boots Riley—an East Bay hip-hop artist and anti-racist community organizer—satirizes the classism, racism, and sexism in the DMEI. Apple TV's *Severance* addresses the worker's alienation in capitalism, and gives expression to the desire to separate work and life in our tech-entangled world of 24/7 labor processes (Flisfeder, 2022; Sowell, 2024).

Whether ideologically backing the status quo or addressing working-class experiences of life and labor in capitalism, the media texts that workers in the DMEI produce can tell their readers, listeners, viewers, and users what topics to think about and how to think about them. *Agenda setting* is a process through which media texts legitimize certain topics for public discourse by telling people what they are supposed to be thinking about, though not necessarily dictating how they think. For example, when the *New York Times* covered the 2023 Writers Guild of America strike, it told its readers that this event was worthy of their attention and thought. Similarly, CNN's coverage of challenges faced by gig economy workers on platforms, such as Uber, tells the viewer this is indeed an important issue to ponder. When a prominent BreadTuber rages against workplace racism and sexism at major tech companies, they draw their community's attention to intersectional inequities prevalent in Silicon Valley. In contrast to agenda setting, *Framing* refers to how media texts may influence how people think about and interpret what is represented. When a news story about a workers' strike against Verizon quotes management's justification for outsourcing and cuts to benefits and pensions and excludes the workers' voices, it subtly suggests that Telco capital's viewpoint is more legitimate than that of the labor force, thereby shaping the reader's perception of the event, and cuing the right side to take in the conflict. Similarly, when an ad for Uber portrays its drivers as upwardly mobile and freewheeling entrepreneurs, it glosses over the perils and pitfalls of laboring for and through this app in the so-called "gig economy," such as these workers' misclassification as independent contractors, inconsistent income streams, and lack of benefits (Rodino-Colocino et al., 2021; Schor, 2020; Woodcock & Graham, 2019).

In summary, workers within the DMEI are not only shaped by whole organizational ways of labor and life but also produce and circulate a wide range of media texts that engage in agenda setting (telling people what topics to think about) and framing (telling people how to think about these topics). In this way, the worker labor practices that make texts about culture and society may shape culture and society. Their labor is sometimes even hired to produce stories about and images of work within the DMEI, and across the whole economy. Overall, work matters to culture; it is part and product of a whole way of life (and of organizational work cultures) and is also the source of innumerable texts that say something about the world (including the world of work).

How Does Work Connect to Time and Space?

In addition to being "cultural," work matters because it shapes and reshapes the worker's relationship to time and space, two fundamental dimensions of the human experience.

Work and Time

Every occupation, career, job, and gig is structured around or presumes a specific temporal order or time-sensibility, and these influence workers' labor processes and experiences (Brogan, 2021; Cote & Harris, 2021; Crary, 2013; Gregg, 2018; Hester & Srniceck, 2023; McCallum, 2020; Sharma, 2014; Vernace, 2020; Wajcman, 2016, 2019a, 2019b; Weststar & Dubois, 2022). Timekeeping was once predominantly based on natural phenomena, such as the position of the sun, but the Industrial Revolution brought fourth clock time and the social construction of universal standard units of seconds, minutes, and hours, furnishing capital with a way to manage labor's work time (Hermann, 2014; Thompson, 1967; Wajcman, 2016, 2019a, 2019b). Clock time ticked in mechanical and pendulum clocks and then the large factory clocks that loomed over workers, subordinating them to capital's new regime of measurable labor-time. Time recorders, where workers punched in and out at the start and end of each shift at the factory, further emphasized capital's time control, while tower clocks extended time discipline beyond the walls of the factory to encompass entire communities. These timekeeping technologies were wielded by companies to instill time discipline in workers, to regulate and control labor processes, and to ensure one's punctuality supported another's profit. Managers conceptualized tasks as functions of time, standardized them, scheduled them, and monitored their execution by workers. Pay for work itself was based on time units, such as hourly or daily rates.

The Industrial Revolution introduced a fundamental shift in the social experience of time and today, capitalism's clock, incessantly ticking, now dominates globally, with corporations applying more invasive technologies to workers to monitor and control labor-time: biometric clocks employing facial, voice, or fingerprint recognition, timed task tracking software, apps that record keystrokes, web search and site visits and wearable tech that records the workers' heartbeats to breathing patterns. Some workers will opt into these labor-time surveillance systems, especially those who embrace the self-mastery of time as a virtue, "a framework for living ethically through work" and ensuring hyper-productivity to fill "the spiritual void of profit-driven corporate culture" (Gregg, 2018, pp. 8–9). In the DMEI, time-based waged labor is still paramount. But pay for time exists alongside pay for task. In this model, workers are compensated for specific tasks or project milestones, rather than the hours spent. This is common among freelancers like writers, graphic designers, and coders on platforms like Upwork or Fiverr, where payment is tied to the completion of a task rather than time spent doing it.

Whether paid for time put in or task put out, workers are expected by corporations to devote more and more of their lifetime to laboring in exchange for the money they need to make their way in the world. In a 1748 essay titled "Advice to a Young Tradesman, Written by an Old One," Benjamin Franklin declared "time is money," and the idea that much of lifetime should involve laboring for money continues to be widespread

(Chayka, 2017). Furthermore, the experience of labor-time has for many workers been one of speeding up, with corporations demanding faster and faster production (Gleick, 1999). "Turnover time" is the duration it takes for corporation to complete a cycle of investment and return, and in pursuit of maximal profit, corporations are striving to minimize the time between production (the time it takes to produce a good or service) and circulation and consumption (the time it takes for the commodity to be sold). As corporations compete for profit with others, they speed up labor processes, pressing workers to complete more tasks in shorter timeframes (McCallum, 2020). Workers are laboring at higher speeds or faster paces to tighter and tighter deadlines, a clear intensification of the labor process for millions perhaps billions, especially those workers networked with ICTs (Wajcman, 2015, p. 95). Software developers iterate code quickly to keep up with shrinking update cycles, movie crews compress shooting schedules for faster content production, and YouTubers record, edit, and release content at a quickening pace to stay relevant. To keep up with these intensifying labor processes, workers are also adopting time-saving tactics, subscribing to self-help for efficient task management, opting for meal prep kits to reduce unpaid cooking time so more is leftover for paid tasks, and taking on back-to-back virtual meetings through scheduling apps that "codify contemporary ideals about efficient time management" (Wajcman, 2019a, p. 1272).

While it's true that labor processes are accelerating, time—whether objectively imposed by management or subjectively experienced and even resisted—is rarely one-dimensional (Sharma, 2014). Different corporations design occupations with distinct "time orders" to be adhered to by workers, shaping their experiences and expectations around work time and tasks. For example, software designers often operate under project-based timelines with milestones, movie and TV producers adhere to strict shooting schedules with set start and end dates, and PR specialists juggle short-term responses to immediate media inquiries and long-term campaign planning. Time may always be a "problem" in the study of society (Bergmann, 1992), but regardless of its complexity, in capitalism, the labor processes of billions of workers are structured by capital's ticking clock. Yet, time is also a site of conflict between managers and workers, marked by disagreements and clashes over the value of time-based labor, work hours and overtime, time-monitoring technologies, scheduling practices, leave policies, and the pressure to maintain a fast-paced work environment without adequate breaks or rest.

Work time has long been a site of contestation and conflict between capital and labor. Unions used time-slogans like "Eight Hours for Work, Eight Hours for Rest, Eight Hours for What We Will!" to advocate for the 8-hour workday and "A Fair Day's Pay for a Fair Day's Work" to demand compensation commensurate with the workers' effort exerted in a day's labor-time. Workers' movements have achieved significant time victories, such as the 8-hour workday, the weekend, paid vacation, sick leave, maternity and paternity leave, and more. Yet, the battle over time continues. Despite technologically determinist dreams of increased leisure time thanks to automation, workers are laboring more not less than before (McCallum, 2020). In the US, the 1938 Fair Labor Standards Act established a 40-hour workweek, yet today, American workers, on average, clock around 1750 hours annually. Workers in some countries like China and India exceed 2100 hours per year! (International Labour Organization, 2023). The corporation's attempt to exert greater control over the worker's labor and lifetime has diminished the modicum of a "work-life" balance. Many find themselves burdened with extended work hours, while simultaneously struggling to adapt to their employers' just-in-time scheduling practices and more recently, zero-hour contracts. The expansion of labor-time has also eroded the workers' civic time, shrinking the time available to meaningfully and purposefully participate in democracy (McCallum, 2020). In response, there is a demand for a reduction of work time and increase in pay, new work-sharing arrangements to spread work between more workers, and a shorter working week with ample time for meeting social needs (Stronge & Lewis, 2021).

Work and Space

Just as work matters because it is intertwined with a society's hegemonic concept of time, it also matters because it is interconnected with the social relations of space and place (Coleman, 2016; Gregg, 2011; Hester & Srniceck, 2023; Hochschild, 1997; Reichenberger, 2018; Saval, 2014). In *The Production of Space*, Henri Lefebvre (1991) argued that space is a social construct and emphasized how spaces are designed, built, experienced, shaped, and reshaped by choices made by humans, some at least. Lefebvre declared that the production of space is not a value neutral project but a political one: "space is political. Space is not a scientific object removed from ideology or politics; it has always been political and strategic.... Space ... is a social product. The production of space can be likened to the production of any particular type of merchandise" (Lefebvre, 1991, p. 341). Lefebvre was concerned with how so many of the spaces produced prioritize relations of production, circulation, and consumption over alternative logics, thereby expanding capitalism and its prevailing class inequities and oppressions and diminishing the spaces in society produced for human emancipation. Lefebvre offered three ways of thinking about space, and these can be adapted for the spatial study of work: *representations of space* (the space of work conceptualized by architect labor: Googleplex was conceived by Clive Wilkinson Architects in collaboration with STUDIOS Architecture); *spatial practice* (the workers' labor practices in a physical workspace: what workers are doing at the Googleplex, in open-plan offices, private meeting rooms, at treadmill desks, and in cafeterias, gardens, art zones, and games rooms); and *representational spaces* (the meaningful and symbolic dimensions of spaces experienced and made by workers: the thoughts, feelings, and perceptions workers have of the space of Googleplex, and the representations they make of it).

All work in the DMEI takes place in produced spaces. Some workers are paid to produce the spaces other workers labor within and struggle over: factories, studios, offices, co-working zones, and more. All too often, the spaces of work express the logics and values of capitalism and play a role in managing the identities and bodies of workers, for ends related to optimal production and maximal profit. But just as different organizations and occupations may exhibit different time orders, the spatial orders of firms and careers are not singular in capitalism, but variable and shifting. Take, for example, the design and configuration of workspaces in motion picture studios and iPhone factories: each workspace as conceived, used, and experienced represents the specific needs and ethos of their respective industries. A motion picture studio is a hub of specialized spaces for film production: soundproofed shooting stages, video editing suites, areas for costume and makeup, props storage, script readings, and rehearsals. An iPhone factory like Foxconn in China epitomizes industrial efficiency: segmented zones for assembly, quality control testing, and packaging. In the online spaces of work—websites, platforms, and digital games—workers labor alone and frequently together from diverse locations, including homes and co-working spaces spread across cities, nations, and continents. The space of remote work has become ubiquitous: through mobile devices and laptop computers, workers are tethered to their employers, contractors, and clients and expected to work "anytime" and from "anywhere." But even when coordinated through the space of Internet apps, websites, and platforms, all work is undertaken by people in concrete places: Turkers toil for Requesters seated at desks in front of computers plugged into outlets wired to specific residential electricity grids; couriers for SkipThe-Dishes on bikes, peddling, moving, steering, eyes on road and digital map, dodging potholes, ice patches, and mud puddles, transporting food directly from restaurants to app users' homes; competitive gamers in Fortnite or League of Legends, eyes fixed on their avatars, hands manipulating joysticks. No labor is truly immaterial or online-only; all takes place in a produced physical space.

Work always happens in a specific location, and workspace design can impact the worker in a range of ways. A well-designed workspace can diminish stress, boost comfort, and foster a positive mood, while a poorly designed one can cause physical and mental strain, frustration, and anger. The workspace design plays a role in the worker's conditions and experiences of labor, their sense of self, and their overall wellness. For this reason, the workspace is not just a practical or value-neutral matter but can be a physical manifestation of the balance of power between capital and labor in an organization, or in society. The workspace design can reinforce the status quo, challenge it, or express a negotiated class compromise. Because workspaces are produced and managed in ways that may side with the interests of capital or labor, they have a politics. Just as workers have long clashed with corporations over matters of labor-time, the space of work is also a perennial arena of class contestation covering everything from on-site health and safety conditions to management's allocation of office space as a status symbol to reward some workers for a job well done and to punish other workers for not doing enough. Furthermore, it is in the place of spaces—shop floors, office buildings, warehouses, retail outlets, and platforms—where labor and capital frequently conflict over all kinds of material and symbolic resources, including space itself.

What Motivates People to Work?

Subsistence: Work to Live

In capitalism, people must work to get the money they need to meet their basic needs. For many, the need to provide for oneself and one's family is a potent motivator for seeking out and doing paid work for others. The worker labors for money, something which has nothing to do with the actual work performed nor the utility or cost of the good or service they produce. Even ostensibly "creative" people frequently find themselves doing what they do because they must, not because it is liberating (Graeber, 2018). Absent a social wage or an extensive social democratic welfare state, people are compelled to undertake waged labor to meet their basic needs. In *The Problem with Work*, Kathi Weeks (2011) scrutinizes this societal expectation to work for wages and the stigmatization faced by those who don't. Even more egregious is how many full-time workers are not paid enough to cover living costs, and so turn to loans and credit cards, only to end up working even more to pay down the debt's principal and interest. In sum, the "dull compulsion of necessity" pushes people into waged work, even in the DMEI. Yet, the motivation to work in the DMEI cannot be solely ascribed to subsistence alone.

Consumerism: Work to Shop

In capitalism, consumption has become a potent driver of production, propelling people into waged work not merely for subsistence but to fulfill an ever-expanding array of manufactured wants and desires (Slater, 1997). Billions in consumer expenditure each year go to non-essential goods that have no connection to real needs. Many people labor intensively, not for essentials they lack, but for non-essentials they believe they want: fast fashion, brand-new cars, the latest iPhone. But as John Kenneth Galbraith (1958) pointed out in *The Affluent Society*, "wants" are not made by consumers but by advertisers, who, on behalf of larger industrial clients, preside over the "machinery for consumer-demand creation": "wants are increasingly created by the process by which they are satisfied." Advertising constructs as opposed to merely reflects the consumer's existing wants and in 2023, corporations spent nearly $875 billion on advertising their goods and services, paying advertising companies for the service of making commodity images for them, influencing the perceptions and behaviors of consumers, and leveraging social media platforms to sell. People will sometimes take extra shifts, work a part-time job on the side of a full-time one, and end up working more, not less, in order to make more money to spend on things they don't need, but have been convinced they want. Workers in the DMEI produce abundant wants—movies, TV series, and games. They also consume them. The irony is not lost when a game developer plays a video game for relaxation, or when a reality TV editor unwinds by watching reality TV. In sum, the many allures and gratifications of the consumer culture is a potent motivator for the daily drudgery and grind of waged work.

Intrinsic-Extrinsic Rewards: Work for Meaning and Compensation

Even still, work is driven by more than wants. People also work in pursuit of a meaningful life. Many who do work for wages, even those who can afford not to, find reasons beyond money to keep at it. People may be drawn to work in the cultural industries, not because it offers high pay or stability but because it offers the possibility of autonomy, self-realization, and recognition (Hesmondhalgh, 2019, p. 352). The motivation to work frequently reflects a balance between *extrinsic rewards*, such as a wage or salary, and *intrinsic rewards*, like the satisfaction derived from a meaningful activity. Reflective of the degradation of so much work in capitalism, a *Harvard Business Review* study found that many professionals would choose to forego a higher salary if that meant more meaningful work (Achor et al., 2018). Of the 2285 workers across 26 fields encompassing a range of pay scales, company sizes, and demographics surveyed, 90% said they would willingly accept a lower income if they could do work that was more meaningful to them. On average, these workers were prepared to sacrifice 23% of their total future earnings for the opportunity to labor in harmony with their values. The study also revealed a big gap between these workers' aspirations for meaningful work and its availability, as a mere 5% of respondents considered their jobs highly meaningful. The phenomena of meaningless work in capitalism is widespread. In *Bullshit Jobs*, David Graeber (2018) lambasted the pointless and inherently useless nature of many waged positions: flunkies, goons, duct tapers, box tickers, and taskmasters. He argues that these types of jobs contribute no real value or meaning to anyone nor society, and yet, they grow.

Love: Work for Passion

The idea of "labor of love," or the prospect of doing what one loves for a living, may also play a role in motivating people to work. Steve Jobs, in his renowned 2005 Stanford Commencement Address, emphasized the importance of loving what you do to achieve greatness. Many people describe their dedication to their professions as "a labor of love," suggesting that what they do for a living is driven by their passion rather than the mere pursuit of the money needed to live. However, in the DMEI, the call to pursue one's passion through work can be used by companies to justify low to no wages, long hours, and precarious employment. "In the Name of Love," Miya Tokumitsu (2014) challenges this "Do What You Love" (DWYL) slogan, prompting us to consider who truly benefits when low to no waged labor for others is perceived by workers who do it as a personal passion project rather than value-adding labor that should be recognized as such and fairly compensated. Tokumitsu says DWYL is classist, as the pursuit of passion over a paycheck is unaffordable to most: "Those in the lovable work camp are vastly more privileged in terms of wealth, social status, education, society's racial biases, and political clout.... For those forced into unlovable work, it's a different story." Brooke Erin Duffy's *(Not) Getting Paid to Do What You Love* (2017) likewise advances a powerful critique of the DWYL ideal through 56 in-depth interviews with "fashion and lifestyle bloggers, video bloggers (or vloggers), do-it-yourself (or DIY) fashion/jewelry designers, participants in fashion networking sites," and "street-style photographers" (p. x). In *Work Won't Love You Back: How Devotion to Our Jobs Keeps Us Exploited, Exhausted, and Alone*, Sarah Jaffe (2021) also deconstructs the DWYL narrative surrounding and mystifying so much work. She states, "The labor of love ethic ensures that we expect to work for the sheer joy of it and makes any work that is not done out of passion suspect." While desiring and pursuing work that aligns with one's passion and love is understandable (only masochists might willingly seek out jobs that are disgusting and loathsome), most people work because they must to survive; unfortunately, real opportunities to love one's labor and get paid are few.

Hope and Aspiration: Work for Future Rewards

"Hope labor" refers to how people may be motivated to work without pay in the present in anticipation of gaining future opportunities for compensation. Kuehn and Corrigan (2013) define "hope labour" as "un- or under-compensated work carried out in the present, often for experience or exposure, in the hope that future employment opportunities may follow" (p. 9). Kuehn and Corrigan (2013) isolate "hope"—the prospect of a future that is more desirable, fulfilling, or better—as something that positively motivates workers to do (and consent to) exploitative unwaged labor in the present (pp. 16–17). They theorize hope dialectically; it is a resource of human emancipation that may motivate workers to imagine and struggle for a future beyond capitalism, and also, an ideology that that may reproduce capitalist exploitation and oppression by motivating workers to chase an ever-elusive better future instead of struggling to transform bad present conditions (p. 17). Another useful temporal concept for understanding what motivates work is "aspirational labour," defined by Duffy (2017, p. 4) as "a mode of (mostly) uncompensated, independent work that is propelled by the much-venerated ideal of getting paid to do what you love." According to Duffy, "aspirational labor" is "both a practice and a worker ideology" that "shifts content creators' focus from the present to the future, dangling the prospect of a career where labor and leisure coexist" (p. 4). Like hope labor, "aspirational labor" instills in workers the expectation "that they will one day be compensated for their productivity—be it through material rewards or social capital" (pp. 4–5). Most of the time, though, this aspirational labor does not "pay off."

Cruel in its optimism and disappointing in outcome, hope labor and aspirational labor abound: unpaid interns labor to gain "experience" they believe will lead to future paid employment; authors write stories and make them accessible to anyone in the hopes that this self-promotion will lead to a paid book contract; on Instagram and YouTube, influencers and creators produce a massive amount of audio-visual content for free, hoping to attract an audience substantial enough to sell merch and generate ad revenue. Within the DMEI, hope and aspiration are hegemonic motivators of maximal self-exploitation. Too often, corporations leverage the worker's dream (or desperation) for a future paid job to serve their bottom line in the present, without ever paying them, deflecting attention away from this cost-saving strategy.

Toward Post-Work? Idleness, Refusals, and Great Resignations

In *The German Ideology*, Karl Marx (1845) described how capitalism established a division of labor in a wide range of companies, confining individual workers to an "exclusive sphere of activity" that they must labor within to make ends meet, and in some ways, trapping humans in rigid roles that limit their potential. Today, a worker might find themselves stuck in the role of a customer support representative, data entry clerk, production assistant, or copy editor, and must remain there if they do not wish to lose their means of making a living. Yet, Marx dreamed of a post-capitalist society in which "nobody has one exclusive sphere of activity but each can become accomplished in any branch they wish," making it possible for people to do "one thing today and another tomorrow," perhaps, to communicate with strangers in the morning, process data after lunch, hang around the movie set in the afternoon, and correct the proofs of great books after dinner but without ever becoming a customer support representative, data entry clerk, production assistant or copy editor. Despite being bolstered by ideals of flexibility, capitalism continues to press many individuals into specific and often rigid occupational roles that rule their lives. Whether someone is a content creator, a social media manager, a game developer, a virtual reality designer, an influencer, a podcast producer, or an Uber driver, they for a large part of their waking and sleeping lives, are reduced to this role in order to sustain their livelihood. However, in a different society, where no one is confined to a single occupation (or compelled to chase many meaningless gigs) to make ends meet, individuals would have the freedom to explore various parts of themselves, and self-actualize. A person could create a YouTube video in the morning, code a game in the afternoon, design a virtual world in the evening, produce a podcast after dinner, and engage in social media strategy late at night, pursuing different interests as they desire, without being permanently reduced to any one job.

Despite its technological advancements, the 21st century's digital society is very far from a post-capitalist utopia where individuals, free from the realm of necessity, explore their potential and self-actualize through their labor process and the products of their labor. In this digital society, a pervasive overwork culture makes it difficult for many to imagine life beyond the confines of specific roles in a division of labor, paid or otherwise. Waged work is a major force in the lives of billions, its grip seemingly tightening with each passing day. This necessity of and obsession with paid work has saturated global consciousness, influencing public education, shaping families, absorbing the pursuit of leisure, and eroding democracy. Business magnates celebrate grueling production schedules as a mark of honor, governments laud the virtues of "industrious families," and entertainment represents self-exploitation as fun and games. Yet, the centrality of waged work to modern life has been contested by thinkers who demand a society without it. Proponents of post-work philosophy argue that a life with less—or even without—waged work could be more fulfilling for all. They trouble waged work's necessity and advance alternative visions of a good life.

In "The Right To Be Lazy," Paul Lafargue (1883) decried waged work, chastising the union movements of his era for fighting to reduce instead of abolish it all together: "It is sheer madness, that people are fighting for the 'right' to an eight-hour working day," he said. In "Useful Work versus Useless Toil," William Morris (1885) envisioned a future without meaningless work. "In Praise of Idleness," Bertrand Russell (1932) argued for the drastic increase of leisure time and reduction of labor-time as the path to human happiness: "Modern methods of production have given us the possibility of ease and security for all; we have chosen, instead, to have overwork for some and starvation for others." In his 1930 essay *Economic Possibilities for our Grandchildren*, John Maynard Keynes (2010) speculated that automation would reduce the time of the workweek to 15 hours, heralding an age of abundant leisure. André Gorz (1982), in *Farewell to the Working Class*, expanded on the possibility of a post-work society supported by automation, arguing that the diminishing centrality of human labor to capitalist production prefigured a post-work future: "The abolition of work is a process already underway…. The manner in which [it] is to be managed … constitutes the central political issue of the coming decades." In "The Abolition of Work," Bob Black (1985) excoriated waged labor: "No one should ever work. Work is the source of nearly all the misery in the world."

In the aftermath of the Occupy Wall Street movement, post-work arguments proliferated. In *The Problem with Work*, Kathi Weeks (2011) scrutinized the societal norm of waged work as an inherent social and political good, and encouraged us to think about life's possibilities, without always reducing them to work. "[W]hen we have no memory or little imagination of an alternative to a life centered on work," wrote Weeks (2011), "there are few incentives to reflect on why we work as we do and what we might wish to do instead." Society's obsession with a waged work-centric life limits our potential and diminishes our capacity to imagine and make alternative futures real. Nonetheless, hope for a world without work is not lost. In *The Refusal of Work*, David Frayne (2015) argued the acceleration of automation and the exacerbation of the global environmental crisis is forcing governments, corporations, and everyone to consider alternative futures, one without work as we know it. Furthermore, a post-work ethos manifested in "The Great Resignation" of the COVID-19 pandemic. The massive number of workers leaving their jobs to reflect upon the meaning of life, and pursue more meaningful opportunities, pointed to people's dream of exodus to a world beyond capital and its control of alienating waged labor. Post-work philosophy is real, in mind and practice, a growing trend among people young and old who are disillusioned with what capitalism has made of work and tried to make of them (Nguyen, 2022). Workers of all ages have experienced bad jobs, bullshit jobs, horrible jobs, and many are becoming vocal about this social problem on the Internet, manifesting in anti-work memes ("Monday Blues"), hashtags (#AntiWork and #WorkSucks) and community forums (Reddit r/antiwork and r/workreform). The Internet has provided many workers with a platform vent labor grievances, seek out and find solidarity, and satirize and subvert the status quo of the corporate workplace.

While post-work philosophy and political practices are expanding, work continues to be a social fact. More so than ever. In this next chapter, we look at the DMEI, an expanding super-sector of work—waged and unwaged, precarious and standard, sometimes creative but mostly standardized, potentially self-actualizing and still alienating, and all the varied experiences of life and labor in between.

2 What Are the Digital Media and Entertainment Industries (DMEI)?

15 Convergent Industry Groups, Central to Work in the Digital Society

Introduction

This chapter opens with a very brief overview of human work and labor in the cultural industries, introduces the "digital society" and defines the digital media and entertainment industries (DMEI) using the North American Industry Classification System (NAICS) codes. The DMEI encompasses 15 interconnected industry groupings: (1) Computer and Electronic Manufacturing; (2) Telecommunications; (3) Computing Infrastructure, Data Processing, Web Hosting, and Search; (4) Software Publishing (Video Games, Apps, and Programs); (5) Broadcasting and Content Provider Industries; (6) Motion Picture and Video; (7) Sound Recording; (8) Advertising, PR, and Marketing; (9) Traditional Publishing (Newspapers, Books, Magazines); (10) Performing Arts, Spectator Sports, and Other; (11) Photography and Image-Making; (12) Toys; (13) Amusement and Theme Parks; (14) Online Creator/Influencer; and (15) Education. The DMEI augments the cultural industries concept to register convergence, the shift from analog to digital, and the digitization of "culture." After defining the DMEI, the chapter describes how the DMEI relates to work as (1) a source of employment, occupations, and jobs; (2) a disruptor of traditional occupations and jobs; (3) an incubator for new and emerging industries and occupations; (4) a producer of new means of production, or new tools; (5) a producer of new tools and systems of managerial control; (6) a demander of new labor power; (7) a catalyst for educational and state reforms; and (8) a supporter of state economic development plans, place-making, and branding.

Culture Inc.: A Very Brief History of Human Work and Labor in the Cultural Industries

For centuries, the production and circulation of informational and cultural goods has relied on the labor of humans, and organizations from states

DOI: 10.4324/9781003131076-3

to religious entities to companies have paid humans to combine their knowledge and skill with various tools to create symbolic works that communicate meaning about society. From the Middle Ages to the Renaissance (5th–15th century), kings, queens, and nobility commissioned artisans to produce artworks representing idealized images of themselves, symbolizing their wealth and status: the Italian statesman Lorenzo "The Magnificent" was painted in 1560 by the artist Agnolo Bronzino on commission to the powerful Medici family. The church also contracted out various creative services, paying artisans to paint religious figures, such as the Virgin Mary, Christ, and various saints. By the late 16th and early 17th centuries, artisans like William Shakespeare were earning a living not only via patronage to elite organizations but also as a shareholder, entrepreneur, and worker for his own company. His King's Men Theatre staged and sold tickets to plays, including comedies like *A Midsummer Night's Dream*, tragedies such as *Hamlet*, and historical dramas like *Richard III*. From the royal court to mass public, these works thrilled audiences and put money in Shakespeare's pocket.

The 18th century's "Age of Enlightenment" saw the growth of capitalism, the common press, and the spread of literacy, undergirding the expansion of modern news and literary publishing industries. Copyright law, established by Britain's Statute of Anne in 1710, recognized the moral and economic rights of authors and publishers and granted them exclusive rights to sell their cultural works in the market for a limited time. Firms owned by prominent 18th-century literary publishers such as Andrew Millar and Thomas Cadell mass reproduced and sold works by authors like David Hume, Edward Gibbon, and Samuel Johnson. In this era, the "author-function" was taking hold, linking texts to specific individuals, responsible for them and their uses. A writer like Daniel Defoe cobbled together a living from many sources: advance payments and royalties from publishers for his *Robinson Crusoe*, fees and commissions for essays written to be sold to newspapers and magazines, and payments for the labor he did as an editor and journalist. From London to Paris, formal art training academies started to grow, cultivating more professional artists keen to produce works for an "art market" comprised of dealers, auction houses, and galleries (the Paris Salon, a notable example). Wolfgang Amadeus Mozart and Ludwig van Beethoven composed classical musical masterpieces, while Denis Diderot and Jean le Rond d'Alembert's *Encyclopedie* spread new knowledge far and wide.

During the 19th century's Industrial Revolution, an age of Euro colonial-imperial conquest and destruction, the rise of factories and mass proletarianization gave rise to a middle and working class with disposable income to spend and leisure time to spare, increasing demand for more cultural and informational goods. More and more "artistic" workers broke their dependence on aristocratic and religious patronage only to become more dependent on the corporate organizations that paid them to produce and distribute symbolic works for sale to markets of mass consumers. Mass circulation newspapers such as *The New York Herald* and magazines like *The Saturday Evening Post* employed many workers, and the literary industries also grew, publishing and marketing novels like Charles Dickens' *Oliver Twist* (1837) and Charlotte Brontë's *Jane Eyre* (1847). The spread of sheet music and the piano in homes, coupled with the building of concert halls, broadened the appeal of music-making as a career path and music-listening as a consumable pleasure. Commercial theater, opera, ballet, and art galleries flourished, and photographers strove to make a living selling their portraiture services to notable people, including artists and authors.

By the early 20th century, the corporatization of the cultural industries intensified (Horkheimer and Adorno, 1995). To land a job in the corporations at the base of them or to set out as an independent artist, people were professionalizing, honing creative and artistic knowledge and skills. A growing number of people sought to become artists and advance their careers by enrolling in art schools across the United States (e.g., the Art Students League of New York, Pennsylvania Academy of the Fine Arts, and the School of the Art Institute of Chicago) and Europe (e.g., the Royal Academy of Arts in London, the École des Beaux-Arts in Paris, and the Academy of Fine Arts in Munich). These schools attracted students from around the world, who frequently aligned their outlook and labor process with the whims and currents of the cultural marketplace.

At the same time, many people were being trained as workers for the new enterprises of the mass media and cultural industries, not by universities or colleges, but on the job. Aspiring journalists often began their careers as apprentices or reporters at newspapers, like *The New York Times* or *The Chicago Tribune*, which ran their own training programs and editorial schools. Budding filmmakers worked as assistants or technicians in early studios, such as those of Thomas Edison or the Biograph Company, while Hollywood's emerging studios served as a key training ground. Aspiring radio professionals gained experience by working at radio stations, such as WEAF in New York, or attending trade schools and programs, such as the Radio Institute of America. Much of the early labor force training for these industries occurred in corporate workplaces and trade schools.

As demand for the labor power of these types of workers increased, radio broadcasting surged, employing technical staff, scriptwriters, journalists, and entertainers to make programs and deliver ad messages to the ear. The photography industries launched new careers in photojournalism. The film industry expanded, transitioning from silent films to talkies, with Hollywood establishing itself as the world's premier movie production hub, entertaining audiences with works like *Modern Times*, *The Wizard of Oz*, and Walt Disney's animations like *Dumbo*. The comic book industry grew as well, with Action Comics introducing *Superman* in 1938, and Detective Comics debuting *Batman* in 1939, hiring writers and illustrators. The advertising industry, led by the J. Walter Thompson Company, expanded to prime consumer demand, and ad workers were paid to make brand images for everything from Rice Krispies cereal to Ford automobiles. From the post-World War II era forward, with the economic and military expansion of the US Empire, the cultural industries continued to grow, along with new occupations in music, TV broadcasting, ICTs, and video games. By the early 21st century, the Internet and social media platforms turned their users into a producer and a consumer of digital content while establishing new careers for online creators and influencers (Cunningham and Craig, 2019, 2021; Poell et al., 2021).

Suffice to say, the production and circulation of informational and cultural goods has always relied on the labor of humans. Humans, whether as independent creators on contract or as salaried workers employed by companies, have produced the communications, informational, media, and cultural environments of society. It has been human labors behind the novels, the paintings, the plays, the magazines, the news stories, the photographs, the posters, the comics, the radio shows, the songs, the movies, the TV series, the video games and the myriad digital podcast series, images and videos. It is humans whose labor results in works that inspire, educate, entertain, and move the hearts and minds of billions. Today, this human-centered idea of symbolic production is imagined to be in jeopardy due to the spread of generative AI systems, and yet, the digital society that we are living in continues to be the result of human labor.

A Digital Society, Made by Workers

Scroll. Click. Stream. Share. In the first quarter of the 21st century, it became common to read that "we" are living in a new "digital society" because digital hardware, software, and content are entangled with so much of what humans do and what happens each day. It is typical to read about how the Internet, personal computers (PCs), smartphones, websites, and apps are driving a "disruption" that is changing the way billions live, work, and play. Yet, access to and the knowledge and skills required to use digital technologies are unequal, and too often, the design of devices and platforms themselves frequently privilege the already privileged while perpetuating longstanding intersecting patterns of inequity and oppression. Nonetheless, in the first quarter of the 21st century, digital technologies *did* become more widely available to more people from all walks of life, and they are now firmly embedded in society, an integral and significant part of its structures and whole way of life.

For one, the gap between those who have access to the Internet and those who don't is shrinking. Even though the digital divide may never be "fully" closed, many more people were using the Internet in 2024 than they were in 2001. After the first dot.com bubble burst and millenarian anxieties about the Y2K bug began to dissipate, 510 million people worldwide were "dialing up" to get online and slowly "surfing the Internet" (8.6% of the global population), but nearing the end of 2024, 5.3 billion people were speed browsing across the Internet's millions of sites via a broadband or wireless connection (67% of the global population). Each year for the past 20 years, Internet usage among Americans in all major socio-demographic categories increased: in 2001, about 50% of the United States' (US) adult population was using the Internet, and by 2024, that grew to 95%. Nowadays, it is habitual for billions of people spanning different class positions, racial ascriptions, sexual orientations, genders, ethnicities, creeds, lifestyles, and locales to be online. The Internet now exercises a soft determinism in society. Even the few that may opt to disconnect still live in a world where the many are online, and for more of their lifetime than ever before. From 2000 to 2018, the time spent online each week by a typical American increased from 9.4 to about 24 hours. During the COVID-19 pandemic, Internet usage went up further, and the typical American now uses the Internet for at least 7 hours each day.

Relatedly, the digital devices people use to access to the Internet are more widespread than ever before. In 2001, a little over half of all US households had one or more PCs, but in 2024, over 95% did. While the early adopters of PCs tended to be American, white, and male, the share of households with a PC has steadily increased around the world, with about 80% in developed countries and 35% in developing countries. PCs have also become more affordable over time: in 2001, one clunky and slow PC typically cost between $3500 and $4500, but in 2023, smaller and faster PCs were selling for around $600–$700. In 2001, mobile phones may have been perceived as luxury goods that rich white men used to flaunt their social status: Gordon Gecko, the ruthless financier in the 1987 movie *Wall Street*, or Patrick Bateman, the serial killer investment banker in the 2000 movie *American Psycho*, come to mind. But by 2023, mobile phones had been reconfigured as necessities for the rich and poor alike. Worldwide, there are nearly 7 billion smartphone users, almost 1.4 billion new units are sold each year, and about 87% of the global human race is talking, reading, watching, texting, and scrolling on one for 3–4 hours each day. For many people, the prospect of everyday life without a smartphone is unimaginable. Glib as it is, the saying "I couldn't live without my smartphone" contains an element of truth—in poll after poll, majorities say their digital devices are necessities and more integral to "life" itself.

This may be because the most universal of our human practices—communication, collaboration, and communion—are increasingly mediated by the screens of digital devices and taking place in the spaces of sites and platforms. As offline and online experiences became evermore enmeshed, social activities that once presumed physical closeness started happening at a distance, through devices and platforms. Nowadays, many teenagers prefer chatting online with friends to hanging out in person; more consumers "go shopping" online and on Amazon while suburban mall after mall closes its doors; more people prefer to stream movies on Netflix than to pay for a ticket to watch one at the local theater while friends separated by town and country join together for online "watch parties"; more students are enrolling in more online college and university programs and courses; more people are meeting with their healthcare providers online instead of taking a trip to the doctor's office; most new couples first meet on online dating apps, then at a coffee shop or bar; career seekers network with prospective employers via LinkedIn; more of us are working remotely and doing our banking online than ever before; the members of Postal Service, Gorillaz, Broken Bells, and Kronos Quartet used the Internet to compose music with each other at a distance, and this is now a common practice; even the activists pushing for social change coordinate multiple in-person city protests online, and tweet and stream these in real time, resulting in global media activist events.

These and many more forms of "digital sociality" are growing, especially for the billions logged in to social media platforms right now. Over the past two decades, social media platforms (e.g., Facebook, YouTube, Instagram, TikTok) have become ubiquitous, part of the body of institutions within which billions of people interact, leading some to describe ours as a "platform society" (van Dijck, Poell, and de Waal, 2018). When they launched in the early 2000s, social media platforms may have seemed to be a fleeting fad or youthful novelty. But by 2024, they were anything but. In 2005, just 5% of American adults were using social media platforms, but in 2011, nearly 50% of all Americans were interacting on them, and in 2024, over 75% were doing so regularly. Although most social media users (as % of the population) reside in the US (302 million), social media platforms extend around the world. In 2023, 72% of China's total population (1.03 billion people) and about 33% of India's population were logged in to social media platforms. While YouTube, TikTok, Telegram, Snapchat, Douyin, Kuaishou, Sina Weibo, QQ are hugely popular, Meta Platforms today owns the most populated platforms, with 3.8 billion people worldwide logged on to least one of its core services (Facebook, WhatsApp, Instagram, or Messenger) each month. Alone and together, countless individuals are now dependent on the Internet, digital devices, and a variety of apps and social media platforms to do what they once did without them.

But that's not all. A lot of people are doing *new* things with digital technologies as well. Not too long ago, large, vertically, and horizontally integrated media corporations were the dominant sources of media and cultural products consumed by society. While these corporations remain influential and continue to expand, their traditional "mass," "one-to-many," and "transmissive" communication model coexists with a new, hyper-customized, "many-to-many," and "dialogical" communication paradigm. Research on emerging "creator cultures" and "platforms of cultural production" shows how mass access to Silicon Valley's tools and services has increased and diversified the sources of media content creation and distribution in the digital society (Cunningham & Craig, 2019, 2021; Poell, Nieborg, & Duffy, 2021). This shift means that almost anyone, not just global media giants like News Corp and the Walt Disney Company, can utilize these platforms to produce and share media content, to inform, entertain, and influence audiences. From the YouTubers live-streaming video content of themselves to hundreds of thousands of subscribers to the Instagram influencers shilling for Sephora and Audible brands, there are an estimated 300 million of these creators around the world harnessing social media platforms to create their own media content and trying to build a paying audience for it. As many as 17 million of these are earning money (though not always nearly enough to live on) (Florida, 2022).

Never has the world ever had so much media "content"—or information—so readily available to consume. Only 600 or so years ago, information was hard to find, because large organizations monopolized it; it was difficult to reproduce (because the technologies of reproduction were not yet around), and it was challenging to distribute (because much was etched in stone or stored away in libraries). Information about the world was mostly controlled by elites, in very limited supply, and something that took a while to travel from one place to another. Today, information is now super abundant. In 2023, X/Twitter users made 200 billion tweets that year, Facebook users shared 4.75 billion posts each day, and YouTubers uploaded 2500 new videos every minute. Over 100,000 new tracks were uploaded to Spotify every day (1 new song per half second), 3 million podcasts circulated, and 4 million e-books were available to read on Kindle. Thanks to digital technologies, information is easily accessed, infinitely reproducible, and it moves instantaneously, from one point on the map to another, with the click of a button. In the past, people may have worried about not having enough information or of being deprived of it by those that did. But lately, it seems that the opposite is true. We don't know how to deal with the glut.

In sum, the first quarter of the 21st century has witnessed the rapid expansion of a digital society, marked by measurable growth in the production, distribution, consumption, and use of digital hardware, software, and media content. Culture is digital. It is undeniable that digital technologies have become deeply entrenched in society and play a significant role in shaping our social lives. But has the proliferation of all things digital made an entirely new and revolutionary "digital society," unlike any that preceded it? A quantitative increase to any one technology in society does not necessarily bring about a qualitative change to society as a whole, nor does it automatically make a society that is one and the same with that technology. There are more pencils and air conditioner units in society now than ever before, but few would boast we are living in an altogether new "pencil society" or "air conditioner society." We should be skeptical of those who claim digital technologies in themselves make an entirely new "digital society." Smartphones and apps are not the primary catalysts for massive social changes, nor are they autonomous actors with their own motives to redefine the way billions of individuals worldwide live, work, and play. No matter how "smart," no TV is an agent with a heart and mind of its own and a will to act upon society in pursuit of goals it decides.

In every civilization, humans have consistently produced technologies that, in turn, have shaped and reproduced the societies of their respective epochs. In today's digital society, nearly every device, application, and piece of content available are direct outcomes of human decision-making and human labor power. An iPhone doesn't design itself. YouTube algorithms do not develop their own ideas about what videos to recommend. Global blockbuster movies and TV series don't script themselves (not yet at least). Generative AI does not generate itself. New digital technologies surely limit and enable human agency, and we make technologies that definitely play a role in making us and our social world, but technologies are themselves in the first instance shaped by human agency, by human knowledge and skill. The CEOs at the top of the biggest tech and media entertainment corporations make decisions about what technologies and content to develop, finance, and market. Silicon Valley's engineers, designers, and programmers make choices about how the apps we log in to operate. Hollywood's executive producers, directors, and scriptwriters shape what movies gets greenlighted, copyrighted, and rented out. While it is reasonable to describe our society as a digital society, it is one produced and reproduced by humans, whose agency is both enabled and restricted by the wider system that shapes it and their collective labors. I call global capitalism's super-sector of industries and firms that employ the workers who make the digital society "the digital media and entertainment industries" (DMEI). This 21st-century concept augments the concept of the cultural industries, which came of age in the 20th century, prior to the ubiquity of digital media in society.

Augmenting the "Cultural Industries": The Work of Classifying the Digital Media and Entertainment Industries (DMEI)

What, then, are the DMEI? To answer this question is to partake in the work of *industry classification*, or the practice of defining companies based on their similarities in the products and services they sell or in the role they play within the overall economy as an "industry." Most often, an "industry" refers to a group of companies that are related based on the main product or service they sell and their largest source of revenue (e.g., the "movie industry" refers to the companies that make movies for sale and whose largest source of revenue derives from movie distribution and exhibition). A "sector" refers to a number of industries that are interdependent in some way (e.g., the movie industry is part of the broader "information" sector, or media and entertainment sector: it depends on theater chains, TV broadcasters, over-the-top streamers, advertisers, and more).

In essence, classifying industries is not just about accurately describing existing industry realities but also involves shaping their identities, setting them apart from others, and determining what falls within their scope. This work of classification can either shed light on or obscure certain aspects of industries, guiding attention toward or away from specific firms, workers, practices, and goods and services. While it is important to be reflexive about the work of industry classification, recognizing the limitations of doing so does not imply we should stop trying to classify or define industries. Industry classifications and definitions can be useful for anyone—policy-makers, firms, unions, academics—interested in researching and analyzing what's up with work within industries. They allow for a focusing of the research eye, collection and analysis of data about labor market dynamics, employment rates, wage patterns, skills, and job growth or shrinkage. They can enable a granular examination of the types of occupations within particular industries, unionization rates, income and wage differentials between workers, and issues of equity, diversity, and inclusivity (EDI). In sum, these classifications and definitions are useful research tools.

Over the past five decades, numerous concepts have been developed to classify the industries and sectors that produce and sell culture, media, information, knowledge, technology, and entertainment goods and services in markets. Key terms include "cultural industries" (Hesmondhalgh, 2019), "media industries" (Holt & Perren, 2009), "information industries" (Noam, 2009), "copyright industries" (Stoner & Dutra, 2022), "creative industries" (Caves, 2002; Flew & Cunningham, 2010), "media and entertainment industries" (United States International Trade Administration, 2021), and "influencer industries" (Hund, 2023). My definition of the DMEI is indebted to all the previous concepts developed by researchers to delimit the boundaries of their object of study and aims to synthesize and augment them, with the most salient of these being the highly influential "cultural industries" concept, which I've used many times before, and continues to have currency in cultural and creative industries policy and research.

The types of companies, industries, and sectors that get bundled together into scholarly concepts of the cultural industries (and related industry classifications) change over time and continue to change with new types of firms, industries, and sectors emerging. In his fourth edition to his landmark work *The Cultural Industries*, David Hesmondhalgh (2019) defines the cultural industries as institutions directly involved in the production of social meaning, primarily dealing with the industrial production and circulation of copyrighted texts (pp. 14–15). Hesmondhalgh categorizes these industries into core groups like television, radio, film, music, publishing, video and computer games, advertising, marketing, public relations, and web design. He contrasts this "core" with "peripheral" groupings such as traditional fine arts and live performances, which have less reach and influence due to their semi-industrial production methods and smaller audiences (p. 16). Hesmondhalgh also identifies neighboring or "borderline" industries, like telecommunications, consumer electronics, and the ICT industries, which often compete and collaborate with cultural industries (pp. 18–21). He notes that technology companies like AAMAM (Alphabet-Google, Apple, Meta Platforms, Amazon, and Microsoft) are distinct from the cultural industries because they are not primarily focused on producing texts (p. 22). Additionally, Hesmondhalgh says fashion, sport, design, and social media platforms are also borderline groups despite having a strong cultural component (p. 23). Hesmondhalgh (2019) defines cultural industries primarily as producers of copyright texts, establishments directly involved in the making and circulating of everything from books to movies that are meant to inform or entertain (p. 466). He cautions against viewing old media as eclipsed by new digital media, highlighting the continued relevance of TV broadcasting and popular music in people's lives, despite the rise of Big Tech (p. xxiii).

While Hesmondhalgh's classification of the cultural industries remains relevant, the telecommunications, electronics, and ICT industries have moved beyond being mere "borderline" players. They have now merged and converged with others, becoming integral to the core cultural industries. For example, Comcast Corporation, one of the biggest telecommunications and media conglomerates in the world, has business operations in many of the core cultural industries. Its Xfinity sells telephone, broadband Internet and cable and streaming TV services, while its NBCUniversal makes news and entertainment texts for TV, radio, and the Internet. Google sells hardware like Pixel phones, dominates Internet search and software services, and owns YouTube, the biggest video sharing platform in the world. Apple is a titan of computer electronics but is also into music streaming (Apple Music) and audio-visual entertainment, releasing hits such as *Severance, Ted Lasso, Beastie Boys Story,* and *Swan Song* (Apple TV+). Meta Platforms is a hardware, software, and advertising services company, whose platforms are used by billions to produce and circulate their own texts. Amazon controls over 50% of the print book market and more than 80% of the e-book market, but is also a publisher (Kindle Direct Publishing), into big data and information services and online advertising (Amazon Web Services, AWS), and a popular TV and movie

What Are the Digital Media and Entertainment Industries (DMEI)? 63

producer (Amazon Studios) and distributor (Prime Video) of copyrighted texts such as *The Boys*, *The Marvelous Mrs. Maisel*, *One Night in Miami*, and *The Report*. Microsoft, a longstanding giant in software and ICT, has also established itself as a major player in digital gaming through its Xbox console and game publishing arm. In 2023, the company further solidified this position by acquiring Activision Blizzard, the world's largest game developer. Sports entertainment firms—MLB, NBA, NFL, NHL, as well as WWE and UFC—produce and sell texts of live events for broadcast and online streaming by numerous companies. All these examples indicate the extent of the integration that has occurred between core, peripheral, and borderline cultural industries and show how porous previously discrete industry groupings have become. In the first quarter of the 21st century, the cultural industries' core, peripheral, and borderline groupings converged, and with the digital media hardware, software, and content their corporations and labor force have brought into the world, and the ubiquity of digitization everywhere and in everything, it has become common to describe the society of the present as a new "digital society." The concept of the DMEI attempts to capture these transformations.

Defined broadly, the DMEI encompass all establishments, ranging from global media giants like Walt Disney and Comcast to tech titans such as Google and Apple to the contractor networks of smaller media companies and tech startups to the entrepreneurial online creators trying to make their way on platforms. But the core of the DMEI are the vertically and horizontally integrated corporate titans whose holdings and operations spread across the traditional cultural industries, as well as telecommunications, hardware, and software industries. Far from being marginal or secondary to history's biggest industries (e.g., Big Auto or Big Oil), the DMEI's corporations are among the most powerful, next to the global financial sector. Apple's 2024 market capitalization of over $3.25 trillion underscores the immense economic weight of these. The Forbes 2023 Global 2000 list highlights the world's ten largest media companies: Comcast Corporation, Walt Disney Company, Charter Communications, Warner Bros. Discovery, Publicis Groupe SA, Omnicom Group, Fox, DISH Network, WPP Plc, and Paramount. It also notes the ten largest tech companies: Alphabet Inc. (Google), Microsoft Corporation, Apple Inc., Samsung Group, Meta Platforms, Tencent Holdings Ltd., Taiwan Semiconductor Manufacturing, Sony Corporation, Oracle Corporation, and CISCO Systems. These and a number of other large, mid-sized, and small corporations undergird the for-profit production and accumulation of intellectual property (IP), including copyrighted content (e.g., books, TV series, movies, music, and games), patented devices (e.g., PCs, smartphones, and consoles) and software (e.g., algorithms, user interface [UI] designs, video processing techniques, or other proprietary designs that make apps and platforms function in a distinctive way). The DMEI concept flags the convergence of once discrete industry groupings into a massive overlapping super-sector whose corporations employ the labor of in-house waged workers and cross-border networks of out-of-house contractors and gig workers, to produce the digital society, and turn a profit.

The DMEI concept relies upon the latest North American Industry Classification System (NAICS 51) codes. NAICS is the standard statistical framework used in North America for categorizing companies into industries and sectors, and it is used for collecting, analyzing, and publishing up-to-date data about these industries and sectors in the US, Canada, and Mexico. NAICS codes are widely recognized for their statistical legitimacy and can provide detailed information about various industry groups, including their labor force. Built with NAICS codes, the "DMEI" serves as a useful heuristic tool for defining the boundaries of this extensive global super-sector, including its various sub-groups and companies. The "DMEI" broadens and deepens the scope for scholars conducting research on work and labor in the digital society, extending it beyond the conventional and sometimes limited range of occupations studied in the "cultural industries" tradition. The scope of the DMEI includes 15 specific industry groups, and a range of companies that operate within and across those boundaries and conduct themselves with the labor of an in-house and out-of-house workforce.

The DMEI encompasses 15 often economically and technologically convergent and international industry groupings: (1) Computer and Electronic Manufacturing; (2) Telecommunications; (3) Computing Infrastructure, Data Processing, Web Hosting, and Search; (4) Software Publishing (Video Games, Apps, and Programs); (5) Broadcasting and Content Provider Industries; (6) Motion Picture and Video; (7) Sound Recording; (8) Advertising, PR, and Marketing; (9) Traditional Publishing (Newspapers, Books, Magazines); (10) Performing Arts, Spectator Sports, and Other; (11) Photography and Image-Making; (12) Toys; (13) Amusement and Theme Parks; (14) Online Creator/Influencer; and (15) Education. Each of these industry groups is briefly described in what follows.

The *Computer and Electronic Manufacturing Industries* (NAICS Codes 334–335) refer to firms that employ workers to produce and sell computers, smartphones, communication equipment, semiconductors, and other electronics. Some companies in this industry include Apple Inc., Samsung Electronics, Dell Technologies, HP Inc., Cisco Systems, Intel Corporation, Texas Instruments, Western Digital, Seagate Technology, Prysmian Group, and Nexans. The *Telecommunications Industries* (NAICS Code 517) are key to the DMEI, and their workers produce and sell infrastructure and services for national and international communication and connectivity. Major companies are AT&T, Verizon Communications, T-Mobile US, Comcast, DirecTV and Dish Network, MagicJack, and Vonage.

What Are the Digital Media and Entertainment Industries (DMEI)? 65

The *Computing Infrastructure, Data Processing, Web Hosting, and Search Industries* (NAICS Code 518/519) produce and sell computing infrastructure and data processing services, enabling businesses to store, manage, and process data. They also sell web hosting services and run Internet search portals. Prominent companies include Amazon Web Services, Google Cloud Platform, and Microsoft's Bing. The *Software Publishing Industries* (NAICS code 511210) encompass a range of companies whose workers' labor is employed to develop and publish software. Prominent video game publishers in these industries include Electronic Arts, Activision Blizzard, Ubisoft, and Take-Two Interactive. Other industry leaders include Microsoft and Adobe Systems. These industries also cover companies like Oracle, SAP SE, Intuit, and Salesforce.com, which sell "enterprise solutions."

The *Broadcasting and Content Provider Industries* (NAICS code 515/516) include companies whose workforces are primarily engaged in the labor of producing and broadcasting radio and TV programs, with iHeartMedia, ABC, Fox, CNN, CBC, and BBC being exemplary. Additionally, Media Streaming Distribution Services, Social Networks, and Other Media Networks and Content Providers refer to over-the-top (OTT) video streaming platforms like YouTube, Netflix, Hulu, and others. The *Motion Picture and Video Industries* (NAICS Code 5121) represent movie and video production, distribution, exhibition, and post-production services: Hollywood studio-distributors like Walt Disney, Warner Bros, Paramount Pictures, post-production companies such as Industrial Light & Magic, and theatrical exhibitors such as AMC Theatres and Regal Cinemas. The *Sound Recording Industries* (NAICS Code 5122) cover music production, distribution, and publishing, and the workforces of companies like Sony Music Entertainment, Warner Music Group, Universal Music Publishing Group, and Interscope Records, as well as independent recording artists, musicians and bands.

The *Advertising, Public Relations, and Marketing Services Industries* (NAICS Code 5418/5419) register global advertising giants like WPP plc, Omnicom Group, McCann Erickson, and MediaCom, whose labor force produces a range of ad services from media buys to branding campaigns. Some of the biggest PR agencies are Edelman and Weber Shandwick, while marketing research and public opinion polling cover ratings companies like Nielsen, whose workers produce and sell qualitative and quantitative demographic data about media audiences, and Internet and social media users.

The traditional *Publishing Industries* (NAICS Code 513) refer to Newspaper, Periodical, Book, and Directory Publishers: the workers of companies like Penguin Random House and Simon & Schuster, *The New York Times* and *Forbes Media*, *The Guardian*, Conde Nast, all play a major role in the news and literary world. Workers in the *Performing Arts, Spectator Sports and other Recreation Industries* (NAICS code 711) produce and stage cultural productions and live performances: Cirque du Soleil, for circus arts;

Broadway Theatre, for theatrical performances; the Metropolitan Opera, for operatic spectacle. In spectator sports, Manchester United F.C., the New York Yankees, Dallas Cowboys, and Los Angeles Lakers stand out as icons in football, baseball, and basketball. The *Photographic and Image Industries* (NAICS code 54192) specialize in photography services and video production, with companies like Getty Images and Shutterstock selling visual content and stock media.

Toy Industries (NAICS code 339930) have expanded from traditional toy manufacturing to integrate with other industry groups in the DMEI. Companies like Mattel and Hasbro now offer interactive, technology-integrated toys with features like app compatibility and augmented reality (AR). Toy manufacturers and their products now appear in the content of video games (e.g., LEGO *Star Wars: The Complete Saga*) and blockbuster movies (e.g., Mattel's *Barbie*). The *Amusement and Theme Park Industries* (NAICS code 713110) include iconic parks like Walt Disney World and Six Flags Magic Mountain, which sell live show and ride experiences based on popular movies, TV shows, and video games. Visitors to Disney parks might pay for the thrill of rides like Guardians of the Galaxy: Cosmic Rewind and Star Wars: Hyperspace Mountain, or a selfie with a low-waged worker dressed up as the characters Gamora or Rey.

The Online Creator/Influencer Industries does not currently have its own NAICS code, but might fall under the Internet Broadcasting and Web Search Portals (NAICS code 519130) and be cross-referenced with other codes as well that capture facets of the Broadcasting and Content Provider Industries, Advertising, Public Relations, and Marketing Services, and Publishing Industries. In general, these industries include the companies, websites, and wide range of entrepreneurial individual and groups of creators engaged in the financing, production, publishing, distribution, marketing, and monetization of videos, live-stream performances, symbols, and digital cultural goods within and across the Internet. These industries and their products are made by millions of "influencers," "social media entertainers," "online creators," and "platform cultural producers" (Cunningham & Craig, 2016, 2019, 2021; Florida, 2022; Hund, 2023; Poell, Nieborg, & Duffy, 2021).

The *Educational Services Industries* (NAICS code 61) is often frequently invisible but essential to the DMEI. It encompasses all the public and private colleges and universities engaged in labor force training, research and development, IP and techno-transfer, and the development of firms, entrepreneurs, and workers for the DMEI as a whole. Harvard University and Stanford University, the Wharton School and MIT Sloan School of Management, Universal Technical Institute and Lincoln Tech, Juilliard and Berklee fine arts scholars are but a few entities in this grouping, but arguably all universities and colleges nowadays play a role in global capitalism (Mirrlees & Alvi, 2020). After all, they employ the professors who

What Are the Digital Media and Entertainment Industries (DMEI)?

research and write all the copyrighted texts (books, journal articles and chapters) that are being produced and sold for profit by the global academic publishing oligopoly of companies such as Taylor & Francis, SAGE, Springer, and others. While one might disagree with the neoliberal state and global capital's reduction or instrumentalization of the education services industries to base economic functions, any effort to alter this real configuration of power must begin with recognition of what it has become, and a reckoning with what it's now designed to do. In an era of right-wing attacks and governmental cutbacks, departments and disciplines in communication, media, culture and creativity have emphasized their utility to capital, promoting their vital role in labor force training and IP development for the DMEI (British Academy, 2024)

The DMEI's 15 Industry Groups/NAICS Codes

NAICS Code	Industry Group
334/335	Computer and Electronic Manufacturing Industries
517	Telecommunications Industries
518/519	Data Processing, Hosting, and Related Services Industries
511210	Software Publishing Industries (Video Games, Apps, Programs)
515/516	Broadcasting and Content Provider Industries
5121	Motion Picture and Video Industries
5122	Sound Recording Industries
5418	Advertising, PR Marketing, and Related Services Industries
513	Traditional Publishing Industries (News, Books, Magazines)
711	Performing Arts, Spectator Sports and other Recreation Industries
54192	Photographic and Image Industries
339930	Toy Industries
713110	Amusement and Theme Park Industries
TBD	Online Creator/Influencer Industries
61	Educational Services Industries

Why the "D" in the DMEI? Foregrounding the 'Digital'

Over the past few decades, the DMEI has been at the center of the transformation of society, while also being impacted by the new technological forces and relations of production its companies and workers unleashed, bringing forth what is sometimes conceptualized as the "digital society."

Digitization

This brings me to a brief explanation for why the word "digital" is prominent in the DMEI concept. "Digital" is not itself a specific industry grouping but is integral to every grouping in the DMEI. I use "digital" as a prefix for the contemporary media and entertainment industries (the "D" of the "MEI") to recognize the dominance of *digitization,* how nearly all forms of information and culture exist in a digital format (a binary code of ones and zeroes understandable by computers and smartphones). As a result of digitization, all major media—news, ads, TV series, movies, games—is produced and circulated as digital media content compatible with digital hardware and software. Furthermore, all digital media content is distributed and exhibited through the Internet and World Wide Web and is accessed, consumed, stored, shared, and interacted with via digital devices, websites and platforms. Although the word "digital" may seem redundant given its ubiquity, the "DMEI" acronym underscores how important digital is to every major media form. Nearly all growth in media and entertainment revenue now comes from digital hardware, software, and content, and all 20th-century products deemed "cultural" are now also "digital."

From Analog to Digital

Analog media formats have declined in prominence and all texts associated with the "cultural industries" are produced in digital forms and are circulated through the Internet and World Wide Web as such. Walt Disney and Marvel.com engage users online, showcasing their extensive IP content libraries. Newspapers like *The New York Times* and the *Times of India,* along with magazines such as *Vogue* and *Sports Illustrated,* run digital editions. Books, once handwritten or typed on paper, are now primarily composed using word processing software and get read on e-readers like the Amazon Kindle and Kobo. Kodak and Fujifilm instant cameras have given way to digital selfies snapped with smartphones, and family photography albums have been replaced by digital photo albums. Vinyl records and cassette tapes, though cherished by collectors and hipsters, have been surpassed by MP3 and streaming services, from Spotify to Apple Music. Analog film reels and VHS tapes have been replaced by digital files for digital theatrical projectors and screens. TV broadcasting, once reliant on analog signals, has transitioned to digital television (DTV). While cable and satellite TV still prosper, streaming platforms, like Netflix and Prime, have expanded. Even traditional radio has been complemented, if not surpassed, by Internet radio and podcasting. Art creation has taken a digital turn with the use of software like Adobe Photoshop and Illustrator, and digital galleries persist on blogs and websites long after in-person exhibits have closed. Works of theater, operas, and concerts are being produced and streamed by companies with online subscribers in mind. Millions of online creators use platforms like Instagram and TikTok to share their work and try to earn an income. Around the world, advertisers have shifted expenditures from traditional print and broadcast media to the Internet, with firms such as Google-YouTube and Meta Platforms selling billions in ad targeting services each year. Moreover, everyday communication with co-workers, friends, and family members now occurs through smartphones and platforms such as WhatsApp, Google Meet, and Zoom. This total digital media and entertainment environment is shaped by *economic* and *technological convergence* processes.

Economic Convergence and Technological Convergence

Over the past 40 years, companies in telecommunications, electronics, ICT, and cultural industries have merged and converged, resulting in a blurring of lines between once discrete industries, products, and services. Prior to economic convergence, companies like Time Inc., News Corporation, and Viacom operated within distinct industries like publishing, news, and TV, constrained by regulatory frameworks and antitrust laws that limited ownership concentration. However, from the 1980s onward, companies in these industries began to converge. Big companies embarked on a spree of takeovers across once-isolated industry segments, joining with other companies, and growing even bigger. The barriers that once separated industry groups started to crumble. Due to economic convergence, one corporation's holdings now span across many industry groups and many firms. Corporations are no longer confined to traditional industry boundaries, instead presiding over integrated ecosystems for digital media production, distribution, exhibition and consumption. The "DMEI" captures this economic convergence, highlighting how companies have expanded their operations and subsidiaries to include a comprehensive range of activities from telecommunications services to hardware and software production to the complete circuit of producing, distributing, and exhibiting copyrighted content.

The economic convergence process has been accompanied by *technological convergence*. Historically, many devices were designed with a single function or limited utility in mind, such as landline telephones for voice communication, pagers for text messages, typewriters for document creation, TV sets for audio-video display, radios for audio broadcasts, film cameras for photography, the Walkman for cassette playback, VCRs for video recording and playback, and game consoles for gaming. But technological convergence is a process where these old devices are made obsolete by multi-purpose devices that integrate many previous functions and utilities. For example, one iPhone or high-end Android device amalgamates a range of functions once fulfilled by multiple gadgets. The smartphone converges a telephone, camera, music player, radio, television, GPS, PC, gaming console, e-book reader, voice recorder, alarm clock, calculator, calendar, flashlight, stopwatch, timer, and fitness tracker. Video game consoles like the PlayStation 5 and Xbox

Series X also exemplify convergence. While consoles were initially just for gaming, they now function as multi-media entertainment hubs, offering disk playback, movie and TV show streaming, music streaming, Internet browsing, digital media storage, social media access, voice and video communication, and integration with other home media devices.

In sum, the DMEI encompasses 15 industry groups, foregrounds the "digital" in everything, and represents an amalgamation of the core and peripheral cultural industries and borderline industries to highlight the range of establishments involved in the production and circulation of cultural texts and the digital hardware and software that enable texts to flow from producer to consumer. The concept of the DMEI acknowledges that the 15 industry groups within the DMEI are not entirely separate or bounded entities but are deeply interwoven and interconnected. This integration is not only due to their interdependence as a "super-sector" but is also driven by ongoing processes of economic and technological convergence, as evidenced by corporate ownership concentrating mergers and acquisitions and the design and everyday use of multi-purpose devices. Furthermore, for the purposes of research on work, the DMEI flags a much bigger labor force than is recognized, theorized, and analyzed in most studies of work in the cultural industries. The concept maintains the longstanding focus on content producers but also points to a much larger spectrum of occupational roles and labor processes in the digital society. Having defined the DMEI, the next section considers the DMEI's relationship to work.

How Is the DMEI Significant to Work in the Digital Society?

The DMEI are of great significance to work in the digital society. They are: (1) a source of employment, occupations, and jobs; (2) a disruptor of traditional occupations and jobs; (3) an incubator for new and emerging industries and occupations; (4) a producer of new means of production, or new tools; (5) a producer of new tools and systems of managerial control; (6) a demander of new labor power; (7) a catalyst for educational and state reforms; and (8) a supporter of state economic development plans, place-making, and branding.

The DMEI are a *source of employment for workers worldwide*. As key employers and also fields of self-employment, the DMEI are the source of a wide range of occupational roles: actors, writers, directors, coders, programmers, designers, technicians, marketers, influencers, and more. The magnitude of employment is substantial. Employment data from the US Bureau of Labor Statistics for May 2022 provides insight into the number of workers employed by specific industry in the DMEI. In the Computer and Electronic Manufacturing Industries: 20,760 computer hardware engineers, 23,300 electrical and electronic engineering technicians, 119,820 electrical and electronic equipment assemblers, and 22,520 semiconductor processors.

What Are the Digital Media and Entertainment Industries (DMEI)? 71

The Telecommunications Industries: 50,030 customer service representatives, 19,830 electronics engineers (excluding computer), and 105,440 telecommunications equipment installers and repairers, among others. In the Data Processing, Hosting, and Related Services industries: 4480 computer programmers and 21,930 computer support specialists. The Radio and TV Broadcasting industries accounted for 203,190 jobs. Additionally, Advertising, PR, and Related Services had a workforce of 480,540. The Motion Picture industry employed 417,620 workers. Worldwide there are millions of creators trying to make a living on platforms like YouTube.

In addition to being a source of employment, the DMEI drive new innovations that *disrupt traditional occupations and jobs*. Video rental stores and their clerks, once a staple of Hollywood exhibition in every small town, have been rendered obsolete by video streaming services like Netflix and Prime. The traditional TV broadcasting business model has been disrupted by social media platforms which suck up more and more ad revenue, leading to layoffs. The music retail and distribution sector was challenged by Spotify, and the heyday of Tower Records, Virgin Megastore, and HMV is long gone. Brick-and-mortar bookstores close and public libraries get defunded, while Google Books and online retailers like Amazon accumulate data and profit. Video games are digitally downloaded direct to user console in the home, or to PCs through platforms like Steam, bypassing GameStop, and its waning workforce. Smartphones displace the photography studio and the professional photographer at weddings and graduations, while analog film development and processing labs close their doors. The role of projectionist at theaters has been outmoded by automated digital cinema projectors. These are just a few of the disruptive impacts of the DMEI on traditional occupations and jobs.

The DMEI are disrupting the old, but also at the forefront of incubating new industries and firms that are *establishing new occupations that were unimaginable just a few decades ago*. Fifteen years ago, there was no such thing as an "influencer" or "social media coordinator," but nowadays, it seems every organization wants to hire one. Additionally, with user experience (UX) and UI design key to ensuring websites are user-friendly and visually appealing, UX/UI designer careers have grown. The advent of virtual reality (VR) and AR has introduced new occupations in immersive experience creation, 3D modeling, and content development. For a time, the Metaverse demanded the labor power of Metaverse developers, storytellers, and AI ethicists. E-sports gaming once seemed just for fun, but it now employs professional gamers, e-sports coaches, game streamers, and event and tournament managers. Podcasting is also source of jobs: hosts, producers, audio editors, and marketing specialists. Evidently, the DMEI make new industries and a range of new occupations.

The DMEI are *producers of new means of production, or new tools*, that are used by workers to do the jobs they do. These corporations employ workers to develop tools that are used by other corporations and their workers to complete a wide array of tasks, including the development of new tools. They produce the hardware and software that are foundational to the labor processes of countless workers, as so many occupations in the digital society rely on their goods and services. Furthermore, DMEI are the source of tools that are integral to modern work, the core infrastructure of communication, collaboration, content creation, data analysis, and social media management. Also, service tools like email and instant messaging (e.g., Gmail and WhatsApp), video conferencing platforms (e.g., Zoom and Microsoft Teams), collaboration platforms (e.g., Slack and Trello), and social networking platforms (e.g., Facebook, X, LinkedIn, Instagram) are intertwined with innumerable occupations in the digital society, extending and intensifying relations of work beyond the traditional workplace, and into households and spaces of everyday life like coffee shops, libraries, public transit, and more, increasing the time people spend completing tasks, and communicating with managers and co-workers. In sum, the workers of the DMEI's corporations produce the means of production that other workers employed by other corporations use to do their jobs across various industries.

The DMEI are also *the producer of new tools and systems of managerial control.* In pursuit of efficiency and control, CEOs and managers regularly look for and adopt new tools to try to get the most out of the workers they employ. As Andrijasevic, Chen, Gregg and Steinberg (2021, p. x) say, "Through each stage of the evolving relationship between workers and employers ... new media formats produce fresh opportunities for subjectification and control." For example, "the platform" may be "a managerial concept" and media tool of management, "steeped in a history of hardware manufacture, and deeply tied to changing efforts of extracting labor and profit" (Andrijasevic, Chen, Gregg, & Steinberg, 2021, p. xv). Platforms like Microsoft Teams and Google Workspace facilitate continuous management and worker communication and collaboration, but this constant connectivity may infringe on work-life boundaries. Project management software, such as Asana, Trello, Jira, and Monday.com, ostensibly aimed at streamlining work processes, can also intensify the workers' self-management and self-exploitation. Time and task tracking applications, including Toggl, Harvest, and Clockify, may perpetuate a culture of relentless productivity. More overtly, monitoring software, like Hubstaff, Teramind, and ActivTrak, offer managers detailed insights into worker computer usage and Internet activity. Similarly, worker feedback tools like SurveyMonkey, Glint, and Officevibe, though designed to improve workplace satisfaction, can be misused to manipulate worker perceptions or deflect from deeper grievances. The DMEI's production and sale of these media technologies support managerial control over workers and their labor processes. In the DMEI, many workers face the paradox of being employed to create new systems and tools for corporations, which managers then use to exercise greater control over the workers' own labor processes.

The DMEI are a *demander of new labor—of new knowledge and skills—from workers.* The CEOs of most industries now demand that workers possess digital skills, as these are essential to most occupations in the digital society. Writing for *Forbes*, Andriole (2016) encourages all modern corporations to compel their workers to develop digital skills if they wish to prosper amid "shifting markets, demographics and aggressive competitors." To stay competitive, companies are encouraged to "retrain and retool the willing keepers," "rent the others," and "replace some members of the technology team" who refuse to adapt. Over the past decade, "digital skills" have been framed as a new standard minimal prerequisite to landing *any* kind of paid work. As of 2023, upwards of 92% of jobs required digital skills. Firms often complain of a global "digital skills gap" and push workers to take the responsibility of closing it by paying colleges for credentials and EdTech companies for badges that symbolize their readiness for digital capital. To the extent that every company is expected to have a website, a social media presence, and communications personnel that uses the Internet to promote what it sells and interact with customers, every company is now a media company. For all the workers who don't land a salaried or part-time job in one of those, including those who must supplement their low wages by doing some form of "gig" work through smartphone and app-dependent platforms like Upwork, digital skills are now the starting point for subsistence. On top of those, there are all kinds of new skills being demanded by the DMEI: Internet of Things (IoT) expertise, AI and machine learning acumen, data analysis, and ever shifting variations and varieties of "soft skills."

The DMEI are a catalyst for educational and state reforms: its companies have *pressed the state and its public education system to build a knowledgeable and skilled labor force for its present needs and future growth* (Madison, 2014; Mirrlees & Alvi, 2020; Noonan, 2015). In the neoliberal framework, the idea of "human capital" refers to the knowledge and skills that individuals invest in and cultivate to become sufficiently productive for, and thereby valued by, corporations. The state, through its public education system, plays a role in human capital formation by contributing to workforce training, relieving corporations of significant training costs. Here, the state's public investment in education is justified as knowledge and skill training for the future economy and oriented toward teaching learners to invest in themselves as future workers for capital to one day use. As states subsidize global capital's accumulation of human capital, higher education is reduced to a servant of industry, not democracy. Today higher education is openly subordinate to the DMEI, tasked with producing a workforce for its firms. The alignment of higher education with the

DMEI's base labor force needs has led to a diminished valuation of social science and humanities disciplines, despite the "soft skills" they've always excelled at cultivating in learners (and workers). The expansion of university and college programs designed to serve the labor force needs of the DMEI has also produced an oversupply of workers infrequently matched by an equivalent quantity of good jobs for them to do.

The DMEI supports *state economic development plans, place-making, and branding*. The idea—frequently mythical—of the DMEI and their creative and technological workforce is frequently taken up by states at different scales of governance to promote economic development and construct place-based identities, whether national, regional, or local in character. The actual presence of the DMEI and workers in a geographical area sometimes will be flagged by the state—in its policy or in its publicity—to frame that place as an attractive locus of capital accumulation. States and the strategic communications firms they hire mobilize the idea of the DMEI in "place branding" initiatives. These image-making efforts aim to make cities, regions, and entire countries stand out on the global stage, with the goal of attracting foreign direct investment (FDI) in support of economic development and social uplift. While intended for strategic communication, these slickly constructed place brands sometimes interweave with how residents residing in the actual places come to imagine themselves and the identities of their communities vis-à-vis others in a world of other places competing for global capital.

Overall, the DMEI are significant to the production and reproduction of the digital society, as well as the forces and relations of production. But how have scholars gone about researching work in the industry groups and firms linked to the DMEI? What is research? What theories and methods do scholars use? The following chapter opens up and tinkers with the toolkit of labor theory and method.

3 What Is Research on Work in the DMEI?
A Toolkit for Labor Theory and Method

Introduction

This chapter is a look into the theoretical and methodological toolkit scholars pull concepts and approaches from when designing and conducting research on work in the communications and media industries, or, the digital media and entertainment industries (DMEI). This chapter describes and tinkers with: organizational sociology (the "production of culture/ circuit of culture/identity"); the "political economy of communication," "media economics" and "media management"; and, "labor process theory," "workerism," and "history from below." Additionally, the chapter surveys some key methods, including: "labor force research," "case studies," "questionnaires and surveys," "interviews," "oral history," "ethnography," and "participatory action research" and "activist autoethnography." It also makes a case for reflexive "normativity" in research. This chapter describes some of the main theoretical and methodological foundations for research on work in the DMEI. It contextualizes these theories and methods, highlights some exemplary cases, and poses some relevant questions.

To Research!

From Curiosity to Question

Albert Einstein once said "I have no special talents. I am only passionately curious." Angela Carter described "curiosity" as "the most fleeting of pleasures; the moment it is satisfied, it ceases to exist." Besides the material conditions of higher education that press scholars to "publish or perish" and now also "be creative" when transforming their findings or knowledge into new media formats, curiosity frequently acts as a driving force for research, catalyzing questions about something that might matter to them, and to the wider world. The initial question any researcher of work in the DMEI should ask themselves is: *what question do I wish*

DOI: 10.4324/9781003131076-4

to answer? The possibilities are infinite: of the portion of TikTok's 1.1 billion users trying to make a living as "influencers," how many do so? How many jobs in the technical communication field have been displaced by ChatGPT, and what are these workers doing now that their knowledge and skills have been made redundant by generative A.I.? What is the demographic profile of the workers paid to create video games in North America, and how do their conditions compare to workers in China? Just as there are lots of research questions to pose, there exist numerous motivations for doing research on work in the DMEI. So, the second question a reflexive researcher should ask themselves is as follows: *why am I doing this research?* To make a purposeful contribution to knowledge about work in the DMEI? To test and validate or refute and refine some old or new theory of work or the worker? To identify and solve real-world problems pertaining to work? To contribute to law, policy, and regulation in support of workers' rights? To join in solidarity with workers in a struggle to understand and change the world, for the better? To inform non-specialist publics about the topic?

Scale: Micro, Meso, and Macro

Over the past two decades, many scholars have been curious about and asked questions about the conditions and experiences of all those "creative," "cultural," "media," "informational," "tech," and "knowledge" workers in the DMEI. At the *micro-level*, the focus is usually on a specific type of worker who performs a distinctive role in the division of labor surrounding a good or service, such as a content creator or a moderator for YouTube, or a gaffer or boom operator on a Warner Bros. Pictures set or a location scout or talent manager for an HBO Studios TV series. *Meso-level* research on work in the DMEI operates at an intermediate scale, with a focus on groups or teams within organizations such as a software development team in a video game studio, the "creative team" of an ad agency, the acquisitions editor, development editor, copyeditor, as well as the producers, designers, marketers, and legal specialists, who have helped Routledge bring this book to you, the reader. On the *macro-level*, the research scope broadens, encompassing the system of capitalism, as well as the reigning structures and organizations of states and corporations that play a major role in shaping and influencing workers within the DMEI and in society as a whole.

Conscience

When conducting research on work in the DMEI at one or all of these levels, a scholar's curiosity and questions about these material matters is sometimes guided by their *conscience*, or a strong ethical and moral sensibility about what is right and wrong, and by extension, what is good and what is bad about work in the society. A scholar's conscience extends from ethical research practices to the decision to take a side in many of the greatest conflicts of the day. For example, some scholars undertake research on work in the DMEI that is interested in protecting and promoting the labor rights and well-being of workers in the DMEI, whereas others might align their intellect with enhancing or transforming the strategic and managerial goals of companies whose profit-motive frequently comes into tension with such rights and quality working conditions. Some scholars might collaborate with workers and participate in worker-led initiatives to advance solutions to social problems of income and wealth disparities, bad jobs, and rampant precarity, and others might see worker self-organization as a problem they can help companies and governments solve and manage. Scholars might try to understand how a state's communications, media and labor laws, policies and regulations intersect to shape the conditions and experiences of workers, for better or worse, with the goal of upholding the policy status quo or finding techniques for reforming and overhauling it. Scholars concerned with equity, diversity, and inclusivity (EDI) may seek to identify and tear down the sexist, racist, classist, and ableist barriers to accessing jobs in the DMEI, and also, examine and counter problems of workplace discrimination, harassment, and harm. Others may do the opposite. Some may wish to know what workers are represented behind the screens and in-the-scenes of the DMEI and probe how everything from news to entertainment to social media can shape public opinion about workers in society in ways that may support or undermine the interests of workers in the DMEI.

In every case, research on work in the DMEI is driven by *curiosity and questions*, *a sense of scale*, and *conscience*, and all of this is paramount to the selection of one's theories and methods.

Theory and Method

But what is a theory and what is a method and what's the difference? In essence, a theory of work in the DMEI is a systematic framework comprised concepts and propositions that helps scholars begin to understand, explain, contextualize, analyze, and interpret the various causes, conditions, experiences, relations, actions, events, and effects related to work in the DMEI, and in society. While a theory offers a framework or lens through which scholars can look at and try to make sense of the world of work in the DMEI, a method refers to the procedure they use to gather, analyze, and interpret data or information about some facet of work in the DMEI. Across various scholarly disciplines and fields such as political economy, business management, sociology, labor studies, communications and media studies, history, cultural studies, geography, and more, numerous theories and methods are available for conducting research on work in the DMEI. But the selection process can be challenging. After all, there isn't one "best theory" or "best method" for researching work in the DMEI. It is a contested terrain, to say the least. Scholars often choose and stick with specific theories and methods for various reasons: expertise gained through training, familiarity, disciplinary standards and norms, philosophical orientation, personal and ethical convictions, and resource constraints. Some may even establish or sustain a scholarly persona or "brand" based on their chosen approach.

For those starting out or continuing on, what's most important is that a theory and method will support one's specific research questions, motivations, and goals. There is a wide array of super-interesting theories and useful methods available for doing research on work in the DMEI today, and these should not be viewed as mutually exclusive or in competition; instead, they can be seen as overlapping and used in a complementary fashion. There are so many micro-fields and gatekeepers. But new scholars need not confine themselves to a single discipline or seek to establish or perpetuate a quasi-monopoly of knowledge to define and control the boundaries of a field. In many research projects, scholars will combine and mix different theories and methods, resulting in hybrid approaches and sometimes novel findings. Most often, the most interesting research on work in the DMEI is eclectic, as scholars undertake inter-disciplinary research that draws from many fields and makes use of a variety of theories and methods. In what follows, I describe some of these from fields that are pertinent to critical research on work in the DMEI.

Some Theories

Organizational Sociology: Production of Culture/Circuit of Culture/Identity

Going back to the post-World War II era, the sociology of work has entailed the "study of jobs and organizations as well as its links to social stratification and inequality, political economy, and worker power" and encompassed "eight major enduring themes: work organization and the labor process; labor markets and careers; professions and professional work; employment relations; meaning of work; unions and worker power; workplace stratification and inequality; and labor force diversity" (Kalleberg & Leicht, 2021, p. 2). Starting in the 1970s, scholars in organizational sociology and cultural anthropology started conducting research on the "the production of culture." Their focus was on "how the symbolic elements of culture are shaped by the systems within which they are created, distributed, evaluated, taught, and preserved" (Peterson & Anand, 2004, p. 311). This approach can be traced back to two influential collections: *The Production of Culture*, edited by Richard A. Peterson in 1976, and a special issue on the production of culture edited by Lewis A. Coser, published in *Social Research: An International Quarterly* in 1978.

In general, production of culture scholars parted ways with the idea of culture as a "whole way of life" that was organically or functionally symbolized by the stories and images of texts such as novels and movies. They focused instead on the industrial production and circulation of texts by organizations, largely for consumer markets. These early cultural industries researchers focused in on: industry structures (the relations between the specific companies that produce and circulate texts), organization (the structural hierarchies within and differences between text-producing firms), government law, policy, and regulation (everything from ownership laws to copyright and content policies to broadcasting regulations), new and emerging technologies (especially the technologies used by workers to produce and circulate texts), and occupations (the range of careers, labor market trends, the conditions, outlooks, and experiences of workers), and the consumer market (not just effective demand but the ideas and assumptions companies, managers, and workers make about the consumer's identity and their tastes and preferences) (Peterson & Anand, 2004, p. 313).

As the production of culture field grew, researchers challenged the Romantic era's notion of the solitary individual artist by showing how cultural symbols and texts were produced as commercial goods through a collective process by many workers in a complex division of labor spanning production networks (Becker 1974, 1976, 1982; du Gay, 1997; du Gay et al., 1997; Fine, 1992; Hirsch, 1978). They analyzed "cultural entrepreneurship" in the development of "fine art" and symphony orchestras (DiMaggio, 1977, 2004; Horowitz & Levine, 1989), and the work of country music-making (Peterson, 1997), advertising (Turow, 1997), North India's cassette culture (Manuel, 1993), and journalism (Gans, 2012; Gitlin, 1994; Hircsh, 1972; Molotch & Lester, 1974; Tuchman, 1978). They scrutinized the influence of intermediaries and gatekeepers in shaping the career prospects (or lack thereof) of workers (Bielby & Bielby, 1999) and interrogated the practices of racial and gendered inclusion and exclusion in TV production and screenwriting (Bielby & Bielby, 1994, 1996, 2002; Dowd & Blyler, 2002; Tuchman, 1989).

The US-based production of culture research shared an affinity with some developments in the British organizational sociology and cultural studies traditions, most saliently represented by research on the "circuit of culture" advanced by Paul du Gay, Stuart Hall, Linda Janes, Hugh Mackay, and Keith Negus in the 1997 book, *Doing Cultural Studies: The Story of the Sony Walkman*. Somewhat similar to the American production of culture research, British "circuit of culture" scholars strove to understand the organizations, human practices, and ideas, values and beliefs that shape the production, circulation, and consumption of cultural artifacts. As du Gay (1997, p. 8) wrote: "You may not know how a Sony Walkman actually works – to produce one requires a considerable degree of technological 'know-how' but it also requires the design and communication of its cultural meaning." In their pathbreaking book *Digital Play: The Interaction of Technology, Culture, and Marketing*, Stephen Kline, Nick Dyer-Witheford, and Greig de Peuter (2003) creatively adapted the "circuit of culture" approach to analyze the making, marketing and use of digital games—post-Fordist capitalism's ideal commodity form.

When adapted for the study of work in the DMEI—for example, the work of making an Apple iPhone—the "circuit of culture" framework offers a useful way to analyze the labor of making and shaping cultural artifacts across five interrelated contexts: *representation* (the iPhone's initial design, and the cultural meaning given it to by those who work in product design, packaging aesthetics and branding); *production* (the iPhone's actual manufacture, distribution, and marketing by workers in factories, logistics and sales, as well as the organizational ideas, values, and beliefs intertwined with the labor of this production); *consumption* (the iPhone's consumption by working people who spend their wages to acquire the device, and who interact with the artifact and interpret and modify its meanings); *identity* (the iPhone's integration into workers' everyday lives and practices, and the unpaid work of branding that consumers do when performing their status and identity through the use and display of this product in society); *regulation* (the iPhone's governance by those workers who make and enforce the state's laws, policy, and regulations related to IP, patent terms and conditions, copyright, and so on) and societal responses to the artifact that limit and enable its uses and meanings.

Another adaptation of the production of culture approach focuses explicitly on how worker identities are formed and reproduced (Banks et al., 2015; Caldwell, 2008; Mayer, 2009. 2011). Here, scholars adopt something of a cultural anthropological lense and probe the production of identities within specific professional communities of workers surrounding one or more media and cultural products. They focus on "how media producers make culture, and in the process, make themselves into particular kinds of workers in modern, mediated societies" (Mayer et al., 2009, p. 2) and center "the lived realities of people involved in media production as the subjects for theorizing production as culture" (Mayer et al., 2009, p. 4). Their primary interest lay in understanding how workers conceive of themselves, and how they make what they do meaningful to themselves, their peers, and the wider society. These researchers explore the ideas and beliefs workers have about themselves and the work they do, the standards, norms, and values that guide their conduct when making goods and services, and the practices and rituals of their working lives. They consider the practices that provide the glue for the workers' own identification of themselves with their work and wider professional networks (Herbert et al., 2020, p. 50). In *Production Culture: Industrial Reflexivity and Critical Practice in Film and Television*, John Thornton Caldwell (2008) showed how much can be learned about the workings of the cultural industries by examining the "work worlds" of its workforce. He raised questions such as: how do workers in specific companies and sectors make sense of their work? How and why they do it? How do they imagine themselves vis-à-vis others when they are doing such work?

The Political Economy of Communication/Media Economics/ Media Management

The political economy of communication has made substantial contributions to the study of work in the industries and corporations that produce and sell information, culture and media as commodities. For much of the fourth quarter of the 20th century, political economy of communication was loosely linked to historical materialism, or, the tradition of Marxist theory, research, and activism. Karl Marx (1867) is the premier analyst of capitalism, communications, and media labor, and for nearly a decade, Marx himself worked as a freelance journalist for the *New York Tribune*, hustling for writing gigs while suffering precarity and immiseration. From the post-war era to the present day, political economists have analyzed how the structures of capitalism, the state, and ideology interact with companies in the cultural industries to largely perpetuate social class divisions and inequalities (Babe, 2009; Birkinbine et al., 2017; Fuchs, 2014; Fuchs & Mosco, 2015a, 2015b; Hardy, 2014; McChesney, 2008; Meehan & Wasko, 2013; Mosco, 2009; Mirrlees, 2016a, Pedro-Carañana et al., 2024; Schiller, 2000, 2014; Wasko et al., 2011; Winseck, 2011). Research in the field advances knowledge about how the old and new configurations of capitalism, imperialism-colonialism, the state, and ideology shape patterns of inequity and oppression related to class, race, ethnicity, gender, sexuality, indigeneity, citizenship, disability, age, and other relations. They also foreground the agency of activist movements and workers' organizations to drive societal transformation for the better (Thomas & Vosko, 2019, p. 4).

Some of the *key points of research focus* in the political economy of communication tradition include but are not limited to: capitalism, ownership and concentration, and market structures; how the corporate ownership and market orientation of the cultural industries, including the production and circulation of texts for markets of audiences/advertisers, influences what texts get made, how and for whom; the corporate control and commodification of information and culture, and the use of IP, patents, and copyrights to dispossess workers of their creations; how and why the textual output of the cultural industries frequently carry images and messages that tend to conform with the ideological status quo, though may sometimes push back against it, or become a terrain of struggle between warring political blocs; the centrality of advertising to the business models of the cultural industries, and the "audience commodity" of radio, TV and Internet and online platforms; the state's role in facilitating and legitimizing capitalist accumulation in the cultural industries with policies, laws, and regulations that are frequently shaped by corporate lobby groups and trade associations; the importance of public media and culture to the needs of a self-governing democracy and civic life; continuity and change in the history of Empire and the cultural industries, focusing on power asymmetries in global communications and media, and old and new dynamics of imperialism; activist media organizations, strategies and tactics, as well as old and new social struggles in and around the media and cultural industries to bring about reforms, even revolutions.

Political economists of communication were among the first to undertake research on labor in the media and cultural industries. In 1983, Vincent Mosco and Janet Wasko co-edited *Critical Communications Review: Volume I: Labor, the Working Class, and the Media*. This volume, featuring essays by scholars including Stewart Ewan, Elizabeth Ewan, Jennifer Daryl Slack, Kevin Robins, Frank Webster, and others, focused on the historical relationship between the working class and the media industries, media unions, the portrayal workers and unions in the media, and the effects of new information and communication technologies (ICTs) on workers and workplaces. Gerald Sussman and John A. Lent's (1998) co-edited volume *Global Productions: Labor in the Making of the "Information Society"* was another major contribution to this field. Sussman and Lent (1998, p. 1) assessed the "global structures of communication, information and media through which pass daily transmissions of voice, data, text, and visual images—from the perspective of the people who actually build them"—and showed the so-called information society to be based on a "new international division of labour" (NIDL). Despite these important contributions to the labor turn, for much of the 1980s and 1990s, scholars focused less on actual waged work in companies and more on the unwaged work of the audience. Some insisted that the audience performed unpaid labor for media corporations and the wider capitalist system by listening to broadcast programs, watching TV shows and being exposed to ads for other products and services (Jhally, 1982; Jhally & Livant, 1986; Smythe, 1977). Others argued that the idea of audience work distracted from the real value-adding labor being done by the waged workers employed by radio and TV corporations, as well as by those toiling for the ratings and advertising corporations they served (Maxwell, 1991; Meehan, 1984, 1990, 1999; Murdock, 1978).

Nonetheless, this tradition exhibits a set of tenets that characterize its approach (the social totality or holism, history, moral philosophy, and praxis) (Mosco, 2009; Wasko et al., 2011), and it is possible to fashion these into a "political economy of communication" approach to work in the DMEI: *holism* (the study of work's shaping by conditions, practices, meanings, and outputs in relation to the totality of economic, political, and cultural power structures in society: how capitalism, corporations, markets, the state and governmental laws, policies, and regulations, as well as dominant culture-ideologies and battles for hegemony between political parties, shape the conditions and experiences of work); *history* (the study of work's continuity and change in the history of capitalism and the media and cultural industries: how the structures of the historical periods and conjunctures persist in the present but may also be disrupted and transformed by workers' agency); *moral philosophy* (the study of work informed by a normative framework built with principles and values of a good and just society and oriented to improving conditions and experiences of work for all); *social praxis* (the study of work generates new knowledge about the world and articulates with pro-worker movements and organizations that aim to change the world of work, and the world, for the better). Holistic, historical, moralistic, and praxis-oriented, the political economy of communication approach to work also reflexively takes the viewpoint of the working class with an eye to its heterogeneity and intersectionality, resulting in a counter-narrative to the dominant discourses and framings of work that often prioritize the standpoint of capital and corporations over labor and society.

Whereas political economy of communication scholars approach questions of work with a view to social power relations, media economics scholars focus on the micro-relations between economics, media companies, and consumer markets (Albarran, 1989, 1996, 1998, 2006; Doyle, 2014; Picard, 1989). The *Journal of Media Economics* and textbooks such as *Media Economics: Concepts and Issues* (Picard, 1989), *Media*

Economics: Understanding Markets, Industries and Concepts (Albarran, 1996), *Understanding Media Economics* (Doyle, 2013) and *Media Economics* (Cunningham et al., 2015) provide overviews of this field. Fundamentally, media economics examines how consumer markets shape the decisions made by managers, decision-makers, and workers within media enterprises that finance, produce, and distribute media products. Picard (1989, p. 7) defines media economics as research into "how media operators meet the informational and entertainment wants and needs of audiences, advertisers, and society with available resources." Albarran (1996, p. 5) characterizes it as "how media industries use scarce resources to produce content ... to satisfy various [consumer] wants and needs." Within media economics, a subfield called media management studies (MMS) has emerged (Küng, 2023), and scholars focus on the strategic and operational aspects of managing media companies to position them for success in the marketplace. Often based in business and management faculties and departments, but with cross-over in some communication and media studies programs, the MMS field equips professionals with the knowledge and skills needed for managing media companies. Critical MMS (CMMS), a related subfield, scrutinizes how media company management practices can either reinforce or challenge social power relations and related inequities and oppressions and tends to try to make media companies do better for society by balancing their profit interests with social responsibilities.

While many management-minded scholars are interested in work, their reasons and goals often differ significantly from those of political economists of communication. While the former might study work in a media corporation in relation to a broader structural critique of capitalism, and with an interest in the agency of workers to refuse, resist, and even go beyond it, the later may be inclined to see the workers' labor in terms of the operational requirements, business strategies, and successes and failures of media corporations in markets. For example, Mierzjewska and Hollifield (2006) view "Media Labor Force Research" as a "critical area of research in media management" (p. 55) because of the importance of the media workforce to business. From their point of view, the labor force matters because "personnel is the largest single budget item for many, if not most, media corporations" (p. 55), "because media products are information products, their quality and creativity is dependent on the knowledge, skills, and talents of the individuals who produce them," and these "knowledgeable, talented employees are the most valuable resource that media corporations control" (p. 55). Furthermore, these management scholars note how the "media labor force is also of interest from a public policy perspective," to ensure a society's diverse population demography-psychography is matched by diversity in media organizations and in the resulting representations of society communicated by the media products available for consumption in markets (p. 56). These considerations are undoubtedly top of mind for media managers. However, the portrayal of workers as mere costs, inputs into production for purchase and exploitation, and vehicles for demographic and psychographic diversity in product design for various niche consumer markets, can normalize the corporation's exploitation of these workers. In contrast to this managerial view of labor for capital, political economists of communication try to understand the conditions and experiences of labor from the point of view of workers. They approach workers as complex human beings, people who possess the power to collectively organize, conflict with management, and pursue labor rights and policies.

Labor Process Theory (LPT)/Workerism/History from Below

Labor Process Theory (LPT) emerged in the 1970s as a critique of top-down management thinking that aimed to help corporations control and exploit labor (Blair, 2001; Im, 1997; Kealey, 2023; Qiu et al., 2014; Smith & McKinlay, 2009). A keywork in the LPT canon is Harry Braverman's *Labor and Monopoly Capital: The Degradation of Work in the Twentieth Century* (1974). Contrary to the prevailing optimism of post-industrial society's management theorists, who believed that the growth of a service-centered knowledge economy and middle class would diminish conflicts between capital and labor, Braverman demonstrated the opposite: a deepening of managerial control over workers' minds, bodies, and practices within corporations, and the persistence of class inequities and conflicts in the workplace, and in society. Following Braverman, numerous scholars have refined, and adapted LPT (Smith & McKinlay, 2009; Thompson, 1997; Thompson & Smith, 2009, 2010). LPT research is presented at events like the International Labour Process Conference (ILPC), and scholars aligned with the monopoly capitalism school tradition, represented by *Monthly Review Press* and others, continue to update LPT for our time. A very brief summary of the LPT approach follows.

In its simplest form, the labor process refers to how labor is organized and undertaken by workers in capitalist societies and in specific corporations. Workers purposefully use their knowledge and skills, materials and technologies, to produce goods and services with both use-values and exchange-values. But as LPT researchers show, in capitalism, corporations try to strictly control the workers' labor process with the goal of ensuring maximal efficiency, profit and further expansion. In a corporation, management uses a combination of persuasive and repressive techniques to motivate and compel workers to undertake goal-oriented actions for their ends and coordinate the conversion of labor and tools into tangible products or services, such as a personal computer or a PR campaign. LPT researchers tend to focus on *three* key components of the labor process: *labor* (the knowledge and skills possessed by workers, essential for performing a wide range of tasks and achieving goals, whether it's assembling a PC or executing a PR campaign); *object of labor* (the specific goods and services to which corporations aim to direct and apply the workers' labor, for example, the PC the worker is tasked with assembling or the PR campaign the worker is paid to conceptualize and launch); *tools* (all the technologies that workers use to produce goods and services, in the case of the PC: electric screwdrivers, automated screw feeding systems, soldering irons, pick-and-place machines, labeling machines, packaging machines; for the PR campaign: PCs + software and apps, such as content management systems, graphic design, and video editing software).

LPT researchers argue that corporations and their managers try to control the workers' labor, the object of their labor, and the tools they labor with, instrumentalizing the worker for a much larger capitalist machine. They say the goal of management is maximal efficiency (doing more with less, and for less) for optimal profit (reducing labor costs and increasing revenue). To achieve that end, managers devise ways of exercising maximal control over the workers' labor process. They separate the conception of the workers' task from its execution, appropriating the knowledge and skill workers possess, and dispossessing the worker of the unique insight and technique they initially brought to the object. Furthermore, LPT researchers say that to control workers, corporations codify and enforce bureaucratic rules, undertake constant surveillance and monitoring and even provide inducements to self-manage. Also, they say management constantly acquires and applies new technologies in pursuit of greater control, sometimes even relieving themselves of control by using these technologies to partially or fully automate a labor process. According to LPT researchers, these managerial control practices deskill workers. As Braverman (1974/1998, pp. 24–25) explained,

> The ideal organization toward which the capitalist strives is one in which the worker possesses no basic skill upon which the enterprise is dependent and no historical knowledge of the past of the enterprise to serve as a fund from which to draw on in daily work, but rather where everything is codified in rules of performance or laid down in lists that may be consulted (by machines or computers, for instance), so that the worker really becomes an interchangeable part and may be exchanged for another worker with little disruption.

Although LPT researchers focus on modern management's efforts to control workers, they also attend to the tensions and conflicts between capital and labor that arise as result: workers may refuse and resist management's controls by finding workarounds, slowing down or even sabotaging some part of the labor process. While corporations and their managers may try to control the workers' labor process and deskill workers, workers may assert their autonomy and innovate ways to re-assert control over their labor process.

While LPT research might suggest managers exert control over the worker's labor process to drive changes in their workers' subjectivity and behavior that concord with capital, *Operaismo*, which translates to *workerism*, is a research tradition focused on the autonomy of workers to change themselves, and the world, through anti-capitalist acts of refusal and resistance (Haider & Mohandesi, 2013). Going back to the 1960s, the Italian researchers in this tradition learned from American Trotskyism (the Johnson-Forest Tendency, founded by C. L. R. James and Raya Dunayevskaya) and France's radical libertarian socialist group Socialisme ou Barbarie (associated with Claude Lefort and Cornelius Castoriadis) (Haider & Mohandesi, 2013). The Johnson-Forest Tendency had studied working-class life and struggles within the Detroit auto industry, publishing pamphlets such as *The American Worker* (1947), *Punching Out* (1952), and *Union Committeemen and Wildcat Strikes* (1955). The publication of the Quaderni Rossi (Italian for "Red Notebooks") in the early 1960s marked the emergence of Operaismo in Italy and became its primary source of praxis by intellectuals such as Raniero Panzieri, Mario Tronti, Antonio (Toni) Negri, and others. Over time, workerism was adapted by thinkers such as Harry Cleaver (1989), George Caffentzis (1999), Steve Wright (2002), Nick Dyer-Witheford (1999, 2015), and others. Building upon this tradition were post-workerist or "autonomist Marxist" theorists such as Michael Hardt and Antonio Negri (2000), Franco "Bifo" Berardi (2009), Paolo Virno, Maurizio Lazzarato (1996), and Silvia Federici (2014). A new generation of researchers carries these important traditions forward, creatively adapting them for the 21st century studies of work and labor in *Notes from Below* (https://notesfrombelow.org/) and elsewhere (Brophy, 2017; Chen, Delfanti, & Phan 2023; Delfanti, 2021a, 2021b; Delfanti & Sharma 2019; Englert et al., 2020; Grayer & Brophy 2019; Hughes & Woodcock, 2023; Woodcock, 2014, 2021).

The goal of Operaismo is to understand the real lives and labors of workers, with an eye to the potential of workers to shift from a class in itself (waged workers, toiling for corporations), to a class for itself (class-conscious workers, making history). At its core, workerism emphasizes the agency of workers within the capitalist system to contest and emancipate themselves from it. It positions workers as the central agents in the system and aims to understand the workers' real lives and labor conditions, composition, experience, consciousness, and potential, from their own point of view, and with a sober assessment of the possibilities and limits surrounding the workers' own capacity for self-determination, collective organization, and emancipation. Researchers in this tradition tend to concentrate on expressions of worker autonomy, paying attention to instances of workers organizing themselves—through workers' councils, independent labor movements, and wildcat strikes—instead of focusing solely on bureaucratized unions and political parties. They also tend to be highly critical of traditional political parties and unions for becoming disconnected from the actual conditions, experiences, and potentialities of workers and sometimes bemoan them for having a conservatizing and neutralizing influence on class struggle. Using the concept of "class composition," these researchers study the changing nature of the working class, how it is structured, the conditions of exploitation, the workers' experiences of this, and the possibilities and limits for worker political mobilization. Like many who wish to bridge the gap of theory and practice, proponents of workerism often support or take part in working-class activism, including strikes, factory occupations, and other forms of direct action. Furthermore, workerists probe how new and emerging ICTs are often developed and used by capital to control workers and counteract class struggle but also suggest that ICTs can be taken up and employed by workers to contest capitalist power.

While the situation in Italy that gave rise to workerism experienced a decline in the late 1970s, its spirit has had a lasting influence on workerist and autonomous Marxist researchers worldwide. Some of the key concepts in this tradition are as follows: *immaterial labor* (labor oriented to the production of intangible or non-material goods, such as information, media, communication); *multitude* (the diversity and multiplicity of workers in contemporary capitalism); *commons* (collectively and democratically owned and managed material and immaterial resources); *self-valorization* (how workers not only produce value for capitalists but also seek to create value for themselves); and *social factory* (the idea that capitalism has expanded from the factory, to encompass and commercialize and extract value from all social life—education, culture, health and wellness, family, community, and more).

Another theoretical approach that centers the worker, not the system, the plans of the CEO, or the new technology, is E. P. Thompson's *history from below*: this tradition emerged in the 1950s, influenced by the British Communist Party Historians Group, and the journal *Past and Present*. In the 1960s, the founding of the History Workshop movement at Ruskin College broadened the scope, incorporating women's history and oral history, and including non-academics. Thompson's research moved the study of history by shifting the focus from "history from above," with its obsession with "great men" and the powerful, to "history from below," or, the conditions, experiences, and outlooks of ordinary people, especially the working class (Thompson, 1966, 2001). The essence of "history from below" lies in its commitment to recognizing and preserving the stories and experiences of those who typically did not have the opportunity to author their own narratives—all those who were subalternized. Thompson implored historians to give voice to those not in a privileged position to write their own stories, whether due to being entrapped in a low-paying waged job or precarious work arrangement, or due to systemic barriers to self-expression. In contemporary times, the relevance of "history from below" persists. By centering on marginalized voices, "history from below" emphasizes the role of the working class in not only speaking but sometimes even "speaking truth to power." Thompson's book, *The Making of the English Working Class*, exemplifies this approach. In the preface, Thompson wrote:

> I am seeking to rescue the poor stockinger, the Luddite cropper, the "obsolete" hand-loom weaver, the "Utopian" artisan, and even the deluded follower of Joanna Southcott, from the enormous condescension of posterity. Their crafts and traditions may have been dying. Their hostility to the new industrialism may have been backward-looking. Their communitarian ideals may have been fantasies. Their insurrectionary conspiracies may have been foolhardy. But they lived through these times of acute social disturbance, and we did not. Their aspirations were valid in terms of their own experience; and, if they were casualties of history, they remain, condemned in their own lives, as casualties.

Thompson's "history from below" can be adapted for the study of work in the 21st century and offer a unique view, one that diverges from the tendency in the business press to center new enterprises, CEOs and innovations, and instead, focuses on working-class experience and struggle (Clark, 2020; Denning, 1996; Hunter & Shearer, 2023; Nielsen, 1983; Paterson, 2001; Salamon, 2023a). The history from below of work in the DMEI is in the process of being written by workers and scholars. These workers face formidable challenges: navigating the precarious nature of gig work, fighting for and winning labor rights, trying to unionize and being fired. Their struggles are frequently met with barriers, setbacks and defeats. They do not always succeed, and their aspirations may sometimes seem utopian in the face of corporate and state power, but their struggles, their experiences, their hopes, and their dreams, are valid and demand recognition. The little salter whose Big Tech union plan never gains momentum; the telecommunications strikers that the state turns its back on when siding with an oligopoly; the whistleblower, fired for making transparent the CEO's illegal behavior; the leader of the software firm sit-in who never lands a seat at the bargaining table. The co-op member who initially champions the model, but later, rejects it; the hacktivists who cannot remain anonymous and are arrested and jailed; the anti-apartheid tech and newsworkers fired for their truth telling; the anti-capitalist YouTubers who never gain a following. In recognizing and learning from these workers' labors, strategies, and tactics of struggle, and by contextualizing and analyzing their small victories and many defeats, "history from below"centers these people's importance to the making of the DMEI and history itself.

Some Methods

Having discussed some critical theories for the study of work in the DMEI, I'll now swiftly review some key methods for actually doing the research: "labor force study," "case studies," "questionnaires and surveys," "interviews," "oral history," "ethnography," "participatory action research" and "activist auto-ethnography." Some pertinent examples of research that operationalize these methods will also be touched upon.

A *labor force study* is a research method that gathers data about the workforce of an industry or cluster of companies to take a snapshot of that workforce's demography (e.g., class, race, gender, age, education level, and ideology), the range of occupations and roles played, employment and unemployment rates, wage patterns, the public impression of workers, their hopes and fears, and more. Labor force researchers rely on data from industry-specific employment records, and other statistical sources, like labor ministries and departments. An excellent example of the labor force research method in action is *The Hollywood Diversity Report 2020: A Tale of Two Hollywoods*. Darnell Hunt and Ana-Christina Ramón (2020), researchers at UCLA's Division of Social Science's Hollywood Advancement Project, led the project, analyzing the demographics of the labor force—both in front of and behind the camera—in top movies, as ranked by global box office success. Their study sought to determine if Hollywood's labor force was proportionally representative of the demographic diversity of the US. The US Census data shows that visible minorities make up an increasing share of the US population (41% at present, and projected to become the majority within a few decades), and that women represent a little over half of the US population (51%). The researchers asked: did the labor force of Hollywood's highest grossing movies in 2018 and 2019 proportionally mirror the US's diversity? They examined 140 films released in 2018 and 146 films in 2019, focusing on lead talent, overall cast, and writers and directors. They found a predominantly white and male workforce in top executive, directorial, and writing roles. While more people of color and women had landed lead roles than in the past, they were still significantly underrepresented relative to their portion of the overall US population. Nonetheless, the research found that Hollywood's representations of society are becoming more diverse, and that movies with multi-cultural casts tend to do well at the global box office. Yet, the control of capital, decision-making power, and profits in Hollywood remains predominantly in the hands of white men, in the CEO positions atop the structure. This points to continuity and change: marginal gains in the politics of decision-making authority and wealth redistribution alongside advancements in a politics of recognition and representation.

Workforce questionnaires and *surveys* are a research method that gathers information about workers experiences, thoughts, feelings and opinions, and satisfaction levels, pertaining to the terms and conditions of their work. The method entails several steps: (1) deciding the focus (e.g., the workforce's thoughts and feeling about the new CEO and their recent salary and stock options increase); (2) designing clear questions using formats like true/false and multiple-choice, Likert scales, open-ended, and others (e.g., do you mostly agree, agree or strongly agree that the CEO pay raise has improved the company?"); (3) selecting a target workforce population (e.g., "White Hat Hacker") and sampling method (e.g., "random," "systematic," "stratified," "cluster," "convenience," "snowball," "quota," "purposive"); (4) collecting data via email or online surveys and ensuring the participants have provided informed consent (e.g., "you have been selected for a special questionnaire, please click here if you agree to the terms and conditions"); and (5) analyzing the data to identify patterns (e.g., "83% of the 104 workers who responded to question #1 said the company could make them happier by reducing the CEO's salary and increasing theirs"); and, (6) sharing findings (e.g., publishing them online or in a news story). A recent study that employs the questionnaire and survey method is "Dignity At Work 2" by the Incorporated Society Of Musicians (ISM) (Williams & Bain, 2022). This method has also been used by scholars to learn about the conditions and experiences of art and tech cooperatives (Dreyer et al., 2020), game developers (Weststar et al., 2018), journalists (Willnat et al., 2022), and creative freelancers (Mackenzie & McKinlay, 2021). Surveys have furthermore been instrumental in uncovering the mental health crisis within the entertainment and tech sectors (Cullins et al., 2020; Mentortribes, 2022), the diminishing sustainability of work in games (Plant, 2023), and the precarious patchwork conditions faced by individuals using platforms for service gigs (Huws et al., 2019).

Interviews are a research method that aims to provide in-depth insights into the experiences, opinions, and feelings of workers, and may consist of structured, semi-structured and unstructured formats. Structured interviews follow a set question list for consistency, semi-structured interviews blend fixed and open-ended questions, and unstructured interviews entail a conversational or dialogical style. Scholars have used the interview method in studies of: the accelerating labor process of digital journalists (Cohen, 2018); social media creators and the pursuit of visibility in algorithm-driven platforms (Duffy et al., 2021; Duffy & Meisner, 2023); the changing relationships between travel influencers and destination marketers (Stoldt et al., 2019); film and TV actors with physical or sensory disabilities (Gulka et al., 2022); ageism in the advertising industry (Brodmerkel & Barker, 2019); how Deliveroo and Foodora riders resist app-based algorithmic management (Bronowicka & Ivanova, 2020); and, the tensions between self-realization and self-exploitation in game testing (Ozimek, 2019a, 2019b).

Oral history is a research method that aims to preserve the voices of workers through recorded interviews with all those who labor, and labor in the DMEI. This method records workers speaking, telling stories, and giving testimonies, resulting in an intimate first-hand account of a worker's experiences, and their personal thoughts and feelings about the work they did or are doing. Studs Terkel's *Working* (1974) and *Gig: Americans Talk about Their Jobs at the Turn of the Millennium*, edited by Marisa Bowe, John Bowe, and Sabin Streeter (2000), exemplify this method. Terkel's *Working* contains the voices of a diversity of workers: farmers, miners, factory workers, communication professors, flight attendants, tech developers, parking valets, newspaper delivery boys, firefighters, CEOs, receptionists, hotel switchboard operators, sex workers, writers, actors, salespeople, barbers, dentists, truck drivers, supermarket checkers, bankers, healthcare professionals, educators, musicians, jockeys, and grave diggers. *Gig* includes the voices of a turn-of-the-millennium workforce, in stories by more than 100 workers: flight attendants, UPS drivers, Wal-Mart greeters, telemarketing supervisors, art movers, steelworkers, corporate securities lawyers, long-haul truck drivers, systems administrators, and many others. Both *Working* and *Gig* are great models of the oral history method.

Ethnography is a research method that entails the researchers' deep engagement with the labor undertaken by workers in organizations. Ethnographers immerse themselves in film sets or in digital media companies and gather insights into organizational structures, workplace cultures, worker interactions, and other dynamics. Ethnographers provide a "thick description" of what's going on with work in the DMEI (Bonini & Gandini, 2020). Nick Seaver's *Computing Taste: Algorithms and the Makers of Music Recommendation* (2018a) is an exemplary model of ethnographic research. *Creative Control: The Ambivalence of Work in the Culture Industries* by Michael L. Siciliano (2021) is another great example of the ethnographic method, based on two years of participatory observation in a Los Angeles music studio and a YouTube network. Other scholars have used ethnographic methods and found that: London and Los Angeles-based influencer communities consist of neoliberal creators who endure precarity, stress and burnout, and algorithmic discrimination (Glatt, 2022b); top-ranked bloggers pursue the ideal of "having it all" through various mythical tropes of creative work (Duffy & Hund, 2015); tech worker engineers play "labor games" to construct their masculine selves (Wu, 2020); and, the Independent Workers of Great Britain (IWGB) Game Workers Unite UK (GWU UK) maps power relations within the workplace while protecting its members' anonymity (Ruffino, 2021). Ethnographies are a useful method but can be difficult to do because many corporations refuse to let researchers on site, and many workers do not want to be analyzed. Those that do may be prevented from doing so by non-disclosure agreements (NDAs).

A *case study* research method aims for a contextualized and theoretically informed examination of a specific instance, object, or phenomenon pertinent to the real world of work in the DMEI. Scholars have used case studies to highlight the dynamism of Chinese creative labor practices across TV, journalism, design, and social media (Lin, 2023) and the class barriers to landing a career in the UK's cultural industries (Brook et al., 2023). Also, they've studied the representation of sex workers in entertainment (Kirshner, 2024) and how skill dynamics in digital game design perpetuates the delegitimization of women's work (Harvey & Shepherd, 2017). Additionally, they have used case studies to examine the pathways to visibility for Black gamers, showing how live-streaming is a new space for Black technocultural production (Chan & Gray, 2020) and scrutinized racialized pay gaps among influencers, focusing on the #InfluencerPayGap Instagram account (Christin & Lu, 2023). Moreover, scholars have used case studies to analyze all 22 collective bargaining agreements of the Writers Guild of America, East (WGAE) to glean worker job and life satisfaction (Salamon, 2023c), craft a detailed history of the Hollywood writer's strike (Handel, 2011), and document the rise of new media unions (Cohen & de Peuter, 2021). Through case studies, they've also addressed the unique dynamics of platform cooperativism in Brazil (Grohmann, 2023), mythologies about creative work (Duffy & Wissinger, 2017), Instagram influencer "engagement pods" as a form of resistance (O'Meara, 2019), political influencers on platforms (Riedl et al., 2023), the ideology of tech workers based on their election campaign contributions (Selling & Strimling, 2023), and efforts to turn Galway, Ireland, into a creative hub (Collins & Power, 2019).

For researchers inclined to ally with the communities, networks and organizations that support or try to build worker power, *participatory activist research* (Pickerill et al., 2021) and *activist auto-ethnography*

(Tillmann et al., 2022) are useful methods. Participatory activist researchers conduct research about an activist group from the *outside-in*. They start as an outsider-researcher of an activist group, not a member of it, but then enter the group, ask questions of its members, document what is going on, and produce new knowledge about it. Participatory activist researchers take it as axiomatic that they must take part in an activist community to really understand it and are "committed to going beyond extracting knowledge from communities, by instead actively contributing to the goals of the individuals and groups involved in the research" (Pickerill et al., 2021). By comparison, activist auto-ethnographers undertake research on an activist group from the *inside-out*. They begin as an insider of an activist group, not an outsider-scholar of it, but then ask questions of themselves in relation to the group, document their experiences, and creatively weave their anecdotes, memories, and feelings into a reflexive and highly personalized story. Auto-ethnographic activist researchers write first-person narratives about "what living an activist life-in and outside the academy—requires, means, and does" (p. 1) and try to "bring to life opportunities, challenges, and complexities inherent in academic activists' sustained commitments to liberation and social justice" (Tillmann et al., 2022, p. 1). In researching union formation, collective bargaining, and strikes, researchers in this tradition would work closely with the workers, actively participate in their communities, networks, and organizations, and support their organizing campaigns, strategic communication, negotiations, and strikes. Instead of participating to extract knowledge from the workers' movement to be used in the writing and publication of one more paywalled journal article owned by Taylor & Francis or SAGE, this method is to give one's time, energy, and care to the labor movement, to support its actions, and bring about outcomes that benefit or enhance what it is doing.

For Normativity

This chapter has provided an overview of some key critical theories and methods used in researching work in the DMEI. There is no one best way to conduct research, nor is there one best theory or method for approaching the study of work in the DMEI. Research should not be Taylorized! The research toolkit is large and open, with numerous theories and methods available to tinker and play with. This chapter invites scholars who may be new to the field to take from this toolkit (and others), and build their own. Ultimately, this chapter described some tools for "getting to work" on work in the DMEI. But this getting to work is always, even if unintentionally, an ethical practice, informed by values and judgments of the right and the wrong, the good and the bad, which brings up the fraught topic of *normativity* in research.

Going back to the late 1990s, work within certain industry groups in the DMEI has sometimes been perceived as inherently "good," or at least better than the "bad" work in some other sectors. The DMEI were sometimes touted by policy-makers, corporations, and the public alike as epitomizing the conditions and experiences of "good work," a positive advancement upon the "bad work" prevalent in the Fordist era of factories and heavy industry. For a time, knowledge, cultural, informational and creative work was hailed as a model for good work, leading the way to a better future of work for all (Banks & Hesmondhalgh, 2009; Hesmondhalgh & Baker, 2011). Government cultural policy-makers, corporations, and even workers themselves commonly promoted the virtues of creative work in the DMEI, aligning this work with autonomy and self-realization, and positioning the knowledge and skills required to work in the DMEI favorably against the standardized, routinized, and easily automated labor process of industrial-era jobs. In the most optimistic accounts, work in the DMEI gave the worker freedom over their labor process, let them become who they are through what they do and harnessed their unique talent to produce novel hardware, software, and content that made corporations a lot of money and made the world a much better place than before. The idea that work in the DMEI is good for workers (in terms of the conditions and experiences it offers) and good for the world (in terms of the impact its products and services have in society) is idealistic given what typically happens in reality (exploitation), but nonetheless, represents a useful starting point for sketching a normative framework of good work. Work *ought* to be good for workers and *should* be good for society, but all too often, it is not.

Long ago, David Hesmondhalgh (2010) observed that many studies of work in the creative industries lacked clear definitions of "good work." He argued that this absence limited the effectiveness of critique and called for broader discussions about what might constitute "good work" (231). He stated, "When we undertake criticism, we presumably do so because of some kind of belief that life [and work] might be made better," but noted that some researchers sidelined the question of what good work might entail and how good work might be achieved in the creative industries and in society (243). The meaning of good work is embattled and always will be, but that does not mean it is a useless idea. There is a need to construct an idea of "good work" in the DMEI that might be useful to anyone interested in trying to improve the conditions of work with and for the many around the world who are laboring in this super-sector. That means being positive, not negative. It involves crafting as opposed to crushing a *normative framework* for assessing the quality of work in the DMEI. To evaluate the quality of any job—determining whether it's a "good job" or a "bad job"—we first need to establish a set of clear criteria. This is where a "normative framework" comes into play. Generally, "normative" pertains to value judgments about things. A normative framework can serve as a useful heuristic for identifying the ideal qualities that define a "good job" as opposed to a "bad job" in the DMEI, guiding informed assessments of specific jobs and occupations that workers do.

Hesmondhalgh and Baker (2013) proposed that "good work" in cultural industries should include "decent pay, hours and safety; autonomy; interest and involvement; sociality; esteem and self-esteem; self-realization; work-life balance; and security" (p. 17). Mark Banks (2017) advanced a powerful normative framework for good work in *Creative Justice*. Central to the normative framework sketched here are nine key principles that can serve as benchmarks for distinguishing "good" work from "bad." This framework is a tool for evaluating work and also conveys a positive vision for what might constitute the conditions and experiences of good work. These principles include: fair pay, or equitable compensation; job security, perhaps in the form of standard employment, but maybe flex-security; the dignity of labor; the recognition of workers' identities; a healthy and safe workplace free from discrimination; workplace democracy; maximal self-realization and minimal alienation; creative empowerment; and outputs that contribute positively to society.

This rough normative framework for judging the quality of work in the DMEI may raise some hackles given controversies surrounding "normative frameworks." While we can acknowledge criticisms of normativity, there are also reasons for embracing it. Banks (2017) argues, "the notion of a non-normative social science is not only impossible but also self-contradictory" (p. 12) and "any critical social science deserving of the name must be, to some extent, normative—it must adopt an orientation of evaluation and judgment" (p. 12). This does not mean scholars should forsake reflexivity or ignore or hide their own potential personal investments and political biases. Nor does it advocate for a rigid adherence to one normative approach in the face of contradicting evidence. Even still, without a normative framework, "social science can only describe the status quo and exclude the possibility of theorizing progressive or emancipatory changes" (Banks, 2017, p. 12). Ultimately, Banks calls for a reflexive approach that constructs and employs normative frameworks for judging the conditions and experiences of work, for calling out and criticizing bad work when apparent and for envisioning the possibility of good or at least better work for the majority of people, if not yet realized.

An additional concern with the use of a normative framework is that perceptions of the badness or goodness of a job can vary significantly among workers themselves. What is considered good or bad work may be subjectively perceived, and a consensus among workers on the essence of a job's good or bad quality is not always crystal clear or easy to build. For instance, a job viewed as "good" in one context by one worker might be seen as "bad" by another. Some might argue against the idea of good work, saying this would be to elevate one particular notion of the good at the expense of the others, privileging those who get to do this good work, and ignoring those who don't. That may be a stretch, though. While we can recognize different perceptions of good and bad work exist among workers, it would be surprising to find workers at Walt Disney Company viewing an increase in their annual pay relative to their productivity and corporate profits as a negative occurrence. Similarly, it's improbable that workers in some Foxconn factory would universally regard unhealthy and unsafe working conditions as a net positive (Qiu, 2016a). Despite the variability in perceptions of good and bad work, there are good reasons for developing a normative framework for judging work in the DMEI that is grounded in certain pro-worker principles.

For one, this normative framework can shift the power of judgment from capital to labor. Traditionally, it is the employer that judges the worker and the quality of their work, but this normative framework "flips the script" and allows researchers and workers to critically assess the conditions of work in the DMEI and evaluate the quality of the job or career provided by corporations.

Second, this normative framework represents a significant shift from assessing workers solely for capital's benefit—seeking more efficient and effective management methods—toward a deeper exploration of the conditions and experiences of work in the DMEI. The goal is to uncover radical improvements that can enhance the well-being of workers and, by extension, society as a whole. It is concerned with the "moral economy" of work, of making judgments about work conditions and experiences to try to minimize exploitation and oppression and maximize "the good life" (Banks, 2017, pp. 42–43).

Third, this normative framework may be a useful guide for anyone who wishes to take up the fight to improve the quality of work in the DMEI. Across history, around the world, workers who have struggled for better conditions and experiences of work have always been guided by a normative framework, sometimes explicit and rationally articulated, and at other times, tacit and deeply felt. The concept of a "good job" may be socially constructed and ever-changing, but it's crucial to all those workers who've gained the confidence to call out bad jobs and advocate for better ones. Workers movements have a long history of criticizing bad jobs and struggling for jobs they consider good, and their collective efforts have led to significant workplace improvements such as minimum wage standards, a fairer share of the surplus profit, weekends, paid vacations, health and safety regulations, and benefits. These achievements underscore the practical importance of a normative framework to real-world class struggles and to making policies that improve the quality of life and labor for the many.

Fourth, without a normative framework that takes the well-being of workers as its starting point, the existing far from less-than-ideal labor standards set by neoliberal states and corporations will continue to prevail over workers, and those are biased, tending to greatly favor the interests of capital over labor.

Fifth, this normative framework could serve as a valuable heuristic tool, a measuring stick for supporting tangible improvements in the conditions of life and labor for workers in the DMEI. For research to be truly beneficial to the working class, both within and outside of the DMEI, it must go beyond merely critiquing bad work conditions and exploitative, precarious and alienating experiences. It should also offer concrete guidance on what better work conditions and experiences might entail. That's what normativity enables.

4 What Is Capitalism and How Do Corporations Shape Work in the DMEI?

Introduction

This chapter is an overview of how capitalism and corporations shape the conditions and experiences of work in the digital media and entertainment industries (DMEI). It begins with a review of some key concepts of workers associated with industrial *and* post-industrial or "informational," "creative," "digital," and "platform" capitalism: "white collar workers," "emotional labor," "knowledge workers," "immaterial labor," "artists," "cultural/creative workers," "cybertariats," "tech workers," "digital labor," and "platform workers." The chapter then defines capitalism as a class society, noting its pyramidal structure of upper, middle, and working classes, and the manifestation of this in the organizational hierarchies of many corporations in the DMEI. It elaborates eight fundamental logics of the capitalist system, explains how they are reproduced by the major corporations of the DMEI, and considers how they shape the conditions and experiences of workers: (1) corporate ownership of capital; (2) waged labor, labor markets, and a division of labor; (3) production driven by profit rather than human need; (4) market competition and market control; (5) exploitation: profit maximization, labor cost minimization, and intellectual property (IP) dispossession; (6) crises, cycles of boom and bust, and creative destruction; (7) income, wealth, and class inequality; and (8) class tension and conflict.

The Making of the Industrial Working Class: A Revision

"Blue-collar," "high-school dropout," "low-income," "conservative," "complacent," and "reactionary" are just a mouthful of the clichés often applied to the "working class" by those individuals who overlook how social class exists as a structural relation to capital, not necessarily in what job one does, degree one holds, wage one makes, party one votes for, or ideology one espouses. Some individuals, possibly anxious about the meaning

DOI: 10.4324/9781003131076-5

of their own so-called "middle class" status, use a classist stereotype to deny how they may be "working class" themselves. The concept of the "working class" is neither monolithic nor unchanging; instead, it covers a multitude of billions of people that have little in common except for their lack of ownership or control over capital, their compulsion to sell their labor power to corporations in exchange for a wage, and perhaps, their experience of exploitation (and alienation) as result. This working class in itself is not automatically for itself, ready to rise up and revolt against capital, raring to resist wage dependency, and in solidarity, contesting inequity and oppression. The working class is something made and remade by everyone from parties to unions to activists to theorists to workers themselves. Sometimes, workers articulate a common class interest, build the organizational resources and capacities to give it expression and focus and take concrete political action—union campaigns, strikes, social movements, state reforms, and revolts—to realize it, every so often, making history.

We live in a world where the majority of people are working class, including the majority of workers in the DMEI, and yet, for much of modern history, the idea of the working class has been constrained by a concept or stereotype of the worker associated with the first and second industrial revolutions. During the 19th and early 20th centuries, several major city-centers across the globe, especially within imperial states—Britain, the United States, Russia, Germany, and Japan—emerged as formidable hubs of mass industrial production and consumption and working-class organization. In the British Empire, Manchester was "Cottonopolis," the epicenter of cotton textile manufacturing while Birmingham was the "City of a Thousand Trades" and Glasgow was the core of shipbuilding, with sprawling shipyards and gigantic vessels. In the emerging US Empire, Detroit, frequently synonymous with "Fordism," was home to automotive giants such as Ford, General Motors, and Chrysler while Pittsburgh was branded the "Steel City" for its steel mills and Chicago was the bloody base of slaughterhouses and rail and transportation networks. Several thinkers have formulated their understanding of "the working class" based on the major labor force that emerged in these urban city centers, which included wage earners toiling in factories, operating heavy machinery manually, enduring a highly controlled labor process overseen by managers, experiencing alienation from themselves, their work, fellow workers, and the end product, all while being exploited for the benefit of corporations.

This industrial working class's demography was multi-cultural, multi-linguistic, multi-racialized and multi-gendered. For example, the turn of 20th-century "working class" in major American industrial cities encompassed not only millions of "white Americans" or, descendants of the British settler colonialists and slave owners, but also, millions of

European immigrant workers—Irish, Italian, German, Polish, Greek, and Scandinavian. African Americans, Chinese, Japanese, Filipino, South Asian Americans, and Mexican Americans were also part of the turn of century working class, hired and exploited by industrial capital as such, while also brutalized by racism, segregation, and unequal treatment. Women were part of the working class as well, but due to patriarchy, they earned lower pay compared to men even when doing the same factory jobs, were slotted into gender-stereotyped "feminine" roles within sexist divisions of labor, and were socialized and cajoled to shoulder the unpaid reproductive labors of housework and caregiving—a "double shift" for patriarchal capital.

In this context, the potential for all these workers to transition from being a class-in-itself to becoming a political class-for-itself was significantly constrained by top-down racism and sexism. Elites frequently constructed and manipulated racial and gender differences among workers to sow division and maintain control. Racism and sexism were deliberately and sometimes inadvertently employed to exacerbate tensions among workers, establishing rifts that pitted differently racialized and gendered workers against each other, as racialized and gendered enemies, instead of working-class allies. This undermined the prospects of working-class solidarity, organization, education, agitation, and collective action against capital, and the bosses at the top. Many members of the so-called "white working class" acted as a hindrance to the formation of a cohesive working class for itself, perpetuating racial capitalism's business model. They worked to earn a position within an ostensibly "superior" white national-racial community, prioritizing their white national-racial identity and the privileges it conferred over the political work of building and identifying with a multi-racial working-class international community. White workers might identify their interests with white bosses, imagining themselves as part of a supposedly superior racial group, even though their class interests were fundamentally at odds. Furthermore, many male workers supported patriarchy and benefited from it. Prevailing notions of "masculinity" were intertwined with specific occupational roles rooted in gender stereotypes. Consequently, too many men associated their self-worth with this masculinity and their performance of it with waged labor alongside other men in factories, instead of joining in solidarity with women who worked for lower wages in factories or undertook unpaid labor at home. Gendered divisions of labor, spanning from the factory floor to the household to the office, reinforced patriarchal capitalism and hindered class unity between male and female working-class people. Often, male workers regarded themselves as superior to their female counterparts, even when both were being exploited for the benefit of male CEOs at the top of the class hierarchy.

For hundreds of years, capitalism's working class has been substantively multi-cultural, multi-linguistic, multi-racialized, and multi-gendered, and these differences have been operationalized for both solidarity and subversion. There has nonetheless been a tendency to imagine the "working class" primarily as a group of white male factory workers, a bunch of "blue-collar" proles toiling on some assembly line. The portrayal of the white male wage earner as emblematic of industrial capitalism's working class is *ahistorical*, and the invocation of this stereotype to symbolize the entire working class obscures the profound diversity of the working class, past and present.

The Making of the DMEI's Working Class: Concepts and Figures

The old Fordist stereotype of the industrial working-class was often invoked by social theorists of post-industrial capitalism as a foil for new concepts and figures of the service working class associated with "post-industrial," or "informational," "creative," "digital," and "platform" capitalism. These concepts and figures point to the ostensible newness and distinctiveness of work and labor in companies, industries, and sectors where "information," "knowledge," "communications," "culture," and "media" services are key to the accumulation of capital. I identify and offer a friendly assessment of some of these: "white collar workers," "emotional labor," "knowledge workers," "immaterial labor," "artists," "cultural/creative workers," "cybertariats," "tech workers," "digital labor," and "platform workers."

White collar worker. In *White Collar: The American Middle Classes*, published in 1951, C. Wright Mills (2002) introduced the concept of the "white-collar worker," marking a significant shift in the understanding of labor, from the production of things in factories to the production of services in offices and retail outlets. Mills' white-collar worker encompasses waged and salaried individuals engaged in professional, desk, managerial, or administrative labor, typically in office settings. These workers were not hired for the knowledge or skill required to make tangible goods but paid for their personalities, and their capacity to perform a service related to the circulation of commodities. "In a society of employees, dominated by the marketing mentality, it is inevitable that a personality market should arise" said Mills. He continued: "For in the great shift from manual skills to the art of 'handling,' selling, and servicing people, personal or even intimate traits of employees are drawn into the sphere of exchange, become commodities in the labor market" (p. 182). Mills observed how "Kindness and friendliness" were expected of white-collar workers, and he lamented how this "personalized service" was actually "pretend interest in others in order to manipulate them" (p. 193), "to further the sale of something"

(p. 182) for the corporation. This "personality" labor estranged workers from themselves and from those they were paid to serve. While there are surely many "white collar" workers in the DMEI doing all kinds of "personality work" (customer service is everywhere), the concept of "white collar" does not capture the range of occupational roles in the DMEI. Furthermore, the existence of work that is project-based and remote in the DMEI does not align with white collar's 9-to-5 day at the office, five days a week with weekends off and an annual salary. Nonetheless, personality work is key to all kinds of jobs in the DMEI.

Emotional Labor

While Mills scrutinized the emotionally deadening white-collar world, in *The Managed Heart: Commercialization of Human Feeling*, Arlie Hochschild (1983) revealed how central emotion had become to post-industrial capitalism. In her extensive study of the service work of flight attendants, Hochschild (1983, p. 7) used the term "emotional labor to mean the [worker's] management of feeling to create a publicly observable facial and bodily display; emotional labor is sold [by workers] for a wage and therefore an exchange value." Hochschild argued that when doing emotional labor, workers' emotions are manipulated by both managers, who design emotion scripts for workers to "deep act" in the presence of customers, and by the customers themselves, who believe "the customer is always right." Hochschild argues that when doing emotional service work for a corporation, workers were alienated from both the labor process (emotional labor with or for others) and the product of their labor (the expression of their emotions). The emotional labor process, "socially engineered and thoroughly organized from the top" (p. 8), subjected workers to the Taylorization of their emotions by management. Also, "When the product is a smile, a mood, a feeling, or a relationship, it comes to belong more to the organization and less to the self" (p. 198). The consequence of capital's management of the workers' heart was emotive dissonance, a gap between what the worker really feels inside and the feeling they perform while working for the corporation and servicing its customers. Emotional labor is pervasive in the DMEI. Online creators on Instagram and YouTube craft relatable personas to foster connections with their audiences through expressions of seemingly "authentic" interest and empathy. Customer service representatives for tech giants like Apple and Amazon must sound happy, exhibit patience, and show understanding when addressing customer complaints. TV anchors and pundits for FOX and MSNBC often perform emotional labor when covering sensitive news stories, displaying sadness, concern, anger, and even outrage. PR professionals manage their clients' public images with expressions of emotions, especially in crisis situations. In the DMEI, emotional labor is an integral part of various occupations.

Knowledge Worker

In his 1959 book *Landmarks of Tomorrow: A Report on the New "Post-Modern" World*, Peter Drucker (1996) coined the term "knowledge worker" to describe a post-industrial workforce comprising highly educated professionals engaged in mental or intellectual activities, and whose occupations entailed the creation, circulation, interpretation, and analysis of intangible goods such as information and knowledge rather than tangible goods. These knowledge workers were employed in "professional" fields like medicine, law, engineering, and academia, and enjoyed a high degree of autonomy and responsibility. In his 1962 book, *The Production and Distribution of Knowledge in the United States*, the Austrian-born economist Fritz Machlup (1962) examined the new knowledge economy, documenting how central the new "information" industries were becoming to American capitalism in terms of both gross domestic product (GDP) and labor force size. Machlup referred to knowledge workers as "knowledge transmitters" and "knowledge receivers." In *Knowledge Workers in the Information Society*, a volume co-edited by Catherine McKercher and Vincent Mosco (2007), contributors expanded and refined the "knowledge worker" concept. The DMEI undoubtedly relies upon a lot of knowledge workers: data analysts, software developers, UX designers, video editors, e-sports analysts, and more. However, the knowledge worker concept is sometimes scrutinized for its mental and manual labor binary: all workers, regardless of their employment in manufacturing or services, possess knowledge, rely on intellect, and every workers' labor practice is also corporeal, undertaken in a material or physical environment, and deeply felt.

Immaterial Labor

Critical theorists such as Maurizio Lazzarato, Paolo Virno, Franco Berardi, and Michael Hardt and Antonio Negri advanced the post-Fordist concept of "immaterial labor" to describe how corporations rely upon the workers' cognitive, communicative, and affective labor power when producing and circulating services. In "Immaterial Labor," Lazzarato (1996) defined this as the labor that "produces the informational and cultural content of the commodity" (p. 133). Elsewhere, Lazzarato (2004, p. 205) elaborated: "What organizations produce and sell not only includes material or immaterial goods, but also forms of communication, standards of socialisation, perception, education, housing, transportation, etc.

The explosion of services is directly linked to this evolution." In *Empire*, Hardt and Negri (2000) reframed immaterial labor, positioning it as key to the production of immaterial goods such as information and cultural products. In the copyright-driven machinery of the DMEI, immaterial labor takes center stage, with millions of products existing solely as intangible entities: one cannot drive *The Walking Dead* to work, affix *Oppenheimer* to a B83 nuclear bomb, put Miley Cyrus's "Flowers" behind one's ear, swallow TikTok's recommender system, light Microsoft Office on fire or shake hands with a favorite YouTuber. While the concept of immaterial labor is valuable in emphasizing the production and circulation of intangible goods and services, it may be less effective as a term for the present or the "new." After all, going back to the 19th century, the cultural industries have hired workers to produce intangibles such as copyrighted brand logos and trademarks for products. While much of the DMEI workforce engages in immaterial labor, this labor is always embodied. Workers rely on their eyes to read information, hands to operate keyboards and mouses, and ears to listen to customer feedback. Although corporations employ immaterial labor, the workers' material labor process does not guarantee freedom from necessity or emancipation of general intellect.

Artist

The Romantic concept of the "artist" has long held a prominent place in the social imagination. During the heyday of the New Left, artists were often celebrated as heroic anti-capitalist figures uniquely positioned to critique and rebel against the system. This perception stemmed from their supposed innate pursuit of individual freedom, authenticity, and self-expression in a world marked by controlled living, mass conformity, and commercial imitation (Boltanski & Chiapello, 2005). The cultural industries incorporated this "artistic critique" of capitalism, co-opting the figure of the artist and deploying it in support of accumulation. Ads told consumers they could attain a rebel status through the purchase and display of edgy products; CEOs likely appreciated the cost-savings of those who fought for flexibility against the old standard employment regime (and the salaries, benefits, and rights it delivered) (Boltanski & Chiapello, 2005; McRobbie, 2016; Ross, 2003, 2009). While individual working artists exist, the Romantic artist is out of sync with the fact that most "artistic" people are today waged laborers for companies. They endure regimented divisions of labor and produce copyrighted texts they do not own and for markets that have nothing to do with their own "self-expression" (Pang, 2015). Most writers at Walt Disney Studios are not "artists" in a traditional sense: they are workers paid to service franchises, not pursue individual freedom; they work in teams, not alone; their names may appear in the credits, but the movie their labor made is not a symbol of their own identity. The movie created by these writers' collective intellect is the intellectual property of the corporation that paid for its production and a symbol of that corporation's brand identity and reputation.

Cultural/Creative Worker

The term "cultural worker"—frequently synonymous with "creative worker"—is often used to describe all those who labor in the cultural/creative industries and as a rejoinder to the prevailing myth that everyone in these sectors is a free-wheeling "artist." In *The Cultural Industries*, David Hesmondhalgh (2019) defined "cultural workers" as "symbol creators or symbol makers" who are involved in creating, interpreting, or reworking cultural texts such as stories, songs, and images (p. 9). Hesmondhalgh (2019, p. 351) adapted Ruth Towse's (1992) findings about the characteristics of "artistic" labor, to list a number of things about "cultural workers": "They tend to hold multiple jobs"; "There is a predominance of self-employed or freelance workers"; "Work is irregular, contracts are short-term, and there is little job protection"; "Career prospects are uncertain"; "The distribution of earnings is highly skewed (that is, unequal)"; workers tend to be younger than those in other sectors; and, "The workforce appears to be growing." While the concept of the "cultural worker" can be a useful albeit catchall term for workers in the cultural industries, not all cultural workers are part of the creative precariat. Also, not all occupations in the cultural industries neatly align with the conventional definition of a "cultural worker" (Miller, 2015, p. 319). Are all workers within a company operating in the cultural industries considered "cultural workers," or does the term specifically apply to those directly involved in creating a copyrighted work of culture? For example, IP lawyers and accountants at a Hollywood studio may not be considered "cultural workers" in the same sense as writers or actors. Additionally, in *Theorizing Cultural Work*, Mark Banks, Rosalind Gill, and Stephanie Taylor (2013) question the meaning of the "cultural" in the "cultural worker" (p. 6) concept and prompt us to ask: what does "cultural" refer to and what makes "cultural" work qualitatively different as compared to types of work not conceived of as "cultural"? Furthermore, the term "cultural worker" can often lead to confusion, especially among those not familiar with cultural policy lingo. Often, "culture" is used as a synonym for race, ethnicity, nationality, and religion, rather than being associated with corporations engaged in the production and circulation of copyrighted "cultural works" and the labor force they employ. For those unfamiliar with the term, a "cultural worker" might be imagined to be someone working in the growing corporate diversity training sector or in multi-cultural social work, rather than those in movie production, advertising, or app development. In any case, the DMEI employs many "cultural workers," and the "platform cultural producer" and "online creator" are new concepts for all those engaged in entrepreneurial forms of symbolic production on platforms such as YouTube, TikTok, and Instagram (Cunningham & Craig, 2019, 2021; Florida, 2022; Poell et al., 2021).

Cyber-Tariat/Tech Worker

Over the past two decades, scholars have advanced the concept of a "cyber-tariat," referring to workers in the electronics and ICT industries, as well as those who rely on the Internet and digital hardware and software to do their work. In *The Making of a Cybertariat: Virtual Work in a Real World*, Ursula Huws (2003) coined the term "cyber-tariat" to recognize the embodied human workers "in all their rounded, messy, vulnerable materiality" (p. 151) toiling online. In *Language Put to Work*, Enda Brophy (2017, p. 11) further defined the "cybertariat" as: "call center workers," "warehouse sorters for e-commerce companies such as Amazon," "assembly workers for outsourced electronics manufacturers like Foxconn," "digital microtaskers hired by virtual temp firms such as Mechanical Turk" and Upwork, "outsourced commercial content moderators for social media companies," "journalists producing copy determined by algorithms for online content farms," "retail employees at Apple Stores and wireless carrier storefront operations," "data entry workers" and the many "millions of others upon whose labour communicative capitalism depends daily, yet remunerates inadequately and sometimes not at all." The concept of the "cyber-tariat" introduced a much needed class analysis to the labor force of digital capitalism and posed a counterpoint to those techno-optimists who depicted the new "virtual" or "informational" or "digital" world of work as emancipating. However, the concept of the "cyber-tariat" casts a wide net, catching a diverse range of occupational roles. The "tech worker" concept exhibits a similar breadth (Daub, 2020; Dorschel, 2022; Irani, 2015; Selling & Strimling, 2023; Ziegler, 2022). While companies like Apple and Amazon may be categorized as tech firms, the multitude of roles within them complicates a general definition of "tech worker." Are software engineers at these companies, workers assembling Apple iPhones at FoxConn and boxing products at an Amazon warehouse, and content moderators deleting hate speech from Apple Music forums and Amazon product review pages all "tech workers"? In summary, both the "cyber-tariat" and the newer "tech worker" concepts are important, but may lack precision.

Digital Labor

The concept of "digital labor" initially emerged to characterize unpaid post-Fordist service work carried out by users on social media platforms. In its premier iteration, it was coined to specifically refer to the unpaid labor performed by the users of platforms like Facebook and Twitter (Flisfeder & Fuchs, 2015; Fuchs, 2014; Fuchs & Sevignani, 2013; Jarrett, 2022; Sandoval et al., 2014). These users, by creating and sharing content, and engaging with others on these platforms, drive more user traffic and contribute to "network effects." The effort and time users spend on these interactions also generate valuable data for the corporations that own the platforms, which is essential to their ad revenue models. The platform-owning companies actively monitor, collect, and aggregate this user data into profiles, and then commodify and exploit it for profit. With this data, they attract corporate customers for their targeted ad placement services, who purchase them with the goal of efficiently reaching users with their digital ads. Because the digital labor of social media users was so essential to the profits of social media companies, some argued that these users were actually unpaid "workers" for Big Tech firms. Over time, the concept of "digital labor" expanded to encompass various forms of paid gig work reliant on digital devices and platforms (Scholz, 2013, 2017). This includes freelance writers (Fish & Srinivasan, 2012), artists, graphic designers, illustrators (Alacovska et al., 2022), content moderators (Roberts, 2016), Amazon MTurk workers (Aytes, 2013; Bucher & Fieseler, 2017), and more. While "digital labor" can be a useful critical term when precisely applied, it now seems to range from the unpaid work of social media users to an array of paid online gigs (Gandini, 2020). As Gandini (2020) says, it "appears as though the expression 'digital labour' has acquired some kind of genericity, becoming a sort of umbrella term" (p. 370). Gandini (2020) continues, "Over the years, the expression 'digital labour' has come to be used indistinctly to identify almost all forms of direct or indirect labouring that takes place through the mediation of a digital medium" (p. 372). Additionally, on their LinkedIn profiles and elsewhere, few workers see or sell themselves as "digital laborers." While artistic campaigns like "Wages for Facebook" were brilliant, digital labor's demand has not garnered widespread support among the majority of waged workers in the DMEI.

Platform Worker

The scholarly recognition of all the workers now doing unpaid and paid digital labor while logged in to platforms has given rise to a new concept of the worker, a "platform worker" that encompasses everyone from Uber couriers and drivers to freelance authors chasing writing gigs on Upwork (Anwar & Graham, 2020; Graham & Woodcock, 2018; Grohmann et al., 2023; Lane, 2020; Van Doorn, 2017a, 2017b). "Platform workers" are individuals who rely on digital platforms to do their jobs, and to earn a living (Bader Law, 2023; Lane, 2020). Their "platform work" includes the provision of services such as ride-sharing, delivery, content creation, and more (Bader Law, 2023; Lane, 2020). For example, workers use apps like Uber or websites like Amazon MTurk or Upwork to complete services for clients in return for payment. Although these platform workers are typically (mis)classified as independent contractors, they depend on proprietary platforms to do their jobs, and frequently experience the problems of other workers, such as limited control over their labor process, a pittance of money paid for work, and management by algorithms (Lane, 2020, pp. 1, 5). Unfortunately, their self-employed or independent contractor status excludes these platform workers from the rights and protections that many other workers are entitled to (Lane, 2020, p. 7). While there are arguably millions of "platform workers" in the DMEI, this is in no way a distinct or unified occupational category (Huws et al., 2019). Also, the phrase "platform worker" can be technologically deterministic: the emergence of platforms ostensibly brought a new occupational category into existence, the platform worker! Undoubtedly, workers depend upon the tools of platforms to do all kinds of service work for others, but we do not label workers who must use pencils to do their job "pencil workers," nor do we call workers who depend on an Internet connection for work "Internet connection workers." Furthermore, many workers who use platforms to try to make a living—plumbers, writers, caregivers, drivers, sex workers, gardeners, and coders—are usually working in pre-existing industries, not at the forefront of new "platform industries" or something called a "gig economy." For example, writers using Substack's suite of publishing, payment, analytics, and design tools to earn a living through subscription newsletters are more accurately described as writers rather than platform workers. Similarly, a comedian uploading videos on YouTube to attract an audience with the hope of making it laugh is more aptly conceptualized as a comedian, not a platform worker. Likewise, all the workers who use Uber's apps to perform the labor of delivering goods are not really platform workers, as Uber did not hire these workers' labor to design the patented software of its platforms. Instead, they are couriers, operating within the logistics and delivery industries; the drivers are part of the transportation sector. "Platform worker" does not capture this specificity.

As the DMEI continues to grow, new concepts and figures of the post-industrial service working class will surely be developed. In many of these theorizations, the idea of the worker's distinctiveness seems to derive from (1) ideas about the technology or software a worker uses to do specific jobs or tasks (e.g., "the app gives rise to an app worker," "platforms make the platform worker," and "MTurk makes the Turk-worker"); (2) general notions of the sector that employs them (e.g., "the tech sector employs tech workers," "the media employs media workers," and "the digital games sector employs game workers"); (3) broad postulates about the essence of their labor, or the knowledge and skill they possess (e.g., the creative worker is a creative worker because they possess "creative" knowledge and skills); or (4) generic classifications of the product of their labor process (e.g., cultural workers produce goods deemed "cultural"). While these ways of conceptualizing workers are prevalent in the field, gaining deeper insights into work in the DMEI may require scholars to shift from the application of broad concepts to very different workers, to a more focused analysis of the specific occupational roles workers are hired and paid to perform for firms. This includes taking a closer look at what specific workers do in a real division of labor surrounding the production of a particular good or service for markets, in firms, industry groups or sectors, while also considering the broader system logics of capitalism.

To understand the nature of work in the DMEI, it is essential to understand capitalism—a specific form of class society characterized by several core system logics. Understanding capitalism, as a class society and a system with specific logics, helps us to understand how all workers in the DMEI, regardless of the technologies they use to labor, the firm, industry or sector that employs them, the specific labor they possess and sell, or the nature of the product-type they are paid to make, are shaped by a social order and set of system logics. By beginning with an understanding of capitalism, rather than relying on general concepts of workers associated with new technologies, fuzzily defined industries and sectors, or labor and product categories, we can better grasp the inter-relations between the macro-level social divisions and system logics and the meso and micro-level conditions and experiences of workers in the DMEI. Starting with an understanding of capitalism lets us see the earth, the forest, the trees, and perhaps the roots as well. To this end, capitalism must foremost be recognized as a "class society."

Capitalism: A Class Society, Manifested in the Structure of the Corporation

Mode of Production

A mode of production refers to how people produce the necessities and wants of their lives, and for the past four hundred years or so, capitalism has been the reigning mode of production. This production is carried out

What Is Capitalism and How Do Corporations Shape Work in the DMEI? 111

by numerous corporations that utilize labor power (that they purchase from workers), technology (that they own or acquire from other companies), and earthly energy systems (that they depend upon to power their operations). Capital, essential to this system, can assume various forms: monetary (cash, credit), physical assets (machinery), or inventories of finished products and ongoing projects (IP). While markets—places where goods are bought and sold, from shopping malls to Amazon.com—are central to capitalism, they alone do not define it. Markets have existed in various societies, including in feudal societies, the Soviet Union, the United States, and modern China.

Over the past quarter century, many terms flag the newness, reinvention, or expansion of capitalism (Boltanski & Chiapello, 2005; Giblin & Doctorow, 2023; Harvey, 2011; McChesney, 2014, 2016; Pasquale, 2015, 2016; Piketty, 2014; Reich, 2021; Schiller, 2000; Srnicek, 2017a, 2017b; Stanford, 2015; Thier, 2020; Zuboff, 2019). Yet, old or new, capitalism always establishes and reproduces structurally differentiated and unequal power relations between people based on their ownership of capital, income, and wealth. Capitalism is a hierarchical class society, with a foundational division between the owning class and the working class. At the tiny top of capitalism's pyramidal social structure is an upper or "ruling class"; somewhere in the shrinking middle, an ambiguous "middle class"; and at a massively widening and deepening bottom, a vast, precarious and indebted working class. The primary division is based on the ownership and managerial control of the largest corporations, which have made two main classes: the shareholder-managerial class, who own and manage these corporations, and the middle and working classes, who sell their labor for money to meet their needs and wants.

The Upper or Ruling Class: CEOs and Shareholders

In the class society, "the ruling class" is not just the major shareholders (the owners) but also the executive decision-makers (the managers) of global capital, including corporations in the DMEI. This gradual shift from the ruling class as "owner" to the ruling class as "owner" *and* "manager" has long been of interest to researchers. In *The Modern Corporation and Private Property*, Adolf Berle and Gardiner Means (1933) suggested the ruling class wasn't limited to those who directly own the means of production but included those with significant managerial control in corporations. They observed, "The property owner who invests in a modern corporation ... has exchanged the position of independent owner for one in which he may become merely recipient of the wages of capital ... [Such owners] have surrendered the right that the corporation should be operated in their sole interest ..." (p. 335). In *The Managerial Revolution: What Is Happening in the World*, James Burnham (1941) argued that capitalism had transitioned to "managerialism," where managers, not owners, wield power in both economic and political spheres. In *The New Industrial State*, John Kenneth Galbraith (1967) echoed these thoughts, emphasizing that industrial companies in key economic sectors were governed not by shareholders but by a managerial-administrative body, or a powerful "technostructure."

Recently, Gérard Duménil and Dominique Lévy (2018) in *Managerial Capitalism: Ownership, Management and the Coming New Mode of Production* expanded on this, delineating the managerial class as distinct from traditional property-owning elites, with their income primarily derived from high salaries. However, the current ruling class in contemporary capitalism's class society is a *hybrid* of the owning and managerial classes. CEOs of major corporations, from finance to the DMEI, often combine substantial stock ownership with their decision-making authority and influence, blurring the lines between ownership and management. This convergence has created a hybrid ruling class where individuals wield both ownership power and administrative control, key to the new class society.

In the DMEI, the CEO shareholder-managers are everywhere enriching themselves. Sundar Pichai, CEO of Google, exemplifies this dual role, owning 1,768,500 shares of Alphabet Inc., and as of 2022, valued at $235 million. Similarly, Apple's CEO Tim Cook, with a net worth of approximately $1.9 billion in 2023, holds 3,280,052 shares, about 0.02% of all outstanding shares, translating to a stake worth around $565 million. At Meta Platforms, CEO Mark Zuckerberg's significant shareholding, totaling 350 million shares or 13.5% of the company, bolsters his substantial net worth of $111.6 billion. Amazon's Jeff Bezos, despite transitioning to an executive chair role, remains deeply invested with 1.26 billion shares, 12.3% of the total, solidifying his influence and net worth of $161.3 billion. Bill Gates, former CEO of Microsoft, and current CEO Satya Nadella, collectively represent a significant ownership stake, with Gates holding 103 million shares and Nadella owning 1,337,768 shares. Elon Musk, as Tesla's largest shareholder and CEO, owns over 411 million shares, a 12.95% stake, propping up his staggering net worth of $230.9 billion. Even in companies like Verizon Communications and Walt Disney, CEOs, including Robert A. Iger, Christine M. McCarthy, and Alan N. Braverman, hold substantial stakes, though less than 1% in the case of Verizon. Netflix's managerial elites, including former CEO Reed Hastings and current CEO Ted Sarandos, similarly represent a significant personal investment in their company, with Hastings owning shares worth over $2.2 billion and Sarandos receiving a total compensation of $50.3 million in 2022, including a $20 million base salary, $28.5 million in stock options, and $1.79 million in other compensation. Thus, in the corporations of the DMEI, CEOs are at the helm of management and invested as major shareholders, a seamless integration of decision-making power and capital accumulation.

The position, power and privilege of these and other CEOs, high-earning shareholder-managerial elites, are structurally and socially distinct from the diminishing middle and expanding working classes their firms employ.

Middle Class/Professional Managerial Class (PMC)

In the class society, the idea of "the middle class" is a way to deny a fundamental structural division between classes exists—every politician nowadays seems to address themselves as or to a "middle class" but what is it? The idea dates back to discourse on the petite bourgeoisie and peasantry in the 19th century and developed over time to address the post-war era's emergence of "new" post-industrial service workers. In 1977, Barbara and John Ehrenreich introduced the concept of the Professional-Managerial Class (PMC) to describe "white-collar" professionals who are distinct from both the traditional industrial working class and the old middle class (Ehrenreich & Ehrenreich, 1977, 2013; Press, 2019). Erik Olin Wright's (1997) concept of "contradictory class locations" suggests "middle class" encompasses occupations that embody the intersecting interests of capital and labor, from low-paid managers in firms to non-managerial workers whose knowledge and skill earn high pay. Starting in the 1970s, the PMC has been gradually proletarianized and precaritized, and we see this happening in all groupings of the DMEI. If a PMC exists, its political future is uncertain. Whether this class will align with the working-class or try to maintain a separate class identity remains to be seen.

The Working Class

In the class society, being "working class" is not a lifestyle choice or a performance of the self; it is a fundamental structural relation to capital shared by billions who, out of necessity, must sell their labor power to survive. Workers toil with and through the Internet in digitally networked factories, warehouses, offices, homes, retail nodes, apps, and platforms, forming the productive core of the DMEI, which is owned and controlled by corporations, whose conduct is motivated by profit. Evidently, capitalism has developed into a hierarchical digital class society, with rulers at the top, some in the middle at lots at the bottom. Class is undeniably fundamental to this society, despite attempts by some to deny or downplay its importance or to reduce socio-economics to a university degree or cultural lifestyle choice. In *Class Matters*, Steve Fraser (2018) states, "class is the secret of the American experience, its past, present, and likely future." Class is also the real condition of the DMEI.

Capitalism: Eight Logics at Work in the Corporations of the DMEI

In the DMEI, there are eight key capitalist logics at play which motivate and shape the conduct of corporations in the DMEI and play a role in shaping the general conditions of work that shape the worker's experience: (1) corporate ownership of capital; (2) waged labor, labor markets and a division of labor; (3) production driven by profit rather than human need; (4) market competition and market control; (5) exploitation: profit maximization and labor cost minimization; (6) crises, cycles of boom and bust, and creative destruction; (7) income, wealth and class inequality; and (8) class tension and conflict.

Corporate Ownership of Capital

The ownership and control of assets—capital—is integral to class power in society, and in the DMEI. Privately owned and publicly traded corporations—not states and especially not workers—are the dominant owners of the DMEI. Next to banks, the powerhouses of the world system are those corporations that own the IP rights to significant digital hardware and software, platform and app services, the means of producing, circulating, and exhibiting digital media content, and troves of copyrighted content. Today's largest owning corporations are not Ford or Exxon-Mobil, but Alphabet-Google, Apple, Meta Platforms, Amazon, and Microsoft, as well as Walt Disney Company, Comcast, AT&T, Viacom and Netflix. Despite being composed of many workers, corporations are legally treated as singular persons with distinct rights and responsibilities, affording shareholders, Boards of Directors, and CEOs limited liability for the decisions and actions of the corporation they benefit from.

A corporate *ownership structure* refers to the arrangement of different entities that own a corporation. Walt Disney Company is illustrative: shareholders, ranging from individual investors to large funds, hold equity in Disney, representing their portion of ownership in the company. The oversight of the corporation is managed by a Board of Directors, elected by these shareholders, and they are responsible for guiding key strategic decisions and safeguarding the shareholders' interests. Disney's day-to-day operations are executed by management, including high-paid CEOs, and lower tiers of managers. As a publicly traded company, Disney's shares are available on stock exchanges, contrasting with privately held companies where shares are not publicly traded. Ownership can also refer to the actual assets held by a corporation. For example, Disney owns a wide range of subsidiaries and properties. Its acquisition of Pixar, Marvel, Lucasfilm, and 21st Century Fox expanded its ownership of IP and diversified its copyright holdings. This further solidified Disney's position in the entertainment market and also enabled it to extend its influence into online streaming services with the launch of Disney+. Disney's ownership of theme parks and merchandise outlets also exemplifies the capitalist logic of owning and controlling various assets and segments to maximize profit.

Owners are those who own and control corporations; workers are those who do not, and instead, get paid by these owners and their corporations for the labor they do. This is a foundational class division in the DMEI. Managers are sometimes owners themselves, but even when not, still are contractually obligated to align themselves with owners' interests and to reproduce the class division, and the hierarchy it entails. At Google, the owners include major shareholders, along with shareholding CEOs. They make strategic decisions about the company's direction, investments, and innovations. Decisions regarding new products like Google Assistant and Google Gemini, or expansion into new markets, are made by those at this upper echelon. Below this level, the vast waged workforce, including software engineers and sales teams, executes these directives. They work within the parameters set by management and do not typically partake in high-level decision-making or profit-sharing. The workers are compensated with wages, but the value their labor contributes to Google's overall profitability benefits the owners and top-tier managers far more than themselves. In much of the DMEI, a hierarchical division between owners-managers and workers is clear. The owners-managers control the strategic direction, while the workers are expected to follow while earning a pittance of the overall value their labor helps to produce.

Waged Labor, Labor Markets and a Division of Labor

Waged labor, another logic of capitalism, is ubiquitous in the DMEI. In capitalism, workers are compelled to meet their needs by selling their labor power to corporations in exchange for compensation, usually a wage or salary. Capitalism's gradual transition from forced labor systems such as slavery and serfdom to markets of ostensibly free labor, where workers voluntarily "choose" to sell their labor power to companies in exchange for money, represents the rule of waged labor over life. However, the workers' apparent freedom to sell their labor power to companies is paradoxical. Workers, ranging from writers to coders, "freely" sell their labor power to firms, but out of necessity. Slogans like "live to create" often mask the reality that for many, creating is compulsory to making a living. Employment contracts, while legally representing a free exchange between sellers (workers) and buyers (firms) of labor power in a market, practically impose conditions of unfreedom upon the worker, curtailing the workers' autonomy over their work and its outcome. For example, at Meta Platforms, engineers and developers may earn high salaries for their work, but their employment contract outlines what they are expected to do and how, and stipulates that the IP resulting from their labor process ultimately belongs to the company. In Silicon Valley and the entertainment industry alike, most of the IP created by workers is owned by companies, rather than by the workers they contract or employ. While workers have the "freedom" to sell their labor power to corporations, in doing so, they submit to a situation of contractual unfreedom with corporations, where their labor process is controlled, and the product of their labor, is not their own.

The *labor market*, another feature of the capitalist system, comprises the places and spaces where the selling and buying of a workers' labor power happens. Historically confined to physical locations, in the 21st century, labor markets have expanded across the Internet through platforms like LinkedIn, Upwork, Fiverr, and gig economy platform apps such as Uber and TaskRabbit. The labor market's dynamics are shaped by supply and demand, and by the ebb and flow of class struggle over time and space. Labor markets are the arenas where human labor is commodified, given a price, advertised, sold and purchased. In these markets, corporations seek out the labor required for their productions, while workers, driven by necessity, look for gigs, jobs, and careers that pay. A *slack labor market* is one with an excess of workers and a dearth of jobs; a *tight labor market* is one with more jobs than there are workers available to do them. In a slack market, workers, as "wage takers," are often pressed by companies to accept lower wages and unfavorable terms due to the surplus of labor available for hire. Conversely, in a tight market, workers gain leverage as "wage makers," bargaining for better wages with prospective employers due to the scarcity of the labor these firms demand. For a time, the ICT industry exemplified a tight labor market, especially for specialized roles like software engineers and data scientists. But as higher education and privatized labor force training systems met and exceeded the demand, it has slackened. The entertainment industry typically runs with a slack labor market, particularly for roles like writers, actors, and musicians. The oversupply of talent in these fields feed precarity and low wages. Yet, within the DMEI, there are also elite workers who command high earnings—famous authors, movie celebrities, and star athletes.

The *division of labor* is central to the management of work in the DMEI. Most of the major hardware, software, and content produced, consumed, and used are not made by one worker from start to finish. There are examples of solopreneurs and indie creators who make things like video games (Markus Persson's Minecraft), apps (Dong Nguyen's Flappy Bird), songs (Prince's Purple Rain) and YouTube content (Contrapoints' YouTube channel). But for most major productions, one person usually doesn't possess all the knowledge and skills required to create a product or service from start to finish. Even if they did, it would be a time-consuming endeavor. In capitalism, production has typically been a collective process involving tens to thousands of people, each contributing specific knowledge and skills to a project. Most often, the production of a good or service is divided into separate tasks, and workers who possess the labor required to complete these tasks are hired and assigned to them, resulting in efficiency and effectiveness. For example, the Apple MacBook was not made by one person. Rather, it was made by hardware, software, electrical and mechanical engineers, quality assurance testers, IP lawyers, packaging aesthetics designers, manufacturers, branding experts, and more. *Barbie* was made by producers, directors, screenwriters, actors, casting directors, art directors, custom designers, and editors. Netflix relies on developers, data engineers, content managers, UI/UX designers, marketing specialists, and customer support, among other workers. Much production in the DMEI is project-based: the division of labor demands skill flexibility and specialization but also standardization and routinization.

Production Driven by Profit Rather Than Human Need

Production for profit, more than production for human need, is a fundamental logic of capitalism, a driver of corporate operations in the DMEI. In this system, corporations prioritize profit maximization and are legally obligated to do so for shareholders, often sidelining broader social and human responsibilities. The pursuit of profit drives corporate decisions about where to invest and where to allocate resources. But this drive for profit leads to uneven resource allocation, often favoring the most potentially profitable productions over more potentially socially useful but less lucrative ventures. One more iteration of the same superhero franchise coming soon, one less documentary about the catastrophic impact of global climate change, or what's to be done about poverty featured at the American Multi-Cinema (AMC) Theatre. While the "market" and ideas about consumer tastes and preferences always influence production, corporate decisions are primarily shaped by ideas about those consumers who have the most purchasing power, often privileging the wants of the already privileged, and ignoring poor people. Apple exemplifies this, profiting through the production and sale of "premium" or "luxury" tech goods. But what is profit? In capitalism, profit is the difference between the total cost incurred by a corporation to produce a good or service, and the total revenue generated from that good or service's sale. Let's consider the iPhone 14 Pro Max, which costs Apple approximately $500 to produce one unit (including parts and labor). Apple sells the device for about $1100 at its stores, in the market. In the first six months of 2023, Apple produced 26.5 million units of the iPhone 14 Pro Max (for a cost of around $13.2 billion) and it sold those 26.5 million devices (at a cost of $1100 per unit). In effect, Apple arguably generated about $29.1 billion in revenue. The difference between the total it costs Apple to produce all those iPhones ($13.2 billion) and the total revenue generated from the sale of these to consumers ($29.1 billion) was about $15.9 billion. Ergo, Apple accumulated $15.9 billion in profit on the production and sale of 26.5 million units of the device. In that same year, 823 million people around the world went hungry. In capitalism, and in the DMEI, production for profit, not human need, is the driving logic.

Market Competition and Market Control

Market competition is a key logic of capitalism, and nowhere is this more evident than in the DMEI. Corporations relentlessly compete with one another for consumer attention and expenditure, and companies that fail to compete face a loss of market share, a downturn in revenue, and insolvency. The logic of competition shapes organizational cultures in the corporations of the DMEI. Management compels workers to compete with workers in other firms in support of their companies' success and also, motivates these same workers to compete against one another, to keep or renew their jobs, or get promoted. Workers often internalize the competitive ethos of the system and the corporation that pays them. For precariat contractors, the project-based nature of much production in the DMEI presses them into even more intense competition with one another, as contract renewal is often tied to the market success of the product. Freelance writers face intense competition to secure assignments, build reputations, and engage readers. Similarly, YouTubers produce content in a super competitive platform ecology, vying for viewer attention, subscribes, likes, and brand partnerships. In sum, competition is a fundamental logic of capitalism that drives corporations in the DMEI and also compels managers to motivate workers to compete with one another and themselves.

Paradoxically, the logic of market competition between corporations is coupled with the logic of *market control* strategies. To try to control markets, corporations integrate with others, merging and acquiring new assets, and concentrating their holdings. The rationale is straightforward: more market competition dilutes their market control, while less market competition consolidates it, knocking out rivals. In the DMEI, corporations strive to outdo rivals by acquiring market control over the copyrighted content, the means of production, distribution, and exhibition, consumer attention, and data. In 2018, AT&T merged with Time Warner, creating Warner Media; in 2019, the Walt Disney Company acquired 21st Century Fox; in 2022, Microsoft merged with Activision Blizzard. Such contradictory competitive anti-competitive logics lead to market oligopolies, with a few giant companies towering over the rest. These large entities establish significant barriers to market entry which hinder new firms from competing. For example, these big companies enjoy economies of scale that allow them to operate more efficiently than smaller competitors. Also, they possess tremendous financial means to influence the state's legal, policy, and regulatory frameworks through lobbying. Additionally, they benefit from established brand reputations, which consumers often favor. The DMEI is not a paragon of free-market competition, but an oligopoly of a few large corporations. Platforms are dominated by Alphabet-Google, Amazon, Meta Platforms, Apple, and Microsoft; telecommunications are concentrated in Verizon Communications, AT&T, T-Mobile, Comcast, Charter Communications, and Dish; media-entertainment is presided over by The Walt Disney Company, Comcast (which owns NBC-Universal), AT&T (which owns WarnerMedia), ViacomCBS, Netflix and Amazon Prime Video. This outsized market power not only limits competition, but can also limit innovation, increase prices, restrict consumer choice, and have adverse impacts on workers.

The corporate mergers and acquisitions that result in ownership concentration and oligopolistic markets have negative implications for workers in the DMEI. These changes in ownership and control invariably impact workers' conditions. Corporate mergers and acquisitions often result in workforce shakeups, including layoffs, downsizing, and firings, as companies, looking for efficiencies and also, to pay down the debt incurred to finance the convergence, aim to streamline operations. Newly merged entities pursue efficiency by eliminating overlapping positions: when companies grow in market size they reduce the number of jobs available to workers. The remaining workers may face increased workloads and pressure to do more with fewer resources. For example, when Sinclair Broadcast Group acquired numerous local news stations in 2017 and 2018, the resulting restructuring eliminated many jobs. In 2018, Verizon Media Group laid off around 800 workers after acquiring various media entities such as Xo Communications and Yahoo. Meredith Corporation's acquisition of Time Inc. in 2018 also led to significant layoffs. Microsoft's acquisition of Nokia's mobile division resulted in thousands of job cuts. In early 2024, BCE, a Canadian telco-media conglomerate, fired 4800 workers

(9% of its labor force), all the while increasing pay to CEOs and dividend payouts to shareholders.

> **Media Concentration and Work in Canada: Findings from the Global Media & Internet Concentration Project (GMICP) and Canadian Media Concentration Research Project (CMCR)**
>
> The Global Media and Internet Concentration Project ((https://gmicp.org/), led by Professor Dwayne Winseck, a renowned political economist of communications based at the School of Journalism and Communication (Carleton University), and comprising over 60 international research experts, seeks to answer a salient question: have media industries, both individually and collectively, become more or less concentrated over time? While the project's primary focus is not on the relationship between ownership concentration and work conditions, findings from the *Media and Internet Concentration in Canada, 1984-2022* (Winseck, 2023a) and *Growth and Upheaval in the Network Media Economy, 1984-2022* (Winseck, 2023b) reports suggest some noteworthy connections (Winseck, 2024). During the period from 2021 to 2022, while Shaw awaited regulatory approval for its takeover by Rogers, the company significantly reduced its investment in network infrastructure, hiring fewer reasonably well-paid and skilled workers (Winseck, 2023a, pp. 60–61). The consolidation of the TV industry by telecom giants like Bell, Rogers, Shaw, and Videotron led to closures, cuts, and spin-offs, resulting in a decrease in the number of TV services in Canada from 190 to 160 by 2022, accompanied by job cuts and layoffs (Winseck, 2023a; Winseck, 2024). Many pay TV services, including Bell's CTV Comedy and DHX's Family Channel, now operate with minimal or no staff, and are "ghost operations" (Winseck, 2024). Despite promises of increased investment in Canadian TV and film production following their ownership consolidation, such investments by Canadian media giants have not materialized on an aggregate level (Winseck, 2024). Moreover, the Canadian newspaper industry has suffered as a result of concentration, leading to a decline in the number of journalists employed (Winseck, 2023b; Winseck, 2024). As telecom and media ownership concentration solidifies, Canadian workers, including "platform workers" and "online creators" reliant on affordable telecommunications services to access the Internet and do their jobs, are feeling the price squeeze (Winseck, 2024).

Exploitation: Profit Maximization, Labor Cost Minimization and IP Dispossession

In capitalism, exploitation is a fundamental logic, particularly evident in the way corporations in the DMEI profit maximally by keeping labor costs to a minimum. In response to pressure from shareholders and boards to maximize returns, the CEOs of corporations have a strong incentive to develop strategies aimed at reducing labor costs, thereby keeping production expenses low and profit margins as high as can be. To this end, the management of many corporations choose to outsource tasks to countries with lower labor costs, hire contract and part-time workers without benefits, adopt and implement labor-saving technologies (LSTs) to replace paid employees, and set up unpaid internship positions to supplant roles previously played by paid workers. They set up new models like zero-hour contracts or rely on freelancers to ensure that they have access to sufficiently flexible labor without having to commit to regular salaries and benefits. Many corporations also suppress wage growth, ensuring that salaries do not outpace profitability, and limit investment in employee training, preferring to hire already skilled workers, thereby externalizing upskilling costs to the public education system or to workers themselves. While it may be rational for a corporation, whose legal responsibility is to pay out dividends to shareholders, to cut labor costs in order to boost profitability, what is good for the owners and shareholders here drives immiserating conditions for the workers: low wages, hyper-productivity, super-exploitation, and precarity.

Also, in the DMEI, corporations exploit workers by dispossessing them of their right to benefit from the IP-protected hardware, software, and content their knowledge and skill played a role in creating. Corporations typically claim IP rights over everything created by their labor force, per employment contracts that workers are made to sign, as a condition of securing a waged job or precarious gig with such corporations. While numerous workers contribute to everything from new devices to algorithms to video games to TV series and movies, corporations assert IP rights over these creations, turning them into their capital. For example, software developed by a worker at Microsoft becomes Microsoft property. A TV series made by a team of workers for Netflix becomes Netflix's property. Corporations pay workers to produce goods and services for them, dispossess these workers of the right to morally and financially benefit from the resulting innovations and creations, and then monetize the IP, licensing the use of it to a variety of customers. The revenue corporations accumulate by selling licenses to this IP far exceeds the wages paid to the workers who created it. For example, Amazon Web Services (AWS) may hire a software developer to build new web apps as part of their regular annual salary, and then license the software to consumer markets, generating millions in profit. Yet, the AWS software developer is unlikely to receive any additional compensation, despite the centrality of their labor in creating the app that AWS is licensing. Similarly, a Hollywood screenwriter's contribution to a script may be key to a blockbuster movie's success, but their compensation is often a one-time payment (though, depending on their contract and union agreement, they may receive residual payments for re-runs, syndication, spin-offs, and streaming). Thus, in the DMEI, the workers whose labor is essential to IP often do not enjoy a fair share of the profits the licensing of the IP generates for the corporation that has asserted ownership over it.

Crises, Cycles of Boom and Bust, and Creative Destruction

In capitalism, *crises* is a recurring logic: the system moves from upturn to the downturn, sometimes stalls and slumps in a period of prolonged economic downturn, marked by reduced growth, increased unemployment, financial instability, or even recession. The National Bureau of Economic Research defines a recession as "a significant decline in economic activity spread across the economy, lasting more than a few months, typically observed in real GDP, real income, employment, industrial production, and wholesale-retail sales." Since the 1970s, recessions have been consistent in capitalism, occurring in 1970, 1973–1975, 1980–1982, 1990–1991, 2001, 2008–2009, and from 2020 onwards. The DMEI, like other sectors of the economy, is at once a driver of crisis, and susceptible to economic crisis, a catalyst and a victim. A crisis can be caused by a wide range of factors, all intrinsic to the workings of capitalism. Firstly, the corporate profit motive can lead to overproduction, where more goods and services are produced than can be consumed, leading to market saturation, inventory buildup, price slashing, layoffs, and unemployment, spiraling out into less effective demand overall. Cycles of boom and bust, characterized by investment and growth followed by downturns and crashes, are a constant. Intense competition can prompt corporations to implement cost-cutting measures such as layoffs or wage suppression, resulting in consumers having less to spend. Financialization blows all too many speculative bubbles that burst, bringing many investors and firms to ruin. Shocks, such as the COVID-19 pandemic, and governmental responses to them, can sink industries: movie theaters, live performances, and sporting events were shut down or restricted for public safety while TV and movie production schedules were stopped, putting millions out of a job. War and geopolitics can also drive upheaval: the new imperial rivalry between the US and China, expressed through the restructuring of international technology commodity chains and the emergence of a national industrial strategy in semiconductors, and other sectors, has been disruptive. So-called "globalization," another hallmark of capitalism, leads to interdependence, meaning that crises in one region can quickly spread to another, adversely impacting both. All in all, capitalism is a profoundly crises-prone system, for the economy as a whole, and for the DMEI. As Marx and Engels poetically put it, "All that is solid melts into air, all that is holy is profaned." Thus, "creative destruction" is inherent to capitalism: corporations constantly seek to produce and sell to new markets, disrupting and destroying "the old" and constantly pushing forward (or at least promising) "the new."

Income, Wealth and Class Inequality

Income, wealth and class inequality are intrinsic to the capitalist system. The accumulation of capital favors those with capital. As the old saying goes, "It takes money to make money" (and those who've taken the most money are in an advantageous position to make more money). The income and wealth divide between CEOs and workers is a case in point of this inequality. In capitalism, *income inequality* arises from radically divergent pay scales, with CEOs taking more and workers getting less. Often, they and their Boards choose to reward themselves, not their labor force, for increasing their corporations' profit, ensuring that most of the profit continues to flow to the few at the top. *Wealth inequality*—stemming from the uneven distribution of assets like property, stocks, and savings—further exacerbates this divide. Those with the means to invest accumulate wealth over time, often at a much faster rate than those without. In capitalism, *class inequality* is registered in the income division between the major CEO-shareholders who preside over companies and the workers beneath. Compustat tracks CEO pay at all publicly owned US corporations. Between 1978 and 2022, inflation-adjusted pay for CEOs of the 350 largest corporations grew by 1209%. The CEO-to-worker pay ratio, or, the gap between CEOs and typical worker pay, has widened. In 1965, CEOs were paid 21 times as much as the typical worker. By 2022, CEOs were paid 344 times as much as the typical worker (Bivens & Kandra, 2023). The DMEI is a microcosm of this inequality. In 2021, AT&T's CEO received up to $24.8 million, taking 231 times the typical AT&T worker's annual pay. Netflix's co-CEOs earned around $40 million each, with pay ratios over 190. The Walt Disney Company's executives got over $32.5 million, with one pay ratio reaching 644. This inequality extends to Silicon Valley. In 2022, Apple's Timothy Cook and Alphabet's Sundar Pichai received compensations of $99.4 million and $226 million, with pay ratios exceeding 800 times the median worker's annual pay. The CEO-to-worker pay ratios at Microsoft, Amazon, Broadcom, Oracle, and IBM were about 680 to 1. While CEOs accumulate vast incomes, the inflation-adjusted wages of workers have stagnated, even declined. Despite rising national productivity and GDP, most wealth accumulates at the top of the social hierarchy, failing to "trickle down."

Class Tension and Conflict

Class tension and conflict are inherent in capitalism, including the DMEI, but this is more overt today because of the extreme inequality in wealth and income distribution. This corporate drive for profit maximization, often achieved by reducing labor costs and laying off workers, conflicts with workers' desires for fair wages and stable jobs. In response, workers sometimes come together to discuss shared grievances, and sometimes take collective action to advocate for fairer conditions, leading to tensions and outright conflicts with the corporations that exploit them. Workers' unions and social movements seek to counterbalance the power of capital and push for a fairer distribution of income and wealth in society.

The DMEI has never been characterized by a condition of lasting "peace" between capital and labor. Throughout the 20th century, the American telecommunications industry saw significant class conflicts. In 1947, about 200,000 AT&T workers went on strike, demanding wage increases and better conditions. In 1983, 675,000 AT&T workers went on strike for job security and healthcare. In 1989, 60,000 workers struck against the New York and New England Telephone companies for healthcare and higher wages. In movies, radio, and TV, workers also contested capital. The 1919 Actors' Equity Association Strike, 1935 and 1945 Hollywood set decorators and prop makers strike led to better pay. The 1952 Screen Actors Guild Strike set a precedent for residual payments based upon TV show reruns. Collective action by the American Federation of Television and Radio Artists and the Writers Guild of America in the 1960s and 1980s pushed for fairer compensation and greater residual payments. The American Federation of Musicians and the National Association of Broadcast Employees and Technicians also engaged in significant strikes, advocating for better royalties and working conditions. The 1941 Disney Animators' Strike, the 1962–1963 Newspaper Strike in New York City, and the 1995–1997 Detroit Newspaper Strike were also significant examples of working class action. Even Silicon Valley has had its share of conflict between capital and labor, from the formation of the IBM Black Workers Alliance (BWA) to the present-day resurgence of unions. A Cold War myth about Silicon Valley portrayed it as a family-oriented sector with no need for unions, promising rising living standards and job security based on healthy corporate profits (Bacon, 2011). Over the years, a tech labor movement emerged, and workers have exposed the harsh conditions of the industry and aimed to transform them. More recently, the struggle continues: the 2018 global Google

What Is Capitalism and How Do Corporations Shape Work in the DMEI? 125

walkout, the Alphabet Workers Union, unionization efforts at Amazon, union formation in digital media, union drives at Activision Blizzard and Ubisoft, and in Hollywood, strikes. All of this highlights a growing class consciousness among a labor force that was for a time, imagined to be postworking class.

What side does the state take in these class conflicts between capital and labor? The next chapter examines the significance of the state—its laws, policies, and regulations—to governing the power relations of work in the DMEI.

5 What Is the State and How Does It Govern Work in the DMEI?

Explicit and Tacit Labor Laws, Policies, and Regulations

Introduction

This chapter examines the state's multi-faceted roles in shaping conditions and experiences of work in the digital media and entertainment industries (DMEI). Supplementing the common focus on the capitalist and corporate determinations of work, the chapter examines the state's substantial, albeit frequently overlooked, role in shaping work in the DMEI. Focusing on the US, the chapter highlights the various explicit and tacit roles the state plays in shaping the conditions of work in the DMEI. These roles include the following: neoliberal superintendent; labor law maker, investigator, and enforcer; shaper of communication and media policies and regulations that impact employment; copyright supporter; antitrust authority; and, industry booster with subsidies, job creation, training, and employment programs. By examining these roles, the chapter underscores the state's role in shaping the quantity and quality of work in the DMEI. It offers a comprehensive overview of how the state, far from being a passive observer, shapes the DMEI's conditions of work, with legal, policy, and regulatory institutions and practices that may exacerbate and temper inequitable class power relations.

The Return of the State

In capitalism, many state agencies facilitate and legitimize corporate profiteering in the DMEI and uphold society's class structure. The state is a supporter of most capitalist developments in the DMEI and tends to be partial to the general interests of the CEOs and shareholders of the many corporations that rule it. But the state is not a unity, not one thing, and there are some state agencies that can play a role in upholding and potentially widening the labor rights of workers in and beyond the DMEI. The conditions of work in the DMEI cannot be understood with a one-sided focus on capitalism and corporations alone. While scrutinizing the pervasive power

DOI: 10.4324/9781003131076-6

of corporations over workers within the DMEI is important, it's equally significant to recognize the power of the state, and the politics of governmental laws, policies, and regulations (Banks, 2009; Banks & Hesmondhalgh 2009; Bernstein, 2000; Christopherson, 2004; Coles, 2010; Huws, 2020; Mirrlees, 2013, 2016, 2019).

Everywhere, from the US to China to Norway, states govern economic activities within their "national" territories and also enact a wide range of laws, policies, and regulations that impact the quantity and quality of jobs available. From Departments of Labor to those Ministries and Commissions concerned with "communication," "culture," and "media" not overtly concerned with labor matters, states—at federal, regional, and municipal levels of governance—shape the conditions of work in the DMEI. Yet, the state is under-theorized and under-examined in studies of work and labor in the media and cultural industries, something frequently ignored. The roles of the state encompass: neoliberal superintendent; labor law maker, investigator, and enforcer; communication and media policymaker and regulator; copyright backer; antitrust agent; industry subsidizer and job booster, trainer, and employer.

The State as Neoliberal Superintendent for Capitalism

Throughout modern history, the political and economic spheres, while different, have never been completely separate. Governments and markets have always been intertwined, with the powers of state and political officials and the powers of firms and their owners, intermingling, mostly in mutually complimentary ways, sometimes in ways that pull in opposite directions. Capitalism has never developed or existed anywhere in the absence of a state which claims sovereignty over a defined territory and bolsters economic developments with vast agencies and institutional techniques for governing workforces within its bounds.

States govern capitalism. They establish, enforce and change the laws, policies, and regulations that shape the conduct of corporations in the economy, international trade with other countries, and consumer rights, from product safety to prohibitions on unfair and deceptive market practices. States use fiscal policy to try to manage national economies by taxing and spending, running surpluses and cutting deficits, and allocating monies to everything from subsidies for the rich to social programs for everyone else. Coordinating with central banks, they use monetary policy to manage the money supply, interest rates, and currency value, usually with the goal of controlling inflation and supporting the next projected cycle of economic growth. They also do things like invest in, plan, and manage infrastructure projects encompassing military outposts, public administration, energy and power generation, the water supply, transportation hubs and nodes, telecommunications and digital networks, and public goods and services (e.g., police, fire, welfare, healthcare, libraries, art and culture, broadcasting, education).

States have always played a significant role in capitalism, but since the mid-1970s, this role has become more obvious, as they've more openly prioritized the interests of corporations over the public good. The post-World War II Keynesian welfare state represented a social contract that managed a balance between the interests of capital and labor, but as this "class compromise" began to erode in the mid-1970s and neoliberal ideology started to solidify the idea that "human well-being can best be advanced by the maximization of entrepreneurial freedoms within an institutional framework characterized by private property rights, individual liberty, unencumbered markets, and free trade," many politicians and policy-makers restructured states for global capital (Harvey, 2005, 2006). As states became neoliberal superintendents, they helped the corporations at the helm of the DMEI grow and prosper in the post-industrial "ICT" and "creative" fields while presiding over more income concentration for the 1%, wealth and class inequality, precarious work arrangements, and attacks on unions and labor rights. In turn, the entrenchment of "new public management" thinking pushed public arts, broadcasting, and media-cultural institutions towards market-facing practices. In this context, states continue to make public policies but frequently prioritize private interests, with the DMEI and their numerous lobbies and advocates being highly influential.

When the state policy-making process is theorized by liberals, the state is sometimes idealized as a democratic sphere of pluralistic competition between different interest groups, all vying for influence. *A liberal pluralist* theorist might construe a corporate lobby in the DMEI as one of numerous diverse interest groups exercising influence in a marketplace of policy ideas, competing to persuade the governmental arbiter that its ideas are most beneficial for society while being counter-balanced by other groups, like unions and NGOs, seeking to exert similar influence, and settling for whatever "compromise" results from this contest. A *power elite* theorist would likely view a lobby for a group of companies in the DMEI, along with the Boards of Directors and CEOs of these, as part of small group of interconnected corporate, military and political elites that possess the power to make the most consequential decisions about the social structure and policy framework, without workers' awareness, participation or consent (Mills, 1956). In the Marxist state theory tradition, the state is sometimes conceived of as passive superstructure that reflects and upholds the capitalist base or is treated as an instrument of power, seized, and wielded by the bourgeoisie to dominate the working class (Aronowitz and Bratsis, 2002). In the neo-Marxist tradition, *instrumentalists* would see a corporate lobby in the DMEI as a front for a fraction of the ruling class,

What Is the State and How Does It Govern Work in the DMEI? 129

using the government and policy as tool for sustaining its power over and exploitation of the working class (Miliband, 2009); *relative autonomists* would concede that corporate lobbies exercise influence within state agencies, but emphasize the state's partial autonomy to establish and enforce labor policies that while not always beneficial to the corporations the lobby represents, are integral to the general maintenance of a crisis-prone capitalist system (Poulantzas, 2014). In any case, the state is of utmost significance to governing work in the DMEI, and states play multi-faceted roles in relation to capitalism and the class power relations of the DMEI.

Paradoxically, while states have become neoliberal superintendents for global capitalism, backers of corporate interests, and frequently side with CEOs in clashes with workers, states can be and do other things, sometimes even support and expand workers' rights. Taking note of the US state's *explicit* and *tacit* labor laws and practices, the next sections will underscore how key the modern state is to governing work in the DMEI and flag the gap between labor law and its consistent enforcement.

The State's Explicit Labor Law: Maker, Investigator, and Enforcer ... Sometimes

In *Law At Work: Class, Property, Capitalism,* Harry Glasbeek (2024) argues that the law is not neutral, but structurally biased towards the maintenance of the power of the state and corporations over workers in society. In the historical transition from feudalism to capitalism, the introduction of "free labour" under capitalism promised freedom through private contracts but ultimately perpetuated new forms of subjugation and exploitation. The established legal framework of capitalism, particularly in Anglo-American jurisdictions, has long shaped labor relations to favor the owners of capital at the expense of those they employ, embedding and normalizing inequalities. After all, the freedom of contract for workers is tantamount to the freedom to sell their labor to corporations and enter into conditions dictated by those who manage them. While the legal system upholds capitalism it can also constrain its excesses to maintain social order, and stave off widespread social unrest and manage and neutralize revolutionary energies.

The state plays contradictory roles in capitalism, frequently backing the interests of corporations and their owners, but also, acting as a labor law maker, investigator, and enforcer, sometimes supporting workers rights. The state establishes the labor laws that govern exploitative employment contracts, but can also advance laws that aim to uphold and enhance workers' labor rights vis-à-vis capital.

The state is the locus of *labor law making*, an entity that establishes and enforces the legal framework that governs the contractual relations between capital and labor, corporations and workers, in the DMEI. The specific process for making labor laws varies from one country to another, and the making of these laws is a political process, influenced by the struggles of corporations, labor unions, advocacy groups, parties and broader publics over the state. Usually, labor laws are established through a formal legislative body. This process typically begins with the introduction of a bill by a legislative body member, followed by in-depth committee review, consultations with experts, public hearings, and potential amendments. After committee review, the bill is debated on the legislative floor, where further changes may be proposed before it is voted on. The final step involves approval from the head of state before becoming law, and enforced by the state as such. After enactment, these laws can be revised over time, and may be reshaped by class conflicts, political struggles, and changing cultural views. One of the most important labor laws in US history is the National Labor Relations Act (NLRA) of 1935, also known as the Wagner Act: resulting from sustained labor movement activism, campaigning, demonstrations, strikes, and more, this law, viciously opposed by many corporations, CEOs, and conservatives, recognized and protected the rights of workers to organize unions, engage in collective bargaining with capital, and take strike actions.

In the main, the state plays a central role in establishing and enforcing the legal framework for the employment contracts that govern the power relations between corporations and workers in the DMEI. *Employment contracts* are formal agreements between companies (e.g., film studios, record labels, publishing houses, game development firms) and workers (e.g., actors, directors, musicians, writers, game developers). These contracts are legal agreements that formally empower capital to try to control and exploit labor (Stahl, 2010, 2013, 2021). They legally define and institutionally enshrine the terms and conditions of the workers' employment. Employment contracts in the DMEI serve several key functions for corporations. These contracts: (1) define roles and responsibilities, and outline the duties, tasks, and expectations of the worker; (2) set compensation and benefits, establishing payment terms, royalties, bonuses, and other benefits, often structured to maximize capital's exploitation of labor; (3) stipulate ownership of Intellectual Property (IP), specifying who owns the rights to the finished product, mostly favoring corporate interests over the creators; (4) ensure legal compliance, including clauses that ensure adherence to industry standards and regulatory requirements; (5) manage disputes, providing processes and practices for resolving conflicts between managers and workers, but usually to protect corporate interests.

While employment contracts in the DMEI are subject to negotiation and contestation, especially in unionized environments, they primarily establish and reinforce the power of capital over labor. These contracts ensure that corporations gain and retain significant control over the labor process and its final product, alienating workers from their labor and legally dispossessing them of the products of their work. Also, many contracts include exclusivity clauses that prevent workers from engaging in similar work for rival companies, deepening their dependency. Furthermore, workers are often required to sign non-disclosure agreements (NDAs) as part of the contract, limiting their ability to speak publicly about their work and conditions, thus maintaining corporate power over the worker's own experiences of labor (and pre-empting the researcher's ability to grasp what's happening). Additionally, corporations typically control the terms and conditions of contract renewals and terminations, creating a precarious labor force constantly at the mercy of capital and desperate to prove its value for the hope of renewal or securing new contracts. In the main, employment contracts in the DMEI prioritize corporate power and profits over the rights and interests of workers, diminishing worker autonomy, dispossessing workers of the rights to their products, maintaining precarity, and driving unequal financial returns. The legal apparatus of the state stands behind these employment contracts, upholding the domination of capital over labor, enforcing general conditions that allow employers to extract surplus value from workers' labor (Glasbeek, 2024; Stahl 2010, 2013, 2021).

Nonetheless, there are instances when workers challenge these contracts through the state's legal sphere. Cases like Olivia de Havilland v. Warner Bros. Pictures (1944), Prince v. Warner Bros. Records (1992), and Frank Darabont v. AMC Networks (2013) represent efforts by workers to contest and rewrite capital's contracts to better serve their own interests. Furthermore, as the DMEI expands, new forms of exploitation have necessitated the workers' fight for new labor laws. One example of this is a new state law that protects "kidinfluencers" from their parents (Maddox, 2023).

The Coogan Act and Kid Influencers

The rise of "kidfluencers" on social media platforms, particularly YouTube, contributes to these platforms' profits while generating substantial income for these young content creators. However, due to their age, children's earnings on YouTube are typically managed by their parents or legal guardians (Maddox, 2023). Unlike adult workers, child performers do not enjoy federal labor law protections. Instead, their protection relies on state-level labor laws, which can vary widely. The question of child performers' rights to their earnings dates back to early 20th-century Hollywood. One prominent case involved Jackie Coogan, a silent film star who starred in Charlie Chaplin's *The Kid*. Coogan faced financial hardship when his parents appropriated and spent most of his earnings on their extravagant lifestyle, leaving him with very little as an adult (Maddox, 2023). Coogan launched and eventually won a lawsuit against his parents. The outcome was the Coogan Act, also known as the California Child Actor's Bill, established in 1938 and updated in 2000. This law mandates that a portion of a child actor's earnings be placed in a trust, legally recognized as their property, and be made accessible to them when they reach adulthood. Despite these legal developments, contemporary "kidfluencers" on platforms like YouTube find themselves in a legal gray zone (Maddox, 2023). They are not officially recognized as child actors because the Coogan Act does not extend to YouTube. Nonetheless, states are starting to enact new laws, to protect kidinfluencers (Maddox, 2023). Illinois, for example, introduced a new law, which came into effect on July 1, 2024 (Kindelan, 2024). This legislation aims to ensure that child content creators receive their fair share of earnings when featured in video blogs or online content that generates a minimum of 10 cents per view. To be eligible, the content must originate from Illinois, and children must be featured in at least 30% of the content within a 30-day period. It is possible that other states will pass similar laws in the future.

In addition to being a sphere where new laws can be made, the state can investigate corporations to ensure their compliance with existing labor laws. The U.S. Department of Labor (DOL), for example, operates a number of divisions and agencies responsible for administering and enforcing over 180 federal laws that pertain to labor, including work in the DMEI. The following sections outline the investigative and enforcement roles of some key DOL agencies in relation to work in the DMEI. These include the Wage and Hour Division (WHD), the National Labor Relations Board (NLRB), the Equal Employment Opportunity Commission (EEOC), the Civil Rights Center, and the Occupational Safety and Health Administration (OSHA). Each agency's role and relevant laws are described, accompanied by examples that highlight the state's governance of work in the DMEI.

The Wage and Hour Division (WHD): Fair Labor Standards Act (FLSA): Exempting "Crunch Time" in the Games Industries

The WSH investigates corporate compliance with the FLSA. The FLSA establishes a federal minimum wage and aims to ensure that all workers receive at least this base pay. The FLSA also requires eligible workers to be paid one and a half times their regular rate for overtime work exceeding 40 hours weekly. Additionally, the FLSA encompasses child labor laws, setting age limits and allowable work hours. The WHD investigates and enforces these provisions, handling labor complaints, managing back wage payments, and taking legal action against companies that violate standards. Unfortunately, some companies in the DMEI have found ways around the FLSA and outplayed the WHD's enforcement of the rules, when taking advantage of exceptions and exemptions to the FLSA that serve their bottom line.

For example, game studios have avoided compliance with the FLSA's provisions pertaining to overtime pay by establishing workarounds so that they can get away with exploitative crunch-time labor practices. "Crunch time" refers to a period leading up to a game's release, where developers and other workers often labor for extended hours—sometimes involuntarily—to meet the studio's impending deadline (Bulut, 2020; Cote & Harris, 2021, 2023a, 2023b; Vernace, 2020; Weststar & Dubois, 2022). This practice, marked by long working days, sometimes up to 16 hours per day, seven days a week for months, often without additional compensation, is longstanding. A 2019 survey by the International Game Developers Association highlighted that 40% of workers suffered this crunch time, often exceeding 20 hours beyond their standard workweek, with only a small fraction receiving extra pay (Thomsen, 2021). Several triple-A game studios, including Rockstar Games (*Red Dead Redemption*), CD Projekt Red (*Cyberpunk 2077*), BioWare (*Mass Effect*), and Naughty Dog (*The Last of Us*), have faced public scrutiny for normalizing crunch time practices and super-exploiting workers.

"Crunch time" may seem like a straightforward violation of the FLSA, but it's not entirely clear-cut. Game studios have managed to evade some FLSA regulations by either categorizing workers as independent contractors or taking advantage of exemptions designed for computer professionals. Here's the background. In the early 2000s, games workers launched class-action lawsuits against major gaming companies, starting with the "EA Spouse Case" against Electronic Arts (EA), challenging illegal exemption classifications and unpaid overtime stemming from the crunch (Dyer-Witheford & de Peuter, 2006). This class action led to significant settlements with companies like EA, Sony, and Rockstar, reclassifying workers to nonexempt status and securing their right to overtime pay. However, a 2008 amendment to California's labor laws, signed by then-Governor Arnold Schwarzenegger, lowered the overtime exemption threshold and broadened the exemption criteria, undermining the progress made by the previous class action. Also, both federal and state laws exempt certain computer professionals from overtime pay if they earn above a specific salary, enabling game studios to demand extended hours from these workers without compensating them. As a result, many game workers are left without legal protection against crunch time (Vernace, 2020). Nowadays, studios continue to crunch workers, who afraid of losing their jobs, will often internalize this brutal labor process. Legal action and unionization have not stopped the acceleration of crunch time, though some companies, like Rockstar Games, claim they are taking voluntary steps to slow it down.

The National Labor Relations Board (NLRB): National Labor Relations Act (NLRA): Big Tech, Violating the Workers' Right to Unionize

The NLRB is an independent federal agency empowered to enforce the NLRA, which protects workers' rights to organize, join, or assist labor unions, bargain collectively, and engage in other activities for mutual aid or protection, as well as the right to refrain from these activities. This right is protected under Sections 7 and 8(a)(1) of the NLRA. Section 7 guarantees workers the right to self-organize, join or assist labor organizations, and seek out mutual benefit. Section 8(a)(1) prohibits corporations from interfering with, restraining, or coercing workers who exercise these rights. Unlawful corporate actions include threats against union activity, interrogating workers about their union involvement, creating an impression of surveillance, enforcing work rules that inhibit these rights, denying off-duty workers access to nonworking areas without valid reason, and disciplining or discharging workers for undertaking these protected activities. The NLRB's NLRA aims to ensure workers in the DMEI and other industries can exercise their rights freely without threat of corporate or managerial retaliation or coercion.

Unfortunately, companies in the DMEI have a long history of violating the right of workers to unionize. Recently, the DOL investigated Apple following allegations of retaliation against a worker who raised concerns about workplace harassment and unsafe conditions (Browning, 2021). Ashley Gjovik, a senior engineering program manager, was terminated by Apple after publicly discussing her experiences of harassment, surveillance, and safety issues at the company. She was part of the #AppleToo movement, which collected and publicized accounts of verbal abuse, bullying, and discrimination within the company. She claimed that her dismissal was under a false pretext and resulted from her numerous complaints, which were met with retaliation by management. In response, Gjovik filed complaints with the NLRB, accusing Apple of inhibiting workers from discussing wages and working conditions, and thereby hindering their collective action. Among the incidents cited was an email from Tim Cook warning against leaks of confidential information, which was interpreted as discouraging open communication among workers. Over a year after these charges were filed, the NLRB found that Apple indeed broke the law by interfering with its workers' rights to organize.

In that same year, the NLRB filed a complaint against Google, alleging multiple labor law violations. Google violated workers' rights with illegal surveillance, the retaliatory firing of several workers who tried to unionize, and the blocking of workers from sharing work-related grievances through calendars, email, and a platform called MemeGen (Peters, 2021). Kathryn Spiers, for example, was fired by Google after creating a pop-up notification for workers visiting the website of IRI Consultants, a firm that Google had hired to squash workers' union campaigns (Elias, 2020).

While the NLRB is important to upholding and enforcing the NLRA, the existing legal framework still heavily favors the power of corporations over workers. When workers attempt to organize unions, they often face unlawful termination by corporations, but the consequences for corporations are minimal. For example, the NLRB recently found Elon Musk's Tesla guilty of illegally firing a worker in 2017 due to their union activities, yet as of 2023, the worker who made the complaint was still unemployed. Similarly, Amazon does everything it can to circumvent or deny unions, but faces few penalties. These companies know that the law lacks effective mechanisms to compel negotiation with newly formed unions, allowing them to employ strategies like stalling in hopes that unionists will leave or lose momentum, ultimately weakening class solidarity and collective action. There are efforts to strengthen these laws (such as the PRO Act passed by House Democrats in 2021), but these often falter due to opposition, leaving the capital-labor power imbalance largely unaddressed and workers vulnerable in their struggle to realize their basic union-building rights (Leonhardt & Scheiber, 2023).

The Equal Employment Opportunity Commission (EEOC): Age Discrimination in Hollywood

The EEOC is an independent federal agency that promotes equal opportunity in employment through administrative and judicial enforcement of the federal government's civil rights laws, which aim to protect individuals from discrimination and to promote equal opportunity. The EEOC investigates and enforces civil rights laws against workplace discrimination within the DMEI. Pertinent laws include the Equal Pay Act of 1963, Civil Rights Act of 1964, Age Discrimination in Employment Act of 1967, Americans with Disabilities Act of 1990, and the Family and Medical Leave Act of 1993.

The Age Discrimination in Employment Act of 1967 protects individuals who are 40 years of age or older from employment discrimination based on age. This includes discrimination in hiring, promotion, discharge, compensation, or terms, conditions, or privileges of employment. In 2000, thousands of writers launched a class-action lawsuit against Hollywood, alleging age discrimination in hiring (Verrier, 2010). In 2010, they had reached a settlement. The workers' case, involving major Hollywood studios, broadcast networks like ABC, CBS, NBC, Fox, and talent agencies such as William Morris, Endeavor, and UTA, accused these corporations of systematically sidelining writers over 40 for jobs when hiring younger writers they imagined were better positioned to script texts that spoke to younger audiences. The corporations agreed to pay $70 million in a settlement and established "Fund for the Future" with $2.5 million, intended to support older and senior writers through grants, loans, and pension supplements (Verrier, 2010). Despite settling, the defendants denied any wrongdoing. This class action suit by writers garnered attention for spotlighting ageism in Hollywood. The case also received a crucial boost from the Writers Guild of America (WGA), which provided research supporting the age-discrimination claims.

The DOL's Office of Federal Contract Compliance Programs (OFCCP) and Civil Rights Center (CRC): Gendered Wage Discrimination in Silicon Valley

The OFCCP and CRC investigate and enforce Equal Employment Opportunity (EEO) laws. The OFCCP ensures that corporations engaged in federal government contracts comply with EEO regulations and prohibits employment discrimination based on race, color, religion, sex, national origin, disability, and protected veteran status. The CRC is responsible for overseeing EEO. In the DMEI, the DOL's OFCCP and CRC have conducted several high-profile investigations, enforcing laws against job discrimination.

For example, the OFCCP has investigated several tech companies for *gendered wage discrimination*. In 2015, computer security researcher Katie Moussouris filed a class-action lawsuit against Microsoft. Moussouris, joined by two other women, claimed they were overlooked for raises and promotions and faced biased treatment in performance reviews due to their gender. In the same year, Tina Huang, a former Twitter worker, initiated a class-action lawsuit against her former employer. Huang contended that Twitter's promotion process was biased, favoring male workers over female workers. In 2016, Qualcomm faced a class-action lawsuit representing 3300 female workers who accused the smartphone chipmaker of gender discrimination. Before the trial, Qualcomm opted to settle, agreeing to pay $19.5 million. In 2021, Google agreed to a $3.8 million settlement with the workers who experienced gendered wage and hiring discrimination between 2014 and 2017 (Nagele-Piazza, 2021). This agreement, benefiting over 5,500 Google workers and job applicants, stipulated that approximately $1.35 million be allocated as back pay and interest to the 2565 female workers affected by pay discrimination. A total of $1.23 million compensated the 1757 female and 1219 Asian applicants who were not hired for the jobs. A total of $1.25 million was earmarked for future pay equity adjustments for Google engineers (Nagele-Piazza, 2021).

The DOL's Occupational Safety and Health Administration (OSH) and the Occupational Safety and Health Act (OSHA): Labor Hazards and Whistleblowing

The OSH and OSHA aim to ensure that the conditions of work across the economy are safe and healthy. OSHA also requires corporations to provide training and education about workplace safety and health, inform workers about potential risks to their safety and health, develop emergency action plans for incidents like fires or accidents, and maintain records of workplace injuries, illnesses, and deaths. Adhering to OSHA standards is not only a legal obligation of corporations but also fundamental to safeguarding the health and safety of workers in the DMEI, with a shared responsibility between corporations for hazard mitigation and workers for reporting safety risks.

Despite its glamorous reputation, Hollywood is full of workplace hazards. The death of Brandon Lee during *The Crow* filming due to a firearms mishap, Kristin Chenoweth's injury from lighting equipment on *The Good Wife* set, Channing Tatum's burns during *The Eagle*, Brad Pitt's Achilles tendon tear in *Troy*, and George Clooney's severe back injury in *Syriana*, remind of this. Halle Berry, Nicole Kidman, Joseph Gordon-Levitt, and Ben Stiller have also suffered various injuries when making movies. The 2021 incident on the *Rust* set, where cinematographer Halyna Hutchins was fatally shot and director Joel Souza injured due to a live round from a prop revolver used by actor Alec Baldwin (whose involuntary manslaughter trial was dismissed in 2024), further highlights the health and safety risks of making movies. These incidents flag the embodied dangers workers confront when making Hollywood's immaterial spectacles.

Silicon Valley has faced significant health and safety problems for much of its history as well. Back in 1980 (when some semiconductors were manufactured in the US), workers at Signetics Corporation exposed serious health and safety risks, including inadequate ventilation, leading to a $25 million lawsuit against Signetics' parent company and chemical manufacturers (Pillar, 1980). The workers' case was supported by the Electronics Committee on Safety and Health (ECOSH) and the International Brotherhood of Electrical Workers and United Electrical Workers. In recent years, Silicon Valley companies have continued to battle health and safety lawsuits, particularly from content moderators working on contract for corporations like Facebook and YouTube (Newton, 2019, 2021). Selena Scola, a former Facebook contract worker, filed a lawsuit alleging that Facebook failed to protect content moderators from mental trauma caused by exposure to horrifying content. The lawsuit led to a $52 million settlement from Facebook in 2020, benefiting around 11,250 moderators and promising additional support for those diagnosed with PTSD. Similarly, in 2020, a proposed class-action lawsuit was filed against YouTube, accusing the company of failing to protect its content moderators from psychological harm. The plaintiff, identified as Jane Doe, claimed that the conditions of work led to her mental health crisis. She also argued that YouTube neglected workplace safety, imposed demanding quotas, and silenced moderators using non-disclosure agreements (NDAs). YouTube settled the lawsuit for $4.3 million in 2022, agreeing to provide counseling services, peer support groups, transparent job descriptions, and a whistleblower hotline.

In addition to upholding health and safety conditions for workers in the DMEI, the OHSA also can protect worker whistleblowers. The OSHA's Whistleblower Protection Program enforces the provisions of more than 20 federal laws protecting employees from retaliation for, among other things, raising or reporting concerns about hazards or violations of workplace safety and health protocols. Even still, worker whistleblowers face dangers when trying to speak truth to the power of big companies like Google, Pinterest, and Amazon. Chelsey Glasson, a former Google worker, filed a lawsuit against Google alleging pregnancy discrimination and retaliation (Bhuiyan, 2021; Hern, 2019). Timnit Gebru, an AI ethics researcher at Google, and Aerica Shimizu Banks, a former Pinterest employee, experienced a significant backlash after exposing unethical practices within these companies. The OSHA's Whistleblower Protection Program is important, but there is a need for even stronger safeguards for whistleblowers who put their careers and livelihoods at risk to shine a light on corporate misconduct.

The State's Tacit Labor Law

While the previous section considered some of the US state's "explicit" labor law agencies and investigation and enforcement mechanisms, there are fields of government law, policy, and regulation that, while not explicitly framed as labor law or investigated and enforced by labor departments and agencies, nonetheless can have a significant impact on the quantity and quality of jobs in the DMEI. They should be taken seriously and examined as a site of what I conceptualize as domains of "tacit" governmental labor law, policy, and regulation. In what follows, four zones of tacit labor law are explored: telecommunications and broadcasting policy and regulation, copyright law, competition and antitrust law, and entertainment and tech industry subsidies.

The Federal Communications Commission (FCC): Communication Policies and Regulations at Work

The FCC, established by the Communications Act of 1934, regulates the corporations that own radio, television, wire, satellite, and cable communications. Its responsibility includes overseeing the telecommunications industry and ensuring efficient and effective public communication services.

What Is the State and How Does It Govern Work in the DMEI? 139

While the FCC is crucial for regulating capitalist communications in the public interest, powerful corporate interests have lobbied and turned this state agency into a means for private gain (Forde, 2024; McChesney, 2008, 2013). This is evident in the "revolving door" phenomenon, where individuals alternate between FCC roles and positions in the corporations they regulate. Additionally, telecommunications and media companies exert considerable influence over FCC policies through campaign contributions, and insider connections. This influence is also reflected in the FCC's spectrum auctions, which often favor monopolies. Although the FCC's mandate does not explicitly address work conditions in the DMEI, its policies and regulations significantly impact investment decisions, thereby indirectly influencing job quantity in the DMEI.

For example, The Telecommunications Act of 1996 was framed as increasing market competition but instead jump started media merger and acquisition mania, strengthening oligopoly control of the market. This Act facilitated the convergence of telecommunications and broadcasting, resulting in the formation of large, vertically and horizontally integrated media conglomerates. Although not explicitly a labor policy, the Act's relaxation of media ownership restrictions paved the way for ownership concentration, with larger corporations absorbing smaller entities and laying off thousands of workers. There was also an increase in precarious gigs as workers entered a labor market with fewer standard employment opportunities. Also, the Act's promotion of digital capitalism spurred a demand for new skills, particularly in digital literacy. This shift compelled workers to upskill to remain competitive, initially creating wage disparities between digitally skilled workers and those without such skills in a tight labor market. Over the past few decades, this digital labor market has become saturated, putting downward pressure on wages. The Act's influence on work is still evident today, particularly in the expansion of 5G networks. Major telecommunications companies, such as Verizon and AT&T, employ thousands of workers to build and maintain this new digital infrastructure. In sum, the Act of 1996 though not framed as a labor policy, had and continues to have impacts on work in the DMEI.

The FCC engages in many other activities that tacitly influence job creation in the DMEI. Key among these tacit labor policy activities are the FCC *Spectrum Auctions*, where corporations bid for electromagnetic spectrum licenses and drive investments in wireless infrastructure and jobs. The 2021 Auction 107 for C-band spectrum raised over $80 billion, increasing investments and job growth in network expansion and 5G service development. *Net Neutrality rules*, particularly their contentious repeal in 2017, have profound impacts on the broadband and Internet service provider industry, influencing infrastructure investment decisions and job creation, especially in smaller tech firms and startups. FCC *ownership rules* designed to prevent media consolidation and promote ownership diversity, although relaxed in 2017, initially aimed to maintain a diverse range of job opportunities. More ownership consolidation can lead to fewer jobs, while restrictions on concentrated ownership can foster media diversity and more job opportunities for workers. Changes in *consumer data privacy regulations* also affect digital advertising and online media, undergirding the demand for data analysts and compliance officers in this sphere. Additionally, the *Universal Service Fund (USF)* supports job creation in telecommunications, particularly in rural communities, through initiatives like the Rural Health Care Program and the E-Rate Program. FCC regulations for TV and radio broadcasting, including decisions on *broadcast ownership and license renewals*, affect jobs in the DMEI. Finally, *media content regulations*, such as those against indecent content and mandates for local content, shape production decisions in TV and radio, impacting jobs related to content compliance and creation.

The Copyright Office and Creators

The Copyright Office administers the US copyright system and advises Congress, federal agencies, courts, and the public on copyright law. This law, enforced by the state, shapes the lives and labors of workers in the DMEI. The state's enforcement of copyright can benefit entrepreneurial creative workers by ensuring they are compensated for their creations via royalties and licensing fees, encouraging them to produce new and innovative content, and offering them leverage in negotiations with the larger corporations that hire their labor power and try to control most copyrights. However, the state's strict enforcement of copyright law can be detrimental to these workers. Overly broad copyright claims by large corporations can stifle the creation of derivative and new works. Many creators, especially newcomers, receive a small fraction of the returns from copyright enforcement as compared to the corporations that own and control the most IP. Additionally, individual workers often cannot afford the cost of enforcing their copyrights against violators or defending against infringement claims by bigger players. The extension of copyright durations, the result of corporate lobbying, can limit the creation of new works from older material. The subjective nature of the fair use doctrine leads to copyright infringement risk aversion and potential self-censorship among creators. Most of the time, large corporations in the DMEI shape copyright law to control IP to maximally benefit themselves, not their labor force, and they sometimes weaponize the law to suppress competition and innovation. While copyright can protect creators' rights (and motivate and reward their creation of content), the state's stringent enforcement of it on behalf of powerful corporations perpetuates their power and profit.

The US Department of Justice's Antitrust Division (DOJAD) and the Federal Trade Commission (FTC)

The DOJAD and FTC are key enforcers of antitrust law, which also indirectly impacts work in the DMEI. Antitrust law, otherwise known as competition law, aims to promote fair and competitive markets by preventing anti-competitive practices and restricting the formation of corporate monopolies or oligopolies that could abuse their power to the detriment of other competitors and consumers in the market. The FTC is charged with investigating anti-competitive corporate behavior across industries. When it identifies violations of antitrust law, it may take enforcement actions such as filing lawsuits, seeking injunctions, and imposing fines. The FTC also reviews proposed mergers and acquisitions by corporations to gauge their impact on market competition and can try to protect consumers from unfair and deceptive practices. The FTC's role extends to monitoring markets in the DMEI.

Antitrust law and the FTC's investigation and enforcement actions are not typically associated with workers' rights, but they can play a tacit role in supporting workers in the DMEI. Monopolistic and oligopolistic companies can use their market power to restrict workers' mobility and suppress optimal compensation for their labor. Hence, those concerned with workers' rights should consider the noxious impacts of corporate monopolies and oligopolies on workers, and the corrective potential of antitrust law. Antitrust laws can be used to prevent or curtail the monopolistic and oligopolistic practices by corporations in labor markets, so as to ensure a competitive job market. They can safeguard workers from corporate behaviors that limit job mobility or unfairly suppress wages. In the DMEI, where a few corporations can potentially control much of the labor market, the FTC's enforcement of antitrust laws can support workers in some ways.

The FTC's efforts to halt the Microsoft-Activision-Blizzard merger, cheered on by Senators, unions, and workers, illustrate the opportunities and challenges faced by those who try to leverage antitrust laws for workers' rights. Under US President Biden, Lina Khan, a critic of monopoly power, was appointed to lead the FTC. The FTC's review of the Microsoft-Activision-Blizzard merger, supported by Senators Elizabeth Warren, Bernie Sanders, Sheldon Whitehouse, and Cory Booker, focused partly on workers' rights (Bevan, 2022). These Senators, backed by the Communications Workers of America (CWA), were alarmed about Activision Blizzard's labor rights violations, including union-busting. They scrutinized the company's sexual harassment problems, called out its exploitation of quality assurance (QA) workers, and expressed support for the unionization campaigns by QA testers (Bevan, 2022). The Senators argued that the merger with Microsoft would exacerbate monopoly power and worsen workers' conditions, and so should be opposed. The FTC moved to block the merger on December 8, 2022, but was unsuccessful. Microsoft's $69 billion acquisition of Activision Blizzard went through, followed by a wave of layoffs affecting 10,000 workers across various divisions, including its Bethesda Game Studios and 343 Industries. Microsoft eventually agreed to a labor neutrality agreement with the CWA in June 2022 (Reuters, 2022). Despite the FTC's efforts to block mergers potentially harmful to workers and even with substantial support from numerous Senators, workers, unions, and publics, its authority is often limited. In contrast, the influence of large corporations within the state appears more dominant, overriding the interests of workers.

The State as Subsidizer: The National Endowment for the Arts, The California Film Commission, DARPA, and More

State agencies at federal, state, and municipal levels coordinate a *vast subsidy system* to bolster the growth of the DMEI and employment. For example, The National Endowment for the Arts, along with State Arts Agencies, provide funding to precarious artists, supporting job creation in the arts sector. The Creative Economy Revitalization Act (CERA), introduced on August 13, 2021, by U.S. Representatives Teresa Leger Fernández (D-NM) and Jay Obernolte (R-CA), is a relevant example. Endorsed by over 175 interest groups, CERA was a $300 million grant program aimed at revitalizing the creative industries during the early COVID-19 period. Developed in collaboration with the Get Creative Workers Working coalition, CERA aimed to help some creators make ends meet while driving regrowth in the sector and ancillary services in production, marketing, and distribution. States also subsidize Hollywood with movie production incentives (MPIs) or tax incentives to encourage in-state production of TV series and movies. Proponents of these subsidies argue that the shooting of TV series and movies on location leads to increased economic activity and job creation, pointing to the influx of small business, tourism, and tax revenue. The California Film Commission which runs the MPI program, argues that Hollywood productions that received $1.1 billion in subsidies between 2015 and 2020 generated nearly $8.4 billion in direct spending and contributed to the employment of over 27,000 actors, 36,000 crew members, and 558,000 extras (EP, 2023). However, critics of the MIP program argue that its cost to taxpayers outweighs the workforce benefits. Arguably these subsidies primarily benefit Hollywood and out-of-state workers rather than in-state workers, and don't create new jobs, but just transfer jobs from one state to another. Furthermore, the project-based nature of Hollywood production drives precarious employment, not full-time stable jobs. Nonetheless, around the world, numerous states offer MPIs to globalizing

Hollywood studios in hopes of attracting "runaway" productions, and generating jobs for local workers.

The state has also subsidized Silicon Valley's development, past and present, and contributed to job creation. During World War II, Congress invested in radar development, benefiting Bell Labs, and funded the University of Pennsylvania's development of the first general-purpose electronic computer. The 1950s saw defense-funded advancements like a nationwide computer network, leading to innovations in screen and memory technologies. Pentagon funding in the 1950s and 1960s supported microwave, satellite communications, and the development of core computer technologies, including the first mouse and graphical user interface. In the late 1990s and early 2000s, tech giants like Google and Microsoft benefited from government funding and contracts. In 2018, Amazon decided to establish its second headquarters (HQ2) in Arlington and promised to generate 25,000 high-paying jobs for Virginians, thanks in part to a state provisioned incentive package of $573 million comprised of cash grants and tax breaks. Apple's 2019 plan for a $1 billion campus in Austin, Texas, expected to create initially 5,000 and potentially up to 15,000 jobs, was supported by a $25 million grant from the Texas Enterprise Fund and property tax rebates. Tesla's Gigafactory in Nevada, receiving one of the largest incentive packages in US history at around $1.3 billion, committed to creating 6500 jobs. Google's 2018 investment of $1 billion in a New York City campus, aiming to double its workforce, benefited from the city's handouts. In sum, state subsidies to the DMEI function as a state-to-capital job development program, creating jobs for workers and generating profits for capitalists.

The State as Labor Force Trainer

The state at all levels plays a central role in partnering with corporations in the DMEI to *train the labor force*. There are numerous state programs and initiatives ostensibly designed to train and upskill workers, to equip individuals with the digital knowledge and skills necessary to land a job in the DMEI. However, beneath the veneer of skill-building, the corporations of the DMEI influence state interventions and training subventions, shaping the composition of the labor force to suit its need for an expanding reserve army. Tech Bootcamps and Coding Academies offer intensive training in software development and data science, expanding the ranks of coders who are likely to be displaced by generative AI before they even apply for a paid job. Support for digital content creation, like that offered by the National Endowment for the Arts (NEA), may nurture artistic talent for the online creator economy but may also deflect attention away from platform precarities. Furthermore, the state, through its public education system, provides a massive subsidy to the DMEI when universities and colleges train the workforce for its corporations in specialized undergraduate and graduate degree programs that offer "work-ready" concentrations. These save corporations on training costs while internships and co-op programs inadvertently mask the exploitation of young workers as they toil for course credit with the hope of one day getting paid. Higher education's growing collaborations with behemoths like Walt Disney Company, Adobe Systems Incorporated and Meta Platforms underscore the entanglement of the state and the DMEI.

The State as Direct Employer

The state, through its public affairs, media, and information agencies, also creates jobs and employs workers. These agencies harness the expertise of workers experienced in branding for automobiles, shoes, and fast food, as well as workers who possess storytelling skills honed in Hollywood and news media, to design and execute strategic communication and public relations campaigns for winning hearts and minds to US foreign war policy, national identity and values (Mirrlees, 2016). For example, the Department of Defense's Public Affairs Office and the State Department's Office of Global Social Media not only employ communication professionals from the DMEI but also contribute to job growth by outsourcing media campaigns to advertising, PR, and marketing firms. These state agencies and their workers produce and circulate content, write national narratives, make and manage national brands, and shape public opinion, locally and globally. The growing connections between state agencies and the DMEI's firms are evident and significant in the new US-China global media rivalry, which relies on the labors of Western and non-Western creative and cultural workers to conduct international information and propaganda campaigns.

The Power and Politics of State Matter to Work in the DMEI

The state facilitates and legitimizes capitalism and the power of corporations to exploit workers, but its influence on the relations between corporations and workers extends beyond merely doing that. As seen in this chapter, the state plays a number of roles: neoliberal superintendent, labor law maker, investigator, enforcer, communication and media policy-maker and regulator, copyright supporter, antitrust agent, industry subsidizer, job booster, trainer, and employer. The state plays a key role in governing work in the DMEI, and its institutions possess some capacity to shape the macro structures of capitalism and the meso and micro power relations of between capital and labor.

Evidently, the state—and state power—matters to workers in the DMEI. But parties and movements play a role in shaping the side the state

What Is the State and How Does It Govern Work in the DMEI? 145

may take in battles between capital and labor. Within democracy, political blocs (coalitions or alliances of social classes, groups, and organizations that join together for a common political project or goal) engage in competition and conflict to shape the state to make, enforce, or modify the rules that govern work in society. While class division is embedded in the edifice of capitalism itself and class conflict persists in the digital society, this social antagonism sometimes gets expressed in opaque forms. It may be addressed and taken up by formal political parties, in wars of position and wars of maneuver, for hegemony, for state power, and clashes between conservative and liberal-progressive social movements in society, in so-called culture wars, which may or may not intersect with overt battles between capital and labor, or, class wars.

The state is in no way a neutral arbiter of structural and conjunctural conflicts between capital and labor, but it can be influenced by warring political parties and the coalitions of interest groups they serve. The state takes sides, serving the interests of some, at the expense of others. This again is why state power matters to workers. While the state facilitates and legitimizes capitalism and secures the interests of the corporations and CEOs at the helm of the DMEI, for its legitimacy, the state must also respond to the popular demands and pressures exerted by political parties and social movements upon it, if only in word, though sometimes, in deed. The state, therefore, is an arena of both the consolidation and possible contestation of class power. The state's laws, policies, and regulations that govern work in the DMEI may at core be designed to facilitate and legitimize capitalism and the power of its owning class. But they could be redesigned in support of the interests, needs, and aspirations of workers. Ultimately, it will be politics, not economics alone, that decides the future of the state, and the side state agencies take in battles between capital and labor. In the meantime, within thousands of corporate organizations across the DMEI, managers are doing everything they can to control their labor force, using a combination of persuasion and repression to ensure workers comply with their directives and to neutralize any refusal or resistance. This brings us to the topic of management, whose history and major theories are the focus of the following chapter.

6 What Is the Management of Work in the DMEI?

Putting Leadership Power, Decision-Making Power, Soft Power, Hard Power, and Market Power to Work on Workers

Introduction

This chapter considers the management of work in the digital media and entertainment industries (DMEI). It explores a spectrum of management theories and practices that shape the power relations between employers and employees in the DMEI. It begins with "Management by Great Leaders": the power of individual CEOs over corporate cultures and workforces. The chapter then shifts focus to "Management as Decision-Making Power," highlighting how decisions made by CEOs shape a company's direction and labor processes. The chapter also addresses "Management as Relational Power," discussing Frederick Winslow Taylor's labor process engineering, Lillian Gilbreth's human relations engineering, and Michel Foucault's concept of governmentality. The chapter then highlights "Soft Power" or persuasive tactics in management: bureaucratic control, participatory management, and the use of perks, fun, and games as tools for motivating work and influencing worker conduct. After that, it scrutinizes "Hard Power" or repressive tactics in management: bullying, surveillance, silencing and censoring, no cold call agreements (NCCAs), non-compete clauses (NCCs) and non-disclosure agreements (NDAs), union busting, unfair firing, blacklisting, and canceling. The chapter also conceptualizes the media market as an "Invisible Manager" or invisible form of power over both managers and workers. Overall, this chapter explores how management is a form of power and influence over workers in their labor process, and in the DMEI. Rather than summarizing studies of the management of workers in specific companies within the DMEI, this chapter offers a broad critical overview of some major concepts in the history of management. It considers how these can be used to analyze the management of work in companies of the DMEI, highlighting their potential utility for future critical research in the field.

DOI: 10.4324/9781003131076-7

Management: The Control and Organization of Something, Someone

In the DMEI, management plays a significant role in shaping the meso and micro conditions and experiences of workers. Management can be defined as "the control and organization of something" and "the group of people responsible for controlling and organizing a company or organization." The largest and most significant corporations in the DMEI are managed by CEOs, whose annual pay is vast in comparison to the workers they employ. In 2022, Google's CEO Sundar Pichai was the highest paid, getting $226 million, followed by Apple's Tim Cook at $99.4 million. Microsoft's Satya Nadella received $55 million. Meta's Mark Zuckerberg got $27 million. Amazon's Andy Jassy was paid $1.3 million. In the telecom-media-entertainment sector, Netflix CEO Reed Hastings accumulated $51.1 million and Comcast's Michael Cavanagh took $40.5 million. In the corporations of the DMEI, management is structured hierarchically, a microcosm of the class division in the wider society. Senior managers, including the Board of Directors and CEOs, set strategic goals and policies. Middle managers, such as department heads, relay these strategies to front-line managers, who then oversee the day-to-day labor process of workers, who are also increasingly trained to self-manage.

What managerial theories might undergird and guide the conduct of the managers who manage the labor force? Andrijasevic, Chen, Gregg, and Steinberg (2021, p. x) say that "management is a cultural practice that takes different forms over space and time" and "always manifests through media and through various mediations." In this chapter, I review some key management theories that have emerged over the past hundred years or so. I suggest that these theories may be manifested institutionally through the corporations of the DMEI, in managerial discourses, bureaucratic-organizational practices, hard and soft power strategies and tactics, and media hardware and software systems that intersect with and shape the conditions and experiences of workers.

Management as Leader Power: "Great Leader Theory" (GLT) and Its Discontents

The "great leader theory" (GLT) of management emphasizes the power that individual leaders have in organizations, emphasizing the traits or characteristics that enable these leaders to lead workers effectively toward ends they decide. Thomas Carlyle (1841), a 19th-century writer, contributed to this notion with his "Great Man Theory" in *On Heroes, Hero-Worship, and the Heroic in History*. In the 1922 book *Economy and Society*, Max Weber (2019) introduced the concept of "charismatic authority" to flag a leader's extraordinary personal qualities that inspire loyalty and devotion in followers (including workers). Henri Fayol (2013) outlined

148   *What Is the Management of Work in the DMEI?*

five key management functions of corporate leaders in the 1916 book, *General and Industrial Management*: planning, organizing, commanding, coordinating, and controlling. In his 1954 *The Practice of Management*, Peter Drucker (2006) emphasized the manager's role in setting objectives and developing people. In *Leadership*, James MacGregor Burns (2010) introduced the idea of transformational leadership, differentiating it from transactional leadership. "Transformational leadership" inspires and motivates workers through vision, personal development, and intrinsic rewards, emphasizing relationships, innovation, and proactive change, while "transactional leadership" manages and moves workers through rewards and punishments based on performance and compliance, focusing on tasks, stability, and adherence to organizational procedures. Warren Bennis (2010), in *On Becoming a Leader* (1989), discussed the process of becoming a leader, focusing on self-awareness and the ability to inspire. In *The Leadership Challenge* (1987), James Kouzes and Barry Posner (2002) outlined key practices of exemplary leadership, including modeling the way, inspiring a shared vision, challenging the process, enabling others to act, and encouraging the heart. They emphasized leadership as a behavior that can be learned and modeled. These thinkers have inadvertently shaped the GLT, centering the identity, authority, charisma, acumen, and virtue of individual leaders in corporations, and affirming their strategic labors of leading the way and being followed by workers toward ends they ultimately decide.

Over the past decade, some books have been written about the white male CEOs of the DMEI as Great Leaders. For example, *Steve Jobs* by Walter Isaacson (2011) examines the life of Apple's co-founder, while *Becoming Steve Jobs* by Brent Schlender and Rick Tetzeli (2016) offers an alternative view of Jobs' leadership. Similarly, *Elon Musk: Tesla, SpaceX, and the Quest for a Fantastic Future* by Ashlee Vance (2017) explores Musk's ventures in tech and space capitalism. Jeff Bezos's story is chronicled in *The Everything Store* by Brad Stone (2013), highlighting his leadership at Amazon. *DisneyWar* by James B. Stewart (2006) details the corporate battles under Michael Eisner's leadership at Walt Disney Company while *The Ride of a Lifetime* by Robert Iger (2019) shares the former Disney CEO's leadership insights. *Hatching Twitter* by Nick Bilton (2014) focuses on the leadership dynamics among Twitter's co-founders, including Jack Dorsey. Additionally, books like *Netflixed* by Gina Keating (2012), although not strictly biographical, shed light on Reed Hastings's role in Netflix's rise. Furthermore, titles such as *The Facebook Effect* by David Kirkpatrick (2011), and Microsoft CEO Satya Nadella's (2019) *Hit Refresh* further contribute to this genre of Great Leader biography and organizational triumph. These books, along with others like *Creativity, Inc.* by Pixar president Ed Catmull (2023), and *Shoe Dog* by Nike founder Phil

Knight (2018), may tacitly reinforce the GLT. While these books provide interesting institutional histories of media and tech corporations through the lens of the lives and will power of bourgeois men, they risk equating the corporation with these white male leaders and overlook the system that shapes them, their firms and inequitable class relations.

While the GLT of management has its popular appeal among those that aspire to be CEOs for corporations in the DMEI, it tends to glorify individual leaders, often at the cost of acknowledging the collective labors of diverse workers in the corporations of the DMEI. These are institutional histories of corporations told from the point of the CEOs that run them. They center the identities of CEOs and downplay the lives and labors of the workers. If applied in managerial practice, GLT can create an organizational culture where individual leaders are put on a pedestal and excessively idolized, overshadowing the talent, knowhow and skill of the countless workers whose labor is essential to producing devices, algorithms, movies, and TV series. After all, corporations are built by the collective intelligence and labor of workers, not just on the big dreams and will to power of individual CEOs. Feminist and anti-racist scholars might also critique the GLT for its focus predominantly on white male leaders and marginalization of the myriad contributions made by women and people of color. Too often, white men are constructed as the archetypal leaders in the DMEI, perpetuating the false idea that leadership is linked to a specific racialized and gendered group. This may uphold sexist and racist notions by implying that other groups might be less capable of effective leadership. Additionally, in reality, many supposedly Great Leaders are not great.

In 2019, a report by Strategy&, a part of PwC, highlighted how many white male CEOs were being dismissed or stepping down from the heights of decision-making power due to very bad behavior coming to light (Berger, 2019). Strategy&'s report tracked CEO successions at the world's 2,500 largest publicly-listed companies and found nearly 40% of involuntary CEO exits were due to ethical breaches: fraud, bribery, insider dealing, or sexual misconduct (Berger, 2019). In 2018, there was a record high in CEO dismissals, with about 18% of CEOs being replaced, a significant rise from 12% in 2010. One of the highest profile cases was Harvey Weinstein of The Weinstein Company, ousted for sexual assault, harassment, and misconduct. Scott Thompson of Yahoo! was fired for falsifying his resume. Les Moonves of CBS was removed after numerous women workers went public about being sexually harassed or assaulted. Travis Kalanick's resignation from Uber followed investor pressure due to his fostering of a toxic workplace culture permissive of sexual harassment and discrimination. At FOX, Roger Ailes resigned following sexual harassment allegations by multiple female workers. Mark Hurd of Hewlett-Packard resigned amid a sex scandal. Pace GLT, the former CEOs of many corporations in the DMEI are Not Great Leaders (NGL).

In response to the problem of bad leaders like these, and the exclusionary workplace cultures they presided over, many corporations, HR departments, and management consultants have been implementing policies, training programs, and initiatives to foster more inclusive, diverse, and equitable (EDI) organizations. While EDI can do some positive institutional work, it has also been scrutinized as part of the elite capture of identity politics, where corporations and their CEOs co-opt the language, ideas, and images of social justice movements to present themselves as allies of anti-racist, feminist, LGBTQ, and other progressive causes while conducting business as usual. In these instances, EDI is an insidious form of "woke washing" that deflects attention from the ongoing exploitation of all workers within capitalism (al-Gharbi, 2024; Táíwò, 2022). Alongside the incorporation of EDI into the DMEI's managerial frameworks, recent influential books have encouraged women, particularly women of color, to pursue management roles and lead: Sheryl Sandberg's (2013) *Lean In: Women, Work, and the Will to Lead*, Minda Harts' (2019) *The Memo: What Women of Color Need to Know to Secure a Seat at the Table*, Oprah Winfrey's (2014) *What I Know for Sure*, and Deepa Purushothaman's (2022) *The First, the Few, the Only: How Women of Color Can Redefine Power in Corporate America*, collectively champion the climb of women, especially women of color, into leadership positions in the corporations of the DMEI. These books serve as motivational resources for women trying to break glass ceilings and become better CEOs and emphasize the positive impact women leaders can have on workplace cultures and shareholder payouts.

While the managerial push for EDI-friendly organizations and multicultural meritocracies may be well-intentioned, the efficacy of these initiatives has so far been limited: the leadership of most corporations in the DMEI remains predominantly white and male. In no way is the demographic profile of the top or middle leadership of the major corporations in the United States reflective of the diversity of the actual country, and certainly not the planet. Corporate America is still predominantly run by white men, as evidenced by a recent study of the top 100 publicly traded companies using federal workforce reports, census data, and corporate filings about the S&P 100 (Guynn & Fraser, 2023). Women are outnumbered 5 to 1 in senior leadership roles, holding just 17% of the 533 named CEO positions in S&P 100 corporations. Despite visible efforts to bridge the gender gap, including the promotion of women to executive suites and boardrooms, the top corporate positions and highest compensations remain largely inaccessible to women. There is an even wider disparity for women of color. They are outnumbered by men 26 to 1 in S&P leadership ranks, a gap five times greater than that for white women. Evidently, the top echelons of the most powerful corporations in the US remain largely white and male, while women and people of color are often in lower level positions and paid less. In a report on the top CEOs of the Fortune 500 corporations, only 8.8% were women (Women

Business Collaborative 2022). But, women CEOs in S&P 500 companies now outnumber CEOs named "John"! (Boyle & Green, 2023). In 2023, there were 41 women leading S&P 500 companies compared to 23 CEOs named John (Johns constitute only 3.27% of the US population, while women make up over 50%). No gender parity, at all. Men still lead the biggest corporations in the DMEI and make the biggest decisions.

Management as Decision-Making Power

Decision-making power, or, *the power to decide*, is the capacity to make choices that significantly impact the direction and operation of a corporation. Max Weber (1993) conceived of decision-making power as the "probability that one actor within a social relationship will be able to carry out their will despite resistance, regardless of the basis on which this probability rests." This ability to exert one's will even in the face of resistance is the essence of the decision-making power held by many CEOs—Elon Musk, Mark Zuckerberg, Jeff Bezos—in the DMEI. In *The Power Elite*, C. Wright Mills (1956) posited that a small elite, including top CEOs, holds the power to make decisions within corporations that steer their conduct, and also shape the wider economy and society: "The powers of ordinary people are circumscribed by the everyday worlds in which they live, yet even in these rounds of job, family and neighborhood they often seem driven by forces they can neither understand nor govern," wrote Mills. "Insofar as national events are decided," noted Mills, "the power elite are those who decide them." The CEOs of the top companies in the DMEI are undoubtedly part of society's power elite, and they possess greater decision-making power than the majority of people in society, including the workers their corporations employ.

In the DMEI, *the decision-making power of CEOs and Boards of Directors over workers is substantial.* The CEO, supported by the Board, exercises primary decision-making authority in various areas, including strategic planning, financial management, and operational direction. The Board of Directors, elected by shareholders, supervises the CEO's actions and advises on key decisions. It also holds the power to appoint or dismiss the CEO and top management. The decisions made by CEOs in the DMEI are far-reaching, shaping not only their corporations but also impacting shareholders, workers, customers, and the broader society. The CEO's decision-making power vastly exceeds that of individual workers, even those who belong to unions. The primary authority to decide what a corporation does rests with the CEOs and Boards of Directors, rather than unions, a distinction deeply rooted in the structural and legal frameworks of capitalism. Through collective bargaining and strike actions, unions may impact and reform certain aspects of a corporation's operations, especially those relating to labor conditions, from wages to benefits to workplace health and safety policies. However, the unions' influence typically does not extend to high-level decision-making processes that shape the corporation overall. Ultimately, while unions possess the power to negotiate specific aspects of corporate policy, the biggest strategic decisions about corporate conduct are mostly made by the CEOs and Boards.

A CEO's decision-making power can impact the workforce in multiple ways. Their financial decision-making influences job creation or destruction. Their decisions on product development and innovation directly affect the types of labor power the company will look to hire, and the kinds of projects workers are paid to work on, in complex divisions of labor. When hiring and firing, CEOs can shape the workforce's size and composition. The compensation structures CEOs establish, including salaries, bonuses, and stock options, have a direct impact on the financial well-being of workers. More money for them means less for workers. Additionally, CEOs shape and symbolize the corporate culture and the brand habitus of workers. Furthermore, mergers and acquisitions, often initiated by CEOs, can lead to workforce restructuring, including mass layoffs and cuts. Lastly, CEOs' involvement in politics, and legal, regulatory and policy affairs, can have far-reaching implications for the company's reputation and, consequently, the public perception of its workforce. In summary, the CEO's decision-making power majorly shapes the conditions and experiences of workers.

Management as Relational Power: Engineering Labor Processes and Human Relations

The history of management is intertwined with the history of capitalism and efforts to control a potentially resistant labor force. In *America By Design*, David Noble (1979) historicizes how engineering, traditionally focused on solving mechanical problems, evolved to address and solve business problems, particularly as related to the tendency of workers to refuse and resist owner efforts to control and maximally exploit their labor. Noble (1979, p. 258) argues,

> The corporate engineers played a double role. As engineers, they were professionally charged with the profit-maximizing advance of scientific technology. And as corporate functionaries, they assumed the responsibility for coordinating the human elements of the technological enterprise… to formulate a scientific way of managing that process, a technology of social production.

Much modern management sold itself to factory owners as a solution to the growing "man problem" in industrial capitalism, otherwise known as working-class self organization and collective action, which hindered optimally efficient production and minimized profits. Noble (1979, p. 262) described this problem as "the resistance of the worker to the management's expropriation of the workers' skills and the fruits of their labour and to the gradual usurpation of their traditional authority over the work process." Noble (1979, p. 262) further explains, "After systematically stripping away all the important incentives for diligent and creative work... these managers had to somehow motivate workers, to get them to 'put their hearts into their jobs'" To solve this so-called man problem, corporations hired engineers, or management consultants. Noble (1979, p. 264) points out, "This reflected a shift of focus on the part of engineers from the engineering of things to the engineering of people" or at least, the social relations between people in organizations. This led to a two-phase managerial approach: *labor process engineering* and *human relation engineering*.

Labor Process Engineering (Scientific Management): Fredrick Winslow Taylor

Scientific Management, also known as Taylorism, represented capital's new approach to *labor process engineering*. Developed by Frederick Winslow Taylor in *The Principles of Scientific Management* (1911), this approach to management marked a significant shift in industrial organization. Taylor, transitioning from a mechanical engineer to a management consultant, introduced Scientific Management principles to try to optimize labor process efficiency. Using time and motion studies, Taylorism broke the autonomy workers once had when managing their own labor processes. It aimed to identify the "one best way to do a task," standardize this, and then impose this standard upon workers, adding a system of incentives and penalties to try to ensure worker compliance with this control. Taylorism departed from the old management style that made some space for worker autonomy. As Taylor (1911) stated, "The philosophy of the old management puts the entire responsibility upon the workmen, while the philosophy of the new [Scientific Management] places a great part of it upon the management." Taylor used case studies from Bethlehem Steel and Midvale Steel to convince factory bourgeoisie to buy and implement his advice, promising a boost in productivity and profits. However, Taylorism's labor process engineering method reduced workers to mere cogs in a factory machine, a dire situation mocked in Charlie Chaplin's *Modern Times* (1936). Workers protested against Taylorism's degradation of their labor and disregard for their humanity.

Human Relations Engineering: Lillian Gilbreth

Worker resistance to Taylorism led to the second phase in management's attempt to solve the man problem: *human relations engineering*. This new managerial approach sought to control the human element of production at both the individual and group levels through the study and manipulation of human psychology and behavior. Psychologists and engineers were spearheading this new technique of human relations engineering in the workplace, emphasizing the psychological needs of workers and calling for fairer wages, fewer working hours, and motivational behavioral techniques to get workers to do what capital wanted done. In this context, Lillian Gilbreth, an American psychologist and industrial engineer, was key to bringing the insights of modern psychology into the field of modern management to enhance capital's production efficiencies. In *The Psychology of Management: The Function of the Mind in Determining, Teaching, and Installing Methods of Least Waste*, Gilbreth (1914) explored the psychological impact of management on workers. Challenging Taylorism, Gilbreth encouraged a management style that recognized workers as unique people, not just labor parts purchased and put to use by an inhuman machine. She proposed that a corporation's productivity could be increased if it offered workers both monetary rewards and psychological recognition for their labor. As she said, "The workers must understand…that they add to the perfectness of the entire establishment" (p. 330). Gilbreth thus defined the psychology of management as: "the effect of the mind that is directing work upon that work which is directed, and the effect of this undirected and directed work upon the mind of the worker" (p. 1). Gilbreth's human relations engineering approach to modern management would not only pay the worker for their labor power but recognize the worker as a unique person and try to empower them to responsibilize their role and organizational function, and advance this fusion as a way to boost a corporation's productivity and profits.

Hard and Soft Power Tactics

In the 21st century, most corporations' management framework will enact a combination of labor process engineering and human relations engineering, or, practices that attempt to control what workers do and how they do it, as well as practices that aim to control how workers think, feel and behave. When they are doing this, modern management frequently strikes a balance between incentivizing (carrots) and disciplining (sticks). In this regard, management can be conceptualized as a form of relational power. "Relational power" is the idea that power is the ability of one entity (A) to influence or control the actions of another (B), with or without B's independent will, using a combination of "sticks" or hard power tactics (fear, control, repression), and "carrots" or soft power tactics (attraction, motivation, persuasion). In the DMEI, managerial control frequently relies on a combination of these hard and soft power tactics. On one side, management utilizes incentives, inducements, attractions, and motivational strategies, aiming to empower workers and inspire their alignment with the company's objectives. On the other side, management makes use of threats, punishments, discipline, and coercion. The relational power of managerial persuasion and repression vis-a-vis workers can be conceptualized as "governmentality" within the DMEI, and in capitalism.

Corporate Governmentality: Michel Foucault

Michel Foucault (1991) conceptualized "the art of government"—or "governmentality"—as the organized institutional discourses and practices (the rationalities and techniques) through which a population is governed (where subjects learn to govern themselves). For Foucault, "governmentality" refers not to big structures and ideologies but institutional power relations, the "how" of governing (that is, the means of shaping how a population behaves and acts, the ways of shaping how humans view and conduct themselves) (Dean, 1999). For Foucault, the most successful "governmentality" does not rely upon coercion or threats to get individuals to follow and comply with rules. Governmentality motivates its subjects to willingly and consensually follow the rules, gets people to see, think, and feel themselves to be benefitted by the rules, and motivates them to govern themselves appropriately, in conjunction with the institutional milieu they are in, and the broader structures and ideologies of the society overall. An effective governmentality is a post-sovereign power: subjects feel obliged to agree or a sense of duty to obey the rules without being forced to do so because they see these rules as good for them and for everyone else. But when they don't, the rules may be enforced through discipline and punishment, forms of repression. Some expressions of these hard and soft tactics of management, of corporate governmentality in the DMEI, are sketched out below.

Soft Power at Work: Managerial Control by Bureaucracy, Participation, Perks, Fun, and Games

Management by Bureaucracy: Max Weber

In *Economy and Society* (1922), Max Weber conceptualized bureaucracy as the most efficient and rational form of managing human activity inside and outside corporations. According to Weber, bureaucracies are characterized by a well-defined hierarchical structure with a clear chain of command, where each level controls the level below and is accountable to the level above. Managerial roles within bureaucracies are specialized, with each member responsible for specific tasks, and individual and collective conduct within the organization is governed by a comprehensive system

156   What Is the Management of Work in the DMEI?

of formal rules and standard operating procedures (SOPs). This approach aims to achieve a high degree of precision, stability, and reliability. For Weber, the best bureaucracies are impersonal, where rules and procedures are applied uniformly to all, without bias. Career progression within bureaucracies is based on merit, with promotions based on performance, rather than managerial favoritism or ideology. While recognizing the value of bureaucratic management, Weber also cautioned against its potential downsides. He described the highly bureaucratic organization as an "iron cage," potentially trapping individuals and societies in rigid systems of control, leading to a loss of individuality and freedom. He expressed concerns that bureaucracies, despite their efficiency, could dehumanize workers with their impersonal structures and rules, diminishing the worker's individuality and autonomy.

In the modern world, all major corporations in the DMEI are bureaucratic hierarchies. A well-managed bureaucracy tends to appear to manage itself without the manager, even though it employs many from top to bottom. In the DMEI, key aspects of bureaucratic management might include clear *job descriptions* that outline qualifications for the position, reinforcing hierarchies, and labor specialization. *Employment contracts* formalize the relationship between the corporation and the worker, setting expectations and providing legal safeguards while outlining rules, roles, and responsibilities. *Employment handbooks* offer detailed company brand identity discourse, policies, and guidelines, ensuring workers habituate themselves to organizational norms, standards, and values. *Organizational charts* visually represent the power hierarchy, and SOPs provide specific instructions for the roles and functions workers perform. *Performance review* systems, structured around predefined criteria, support assessments based on an idea of merit. When starting a new job in a corporation that is part of the DMEI, the worker is immersed in that corporation's bureaucracy, and bureaucratization is a form of managerial governance that aims to motivate the workers to govern themselves in concordance with the bureaucracy.

Management by Participation: Elton Mayo, Kurt Lewin, and Rensis Likert

Management by participation encourages and designs worker participation into managerial decision-making processes to try to enhance job satisfaction and self-responsibilized productivity. Elton Mayo, Kurt Lewin, and Rensis Likert laid the foundations for this soft management tactic. Elton Mayo (2010), an Australian-born psychologist, conducted the Hawthorne Studies at Western Electric Company's Hawthorne factory between 1924 and 1932. Mayo learned that worker productivity increased when workers felt like they were involved in making the decisions management made about their work conditions. This included changes in lighting, rest breaks, and meal availability. Kurt Lewin, a social psychologist, introduced the concept of participatory decision-making in the organization. He advocated for collaborative problem-solving and identified democratic leadership as a style that resulted in higher job satisfaction and performance (HDRQ Staff, 2022). Rensis Likert (1961), another social psychologist, furthered this approach in his book *New Patterns of Management*. Likert introduced a framework of four types of management systems (Exploitative Authoritative, Benevolent Authoritative, Consultative, and Participative) and argued that the Participative system, characterized by decentralized decision-making and worker participation, was the most effective. In its early years, Google was touted as being a role model corporation for participatory management: it was associated with a somewhat flat or horizontal organizational structure, a "20% time" policy that allowed workers to dedicate a fifth of their working hours to passion projects, TGIF sessions where workers had discussions with CEOs about policy, open space office design for teamwork and collaboration, and various feedback mechanisms. But Google's ongoing anti-union activities indicate only certain types of worker participation will be tolerated by management. This is one of potentially many examples of how the ideal of participatory management can be contradicted by real CEOs, particularly when workers' participation involves unions or collective action. When such participation is substantive and threatens to influence real decision-making power regarding the conduct of the corporation and the distribution of surplus profits, it often faces resistance.

Management by Perks

A "perk" refers to a benefit a corporation provides to its workforce beyond the regular salary. Management by perks is a persuasive managerial tactic that corporations use to attract and retain talent, foster a positive work environment, and encourage worker brand loyalty and productivity. Google, for example, offers many enticing perks, making it one of the most sought-after places to work. These include: salaries that include bonuses and stock options; healthcare coverage, mental health resources, and access to fitness centers; a flex work environment, allowing for telecommuting and adaptable work hours; office spaces featuring open collaborative areas, game rooms, relaxation zones, and even slides and bouncy balls; on site culinary services, providing workers with free gourmet meals and a variety of snacks and beverages; parental leave policies, including extended maternity and paternity leaves; robust retirement plans, such as 401(k) matching; shuttle services, open-access rainbow colored bicycles and travel benefits; and, educational opportunities for knowledge and skills augmentation. These perks have contributed to Google's great workplace reputation and also persuades the workforce to be maximally productive, and to feel good while doing that for the company's gain.

Management by Fun

Management by fun is a persuasive management tactic that incorporates ostensibly playful and fun activities into the labor process, aiming to boost job satisfaction and productivity (Pardes, 2020). In the DMEI, "management by fun" aims to get workers to work harder, with a smile on their face. For example, Meta Platforms' management organizes various recreational events, outings, game nights, and hackathons, using fun to foster team bonding. Similarly, Salesforce integrates fun into regular team-building events and so does Apple. Management by fun may be used by managers to not only boost worker productivity and satisfaction but also exercise control through an image of empowering workers to "just have fun." As Fleming (2009, p. 56) notes,

> One of the key aspects of the 'just be yourself' management discourse and its quest for personal authenticity is the fetishization of fun and play at work.... The presumption is that fun is part of our authentic personhood and should be celebrated, often involving strange exercises and games. Employees are presumed to be motivated by this.... In order to make work fun a process of mimesis occurs in which non-work gestures are simulated inside the organization ... managed fun is more of a controlling gesture rather than an act of liberation.

As a "controlling gesture," a corporation's "management by fun" can normalize intensified productivity within the rubric of having fun, supercharging workers' self-exploitation by associating that with joy and play. On-site play rooms and recreational events may keep workers from going home, and potentially working over time without ever expecting overtime pay (Ross, 2009). This fun environment can exacerbate structural inequalities, as lower level workers may not receive the same fun opportunities. And when workers managed with fun start to feel sad, stressed, or exhausted by the labor process, they may repress these feelings to maintain a smiley face for the boss. At worse, "management by fun" powers an exploitative and unhappy work culture that compels workers to add to their labor process dubious expressions of personal wellness and performances of happiness. Management by fun tries to make work enjoyable, even when the opposite may be true. This facade of fun work serves to mask the exploitation workers endure. Under the guise of fun, workers may be coaxed into accepting the unfun extraction of surplus value from their labor.

Management by Games

Management by games is a management tactic that employs and embeds game-like scenarios and simulations in the workers' labor process, to try to make it as efficient as possible. It is when management applies "game systems – competition, rewards, quantifying player/user behaviour – into non-game domains, such as work, productivity and fitness" (Woodcock & Johnson, 2018, p. 542). Gamification leverages the psychology of gaming—competition, achievement, and reward—to get workers to immerse themselves in a goal-oriented labor process. For example, Google gamified its bug-tracking process with points and leaderboards. Microsoft gamified customer service call centers to improve agent engagement, satisfaction, and efficiency. While management by games can design a labor process into a play-like experience, it is still a labor process, controlled by managers, for the corporation. Also, the conflation of work and game is dubious: most people volunteer to play games for fun; most workers are compelled to labor by necessity, and it is managers, not workers, who decide on the game's rules and goals. Gamification is Taylorism, repackaged as a game that workers voluntarily play, even though they are usually forced to do so by managers, which is no fun at all. Gamification may also solidify worker competition by privileging and rewarding the best worker-players, and frowning upon those less adept at the playing the "game." Management by games risks reducing labor to a fake form of play where rules are set by management and the winner is always the corporation that rigs these labor process games to win maximal profit. As Woodcock and Johnson say (2018, p. 542), "'gamification' represents the capture of 'play' in the pursuit of neoliberal rationalization and the managerial optimization of working life and labour."

The Humane Workplace of the DMEI

In his book *No-Collar: The Humane Workplace and its Hidden Costs*, Andrew Ross (2003) examines the management style and workplace culture of the creative and digital media industries in New York City during the late 1990s and early 2000s. Through a detailed ethnography of two New York City digital media firms, Ross explores environments that initially offered "oodles of autonomy along with warm collegiality" but ultimately enlisted "employees' freest thoughts and impulses in the service of salaried time" (p. 17). Ross identifies a shift in management styles in these industries, where a "new breed of management guru" in the 1980s and 1990s challenged traditional hierarchies, rules, and rituals of the white-collar office, in theory at least. These thinkers advocated for a "humane workplace," which recognized workers' cultural identities and encouraged free-wheeling self-expression, empowered by open layouts, relaxed dress codes, and lots of participation. However, Ross argues that this model's embrace of subjective "self-expression" while on the job did not equate to objective rewards, like higher wages or greater job security. Furthermore, the management of these "industrialized bohemias" co-opted the aesthetic and counter-cultural ethos of the 1960s for corporate ends, tapping the "artistic sensibility" of workers to get them focusing on intangible rewards like personal fulfillment in lieu of tangible benefits, like fair pay. Simultaneously, the humane workplace's emphasis on personal identity development could also stall a collective, solidaristic identity among workers, potentially impeding union formation. While many corporations today design humane workplaces that are superficially appealing, they may conceal the real structure of class exploitation and inequality.

Hard Power at Work: Managerial Control by Bullying, Surveillance, Silencing and Censoring, NCAAs, NCCs, NDAs, Union Busting, Firing, Blacklisting, and Canceling

Management by Bullying

Management by bullying is a repressive tactic that involves systematic negative actions by those in managerial positions to control and intimidate workers, exploiting power hierarchies to manipulate. Characterized by repetitive, abusive behavior, such as gaslighting, spreading rumors, unwarranted criticism, and humiliation, this tactic erodes the workers' self-esteem, leading to stress, health problems, unhappiness, and reduced productivity. Managers may bully proactively, to get the worker to do something they don't want to do, or bully as a punitive measure, to punish workers for not doing what is demanded and expected of them. Several high-profile cases concerning the CEOs of corporations in the DMEI illustrate this bullying problem. In 2017, Uber's former CEO Travis Kalanick resigned following reports of workplace bullying. WPP's Martin Sorrell, known for presiding over a bullying environment, resigned in 2018. The producers at The Ellen DeGeneres Show were called out for bullying, leading to a public apology from Ellen DeGeneres in 2020. In 2021, Activision Blizzard was sued over allegations of a "frat boy" culture, where bullying and harassment was rampant. Management's use of bullying to try to control workers points to institutionalized coercion within corporations.

Management by Surveillance

Management by surveillance is a managerial tactic that uses information technologies, apps and platforms to closely monitor and control labor processes, often violating workers' privacy and dignity. Workplace surveillance aims to control what workers do and how they do it, enforce compliance with bureaucratic rules and norms, optimize the workers' productivity and efficiency, and deter dissent. Apropos the "panoptic principle," when workers are aware of being monitored or the possibility of being monitored, they tend to adhere to the rules set by management for labor process control (Foucault, 1977; Lyon, 1994). In contrast, when workers believe they are not under surveillance, they may be more likely to assert their autonomy within the labor process, contrary to management's rule. Management's surveillance techniques can vary widely, ranging from in-person supervision to total online monitoring. For example, in the Amazon warehouse, "workers are subject to a system of total surveillance," typified by barcode scanners that register every move workers make, security cameras that record everything they do, and spies to listen in on what they are saying (Delfanti, 2021b, p. 68). Also, artificial intelligence (AI) is used by management "to monitor and analyze various aspects of employee behavior, performance, and activities," and also records the worker's "digital activities, such as emails and online interactions, as well as physical behaviors through tools like video, biometric, or other sensors" (CLJE, 2024, p. 4). Furthermore, management designs "algorithms and automated systems to monitor and control various aspects of [labor] processes," including the "allocation of tasks, scheduling, performance monitoring, and decision-making" with the goal of optimizing "efficiency, resource allocation, productivity, or other objectives" (CLJE, 2024, 4). Management by surveillance uses advanced monitoring and information aggregation, processing and sorting technologies to try to maximize worker productivity and reward or punish workers based on normative criteria that they do not decide or control, frequently infringing upon their privacy, instilling fear and suspicion, decreasing happiness, and leading to alienation and angst. Management by surveillance, by Big Data systems, AI tools, and algorithms quantifies the worker, turning people into data to be controlled and exploited (Ajunwa, 2023).

Management by Silencing and Censoring: The Non-Disclosure Agreement (NDA)

Management by silencing and censoring aims to reduce or obstruct the worker's freedom of speech about workplace problems, grievances and inequities. By restricting speech, management tries to quash dissenting worker opinions, sustain conformity and monopolize the narrative about the company and its brand, both internally and externally. NDAs are a

162   What Is the Management of Work in the DMEI?

common technique for this purpose. Originally meant to protect sensitive information (e.g., trade secrets), NDAs can be misused by management to silence workers who might speak up and to the press about a company's unethical or illegal practices, such as discrimination or harassment. At worst, NDAs curb the worker's freedom to discuss workplace issues with co-workers, or seek external support for harm done to them. It can prevent them from criticizing exploitative practices publicly, even when such criticism is beneficial to democracy and other workers. For example, Fox News used NDAs in settlements involving sexual harassment by Roger Ailes and Bill O'Reilly (Dockertman, 2019). Miramax and The Weinstein Company used NDAs to try to control the speech of the women sexually assaulted by Harvey Weinstein (Farrow, 2019; Kantor & Twohey, 2019). Tesla used NDAs to silence its workers' open discussion about workplace problems (Bolden-Barrett, 2018). WPP CEO Martin Sorrell resigned, with reports of NDAs being used in the internal handling of claims made against him (Goodey & Davies, 2018). Bloomberg LP used NDAs in settling harassment claims. Activision Blizzard's use of NDAs contributed to a toxic workplace culture, protested by workers with walkouts and lawsuits against the firm (Jaeger, 2021). While NDAs may be used to protect confidential information against IP theft, they can also be weaponized by management to censor speech and cover up misconduct.

Management by "No Cold Call Agreements" (NCCAs)

The "no cold call" serves as a managerial tactic aimed at restricting workers' mobility within the labor market, to the corporation's benefit, and at the worker's expense. Cold calling occurs when management from one company reaches out to a worker at another company, enticing them to consider switching jobs. However, to impede a worker's freedom to transition between companies, the managerial elites of two or more firms sometimes enact NCCAs. When doing this, they establish a quasi-monopoly that not only stifles genuine competition within the labor market, where corporations vie to attract talent, but also weakens the bargaining power of workers, who might leverage an offer from a prospective employer to negotiate a better deal with their current one. For example, a major 2010 antitrust lawsuit by the U.S. Department of Justice (DOJ) against six technology companies brought to light a NCCA (DOJ, 2010). Dating back to 2005, Apple and Google had agreed not to cold call each other's workers, with similar agreements between Apple and Adobe, Apple and Pixar, Google and Intel, and Google and Intuit. These NCAAs, brokered by the higher ups, undermined competition between companies for workers' labor and also restricted workers' mobility, depriving them of potential job opportunities. Another major lawsuit pertaining to NCAA took place in 2017, when Walt Disney Company and other companies paid millions to settle a class action suit brought by animators and visual effects workers against them. A number of Hollywood studios had allegedly conspired to suppress wages and restrict the mobility of their workers by agreeing not to poach one another's talent (Cho, 2024). While the prevalence of NCAAs may have receded, workers should be alert to this monopoly tactic for minimizing their freedom and bargaining power.

Management by "Non-Compete Clauses" (NCC) in Contracts

The NCC is a management tactic used to restrict a workers' future career prospects. These clauses, often part of employment contracts workers sign when starting a new job with a corporation, prohibit these workers from laboring in similar professions for corporations in competition with their former employers. When stringent, the NCC limits the worker's ability to seek out and gain employment in any industry that might value their knowledge and skillset, post-employment. Within the DMEI, managers may employ these clauses to maintain control over top talent and prevent competitors from benefiting from the fruits of their labor. This practice also erodes workers' bargaining power. In most cases, workers can leave a job they are unhappy with and find a similar one elsewhere, but NCCs make that difficult. Additionally, workers sometimes threaten to quit in order to negotiate concessions from their employers, but under these contracts, such threats may be perceived as mere "crying wolf." An early example of a non-compete or "exclusivity" clause was in Hollywood's Golden Age: actors signed contracts that bound them to labor exclusively for one studio for a long period of time, and not its competitors. The arrangement provided actors with a regular salary, but restricted their creative freedom and opportunity. As SAG-AFTRA has said, the studio's NCCs "unreasonably constrained our members in taking new employment"(Cho, 2024). The tech industry has also deployed NCCs. In 2015, Amazon had warehouse workers sign a contract that promised that they would not labor for any company where they "directly or indirectly" support any good or service that competes with those at Amazon. In 2019, Netflix sued its former executive Tara Flynn who had left to join Disney's streaming service, Disney+. In the music industry, artists will be compelled to sign on to NCCs in contracts with managers and record labels, locking them in to a company and limiting their freedom to move on. In 2024, the FTC brought NCCs to an end, banning them (Cho, 2024).

Management by Union Busting

Silicon Valley's corporate and managerial elites have long opposed unions: Robert Noyce, Intel's co-founder and a key player in the development of the Valley, once said that "remaining non-union is essential for survival for most of our companies. If we had the work rules that unionized companies have, we'd all go out of business." The anti-union ideology of the Valley's CEOs persisted over time, and companies offered attractive compensation and benefits to workers, as well as perks, to try to deter unionization. Union busting refers to top-down managerial tactics that aim to prevent labor union formation. Often in violation of the workers' right to unionize, managers will spew anti-union messages, hire consultants specializing in union avoidance, surveil union organizers, retaliate against union-friendly workers, and offer anti-union incentives to workers on the fence. Harassment, bullying, exclusion from meetings, and the like are additional repressive tactics managers may use to pressure rank-and-file workers into resigning or deter potential unionists from rising in the ranks. Sometimes managers even resort to firing unionists. Dulles Drywall, a Microsoft contractor, fired 47 workers who were trying to organize a union to contest underpayment. Instacart fired every worker who voted to unionize (Moss, 2023). Tesla, adhering to Elon Musk's anti-union stance, allegedly fired over 30 workers to crush their union campaign (Sainato, 2023). Hopper fired some pro-union workers. Amazon's firing of union organizers like Christian Smalls, further demonstrate the pervasiveness of union-busting tactics.

Management by Firing and Unfair Termination

Management by unfair termination is a tactic whereby managers fire workers for reasons unrelated to their knowledge and skills, but rather due to their dissent against company policies and practices (Elias, 2020; Hern, 2019; Peter, 2021). For example, Dr. Timnit Gebru and Margaret Mitchell from Google's Ethical AI team were fired after raising concerns about the company's AI biases while Google Walkout organizers Meredith Whittaker and Claire Stapleton left the company due to retaliation from management. Apple fired Janneke Parrish, a leader in the #AppleToo movement. Facebook dismissed Sophie Zhang after she shed light on the platform's manipulation of political information. Netflix fired the leader of a Trans-worker resource group who organized a walkout to protest Dave Chappelle's transphobic remarks in the comedy special, *The Closer*. Management's message is clear: workers who challenge company conduct may face termination—a deterrent to others who might wish to do the same.

Management by Blacklisting and Canceling

Management by blacklisting and canceling tends to discriminate against and pre-empt a worker's employment or end an existing employment contract for political reasons, not because the worker is unqualified or poorly performing. Historically, blacklists were secretive no hire lists held by managers. The McCarthy-era's Hollywood Blacklist targeted creatives suspected of Communist affiliations, such as Dalton Trumbo and John Garfield. Legal protections against discrimination challenge traditional blacklisting practices, but with many things, the state's enforcement of these protections is lax and can be evaded. In the 21st century entertainment industry, forms of tacit blacklisting seem to exist when corporations, influenced by CEO and shareholder political ideologies and advertising interests, refuse to hire workers due to their activism rather than lack of skill or talent. Colin Kaepernick has been unsigned since 2016 after kneeling at NFL football games in protest of racial injustice. The musician Natalie Maines of The Chicks faced blacklisting from country radio because of her principled criticism of George W. Bush's role in the United States' invasion and occupation of Iraq in 2003. Hollywood actors Susan Sarandon and Mark Ruffalo have regularly experienced professional troubles due to their outspoken progressive positions on climate justice and Palestinian human rights.

In contrast to management by blacklisting, management by canceling in the DMEI often arises from audience-driven censure or outrage, leading to management's dismissal of workers for insensitive actions or inappropriate statements. This bottom-up consumer pressure, typically advanced through viral social media campaigns on X/Twitter or elsewhere, leads to management canceling the worker's employment contract to maintain a positive corporate brand identity and consumer loyalty. Examples include James Gunn's temporary firing by Walt Disney Company over offensive tweets about pedophilia and rape, ABC firing Roseanne Barr due to her Islamophobic and anti-Black racist tweets, and Shane Gillis' removal from *Saturday Night Live* following the outing of videos in which he conveys a Sinophobic slur. Public opinion, especially on social media, can shape management decisions toward workers. Unlike historical blacklists, these incidents are not industry-wide but while contingent, management by canceling has happened.

Management by Markets: The Invisible Manager

"The market"—real and imagined—acts as a manager of sorts, influencing decision-making by CEOs about the overall conduct of the corporations they direct. Shifting consumer demands and trends often shape product and service success, compelling CEOs and firms to adapt. For example, Netflix evolved from a DVD rental to a streaming service in response to changing consumer preferences, a move mirrored by other industry giants like Apple and Disney when they launched Apple TV and Disney+. CEOs, irrespective of their personal preferences, must be responsive to and constantly adapting to market shifts, to ensure their corporation's success. This market-driven management also influences independent content creators and influencers on platforms like YouTube, Instagram, and Twitch. Their labor is tacitly managed by audiences, sponsors, platform policies, and algorithms, and the need to constantly innovate and adapt to stay relevant and connected. From the heights of Walt Disney Company to the newest Tuber, the market acts as an "invisible manager" of CEOs and creative entrepreneurs, guiding decisions that shape strategy, and content production and exhibition. At least eight key types of "management by markets" come to mind: investor and sponsor decisions, advertising expenditures, mass market demands, niche market tastes and preferences, revenue and monetization models, competition and innovation, user feedback and analytics, algorithms, and happenings and trends in the wider society and culture. Each of these market factors play a role in managing the managers of corporations in the DMEI, who then make strategic decisions that manage their respective workforce, from top to bottom.

Beyond Management? Cooperatives and Unions

The management of corporations is informed by a long history of management theory and manifested in a wide arrange of managerial-governmental power relations, technologies, and hard and soft power tactics that aim to control the conduct of workers. While managers are everywhere, their utility has always been in question. Are managers truly necessary? Do they serve a positive function, or are they instruments of class rule? The rigid hierarchical division of labor in a corporation, with top-level shareholders and Boards appointing CEOs who try to control workers using repressive and persuasive tactics, often undermines the workers' freedom and democracy, not just within the workplace but in society as a whole. Given this, it's unsurprising that critics of CEO-centered and "top-down" management models advocate for pro-worker and "bottom-up" alternatives such as cooperatives and unions, even in the DMEI. These alternatives to business as usual can disrupt entrenched power hierarchies and establish cooperative relations for decision-making and revenue sharing.

Worker cooperatives remain a rarity in the DMEI. Traditionally, cooperatives have thrived in lower-wage sectors like manufacturing and retail or as part of development initiatives in the Global South. However, the cooperative model is increasingly catching on in some spheres of the DMEI, representing a shift from vertical corporate power structures to more horizontal co-management models (de Peuter, 2017; de Peuter et al., 2020; de Peuter et al., 2022; Sandoval, 2016, 2018). These cooperatives are owned and controlled by their members, who collaboratively make decisions and prioritize worker and community wellness over mere profit maximization for shareholders and CEOs. By challenging the dominant managerial paradigm, cooperatives emphasize shared ownership, democratic governance, and social responsibility. In 2023, the United Nations declared 2025 the Year of Cooperatives for the second time, acknowledging their contributions to decent jobs and social development. This recognition underscores the potential of worker cooperatives to enhance work and life quality for many workers. For example, Fairmondo, based in Germany, is an ethical online marketplace operating as a cooperative, offering a fair alternative to traditional e-commerce platforms like Amazon. Owned and controlled by its members, Fairmondo ensures democratic decision-making and equitable profit distribution. It focuses on ethical and sustainable products, supporting fair trade and environmentally friendly practices. Means TV, a US-based cooperative, is a worker-owned streaming service offering progressive and leftist content. It ensures democratic decision-making by its workers, who collectively own and manage the platform. Operating on a subscription-based model, it maintains financial sustainability without relying on traditional advertising. Hypha is a worker-owned cooperative specializing in emerging technologies such as web development, digital strategy, and design. Its democratic governance model where all long-term employees are cooperative members ensures shared ownership and decision-making power. Stocksy is a worker-owned cooperative specializing in high-quality, royalty-free stock photos and videos. Its photographers and videographers are also owners: they receive 50% of Standard License Purchases and 75% of Extended License Purchases. Motion Twin, a worker-owned cooperative, is known for developing video games, including the critically acclaimed *Dead Cells*. Operating on democratic principles, all workers share equal ownership and decision-making power. Motion Twin emphasizes sustainable and ethical business practices, aligning with the values of fairness, transparency, and social responsibility. These and other worker cooperatives in the DMEI exemplify the possibility of creating equitable, democratic, and socially responsible enterprises within a supersector mostly dominated by titanic media giants. They offer an alternative model to the top-down managerial status quo, manifesting the ideal of workers' ownership and control.

Unionization and collective bargaining can also disrupt top-down corporate management practices in the DMEI, with Silicon Valley being a case in point (Bacon, 2011). For Silicon Valley workers, organizing unions has been difficult due to the strong anti-union sentiment fostered by CEOs, who frequently worked in partnership with the military-industrial complex as subservient contractors. Early unionization efforts by electronics workers were met with fierce resistance from companies and their CEOs. Nonetheless, starting in the 1970s, the United Electrical, Radio and Machine Workers of America (UE) began organizing in various semiconductor manufacturing plants. Many union activists were fired. Eventually, health and safety became a focal point for worker organizing. The Santa Clara Committee on Occupational Safety and Health (SCCOSH) and the Silicon Valley Toxics Coalition emerged, advocating for safer working conditions and exposing the tech industry's environmental harms and hazards. The second wave of union organizing targeted contractors and service workers. Janitors launched a successful campaign against Shine Maintenance Co., a contractor for Apple, despite facing retaliation and firings. This campaign, supported by a broad coalition of community activists, led to union contracts for janitors at Apple and Hewlett-Packard, demonstrating the power of community-labor alliances. Workers at Versatronex also organized against sweatshop conditions, culminating in a six-week strike that drew significant attention and support from the local community. However, the company ultimately closed the plant to avoid unionization. Over the years, the Silicon Valley union movement has faced numerous obstacles, but workers' campaigns and strike actions have exposed the harsh realities of the industry and aimed to go beyond them (Bacon, 2011). In recent years, unionization campaigns in Silicon Valley have again gained some momentum. Some of these include the Alphabet Workers Union at Google, Amazon Workers United, Chris Smalls' Amazon Labor Union, Apple retail employees forming AppleCORE, Facebook's content moderators in the Global South seeking union representation, and union drives at Tesla's Fremont factory. While unions do not overturn management structures in the corporations of the DMEI, they can enhance the bargaining power of the worker vis-a-vis the boss, and help address the structurally and institutionally embedded asymmetrical power relations between capital and labor.

Cooperative and unionist alternatives to the status quo of managerial power are gaining traction in some industry groupings and companies of the DMEI, but this is not yet a widespread phenomenon. Cooperatives and unions may not be perceived positively by workers under the sway of meritocracy, an individualistic and individualizing ideology about work in the DMEI that while appealing and sometimes real, most frequently serves to divert attention from the system logics and structures of a deeply inequitable and unfair class society.

7 Is Meritocracy at Work in the DMEI?

Intersectionality and Inequality, with Distinction

Introduction

This chapter focuses on meritocracy and intersectionality in the digital media and entertainment industries (DMEI). It unpacks the idea of meritocracy, probing some of its key assumptions: the just allocation of rewards based on individual performance, the correlation between effort and reward, the notion of equal opportunities for all irrespective of background, the idea of a level playing field in society, and the attainability of social mobility. The chapter then presents an intersectional framework for interrogating classism, racism, sexism, ageism, and ableism at work in the DMEI. After that, it turns to the workers' challenge of preparing for and landing a lucrative career in the DMEI. It considers the interplay of "economic capital," "social capital," and "cultural capital," accumulated in and transmitted generationally by the family, in relation to unequal access to the educational credentials, internship experience, professional networking, and self-branding often demanded of workers by corporations in the DMEI. Touching upon Hollywood's response to Black Lives Matter (BLM), hashtag campaigns such as #SiliconValleySoWhite and #MeToo, and the classism of the so-called Creative Class, this chapter highlights the gap between the meritocratic ideal and the real intersecting inequities and oppressions at work in the DMEI.

"When You Wish Upon a Star": The Meritocratic Dream of the DMEI

The corporations of the DMEI propagate stories that epitomize the American Dream, painting a portrait of a meritocratic capitalism where talent, hard work, and perseverance can elevate an individual from obscurity to stardom. This narrative, akin to the enchanting lyric from the classic *Pinocchio* song by Cliff Edwards, "When you wish upon a star, Makes no difference who you are, Anything your heart desires, Will come to you," crystalizes the meritocratic ideal. It suggests a world where dreams, irrespective

DOI: 10.4324/9781003131076-8

of one's background or class position, can come true, through sheer will and effort. The DMEI persistently tells and sells this compelling tale, portraying "America" as a perfect meritocracy where individuals, through their own pluck, rise from modest beginnings and hardships to global fame and fortune.

Of course, some dreams really do come true. Oprah Winfrey made her way from rural racist Mississippi to the heights of global media ownership. Dolly Parton grew up in a one-room cabin in Tennessee and became a country music celebrity. Leonardo DiCaprio shifted from a low-income neighborhood to an Oscar-winning celebrity. Dwayne "The Rock" Johnson, fought his way from poverty and racism to WWF revere and a Hollywood A-list. Eminem's ascension from Detroit's 8 mile to hip-hop legend. Justin Bieber's leap from a small Canadian town to YouTube to global pop stardom. Viola Davis, Halle Berry, and Lupita Nyong'o—all symbols of Hollywood dreams come true. Steve Jobs and Steve Wozniak, who made Apple in a garage, or Mark Zuckerberg's development of Facebook while studying at Harvard University, highlight how "nerds" can rule (and perhaps take revenge on) the world. The billionaire Whitney Wolfe Herd, who co-founded Tinder and later started up Bumble, is frequently cited as an example of how the tech industry's sexist barriers can be overcome. Arlan Hamilton, a queer Black woman who founded Backstage Capital was once homeless, but now is a venture capitalist, investing in startups for the underprivileged. Tristan Walker, founder of Walker & Company, developed a successful app despite suffering classism and racism.

These inspiring stories paint a picture of the DMEI as a place where dreams really do come true, where "rags to riches" is not only possible but a widely recurring phenomenon. The DMEI's meritocratic ideal is ubiquitous and compelling, motivating millions to imagine themselves one day "becoming what they now see" in the spectacular fictional universe of entertainment, and following in the footsteps of their celebrity icons and their innovator role models. This aspirational culture encourages a vast number of people to devote themselves and their lives to accumulating new knowledge, upskilling and reskilling, and taking risks and leaps, in hopes of one day, being recognized and rewarded, with money and status, for their specialness. Unfortunately, not everyone's American dream comes true. Actors pursuing Hollywood stardom face a disheartening reality: 2% of actors manage to earn a living exclusively from acting while 90% experience unemployment at any given time (Simkins 2019). On reality TV shows like NBC's *The Voice*, John Legend earns $14 million per season, a figure that stands high above the contestants' stipend to cover basic living expenses (Arditi, 2023a). The labor market of skilled and industrious creatives vying for limited spots at the top of the Hollywood hierarchy is over-saturated, making the meritocratic dream of the DMEI out of reach for most. And yet, millions still pursue it! What is the meritocratic ideal, and why is it so pervasive, yet so frequently at odds with reality?

Meritocracy: Ideal and Reality

Meritocracy posits that individuals who are talented, capable, and hardworking should be rewarded by society with success, typically manifesting as wealth and social status. Meritocracy is the idea that social mobility should be based on individual merit—a blend of ability, knowledge, skills, and aptitude—rather than on family background, inherited wealth, or personal connections. Meritocracy means that societal positions and privileges should correlate with one's efforts and abilities, that social mobility is possible if you work hard enough for it, and that class positions are not static, but in flux. Historically, the rise of the meritocratic ideal marked a shift from feudal-aristocratic societies to liberal democratic capitalism, where previously, wealth and status were largely determined by birthright and hereditary privilege. A landlord was a landlord, a peasant was a peasant. That was immutable. The meritocratic move away from that bad thinking gained momentum after the French and American Revolutions, and advocated for personal merit as the basis for social position, challenging the notion of social superiority by heredity or divinity. Meritocracy paved the way for some individuals to change their social positions, inspiring peasants to strive to become lords, the poorest to seek great riches, and workers to become bosses.

Yet, the path to realizing the new meritocratic ideal was frequently blocked for the many, especially those who were not property owning white men. For much of American history, meritocracy has been an aspirational ideal, overshadowed by systemic social discrimination based on the ownership and control of wealth, as well as ascriptions of class, race, and gender. In the US, slavery and post-Civil War Jim Crow laws negated meritocracy for Black Americans. Women were largely confined to domestic roles with scant political or economic power: the suffragettes won voting rights for women in 1920, 144 years after the Declaration of Independence. Euro-colonial policies made meritocracy impossible for the many millions of colonized peoples Empires brutalized with with war, genocide, the slave trade, displacement, exploitation, and oppression. The poor and working class found their prospects for social mobility minimal. While the US glorified the meritocratic ideal, history frequently told a different story.

In the late 20th and early 21st centuries, meritocracy was never something given by the elites to the people, but more of an ideology, or set of ideas and beliefs, that motivated many millions of people to fight for rights denied to them. The Civil Rights movement led to crucial legislative changes and affirmative action policies. Women's rights movements improved women's access to higher education and careers. The labor movements and social democratic reforms broadened opportunities for class mobility. While some progress has been made in reducing explicit legal and systemic barriers to meritocracy, classism, racism, and sexism persist in society, and these inequities and oppressions, along with nepotism and favoritism and sometimes just sheer luck, have hindered the full realization of the meritocratic ideal. As there have always been foundational gaps between the meritocratic ideal and reality, it is important to probe the claims that meritocracy makes and question the assumptions inherent to these. In the following section, I do this, using some examples.

The Meritocratic Ideal: Five Assumptions, Deconstructed

The Just Allocation of Rewards Based on Individual Performance

The meritocratic ideal posits that the allocation of rewards in society—wealth, prestigious jobs, and high salaries—is justifiably based on individual performance and achievement. In this view, those at the top of the social hierarchy, at the commanding heights of the DMEI, being the richest, most famous, or most influential, have rightfully earned their place, while those at the bottom supposedly merit their lesser positions. But does this hold up under scrutiny? Is it true that the super-rich and the working poor have unequivocally "earned" their respective class positions in society? Not quite. Some individuals succeed not solely through their abilities and efforts but because they were *born into wealthy families* that afforded them additional resources and privileges to help them succeed while most other people strive and strive with little to no help at all. As Nicole Aschoff (2019) writes, "While meritocracy instead of inheritance certainly sounds appealing, it doesn't quite fit reality." Instead, continues Aschoff (2019), "Most wealth … continues to be transferred from elite parents to their elite children, and is highly skewed according to race, class, and gender." As income inequality rose sharply in the U.S. around 1980, intergenerational class mobility began to fall; nowadays, the US "has relatively low rates of intergenerational income mobility, especially when compared with other advanced economies" and "Black families are disadvantaged relative to White families when it comes to both upward mobility from the bottom and downward mobility from the top" (Mazumder, 2022). Several CEOs of companies in the DMEI come from wealthy families. Bill Gates, co-founder of Microsoft, was born into a family with a father (William H. Gates Sr.) who was a renowned lawyer, and a mother (Mary Maxwell Gates), who was well-connected to corporate America. Rupert Murdoch, CEO of News Corporation, inherited a newspaper from his father, Sir Keith Murdoch, and Rupert's sons Lachlan and James Murdoch, inherited positions within the media conglomerate their father and grandfather built. Similarly, Sumner Redstone passed his wealth on to his daughter, Shari Redstone, who is now chairwoman of Paramount Global, president of National Amusements, and the former vice chair of CBS and Viacom. In the case of Comcast, billionaire Brian Roberts followed in the footsteps of his father, Ralph J. Roberts, the company's co-founder, to become its Chairman and CEO. Katharine Weymouth became CEO of *Washington Post Media*, continuing a family dynasty that included her great-grandfather and grandmother. Being born into extraordinarily wealthy families that own corporate empires, and the enjoyment of rewards that flow from this luck (e.g., an inheritance or a promotion), are in no way based solely on individual performance and achievement.

The Correlation Between Effort and Reward

The meritocratic ideal posits that the hardest workers receive the greatest rewards. The idea here is that those with a "strong work ethic" will be rewarded, and this should motivate individuals to strive for maximum rewards through hard work. The assumption here is that rewards will be proportionally allocated to people based on the level of hard work they do and that those in possession of many rewards have earned them, while those lacking such rewards, have simply not worked hard enough. But how accurate is this assumption? Does hard work invariably lead to commensurate rewards? Are workers universally paid what they're worth? Not really (Rosenfeld, 2021). The Economic Policy Institute's study on *The Productivity-Pay Gap* (https://www.epi.org/productivity-pay-gap/) found that "The gap between productivity and a typical worker's compensation has increased dramatically since 1979." The productivity of workers has grown, but the wages paid to them have not. The discrepancy between the ideal of hard work resulting in great rewards and its opposite in the real immiseration of the many is further illustrated by the millions of minimum-waged workers who labor tirelessly every day but are not paid a high enough wage by their employers to meet their basic needs. The National Law Income Housing Coalition's 2021 Out of Reach report (https://nlihc.org/oor) found that people working a full-time minimum wage job could not afford a two-bedroom apartment in any state in the US. If the hardest workers are not reaping the greatest rewards, who is? In *Capital in the Twenty-First Century*, Thomas Piketty (2014) demonstrates how those who already own capital, who have inherited wealth, accumulate more and more rewards, mostly through capital gains, while most waged workers (with the exception of top shareholder-salatariat CEOs), receive a shrinking portion of the economic "pie." Piketty states, "When the rate of return on capital exceeds the rate of growth of output and income ... capitalism automatically generates arbitrary and unsustainable inequalities that radically undermine the meritocratic values on which democratic societies are based." Consider the so-called "millennials": despite being the most educated generation in US history, investing unprecedented time, energy and money in preparing themselves for the labor market, these workers are in a more precarious class position than previous generations—poorer, in debt, and with a shrinking social safety net (Harris, 2017). They work hard but are not sufficiently rewarded. Furthermore, the idea that the hardest work receives the greater reward is also challenged by the fact that Boards of Directors frequently reward CEOs for making decisions that keep workers' productivity up and labor costs down, so as to ensure that super-exploitation happens, profit accumulates, and increasing dividends to shareholders get paid out (Rosenfeld, 2021). In 2021, the pay ratio of Elon Musk's compensation to the median compensation of a Tesla worker was 18,043-to-1. When appearing on Saturday Night Live and ranting on Twitter that year, was Musk really working that much harder than all those workers in his Gigafactory, assembling Tesla vehicles?

Equal Opportunities for All Irrespective of Background

The meritocratic ideal posits that everyone has equal opportunity to pursue rewards such as wealth, prestigious jobs, and high salaries, irrespective of their family background, class, gender, race, ethnicity, age, disability, or religion. While everyone should have an equal opportunity to pursue rewards without discrimination, is it true that everyone has the same opportunity to pursue rewards, regardless of their starting point? Social history shapes starting points, and some people have long enjoyed greater opportunities than others to pursue rewards, not only because they are wealthy but also because they are beneficiaries of a society that has repeatedly included them and excluded others from the range of opportunities available. For much of history, middle and upper class white men have been favored for occupational roles in the DMEI while the poor and non-white folks and women have been subjected to discrimination in both the job market and corporate workplaces. In the post-World War II era, major literary publishers like Random House and Simon & Schuster were run by white men, despite strides made by women such as Blanche Knopf and Margaret K. McElderry. The PR and advertising industry of the 1950s and 1960s was largely controlled by white men, with women often relegated to lower level roles: figures like Mary Wells Lawrence and Shirley Polykoff were rare. Television in the 1960s and 1970s was largely dominated by white men in leadership. In the 1970s and 1980s, most tech firms were run by white men, and despite the brilliance of Grace Hopper and Katherine Johnson, Silicon Valley's CEOs were predominantly white and male. The video game industry of the 1990s and early 2000s continued this trend of whiteness and maleness, marginalizing women and people of color. The Internet and social media industries have also been mostly run by lots of white and male CEOs. Pick any decade and any of the DMEI's core industries, and you will likely find a capitalist class and working class that do not proportionally represent the demographic diversity of American society as a whole because opportunities have not been genuinely equal for all, nor free of discrimination. While there are strides in EDI management, history's inequities and oppressions weigh on the present. Opportunities have never been substantively "equal" for everyone.

Society is a "Level Playing Field"

The meritocratic ideal presumes that society is a "level playing field," a situation in which everyone has a fair and equal chance of succeeding. The "level playing field" is a nice idea borrowed from economics, but it does not really reflect what happens in the real world. There are many cheaters and rule-breakers in capitalism. Corporations in the DMEI may try to make the market rules and manipulate or break them for their gain. Corporations are known to evade taxes, underreport income, hide assets in offshore havens, distort competition, and deprive governments of revenue for the public services people need. When applied to the labor markets, the "level playing field" does not capture reality. Access to CEO roles in corporations should be a level playing field, but this has not always been the case. A level playing field suggests there is no unfair or unequal advantage due to family or personal connections. But what about nepotism? Who your parents are, and who they know, can be central to launching a career, and leapfrogging over the barriers faced by other market entrants, into the spotlight. The phrase "Nepo babies," or, those who gain career advantages as a result of family wealth and professional connections, sums up how some people start at the top of the Hollywood ladder. For example, Dakota Johnson (daughter of actors Don Johnson and Melanie Griffith), Sofia Coppola (Francis Ford Coppola's daughter), Gwyneth Paltrow (daughter of actress Blythe Danner and producer Bruce Paltrow), Drew Barrymore (born into the iconic Barrymore family), Miley Cyrus (daughter of Billy Ray Cyrus) and many more celebrities had a head-start. None of this is to suggest these people lack sufficient talents or a strong work ethic, but it is to suggest that their class and familial ties played a role in making more connections for them, giving them advantages not enjoyed by the millions of people that start at the bottom of Hollywood's career ladder.

The Attainability of Social Mobility

The meritocratic ideal suggests that social mobility is universally achievable and implies that even the poorest can climb out of one class position and into a higher one. But how common is it for people living in abject poverty to collectively become comfortably "middle class?" Is there even any evidence to suggest that people who start in one class position regularly climb up to another? No, the data suggests the opposite is true: "Americans are quite unlikely to move far up (or down) the wealth ranks early in life, and their chances decrease with age" (Smith et al., 2022). Over the past 50 years, there has been a decline in upward social mobility (Lu, 2020), and the recent trend seems to be downward mobility. It is unlikely that most children will outearn their parents. While 90% of children born in 1940 achieved that "American Dream," from the 1970s forward, fewer and fewer people being born into society are surpassing their parents' earnings (Kelley, 2020). Capitalism is a class society, with a division between wealthy owners and workers. As a result, achieving universal social mobility within capitalism is impossible. As more and more young people experience structural barriers to class mobility, they will question, if not outright mock, the meritocratic ideal. "Intersectionality" provides a better starting point than the ideal of "meritocracy" for understanding the power relations at work in the DMEI, and in the political economy more broadly.

Intersectionality: Class, Race, Gender, Age, and Ability at Work in the DMEI

The present is not a "blank slate" for everyone in tabula rasa, but a congealment of history's intersecting inequities and oppressions, including struggles by those who bore the brunt of history's hardships, to improve their conditions. When we talk about inequity and oppression, history hurts and is a source of both. History is a necessary reminder of why the past persists in the present, but also, how past struggles continuing in our time, may point the way toward better different futures. Despite recent equity, diversity and inclusivity (EDI) initiatives in the corporate world, forms and experiences of classist, racist, and sexist inequity, oppression and discrimination exist in the DMEI (Banks, 2017; Bielby, 2009; Bristol Creative Industries, 2021; Brook, Miles, O'Brien, & Taylor, 2020, 2023; Carey, O'Brien, & Gable, 2021; Coles, Ferrer, Zemaityte, & Banks, 2022; Harrison, 2019; Hesmondhalgh & Baker, 2015; Williams & Bain, 2022; Johnson, 2019; O'Brien & Oakley, 2015; O'Brien, Laurison, Miles, & Friedman, 2016; Stone, 1987, 1988; Swyngedouw, 2022; UCLA, 2020; van Doorn, 2017a; Williams & Bain, 2022).

Intersectionality is a concept for identifying and explaining the complex and historically entrenched power relations between individuals and groups in society that sustain and perpetuate hierarchies of inequity and oppression, in the home, the school, in the mosque, synagogue and church, in the government, on the Internet, and in the corporations of the DMEI. First conceptualized by Kimberlé Crenshaw (1989, 1991, 2006), "intersectionality" centers on how different aspects and ascriptions of identity—such as class, race, gender, age, and ability—intersect and shape one's experiences of social privilege and lack of it, resulting in equality and discrimination, inclusion and exclusion, equity and inequity, and empowerment and oppression. Against the idea that one form of inequality and oppression is foundational to or determining of all others, "intersectionality" is a way of saying one cannot understand classism without also understanding racism, understand racism without also understanding sexism, understand this trinity of classism, racism, and sexism, without adding into this matrix ableism and ageism, and many other overlapping factors that may empower and disempower individuals and groups (Noble & Tynes, 2016). As Crenshaw says:

> Intersectionality is a lens through which you can see where power comes and collides, where it interlocks and intersects. It's not simply that there's a race problem here, a gender problem here, and a class or LBGTQ problem there. Many times that framework erases what happens to people who are subject to all of these things.
> (Columbia Law School, 2017).

Drawing from these insights, an intersectional theory of work in the DMEI is broad, and brings together specific traditions in the study of work, from anti-racist, anti-classist, anti-sexist, anti-ageist, and anti-ableist theory, research, and social movement and labor politics. An all too brief sketch of this follows.

Class and Classism

The study of class and classism in the DMEI takes it as axiomatic that class is foundational to capitalism and its hierarchical division of social classes, of owners and workers (Amrute, 2016; Aronowitz, 2004; Artz, 2006; Bristol Creative Industries, 2021; Carey, O'Brien, & Gable, 2021; Davis, 2020; Dworkin, 2007; Edgell, 1993; Eidlin, 2016; Fantasia, 1989; Fraser, 2018; Grindstaff, 2002; Grusky & Sørensen, 1998; Hesmondhalgh, 2017; Huws, 2014; Kendall, 2005; Lebowitz, 2003; Martin, 2019; Panitch, 2020; Pincus & Sokoloff, 2008; Polson, Schofield Clark, & Gajjala, 2021; Reagan, 2021; Skeggs & Wood, 2011; Standing, 2011; Wright, 1997). Arising from the class structure, classism takes form in systemic prejudices against individuals or groups based on their socio-economic status. In capitalism, social class is often determined by economic status, income, and wealth, resulting in a society where advantages and disadvantages are unevenly distributed. Capitalism empowers certain classes over others, privileging the upper classes who control the capital, and underprivileging individuals from poor and working-class backgrounds, who face barriers to accessing education, healthcare, and good jobs, limiting their social mobility. In the DMEI, class divisions significantly influence work and the worker. The undeserving rich of the upper class occupy CEO positions and exercise control over the workers and labor processes, profiting from production, and the exploitation it always entails. Classism also manifests in the DMEI through biased hiring practices, unequal promotion opportunities, and a general disregard for the experience and self-emancipation activities of working-class people. Class roles, defined by stereotypes associated with different social classes, frequently shape professional interactions and perceptions of people's "fit" with careers in the DMEI. These roles often favor individuals who perform an upper-class cultural habitus, further expressing and solidifying class divisions at the cultural level. By acknowledging and scrutinizing these class-based power relations, research on work in the DMEI can move towards recognizing working-class people, dignifying what they do, and supporting their individual and collective actions to improve their conditions. The study of classism in the DMEI takes it as axiomatic that social class, though frequently excluded from EDI frameworks, is a salient determinant of inclusion and exclusion. It also recognizes that one cannot end classism altogether without also reforming or pushing beyond capitalism.

Race and Racism

The study of race and racism in the DMEI focuses on how racialization and systemic racism shape the workings of work (Amrute, 2016; Benjamin, 2019; Chan & Gray, 2020; Christin & Lu, 2023; Dowd & Blyler, 2002; Herman, 2020; Hunt, 2017; Jhally & Lewis, 2019; Martin, 2021; McIlwain, 2019; Nakamura, 2009; Noble and Tynes, 2016; Saha, 2018; Smith, 2013; Stevens, 2022). Race, though a social construct, permeates all aspects of society and has real embodied effects and consequences in the DMEI. Racism assigns superiority or inferiority to people based on ascribed or perceived racial characteristics, interacting with other forms of oppression like classism and sexism. In the DMEI, racism manifests in individual racist prejudices, institutionally racist policies, and structural racism. The concept of "racial capitalism" highlights how the historic and continuing construction, exploitation, and marginalization of racialized groups have been integral to capitalism, which emerged through colonialism, imperialism, and the transatlantic slave trade, all of which needed racism. Within the DMEI, racism manifests in discriminatory racial barriers to labor market participation, systemic underrepresentation of racialized people in executive positions and labor forces, racialized pay gaps, and racist stereotypes and jokes. Researchers of work in the DMEI consider continuity and change in the history of white supremacy, racialization and racism as related to labor market entry, labor processes, and media and cultural products. Recognizing and challenging racism is essential for transforming work in the DMEI. It involves not just acknowledging but actively working to dismantle racial capitalism's old structures and new manifestations.

Sex, Gender and Sexism

The study of sex, gender, and sexism in the DMEI examines the enduring problems of patriarchy and sexism (Consalvo, 2008; Cannizzo & Strong, 2020; Duffy, 2015a, 2015; Gregg & Andrijasevic, 2019; Handy & Rowlands, 2014; Hill, 2014a, 2014b; Huws, 2015; Jarrett, 2016; Jones & Pringle, 2015; Kantor & Twohey, 2019; Liddy & O'Brien, 2021; Mayer, 2013; Milestone, 2015; O'Brien, 2019; Ryan, 2023). Patriarchy, a system where men rule and hold primary structural power over the state, economy, and civil society, to the detriment of women, has long been part of capitalism and shaped conditions of "women's work," paid and unpaid, to the benefit of men. In the DMEI, this history of patriarchy extends from governments to industries, boardrooms to bedrooms, largely putting men in a position of owning and controlling resources, and privilege in labor force participation, leadership opportunities, moral authority, decision-making power, and pay scales not shared equally with women. Sexism, rooted in the patriarchal idea of male superiority, is intertwined with the social construction of stereotypical gender roles that normalize men's dominance and women's subordinance in the DMEI. Too often, women are relegated to low-paying and precarious jobs, reflecting a systematic devaluation of their work. In the DMEI, this is evident in the "glass ceiling," which hinders women's career progression to top leadership roles and the gender pay gap, which keeps men wealthier despite doing the same job as women (and sometimes not doing as much at all). Also, patriarchal workplace cultures devalue women's contributions and adversely affect women's health and wellness. Countering sexism in the DMEI requires an understanding of how patriarchal patterns and gendered power relations persist at work, and supporting worker efforts to change that.

Age and Ageism

The study of age and ageism in the DMEI focuses on the social construction of age and forms of discrimination toward individuals based on their age (Ayalon & Tesch-Römer, 2018; Baum, 2018; Berg, 2021; Brodmerkel & Barker, 2019; Nelson, 2002; Rosales & Fernández-Ardèvol, 2020; Rosales & Svensson, 2021; Schaffer, 2023; Sufit, 2023). This form of prejudice can impact both older and younger people by establishing or sustaining barriers to workforce participation and employment opportunities. In the DMEI, ageism often reflects a capitalist bias that emphasizes energy and novelty, stereotypically associated with youth. This leads to the stereotyping of older workers as being out of touch with "the now" and "the new." Ageism can also discriminate in hiring, retention, and promotion practices. In Hollywood, older actors, especially women, experience limited opportunities for leading roles, with so many roles made for men, or for youth. The tech industry also exhibits ageism, often favoring younger people who are perceived as more technologically savvy than older people. Despite studies showing that successful founders of tech companies are often older, the tech industry's youth-centric culture persists, eroding fair treatment for workers of all ages.

Disability and Ableism

The study of disability and ableism in the DMEI focuses on discrimination or social prejudice against individuals with disabilities (Campbell, 2009; Cherney, 2011; Elber, 2018; Ellis, 2016; Galer, 2012; Goggin & Newell, 2002; Harpur, 2020; Goodley, Lawthom, Liddiard, & Runswick-Cole, 2019; Gulka, Macleod & Gewurtz, 2022; Kashani & Nocella, 2010; Lall, 2020; Nario-Redmond, 2019; Preston, 2016; Pullin, 2009; Shakespeare, 2013; Tucker, 2017). This discrimination encompasses attitudes, behaviors, and practices that devalue people with physical, intellectual, or psychiatric disabilities, often promoting the belief that these individuals are inferior or need to be "fixed." In the DMEI, ableism manifests in explicit discrimination to more subtle biases, leading to limited access to jobs and underrepresentation in key roles. Capitalism's emphasis on productivity and profit exacerbates ableism, often incentivizing corporations to assess an individual's potential value as a worker based on their ability to produce as efficiently as it demands, implicitly disadvantaging those with disabilities, and denying them the right to appropriate workplace accommodations. As a result, people with disabilities face lower employment rates and are often marginalized in the labor market. In the DMEI, disabled people are underrepresented in the upper echelons of management, and in lower technical and service roles. Discriminatory hiring practices, physical inaccessibility, and technological barriers further limit the participation of disabled people in the DMEI's workforce.

In sum, the concept of intersectionality, which examines how overlapping facets and ascriptions of identity in society—such as class, race, gender, age, and ability—interlink with varying forms of social privilege and under-privilege, is helpful for understanding the dynamics of equality and discrimination, inclusion and exclusion, equity and inequity, and empowerment and oppression, at work in the DMEI. It provides a useful lens for looking at how overlapping and intersecting inequities and oppressions in society shape the DMEI's conditions and experiences of workers in both similar and different ways. It is a salient counterpoint to the meritocratic ideal of the DMEI, and of capitalism itself.

Do Black Lives Matter (BLM) to Hollywood's White Owners?

In response to the BLM protests, every major Hollywood studio expressed support for Black Americans. The 20th Century Studios posted on Facebook "We believe Black lives matter and that this message is one that everyone should hear." Paramount CEO Jim Gianopulos sent an internal memo to employees, expressing that "Too many members of the Black community have had their breath stolen from them through racial injustice" and pledged to use Paramount "platforms to shine a light on the realities of racial injustice and call for equality," "amplify the voices of the communities we serve and provide a call to action for change," and "foster a culture that deeply values and respects diversity and inclusion" (Low & Yap, 2020). Universal Pictures issued a similar statement while Sony Pictures launched "Sony Pictures Action" to donate to racial justice organizations and to augment its existing diversity and inclusion human resource programs (Comtois, 2020). The Walt Disney Company and ViacomCBS donated a total of $7 million to NAACP and other liberal Black organizations and Marvel Entertainment tweeted it "stands against racism." After posting "We have a platform, and we have a duty to our Black members, employees, creators and talent to speak up," Netflix curated a "Black Lives Matter" collection of films, TV series, and documentaries to help viewers "learn more about racial injustice and the Black experience in America." NBC-Universal declared that new episodes in its 2021 season of *Law & Order: SVU* would address the problem of police racism and violence in allusion to the killing of George Floyd. HBO Max temporarily canceled *Gone With the Wind* and then re-released it with a special preface about its racist context. TV networks from NBC to FX purged episodes that feature blackface from series such as *30 Rock*, *Community*, and *The Office* (Herman, 2020). Despite these gestures of support for BLM, the CEOs of the major Hollywood studios were all white men: 20th Century Studios (Steve Asbell), Paramount Pictures (Jim Gianopulos), Universal Pictures (Jimmy Horowitz), Sony Pictures (Tony Vinciquerra), and Walt Disney Studios (Bob Chapek). "It's easier to get a Black president than a black studio head," says Spike Lee (Coyle 2020). Even still, in the 21st century, a Black entertainment bourgeoisie (e.g., Oprah Winfrey, Tyler Perry, Tara Duncan), Black TV networks (Black Entertainment Television), many Black directors (e.g., Ryan Coogler, Spike Lee, Millicent Shelton, and

Boots Riley), and popular TV shows and films with predominantly Black casts (e.g., *Black Panther, Black-ish, Da 5 Bloods, Sorry to Bother You*) exist. Also, Hollywood initiatives to recognize, incorporate, and reward Black entertainment workers have begun to overtly celebrate Black Excellence in directing, screenwriting, and acting. UCLA's *Hollywood Diversity Report 2022* found the percentage of leading roles played by people of color in 2022's top 200 films nearly quadrupled since 2011; their share of writing credits has more than quadrupled; and their percentage of directing jobs has nearly tripled (Wilson, 2022). The Academy of Motion Picture Arts and Sciences expanded and diversified its voting body, and there are more Black Oscar nominees and winners. Nonetheless, with regards to corporate ownership, authority, decision-making power, and control of surplus profit, Hollywood's upper echelon remains much whiter than the multicultural society in which it is based.

#SiliconValleySoWhite

Alphabet-Google, Apple, Meta Platforms, Amazon, and Microsoft (or, the "AAMAM") are the world's largest tech corporations, and their profits, market capitalization, scale of operations, and user base are unrivaled. Apropos the hashtag #SiliconValleySoWhite, they express the inequities of racial capitalism. In *Black Software*, Charlton McIlwain (2019) exposes the collaboration between the US federal government, the computing industry, and elite science and engineering institutions, beginning in the early 1960s, as a calculated effort to use new computer technologies to contain, profile, and detain Black Americans, reinforcing systemic racist oppression and capitalist exploitation. In the early 1980s, a nearly all-white class of investors, inventors, and entrepreneurs populated Silicon Valley and absorbed 80% of its income (McIlwain, 2020). Despite the many innovations made for Silicon Valley by African American computer networking and Internet creators (McIllwain, 2019), Silicon Valley is still disproportionately populated by a white bourgeoisie and workforce, and white privilege pervades the companies that own the world's greatest gadgets, apps, and platforms (Rangarajan, 2018). Most of the ownership class in Big Tech remains predominantly white and male, and the prominent figures representing the digital age continue to be billionaires like Elon Musk,

Jeff Bezos, and Mark Zuckerberg. While there are some Black CEOs in Silicon Valley, their numbers are significantly lower compared to their white counterparts at the helm of the industry. Despite their class privilege compared to Black and white workers, some Black CEOs report instances of racial discrimination from white economic elites. These elites sometimes question their suitability for leadership roles and may elect to partner with white business associates in an attempt to gain the confidence of white venture capitalists, who might otherwise discriminate (Anand & MacBride, 2020). Big Tech companies tend to over-represent white workers in their labor force. In 2016, Black employees accounted for only 3% of the workforce in Silicon Valley's top 75 firms. In 2019, Facebook's workforce was 3.8% Black, and at Google, only 1% of employees were Black women (Harrison, 2020). Additionally, some Black workers in Big Tech report on the job racial discrimination. For instance, Black Facebook workers have mentioned being "Zucked" or censored when discussing racism (Guynn, 2020). While Silicon Valley reproduces racial capitalism, the telecommunication industry props up a racialized "digital divide": poor whites are "more likely to have internet access than poor Blacks" (Gustin, 2016). The Black people who are serviced may experience "data discrimination" when using platforms whose racially biased search engine algorithms are frequently designed or programmed to privilege the identities, tastes, and preferences of white people (Noble, 2018).

Unequal Access to Work in the DMEI: Whose "Cultural Capital"?

Poking holes in the meritocratic ideal does not explain why some corporations in the DMEI seem to privilege relatively economically privileged workers for careers while keeping less economically privileged workers, out. To try to explain this phenomenon, we need to develop a more robust understanding of the conditions that may enhance or limit a worker's chances of landing a career in the contemporary DMEI. To this end, we can revisit the work of Pierre Bourdieu (1984, 1986), the prominent French sociologist who elaborated on how the accumulation of "economic capital" often serves as a prerequisite for the accumulation of "cultural capital" and "social capital," which both play a significant role in helping or hindering workers' preparation for and access to employment in the DMEI.

Economic Capital, Cultural Capital, Social Capital, and the Family

Economic capital refers to the assets and wealth an individual or family owns and controls: this "is immediately and directly convertible into money and may be institutionalized in the forms of property rights" (Bourdieu, 1986). *Cultural capital* refers to one's possession of things like knowledge about society and how things work based upon legitimized or authoritative sources and thinkers, a proficiency with speech and dialogue, a demonstration of good manners and relevant tastes, as well as institutionally recognizable qualifications and accolades, such as university degrees and awards. Cultural capital "is convertible, on certain conditions, into economic capital and may be institutionalized in the forms of educational qualifications" (Bourdieu, 1986). *Social capital* refers to the social connections and networks one has or accumulates, "which are convertible, in certain conditions, into economic capital" (Bourdieu, 1986). Social capital refers to the "aggregate of the actual or potential resources which are linked to possession of a durable network of more or less institutionalized relationships of mutual acquaintance and recognition – or in other words, to membership in a group." And, the volume of the social capital possessed by a given individual thus depends on the size of the network of connections they "can effectively mobilize and on the volume of the capital (economic, cultural or symbolic) possessed" in their "own right by each of those to whom they are connected." For Bourdieu (1986), property, wealth, and high incomes, are the most significant form of capital, as this "economic capital is at the root of all the other types of capital." Bourdieu conceptualizes cultural capital and social capital as "disguised" expressions of economic capital: one who possesses abundant economic capital frequently also possesses the means to distinguish themselves culturally and establish or perpetuate social connections to other influential individuals and groups.

The family is viewed by Bourdieu as the key site for the accumulation, transmission, and reproduction of forms of economic, cultural and social capital. As Bourdieu (1986) writes, "the precondition for the fast, easy accumulation of every kind of useful cultural capital, starts at the outset, without delay, without wasted time, only for the offspring of families endowed with strong cultural capital...It follows that the transmission of cultural capital is no doubt the best hidden form of hereditary transmission of capital." Furthermore, Bourdieu (1986) explains how "the social capital accruing from a relationship is that much greater to the extent that the person who is the object of it is richly endowed with capital (mainly social, but also cultural and even economic capital), the possessors of an inherited social capital, symbolized by a great name...". While capitalism is an inherently class-divided and class-unequal system, family units within capitalism play a key role in reproducing social classes, transmitting economic, cultural and social capital, and conferring privileges across generations.

Children born into families with significant economic capital often begin accumulating wealth from birth, placing them in an advantageous position for making further economic gains. Early on, they also start accumulating cultural capital, which further strengthens their capacity to accumulate more cultural capital. They will also be privileged with social capital, and invited to make even more social connections. These kids are immensely privileged: they start ahead furnished with the means to get ahead. Conversely, kids who grow up in poor or working-class families with limited economic capital will not enjoy an inheritance, nor even start the quest for economic capital until much later in life, if they manage to climb out of poverty or low-income living that is. These kids may be discouraged by parents and communities from reading, learning about the world, communicating about the world, analyzing the world, but eventually amass some standard operational cultural capital, thanks to public education systems. But they always start at a disadvantage compared to their wealthy counterparts who have access to both economic and cultural capital from early on, and lots of social connections that support their further accumulations down the road. Wealthy families often pass down economic, cultural and social capital to their children, providing them with privileges that are typically unavailable to those from poorer or working-class backgrounds, whose parents and grandparents never received such class privileges and cannot easily pass much on to the next generation.

Education is a microcosm and mechanism of society's class system (Cooper, 2023; Cornwall, 2023; McCluskey, 2023; Rosalsky, 2023). Children from families in the top 1% are more than twice as likely to attend elite universities—Ivy League Plus schools such as MIT, Stanford, Duke, and the University of Chicago—than those from the poor working class. This disparity stems from these families' possession of economic capital to afford high tuition fees, cultural capital to prepare their children with the advanced knowledge required for admission, and social capital that aids in the admissions process. Additionally, Ivy League schools often prioritize applicants from affluent families, anticipating future alumni donations. Once enrolled, these wealthy students from capital-concentrating families further expand their knowledge, reinforce their cultural distinction, and fortify elite social connections, accumulating more cultural and social capital along the way. This process enhances their ability to perpetuate and further profit on the economic capital they've inherited, enabling them to establish new families with similar class privileges. Consequently, graduates of Ivy League schools are overrepresented in the upper echelons of the corporate world, often achieving top 1% income levels while kids from the public schools graduate with debt to pay. The accumulation of economic, social, and cultural capital begins with the privileges of ruling-class families. These advantages extend through education and into society, reinforcing a class hierarchy and perpetuating forms of privilege within the broader economy. Ultimately, those who start with economic, cultural, and social capital are better positioned to accumulate more capital than those who start with little to none. Those who begin with class privilege frequently sustain and enhance that privilege. For those with little to none of the forms of capital that animate it, life is an uphill battle, with many losses, few wins.

One's family capital is undoubtedly a privilege, but it does not strictly cause or always determine one's cultural or social capital. There are instances when individuals from elite backgrounds make poor decisions and squander their privilege and opportunity, resulting in diminished capital. Hunter Biden, Cameron Douglas, and Tori Spelling come to mind, though their families often rescue them from peril and maintain their upper-class lifestyles. There are some cases of kids from poor and working-class backgrounds who possess almost no economic capital at all, who strive to accumulate substantial cultural and social capital, and do that, eventually becoming rich and famous. Justin Bieber, Cardi B, and Jay-Z are frequently cited in these "rags to riches" stories. Yet, in the 21st century digital society, where people are more educated and more connected than ever before, the possession of cultural and social capital does not necessarily or even frequently translate into the accumulation of economic capital. A recent graduate from a public university who did everything they possible could to learn to show off their insight into Murakami's latest novel, distinguish a Banksy from a Basquiat, and advocate for a net-zero lifestyle at a dinner party while teaching their elders about TikTok intersectionality might earn them a gold star among those who value this type of cultural capital, yet such cultural distinction may not lead to or correlate with their accumulation of capital, in the form of a high income. Also, possession of online social capital, such as a giant Facebook friend following of 5000, does not translate to friendship with Mark Zuckerberg and others with real influence. One can be popular on Facebook and boast a vast network of friends, yet without connections to those who hold economic power, the social capital amassed on Facebook does not lead to fame and fortune. Nonetheless, the interplay between economic, cultural and social capital is a useful heuristic for considering the inequities in access to the resources required to prepare for and land a career in the DMEI. This interplay undergirds unequal access to educational credentials, internship experience, professional networks, and self-branding rituals that are often key to landing a job in the DMEI.

Unequal Access to Education

Economic, cultural and social capital significantly shape access to the informal and formal educational opportunities that are integral to preparing oneself for and landing a career in the DMEI. While those with economic capital typically have access to abundant pristine educational opportunities, people from poorer socio-economic backgrounds do not. Also, the possession of economic capital affords the luxury of free time and space without waged work, which is often crucial for self-teaching, self-training and creative exploration, the honing of knowledge and skills related to a career in the DMEI. Conversely, those with limited economic capital must juggle between waged work and unwaged reproductive labor, leaving less time for educational activities unrelated to immediate necessity. In terms of formal education, economic and social capital puts one in a position to afford to access prestigious, often private Ivy League universities and colleges known for their arts and STEM programs. These institutions' curriculums, faculty, and industry connections help those who can afford to purchase their degree from these providers. In contrast, individuals from poor and working-class backgrounds are more likely to attend underfunded public colleges, if any. Moreover, access to prestigious educational institutions is sometimes bought and paid for by wealthy parents, not earned by applicants. The College Admissions Scandal of 2019, involving actors Lori Loughlin and Felicity Huffman, highlights how the wealthy can manipulate who gets access to elite education and who cannot, and how those in possession of lots of economic and social capital can rig the opportunity for their children to accumulate cultural capital. Moreover, academic selection processes can be influenced by homophilic tendencies, perpetuating class discrimination, exclusion, and divisions within education institutions. The *Elitist Britain?* study by the Sutton Trust and Social Mobility Commission further illustrates this point, revealing a disproportionate representation of private-schooled individuals in influential positions in the media and creative industries (The Sutton Trust, 2019).

Unequal Access to Internships

One's economic and social capital plays a significant role in facilitating access to cultural capital accumulation opportunities and by extension, career opportunities, particularly through internships. Paid or unpaid, internships often serve as means for young workers to accumulate the "experience" (code for a bundle of knowledge and skills) that so many corporations across the DMEI ask for in their job postings. Internships are supposed to offer those who do them real-world experience, knowledge acquisition, skills training, and networking opportunities. However, the unpaid internship system privileges those who can afford to work without pay, often for extended periods, while economically discriminating against those who cannot (Banks, 2017). Few can afford to forego a wage in pursuit of an experience to put on the resume. As de Peuter, Cohen, and Brophy (2012) explain, "few people can afford to work for free." As Hesmondhalgh (2019, p. 353) avers, unpaid internships put "young people from less privileged backgrounds at a significant disadvantage." Furthermore, lucrative internships at prestigious companies in the DMEI are often more accessible to rich kids whose families' social connections can open doors, compared to those without keys to such doors. Elite internships may go to individuals with ties to company executives or personnel, a form of class discrimination that favors the well-connected over merit-based selection. Thus, individuals who possess economic and social capital are in a privileged position to accumulate more cultural capital through unpaid internships with corporations in the DMEI. Those without these forms of economic and social capital may be unlikely to acquire the experience demanded by those same corporations. The unpaid internship not only reproduces class privilege in developing a CV requisite to applying for jobs but also perpetuates a labor market that includes the rich and excludes the poor.

Unequal Access to Professional Networks

In the DMEI, the maxim "you are who you know" encapsulates the role of social networks in shaping career opportunities and trajectories. This phrase underscores a truth: one's professional connections, often a reflection of ones possession of pre-existing economic and cultural capital concentrated in the family, significantly impacts one's employment opportunities, or at least a chance to "get a foot in the door." Those who possess economic capital usually have the means to engage in habitual social networking activities, like attending key industry events and building relationships with gatekeepers and intermediaries. In contrast, people from poor and working-class backgrounds are often too busy working for wages to enjoy the luxury of schmoozing with wealthy and influential people or cultivating networks. While platforms like LinkedIn have made networking more accessible to more working people searching for jobs, this practice itself requires a great deal of time, time that many don't have. But time is not the only factor. Frequently, individuals born into families with economic capital benefit from pre-existing professional social networks, affording them a substantial advantage. In contrast, those without economic and social capital often find themselves needing to proactively reach out to various individuals in a sometimes disappointing and humiliating hustle to make professional connections that could be beneficial in the long run, which might lead to some other connection, that might open the door to a job, or maybe a gig, or maybe another connection.

Unequal Access to Time for Self-Branding

Abundant career advice literature, labor-market help experts, and counselors encourage workers to cultivate a distinctive brand image or persona for themselves, and to communicate that self-brand far and wide, as a way to get noticed, maybe even hired (Gandini, 2016). Self-branding is a means to display cultural and social capital, and to make oneself visible, which is integral to securing employment and in turn, accumulating economic capital. Frequently, many "precariously employed workers do feel pressured to incorporate personal branding into their orientations toward both self and work" (Vallas & Hill, 2018, p. 297). Millions are actively developing self-brands in pursuit of waged work, and doing so may be a form of unpaid work (Hearn, 2008a, 2008b). In the past, companies might "invest" in their labor force; now, workers are socialized to invest in themselves, train themselves, brand themselves, for a chance at waged employment. This can be an arduous process, as the work of making a self-brand demands not only knowledge and skill but also a substantial investment of time and energy. Crafting and circulating a consistent brand image of oneself across various social media platforms requires continual content creation and interaction with people, which is time-consuming and can be exhausting. The labor of self-branding is demanded of everyone and has largely become a new norm that corporations in the DMEI expect of all workers who aspire to enter its labor force. And yet, those who possess greater economic, social and cultural capital than others tend to enjoy a competitive advantage when self-branding. They possess not only the financial means but the established social connections and bundle of knowledge and skills, as well as time, to successfully build and project self-brands, and manage reputations online. Individuals from underprivileged class backgrounds may already be working waged jobs and doing unpaid reproductive labor for the family, making the unpaid work of self-branding unfeasible, further putting them at a disadvantage in an industry that puts a premium on digital image-making and networking. The labor of self-branding belies a fundamental inequality within the DMEI, where success in self-branding, and by extension, landing a job, is closely tied to one's existing economic, social and cultural capital.

Unequal Access to Equal Opportunity: Discrimination in Hiring

In the DMEI, the ideal (and legal precedent) of equal opportunity to a job is often overshadowed by deep-seated discrimination and bias in hiring processes. The inequities in economic, social and cultural capital play a significant role here. Cultural capital might lead to greater success in job interviews, where an individual's ability to "fit" the role is often assessed based on subjective criteria that favor those from certain class backgrounds, and the cultural habitus stemming from them. This bias extends beyond just the interview phase; it permeates the entire professional culture, advantaging those who are adept at "playing the professional part" and aligning with the industry's predominant way of work life. Also, one's possession of social capital, such as a pre-existing relationship to a CEO or top personnel at a firm, can lead to bias and discrimination in the hiring process by giving undue advantage to well-connected candidates, thereby excluding equally or more qualified applicants without such connections. Furthermore, the barriers to entry to employment in the DMEI are compounded by issues of *ascription biases*. There's a historical tendency in capitalist societies to associate certain jobs with specific demographic groups—a practice that results in occupational segregation by class, race, gender, age and ability. For instance, directing a movie or creating a video game was long perceived as something white men were uniquely suited to do, even though that's not the case. Ascription bias involves prejudging or stereotyping individuals based on attributes such as class, race, gender, age, or disability, rather than evaluating their qualifications for a position based on their actual knowledge and skills. *Affinity biases* in hiring practices within firms and occupations in the DMEI are another barrier to employment. These biases, often subconscious, can lead to favoritism toward candidates who share similar backgrounds, interests, or appearances with hiring managers. These discriminatory practices are being extended by *algorithmic bias* in AI-based hiring systems. While these automated systems are often touted as objective, their algorithms can reinforce existing prejudices, essentially "coding" the classist, racist, sexist, ageist, and ableist biases of society and corporations into the hiring process (Chen, 2023; Jackson, 2021; Prince & Schwarcz, 2019; Raghavan et al., 2020). For example, ChatGPT is being used by some companies to help them with their job recruiting. Yet, "When asked 1000 times to rank eight equally-qualified resumes for a real financial analyst role at a Fortune 500 company, ChatGPT was least likely to pick the resume with a name distinct to black Americans" (Wright, 2024). Modern AI may appear neutral but can and does discriminate against certain people in the hiring process.

The Classism of the "Creative Class"

In *The Rise of the Creative Class*, Richard Florida (2004) argues that the economic success of cities and regions is largely driven by the presence of a "creative class." This "new" class of artists, scientists, engineers, and business professionals is supposedly engaged in labor processes that involve creativity and innovation, leading to new IP. While Florida highlights the economic and cultural benefits supposedly brought to cities by the creative class and acknowledges some of the inequities that exist in the creative economy, he doesn't consider the classism prevalent in the creative industries. According to "Social Mobility in the Creative Economy: Rebuilding and Levelling Up," a report from the Creative Industries Policy and Evidence Centre (Carey, O'Brien, & Gable, 2021), the UK creative economy is classist. Individuals from socio-economically privileged backgrounds are more than twice as likely to secure creative roles as those who are socio-economically underprivileged. Data from the Office for National Statistics' Labour Force Survey points to how in 2020, 52% of the creative workforce came from high socio-economic backgrounds, markedly higher than the 38% average across all industries. The underrepresentation of people in these industries from working-class backgrounds is notable, with only 26% of creative jobs held by individuals from these backgrounds in 2020. The sector's expansion since 2014, adding over 400,000 jobs, has predominantly benefited those from upper-middle-class origins, with minimal increase in working-class representation. Furthermore, the COVID-19 pandemic exacerbated these class-based exclusions, particularly in film, TV, design, and performing arts. This class-based exclusion in the creative industries, which intersects with sexism, racism, ageism, and ableism, highlights the need for concerted efforts to put class into the broader EDI agendas for the creative industries, as well as creative policy frameworks. If not, the whole creative class thesis, and the neoliberal state urban development plans based on ideals of creativity, will likely continue to be classist, and of service to the upper-class. Perhaps the "creative city" thesis itself is inherently classist. It idealizes a narrow band of globe-trotting professionals associated with creativity, while marginalizing the essential contributions of workers in local industries. By prioritizing the attraction of the so-called creative class to immiserated urban areas, the thesis exacerbates economic disparities and fuels gentrification,

> displacing lower-income residents who cannot afford the resultant spike in living costs, let alone the artisanal baked goods, organic carrots, and craft beer sold by entrepreneurial creatives. It promotes elitism, suggesting that a city's success hinges on the migration of talent rather than investing in and empowering existing communities, thereby reinforcing social and economic hierarchies and neglecting the working class.

Meritocracy as Ideology

Meritocracy has always been more of an ideal than a reality. Capitalism, class relations, and enduring historical and social problems such as classism, sexism, racism, ageism, and ableism, along with radical disparities in economic, social, and cultural capital, ensure that this remains the case. Within the DMEI and beyond, the meritocracy ideology obscures the historical and ongoing structural social divides in capitalism between owners and workers, the intersecting inequities and oppressions of classism, racism, sexism, ageism, and ableism, as well as the advantages accruing to those who possess the greatest economic, social, and cultural capital, and the disadvantages befalling those who have very little to none at all. Consider my revised lyric to the *Pinocchio* song: "When dreams fade in the light of day, your social history paves the way; hard work alone may not suffice, in a world where capital dictates the roll of the dice."

In *The Meritocracy Trap*, Daniel Markovits (2016) asserts: "Meritocracy ideology frames what is in fact structural inequality and structural exclusion as an individual failure to measure up." Similarly, Jo Littler (2017) in *Against Meritocracy: Culture, Power and Myths of Mobility*, critiques the ideology of meritocracy, showing how it props up wealth and income disparity with "a familiar social story" of hard work leading to success getting "insidiously spun back on us" (Littler, 2017). Even though the ideology of meritocracy may distort reality, its narrative is deeply ingrained in the DMEI, leading millions to misunderstand how the system beneath actually works and the reasons behind income and wealth inequality. In this way, meritocracy may be a ruling class ideology, a set of predominantly illusory beliefs that not only distorts the true workings of the system but also persuades those most exploited and oppressed by it to keep believing that if only they work harder, they too can be rich and famous. By calling out this meritocratic ideology's covering up of myriad intersectional inequities and oppressions, we can begin to envision a more truly equitable, diverse, and inclusive DMEI.

8 What Is the Globalization of Work in the DMEI?

Outsourced Hardware, Software, Content, and Service

Introduction

This chapter examines the globalization of work in the digital media and entertainment industries (DMEI). The chapter opens by situating "globalization" or "global capitalism" within a historical framework of Empire and imperialism. It then focuses on how the corporations of the DMEI are hiring the labor of workers around the world to produce their hardware, software, content, and services in a new international division of labor (NIDL). The chapter highlights some current cases of this globalization of work, or corporate outsourcing, focusing on the cross-border making of digital devices, Hollywood movies, and video games. It also explores the labors of global call center work, remote work, social media content moderation, and micro-tasking across the Internet and platforms. Having shown the trans-nationality of digital media and entertainment production, the chapter complicates the idea that any piece of digital hardware, software, or content is essentially or exclusively "national" in character. It concludes by weighing the pros and cons of the globalization of work in the DMEI, flagging social problems such as the "race to the bottom," global labor arbitrage, the erosion of workers' rights, the normalization of precarious gigs, and growing economic inequality and wealth concentration. It also considers the barriers to and openings for novel mediated forms of international labor solidarity among workers in the global DMEI.

Empire, Globalization, and the Nation-State

Capitalism did not originate with free and equal individuals—owners and workers—buying and selling labor power in markets, nor did it develop on a national island with no connection to a wider world. Rather, the history of capitalism is intertwined with the rise of Empires. While the shift from feudalism to capitalism happened in England, this transition relied upon the brutal colonial conquests by Spain, Portugal, Holland,

DOI: 10.4324/9781003131076-9

France, and England in the 15th, 16th, and 17th centuries. In a chapter in *Capital* entitled "The Modern Theory of Colonization," Karl Marx (1990) explained *why* colonization was so essential to laying the groundwork for industrial capitalism. Marx showed "the genesis of the industrial capitalist" to be the Euro-colonial conquests of the Americas, Asia, and Africa and framed these as the "chief moment of primitive accumulation" (p. 915). The Euro-colonial conquests established "the basis of the capitalist mode of production" (p. 934) and this "primitive accumulation" propelled this mode of production into the world, "dripping head to toe, from every pore, with blood and dirt" (p. 926).

The globalization of capitalism has always occurred within a world system of shifting imperial centers (the countries that possess the greatest power to drive global transformation) and peripheries (the countries in subordinate positions to these Empires, as formal colonies or a post-colonial ally or proxy states). Until the 17th century, the mercantile Empires of Spain, Portugal, and Holland dominated world trade, but by the mid-18th century, England had become the most powerful Empire in the world. Even still, the power structures of the world system are not static, but dynamic: Empires rise, sustain, and fall while once peripheral countries can become imperial centers. During the mid-19th century, the US, formerly a colonial periphery of the British Empire, revolted and over time, transformed into a new imperial center. From the post-World War II era onward, the US became a new post-colonial Empire for global capitalism, superintended by its neoliberal super-state and backed by many other national states and internationalizing corporations worldwide. The expansion of any Empire—its imperialism—is driven by a convergence of economics and geopolitics, the de-territorializing economics of capitalist accumulation (the production, trade, and investment practices of corporations as they seek to turn a profit in markets across nation-state borders), and the territorial geopolitics of a powerful state (the diplomatic, political and military strategies of a superpower or hegemon as it struggles to assert its interests and achieve its goals vis-à-vis other states and peoples) (Mirrlees, 2013, 2016, 2023b, 2023c, 2024). Empire and imperialism have played a central if not primary role in shaping the world system and still persist in old and new forms of "globalization" today.

Capitalism has always been part of a world system, with Empire and imperialism as its geopolitical agent, but starting in the 1990s, scholars started using the word "globalization" to name a totally new agent or set of processes that were interlinking and connecting the world. Giddens (1990, p. 64) defined globalization as "the intensification of worldwide social relations which link distant localities in such a way that local happenings are shaped by events occurring many miles away and vice versa." Tomlinson (1999, pp. 1–2) construed globalization as "an empirical condition" characterized by "complex connectivity" between all polities, economies, and cultures. Robertson (1992, p. 19) described globalization as "the compression of the world and the intensification of the consciousness of the world." In some of the post-Cold War research on globalization, and in the heyday of America's unilateral moment, scholars imagined the world system of national polities, economies, and cultures was over, and yet, in our time, the structures of the old have endured but also exhibit some salient changes.

Capitalism is global, corporations coordinate the production, distribution, and circulation of goods and services within and across borders, and cultures are always already hybrids, but the world system has not as a whole evolved beyond or ruptured with the longstanding nation-state paradigm. Instead, powerful states from the US to China, backed by their political allies and business interests elsewhere, have been key to the making of global capitalism, and they support the internationalization of corporations, technologies, and entertainment media with their "national" strategic plans and policies. There may now be a nascent or full blown inter-imperial rivalry between the US and China, with the global DMEI a significant economic, geopolitical, military, and cultural-ideological battleground (Mirrlees, 2013, 2016, 2023b, 2023c, 2024). While the Internet, smartphones, and global media events, from the World Cup to the latest Marvel blockbuster movie, have fostered a sense of a shrinking planet or "oneness," the world system is still one in which nation-states exist and exert sovereignty of the affairs of their respective territories, establish and enact legal, policy, and regulatory frameworks to govern working populations, and expand, through the DMEI, into other countries, influencing them in subtle and profound ways. Even special economic zones (SEZs) are state-authored, with governments often loosening labor standards, crushing unions, and dolling out tax breaks to globalizing corporations, offering the local labor force up for exploitation.

The contemporary world system is not flat but a hierarchy of numerous competing, conflicting, and collaborating nation-states that support global capitalism and facilitate and legitimize the operations of corporations, including those corporations that comprise the DMEI. Even though these corporations are headquartered in territorial nation-states (mostly in big cities), their financing, decision-making, and production, distribution, and marketing of goods and services, stretch across national borders and territories, and rely upon the mobilization and appropriation of the knowledge and skills of sub-contractors and workers around the world. The production and circulation of digital hardware, software, and content by corporations is a worldwide affair connecting many companies and many workers across countries, regions, and cities. In this regard, even though a world system of nation-states endures, the notion that any piece of digital media hardware, software, or content is exclusively "national" can be troubled by showing the international or trans-national labor force, mobilized for its making.

Global Productions: Labor in the Making of the "Information Society", co-edited by the political economists of communication Gerald Sussman and John A. Lent (1998), marked a premier critical study of global capitalism's labor force and cross-border commodity chains. In this volume, Sussman and Lent (1998, p. 1) assessed the "global structures of communication, information and media through which pass daily transmissions of voice, data, text, and visual images—from the perspective of the people who actually build them"—and show the digital society to be based on a "new international division of labour" (NIDL). Contributors to the volume focused on power asymmetries between global corporations and local workers. As Sussman and Lent (1998) summarize: "Assembly workers in Hong Kong who manufacture the ... components" receive no royalties (p. 1), the "people who build film and television sets" win no Oscars (p. 2), and the "workers who produce information and images that frequently accords with the status quo," "have little or no say over" what they are made to do (p. 4). Also, the volume's contributors examined the rise of global media and tech corporations, and their outsourcing of electronics manufacture, animation, TV and movie production, and information services to low-paid and non-unionized workers in developing countries. Furthermore, they scrutinized the whiteness of Silicon Valley's tech elites and forms of racist and sexist discrimination that put and kept people of color, largely women and immigrants, in low-paid positions. Additionally, they showed the role of all nation-states and their political elites and business leaders, in the North and South, in supporting the cross-border business operations of media and tech corporations. Importantly, they encouraged union campaigns to contest the bad conditions of work and foregrounded the struggles by workers using ICTs as a "new means for internationalizing their potential collective strength" in pursuit of "democratic participation and a decent and sustainable quality of life" (p. 11).

The Globalization of Work in the DMEI: A World Labor Market, for Corporations

At the core of today's DMEI are corporations that span across borders, supported by neoliberal states, which facilitate and legitimize their accumulation. Some of the largest US-based corporations, both major and minor players in various groupings of the DMEI, are primarily headquartered in and around Los Angeles and Palo Alto, California, colloquially known as "Hollywood" and "Silicon Valley." But in pursuit of financial investments to make, labor to hire, consumers to sell to, and data to aggregate, Walt Disney, Apple, and Google, all expand beyond the locales in which they are headquartered. These corporations navigate the world labor market in search of "cost-efficient," yet knowledgeable and skilled workers, to hire on to the productions of hardware, software, content, and services. The global media and tech giants centralize capital ownership, decision-making, and IP control while decentralizing and contracting out tasks to workers in many locales, resulting in divisions of labor that criss-cross countries, regions and cities. Work in the DMEI is undertaken across transnational production networks and commodity chains comprising in-house agencies, subsidiary firms, and independent contractors. Tasks that may have been assigned to a single urban, regional or national workforce are being routinely distributed across a multinational or international workforce. Cities across the world, each fostering its own ecosystem of industrial districts, distribution chains, and content creation hubs, concentrate much of this production. However, the world system still exhibits historical and geographical unevenness, reflecting longstanding asymmetrical power relations among imperial and post-colonial states. Corporations in countries like the US (and increasingly, China) sit at the apex of this hierarchy (Mirrlees, 2023b, 2023c, 2024). Contrary to the idea that the world is "flat," the world labor market is unevenly developed, historically and geographically, and characterized by a complex web of interdependencies and enduring and novel imperial power asymmetries. The following sections consider some cases of the globalization of work in the DMEI.

AAMAM Goes to China: "Dying for an iPhone"

Silicon Valley's coordination of cross-border commodity chains and supply networks of hardware and electronics manufacture stand as a disturbing case of the globalization of work in the DMEI. The AAMAM (Alphabet-Google, Apple, Meta Platforms, Amazon, and Microsoft) have consistently prioritized high profits and low labor costs over the integrity of their liberal democracy brands when outsourcing hardware assembly to authoritarian contractor factories in China (Ross, 2007). Apple relies extensively on China-based contractors like Foxconn for the manufacture of its flagship products, including the iPhone, iPad, and Mac computers. The rationale behind this outsourcing is clear: to leverage China's efficient factory systems and lower labor costs, which in turn maximizes profits for Apple and its owners. Google also contracts manufacturing to China for its hardware products like the Pixel smartphone. Meta Platforms relies on China's workers to assemble hardware products like Oculus VR headsets. Amazon outsources the production of Kindle e-readers and Echo smart speakers to China and Microsoft does the same for its Surface devices and Xbox gaming consoles. Overall, AAMAM's outsourcing practices in China are a grim expression of global capitalism, where chasing low labor costs to secure high profits is paramount. AAMAM's riches have relied on the super-exploitation of Chinese workers, some of whom have committed suicide due to what are scrutinized as slavery-like life and labor conditions (Qiu, 2016a).

Dying for an iPhone: Apple, Foxconn, and the Lives of China's Workers by Jenny Chan, Mark Selden, and Pun Ngai (2020) provides an unsettling study of the brutal labor regime endured by Chinese workers at Foxconn, the principal manufacturer of Apple's iPhone. Apple, China's party-state, Foxconn, and global consumers all drive this process, with Apple searching for low labor costs, the CP embracing foreign direct investment, Foxconn taking a cut, and consumers blissfully oblivious to the workers' sweat, blood, and tears on the iPhones they are living through. This is not a straightforward case of US-centered platform imperialism. The Chinese party-state is a willing accomplice to Apple and Foxconn's exploits, and its CP officials favor the interests of these corporations, much more so than the workers it prevents from forming independent unions. Many Foxconn workers live in on-site factory dormitories which Foxconn owns. Part of the wage paid to them by Foxconn goes back to Foxconn, which is also their landlord. In despair, some workers kill themselves or at least try. To catch the workers who try to jump to their death from dormitory windows, Foxconn installed nets just above the factory floor. *Dying for an iPhone* not only exposes the underbelly of Apple's outsourcing to Foxconn but also calls for a reevaluation of the global manufacturing and consumption model itself.

Global Hollywood: Local Precarity

The cross-border production of Hollywood movies and TV series is another significant illustration of the globalization of work in the DMEI. Hollywood, once understood to be a uniquely "American" industry, has become a globalized trans-national content production factory, with US corporations and their owners the greatest beneficiaries of the IP and the profits accruing to them (Curtin & Sanson, 2016, 2017; Elmer & Gasher 2004; Johnson-Yale, 2008, 2017; Mayer, 2017; Miller, 2016; Miller et al., 2005; Mirrlees, 2013, 2016a, 2018; Pendakur, 1998; Scott, 2005). Hollywood's major studio-distributors, owned by even larger global media conglomerates, are the flagships for cosmopolitan and international business partnerships that bring together the knowledge and skills of entertainment workers from across the globe. Hollywood studios sub-contract various aspects of production to locations worldwide, integrating workers and firms based in other countries into their expansive production networks, all the while gobbling up subsidies from national states and even municipalities. Countries, regions, and cities compete to give global Hollywood financial incentives to localize, and those that give Hollywood the most subsidies tend to win short-term production contracts and precarious jobs. As result of their generosity, Toronto and Vancouver are sometimes called "Hollywood North." They attract a number of "runaway productions" from Los Angeles, often to the chagrin of American workers. However, while a local movie industry's role as a dependent servicer of global Hollywood production generates jobs, these are mostly short-term contract gigs, not a path to long-term prosperity for nations, industries, or workers. Additionally, these global productions usually make over local landscapes into simulacra of American cities. Toronto becomes New York City. Vancouver is remade into Seattle. Yes, these productions inject some monies into the local economy, but the real profits are accrued by the Hollywood studios that control the IP rights to the finished product, highlighting the asymmetric power relations between the local and the global in this arrangement. Nonetheless, worldwide, state after state giddily competes to win Hollywood production contracts, increasing subsidy offers and decreasing labor's bargaining power, hoping to create "creative jobs," stimulate the service sectors, and maybe even parlay the star vibes into the making of a tourist hotspot. The ensuing race to the bottom, driven by this competition, puts downward pressures on wages while cash flows up from the public to the state to the studios and their corporate owners.

In *Precarious Creativity*, Michael Curtin and Kevin Sanson (2016) and contributors to this exceptional volume provide a detailed look at the unglamorous reality of global Hollywood studios' relentless quest for high-skilled yet low-cost talent—a pursuit that is reshaping and degrading labor conditions worldwide. They examine how Hollywood, once the beacon of aspiration for screen media workers, from actors to gaffers, has internalized a cost-cutting ethos that, since the 1990s, has increasingly led to the outsourcing of production to locations with cheaper labor rates and lax regulations. Globe-trotting studio bosses take advantage of locally provisioned production incentives like tax breaks and subsidies. No single production hub becomes a Hollywood favorite when studios "keep scouring the globe for lower labor rates and less regulated environs" (Curtin & Sanson, 2016, p. 1). This global mobility of production has deflated wages, eroded benefits, and diminished job satisfaction for workers, leaving them to endure "severe financial, physical, and emotional strain" (Curtin & Sanson, 2016, p. 2). In right-to-work states such as Louisiana, Georgia, and Florida, and in union-weak cities like Prague, workers succumb to precarity, often taking "a small fraction" of the earnings compared to their unionized counterparts (Curtin & Sanson, 2016, p. 3). Even in union-strong cities like Toronto, Vancouver, and London, concessions are made to woo Hollywood productions, cutting wages and undercutting labor standards. The resultant jobs, while skilled, tend to be temporary. From Hollywood North to Bollywood and Nollywood, the pattern of precarity repeats. Even still, workers around the world, in a multiplicity of nationally situated movie industries, campaign for improved conditions (Curtin & Sanson, 2016, pp. 3–4).

Global Hollywood's *Suicide Squad*: Made in Canada, for Warner Bros

Warner Bros. Pictures is one of the world's largest studios. Though based in the US, it travels the world when making movies, often outsourcing production tasks and shoots to cities in Canada. A Hollywood flick that was partially made in Canada is Warner Bros' *Suicide Squad* (2016). This D/C comic book-inspired film is about a secretive US security state agency that puts together a team of super-criminals (the new "heroes" of Empire?). This shadowy agency gets the team to carry out "black ops" alongside US Navy SEALs against an evil witch-goddess called the Enchantress in exchange for reduced prison sentences. *Suicide Squad* gave its viewers lots of explosions and crashes and fights and unfunny one liners. Panned by most reviewers, *Suicide Squad* was nonetheless a global box office success, and another example of how a socially useless cultural product can make its owners big bucks. With a budget of $175 million, *Suicide Squad* took $637 million from viewers all over the world in August 2016. This put a profit of $462 million into Warner Bros' pocket. *Suicide Squad* made Warner Bros a lot of money—and a Canadian labor force helped to make it. Much of *Suicide Squad* was shot on-location, downtown Toronto. When watching spectacular sequences—like the one in which the Batmobile chases the Joker and Harley Quinn or the climactic final battle between the Squad and the Enchantress—viewers may glean Toronto locations like Dundas Square and the Bay Street Subway Station. But probably not because these and other Canadian sites were made over into "Mid-Way City," a fictional American city loosely based on Illinois. The performances of the Joker and Deadshot by American celebrities Jared Leto and Will Smith generated a lot of buzz for the flick. But behind the scenes, about 4000 Canadian workers played less glamorous but still important roles in the movie's division of labor. Employed by Toronto-based firms like Pinewood Studios, Speed Fastening

Systems, Demtra Sheet Metal, and Tommaso's Trattoria, they built sets, lit stages, created special effects, coordinated electricity, and fed the cast and crew. *Suicide Squad* was also a big budget Hollywood production subsidized by the Canadian government's cultural policy agencies. In the film's credit roll, Warner Bros thanks Toronto, Ontario, Quebec, British Columbia, and the Canadian Federal Government for big tax credits that made its labor costs a lot smaller. The Motion Picture Association—Canada (MPAC), the lobby for Hollywood's big six, says Warner Bros' production of *Suicide Squad* contributed $80 million to Ontario's economy. Zombie economics. But even if so, that's a pittance compared to the super profits that filled the coffers of Warner Bros, the film's copyright owner, and primary beneficiary. Warner Bros made *Suicide Squad* with Canadian places, workers, and public funds and made a huge return on investment. *Suicide Squad*'s value to the development of a strong Canadian film industry is uncertain, and its contribution to Canadian culture and global knowledge about it is miniscule.

The "McDonaldization" of Creativity?

In *The McDonaldization of Society*, George Ritzer (1983, 2009) introduced the concept of "McDonaldization" to describe the logics of a process whereby society comes to adopt and reflect the characteristics of the world's most famous fast-food restaurant—McDonald's! Ritzer's model of McDonaldization entails four key logics: *efficiency*, focused on minimizing time, exemplified by the quick service model of McDonald's (on average, it takes the worker about 60 to 90 seconds to assemble a Big Mac from start to finish: this includes placing the beef patties, sauce, pickles, lettuce, onions, and cheese on the buns, and then wrapping and serving the sandwich to the customer); *calculability*, emphasizing quantifiable outcomes like sales over subjective preferences like taste, promoting the idea that quantity is quality (Supersize it! Big Macs go better with Large Fries and Giant Coke!); *predictability*, ensuring standardized and uniform services and products across all locations (standardized recipes, production methods, and training and quality control regimes ensure that every cheeseburger tastes the same, whether made in Shanghai, New York City, Tokyo, or Paris); and *control*, achieved through standardized tasks and the substitution of human labor with technology (a wickedly Taylorized labor process plus automated cooking equipment, inventory management, and self-service kiosks and apps ensures management's control of workers). McDonaldization, while hyper-efficient within global fast-food operations, results in a homogenization of social and cultural practices and a "mind-numbing sameness." Applying George Ritzer's concept of "McDonaldization" to the production of media provides an interesting view of the degradation of the labor process and product in some quarters of Hollywood spectacle entertainment-making.

In the production of blockbuster action movies, efficiency is evident in streamlined production schedules and contractual timelines aimed at cost-effectiveness. Hollywood studios employ project management techniques, including detailed scheduling, budgeting, and resource allocation, to ensure each phase of the movie-making process is completed on time and within budget. Calculability is apparent when a movie's potential for success is measured in terms of quantifiable box office earnings and audience reach, rather than qualitative registers of artistic merit or novelty. Consequently, workers are hired to create movies designed to achieve box office success by appealing to the lowest common denominator, prioritizing mass appeal and profitability over everything else, as seen in formulaic franchise blockbusters like every installment of the *Transformers* series. Predictability is reflected in the repetitive structure of action movies, with writers tasked with crafting near-identical narratives and plots, rehashing sequences such as high-speed chases and heroic protagonists overcoming obstacles. Examples include the simultaneous releases of *Armageddon* and *Deep Impact* in 1998, both revolving around averting an asteroid collision with Earth, and *Olympus Has Fallen* and *White House Down* in 2013, both spectacular assaults on the White House and subsequent heroics to save the President. Control in the Hollywood labor process for action movies is achieved through Taylorism and technology by standardizing tasks and optimizing workflows to maximize efficiency and productivity. Filmmaking is broken down into specialized activities, while many aspects of the process are automated using advanced computer-generated imagery (CGI) and motion capture technologies that streamline the creation of spectacular sequences, reducing reliance on practical effects and stunts, and allowing precise control over the final product. Digital editing tools enable filmmakers to quickly revise scenes in response to shifting consumer attitudes and to localize the product for national markets, such as complying with PRC censors.

What Is the Globalization of Work in the DMEI? 203

> Even YouTube influencers' reaction videos to action movie previews seem McDonaldized. Efficiency is key in these videos, with creators employing a quick production process involving real-time reactions and summaries, timing their YouTube release with the studios' PR campaign schedule. Calculability is apparent, with success measured through views, likes, and subscriber growth. Predictability is also present, with viewers expecting certain types of emotional reactions to blockbuster content: "This looks epic!" with wide eyes and raised eyebrows, nodding in approval while saying, "I can't wait to see this!" Control is exercised in production, with repeatable gimmicks and setups optimized for YouTube's algorithms. In sum, Ritzer's concept of McDonaldization is a valuable lens for understanding how the logics of efficiency, calculability, predictability, and control shape the production of Hollywood action movies, and perhaps even some of the creators of "reaction" videos.

Global Games Making: Multinational Credit Roll

Like Hollywood, the video game industry's globalization happens across an expansive cross-border division of labor, with major US-based corporations outsourcing various game development tasks, as well as quality assurance, testing, and customer support, to countries where skilled labor is plentiful, and costs are lower than what they'd have to pay in their respective "home" labor markets (Bulut, 2015; Dyer-Witheford & de Peuter, 2009, 2020; Hammar, 2022; Hammar et al., 2021; Ozimek, 2019a). The outsourcing of video game development work by major companies like Ubisoft, Electronic Arts (EA), Activision Blizzard, and Rockstar Games is telling. Ubisoft, creator of *Assassin's Creed* and *Far Cry* franchises, extends its game development labor process across international studios and contractors, hiring workers from Romania to India. EA, behind titles like *FIFA* and *Battlefield*, leverages global labor in urban locales in Canada to India to Singapore, while Activision Blizzard, famous for *Call of Duty*, presides over a network of global studios for a range of specialized game production tasks, from design to testing. One may watch the credits roll at the end of games to grasp the expansive multinational labor force marshaled by companies.

While high-level game design, core development, and copyright often remain within the flagship studios headquartered in the US and Europe, these studios rely on international contractors and their workforces for tasks like 3D modeling and animation (Thomsen, 2018). For example, Virtuos, headquartered in China, contributed art and level design for titles like *Horizon: Zero Dawn* and *NBA 2K18* (Thomsen, 2018). Keywords

Studios, headquartered in Ireland, is another player in this outsourcing landscape, selling services from art production to player support to firms across various countries. This global outsourcing model may empower video game corporations in the Global North to produce triple A games at scale but also thrives on massive disparities in pay scales (Ozimek, 2019). While many global games workers are precarious, some are organized and organizing unions (Ruffino, 2021).

Global Call Centers: "Englishization" and "Callcentrification"

Call center outsourcing is a widespread practice among Silicon Valley companies, another case of the globalization of service work in the DMEI. Numerous companies outsource customer service work, technical support, or telemarketing, to networks of contractors around the world (Boussebaa et al., 2014; Brophy, 2017; Glover, 2022; Woodcock, 2016). For example, Microsoft, Dell, and AT&T outsource customer service and technical support to India, capitalizing on its large English-speaking workforce. The Philippines, with its strong English language proficiency and longstanding neo-colonial subordinance to the US, hosts call centers for Amazon. Across Eastern Europe, IT customer service support in countries like Poland, Romania, and Bulgaria present the value-proposition of skilled labor and geographical proximity to Western Europe, attracting contracts from companies like IBM and Oracle. Costa Rica, Mexico, and Brazil have become favored destinations for the "nearshoring" of call center service work by US-based firms such as Apple and HP. Big and small corporations in the DMEI provide round-the-clock customer support to their consumers and service users by positioning their call centers in various time zones, thus harnessing the labor of a geographically distributed workforce that is always on, and that must speak English as a prerequisite to getting hired and being paid low wages.

Globalized call center work is marred by a range of labor hazards and harms (Boussebaa et al., 2014; Brophy, 2017; Glover, 2022; Woodcock, 2016). Workers in these centers often experience strenuous working conditions, including long, irregular hours and stringent performance metrics, leading to significant physical and mental health issues such as stress, burnout, and repetitive strain injuries. Compounding these problems are the relatively miserable wages paid to call center workers. Job insecurity is another problem, as outsourced work is unstable due to fluctuating whims and demands of the corporations that pay for the contracts. Moreover, workers in non-English-speaking countries are compelled to not only learn English but to frequently undergo a training process of "Englishization." Workers adopt new Western names, speak with Midwestern American or British accents, and perform cultural identities to make the Western customer comfortable and feel like they are speaking to a worker, close to home. These "Englishized" workers then get evaluated by their comprador class managers, with their performance for the customer, praised or put down (Boussebaa et al., 2014). Furthermore, management's intensive labor process monitoring and surveillance practices in call centers, where calls are continuously recorded, listened to, and scrutinized to ensure that workers are adhering to scripts and service protocols defined by others, undercut their privacy and autonomy. Additionally, career advancement opportunities for workers in call centers are often limited, with a rigid hierarchical structure that offers few pathways for professional growth. Globalized call center work is tough on the body and the mind, but millions worldwide are doing it right now, and some of those millions are organizing unions and refusing and resisting exploitation.

Enda Brophy's (2017) extensive research on call centers, detailed in *Language Put to Work: The Making of the Global Call Centre Workforce*, foregrounds the plight and the empowerment of call center workers. Brophy (2017, pp. 229–230) notes, call center work is "one of the fastest-growing forms of employment, and has become emblematic of processes that have characterized the broader transformation of work in communicative capitalism." Brophy coins the concept "callcentrification," a neo-Taylorist managerial practice that standardizes and routinizes communicative labor processes at the expense of worker autonomy. While call centers lead to "proletarianisation rather than professionalization," call center workers are also organizing. Brophy's extensive research foregrounds diverse tactics by call center workers to collectively contest the terms and conditions of their exploitation: dis-identification with management, slacking, quitting, pickets, strikes, and even novel forms of digital sabotage. While unions are important, Brophy shows other organizations, such as Italy's Atesia workers, as well as "nomadic" and "free-market unionisms," to be alternative models. Jamie Woodcock's (2016) *Working the Phones: Control and Resistance in Call Centres* is another important ethnographic study of the global call center industry and its labor force. It focuses on the exploitative conditions of work in high-volume UK call centers characterized by low pay and high turnover. In these call centers, management engages in intense surveillance of workers to ensure strict adherence to call scripts while workers struggle to keep up and face ethical dilemmas when hocking insurance to the vulnerable. Like Brophy, Woodcock foregrounds worker resistance in the call center beyond traditional trade unions, lauding subtle acts of worker defiance.

Global Remote Work: Down with Upwork

Global remote work is another example of the globalization of work in the DMEI, and heralds a shift in white collar service labor from city-based office places, to the networked spaces of the Internet and platforms. Companies seeking high skilled and low cost labor beyond their local and national geographical confines are finding it in a massive international labor force of remote workers, on the Internet. For example, GitLab and Basecamp mostly operate remotely, with their workforce distributed globally. Amazon and Shopify hire remote customer service workers. PR and advertising firms hire freelancers for global creative projects via platforms like Upwork and Freelancer. In this new model, corporations are searching out and hiring workers from a 24/7 trans-national online labor market. Some workers relish in the opportunity to work from virtually anywhere, at any time. This flexibility, however, often blurs the line between work and personal life, leading to an "always on" work culture, and like other outsourcing regimes, remote work has become central to global capitalist accumulation.

Previously, Silicon Valley companies would establish secondary headquarters in other countries to access the labor force. However, the new remote work paradigm has enabled the same companies to search out and hire labor from countries like the Philippines, Argentina, Brazil, and India, without having to establish subsidiaries (Elliot, 2022). Companies like Coinbase and Shopify hire software workers outside the US, and firms like Terminal and Telescoped are "remote-sourcing" developers. Latin American developers are particularly sought after by Silicon Valley firms due to shared time zones with the US and presumably lower salary expectations compared to US-based engineers. Developers often face the dilemma of choosing between higher paying but unstable contracts with US startups and lower paying but relatively stable jobs with local companies (Elliot, 2022). In Argentina, for example, some software developers will sign on as independent contractors, captivated by the allure of earning US dollars in a context high local inflation.

Upwork Global Inc. is at the forefront of global remote work, epitomizing an online platform that connects clients and freelancers, from almost anywhere, at any time. Originating from the 2013 merger of Elance Inc. and oDesk Corp. and rebranded as Upwork in 2015, the company is headquartered in Santa Clara and San Francisco, California. Its model is straightforward: clients post ads for jobs with defined budgets, and freelancers, from anywhere in the world, apply to these jobs, get interviewed and reviewed, and may be hired or given a pass. The flexible relationship temporarily formalizes with a contract, setting clear parameters on work hours, pay, and deadlines. This Upwork platform is part of a global freelancing boom, with a reported 43% of millennials turning to freelance work, for flexibility but mostly out of necessity in an age when standard employment is no longer the norm, and hustling is the way of the world (Kempton, 2023).

There is much precarity in this online piecework due to fluctuating skill demand, unreliable and sometimes abusive clients, and cutthroat competition between workers for gigs (Popiel, 2017). Also, high wages are often elusive. The platform's $3 minimum rate, while intended as a safeguard, impacts only a fraction of its workforce (Popiel, 2017). Furthermore, UpWork itself appropriates a percentage of freelancers' earnings, prioritizing its own wealth over the financial health of its somewhat dependent contractors. Nevertheless, for some workers, the benefits outweigh the costs. D'Cruz and Noronha's (2016) study highlights the positives of Upwork, particularly for Indian freelancers looking for job opportunities, pursuing skill development and career advancement, and seeking validation and recognition for a job well done. In India's labor market, Upwork is the best of a not-so-good situation for many workers (D'Cruz & Noronha, 2016). In sum, Upwork is a vast borderless labor marketplace, connecting freelancers with clients across the globe. Yet, Upwork places its contractors in a situation of unpredictable job opportunities, intense competition with others, and low and sometimes no pay, privileging the platform's owners' profits over the welfare and well-being of its distributed workforce.

Commercial Content Moderation (CCM): Facebook, Sama, and Neo-Colonialism

The growth of global content moderation companies, which sell services to Silicon Valley and the world's largest platform companies, is another example of the globalization of work in the DMEI. Far from being bastions of absolute user freedom, social media companies like Facebook and YouTube establish and enforce policies that govern user behavior and freedom of expression (Gillespie, 2017, 2018; Mirrlees, 2021). As Tarleton Gillespie (2018, p. 5) explains in *Custodians of the Internet: Platforms, Content Moderation*, and the *Hidden Decisions That Shape Social Media*, no Internet service exists "that does not impose rules" upon users. These companies secure their users' consent to their rules of communicative conduct through "terms of service" and "community guidelines" that users must agree to as a condition of signing up and logging on (Gillespie, 2017, 2018). All major platform companies now have and enforce "community standards," and these behavior and expression control regimes prohibit things like hate speech, nudity, violence, spam, disinformation, and bullying to keep users "safe" and global brand reputations secure. However, the practical enforcement of these content policies falls to unpaid users and paid invisible workers employed by the commercial content moderation (CCM) industry. These paid CCM workers do the dirty work of keeping the users' social media feeds, profiles, and screens clean, and suffer many psychological harms (Breslow, 2018; Chen, 2014; Chotiner, 2019; Jereza, 2022; Newton, 2019, 2020; Perrigo, 2022, 2023a, 2023b; Roberts, 2016, 2019).

In *Behind the Screen*, Sarah T. Roberts (2019) shows how the labor commercial content moderators perform in exchange for pay impacts them both professionally and personally. Roberts' extensive interviews with moderators reveal a workforce that spans from Silicon Valley to the Philippines and highlight the meager wages, subpar working conditions, and psychological distress these workers frequently endure when on and off the job. Content moderators review flagged content and make split-second decisions on whether that content should remain on a platform or be removed, based on the community guidelines and internal content policies of the company that contracts their labor. This work is usually short term, fraught with high turnover due to burnout and psychological distress. A lack of health and wellness benefits compounds the precarity of these jobs, and some moderators develop PSTD while at work. The mental toll is heavy, as moderators are ritually exposed to horrifying and violent images of suicide, murder, hatred, terrorism, and even torture. To cope with or manage the disturbing intrusions of these terrible images into their personal lives, some develop drug and alcohol addictions (Chen, 2014; Kulwin, 2017). The CCM industry's miserable conditions are magnified when Silicon Valley outsources these jobs to low-cost labor markets with minimal protections for workers. Indeed, content moderation tasks frequently land on the laptops of low-paid workers in the Global South (Chen, 2014; Kulwin, 2017; Read, 2019).

A notable example of such neo-colonial exploitation was Meta's outsourcing of content moderation for Facebook to Sama, a supposedly "ethical AI" company based in California, which professed a commitment to alleviate poverty by offering "dignified digital work" to people in poor countries (Perrigo, 2023a, 2023b). Near a slum on the outskirts of Nairobi, Kenya, approximately 200 young Africans were hired by the US-based Sama as content moderators for Facebook. Yet, Sama paid the workers as little as $1.50 per hour to sift through and remove disgusting and disturbing content, all the while suffering intimidation and threats by their anti-union managers. The workers planned a strike in 2019 to demand better labor conditions, and Sama responded by dispatching executives from San Francisco to quash the collective action and fire the strike's leader, Daniel Motaung. By early 2023, following international controversy and brand reputation damage, Sama ceased selling its content moderation services to Facebook, laying off 3% of its labor force, mostly in Nairobi. Meta then reportedly contracted out content moderation services to another contractor outpost in Africa whose labor conditions were even worse than Sama's (Perrigo, 2023a, 2023b). So much for Meta's mission to "give people the power to build community and bring the world closer together."

Whether outsourced to companies operating in the Global North or the Global South, the labor of content moderation is extraordinarily alienating, with CCM workers reviewing "hundreds of pieces of pornographic, violent, disturbing, disgusting, racist, sexist, and homophobic content" that is antithetical to their own identities, principles and values, and cultures (Newton, 2019). Racialized workers may be compelled to moderate white supremacist hate speech and "are disciplined in ways that leave them no choice but to align with Facebook's post-racial approach" (Jereza, 2022, p. 14). Silicon Valley's sub-contracting of this work to the CCM industry not only shields the biggest tech companies from direct accountability but also obscures the workers' plight, including their exposure to traumatizing material and the meager compensation paid for their services compared to workers formally employed within the same companies. The CCM industry is paradoxical: content moderators must protect the brand of their client while also considering the potential value in viral sensational content to its platform, a balancing act between abiding by community guidelines and enabling platform profit (Roberts, 2019). Improving the lives of these workers requires greater recognition and respect for what they do, and greater redistribution of the profit, so they get paid fairly.

> **The African Content Moderators Union**
>
> The African Content Moderators Union was established on May 1, 2023, in Nairobi, Kenya, by over 150 workers employed by third-party outsourcing companies to moderate content for major tech firms like Meta, Bytedance, and OpenAI (Bhalla, 2023; Haskins, 2024; Hendrix, 2023; Perrigo, 2023c). These workers, among the lowest-paid in the global tech industry, earned as little as $1.50 per hour and faced severe mental health consequences due to their labor of moderating toxic, hateful, and traumatic content. Their push for unionization began in 2019 when Daniel Motaung, a Facebook content moderator, was fired by the outsourcing company Sama for attempting to organize a workers' union called the Alliance. This set the stage for Motaung's establishment of the African Content Moderators Union, which aims to fight global Silicon Valley exploitation by locally advocating for better wages and mental health support, improving working conditions, dignifying labor, unionizing more workers, providing a collective voice to protect their rights, and compelling platform giants to comply with local labor laws and stop union-busting practices. The African Content Moderators Union faces organizing challenges, such as workers' precarity and their position as their families' primary breadwinners, workers' fear of joining due to retaliation by union-busting employers, and legal battles with tech

companies that often violate court orders and appeal lawsuits to block progress. Nonetheless, the union's membership has grown to around 400 since its formation, including workers from various African countries. The union's successful legal actions against Meta in Kenya may set a new precedent. It has gained international attention through social media outreach and high-profile news coverage, helping to amplify the workers' struggle and pressure tech companies to negotiate. James Oyange Odhiambo, a union member, expressed optimism about the union's potential impact: "People should know that it isn't just Meta—at every social media firm there are workers who have been brutalized and exploited. But today I feel bold, seeing so many of us resolve to make change." Overall, the African Content Moderators Union is an immensely positive development. The fight for better working conditions, fair pay, and adequate mental health support is not only a local issue but a global one, and labor internationalism is more important than ever (Bhalla, 2023; Haskins, 2024; Hendrix, 2023; Perrigo, 2023c).

Global Micro-Tasking and Ghost Work on Global Labor Market Platforms

Corporations are further dividing complex divisions of labor into greater complexities by breaking down the production of a complete good or service into ever more specialized tasks and hiring a large number of workers to do them. This is often referred to as "micro-tasking," where companies outsource small, cognitive tasks that are too basic for skilled labor but too complex for AI systems to workers logged into various apps and platforms (Cushing, 2012; Dubal, 2020; Gray & Suri, 2019; Jones, 2021; Lotz, 2022; Moreschi et al., 2020; Semuels, 2018; Press, 2021; Shestack, 2021). The workers who are hired to complete these tasks, often for minimal pay, are frequently referred to as micro-workers or digital pieceworkers. Companies post micro-tasks on platforms like CrowdFlower, Clickworker, Toluna, and Amazon Mechanical Turk, and some workers are contracted to complete them (Semuels, 2018). These platforms are interested and exploitative intermediaries between corporations and these micro-task contractors, and their owners take a cut from transactions (Jones, 2021). Google and Facebook might contract micro-taskers to complete tasks related to the training of their AI systems, image annotation for drone navigation, or chatbot programming.

In *Ghost Work: How to Stop Silicon Valley from Building a New Global Underclass*, Mary L. Gray and Siddharth Suri (2019) explore the lives and labors of these micro-taskers, or what they call "ghost workers." They refer to all those who do micro-tasks as "ghost workers" due to their mostly invisible presence on platforms and the non-recognition or undervaluing of their labors by companies and consumers alike: "the human labor powering many mobile phone apps, websites, and artificial intelligence systems can be hard to see. In fact, it's often intentionally hidden" (Gray & Suri, 2019, p. 7). Gray and Suri provide historical context for these workers, drawing parallels between what they do online today and the factory and home-based piece work that many workers did in the 19th century. From tagging images for machine learning algorithms to moderating social media content, these ghost workers complete many tasks, but are poorly compensated by their clients. All too often, these workers are dehumanized and exploited, treated as expendable parts of a larger profit-making machine. Nonetheless, these ghost workers are also often resilient. They form communities and share knowledge about their conditions and experiences, and some may also participate in collective campaigns for greater recognition, protection of their rights, and fairer pay. In *Work Without the Worker: Labour in the Age of Platform Capitalism*, Phil Jones (2021) also examines the precarious nature of all those workers engaged in the labor of micro-tasking. This type of labor is primarily done by workers in the Global South who are hired by companies and clients in the Global North. Workers are compensated per task rather than for the time spent on them, often receiving less than 20 cents per micro-task. Consequently, some workers earn as little as $2 per hour (Jones, 2021). Micro-task workers endure unpaid time searching for tasks to do, a constantly accelerating workflow, and algorithmically driven control systems. Furthermore, while workers who live and labor in specific locations often build collective identities and camaraderie, the millions doing ghost work from many different points on Earth tend to experience isolation. Nevertheless, some of these workers are trying to organize and take collective action, evident through small but significant expressions of solidarity and mutual support across platforms, including pro-worker platform initiatives such as Turkopticon and FairCrowdWork.

Amazon Mechanical Turk (MTurk)

Since its launch in 2005, Amazon Mechanical Turk (MTurk) has been a lead platform in the precarious world of ghastly and ghostly micro-work (Aytes, 2012; Bucher & Fieseler, 2017; Cushing, 2012; Grohmann & Araújo, 2021; Irani, 2015). MTurk is a crowdsourcing marketplace operated by Amazon Web Services. It enables individuals and companies (known as Requesters) to outsource tasks to a distributed workforce (known as Turkers or Workers). These tasks, known as Human Intelligence Tasks (HITs), are simple and repetitive activities that require human intelligence to complete, such as data entry, image tagging, surveys, content moderation, and transcription. Requesters can post tasks that can be completed by a large number of Turkers from around the world, leveraging the power of the so-called global digital crowd to accomplish tasks efficiently. Tasks posted on MTurk are typically those that are difficult for AI systems to do accurately but are relatively simple for humans, such as recognizing objects in images or transcribing audio recordings. Workers are compensated based on the completion of tasks, not the time it takes to do them. The payment for each task is determined by the Requester and can vary depending on the task. MTurk is used by a wide range of organizations, including academic researchers and companies, to collect data, conduct research, and perform various types of analysis that require human input. MTurk's labor model enables various Requesters to outsource work to independent contractors without providing traditional employment benefits or assuming liability for their wellness. This model allows Requesters to set low task prices, often resulting in minimal pay for the Turkers. Workers on MTurk can try to earn money from anywhere with an Internet connection. Sometimes, they earn less than $1 per hour and experience super-exploitation (Semuels, 2018). The platform's uptake by many corporations around the world underscores their exploitation of low cost human labor to increase their profits. In response to this, workers have communicated their struggles and shared their conditions and experiences on platforms such as Turkopticon, TurkerNation, and MTurkForum (Moreschi et al., 2020; Zyskowski & Milland, 2018).

Toward a New Labor Internationalism in the DMEI?

Most of the workers in the digital chains and circuits of the DMEI's trans-national production and distribution of digital hardware, software, and content are not autonomously producing for themselves, or with others in guilds, cooperatives, or workshops. They are foremostly workers, employed—contingently, part-time, and full-time—by some of the world's largest corporations and their cross-border networks of mid-sized contractor and smaller sub-contractor firms. All of these corporations, in turn, are motivated by the system of capitalism, which is governed by states and usually backed by national laws, policies, and regulations. States, whether in the US, China, or elsewhere, facilitate and legitimize trans-national corporate accumulation while proactively and reactively managing the system's many crises. The world market that the DMEI expands across is marked by widespread unmet basic needs and a growing disparity between the super-rich and everyone else. Poverty and precarious employment are increasing, and in affluent countries, even the US, life expectancy is declining. Concurrently, far-Right political parties are gaining ground, driven by xenophobia, sexism, racism, and ethno-nationalism, posing a significant threat to democracy. The world faces escalating international conflicts and wars, while global climate change affects all species. The DMEI is not solving these problems. After all, one cannot eat a selfie to survive, watch self-help videos on YouTube to stop fascism, or use X/Twitter to make Elon Musk stop war and climate catastrophe.

Nonetheless, corporations in the DMEI continue to prosper, and their outsourcing and sub-contracting out of work—iPhone assembly, Hollywood movie-making, digital games development, call center service work, remotely coordinated IT and software servicing, freelancing, CCM, and micro-tasking—relies on the labors of millions of workers from numerous countries. The cross-border production of digital media hardware, software, content, and service by so many corporations and workers in so many countries, regions, and cities complicates nationalistic notions of digital media, even though all of this production, exploitation, and profit happens in a world system of nation-states.

The globalization of work in the DMEI can be criticized for the bad conditions of life and labor it expects and reproduces. First, there's the *exploitation of labor*, exemplified by practices like outsourcing manufacturing jobs to countries with lower wages, as seen in AAMAM's outsourcing of hardware manufacture to Foxconn in China. The globalization of Hollywood movie production has also impacted local economies and jobs, particularly in Hollywood, where the studios' expansion to global locations offering tax incentives has led to local job losses, all the while encouraging precarious jobs elsewhere, subsidized by national governments. Additionally, the globalization of games development, call center service, and software and IT tasks underscore *income and wealth inequality*, where the CEOs of corporations amass big returns, while many workers receive minimal compensation. Moreover, there is *no universally accepted labor law framework* governing these cross-border production relationships, nor a global state or authority to enforce such labor standards. Consequently, workers are subject to a patchwork of legal principles and policies established by various nation-states, resulting in uncertain or insufficient protection of their labor rights, which ultimately empowers global capital to be a determiner and decider of these, locally. Furthermore, the practice of *global labor arbitrage*, where companies take advantage of cost differentials in labor markets across different countries and regions, outsourcing tasks to wherever the labor costs are lowest and driving down labor standards and expectations, results in immiserating working conditions and lower wages for workers everywhere. Last, *intensifying competition* between workers for contracts and gigs and tasks on these platforms can lead to a race to the bottom, where workers, compelled to outbid one another in hopes of securing a chance to get paid, accept lower and lower compensation, degrading and devaluing everyone's labor in the process. For all these reasons, the study of the globalization of work in the DMEI must attend to the asymmetrical power relations between the CEOs doing the globalizing and the workers whose local labor power their companies organize, hire, exploit, and fire. It is in these power relations that the hierarchical structure of the world system becomes clear: the post-colonial era is a neo-colonial one, where old and new imperial relations exist.

The everyday lives and labors of workers everywhere are more than ever interlinked into a global network of production relations, part of a web of local and global connections between companies and contractors in the DMEI, near and far. These workers are brought together by production relations coordinated by corporations across borders and time zones but dis-united as a working class for itself. One reason for this is geographical separation, as workers are dispersed across different countries and time zones, making coordinated collective communication, organizing and class action difficult. Another reason is the hodgepodge of national labor laws, policies, and regulations in each country, which make it difficult for workers to appeal to and benefit from a truly universal or collective labor right. Yet another reason are the cultural and language barriers, along with old atavistic and reloaded nationalist animosities, fears and passions, which may further stymie the communicative and social basis for international identifications and solidarities between workers. And the final reason are the entrepreneurial and freelancer ways of life and forms of hyper-individualization that may undercut the basis for workers' cooperation and collective identify formation and identification as a working class for itself.

Everyone interested in the globalization of work in the DMEI should shine a light on what global capital is doing to disorganize local labor but also, highlight challenges and opportunities faced by workers who are, against all odds, collectively contesting what capital is doing. Though a global class consciousness is constrained and deflected, there's imminent possibility for forging common ground between workers around the world through the globalizing DMEI. These new cross-border production networks hold opportunities for cross-cultural communication, the sharing of similar and different experiences of exploitation and oppression, the multitude of strategies, tactics and struggles, and the making of new collective identities, and solidarity (Woodcock, 2021). International labor organizations can play a role in linking workers across national boundaries and advocating for global labor standards and rights. Cross-border solidarity movements and social media campaigns can support worker rights in different countries and regions, while maintaining a focus on global capital-labor problems. Workers can use the platforms that exploit their labor as a means of pro-worker communication, organization, and resistance (Woodcock, 2021, p. 3). With pro-worker unions, social movements, organizations, and parties locally rooted within specific regions and countries, globally reaching out, weaving themselves together in solidarity with like-minded allies and affinity groups elsewhere, the possibility for building a world free from the cage of the DMEI and the inter-state system that entraps human potential becomes imaginable. With so many global social problems that no single state can solve alone, there is a real need for renewed workers' internationalism, and the DMEI is one space to organize that.

9 What Is the Platformization of Work in the DMEI?

Online Creators, Cultural Producers, and Influencers

Introduction

This chapter is an overview of the conditions, characteristics, and experiences of online creators, cultural producers, and influencers in the digital media and entertainment industries (DMEI). After describing the platform society, the platform giants, and core platform mechanisms ("datafication," "commodification," and "selection"), the chapter considers the rise of the "Creator Economy" and the labor processes and products of online creators, cultural producers, and social influencers. It then ponders the peculiar occupational status of these figures, showing how they don't quite fit into any pre-existing occupational categories (worker-employee, small business owner-entrepreneur, and self-employed freelancer). Although the online creator, cultural producer and influencer represent a relatively novel occupational role (and one performed by millions worldwide), the chapter shows how the labor these workers undertake for themselves or for their clients nonetheless supports the structural and relational power of Google, Meta Platforms and Amazon (GMA)—significant corporations in the DMEI. That said, the new platformization of work expresses a dialectic of continuity and change in Creator Capitalism, as well as a new creator labor politics whose history and future is in the making.

Platforms and Society

In *Keywords*, Raymond Williams (1976) defined society as the total social world in which we exist, or, "the body of institutions and relationships within which a relatively large group of people live" (p. 291). Over the past two decades, social media platforms (e.g., Facebook, YouTube, and TikTok) seem to be embedded everywhere, part of the body of institutions and relationships within which billions of people interact. While the traditional cultural industries and one-way transmissive media systems still exist (e.g., TV broadcasting), the Internet and World Wide Web support many-to-many

DOI: 10.4324/9781003131076-10

communications and enable their users to produce and consume content. With an increasing number of people all over the world logging into and using the services of websites and apps for an increasing amount of their life and work time, platforms have come to interweave with every facet of modern society, from the economic structure of capitalism to the politics of state and civil society to everyday cultural relations and practices. The concept of the "platform society" points to how integral platforms have become to society, and how platforms "are gradually infiltrating in, and converging with, the (offline, legacy) institutions and practices" through which democratic and authoritarian societies are organized (van Dijck et al., 2018, p. 2).

But what exactly is a platform? The term "platform" is multifaceted, connoting a wide range of objects, systems, and practices. It includes the foundational software that supports and enables various applications to run, such as operating systems. Additionally, platforms extend to social networking sites and services designed for social interaction, content sharing, data aggregation, and advertising, as well as to online content creation, publishing, distribution, and streaming services. In *Platform Capitalism*, Nick Srnicek (2017) describes platforms as intermediaries between different users, customers, advertisers, and service providers. Contrasting this, Jose van Dijck, Thomas Poell, and Martin de Waal (2018) show in *The Platform Society* how platforms are not neutral but are interested mediators that actively shape users' interactions. In *Platforms and Cultural Production*, Thomas Poell, David Nieborg and Brooke Erin Duffy (2021, p. 5) define platforms as "data infrastructures that facilitate, aggregate, monetize and govern interactions between end-users and content and service providers." Owned by some of the world's largest corporations, platforms are at the economic core a proprietary or "privatized infrastructure" designed to generate revenue (Andrejevic, 2012; Gillespie, 2018; Jin, 2015; van Dijck et al., 2018).

Most of the world's largest social media platforms are under the ownership of major corporations like Alphabet-Google (owner of YouTube), Apple (owner of AppStore, Messages and FaceTime), Meta (owner of Facebook, Instagram, and WhatsApp), Amazon (owner of Twitch), and Microsoft (owner of LinkedIn and GitHub). These US-based companies, along with their growing and globalizing counterparts in China (WeChat, Sina Weibo, Douyin, Bilibili), significantly influence the economic models, hardware and software infrastructures, and political and ideological superstructures of the world platform ecosystem, shaping the framework through which billions of users interact with one another (van Dijck et al., 2018). These corporations are leading figures in "information capitalism" (Fuchs, 2010, 2014), "platform capitalism" (Srnicek, 2017), and "surveillance capitalism" (Zuboff, 2019). Their platforms are designed for the systematic collection, algorithmic processing, and monetization of user data (van Dijck et al., 2018). They use mechanisms of "datafication" (turning various aspects of social life into quantifiable data), "commodification" (transforming user data into commodities), and "selection" (using algorithms to steer user interaction based on inferred personal interests) (van Dijck et al., 2018, pp. 31–48). These platforms are also key to the rise of the "social media entertainer," "influencer," and "platform cultural producer" (Bishop, 2022; Cunningham & Craig, 2016, 2019, 2021; Poell et al., 2021), new occupations which are part of novel industry groups in the DMEI being defined and redefined right now.

The Rise of the Creator Economy: Social Media Entertainment and Platforms of Cultural Production

In 2016, Stuart Cunningham and David Craig (2016) identified a new globalizing social media entertainment (SME) industry. Their research, conducted over two years and involving over 135 interviews with executives, content creators, and various managers and analysts, found a "proto-industry" taking shape across "global online screen entertainment platforms" (Cunningham & Craig, 2016, p. 5412). This burgeoning SME industry was founded on the "technological, networking, and commercial affordances" of social media platforms and comprises a "rapidly professionalizing and monetizing wave of diverse, multicultural, previously amateur content creators" from across the globe who use platforms to develop their media brands, create, and publish all kinds of content, and cultivate massive, trans-national fan communities (Cunningham & Craig, 2016, p. 5412). In *Social Media Entertainment: The New Intersection of Hollywood and Silicon Valley*, Cunningham and Craig (2019) tracked the lives and labors of many of these new entrepreneurial creators. In their follow-up edited volume *Creator Cultures*, Cunningham and Craig (2021) staked claim to an interdisciplinary field of "Creator Studies" and showcased the labor and products of a diversity of online creators—YouTubers, Twitch gamers, Instagram influencers, TikTokers, among others. From the US to China, online creators are entrepreneurial individuals who produce and publish digital media content and engage with their clients and communities on major social media platforms.

A related landmark contribution to an understanding of the new occupational roles and labor processes unfolding across social media platforms was advanced by Brooke Erin Duffy, Thomas Poell, and David Nieborg's (2019) special issue of *Social Media + Society* on the "Platformization of Cultural Production." As they point out, "contemporary platforms" are "reconfiguring the production, distribution, and monetization of cultural content in staggeringly complex ways" (1). They attended to the "transformed nature of cultural production" (1) in the society of platforms. In *Platforms and Cultural Production*, Poell et al. (2021) present a systematic overview of new and emerging forms of cultural production on platforms. For these researchers, platform "cultural producers" refer to a "broad range of actors and organizations engaged in the creation, distribution, marketing, and monetization of symbolic products" within and across these platforms (Poell et al., 2021, p. 180). They present a comprehensive framework that highlights the opportunities and challenges faced by platform cultural producers, as related to continuity and change in the cultural industries, law, policy and regulation, precarious work and labor processes, technological affordances and algorithms, and democracy.

Richard Florida (2022), renowned and notorious for coining the term "creative class" and advising elites in government culture ministries, creative industries, and academia on how to build creative cities, examines the new dynamics of the SME and platforms of cultural production in his Meta Platforms-funded study, "The Rise of the Creator Economy." Drawing from a thorough review of over 75 reports, studies, articles, and books, along with interviews with researchers, thought leaders, and creators, Florida defines the "Creator Economy" as the broad economic and social infrastructure supporting creators: the training institutions, networks of startup companies, intermediaries, and advertisers, digital tools, and platforms like Facebook, YouTube, Instagram, TikTok, Substack, and Patreon (Florida, 2022, p. 3). Florida introduces a potential new occupational category, defining "Creators" as individuals who are getting entrepreneurial when using digital hardware and software to innovate, produce, and publish creative content such as video, art, music, design, text, games, or other media. These Creators monetize their work through memberships, subscriptions, digital tips, advertising, brand partnerships, endorsements, direct platform funding, and other digital payment forms (Florida, 2022, p. 3). The Creator Economy is mostly concentrated in the US, with significant hubs in the San Francisco Bay Area, Los Angeles, and New York City. However, it is expanding both nationally and internationally, as indicated by creator startups in over 65 cities around the world (Florida, 2022, p. 3).

In the Creator Economy, the most famous Tubers and TikTokers are followed by millions of people around the world (Bruce, 2021), and they are not only influencing minds on behalf of their respective clients and communities but also inspiring new career paths for young people to follow (MacDonald, 2022; Min, 2019). Many teens reportedly dream of becoming a "social media star" and a 2021 YouGov survey found jobs like YouTuber, streamer, or vlogger ranking in their respondents' top five career choices. The Creator Economy is a vast labor force, now encompassing anywhere from 30 to 85 million Americans and approximately 300 million people worldwide (Florida, 2022). Signal Fire estimates there are about 50 million creators globally, including 2 million professionals and 48 million amateurs (Yuan & Constine, 2020). Citibank projects there are over 120 million creators, and a 2023 Goldman Sachs report predicted that the Creator Economy would double in size, from US$250 billion to $500 billion, by 2027. Moreover, Bishop (2022) argues that the knowledge and skill related to being an "influencer" is creeping out of the Creator Economy and into professions across numerous industries: "Influencer creep can be felt most keenly in sectors that operate on freelance and insecure labor," where workers do unpaid promotional work try to make a positive image of themselves for a variety of prospective constituents. As Bishop (2022) explains, "Workers must play to audiences, clients, bosses, and platforms all at the same time, with no guarantee that any of it will pay off."

The Creator Economy is not an island unto itself; it is now deeply interconnected with and influences all industries and sectors. The laws, policies and regulations for governing the Creator Economy continue to be a work in progress, with different nation-states developing common and unique governance frameworks. The US state has historically taken a relatively hands-off approach to governing the global Creator Economy, allowing companies like YouTube, TikTok, and Instagram to operate with significant autonomy to determine the terms and conditions that govern their platforms and billions of service users. However, the Federal Trade Commission (FTC) has recently implemented guidelines to ensure transparency in influencer marketing, requiring creators to disclose sponsored content clearly. Additionally, the proposed American Innovation and Choice Online Act and the Open App Markets Act represent a potential shift toward more robust creator economy regulation. In China, the party-state governs its Creator Economy through stringent regulations enforced by the Cyberspace Administration of China (CAC), requiring creator laborers to follow content guidelines, register their names, and sometimes promote content convivial to the state's national culture. In Europe, the Digital Services Act (DSA) and the Digital Markets Act (DMA) represent regulatory frameworks that aim to enhance transparency, accountability, and fairness in the Creator Economy. The DSA focuses on content moderation, user rights, and platform accountability, while the DMA aims to curb the market dominance of major American tech platforms, fostering a more competitive and equitable environment for smaller creators. In Canada, Bill C-11, also known as the Online Streaming Act, aims to regulate platforms like YouTube and TikTok, requiring them to contribute to the creation of Canadian content and adhere to Canadian broadcasting standards. This legislation seeks to level the playing field between Canadian-owned broadcasters and US-based platforms while ensuring Canadian content creators receive fair compensation and visibility. For some time, US-based neoliberal legal, policy, and regulatory standards, norms, and values governing the general Internet and digital communication system constituted the tacit governance framework for the global Creator Economy. But as millions from around the world entered the creator economy, the laissez-faire approach has gradually given way to stronger intervention by territorial nation-states, which seek to design and enforce their own public interest and cultural and techno-nationalist frameworks for governing the conduct of US platforms and their service users. In any case, anyone who pursues a career as an online creator will have their labor shaped by the economic structure of global digital capitalism and the political structures of nation-states, as well as the specific organizational and institutional frameworks of the corporations that own and control the platforms.

Although star and celebrity content creators (MrBeast, Charli D'Amelio, Cristiano Ronaldo, etc.) are frequently seen as the faces of the Creator Economy, millions of ordinary workers are learning that online creator gigs are in demand and growing across the economy. In the healthcare industry, medical professionals are working with influencers to share public health information and combat disinformation and misinformation. In finance, content creators are being employed as digital storytellers for bank brands. Even manufacturing and agricultural firms hire influencers to connect with their consumers. Governmental agencies are also leveraging online creators for strategic communications, public affairs and community engagement. Political parties employ influencers to reach their constituents and move citizens to vote for their leaders (Racker, 2022; Riedl et al., 2023). Non-profit, non-governmental, and advocacy organizations, as well as social movements, partner with online creators to raise consciousness about social problems. These "Creators for Change" (C4C) (https://creators4change.com/) encompass "all the individuals, groups, and movements concerned with social justice that harness platforms to creatively agitate and advocate for social change" related to environmental sustainability, EDI, democracy, human rights, and more. Spitfire Strategies (https://www.spitfirestrategies.com) suggests current and future growth in partnerships between online creators and social advocacy organizations.

In addition to the creative entrepreneurs working independently to try to make a living through their own channels and social media handles, there's significant increases in the Creator Economy labor force due to cross-sectoral demand for workers who possess the knowledge and skill of utilizing digital hardware, software, and social media platforms for engaging and informing audiences, as well as shaping public perceptions and thoughts on wide range of things and topics, from smartphones to energy policy. Over the past eight years or so, research on those who labor for the Creator Economy's industries of SME, influence, and platform cultural production has boomed. This is showcased by the most comprehensive and up-to-date reading list on the "Influencer Industries & Creator Culture" field, generously and continuously updated by Dr. Zoë Glatt (2024). Researchers in the field have examined: influencers on Instagram and other platforms (Abidin, 2018; Arriagada & Ibáñez, 2019, 2020; Bishop, 2022; Carman, 2020; Cong & Li, 2023; Duffy, 2020; Glatt, 2022b, 2023; Hearn & Schoenhoff, 2015; Hudders & Lou, 2023; Hund, 2023; O'Meara, 2019; O'Neill, 2019; Psarras et al., 2023; Salamon, 2015; Stevens, 2022; Stoldt et al., 2019; Trujillo, 2016; Wellman, 2020, 2021); YouTubers (Andrejevic, 2009; Bishop, 2018a, 2018b, 2019; Cunningham & Craig, 2017; Glatt,

2022a; Glatt & Banet-Weiser, 2022; Marwick, 2015; Postigo, 2016; Siciliano, 2021); and all kinds of online creators, social media entertainers, and platform cultural producers (Chayka, 2021; Carpenter & Lertpratchya, 2016; Cunningham & Craig, 2016, 2019, 2021; Duffy, 2017; Duffy et al., 2019, 2021; Florida, 2022; Glatt, 2022b, 2023; Hund, 2023; Lin, 2023; Mirrlees, 2020, 2023; Nieborg & Poell, 2018; Poell et al., 2021; Su, 2023; Yuan & Constine, 2020). Using questionnaires, interviews, case studies, digital ethnographies, participant observation, and discourse analysis, researchers have probed on the meso and micro conditions, experiences, challenges, and opportunities of laboring in the Creator Economy.

While some of the individuals who are learning to labor as influencers and creators are driven by intrinsic rewards like a passion for a topic and care of community rather than external incentives like fame and fortune, many individuals leaping into the creator labor market are self-conscious professionals. They are "getting entrepreneurial" with the goal of not only making ends meet but also making a solid living, maybe even making it rich. Yet, the Creator Economy is not a meritocracy. While a few of these creators end up accumulating millions, most do not. Although platforms like YouTube and TikTok ostensibly "democratize" content creation, not all creators enjoy equal opportunities for success. Creators from privileged backgrounds have an advantage over those from vulnerable or already marginalized groups, and society's intersecting inequities and oppressions of classism, racism, sexism, ableism, and ageism don't disappear on platforms. Algorithmic biases on these platforms can reproduce or even exacerbate existing inequities and oppressions by favoring certain creator identities and types of content over others, benefiting those who've already benefitted. And whether rich or poor, an avatar for a majoritarian or minoritarian positionality or worldview, all creators must abide the mechanisms of platform capitalism. When making and trying to monetize their content within platform markets not of their own choosing, creators must—out of necessity—compete with one another for visibility, subscribers and followers, advertising partnerships, corporate sponsorships, merchandise sales and donations (Cunningham & Craig, 2022; Poell et al., 2021). In effect, many of these workers conduct themselves as small businesses, competing against others in attention economies characterized by precarity, winner-take-all for the few, low to no pay for most, work-life boundary blurs, and rampant burnout (Duffy et al., 2021; Glatt, 2022a, 2022b; Poell et al., 2021). These workers' livelihood rests on their entrepreneurial acumen and ability to flexibly re-adjust their "authentic" personas, branded content and practices to every platforms' monetization model, tools, interfaces, community guidelines, and algorithmic regime (Poell et al., 2021, p. 180).

Virtual Influencers: Automating Creators?

Lil Miquela has 3.5 million followers on TikTok and another 2.6 million on Instagram. Since her debut in 2016 she has earned an average of $2 million annually by talking up brands including Dior, Calvin Klein, and BMW. In 2023, she was paid approximately $10,000 per Instagram post (Hwang, Zhang, Liu, and Srinivasan, 2024; Nguyen, 2023). Lil Miquela is far less likely than traditional influencers to burnout and berate her sponsors or followers, because she's a computer-generated avatar, programmed and controlled by a marketing company called Bruds. Virtual influencers—digital avatars that captivate millions with always-available personas—are transforming content creation, marketing and consumption online (Hwang, Zhang, Liu, and Srinivasan, 2024; Nguyen, 2023). Virtual influencers are produced using CGI (computer-generated imagery), motion-capture technology, and AI systems, and are rented and deployed on behalf of brands to target and resonate with specific audiences. They can be categorized into three main types: non-humans, animated humans, and life-like CGI humans. Dating back to the Japanese "virtual idol" Kyoko Date, today's virtual influencers offer unique advantages to brand marketers, from their ageless and scandal-free existence to their ability to communicate in multiple languages anywhere at any time, all the time (Hwang, Zhang, Liu, and Srinivasan, 2024; Nguyen, 2023). For many brand marketing companies looking to keep costs low and profits high, virtual influencers are a cost-efficient or cheap alternative to the labor of human influencers. While human influencers with millions of followers may demand hundreds of thousands of dollars per post, the virtual influencer Lil Miquela's 2020 rate per post was approximately $12,600. There are a number of concerns surrounding virtual influencers, the first being transparency. As they become more human-like, distinguishing them from real people online pose challenges, raising fears that consumers will be deceived and manipulated. Also, the industry's use of virtual replicas of real people, including deepfakes, the absence of the consent of the individual being simulated, and the exploitation of their image or likeness, is surrounded by controversy. Furthermore, the rampant hiring of virtual influencers impacts the job prospects of human content creators and disrupts the broader labor market. Human influencers now face competition from their digital counterparts, and with a reserve digital army of virtual influencers paid less than humans, this pushes down the cost of labor, sometimes even eliminates the need for it by automating the work of influencing. For example, brand marketers for companies including Prada, Cartier, Disney, Puma, Nike, and Tiffany now use the service of virtual influencers to promote their products. While the design and management of virtual influencers creates new job opportunities for those skilled in this area and generates revenue for the companies that own these, the rise of virtual influences reduces labor market demand for human influencers. They represent a significant development in the online Creator Economy, and it is likely that the coexistence of virtual and human influencers will shape the future of influencing (Hwang, Zhang, Liu, and Srinivasan, 2024; Nguyen, 2023).

What Is the Occupational Status of a Creator?: Not Quite a Worker-Employee, Small Business Owner-Entrepreneur, Self-Employed Freelancer

The occupational status of online creators is an expansive grey zone, an ambiguous, indeterminate, or undefined area that falls between clear-cut definitions and classifications. They are sometimes described as creative workers or cultural producers, small-business owners and entrepreneurs, or self-employed freelancers. Yet, none of these old occupational concepts fully captures the specificity of the online creator. I'll unpack each of these occupational categories, showing why the creator does not fit directly into any of them.

Worker-Employee

Online creators are sometimes described as workers, which might connote employment with a company in the DMEI. Yet, a YouTuber or Instagram influencer typically does not fit the traditional classification of a worker or employee for several reasons. Unlike traditional waged workers or employees, YouTubers and Instagram influencers do not have a formal employment relationship with the companies that own the platforms they labor on (e.g., Google for YouTube, Meta Platforms for Instagram). They are not hired by these companies under contract, do not receive a regular salary, and do not enjoy the same labor law protections, nor the benefits that come with formal employment, such as health insurance, pension contributions, or paid leave. As result, they are legally classified as independent contractors, not employees. Also, creators arguably enjoy slightly more autonomy over their labor process and output than most waged workers, whose activities and products are typically directly controlled by their employers. While consumer markets and algorithms do influence creators' decisions, they may have more freedom than employees at companies like Wal-Mart or Fox News, who must adhere to corporate directives and objectives, production regimes, schedules, and brand ideology. Compared to waged workers for big corporations, creators arguably enjoy more flexibility in choosing what to produce, how to produce and deciding their work schedules. Relatedly, creators are mostly "remote workers" who labor from their own homes or rented studio spaces; unlike many waged workers, who go to a place of work, at a specific company, the companies that own the platforms do not provide creators with a physical workspace. Furthermore, unlike the waged worker, the creator's income is not fixed or predictable; instead, it's primarily generated through advertising revenue, sponsorships, merchandise sales, and other forms of monetization that are directly tied to their personality and their product's popularity. The waged worker is not compelled to directly take responsibility for the employer's customers and sales; but the creator must carry the burden of financial risk and constantly produce content that builds and retains an audience to maintain or increase their income. Additionally, whereas the relationship between employers and employees is governed by employment contracts, the relationship between the companies that own the platforms that creators depend on to do their work, and the creators themselves, is usually governed by terms of service agreements. These agreements do not establish a legally binding employer-employee relationship but instead outline the terms and conditions of using the platform and how revenue generated from content is parsed out. For all these reasons, creators don't reflect the occupational category of a waged worker or employee.

Small Business Owner-Entrepreneur

Online creators are frequently described as entrepreneurs or small business owners. Alone or with a small team, they develop a brand, create content, and monetize it. They "get entrepreneurial." While many YouTuber or Instagram creators do identify as business owners or entrepreneurs, they might not always fit a strict or traditional classification as such. For one, corporations and even small businesses usually own and control capital assets and employ workers to do jobs for them. But creators frequently operate without much capital overlay, and they labor independently or with a small team of likeminded producers. Also, it would be unusual to find a large or small business dependent exclusively upon another for its very existence, and yet, the business model of creators heavily relies on third-party platforms owned by the most powerful corporations in the world to publish content and generate income. The creator's dependency on another corporation's means of production and circulation makes them seem more like dependent contractors to that corporation and its infrastructure rather than a full-fledged business that owns and controls its means of production and distribution outright. Furthermore, traditional media businesses sell their products and services directly to consumers: a cable TV broadcaster sells subscriptions to its content service and also sells scheduled space and time to advertisers, looking to reach that company's viewing audience. But creators do not "sell" their core product or service to the majority of people who view and consume it. Instead, they sell their service of informing, entertaining, and influencing people to corporate sponsors (brand advertisers) and advertisers (ad revenue sharing agreements with platform companies) and may also sell ancillary goods like merchandise to their followers and fans. For these reasons, the creator does not fit directly within conventional categories of the small media business owner or media entrepreneur, and yet, their habitus and practices express entrepreneurial norms and values. They must invest in capital, identify a market (of clients and consumers), develop a product (the content they create), build a brand that is attractive and authentic-seeming, attract an audience, engage in multi-platform marketing, and strive to make money, much like a business owner.

Self-Employed Freelancer

Creators are sometimes considered to be self-employed freelancers because they work on a project basis for branding, advertising, and marketing firms who've been contracted by larger corporate clients to put the image of their product or service in front of the target consumer. As self-employed freelancers, they work for themselves, engage in self-branding, search for and secure contracts or "gigs," negotiate contracts for sponsorships and other partnerships with clients, manage their own labor process in concordance with project timelines, and earn income from the sale of their communication, personality, and influence services to those who demand them. While YouTubers and Instagram influencers share some characteristics with self-employed freelancers, there are nuances. First, these creators are dependent on the services of one or a few major corporations' platforms to publish their content, attract and reach an audience, and generate income. In contrast, many self-employed freelancers make themselves visible and readable on a diverse array of platforms—or none at all—to find or attract clients and eventually sell their services. This means a creator's labor process is frequently intertwined with a specific platform, whereas freelancers have the flexibility to choose from multiple platforms or directly engage with clients. The key distinction lies in the income source: creators primarily earn from their service labor on one or a few platforms, while freelancers assemble their income by selling their service across various platforms to multiple clients. Also, creators and freelancers do not always share the same business model. For example, YouTubers and Instagram influencers typically generate their income through ad revenue, sponsored content, affiliate marketing, and merchandise sales, through the platform. In contrast, freelancers are usually paid directly by clients for the specific services they produce. Furthermore, creators must labor under the terms and conditions set by the platforms, meaning there are significant restrictions on what they can produce and how they can monetize it. The fear of the platform going under or of being de-platformed always looms large. In contrast, freelancers may have more control over their labor process, and greater flexibility to select projects from clients who demand their knowledge and skills without the same level of restriction from a third-party intermediary, with its own vested profit interests in serving advertisers. Additionally, the relationship between creators, freelancers, and their clients may be distinctive. Creators might work through intermediary agencies or the platforms' built-in advertising and sponsorship mechanisms to secure lucrative partnerships or brand deals with clients. Freelancers may work directly with clients, not intermediaries or platform infrastructures, and negotiate the contracts, deliverables, and payments directly with the clients. In sum, while online creators may be viewed as independent contractors providing services to other businesses, they are not exactly the same as self-employed freelancers.

Overall, the occupational status of the creator is a grey zone, not only because creators do not easily fit the category or classification of worker-employee, small business-entrepreneur, and self-employed freelancer but because the creator itself does not frequently have a stable referent in an industry grouping that most entities responsible for gathering information and data about labor force dynamics recognize. At the present time, one is unlikely to find the category of "creator" mobilized consistently if at all by most government labor ministries, agencies, or bureaus that collect and publish data about industries, labor markets, and occupations, nor by the tax authorities that have us all declare our employment status or occupation on annual tax return forms. There is no clear online creator or influence industry code in the NAICS. In AAMAM transparency reports, industry literature, academic research, and creators associations, occupational concepts for creators continue to be in flux, despite many attempts to craft a stable definition. Whether defined as a worker, an entrepreneur or a freelancer, or something else altogether, all creators work within a capitalist system and are shaped by the system's old and new logics, and labor hazards. With an eye to continuity and change, I provide a broad overview of the eight core capitalist logics undergirding the "Creator Economy," or GMA's "Creator Capitalism."

Creator Capitalism: Google-Meta-Amazon (GMA) Rule: Structural and Relational Power

Alphabet-Google, Amazon, Meta, Apple, and Microsoft—collectively known as AAMAM—are among the most powerful corporations in the world, wielding significant platform influence that is ubiquitous and which intersects with the life-labor process of millions of creators around the world. Some of the key AAMAM players in the Creator Economy include Google, with its platform YouTube; Meta, through Instagram and Facebook; and Amazon, via Twitch.

To fully understand the magnitude of GMA's platform power vis-à-vis creators, we can conceptualize power as both "structural" and "relational" (Mirrlees, 2021). GMA possesses vast *structural power*, encompassing ownership and control of capital assets, including the proprietary platforms that creators labor through, as well as market capitalization, revenue, and IP portfolios. While structural power provides a meso-level understanding of GMA's influence over creator labor, *relational power* is useful for probing micro power relations between GMA and their many service users, including creators. Here, power is a dynamic relationship between at least two or more entities, with one of those willfully acting to try get the other to act in ways that align with their strategic goal. As Michel Foucault (1982) famously put it, "The exercise of power consists in guiding the possibility of [a subject's] conduct and putting in order the possible outcome." GMA not only elicits the willing and consensual participation of creators through user agreements and mobilizes their consent to service terms and conditions and community guidelines but also employs repressive techniques to punish creators who break the rules. GMA's structural and relational power plays a significant role in shaping the framework of creator labor, but as GMA are shaped by the broader logics of capitalism, they matter too. GMA's combined power, plus the eight core logics of capitalism, are key to understanding the material conditions undergirding creator labor, as well as the possibilities and limits of creator empowerment.

Corporate Ownership of Production, Distribution, and Exhibition

The GMA own many of the platforms that creators use to labor. At the same time, these creators must invest in their own content production tools: high-performance computers, quality cameras, microphones, stabilizing equipment, and lighting setups, as well as software tools for image, video, and audio editing. The power relationship between GMA and creators is asymmetric, with corporations exercising considerable influence over creators, and creators having very little influence over decisions made by these firms. Corporations decide the user agreements and community guidelines that creators agree to, which limit what creators do and how they do it, and outline consequences for dissent. They decide the general business models creators rely on to try to earn a living, and the algorithms they play to. While GMA own the platforms that underpin creator content distribution and exhibition, content creators own a very small means of production.

Division between Owners and Workers

In GMA, there is a clear organizational and hierarchical division between owners and workers, with Boards and CEOs at the top, and waged workers from top to bottom. There is also a structural division between those who own GMA, and all those millions of creators laboring on the platforms, even though they are not formally employed by them. In some ways, the CEOs and the higher tier labor force of the GMA are the invisible "managers" to creators, because it is they who make the major decisions about the platform's monetization models, infrastructure and interface designs, and algorithms that weight upon creator labor processes and products. In this regard, there is still a division between the owners of the platform (GMA and their CEOs) and creators who in many ways are working for these companies, and apropos "network effects," absolutely essential to the popularity and profitability of their platforms.

Waged Labor, Labor Market, Division of Labor

The relationship between GMA and creators is not based on the traditional wage relationship. The GMA do not hire creators and pay them for their knowledge and skill, nor do they pay them to make videos and post content on their platforms. These Silicon Valley firms don't pay creators for the labor of content creation but, instead, provide these creators with services that they may try to use to get paid through ad revenue sharing, sponsorships, viewer donations, and merchandise sales. The establishments that may pay for the creator's labor include a wide variety of intermediaries and sponsors, such as ad firms, non-profits, and even government agencies. Also, the audiences amassed by creators may also indirectly pay for the creator's labor. For example, on YouTube, ad revenue is directly linked to audience engagement with the creator's content, and the individual followers of creators may donate to the creator or purchase some merchandise from them. Furthermore, whereas the traditional division of labor in GMA involves splitting the labor process of making a product or service into many tasks, with a number of workers hired to play specific roles, in the GMA's platform framework, a creator frequently plays multiple roles covering a total labor process: conceptualizing, writing, acting, filming, editing, and marketing videos, and then interacting with audiences.

Production for Profit, Not for Human Need

GMA are all profit-seeking corporations, and they are foremostly interested in producing goods and services that will support their bottom line. Regardless of the personal motivations of the millions of creators—passion, self-expression, altruism, or community engagement—their knowledge and skill contributes to the profit interests of the GMA. The GMA's revenue strategies depend significantly on the labor of content creators, labor they do not pay for. For example, advertising revenues are driven by creators attracting audiences to the platform. Ad revenue-sharing models encourage more content production but often favor the platform owners' revenue accumulation. Premium features and subscription services also benefit from the creators' labors to produce exclusive content. User data generated by creators' audience engagement is monetized as well, underscoring creators' indirect contribution to platform data monetization. Sponsorships and e-commerce features facilitated by platforms rely on creators' own brand building and audience engagement. While individual creators may have diverse motivations, the corporations that own the platforms put the creators' labor to work for their profit.

Market Competition and Market Control

While GMA exercise something of an oligopoly or monopoly over a large chunk of the Creator Economy, creators themselves often engage in fierce market competitions with one another for audience attention, likes, follows, shares, ad revenue, and algorithmic favoritism. Creators not only produce engaging content in competition with others but also cultivate a distinct personal brand and cross-promote it everywhere to stand out in a glutted market. While this cutthroat individualistic competition between creators produces network effects for the GMA, bolstering their bottom line, the "market competition" between creators occurs within a platform market structure that is oligopolistic and monopolistic, pretty much ruled by the GMA and their subsidiaries. The paradox? Competition between creators is fierce, but competition between the owners of the platforms they labor through is not.

Exploitation

In GMA, exploitation typically revolves around workers being compensated with wages that do not equate to the full value they create. The surplus value generated from their labor is accrued by the corporation

What Is the Platformization of Work in the DMEI? 231

as profit. While GMA exploit their waged labor force in old-fashioned ways, their exploitation of creators differs because of the absence of the traditional employer-employee wage relationship. The GMA use their service users, or creators, for their ends, and this can be conceived as *exploitation*. Creators invest an immense amount of knowledge and skill, and time and effort, into producing content for distribution and exhibition on GMA's platforms. But these creators are not compensated for this labor, nor its product. While some eke out a living, most earn a pittance or nothing at all. Millions of creators give billions of hours of unpaid or under-compensated labor to platforms that serve GMA's bottom line. After all, creators are essential to the business models of these platforms: no content uploaded to platform, no users attracted to platform, no data accumulated, no revenue generated by platform's ad service sales. While many creators grapple with low to no-waged work and financial precarity, the elite of GMA, including their CEOs, are some of the wealthiest people in the world. Corporate profits swell exponentially as a direct result of the collective labor of creators, who are all too often left coping with immiseration.

Crisis and Cycles of Boom and Bust

GMA are impacted by the crisis tendencies of capitalism, and the system's disruptive boom and bust cycles, but creators are impacted much more harshly than these firms because of their precarious predicament. In capitalism, economic booms often lead to increased corporate spending on advertising and consumer spending in media, benefiting creators through more partnership deals and monetization opportunities. But during economic downturns, advertising and consumer spending diminishes, corporate branding budgets are cut and consumer dollars flow to essential goods, reducing creators' incomes. Downturns hit creators hard, harder than the corporations that own the platforms they labor on. Unlike the full-time employees of GMA, creators lack regular pay and labor protections.

Class, Income, and Wealth Inequality

In GMA, there are significant pay gaps between CEOs and workers, but most creators who work on platforms owned by GMA are at the basement floor of income and wealth distribution. While CEOs such as Mark Zuckerberg, Adam Mosseri, Sundar Pichai, and Neal Mohan control fortunes, many creators, despite their entrepreneurial outlook and work ethic, are part of the working poor. The top 1% of creators amass 99% of total income, while two-thirds make less than $25,000 annually, and over a quarter earn less than $1,000 (Florida, 2022). Less than 4% of creators make over $100,000 a year. The multi-million annual earnings of top YouTubers like MrBeast, Markiplier, Unspeakable, Like Nastya, and Ryan's World contrast with the multitude of creators struggling to earn something close to a livable wage. A mere 3% of top-viewed YouTube channels garner significant revenue, while many YouTubers earn below the poverty line (Bärtl, 2018). For every PewDiePie and middling TikTok celebrity, there are tens of thousands of creators barely make a living. Inequality exists between the CEOs of the platforms that creators toil on, and also, between a small group of elite creators, and everyone else.

Class Tension and Conflict

Class tension and conflict exist within GMA: Alphabet Workers Union covers Google employees; Meta Platforms workers are not unionized, but many engage in labor activism, overt and covert; Amazon is a flashpoint of contemporary class struggle and union campaigns. In formal employment relations, class tensions and conflicts between capital and organized and disorganized labor emerge around working conditions, wages paid, benefits, and more. In the Creator Economy, creators are not formally employed by corporations, so cannot directly bargain with owners over the terms and conditions of work, and lack a collective labor voice on platforms. Nonetheless, some creators have tried to organize and collectivize, to strengthen their power vis-à-vis GMA, and there is an emerging collective creator labor politics. Some creators also coordinate collective log outs from and boycotts of platforms to dissent against GMA. Some creators exit GMA's platforms and seek out alternatives or forge new cooperative networks.

Labor Hazards of Creator Capitalism: Creator Collective Action and Class Struggle

While Creator Capitalism offers some new opportunities for paid and unpaid work, it, like the wider DMEI, has several labor hazards. Like many careers in the DMEI, the creator field is stratified by class differences and intersectional inequities. Creators from affluent backgrounds possess the means to acquire high-quality production tools and pay for advanced training and skills development, which may give them an advantage over their less privileged creator counterparts. Also, wealthy creators can leverage their existing monies and professional connections to open doors that remain locked to the poor. Most creators experience precarity, and frequently labor for little to no pay. They put lots of time and energy into their labor process and digital products, with uncertain and inadequate returns. Additionally, the creator labor market is oversaturated with highly skilled and talented individuals competing for limited contracts with sponsors, and ever thinner and segmented slices of the online demographic pie: the abundance of creators available for work translates into reduced standards and diminished bargaining power for all. Corporations now have more online "personalities" to partner their brands with than ever before, reducing the value of each. Furthermore, creators lack the governmental labor protections of regular employees. Classified as independent contractors, they do not have access to benefits and the costs of healthcare insurance pile up quick. Meanwhile, the personal and psychological consequences of being a creator are many. "Instagram-perfect" images belie a massive mental health crisis. Burnout is also rampant. YouTubers endure exhaustive production schedules that consume weekends and holidays, while Instagram influencers blur life and work, curating their feeds and engaging with followers, often feeling guilty for any time spent alone or in worry of missing an opportunity to engage and potentially, get liked or followed. Despite its meritocratic shine, the Creator Economy discriminates: creators of color and LGBTQ+ folk have been found to be paid less for labor than their white cis counterparts by the same brand sponsors. Also, creators from minority groups are often targeted with hate and harassment, even death threats. This can have profound mental health consequences, leading to anxiety, stress, and fear, and in extreme cases, creators just quitting the platform.

While the Creator Economy may appear to offer a new way for countless people to level the playing field and level up, its meritocratic ideology can also conceal substantive unfreedom and inequality that is consistent with the history of capitalism. As such, the Creator Economy represents the labor movement's next organizing opportunity (Curl, 2022), and many online creators, even the best remunerated, are becoming interested in unions (Craig & Cunningham, 2023; Stanley, 2024). Creators, often working in isolation from one another and embracing entrepreneurial and meritocratic ideologies, were initially slow to embrace the idea of collective organization and action. However, a growing awareness of the structural and relational power disparities between GMA, advertising companies, a wide range of sketchy intermediaries, and creators, has sparked an attitude change among these workers. Kajabi, the creator commerce platform, surveyed 2,000+ high-earning creators across the world who make over $100,000 per year. Overall, 46% of the creators surveyed declared they'd join a union in the future and another 37% said they would "consider" joining a union (Stanley, 2024). "Even top-tier creators understand the precariousness of a platform-dependent career," says Brooke Erin Duffy. "Unionization represents an important way that they can exert control amid a wildly unpredictable work culture" (cited in Stanley, 2024). A significant hurdle for creator unions is the classification of creators as independent contractors rather than employees. Under the National Labor Relations Act (NLRA), only employees have the right to unionize, and efforts to reclassify creators as employees have faced resistance from platform owners, which prefer to maintain the current independent contractor model, which suits their bottom line.

Nonetheless, creator labor organizations are growing. In 2016, the Internet Creators Guild was founded by YouTuber Hank Green, and in 2019, the YouTubers Union was also launched by Berlin-based YouTuber Jörg Sprave, the famous slingshot artisan. These died out, but creators have nonetheless been regrouping (Craig & Cunningham, 2023). Over the past few years, collective creator organizations, including unions, have sprung up in direct response to the precarious conditions that individual creators face: unpaid labor, lack of standardized contracts, and significant pay disparities. The Creator Union, launched in the UK in 2020 by fashion influencer Nicole Ocran, aims to amplify the voice of creators and provide a safe virtual space for collaboration and mutual aid. It tackles the absence of contracts, the unauthorized use of copyrighted content, and severe pay gaps across creator demographics. The union offers educational resources, including legal advice, contract templates, and fair pricing guidance, fostering a supportive community for creators. Founded in June 2020 by Chriselle Lim, Aliza Licht, and others, the American Influencer Council (AIC) focuses on educating and supporting US-based creators through mentorship, small business development, and ethical conduct standards (Blackburn, 2024). Platforms like F* You Pay Me (FYPM), co-founded by former influencer Lindsey Lee Lugrin, provide creators with transparency on brand collaborations and rates of pay, helping them negotiate fair pay by anonymously sharing their experiences with various clients (Liederman, 2024). In late 2022, TikTok creators began chatting up unionization through a Discord group while The Twitch Unity Guild pushed for more community and professional development (Craig & Cunningham, 2023). In 2021, SAG-AFTRA expanded to include TikTok, Twitch, Snapchat, and Instagram creators with its Influencer Agreement, highlighting the Hollywood union movement's growing recognition of creator labor and labor rights (Haring, 2023; Lorenz, 2021). The Creators Guild of America (CGA), launched in August 2023, is a non-profit organization dedicated to providing resources, recognition, and community support for creators at the cost of $99 per year. It offers campaign accreditation, educational programming, and advocates for fair compensation and content ownership, with members like YouTube influencer Justine Ezarik and Triller's Head of Talent, Jason Davis (Stanley, 2024). All of these forms of collective association by creators are positive, but the path to formal unionization for creators remains fraught, not least because the corporations that own and control that platforms creators depend on are vehemently anti-union and possess a managerial toolkit for union deterrence, avoidance, disruption, and destruction. Nonetheless, the conditions of Creator Capitalism have resulted in many creators developing a class consciousness. In the future, many more creators will unite and forge new solidaristic associations, including unions, to advocate for their interests and win greater labor rights.

10 What Is the Automation of Work in the DMEI?

Generative AI and Labor-Saving Technologies (LSTs)

Introduction

This chapter explores the automation of work in the digital media and entertainment industries (DMEI), focusing on labor-saving technologies (LSTs) in the age of generative Artificial Intelligence (AI) services such as ChatGPT and DALL-E. It contemplates the recent threat posed to the longstanding centrality of the humans in informational and symbolic production by generative AI and AI Art. Shifting from existential questions about the essence of the artist and anthropocentric artworks to the power wielded by the corporations that own and control AI systems, the chapter suggests generative AI is a new LST in the DMEI. The chapter considers the capitalist determinations and class politics of LSTs and presents a useful heuristic for contemplating the stages in which LSTs impact the worker's labor and life: *deskilling*, *dependency*, *displacement*, *depression*, and *development*. The chapter engages the longstanding and renewed debate about "technological unemployment" in capitalism and highlights the agency of workers to contest LSTs, with the 2023 Hollywood writer's strike a case in point. The chapter concludes with snapshot of some of the utopian dreams and dystopian nightmares of a totally automated future and highlights some of the ways AI-LSTs are being contested with ethical frameworks, neo-Luddism, online campaigns, art, legal action and new policy and regulatory ideas.

Generative AI and AI Art: The Death of the Artist and Art, for AAMAM?

New generative AI programs are being used to automate a wide variety of labor processes that were once thought to be exclusive to human workers. *Generative AI* is a type of AI software capable of generating or producing texts, images, audio, or video, based on patterns and data it has been trained on by humans. The most well-known examples of

DOI: 10.4324/9781003131076-11

generative AI being used by some humans to supplant others these days are ChatGPT for text generation and DALL-E for image generation. These new AI services are said to be the latest technological means of bringing about the automation of creativity, or, the use of advanced technology to emulate, and potentially replace, the value of human-centered labor power. While the real existence of AI is widely debated, generative AI services are being used by many to produce what is being socially recognized as "creative" work—stories, images, songs, and videos—with minimal prompts, or, to augment or substitute "creative" labor processes once believed to be exclusively human, and not the domain of machines. The result is sometimes referred to as "AI art", and two examples of this come to mind.

Stephen Marche is a Canadian novelist and essayist known for his contributions to *The Atlantic* and *The New York Times*. Marche has long been interested in the relationship between digital technology and literature, the impact of AI on the traditional idea of the author, and the role that AI can play in the practice of fiction writing. A few years ago, Marche started using AI to "co-write" works of fiction and, in 2023, Pushkin Industries published *Death of an Author*, a murder mystery novel, which Marche co-authored with three AI programs: ChatGPT, Sudowrite, and Cohere (Garner, 2023; Comitta, 2023). Marche employed ChatGPT to develop the novel's narrative and plot, Sudowrite for the prose, and Cohere for similes and metaphors. Despite acknowledging his use of AI to generate the novel in its entirety, Marche considers himself the source of this artistic work, and his publisher Pushkin Industries is selling it as an ebook and an audio-book on Amazon.com and elsewhere (Garnder, 2023; Comitta, 2023). Another artist who is using AI to create ostensibly "new" AI artworks is Jason M. Allen (Roose, 2022; Vallance, 2022). Allen started playing around with Midjourney, an AI program that turns text prompts into hyper-realistic images. Allen used this AI system to prompt hundreds of images into existence. Soon after, he decided to submit one of these Midjourney images to the Colorado State Fair, which had a division for "digital art/digitally manipulated photography." Several weeks later, Allen saw a blue ribbon hanging next to his piece, "Théâtre D'opéra Spatial". Allen had won the division and a $300 prize, perhaps the first instance of AI-generated art receiving such an award. In response to critics, Allen defended his use of AI, saying that it did not break any rules. Marche's AI-written novel and Allen's AI-generated digital painting challenge traditional notions of the author and artist: if AI can generate this creative content, who is the true creator—the machine, the person who inputs the prompts, both, or neither? As more and more people use AI systems to co-create new digital artworks, we constantly read that the history of human-centered art has come to an end, and that the anthropocentric idea of the artist as we've known it for all of recorded history is finished. The headlines everywhere tell us that "The Artist is Dead and AI Killed Them," or "The Death of Art: The AI Revolution."

The notion that AI has "killed" or will "kill" both the artist and their art represents a metaphor for the deep-seated anxieties workers in the DMEI harbor regarding AI's immediate and future effects on their professions, and capacity to labor for pay, for a living. These workers' concerns extend beyond philosophical ruminations about the essence of the artist and art and exceed existential questions about what will become of humanity when humans no longer imagine themselves to be in possession of a monopoly on creativity. The workers' fears primarily stem from the looming possibility of their labor power's devaluation by AI, and capital's use of generative AI to render them unemployable. Given that the labor sold by these workers to corporations has not only been essential for the DMEI's growth but also considered resistant to the threat of automation, the proliferation of generative AI disrupts this status quo. As generative AI becomes integrated with and used by corporations across the DMEI, numerous workers—both full-time and contractual—have legitimate reason to worry about their future employment prospects and the devaluation of their knowledge and skills. Generative AI's ability to generate texts, images, and videos with minimal human prompts and in a fraction of the time required by pre-existing labor processes, threaten to erode the professional identities of workers, and devalue their labor.

Yet, it must be remembered that generative AI systems, which are heralded as disruptors of the DMEI and destroyers of millions of jobs in the DMEI, are currently being researched and developed, designed and managed, owned and controlled, by firms in the DMEI, where humans toil for wages. As Lewis (2024) explains:

> AI was not dreamed into existence by celebrity tech moguls in underground mansion bunkers. It is borne of human intelligence, the result of the collective labor power of millions of workers across a century and around the globe: computer scientists, roboticists, software engineers, mathematicians, geoscientists, ocean cable technicians, underground miners, landfill workers, equipment installers, teachers, data annotators, semiconductor processors, and the millions of paid and unpaid careers who maintain them.

While it is human labor that is bringing AI into existence, the workers who sell the knowledge and skills required to produce AI are frequently employed or contracted by the biggest tech corporations. The AI Now Institute, a collective of esteemed AI researchers and policy experts, describes modern AI as foundationally dependent on the infrastructure, hardware and software of Silicon Valley's tech giants, notably Alphabet-Google, Apple, Meta Platforms, Amazon, and Microsoft (or, the AAMAM). These companies not only operate vast AI subsidiaries but are also the biggest owners of AI firms. At the beginning of 2024, Statista reported nearly 80 AI sector startups had been acquired by AAMAM since 2010: 29 projects for Apple, 15 for Alphabet, 13 for Microsoft, 12 for Meta, and 7 for Amazon. Also, these companies enjoy a unique advantage in developing and refining AI models, thanks to their access to vast datasets harvested from billions of users worldwide. Such data, integral for training machine and deep learning AI systems, also solidifies these companies' profitability through the sale of their targeted advertising services. Furthermore, the AAMAM lead AI R&D agenda setting; they set the direction and the pace for innovation through influential research papers, open-source projects, and major AI conferences. AAMAM already enjoy something akin to an Internet or platform oligopoly, and they are now extending that market power to AI. They license the use of these AI services to individuals and corporations across the whole economy and roll out freemium versions in support of their data-veilance business models, accumulating profit along the way. Even ostensibly non-profit AI companies are partnered with AAMAM. OpenAI, which runs ChatGPT and DALL-E, is branded as a "non-profit" entity and packaged with platitudes of AI for universal human uplift. But since 2019, OpenAI has run a for-profit subsidiary, OpenAILP, to attract investment and monetize its services. In 2024, OpenAI was valued at around $80 billion. Microsoft has a big piece of that. In fact, Microsoft is OpenAI's major investor, backing it with $13 billion or so.

When we recognize AAMAM's immense ownership over generative AI, and AI IP, platforms and services, we can grasp the legitimate fears that many workers across the DMEI have: that generative AI may be capital's latest and most disruptive labor saving technology (LST) (or, labor killing technology). Generative AI can be conceptualized as a new LST, produced by AAMAM, and sold to other corporations looking to acquire and implement new tools designed or intended to reduce or replace human labor to reduce production costs and increase revenue. The impact of generative AI on workers in the DMEI is vast and growing. To understand why so many corporations are subscribing to this LST, let's look at what capitalism motivates them to do with new LSTs, and how what they do adversely impacts the worker's labor process and life.

Capitalism and LSTs

In capitalism, corporations are always searching for ways to reduce production costs associated with wages paid to workers. LSTs give capital a means to significantly reduce, if not eliminate, certain types of knowledge and skill possessed by workers, thereby freeing corporations from their dependency on the human labor necessary to perform or accomplish specific tasks related to the production of a good or service. Some corporations hire the labor of some human workers to produce and sell LSTs to other corporations, which consume and use them for their own ends, to stay competitive with rivals in the market, to reduce labor costs and maximize profits. LSTs are produced and sold, purchased and consumed, by corporations, but they are in no way "value-neutral" tools that represent a universal interest. LSTs are made by some companies that hire and exploit waged human labor to make profit and, also, to help other companies looking to relieve themselves of waged human labor, to profit-maximize. Thus, we can distinguish between the companies that hire and pay human labor to produce LSTs, including generative AI systems, and the companies that purchase LSTs and related automation services as commodities, to displace or replace paid human labor. By design, many LSTs represent the interests of capital, not labor (Aronowitz & DiFazio, 1995; Carr, 2015; McChesney & Nichols, 2016; Nobel, 1979, 1984; Ovetz, 2023; Rifkin, 1995). LSTs are everywhere.

The factories of the world are filled with fewer blue-collared workers and more robots programmed to assemble everything from Ford and GM automobiles to Nike and Adidas sneakers. Distribution warehouses, like those run by Amazon, employ workers who labor alongside robotic dollies to fill and carry shelves of books and beauty accessories to meagerly paid packers that nimbly bundle these commodities into the boxes shipped directly to our doors, sometimes by drone. Google's self-driving cars may one day cut cabbies and Uber drivers out of the transportation market, while customer service jobs are designed away by user-friendly interfaces that shift tasks once done by paid workers to unpaid consumers: order your own Happy Meal at a McDonalds kiosk resembling a gigantic iPad; be your own travel agent on Expedia.com; self-checkout your IKEA box and then assemble its contents into a bookshelf from the comfort of your home. Wall Street traders square off against algorithmic finance bots and robo-advisors, and data entry specialists are displaced by advanced data entry software. Proofreaders and paralegals are rivaled by intelligent machines, as are other white-collar workers. Junior computer software engineers are being told by former mentors that they will soon be replaceable by the AI systems they built. Corporations in the DMEI have begun eliminating various jobs, occupations, and careers through the acquisition and implementation of generative

AI systems. Content writers and copywriters face obsolescence by AI systems that produce and edit articles, blog posts, and marketing copy. Graphic designers and illustrators are compromised by AI-driven design software, video editors compete with automated editing tools that perform tasks they were trained and paid to do, and sound engineers find their utility diminished by AI music composition software. Social media managers witness AI tools absorbing their content creation, scheduling, posting, and data analytics skills while customer support workers are replaced by AI chatbots.

Overall, LSTs offer significant advantages to corporations. As Lewis (2024) explains, "Capital is not aiming to produce self-aware machines... The hope seems to be for obedient, cost-cutting, productive things." LSTs can often execute repetitive and complex tasks more swiftly and with greater precision than human workers, who are susceptible to physical and psychological fatigue. Additionally, LSTs do not ask corporations to abide by governmental labor laws, policies, and regulations that protect workers' rights, expect wages, benefits, and perks, form unions in response to exploitative conditions, or go on strike. Despite the benefits of LSTs to corporations, a corporation's financial investment LSTs is frequently considerable. Furthermore, competition with rivals demands continuous updates and replacements to LSTs. Workers refusals and collective action and strikes in protest of LSTs, followed by layoffs and restructuring, can pose managerial dilemmas and brand reputation challenges. After all, pro-labor citizens might forcefully disagree with a company's decision to use LSTs to automate their neighbor's livelihood. The potential benefits of LSTs to workers include relieving them from menial tasks they don't want to do, or helping them to do tasks they must do or want to do with greater efficiency and efficacy. However, the costs of LSTs to workers are profound. Workers may go to college or university to develop the knowledge and skills needed for a specific occupation or career and then discover that the job they spent thousands of dollars and years preparing themselves for has been automated away the moment they they graduate into the labor market. The workers who have enjoyed a long and stable career may be laid off or fired by a company that has chosen to acquire LSTs, and their loss of income to LSTs is frequently coupled with a loss of a sense of self, as well as a loss of social status.

LSTs and the Workers' Labor and Life Process: Five Stages

When capital acquires LSTs, its impact on the worker's labor and life process tends to unfold over five distinct but interrelated stages: *deskilling*, *dependency*, *displacement*, *depression*, and *development*. This is not a linear nor inevitable process: workers can contest what capital does with LSTs in each stage.

Deskilling

Deskilling represents the initial stage when a corporation acquires and implements LSTs. In this stage, capital embeds the knowledge and skills required to complete specific tasks into the technology itself. Consequently, the worker is now in competition with the tool that has absorbed their labor. This diminishes the value of the workers' labor and transforms the worker from being an empowered tool user to being a somewhat anxious competitor with the tool.

Dependency

The second stage is dependency, where workers become increasingly dependent on the new LST to do their job. The workers' role changes from independence to semi-independence to deep dependence upon the LST. This dependency is not solely physical but also mental; workers must know how to use or operate the tool to complete the job they are expected to do. They become integrated with the new machine, a human-machine system of sorts. Here, managers exercise greater control over the workers' labor process. It is no longer the worker who employs the technologies of work, but rather the technologies of work that employ the worker. The dependency stage is marked by a shift in the nature of work, where workers become integrated with tools and compelled to use such tools to do what they do and do it as they are told.

Displacement

In this third stage, the corporation employs the LST to replace the worker, automating tasks the worker had previously been paid to do as a tool user or as part of the human-machine system. The tool becomes the new worker. The LST advances from being a tool integrated with the worker's labor process to an autonomous entity set apart from it and capable of performing the workers' total role, on its own. As a consequence of the uselessness of the workers' labor power to the corporation, which has hired the LST in place of it, the worker is fired, no longer the recipient of the wage they need to live.

Depression

The fourth stage is depression. The workers who have been put out of paid work due to their previous employer's decision to displace and replace them with the LST, experience great psychological and emotional hardship, on top of the financial strain. The worker joins capitalism's "reserve army of labor," a segment of the workforce that is unemployed or underemployed, essentially available for work, but out of it, and out of a wage. These workers have lots of experience, but the knowledge and skill they possess is no longer of value to capital. The workers realize they cannot compete with the tools that corporations hired when firing them. They may search for other jobs, advertising the sale of their labor power on the labor market, but fewer and fewer corporations demand the labor they supply, leading to their immiseration and despair. This stage also represents a chance to politicize LSTs: as the human cost of the tool becomes all too apparent to workers, they may educate, agitate, and organize with others, raising consciousness about and contesting capital's machines.

Development

The final stage is development. This stage entails the workers eventual response to technological unemployment. The worker may protest and engage in some activist politics, but in the absence of organizations or parties that will support their struggle for a different world, or impose regulations upon capital's latest LST, they will, pressed by necessity, likely immerse themselves in new education and training practices, reskilling or upskilling. The worker develops new skills in a desperate attempt to climb up from the ranks of the reserve army and back into a paid position; with new skills integrated into their labor power, they re-enter the labor market as a seller looking for a buyer, and compete with other workers for jobs. The development stage entails workers doing more than just acquiring new skills or learning how to use new tools. Workers may try to reinvent their professional identity and advertise their labor to prospective employers. Development is a stage of strategic adaptation, where the worker searches out positions that may be less susceptible to automation, at least for the short term. Development presents its own set of challenges, including the workers' need for resources and access to training. Sadly, many workers who try their best to augment their labor power and renew their identities remain unemployed, stuck in the reserve army, and for no fault of their own.

This five-stage model is useful heuristic for grasping the impact of LSTs on the worker's labor-life process. However, the staged process—deskilling, dependency, displacement, depression, and development—is not predictive nor is it destiny. In some stages, LSTs may complement workers' skills rather than diminishing them and change the nature of the job rather than destroying the skill required to do it. Workers are not passive victims of LSTs. At every moment in the history of capitalism, workers, and their collective organizations, have tried to insert themselves into the making of new tools and the shaping of capital's application of these to the labor process and to society. Class struggles around LSTs ebb and flow. As the history of Luddism reminds, workers have sometimes outright refused new tools and even rebelled against and smashed the machines that corporations brought in to deskill them and diminish their autonomy. In each stage, workers may contest capital's plans to kill their labor's value and throw a metaphorical monkey wrench in the gears (Jones, 2006; Merchant, 2023a; Mueller, 2021).

For example, workers may contest deskilling by advocating for the preservation of their skills and occupations within their respective industries and firms. To counteract technological dependency, workers might focus on continuously developing and maintaining a diverse skill set that extends beyond operating machinery or software. By diversifying their skills, they reduce their reliance on any single tool and expand their general intellect. To resist displacement, workers might engage in union campaigns and forms of collective action and bargaining to negotiate new terms that protect their jobs against automation. They might also advocate for corporate or state policies that prioritize human labor for certain tasks or that slow the new tool's diffusion in society, making time to regroup, or to retrain for what's next. In the depression stage, workers may, in solidarity with others, form mutual aid groups or join activist campaigns that try to change the capitalist system that brought into existence the LST that management was motivated to use against them. During the development stage, worker resistance is more about adaptation than refusal, direct action and outright opposition. Workers focus on reskilling and upskilling, augmenting their labor power. Practices of networking and learning become tactics for workers to rebuild the sense of agency they lost when their previous employer imposed its new tool, rebuild the dignity that was destroyed by the machine, and re-enter the labor market, facing capital once again, but now in competition with other workers for a waged job.

While workers have agency to adapt, negotiate, organize, refuse, reject, and resist the LSTs that corporations and their managers acquire and impose upon them and their labor-life process, history suggests corporate managerial elites, not workers, have by and large driven disruptive technological changes, and made the main decisions that have shaped the application of new technologies to labor-life processes. This is due in part to the dearth of strong pro-worker organizations and political parties that possess the resources and capacities for counter-balancing capital's technological power at a massive scale. Nevertheless, workers and labor researchers should always be mindful of capital's new and emerging LSTs, and, always, reveal the class *politics* of these, the power relations designed into and afforded by these.

Self-Realization and Alienation at Work: Four Types of Estrangement in Capitalism

In "A Theory of Human Motivation," Abraham Maslow (1943) placed "self-actualization"—the realization of one's talent or potential—at the pinnacle of the hierarchy of human needs. Maslow posits that once the human species' subsistence and fundamental needs are met, self-actualization emerges as a vital driving force, characterized as "the desire to become more and more what one is." Karl Marx (1844, 1845, 1867) posited the individual could, if the conditions were right, realize themselves and their humanity, through their labor. But conditions in capitalism make this impossible. For Marx, the system's logics, the capital-wage relationship, and the management of the labor process, hinder the workers' self-realization and instead *alienate* them (Healy, 2020). In *The Tyranny of Work: Alienation and the Labour Process*, sociologist James Rinehart (2006, p. 14) defines alienation as involving "human estrangement—from persons, objects, values, organizations, or from oneself." Building upon this foundation, there are four types of alienation the worker might experience in the DMEI: (1) estrangement from the products of their labor; (2) estrangement from the labor process; (3) estrangement from their essence, their sense of self or potential; and, (4) estrangement from other workers. This alienation is not merely a personal feeling but is the result of what capitalism and corporations do to workers.

First, workers are alienated from the products of their labor. Workers relate to the products of their labor as to an alien object. In the DMEI, the iPhone has nothing to do with the personality of the Foxconn worker who assembled a part of it. The formulaic advertisement for the latest gas-guzzling truck in no way expresses the sustainability mindset of the worker who created it. Furthermore, the worker's very act of making the iPhone or the ad undergirds their own impoverishment, as their hand and mind benefit the corporation that pays for it, more than themselves. Second, workers are estranged from the labor process. In the DMEI, so many monotonous and repetitive tasks are designed in advance of the worker, for the worker to fulfill, at a pace and timeline, other-directed, reducing them to cogs in a machine. The practice of laboring itself becomes external to the worker, a dispiriting activity that estranges the worker from what they are doing. The news anchor may loathe the same teleprompter message they are paid to read at exactly the same time in the nightly schedule to thank their employer's corporate sponsors, but they must do it anyway. The actor who declares Swiffer has revolutionized the household while perpetuating some dated gender stereotype may feel ashamed of the act. Third, alienation manifests in workers' estrangement from their species-being. Under capitalism, work is reduced to survival, stifling personal creativity and community. Workers feel at one with themselves when they are not laboring for others, but most of the time, they endure this, disconnected from their humanity. The machine learning engineer who spends their days and nights developing, training, and fine-tuning GPT models that will eventually make the value of their own labor power obsolete may want more from life, might even fear what this new generative-AI system will do to society, but does it anyway. Finally, alienation affects workers' relationships with one another, turning potential collaborators into competitors. This competition for jobs, for higher pay, in service to a corporation that wishes to exert monopoly power over the market, undermines solidarity among workers, leading to a loss of comradery. Competition among influencers exacerbates alienation as individuals commodify themselves and their personalities, staging and performing authentic emotional expression and interpersonal connection to solidify their position in an attention economy. In sum, if one takes Marx seriously, capitalism overwhelmingly alienates humans from what they produce, how they do it, their deepest nature and sense of self, and from other humans.

Unemployment and "Technological Unemployment"

One of the big old political questions surrounding new technologies is: do they cause *unemployment*? Before we address that question, it should be recognized that most corporations and governments take a degree of unemployment for granted, accept it as the status quo, even encourage it. Speaking at the Australian Financial Review's property summit, Tim Gurner, a property developer with a net worth of $584 million, actually called for an increase in unemployment: "We need to see unemployment rise. Unemployment has to jump 40%, 50%," he declared, adding that this would serve to remind workers of their place in the capital-labor hierarchy and combat workers' militancy (Downie, 2023). Gurner's comments are consistent with the worldview of free-market ideologues, corporations, and governments that advocate for sustained and somewhat high unemployment as a disciplinary measure against workers' power (Downie, 2023; Ozimek, 2023; Vicks, 2021). Advanced by the Chicago School economists, this "neoliberal" approach to fiscal management enforces notion of a non-accelerating inflation rate of unemployment (NAIRU). It posits that a certain level of unemployment is essential to prevent wage-driven inflation, implying that workers must endure a perpetual state of precarity to maintain a country's economic stability. This keeping of workers in a state of dread about employment deprivation and desperation to secure a job can also lower their life expectations and have the inadvertent consequence of de-politicizing them. As many neoliberal states have normalized fluctuating unemployment rates, veering away from the goal of full employment enshrined in the Keynesian welfare state, supply-side labor market dynamics have come to predominate, with both firms and states placing an emphasis on higher education to produce a surplus of workers for jobs that may not even exist. The result? Too many knowledgeable and skilled workers looking for jobs, and too few good jobs for everyone. In the DMEI, and elsewhere, the oversupply of workers and under-supply of well paid and meaningful jobs are all too common. In effect, corporations become the wage makers, and workers, the wage takers.

In this neoliberal model, a lot of people will always be unemployed. According to the Organisation for Economic Co-operation and Development (OECD), "unemployment" refers to individuals above a certain age (usually 15), who are not in paid employment or self-employment but are available and actively seeking paid work. A country's *unemployment rate* is the percentage of the labor force that is unemployed. In the US, about 6.4 million people were unemployed in 2024. Worldwide, there are between 220 and 235 million unemployed. Since the 1970s, economic stagnation and recessions have led to higher unemployment rates, and recoveries often lag in restoring employment to previous levels. However, the official unemployment rate does not account for *hidden unemployment* – all those people who have stopped searching for a job. *Real unemployment* includes both the officially unemployed and the hidden unemployed. Additionally, the rate does not reflect job quality, an important aspect of the workers' well-being. A corporation may hire many workers for many jobs, but not necessarily good-paying or deeply meaningful ones. In any case, unemployment is caused by a wide range of factors, from the overall state of the economy to the policies and decisions corporations and governments make, but technologies, especially LSTs, definitely play a role.

The precise relationship between LSTs and unemployment has long been a focal point of scholarly debate. John Maynard Keynes, in 1930, introduced the concept of "technological unemployment," defining it as unemployment caused by LSTs outpacing the creation of new jobs. Forty years ago, André Gorz (1985, 1989), predicted LSTs would diminish capital's need for a waged labor force. In his book *Paths to Paradise*, Gorz (1985) declared the outcome of LSTs would be the establishment of a small class of "elite waged workers" and a large group of "unemployed and precarious casual workers," a bifurcated workforce. Predictions of total technological unemployment have intensified with each major LST.

In *Millennium*, Jacques Attali (1991) that "Machines are the new proletariat—the working class is being given its walking papers." In *The End of Work*, Jeremy Rifkin (1995) declared the phasing out of "mass work" across industrialized nations due to LSTs. The rapid integration of LSTs by corporations, while economically rational in the short term, risks undermining the very foundation of the capitalist system over the long term. Arguably, when all corporations acquire and implement LSTs to relieve themselves of having to pay for human labor to produce their goods and services, they also paradoxically reduce the number of consumers who can afford to purchase the commodities automatically produced for the market. This portends an overproduction crisis (too many goods supplied, not enough effective demand for them), a fall in the profit rate, and stagnation, even collapse.

This concern may not be only theoretical. Recent studies of LSTs paint a gloomy picture of the future of work. In *Race Against the Machine*, Erik Brynjolfsson and Andrew McAfee (2011) note that despite increases in corporate output, productivity, and profit, there hasn't been a corresponding boom in employment. In 2017, the consulting behemoth McKinsey projected that up to 60% of all jobs were susceptible to some level of automation, potentially rendering 400–800 million workers redundant by 2030. The Organization for Economic Cooperation and Development (OECD) chimed in with a sobering statistic: "27% of jobs are in occupations at high-risk of automation," notably in highly skilled fields such as finance, medicine, and law. However, not everyone agrees with the idea that LSTs are the primary driver of current and future mass unemployment trends. In *Automation and the Future of Work*, Aaron Benanav (2020) acknowledges capital's increasing use of LSTs. Still, he challenges the premise that automation is fundamentally responsible for declining jobs and wages, pointing instead to de-industrialization, systemic underemployment, sluggish growth in labor productivity, and lowered manufacturing output. In *Smart Machines and Service Work: Automation in an Age of Stagnation*, Jason Smith (2020) also challenges the idea that we are fast approaching a totally automated future society, explaining that it is highly unlikely that corporations would collectively and uniformly apply a total automation system across all industries and sectors, completing wiping out their need for waged labor. Corporations only acquire and implement LSTs when they promise profit. Not all do, at least not in the short term. This selective development, adaptation, and application of LSTs by corporations results not in total automation, but uneven geographical and temporal developments in automation across sectors and industries. Where human labor remains cheaper than LSTs, corporations will search out and exploit waged workers. Where LSTs become more cost-efficient than human labor, corporations will invest in and implement LSTs, to relieve themselves of having to pay wages to humans. While LSTs are used by capital to eliminate many waged jobs in some sectors and industries, the likelihood of every waged job being displaced and replaced all at once in every sector and industry everywhere is improbable. That's not what's happening at the present time anyway. Even still, over the past few years, many have argued that generative AI represents a paradigm shift, and that capital will use it to destroy millions of waged jobs.

Accelerating Technological Unemployment by Generative AI? Pumping the Breaks in Hollywood

The predictions about what generative AI will do to the modern labor force are staggering and distressing. A Deloitte study found that over 50% of organizations planned on incorporating the generative AI in 2023 (Gibbons, 2023). The International Labour Organization (ILO) says generative AI is poised to automate millions of clerical jobs, leaving a trail of deskilled and unemployed office workers in its wake. Economists at Goldman Sachs (2023) declare that generative AI could displace 300 million full-time jobs globally in the coming years. The World Economic Forum predicts that a significant percentage of workplace tasks will be automated by 2027, leading to mass job elimination and unemployment. Researchers from OpenAI suggest that 80% of American workers could see up to 10% of their work automated. The upshot for corporations is a boost in productivity among the few workers they retain and "augment" with AI. The workers' increased productivity will not be met with increasing wages; as usual, the surplus will be funneled into higher profits for the corporations rather than bigger monthly deposits into workers' checking accounts.

The DMEI, which are deeply class divided, will be made even more so as more and more corporations embrace generative AI. The creative class was supposed to produce a new economy that revitalized urban centers and made the world a better place for all, but it seems that some of these workers produced AI systems to render jobs done by many other creative workers obsolete. Corporations across the DMEI have been hiring and deploying generative AI systems to perform tasks related to communication and creativity once thought to be uniquely "human." These AI platforms and services are being harnessed by CEOs to cut costs associated with labor across various occupations in the DMEI: software developers, scriptwriters, actors, illustrators, video editors, web designers, journalists, marketers, copyeditors, and more (Merchant, 2023b; Zinkula & Mok, 2024). As generative AI continues to be incorporated into the operations of firms across the DMEI, the future of many careers, occupations, and professions once thought un-automatable may be in jeopardy (Flew, 2023). In most cases, the rapid uptake of generative AI by corporations in the DMEI not only threatens to make the labor power of millions of workers valueless but also expand the already vast reserve army of creative and cultural workers. At worst, generative AI will further intensify competition between workers, drive down bargaining power and wages for all, and empower capital over labor even more. This is probable but not inevitable: some workers are contesting generative AI.

Over the past few years, Hollywood became a flashpoint for larger societal debates about and worker struggles to pump the breaks on the accelerating diffusion and disruptive impacts of generative AI. The adoption of generative AI by major studios was quickly recognized by workers as a significant threat to their careers. Hollywood writers, for one, fear replacement by AI. While ChatGPT has limitations, particularly in nuanced dialogue and character development, studios seem to now view writing as a function that can be automated or outsourced, and as they embrace AI, they diminish the value of writer labor. Hollywood actors are also worried about being automated out of a job by AI. Studios now use advanced AI systems, including deepfake techniques, to simulate actors or their likenesses in movies. This was evident in the *Star Wars* franchise, where CGI was used to recreate the late Peter Cushing's character Grand Moff Tarkin in *Rogue One: A Star Wars Story* and to simulate a Carrie Fisher as Princess Leia in *The Rise of Skywalker*. In these blockbuster productions, AI was used to digitally simulate dead actors, with audiences frequently not discerning the difference between the real actors and algorithmically reproduced copies. Hollywood visual effects (VFX) and animation specialists are also concerned about the studios' automation of their jobs with generative AI.

Some Hollywood workers are fighting back against the studios' embrace of generative AI, recognizing the threat it poses to their crafts and livelihoods. Notably, generative AI became the site of capital-labor conflict in the Writers Guild of America (WGA) and SAG-AFTRA strikes in the summer of 2023 (Hart-Landsberg, 2024). These unionized Hollywood workers pushed back against the use of AI systems by Hollywood studios represented by the Alliance of Motion Picture and Television Producers (AMPTP) (Universal, Paramount, Walt Disney, Netflix, Amazon, and Apple). The workers pressed for restrictions on these studios' use of AI to protect their crafts, careers, and livelihoods. The Writers Guild of America (WGA), representing around 12,000 screenwriters, struck against studios for five months. Initially, the WGA proposed that studios should not use AI to generate original scripts. When studios rejected this, the union took a firmer stance against AI. During the strike, the WGA organized meetings on AI for workers in related industries, rallying broader workers' support for their cause. The strike concluded with a new contract prohibiting the studios' use of AI systems to write or rewrite scripts or as source material, while allowing writers to use AI if they choose.

The contract also prevents studios from using writers' material to train AI systems. The WGA's contract set a positive precedent on AI-LSTs: studios cannot use AI to remove humans from the scriptwriting process. As Adam Conover, a member of the WGA negotiating committee, explained: "Studios cannot use AI to write scripts or to edit scripts that have been written by a writer" (Anguiano & Beckett, 2023). Similarly, the Screen Actors Guild-American Federation of Television and Radio Artists (SAG-AFTRA) went on strike two months after the WGA, and took on the studio's use of AI to simulate and automate actors out of a job. Their new contract mandates that producers must negotiate with the union before using "synthetic performers" instead of hiring human performers. It also requires consent from performers when studios use AI to simulate their recognizable likenesses in digital forms. The WGA and SAG-AFTRA's contracts are among the first to establish protections for workers against capital's use of AI to automate their labor power (Anguiano & Beckett, 2023; Coyle, 2023). The general win for workers in the recent Hollywood strike points how the effect of new LSTs is not always inevitable. Studios wanted to use generative AI to automate parts of entertainment production, but workers' collective action disrupted that plan. The workers revealed the class politics of generative AI and organized to constrain the studios' power to use these new LSTs to adversely impact their livelihoods.

Likeness Licensing, AI, and Celebrity Deepfakes: Scarlett Johansson vs. Open AI

"Likeness licensing" is a legal agreement that allows a corporation to use a person's likeness and their qualities in exchange for compensation. It transforms a person's appearance, voice, and even their quirks into valuable commodities that can be copyrighted, bought, and sold in an expanding "likeness market." For example, the sports industry and various team franchises have long capitalized on likeness licensing, with athlete likeness rights sold to software developers for games like FIFA, NBA 2K, and John Madden Football. However, the rise of AI-generated likenesses has introduced new labor and legal issues. Celebrity actors are increasingly worried about losing control over their digital likenesses and being exploited by studios and malicious entities. Lesser-known actors fear being automated out of existence entirely by AI likeness simulators. Hollywood is now a battleground for disputes over who owns the digital likeness of an actor and concerns surrounding the actor's right to consent to the creation and use of their digital likeness in various digital media and entertainment products. Companies sometimes argue that because they financed the movie that the actor appeared in and own the copyright to the content, they also own everything it includes, including the actor's likeness. The right to publicity, which is recognized in about 38 states for the living and around 20 states for the dead, prevents the unauthorized commercial use of an individual's name, likeness, or other recognizable aspects without their consent. Yet, the First Amendment and copyright preemption defenses often limit the applicability of right to publicity claims, particularly in cases involving expressive uses of likenesses in digital media and entertainment products. As a result, many actors are vulnerable to likeness exploitation: their likenesses can be used without their consent in ways that can dispossess them of payment for the use of their image and damage their reputations and livelihoods. For example, generative AI systems are being used by studios to create deepfakes of celebrity likenesses and malicious entities are doing the same, without the consent of the workers whose likenesses are being simulated and manipulated. In 2021, deepfake videos of Tom Cruise saying things he never said went viral on TikTok, while deepfake pornography videos of Gal Gadot spread across the internet. Recently, Scarlett Johansson challenged Open AI for using her voice's likeness without her consent (Cho, 2024). OpenAI asked Johansson if it could license her voice for their ChatGPT 4.0 system. Johansson refused, but OpenAI went ahead and created a voice named "Sky" that closely mimicked hers anyway. To challenge OpenAI's blatant disregard for her consent to simulate her voice, Johansson took legal action against the company, pushing for transparency about how the "Sky" voice was made. In response, OpenAI removed the "Sky" voice from its ChatGPT 4.0 system. This case epitomizes the "ask forgiveness, not permission" attitude prevalent in Silicon Valley, where tech companies often flout laws and ethics, until they are called out for their bad behavior, fueling conflict between AI firms and workers and intensifying public distrust. Clearly, there is a need for new or stronger laws to protect working actors from such unauthorized simulations and abuses of their digital likenesses (Cho, 2024; Davis, 2023; Lee, 2023; Pulver, 2017; Schomer, 2023; Stanton, 2023).

**Utopian Dreams and Dystopian Nightmares of
Totally Automated AI Futures: What's Being Done About the
Automation of Work in the DMEI? (AI Ethics, Neo-Luddism,
Online Campaigns, Legal Action, Principled Regulation)**

Throughout capitalism's history, and the history of the DMEI, waged labor by humans has so far been fundamental to the system, deeply ingrained in ways of life and work. However, generative AI has renewed a debate across the political spectrum about the necessity of waged labor to the system. As corporations develop, acquire, and use new LSTs that have been designed to displace waged human workers, more occupations and labor processes are threatened with obsolescence by automation, even those in the DMEI. This was not how the digital society was supposed to turn out. In the 1960s and 1970s, proponents of the post-Fordist service economy assumed that white-collar knowledge workers would be immune to automation, in contrast to blue-collar manufacturing workers. In *The Coming of Post-Industrial* Society, Daniel Bell (1999, p. xvii) declared: "An industrial society […] is founded on a labor theory of value, where the advancement of industry is achieved through labor-saving devices, effectively substituting capital for labor." Contrasting this old Fordist regime with the post-Fordist new, Bell elaborated: "A post-industrial society is underpinned by a knowledge theory of value. Here, knowledge becomes the primary driver of invention and innovation" (xvii). What Bell and his liberal contemporaries overlooked was the possibility that capital would utilize the knowledge of these workers to innovate LSTs that would ultimately lead to their own deskilling and eventual redundancy. Bell and others did not seem to recognize how capital would learn to leverage the labor of highly educated individuals, ranging from university graduates to PhD students and professors, to develop new LSTs that would eventually be used by corporations to put knowledge workers out of a job (Lowrey, 2023).

What might the future of work look like in a world where LSTs supplant occupational roles that currently require the waged labor of humans? There is no consensus that the total automation of the economy or the DMEI will happen in the future, nor is there any evidence that an automated future is what the majority of the world's workers want. The future of AI LSTs at work is without guarantees. In *AI and the Future of Creative Work*, Michael Filimowicz (2023, p. xiii) explains how the "future of creative work will be more complicated than 'the robots will take our jobs'", as many future workplaces may become "hybridized with human and computational labor complementing each other" alongside changes in "cultural conceptions of what it means to be a creative worker" due to fusions of "human-machine labor." Nonetheless, the global discourse on the future impact of LSTs on the world economy and across the DMEI seems to vacillate between utopian dreams and dystopian nightmares. The narrative swings from hopes of a radically better future to fears of a profoundly worse one. In the optimistic story, the utopian vision is of a totally automated techno-culture, a future where LSTs are used to liberate humanity from the grind and alienation of waged labor, heralding a brave new world of abundance, leisure, and creative self-realization for all. In the pessimistic tale, the dystopian scenario is a Matrix-like hellscape where AI-systems dominate humanity, all the while using authoritarian command and control systems and super-charged weaponry to repress and control destitute and revolting populations. In the dream of a fully automated AI-utopia, humans finally get to realize their humanity through creative, self-actualizing labor. In the nightmare of AI dystopia, humans and their creativity don't matter. They and their "humanity" are useless and without value, economic or otherwise. These utopian and dystopian visions of the future give expression to popular hopes and fears about LSTs, but they are not entirely new. Throughout history, each disruptive change to society brought about by the newest LSTs has elicited awe and shock from workers. Worker's struggles, not LSTs in themselves, always play a role in shaping the future.

Even still, the future of work in the DMEI is at a critical juncture. It is imperative that workers be empowered to actively shape their relationship to generative AI, rather than passively being shaped by this new LST and its makers. The benefits of LSTs to corporations in the DMEI are costly to workers. What, then, is being proposed in response to AI's disruption of work in the DMEI?

At the philosophical level, Lewis (2024) proposes a critical "AI realism." This way of thinking about AI moves beyond the technologically determinist hype and opens the black box of human-generated AI systems. It aims to understand how AI actually works, contextualize it, and critically examine the corporate, military and government institutions shaping AI for their ends. Also, many people are proposing and pursuing "AI Ethics", seeing this as in some way protecting workers from the impacts of LSTs. The widespread discourse on AI Ethics involving industry stakeholders, policy-makers, and academics tends to overlook the class and labor politics of generative AI, focusing instead on consumer rights and user data privacy. Furthermore, ethical AI frameworks, if not already under the ethics-washing influence of AAMAM, tend to be reactive and politically idealist. Chastising a corporation for using generative AI to automate jobs, bemoaning that business application of AI as "unethical," or "wrong" or "bad," ignores the capitalist system logics driving that corporation to adopt LSTs in the first place. When confronted with such ethical finger wagging, the Board of Directors and CEO of such a corporation may argue that their primary obligation is to generate profits for shareholders.

That is mostly true. Moralizing about AI misses the point when not also moralizing about capitalism. Additionally, despite all the talk of AI Ethics, AAMAM continue to concentrate control over these AI systems, while global capital harnesses and employs AI in ways that deskill, degrade, and displace labor. The belief that an AI system, designed to supplant human labor, can be used "ethically" is not just naive but also a diversion from its actual, intended use, by capital for capital. As Molly Crabapple says, "There is no ethical way to use the major AI image generators...all of them are built for the purpose of deskilling, disempowering and replacing real, human artists" (Merchant, 2023a).

While AI Ethics is an important way of raising a social consciousness about AI, thinking about the system beneath the AI industry, the class and labor politics shaping these LSTs and strategic and tactical worker responses to those is paramount. Too often, commentators represent AI and all LSTs as though these have a will to power of their own, deflecting attention away from the corporations that design and own and sell the right to use them, and the many other corporations that are buying these new services to take work away from the worker. There is value in democratic debate on the role of LSTs in society, and a need for human agency in shaping new technological developments for the collective and public good rather than for narrow and disruptive profit-driven interests. After all, the politics driving the development and diffusion of LSTs poses a significant challenge to the labors and livelihoods of millions of workers. It is only through naming those class politics, deliberating about what should and can be done in response, building organizational resources and capacities for doing it, and supporting the collective actions of workers, that society can begin to mitigate the adverse consequences of LSTs and safeguard the dignity, rights, and livelihoods of workers experiencing technological obsolescence.

Drawing inspiration from the Luddites, authors like Gavin Mueller (2021), in *Breaking Things at Work*, suggest that breaking LSTs still holds tactical value for workers' movements. The Luddites were members of a 19th-century movement of English textile workers who rejected and even smashed certain types of machines that had been designed to deskill and displace their labor. The term "Luddite" originates from their symbolic leader, Ned Ludd, an apocryphal figure whose name was used in the threats by skilled craftsmen against mill owners and government officials. The movement, which began in Nottingham and spread across England between 1811 and 1816, saw textile workers engaging in clandestine raids in factories to destroy machinery that was being used by the bourgeoisie to drive down wages and put them out of a job. The British state responded to the Luddite uprising with military force. In 1813, "machine breaking" was declared a capital crime. Following a mass trial, numerous Luddites were jailed, executed, or exiled to the penal colony of Australia. Over time, the term "Luddite" has been used as a shorthand for anyone who opposes technology. But this misses the point. The Luddites' actions, from machine breaking to public demonstrations and letter-writing campaigns, were heroic efforts to preserve their skill and dignity in protest against their deskilling and displacement by capital's new machines. Despite being suppressed, their legacy endures as a symbol of worker resistance to LSTs and automation systems. The ghost of Ned Ludd haunts the AI present (Graham, Cant, Muldoon, 2024; Jones, 2006; Merchant, 2023a; Mueller, 2021).

As mentioned previously, the WGA and SAG-AFTRA strikes contested the studios' potential uses of generative AI to the detriment of workers. Online campaigns are also contesting capital's newest generative AI machines. The Center for Artistic Inquiry and Reporting released an open letter calling on organizations to "restrict AI illustration from publishing" altogether (Crabapple, 2023; Klein, 2023). Signed by thousands of workers in the DMEI, the open letter, co-authored by artist Molly Crabapple and journalist Marisa Mazria Katz, called out Big Tech's attempt to automate creativity: "While illustrators' careers are set to be decimated by generative-AI art, the companies developing the technology are making fortunes." The Artist Rights Alliance (ARA), an artist-run, non-profit organization co-founded by GRAMMY winner Rosanne Cash, is advocating for the rights of songwriters and musicians in the face of AI's use to subvert them. ARA recently released an open letter, endorsed by over 200 artists, including Billie Eilish, Nicki Minaj, Katy Perry, and the estate of Frank Sinatra, calling on AI companies and digital platforms to cease "the predatory use of AI to steal recording artists' voices and likenesses, violate creators' rights, and destroy the music ecosystem" (Artists Rights Alliance, 2024). This letter chastises two particularly harmful practices: the unauthorized use of musical works by AI developers to train and produce AI-generated music, and the use of AI-generated sound to reduce royalty obligations to human artists (McMahon, 2024). As Jen Jacobsen, Executive Director of ARA, says: "Working musicians are already struggling to make ends meet in the streaming world, and now they have the added burden of trying to compete with a deluge of AI-generated noise. The unethical use of generative AI to replace human artists will devalue the entire music ecosystem — for artists and fans alike" (Artists Rights Alliance, 2024). While these interventions have caught the attention of policy-makers, artists are collaborating to create symbolic goods that highlight the power of workers to challenge AI systems. The DAIR Institute, Collective Action School, and Collective Action in Tech (2024) produced a digital zine called *Bits in the Machine: A Time Capsule of Worker's Stories in the Age of Generative AI*. Unlike top-down state and corporate policy reports on AI's impact on workers, this zine provides a bottom-up perspective, emphasizing grassroots worker organizing to resist AI while demanding worker participation and ownership of new AI systems.

These high-impact strikes, campaigns and creative initiatives are being accompanied by workers outright suing AI companies for copyright infringement. For many artists, AI-generated art often constitutes large-scale plagiarism and copyright infringement of their works. This is primarily because such art is created by algorithms trained on datasets comprising millions of copyrighted works, utilized by companies like OpenAI without creators' consent or compensation. In response, The Authors Guild has advocated for legal and policy measures that both foster AI development and safeguard human authorship. Ethics, machine breaking, strikes, online campaigns, creative interventions, and legal action, while purposeful, can only achieve so much and usually does not yet constitute a coherent politics for fundamentally challenging finance capital and Silicon Valley's accelerating automation of more and more occupations across the DMEI. The march of AI may seem irresistible, but it doesn't have to preclude a labor politics for making fairer and more just future of work. In *Feeding the Machine: The Hidden Human Labor Powering A.I.*, Mark Graham, Callum Cant and James Muldoon (2024) outline four pro-worker principles to guide AI's regulation. First, they say we must build and connect organizations that amplify workers' collective power, institutionalizing local unions and fostering transnational campaigns that unite blue and white-collar workers across global AI production networks. Second, civil society and social movements should pressure companies to guarantee fair pay and conditions for all workers throughout the supply chain, as AI is often embedded in consumer goods and services. Third, states should regulate companies to ensure minimum labor standards (despite the risk of tasks flowing to less regulated areas) through global agreements like an International Labour Organization (ILO) convention and regulations such as the EU's supply chain directive, which mandates ethical and environmental standards in AI. Fourth, worker-led interventions are needed to establish workplace democracy, including cooperatives where workers own and manage organizations and company boards with equal worker representation.

11 Is Work in the DMEI "Free?"

Advertising, Audience Commodities, Social Media Users, Brand-Loyal Fans, Crowdsourced Task-Takers, Interns, and Athletes

Introduction

Free or unwaged work refers to the labor undertaken by people for profit-seeking companies without monetary compensation. While most people are compelled to labor for corporations in exchange for wages necessary for their subsistence, some people labor for corporations without pay, sometimes even unaware that what they are doing with their time, activity, and energy, is value-adding labor for these corporations (Brabham, 2012, 2013; Cohen, 2008, 2013; Fast et al., 2016; Fuchs, 2010; Hesmondhalgh, 2010c, 2016; Huws, 2010; Ross, 2009, 2014; Jarrett, 2022; Terranova, 2000, 2004). This chapter considers the prevalence of "free" or unpaid forms of labor within the digital media and entertainment industries (DMEI). The chapter begins by foregrounding the central role of advertising in the DMEI and then reviews the concept of the "audience commodity," as produced by TV-radio broadcasters, "the commodity audience," made by ratings and market research agencies, and the "prosumer commodity," of social media platforms. The chapter also considers the "free labor" of brand-loyal fans, crowdsourced task-takers, interns, and indentured laborers. By considering these different forms of unwaged work in the DMEI, the chapter sheds light on the ways corporations leverage the labor of billions to add value to their products and services without paying for it. The final section of the chapter presents a broad overview of the threats to workers' freedom of expression, while laboring for pay or without it, in the DMEI.

TV's Audience Commodity, Ratings' Commodity Audience, and Social Media's Prosumer Commodity

Capitalism, Advertising and the DMEI

In the DMEI and in capitalism more broadly, advertising plays a central role in sustaining the cycle of production and consumption and the wider culture of consumerism that pervades everything. Corporations must sell

DOI: 10.4324/9781003131076-12

their goods and services to realize profits. However, this process depends on consumer demand, which advertisers help to create. When producing and paying to place advertisements in various media—from billboards to TV spots to social media platforms—these workers construct and inform people about brands, persuade people to consume them, and socialize people to perceive themselves as consumers. Advertising workers help corporations differentiate their products and services from those in a market flooded with similar commodities. By driving consumerism, advertising ensures the continuous cycle of production and consumption necessary for the survival of capitalism itself.

Advertising Corporations

The contemporary advertising industry is highly concentrated, dominated by a few major global companies selling extensive services and wide-reaching influence. WPP plc, headquartered in London, stands as one of the largest, offering a myriad of marketing, communication, and advertising services through its network of agencies. Omnicom Group, based in New York, is another, providing advertising, marketing, and corporate communications services worldwide. Publicis Groupe, a French multinational, and the Inter-Public Group (IPG) from the US, runs several leading public relations (PR) and marketing agencies, while Dentsu Inc., based in Tokyo, is Japan's largest agency. Additionally, Havas, part of the Vivendi group and headquartered in France, operates in over 100 countries. These corporations not only dominate the global advertising services industry but also shape the meaning, presence, and performance of countless brands across the globe and across platforms. The relationship between these global advertisers and companies in the DMEI that depend on ad revenue is symbiotic. Advertising agencies pay to use the ad placement services sold to them by media companies with the goal of capturing audience attention and moving it toward ads for their clients' branded products and services. Media companies provide these agencies with access to their audience base, relying on advertising contracts to cover operational costs and generate profits for their owners.

Advertising Business Models

Advertising agencies and their expenditures have long paid for most modern media. The workers for these agencies purchase ad space from newspapers and magazines (front page ads, full cover ads, and special inserts being lucrative). They buy airtime from radio broadcasters (drive time slots, shows featuring popular hosts, and more). They consume time and space in the daily schedules of TV networks (prime time slots and special events, like the Super Bowl, Olympics, or Oscars). They spend to place targeted ads across

Google's platforms, frequently engaging in bidding wars with one another to try to win access to the most lucrative batches of users. They bid for and purchase ad space and targeted services from platforms like Facebook, X, and TikTok, utilizing them to access and algorithmically target user attention by placing ads in feeds, stories, and as sponsored content. Advertisers are also increasingly tapping into over-the-top (OTT) video-streaming platforms, which have shifted from exclusively subscription-based revenue generation services to a dual revenue model that now relies upon advertising services. Netflix's ad-supported tier is "Basic with Ads." Disney+ launched "Disney+ Basic" Amazon Prime Video launched an ad-supported tier and has become a major seller of advertising services, with advertising companies worldwide paying Amazon Web Services (AWS) to access its massive user base, leveraging its Sponsored Products, Sponsored Brands, and Sponsored Display Ads.

The Advertising-Media Symbiosis: Valuing the Audience

There exists a symbiotic relationship between advertisers and all kinds of media corporations, old and new: advertising corporations depend on the media to access audience attention and expose people to ads for branded products and services; media corporations rely on advertising revenue to cover costs, and turn a profit. The commercial value of advertising space and time offered by media corporations to advertisers is shaped by the quantity and quality of the audience or user base they can deliver. A larger audience equates to more potential customers seeing the ads, thereby increasing the value of the advertising space due to the higher likelihood of engagement and sales. Equally important is the demographic profile of this audience, as advertisers are willing to pay a premium to reach specific segments that are more likely to be interested in their products or services. The ability of the media corporation to effectively deliver this targeted audience's attention—through high engagement rates, relevant content, and strategic ad placement—further enhances the value of its advertising services. In this cybernetic system, the audience is not just a passive receiver but a crucial asset; their engagement and demographic profiles are key in determining the attractiveness and valuation of the media space for advertisers. Whether in traditional media like newspapers and broadcasting or new media platforms like the Internet and social media, the audience's size and demographic profile underpin the media company's ability to attract advertisers and generate revenue. No audience, no ad dollars. The audience size and demography attracted to a media corporation's product or service shapes its capacity to attract global advertisers and command higher prices for ad space. Without an audience's presence, characterized by both substantial size and specific demographic attributes sought after by advertisers, media companies would struggle to generate ad revenue and stay in business.

The importance of the audience necessitates a radical reimagining of their function within the DMEI. Rather than merely conceptualizing them as consumers of media content, can we reconceptualize them as "workers" for corporations? This is precisely what political economists studying the audience commodity, the commodity audience, and the prosumer commodity have done.

The Audience Commodity: Watching TV as Working

The idea that the TV audience itself has become a commodity was proposed by Dallas Smythe (1977, 1978, 1981). In "Communications: Blindspot of Western Marxism," Smythe (1977) first introduced the theory of the audience commodity, arguing that media audiences performed unpaid labor for radio and TV companies and advertisers. Challenging the rigid separation of labor time and leisure time in capitalism, Smythe argued that "Work time is not only the time people are on the job [laboring for wages] but also the time they are exposed to advertising on radio and television [consuming, undertaking unwaged leisure activities]" (p. 5). Smythe contended that TV and radio companies produced audiences "with predictable [demographic] specifications who will pay attention in predictable numbers and at particular times to particular" TV and radio shows (p. 6), and sold the scheduled attention of these active audiences to advertisers, who bought access to this audience's attention from the TV and radio companies. Smythe posited that "because audience power is produced, sold," by media corporations, and "purchased, and consumed," by advertising corporations, "it commands a price and is a commodity" in an audience labor power market of sorts (p. 4). In essence, Smythe argued that audiences did value-adding work for media corporations when they watched specific entertainment shows and ads at specific times; Smythe also contended that "audiences work [for the capitalist system as a whole] when they learn to buy goods and to spend their income accordingly" (p. 8), as this consumption helps corporations realize profit, thereby reproducing the relations of production.

Presently, TV broadcasters like NBC, CBS, and ABC purchase the rights to exhibit TV series and movies from studios, but their primary goal isn't just to schedule and showcase this content. Instead, their business model is about attracting an audience to this content, and, in turn, selling this audience's attention to advertisers. In 2023, the cost of a 30-second advertisement spot during primetime TV slots reflected the high value placed on audience attention. A 30-second spot during *The Masked Singer* cost $80,699, while *Bachelor in Paradise* commanded $96,782. More expensive spots were in *Survivor* at $99,780, *Dancing with the Stars* at $104,954, and *60 Minutes* at $117,939. Even more expensive were spots were "The Voice" on Tuesday at $122,899 and Monday at $125,833. However, it was the football nights that fetched astronomical prices, with "Thursday Night Football" at $440,523, "Monday Night Football" at $562,524, and "Sunday Night Football" at a whopping $882,079 (Herren, 2023). Clearly, TV broadcasters continue to commercialize audience attention, and advertisers, even though shifting online, are still willing to spend heavily to capture attention for their clients during prime-time TV broadcasts. Given how TV broadcasters rely upon the audience watching TV shows (and ads) to make money by selling that audience's attention to advertisers, scholars contend that "when the audience watches commercial television it is working for the media," producing both value and surplus value (Jhally & Livant, 1986, p. 135). "This is not meant as an analogy," Jhally (1987, p. 83) argued, "indeed watching is an extension of factory labour, not a metaphor." In the theory of the audience commodity, the act of viewing ads for products and services is considered unpaid work performed by audiences, a form of uncompensated but value-creating labor that viewers of TV must engage in as part of the entertainment experience.

While fascinating, the theory of the audience commodity is not without its critics. Lee McGuigan and Vincent Manzerolle (2014) bring together many of the key contributors to the longstanding "audience commodity" debate in *The Audience Commodity in a Digital Age: Revisiting a Critical Theory of Commercial Media*; the book includes Dallas Smythe's original essay, some influential critiques (by Graham Murdock, Eileen R. Meehan, and Sut Jhally), and recent developments of this theory in relation to social media platforms (by Mark Andrejevic, Edward Comor, Christian Fuchs, and more). Overall, the audience commodity is a provocative and generative key concept in studies of unpaid work and free labor in the DMEI (Andrejevic, 2004, 2007, 2008; Caraway, 2011; Cohen, 2008, 2013; Crain, 2021; Dolber, 2016a, 2016b; Fisher, 2015a, 2015b; Flisfeder & Fuchs, 2015; Fuchs, 2010, 2011, 2012a, 2012b, 2014, ; Gandy, 1993, 2003, 2004; Jhally, 1982; Jhally & Livant, 1986; Lebowitz, 1986; Lee, 2011; Livant, 1979; Maxwell, 1991; McGuigan, 2012, 2023; Meehan, 1984, 1990, 1999, 2000, 2005, 2007, 2018; Meehan & Wasko, 2013; Murdock, 1978, 2000; Napoli, 2010; Svec, 2015).

The Commodity Audience: Ratings Workers Are Watching

Researchers contributed to the audience commodity debate by emphasizing the importance of ratings to the production of the audience (Maxwell, 1991; Meehan, 1984, 1999, 2000, 2007; McGuigan, 2023). To attract advertisers to their services, TV broadcasters must attract large audiences for advertisers to target and also convincingly demonstrate the actuality of the audience working for them to advertisers. To achieve this, TV broadcasters pay ratings companies to pay workers to measure the size and composition of their audience, and produce information about the audience, which advertisers demand. Maxwell (1991) criticized Smythe's "watching as working" formulation, noting that the real productive labor within the media industry is performed "within the ratings industry, advertising and broadcast marketing firms, and other areas of the image and information industries" (p. 32). From this angle, the world's largest media ratings companies and their labor force are key to making and selling the people, as a commodity audience (McGuigan, 2023). Leading the pack is Nielsen Holdings plc, selling its ratings, measurement, and analytics services across TV, radio, and digital media. Kantar Media, a division of WPP plc, sells media monitoring services, including television audience measurement, radio listenership, and online and social media interactivity analysis. The waged workers employed by these and other companies use everything from traditional surveys to advanced digital tracking technologies to furnish TV broadcasters and advertisers with information or data about the size and scope of audiences watching and interactively and affectively engaging with a variety of digital media works. TV broadcasters and other media and online corporations, purchase and use this information to determine the economic value of ad services, and charge advertisers accordingly for access to audience or user attention.

Take a popular prime-time television show like *This Is Us*, which consistently achieves high Nielsen ratings. This large viewership lets NBC increase the cost for a 30-second ad spot during the show's schedule, as advertisers are willing to pay a premium for the extensive audience reach and engagement. Similarly, TV events like the Super Bowl garner an exceptionally big audience, helping broadcasters drive up prices for ad spots into the millions. In the case of news TV programs, a slot in the evening news with high ratings yields a bigger return than one with low ratings, because advertisers want to reach a lucrative demographic. In every case, advertisers rely on ratings as these provide insights into audience size, demographics, and engagement, helping them to make informed ad spot (and audience attention) purchasing decisions. Ratings inform advertisers about the number of people watching a show. This quantitative data paired with qualitative demographic information about age, gender, income level, and interests of people watching, allows advertisers to target their ads. For instance, a brand catering to young adults will seek TV series popular within this demographic. Moreover, ratings offer a window into audience engagement, indicating how attentive viewers are to the content, and consequently, to the ads shown. This helps advertisers in assessing the cost-effectiveness of ad spots, and gives them confidence that they are investing in media venues that offer the best return on investment. Overall, ratings are key to deals between TV broadcasters and advertisers.

In her pathbreaking revision of audience commodity theory, Eileen Meehan (1984, 1999, 2000, 2007, 2013, 2018) introduced the concept of the "commodity audience," emphasizing how rating companies and the workers employed by them for a wage construct and valuate viewers: "It is not the viewers who work, but rather the statisticians" (Bolin, 2009, p. 357). Meehan (1984) argues that the work of gathering data about audiences undertaken by media ratings corporations is not a neutral practice, but selective and motivated. Meehan (1990) says TV networks are only interested in appealing to audiences that will be of interest to advertising firms and their clients, and so TV networks pay ratings firms to count the audiences that count for them, which are most of the time, the most affluent. In effect, "ratings do not count the [totality of] viewers, but only the commodity audience which is saleable [at the highest price] to national advertisers and networks" (p. 118). Therefore, we can say that "both intellectuals and masses have been defined out of this market and out of the audience. Neither intellectuals nor masses count" (p. 118). Consider a luxury car brand like BMW seeking to advertise its latest model: ratings firms like Nielsen might prioritize the rating of TV shows popular among higher-income households and focus on consumers with disposable income that advertisers want most to reach and sell the BMW to. Also, a sitcom popular with young adults might be valued higher for advertising, even if it equally appeals to older audiences, because advertisers wish to sell products to this demographic. Additionally, ratings assign different social values to audience groups based on their perceived economic value. A daytime talk show with a large audience but perceived lower disposable income will fetch cheaper advertising spots compared to a prime-time show with a smaller, wealthier audience. In sum, ratings companies and their waged workers produce and sell information about the diversity of people assembled into audience groups, and put these "commodity audiences" to work for their owners' profit.

The Prosumer Commodity: Working While Posting, Liking, Sharing

In the DMEI, the Internet has blurred the once-distinct roles of producers and consumers, ushering in the "prosumer" (Bruns, 2006, 2008; Napoli, 2010; Ritzer & Jurgenson, 2010). This term, first coined by Alvin Toffler in *The Third Wave* (1980), suggests media consumers are also media producers, engaged in the practice of "prosumption": on the Internet and social media platforms, digital media content is now regularly produced by the same people that consume it (Ritzer & Jurgenson, 2010). In this "prosumer capitalism" model, "there is a trend toward unpaid rather than paid labor and toward offering products at no cost, and the system is marked by a new abundance where scarcity once predominated" (Ritzer & Jurgenson, 2010, p. 14). *In Network Culture: Politics for the Information Age*, Tiziana Terranova (2004, p. 78) conceptualized the Internet user's prosumption as a form of "free labor", a moment where the "knowledgeable consumption of [digital] culture is translated into productive activities that are pleasurably embraced [by users] and at the same time often shamelessly exploited [by Web 2.0 social networking firms]." Numerous political economists have conceptualized this Internet platform prosumer as an unpaid worker (Andrejevic, 2008, 2009; Arvidsson, 2008, 2009; Cohen 2008, 2013; Fisher 2015a, 2015b; Flisfeder, 2016; Fuchs, 2011, 2012a, 2012b, 2014; Jarrett, 2022). The key thinkers in this "digital labor" tradition, argue that "the dominant capital accumulation model of contemporary corporate Internet platforms is based on the exploitation of users' unpaid labour, who engage in the creation of content and the use of blogs, social networking sites, wikis, microblogs, content sharing sites for fun and in these activities create value that is at the heart of profit generation" (Fuchs & Sevignani, 2013, p. 237).

The idea that "if you don't pay for a product, you are the product," has long been a pop e-business axiom. The phrase speaks to the platform capitalist business model of many Silicon Valley companies, especially those like social media platforms and search engines that seem to offer "free services" to users. We don't pay to search for the meaning of "prosumer" on Google's search engine. We don't pay to log in to Facebook to check out what our friends might say about this concept. The meaning of "If you don't pay for the product, you are the product" is that when an Internet corporation offers a service for free to users, it has found some other way to generate revenue from what you do with that service. Often, Internet corporations collect data about their users—their behaviors, preferences, interests, and other personal information—and then monetize it (Cohen, 2008, 2013). This monetization typically happens through selling the user data and/or access to user attention on the platform to advertisers looking to engage in targeted advertising. In such "freemium" business models, the users themselves, or more specifically, their data and attention, become the product that the company sells, or at least depends upon, to generate ad revenue. A twist on this trope is this: "If you don't pay for a product, you are an unpaid worker for its platform."

The first political economist of communication to examine how Facebook was using (and exploiting) the free labor of millions of users logged on to and prosuming content on the platform was Nicole Cohen (2008). In "The Valorization of Surveillance: Towards a Political Economy of Facebook," Cohen (2008) explained, "Like other Web 2.0 businesses, Facebook is engaged in the commodification of what can be understood as free labour, or what has been called immaterial labour" (p. 8). Furthermore, she noted, "The business models of Web 2.0 ventures depend on the performance of free labour; without it there would be no content and therefore no profit" (p. 8). On Facebook, almost all member activity can be conceived of as immaterial labour that benefits the company" (p. 10). In "The Political Economy of Privacy on Facebook," Christian Fuchs (2012), another significant political economist of communication, elaborated on how Facebook users do unpaid or free labor for the corporation. Fuchs argues that when Facebook users productively prosume on the platform, the resulting user-generated content is not only owned by Facebook (read the IP clause of the user agreement) but also adds to a user's data profile, which Facebook controls and exploits for its own commercial gain. Facebook users are both the producers of content they do not own and contributors to the data Facebook monetizes to rake in billions in ad revenue each year. Fuchs (2012, p. 146) notes, "Facebook surveillance creates detailed user profiles so that advertising clients know and can target the personal interests and online behaviors of the users." Facebook users, although they are the creative source of the content and data, do not own what they create and do not monetarily benefit from the production and market exchange of these commodities; they are thus exploited. In essence, users' prosumption time, interaction and attention, given freely to the platform, scrolling, clicking, liking, sharing, posting, commenting, and watching, is the "free labor" that is key to Facebook's bottom line. In this way, Fuchs conceptualizes social media use as a new form of unpaid work (and exploitation).

Extending or posing an alternative to the widespread notion that Facebook depends on and exploits the free or unpaid labor of its billions of users for profit, the platform can be conceptualized as digital property or territory. In this view, Facebook acts as a corporate landlord of sorts, renting out space and time on the platform to clients for various purposes, including advertising to the billions of people hanging out on its turf. In this model, user activity on Facebook is not akin to labor being put to work to produce actual goods and services, but rather, likened to unpaid promotion and marketing that elevates and enhances the perceived value of the platform as a great space to commune, collaborate and communicate with others to everyone else, enticing more and more users to sign up and log on. Although prosumer activities undeniably make Facebook more attractive to advertisers (hence allowing Facebook to "charge rent" for ad space and time), the users themselves are not laboring in the traditional sense but rather enhancing the value of the platform and its services to advertisers through their presence and interactions. If the "free labor" of Facebook users produces anything, it is not a tangible or intangible commodity, but rather, a "network effect": the more users that join and engage on the platform, the more attractive it becomes to potential new users. This phenomenon can be compared to a business tower, shopping mall, or sports stadium that charges premium rates for renting space and time when these locations are bustling with people. Similarly, Facebook capitalizes on the network effect by attracting more users, which in turn makes the platform more appealing to advertisers and other clients, who pay premium rates for Facebook's suite of services. Essentially, as Facebook's user base grows, so does the value of the platform, creating a cycle that continuously draws in more users and advertisers, and sales and revenues.

In sum, the audience commodity of TV broadcasting, the commodity audience of ratings, and the prosumer commodity of social media platforms are of great significance to conceptualizing the free or unpaid labor of media audiences and Internet users in the DMEI. They point to how the audience's (inter)activity is central to the business models of old and new companies, and how everyone from TV viewers to Facebook users can be conceptualized as doing free but valuable labor just by watching, existing for or interacting with media.

Wages for Facebook (http://wagesforfacebook.com)

Launched in January 2014 by curator Laurel Ptak at the University Art Gallery at the University of California, San Diego, "Wages for Facebook" posed a provocative question: are Facebook users doing unwaged work for this massive global corporation? In the exhibition's reception area, a big iPad showcased a website that conveyed Ptak's answer: "THEY SAY IT'S FRIENDSHIP. WE SAY IT'S UNWAGED WORK. WITH EVERY LIKE, CHAT, TAG OR POKE OUR SUBJECTIVITY TURNS THEM A PROFIT. THEY CALL IT SHARING. WE CALL IT STEALING." Ptak's "Wages for Facebook" installation was inspired in part by her contemplation of Mariarosa Dalla Costa, Silvia Federici, Brigitte Galtier, and Selma James' "Wages for Housework" campaign, which raised consciousness about the unpaid labor done by women in the household to reproduce the relations of capitalist production, mostly to the benefit of male CEOs. Adapting the ethos of this 1970s Marxist-feminist campaign, "Wages for Facebook" demanded wages for unpaid social media labor. It argued that user activities on the Facebook platform are a form of value-adding labor for the corporation that owns it, yet users receive no monetary compensation. Ptak's art installation and campaign included a manifesto website, campus-wide promotions, and workshops. It sparked widespread discussions about the transformation of work and labor in the age of social media platforms (Jung, 2014).

Brand Equity: Brand Loyalty and Franchise Fandom as Unpaid Work

Valuing Brand Equity

Do a consumer's perceptions of a company and its products and services constitute a source of economic value? Moreover, how does the "brand" of a company, as intertwined with consumer perception, contribute to its valuation in capitalism? Brand equity, or, the intangible assets of a brand, is indeed a measure of real economic value, influenced by consumer perception. This value manifests in many benefits to the corporation that controls the brand. First, a robust brand image fosters *consumer loyalty* to a corporation over its competitors. This loyalty translates into increased sales and market share, and ultimately, contributes to the economic value of the corporation. Second, strong brands command a *premium price* for their products, supporting higher profits. Third, established brands often incur *lower advertising expenses* for the same visibility because they are already embedded in society and culture, as well as in the consumer mind. Fourth, recognizable brands can extend their reach to new products and markets more easily, leading to *diversified revenue streams*. Fifth, a distinguished brand image serves as a *barrier to entry* for new competitors. Sixth, a reputable brand image bolsters *investor confidence*, often resulting in higher stock valuations. In the DMEI, brand equity matters, and companies like Apple, Disney, and Netflix, exemplify how brand strength can strengthen their financial valuations and oligopolistic profit powers in the market.

The Work of Brand-Loyal Consumers

A significant producer of a corporation's brand equity is the *brand-loyal consumer*. The perceptions and feelings consumers have about brands, and the actions they undertake in relation to brands, can be conceptualized as a form of unpaid labor for corporations. This unpaid labor involves consumers ritually engaging in social and emotional activities that enhance brand equity without being directly paid or compensated for their work. West (2017, p. 250) explains how brand-loyal consumer activities—from habitual purchasing and product use to advocating for the brand on social media and participating in brand events—constitute "affective labor." The time, energy, activity, perceptions, and feelings of brand-loyal consumers significantly contribute to brand equity and the corporation that prospers as result of it. Through what practices does the labor of brand-loyal consumers manifest? Enthusiastic consumers voluntarily promote the brand, effectively serving as unpaid word-of-mouth marketers. Loyal customers create content like reviews and tutorials, providing authentic endorsements without direct compensation. They give a lot of customer feedback that may factor into product innovation—a form of unpaid research and development (R&D). Consumers often form communities around brands, enhancing the brand's popularity and presence in society. In times of crisis, loyal customers defend the brand, protecting its reputation from those who may sully and tarnish it. Loyal customers provide predictable, long-term revenue through repeated purchases and brand advocacy. For example, Apple's billions of brand-loyal consumers perform various types of unpaid labor for the corporation: they talk up the latest iPhone with friends and acquaintances, enthusiastically write and share product reviews online, send feedback to Apple about their likes and dislikes, voluntarily help troubleshoot problems in online forums, and try to persuade others that Apple products and services are the best. These labors of the Apple loyal consumer go uncompensated but nonetheless cultivates and nourishes Apple's brand equity. In this context, the Apple loyal user plays a dual role for the corporation—as a predictable consumer of its branded goods and services and as a productive contributor to its brand equity.

Fandom for Franchises as Unpaid Work

A pertinent type of brand loyal consumer that has come to play a significant role in boosting the brand equity of corporations in the DMEI is the entertainment franchise fan. Far from being mere passive consumers, fans are deeply invested in franchises—TV shows, films, and video games—often transforming their passion into producing derivative or novel media content. This unwaged fan production can take various forms: online fan community posts, fan fiction, fan art, and fan video tributes. Fans often form fandoms in the hundreds of thousands to millions, people united by their shared love for an entertainment franchise and its fictional world. In essence, fans are super brand loyal consumers, and their labors contribute significantly to the brand equity of the corporation that owns the IP to their beloved franchise. In the 1990s, media corporations began to recognize the potential of fans as boosters of their brands, and a source of unpaid labor for viral publicity campaigns. Fans, with the branded cultural capital and forms of distinction they accumulated and performed to others through their knowledge of fictional universes and popular cultural happenings wrapped in copyright, were marshaled as part of the global entertainment industry's selling campaign. Their unpaid labor helped corporations shape and steer consumer tastes and trends in the media market. Fans were perhaps the first "influencers." Unpaid fan activities--public expressions of passion, desire, and enthusiasm for some new installment of a franchised movie, TV series or video game--tacitly paralleled the paid work of guerrilla marketers. No longer a niche subculture, fandom was had become a mainstream phenomenon, something corporations tried to design and build into every marketing cycle for the latest blockbuster movie, TV series, or triple-A video game they pushed. At present, many fans work without pay for their favorite franchises and their owners. Fan events such as Comic-Con are lucrative, especially with fans doing the free labor of bolstering the brand equity of the corporations whose franchises they celebrate and spend much of their lifetime making meaning within. Additionally, fan-maintained online platforms and wikis, serve as both information repositories and community-building spaces. In so many ways, the labors of brand-loyal fans boost the brand equity of entertainment franchises, all without compensation.

> ### Entertainment News Platforms and Unpaid Fan Labor
>
> Online platforms for sports and entertainment fandoms rely on the unpaid labors of fans who create and share content. FanSided, a network of fan-driven sports and entertainment sites, depends on unpaid fans who produce and spread content about their favorite sports teams and topics. TV Tropes is a wiki-style website built on contributions from volunteers who curate a vast database of media "tropes." Reddit hosts various subreddits where fans share their analysis, reflections, and arguments about entertainment. The business models of these platforms revolve around monetizing user-generated content. FanSided primarily earns through advertising and, in some cases, sponsored content or partnerships. TV Tropes accumulates ad revenue and donations from users. Reddit generates revenue through advertising, premium memberships like Reddit Gold, and a microtransaction system. These platforms capitalize on the labors of sports and entertainment fans and their user-generated content to attract a large, diverse audience, making them attractive to advertisers and sponsors.

Crowdsourcing and 'Crowdsourced' Free Labor

As discussed above, the Internet has blurred the traditional boundaries between leisure and labor due to efforts by corporations to transform what were once leisure activities into value-adding labor practices that support their bottom line. This is encapsulated in the term "crowdsourcing," coined by Jeff Howe in his 2006 *Wired* article. Howe (2006, 2008) posits that leading Internet companies are structured to exploit the "spare processing power of millions of human brains" across a global virtual market. This strategy transforms the knowledge and skill of amateurs, hobbyists, part-timers, and dabblers into valuable production inputs, thereby reducing labor costs for firms. Unlike traditional outsourcing or offshoring, crowdsourcing taps into a networked "crowd of prosumers" (Howe, 2006). Brabham (2012, p. 395) defines crowdsourcing as an online, distributed problem-solving and production model: "All crowdsourcing applications consist of an organization that issues a task to an open online community, and the community participates in accomplishing the task for the benefit of the organization." In this model, corporations try to tap into and leverage the collective intelligence of an online community for specific tasks, blending traditional product management with innovative, open-source processes (Brabham, 2012, p. 395). Scholz (2017, p. 18) further expands on this concept, noting that the practice of "Crowdsourcing has the goal of distributing the workload from one, sometimes paid, individual to many, frequently unpaid or underpaid volunteers." Former *Wired* editor Chris Anderson said of this practice: "Users happily do for free what companies would otherwise have to pay employees to do." Crowdsourcing has been employed by a number of corporations in the DMEI to tackle an array of tasks, at little to no cost. Indeed, "The productive power of the network [of unwaged crowdsourced workers] becomes a dynamo for profits" (Scholz, 2017, p. 23).

Crowdsourcing has emerged as a lucrative strategy across various industry groupings in the DMEI, where companies solicit, mobilize, and exploit the crowd's unpaid work or free labor for commercial gain. Crowdsourcing is happening in advertising, movie-making, television production, digital photography, music, video gaming, news journalism, and software and hardware R&D. In advertising, companies like Coca-Cola, Doritos, Lay's, Heinz, and Budweiser have tapped the collective creativity of their consumer base: campaigns like Coca-Cola's personalized bottles, Doritos' "Crash the Super Bowl," and Lay's "Do Us a Flavor" make consumers into active promoters of the product. Hollywood has also embraced crowdsourcing, with films like *Life in a Day* (2010) relying on 80,000 video submissions from people spread across 192 countries, and *The LEGO Movie* (2014) inspired by fan-created stop motion films, or Brickfilms. Television production has similarly turned to crowdsourcing, transforming viewers from passive audiences to active content contributors. *America's Funniest Home Videos* and *American Idol* draw upon viewer submissions and contestant performances, reducing production costs by capitalizing on the free labor of viewers, who submit the home-made content that appears in the show (e.g., a video of a goat on a farm making strange noises), and contestants, who sing and perform hit songs (e.g., Adam Lambert's rendition of "Mad World"). In digital image-making, platforms like Instagram, Unsplash, Flickr, and 500px thrive on user-contributed photographs, offering exposure to users but using their creative content for driving network effects. In the music industry, artists like Taylor Swift, Adele, and Coldplay have recruited their fans into the songwriting process. In the video gaming industry, modding and community moderation represent a treasure trove of unpaid labor. As the news industry continues to decline in profits, companies leverage the free labor of citizen journalists while laying off and precaritizing professional journalists who previously earned a salary. In the software and tech sector, companies like Eli Lilly, Boeing, and Google have used crowdsourcing for R&D. Platforms like InnoCentive, open-source projects like Linux, and user-driven apps like Waze also point to how companies harness the intellect, creativity and expertise of a global community, the labor power of a vast crowd, often without paying for it.

Apprenticeships, Internships, and Indentured Labor

Apprenticeships have long been part of occupational training going back to antiquity. An apprentice typically served a term under a master craftsman, during which time they were taught a trade. In exchange for their service, apprentices received board and lodging but were seldom paid. Although training for the crafts have developed over time, apprenticeships persists. Modern apprenticeships still involve individuals being trained in a specific trade. However, unlike regular employees, apprentices are not usually paid for what they do. They occupy a transitional position, with their future employment contingent on the quality of their performance during the training period.

Internships in the DMEI are everywhere (de Peuter et al. 2015; Perlin, 2012). Ideally, internships are training grounds for aspiring professionals, offering hands-on experience in real-world settings, relevant skills, and mentorship. An effective internship should provide regular feedback, meaningful interaction with supervisors, and ample networking opportunities, setting the stage for future career success. However, the term "internship" often obscures the value-adding labor of interns, who frequently do work for corporations without compensation. Although interns are typically distinguished from employees, this distinction becomes blurred when they perform substantial, value-adding work. We can observe the exploitation of interns' free labor by corporations across the DMEI, with the reality-TV industry being a particularly shameful example. In *Intern Nation: How to Earn Nothing and Learn Little in the Brave New Economy*, Ross Perlin (2012) observed, "reality TV truly embraces the intern" (p. xii). Mirrlees (2015) showed the profit squeezed out of this embrace in a study of how 20 reality TV intern job ads for 19 different reality TV studios represent the work of interns and internships. By interrogating how the job postings depict the work that reality TV studios expect interns to do, the skills that TV studios expect interns to possess as a prerequisite to considering them eligible for mostly unpaid positions, the asymmetrical power relations between studios and interns, and the studios' utilization of "hope" for a career-relevant experience to recruit interns, Mirrlees (2015) found that many reality TV interns are actually misclassified workers whose labor adds to the production of copyrighted TV shows, but goes uncompensated. To add insult to injury, many internships across the corporations of the DMEI, do not lead to any form of gainful employment, but to more unpaid internships. Internships should act as stepping stones to employment rather than as a means for companies to reduce labor costs by exploiting the hopes and unpaid labors of young workers. Unfortunately, all too often, internships lead back to unemployment and violate labor laws.

In the US, the legality of unpaid internships hinges on several criteria. An internship must mirror the kind of training provided in an educational environment and primarily benefit the intern, not the employer. Interns cannot replace regular employees or provide immediate advantage to the employer. Additionally, the intern must be made aware that they are not entitled to wages, nor to a job with the corporation following the termination of their internship experience. Yet, many internships fail to abide by these laws. When interns do value-adding labor for corporations, they should receive at least minimum wage. In response to the spread of illegal and exploitative internships, interns have spoken out about their experiences, some unions have attempted to organize interns, and lawyers have filed class action lawsuits on behalf of interns against companies such as Fox Searchlight Pictures, Warner Music Group and Condé Nast (Cohen & de Peuter 2013; de Peuter et al., 2012; Perlin 2012).

Internships have sometimes been described as indentured labor, a system where individuals are bound to work for a specific employer for a set period in exchange for non-monetary benefits, like training. But this phrase has been increasingly applied to the relationship between college and university sports teams, and athletes, who are not paid for playing the game, but whose labor makes millions for the teams. These athletes in the National Collegiate Athletics Association (NCAA) typically receive scholarships covering tuition, room, board, and other expenses, which are certainly valuable. However, beyond these provisions, they are not compensated, nor allowed to profit from their name, image, or likeness (NIL). Critics of this system have likened it to "slave" labor or indentured servitude. Undoubtedly, college athletes contribute substantially to the business models of their respective schools. Their athletic performance is what drives ticket sales, TV distribution deals, merchandise sales, and more. Despite their labor's value, athletes are compensated only through scholarships and earn no cut of the revenue they help generate for their teams (Branch, 2011; Nixon, 2014; Nocera & Strauss, 2016). While the public and legal debate is ongoing, the growth of a class consciousness among athletes and the NCAA's rethinking of NIL rights suggest a shifting sports labor politics.

Freedom from Free Labor in the DMEI? Threats to Workers' Freedom of Expression

In the DMEI, there are a growing number of individuals, driven by oblivion, compulsion, pleasure, loyalty, play, hope, and aspiration, doing unpaid labor for large and powerful companies. Free or unpaid labor—watching TV or being turned into a ratings commodity, using social media platforms, fawning over a franchise, doing crowdsourced tasks, and interning—has become interwoven with the DMEI. The existence of free labor in the DMEI raises ethical questions and arguments for and against it (Hesmondhalgh, 2010c, 2016). Some forms of free labor in the DMEI can play a role in a worker's development of new knowledge and skills, and potentially expose them to paid jobs at some later date. Even still, unpaid labor, particularly when it benefits large corporations financially, is exploitative. This practice devalues labor and can perpetuate systemic inequalities, as it favors individuals who can afford to work without pay, thereby excluding those from less privileged backgrounds. Moreover, free labor can be illegal if it violates labor laws. While often packaged as consensual, free labor obscures the asymmetrical power relations between profit-seeking companies and unpaid workers desperate to make their way. The ubiquity of free labor exacerbates the class division in society, funneling profits to the wealthiest, often at the top echelons of the DMEI. While working for free might offer some benefits to those who choose or feel compelled to do it, it often comes at the cost of paid training opportunities, well-paid jobs, and equality.

The problem of free labor in the DMEI is real, but there are other ways to conceptualize problems related to labor's freedom (or lack thereof) in the DMEI. For instance, freedom of expression is a cornerstone of human rights, but how free are workers in the DMEI to express themselves, while laboring, when producing hardware, software, services and content? According to Article 19 of the Universal Declaration of Human Rights (UDHR), adopted by the United Nations General Assembly in 1948, "Everyone has the right to freedom of opinion and expression; this right includes freedom to hold opinions without interference and to seek, receive and impart information and ideas through any media and regardless of frontiers." While freedom of expression is a universal human right, workers' rights to express themselves in an employment relationship to a corporation are frequently limited, even in the DMEI, which are often imagined as the ultimate bastions of freedom of expression. In concluding this chapter, I will quickly address some political and economic conditions that can radically limit and even directly threaten workers' right to freedom of expression in their labor process and product.

Government censorship continues to undermine the freedom of expression of workers around the world. In China, news workers and online creators are unable to freely give expression to workers' collective actions, strikes, protests and uprisings, as internal class conflict and struggle is heavily censored by the state. The Chinese party-state maintains strict control over the media and Internet, often suppressing content that could portray the country in a negative light or incite revolution. Media workers who attempt to freely give expression to dissent are deemed politically incorrect by the party-state and are not only censored, but often face harassment, deterrence, detention, and at worse, a jail sentence. In Turkey, numerous media workers were arrested and media outlets shut down following the 2016 coup attempt; similarly, Russia exerts tight control over media, and in Saudi Arabia, media workers are prohibited from criticizing the monarchy and its human rights violations. Despite the First Amendment, the United States is home to all kinds of censorship of workers' expressions, on the Internet, across workplaces, and in the media.

Around the world, state censorship regimes not only restrict the informational and creative labors of workers but also erode their human right to freely express themselves. While states can and do impose laws and regulations that restrict freedom of expression in society, and in the DMEI, the censorship of workers is also undertaken by corporations, even in ostensibly "open" and "free" and "democratic" countries. While neoliberals often portray states as the primary censors, markets as fountains of free expression, and corporations in the market as the great enablers and defenders of this human right, this libertarian free market populist notion overlooks—and sometimes deliberately obscures—the reality that censorship can be hardwired into the capitalist system and the conduct of corporations. Owners, branded business models, advertisers, employment contracts, and society can act as censors.

The owners of the means of media and communication in society can exercise a proprietary right to restrict the workers' right to freedom of expression in their labor process and product. A media company owned by a CEO with a strong political ideology might enforce editorial guidelines that align with that ideology, censoring the workers' development and publication of any content that contradicts it. At Fox News, the conservative ideology of its owners, particularly Rupert Murdoch, influences the TV network's editorial agenda, pressuring news workers to align their work with the network's ideology.

Yet, corporate censorship is more complex than partisan owners dictating the ideology of the content the workers they employ produce and circulate. Sometimes, the branded business model of a media corporation is designed to be politically biased, partial to one ideology assumed to also be held by the audience group or audience commodity of readers, listeners and viewers, it wishes to attract to its products. The Sinclair Broadcast Group routinely runs TV segments with a specific right-wing slant across its numerous local TV stations, aiming to reel in and deliver the conservative audience commodity to ads. In these business models, workers are expected to conform to and perform for the brand's skewed ideology.

Advertisers can also act as censors of the worker's freedom to express themselves through their labor and its product. Because media corporations, rely heavily on advertising revenue, they are often pressured to tailor their content to meet the demands of their advertiser clients and those entities' larger corporate clients. This financial dependency can lead to *direct censorship* (where management prohibits workers from creating content that might be or be seen to be in opposition to the advertiser and their client), and *self-censorship* (where workers avoid topics or frames that might displease the advertiser and their client). For example, fossil fuel advertisers have historically pressured media outlets to minimize coverage of climate change. TV and movie studios may alter storylines to please product placers while YouTube creators that clash with consumerism may be made algorithmically invisible.

Sometimes, however, censorship can be imposed upon workers, from the moment they sign an employment contract. In many corporations, workers are expected to adhere to company policies and codes of conduct that may proactively curb or limit certain forms of expression deemed detrimental to the company's interests or brand. Often, the worker's freedom of expression is constrained by non-disclosure agreements (NDAs). In Hollywood, NDAs were used by The Weinstein Company to try to silence victims of Harvey Weinstein's sexual harassment and abuse. Many tech workers are also muzzled by NDAs.

Threats to the workers' freedom of expression can also come from outside corporations, by mobs of people that use intimidation, bullying, threats of violence, and violence itself, to try to silence the worker. Several workers in the DMEI have been targeted with threats and abuse by far-right white supremacists. Anita Sarkeesian, creator of the web series "Feminist Frequency," suffered extensive online harassment, including death and rape threats, during the "Gamergate" controversy due to her critique of sexism in video game cultures. The comedian Leslie Jones was afflicted by severe online harassment, including racist misogynistic attacks, and the hacking of her private information, following her role in the 2016 reboot of *Ghostbusters*. Global icon Beyoncé was attacked by white supremacist groups for speaking out against racism at her Super Bowl performance of "Formation." Additionally, journalists covering the global far-right's so-called Freedom Convoy were met with threats and violence from its members.

Around the world, in authoritarian capitalist and nominally liberal democratic capitalist societies, the workers' freedom to express themselves through the communicative and media labor process and product is constrained, whether by formal state censorship regimes, corporate censorship regimes, or a combination of both. Robust international and national legal protections, supportive unions, and a civic culture of informed public dialogue and progressive activism can empower workers to conscientiously speak out against social injustices and support movements to understand and change the world for the better. The next chapter recognizes the vibrant workers' movements and expressions of collective action in the DMEI.

12 What Are Workers Doing to Make the DMEI's Future of Work Better for All?

Collective Action!

Introduction

This chapter explores what workers in the digital media and entertainment industries (DMEI) are doing to make a better future of work. Diverging from top-down future forecasts by governments and corporations, it centers on grassroots collective actions, strategies, and tactics that workers in the DMEI are employing to define their own futures of work. The chapter recognizes the barriers to workers organizing collectively, such as employer loyalty, wage dependency, internal class and occupational divisions, geographic dispersion, dominant ideologies, corporate and state repression, and an education system favoring individualism. Despite these challenges, the chapter highlights collective actions by workers in the DMEI: unionization, cooperatives, and pro-worker social media campaigns like "Make Amazon Pay," "#MeToo," and "#OscarsSoWhite." Workers' collective action extends to class action lawsuits, and advocacy for Universal Public Goods (UPGs) and Universal Basic Income (UBI). Furthermore, workers are recognizing the significance of state power, political parties, and policy-making as an asymmetrical battleground that must be engaged. This overview of what workers are doing to make a better future of work in the DMEI not only addresses the challenges but also illuminates the opportunities for collective action to change the world for the better.

The Future of Work, from Below

This book has shown how the continuing logics of the capitalist system, as well as new Silicon Valley and Hollywood business models, have bolstered corporate power in the US and around the world, often at the expense of workers. As we ponder the "Future of Work," we encounter a plethora of predictions and projections, predominantly shaped by powerful entities such as corporations, governments, and the consulting firms they hire.

DOI: 10.4324/9781003131076-13

McKinsey, Deloitte, Accenture, and Catalant promulgate future scenarios emphasizing endlessly disruptive, technology-driven changes. Financial institutions like the Bank of America and Barclays, along with the business press, including *Fortune*, *Forbes*, and *The Economist*, are vocal proponents of this technologically determined future of work. For capital, the preferred future of work is one where workers will be compelled to continuously upskill, endure a life marked by uncertainty and precarity, and embrace an entrepreneurial mindset. This future offers no hope for security. The message from capital to labor seems to be this: adapt and compete in the economy we rule, or find yourself destitute, with no right to a good life, and no chance at making one.

Over the past several decades, corporate and state restructuring has weakened the power of the working class in the DMEI, and in society as a whole. Although there was never a "golden age" of work, the previous 50 years of state and corporate restructuring have made life more precarious for workers across all sectors of the economy. In the first quarter of the 21st century, workers have endured the globalization of capitalism, de-industrialization and the outsourcing of manufacturing, service, and media-tech jobs, unending wars that cost the taxpayer trillions and killed millions, a global financial crisis and slump, the COVID-19 pandemic, mental health crisis, the consequences of global climate change, the automation of an increasing number of occupations by generative AI, the proliferation of precarious gigs, widespread unemployment and homelessness, topped off by a rollback of the state's capacity and willingness to fund and provision the vital social programs and public goods that most people need. The transformation of the social democratic welfare state into a neoliberal corporate state has resulted in policies that often prioritize private interests, at the expense of the public good. Wealth inequality between society's super-rich and everyone else has resultantly reached an unprecedented extreme, while real wages have steadily stagnated over time and debt has become a new way of life for most. For many in the working class, social progress feels to have stopped. There is no hope for change when soaring income and wealth inequalities empower the top 1% to distance themselves from the majority, when basic necessities of life are commodified and tough to access, and life expectancy even in the richest country continues to decline. Social democratic parties, unions, and working-class social movements still exist, but are frequently in a compromised or defensive position, struggling to parry the blows of the neoliberal center and fascist far-Right while holding on to the diminishing wages, social provisions and protections, and labor rights that took a century of class struggle to win. Unless there are major structural changes, it is hard to look forward to the future. And yet, we must not stop laboring for something different. As Lewis (2024) says:

> Capitalism is an operating system. Operating systems can be changed. All we have is each other, the earth, the sky, our animal co-inhabitants, and these machines we've created. Humanity's legacy should not be exploitation, the reduction of life into ingestible data sets, and the rationalization of genocide. Our current operating system has brought the world to its present state, but we are creative and resourceful beings. We can do better. And it is up to us. There is no technological solution because we are the origin of all technology. The future is our responsibility.

In these dire times, the history of working-class movements and their remarkable achievements offers a glimmer of hope, as can all of the present and emerging workers' organizations and collective actions. While capital continuously tries to monopolize the narrative of the future of work and impose it upon workers, workers, collectively organized, struggle to continuously rewrite and reshape that future of work, for themselves, and their communities. Thus, the future of work isn't predetermined; in the past, as in today, it is a battleground that will be shaped by class struggle. In this regard, instead of asking "what is the future of work?", a more pertinent question is: "whose vision of the future of work will win?" The DMEI is ground zero in this struggle over the future of work. These workers' labor is the source of the intellect, creativity, and innovation that made the digital society, and if united, these workers could drive post-capitalist transformation. Yet, there are significant structural, institutional, and ideological barriers standing in the way of making a better and different future, and always a big gap between just being working class and becoming a working class united.

Barriers to Collective Action in the DMEI

There is a working-class "in-itself" and a working-class "for-itself." What are the barriers that impede workers from taking the leap from being a class in-itself to one for-itself?

First, corporations in the DMEI play a central role in shaping workers' identities and loyalties, often leading them to closely identify with their brands, as opposed to viewing themselves as part of a broader working-class collective. Workers are typically organized into highly competitive units within their respective corporations and encouraged to align their interests and well-being with those of the employer. The worker's dependence on a salary, wage, or gig payment cements this identification, motivating them to work diligently in support of their employer's strategic goals. As a consequence, workers are encouraged to compete not only against workers in other corporations but also against their peers within the same corporation, diminishing the basis for intra-organizational and cross-organizational solidarity. The result is that workers' allegiances are often more closely tied to their employers rather than to a political idea of the working class a whole.

Second, the internal division of labor within corporations of the DMEI can impede working-class solidarity by creating distinctions among workers in terms of status, pay, and decision-making power. For example, in a typical movie production company, a clear hierarchy is observable, sometimes captured by the "below-the-line" and "above-the-line" distinction: high-paid executives and producers who make crucial decisions and issue orders contrast with lower paid technical staff like editors, sound engineers, and camera operators. In Silicon Valley, engineers and developers often enjoy big salaries and extensive benefits, whereas electronics factory workers in other countries, tasked with assembling the devices designed in Cupertino, toil in brutal conditions for substantially less pay. Despite contributing to the same end product, these workers experience vastly different labor processes. Within one corporation, differences in wages, working conditions, and decision-making power establish a hierarchy that diminishes the ability of workers to view themselves as part of a unified class with shared interests.

Third, the global production chains of the DMEI in a world system still structured as territorial nation-states make collective class identification in a truly internationalist sense extremely challenging. In the DMEI, corporations often coordinate the production of hardware, software, and content across international borders, hiring a multitude of workers from various contractor firms in multiple countries, regions, and cities to complete specific tasks or components of the final product. A major tech company might design a smartphone in the US, manufacture its components in several Asian countries, and then assemble it in Europe, paying for the labor of many workers who never meet. Each group of workers operates under separate patchworks of global, regional and national labor laws and social conditions, making it challenging to establish a unified approach to labor rights and collective action. This fragmentation is accentuated by the varying levels of unionization and labor organization in different countries. While workers in one country or region might have strong union support and collective bargaining power, their counterparts in another country or region may lack such strength entirely. This geographical dispersion of tasks and the differences in labor rights and protections across local and national borders is a significant barrier to global or international working-class solidarity. Internationalism is especially difficult to achieve in contexts where populist autocrats and demagogues reimagine the nation in the most reactionary and regressive ways. They construct and solidify distinctions between Us and Them, Self and Other, and socialize workers to view themselves as members of a national ethno-people with shared interests alongside the national business elites and state leaders who govern (or rule) them.

Fourth, the dominant ideology presents a formidable barrier to working-class unity in the DMEI. Workers are often encouraged to view themselves as lone entrepreneurs engaged in dog-eat-dog competition with one another, rather than as part of a working class capable of improving its conditions. The DMEI's corporate cultures promote a meritocratic ideology where success is attributed to individual hard work, talent and luck, and the American Dream narratives surrounding many CEOS and celebrities exemplify this. The dominant ideology is reinforced by the Right's anti-worker propaganda, which dismisses the concept of a "working class" and champions the "middle class." Also, the slogan that "there is no alternative" to free-market capitalism, while unappealing to many, is infrequently countered with proposals and prospects for a viable alternative to the system capable of motivating hope and moving people to action. Related delusions such as "free markets are essential for freedom and democracy" or "a rising tide lifts all boats" are often accepted without question, further entrenching the dominant ideology. These ideological barriers stand in the way of the unity of the DMEI's multitudinous working class. At the same time, the inequities and oppressions stemming from institutional discourses and practices of classism, racism, sexism, ageism, and ableism persist, while liberal EDI frameworks and identity politics get misread by the Right as a "cultural Marxist" conspiracy and called out by the Left for "woke washing" corporate power.

Fifth, the repression of working-class organization, solidarity, and struggle by states and corporations is a major problem. Governments have taken direct actions against labor movements in countries, outright banning or heavily restricting independent union formation and collective action. In countries where unions are permitted, states often exhibit a bias toward corporate interests. Even when workers go on strike, governments may weaponize back-to-work legislation to force workers back to the daily grind, claiming it is in the public or national interest. Corporations, too, play a crucial role in suppressing working-class solidarity. They and their managers may use harassment, wrongful termination, bullying, pervasive surveillance, and harsh discipline to intimidate workers, dissuading them from starting a union or taking collective action. In sum, state and corporate repression disrupts class solidarity in the DMEI.

Despite the numerous barriers to working-class solidarity both inside and outside the DMEI, workers demonstrate remarkable resilience and ingenuity in developing collective resources and capacities and strategies and tactics to contest the rule of capital over their lives and labors.

Openings to Collective Organization and Action in the DMEI

Unions

Unions play an undeniable role in backing workers' rights and expanding them further. A union is essentially an association of workers that forms a legal unit or legal personhood, often referred to as a "bargaining unit." This unit acts as a bargaining agent and a representative for a group of workers in all legal matters related to or arising from the administration of a collective agreement. In the early 20th century, unions grew very rapidly in many countries, but over the past 50 years, they have shrunk. In North America and across Europe, the number of unionized workers is at an all-time low. In 2022, the US's unionization rate stood at around 10.1%, Canada's was approximately 30%, and across Europe, countries such as Sweden and Denmark boasted higher rates exceeding 60%, while others like Germany were closer to 20% or lower and France around 12%. Despite the decline of unions, more and more working people want to start or join one (Saad, 2023). There's good reason for this. Unions organize, fight for and win a wide range of rights and benefits for workers. Among the major achievements of unions are fair wages, workplace health and safety, the 40-hour workweek (and overtime pay), healthcare benefits, pension plans, paid leave benefits (e.g., sick leave, vacation time, and parental leave), job security, collective bargaining rights, anti-discrimination measures, and grievance mechanisms. Beyond the workplace, unions have engaged in political advocacy to fight for and win labor laws, policies and regulations that benefit the working class, improving conditions for all workers.

Over the past decade, there has been a union resurgence across the DMEI. In Silicon Valley, Google workers formed the Alphabet Workers Union in partnership with the Communications Workers of America (CWA). Apple Store workers in Towson, Maryland, initiated unionization within the company's retail sector. ZeniMax workers have also unionized under the CWA, marking the first official union linked to Microsoft. Amazon warehouse worker unionization efforts are bold, from Staten Island to Alabama and Chicago. Collective Action in Tech (https://data.collectiveaction.tech/), led by Ben Tarnoff and Clarissa Redwine, documents over 542 worker actions in and around Silicon Valley. Nicole Cohen and Greig de Peuter's (2020) book, *New Media Unions: Organizing Digital Journalists*, and the "Digital Media Unionization Timeline" (https://culturalworkersorganize.org/digital-media-organizing-timeline/) of the Cultural Workers Organize project, showcase the massive wave of new media unions. Part of CWA, The Digital Media Workers Association promotes fair labor practices and equitable treatment in the industry. The gaming industry, too, is experiencing a rise in unionization, with Raven Software's unionization under the CWA impressive. In the US, Corsair Gaming and Halo Infinite and Forza Motorsport QA workers have sought a union (Carpenter, 2023; Keogh & Abraham, 2022). Some Marvel VFX artists are unionizing too. As are podcasters: workers at Lemonada Media, the podcast network behind titles such as *Wiser Than Me With Julia Louis-Dreyfus* and *Fail Better with David Duchovny* unionized under the Writers Guild of America East (WGAE). So have workers at Crooked Media, the iHeart Podcast Network, Pineapple Street Studios, Pushkin Industries, The Ringer, and Spotify Studios. There are also a variety of worker organizations, associations, and activism networks that advocate for labor rights, despite not being traditional labor unions. The Tech Workers Coalition (TWC) aims to build community among tech workers and support discussions on workers' rights and interventions in support of ethical tech practices. Game Workers Unite advocates for the rights of game workers, the Freelancers Union is a non-profit that champions independents, and the Creators Guild of America supports content creators. The renewal of the union movement in the DMEI is a positive development, but for those looking to build a future beyond capitalism, other types of openly political organizations are also needed.

Strikes are a powerful expression of collective action by unionized workers who temporarily refuse to labor to demand better conditions, fairer wages, and other employment-related rights from their employers. This form of collective action epitomizes working class solidarity, as workers unite to achieve workplace improvements that would be impossible to secure individually. Strikes provide immense leverage workers struggles against management, as halting production, slowing or stopping the labor process itself, directly impacts a corporation's profits, forcing management to take workers' demands seriously. Strikes also shine a light on the exploitative and oppressive conditions workers endure, raising public awareness about what's going on in an industry or sector, and potentially, garnering public support for the workers' cause. Also, when workers participate in a strike, they may solidify their class consciousness and sense of collective strength. This can empower workers by showing that they are not alone and powerful when united. Furthermore, strikes can be a tool used by workers to defend themselves against a corporation's violations of their labor rights and to advocate for new protections, often sparking significant state-level legislative, regulatory and policy changes that benefit the entire working class. Historically, workers' strikes have been key to achieving major reforms. They are a shining example of the power and promise of worker-centered collective action.

Fairness in Factual TV Campaign

The Fairness in Factual TV campaign (https://fairnessinfactualtv.ca/) is a worker-led initiative seeking to improve working conditions in the non-fiction TV and film industry, covering genres like reality, lifestyle, and documentary. Launched in 2015 with support from CWA Canada and the Canadian Media Guild (CMG), the campaign's main goals include fair pay, safe working conditions, understandable rules, portable benefits, and proper onscreen credits for workers. The IATSE joined the campaign in 2019, expanding its reach across North America. Over 400 workers have joined the movement, resulting in notable achievements such as the development of an industry guidebook, data collection on pay rates, community-building events, advocacy for labor law changes, and significant legal action against Cineflix by CMG's law firm, Cavalluzzo LLP, for unpaid holidays and overtime. The campaign focuses on securing industry-wide contracts that cater to the diverse needs of workers in production offices, on set, and in post-production. Key objectives include setting basic minimums for each job role, regular wage increases, ending wage theft, enforcing health and safety standards, providing paid sick days and health benefits, ensuring work/life balance by giving workers the right to accept or refuse overtime, and eliminating arbitrary unpaid hiatuses. The Fairness in Factual TV campaign represents a positive step toward transforming the non-fiction TV and film industry into a fairer, safer, and more equitable environment.

Cooperatives in the Arts and Tech

Cooperatives go back to early industrial capitalism, a foundational example being the Rochdale Society of Equitable Pioneers, established in 1844. In *Sharing Like We Mean It: Working Co-operatively in the Cultural and Tech Sectors*, de Peuter et al. (2020) define a "co-operative" as

> an organization collectively owned and democratically governed by its members. A worker co-op, for example, is a business owned by the people who work in it, while a consumer co-op is owned by the people who purchase from it. Co-ops can be for-profit or not-for-profit, a small-scale operation or a vast enterprise. Co-ops are created to satisfy an unmet need among their members, whether it's a need for a sustainable livelihood or affordable rent. Conventional companies are driven to maximize profit. In contrast, the co-operative tradition is rooted in mutual aid, dignity, local economies, and

What are Workers Doing to Make the DMEI's Future of Work? 285

service to community. In a co-op, big decisions are not made single-handedly by a boss, a venture capitalist, or the largest shareholder. As democratic organizations, co-ops uphold the principle of one member, one vote.

(p. 6)

According to de Peuter et al. (2020), cooperatives are guided by *seven fundamental principles*. First, they offer *voluntary and open membership*, welcoming individuals from all backgrounds without discrimination. These members actively exercise *democratic control*, having equal voting rights and participating in decision-making and policy formation. *Economic participation* is also key, with members contributing to and having democratic control over the cooperative's capital. Cooperatives remain *autonomous and self-reliant*, even when entering external partnerships, ensuring that member control is always preserved. *Education and training* are provided to members and employees, enhancing their contribution to the cooperative's growth, while also informing the public about the cooperative model. A spirit of collaboration is fostered through *cooperation* among cooperatives at various levels, enhancing service and movement strength. Last, a deep *concern for community* is central, with cooperatives working toward sustainable community development through member-approved policies. These principles collectively ensure that cooperatives operate in a manner that is inclusive, member-focused, and community-oriented (de Peuter et al., 2020, p. 10).

Worker cooperatives in the DMEI present innovative alternatives to traditional business models, focusing on democratic control and worker empowerment (Boyle & Oakley, 2018; de Peuter, 2017; de Peuter et al., 2022; Sandoval, 2016, 2018). In their study of coops in the creative industries in Canada, the US, and the UK, de Peuter et al. (2020) found "a small but vibrant co-operative landscape in the cultural and tech sectors, from co-operatively run art galleries to co-op advertising agencies, web development companies, architecture firms, coworking spaces, ceramic studios, and film production rental services" (p. 7). The researchers identify many pertinent examples of coops. For example, KO_OP in Montreal and Meerkat Media in Brooklyn are worker co-ops in digital games and media production. Lower Town Lofts in Saint Paul offers live-work studios for artists, while Means TV in Detroit streams film and news. The New Internationalist in Oxford, a multi-stakeholder co-op, engages in publishing, and Openflows in New York develops open-source software (de Peuter et al., 2020, p. 20). The researchers also describe the challenges of working in coops (de Peuter et al., 2020, p. 42). While prioritizing people over profit and eschewing competitive logics, cooperatives are politically constrained when operating within capitalist markets that pressure all entities to focus on the bottom line and growth. "Co-ops are not a magic solution to systemic work problems," but the "co-op model, in conjunction with other pro-worker policies and organizations, holds potential to democratically remake work in ways that have yet to be fully realized or widely tested in creative industries" (de Peuter et al., 2020, p. 7).

Platform cooperatives, or platform co-ops, represent cooperatively owned and democratically governed platforms, such as websites or mobile apps (Duda, 2016; Grohmann, 2021, 2022, 2023; McCann & Yazici, 2018; Muldoon, 2020, 2023; Nicoli & Paltrinieri, 2019; Sandoval, 2016, 2018, 2020; Scholz, 2016; Scholz & Schneider, 2016; Schor, 2020). In *Platform Cooperativism: Challenging the Corporate Sharing Economy*, Scholz (2016) argues that we can draw from the history of cooperatives and infuse cooperative principles into the redesign of the Internet and platform ecology. Scholz (2016) introduces the concept of "platform cooperativism," a model that advocates for new ownership structures on the Internet that entail democratic governance and solidarity. Currently, "platform capitalism" is predominantly shaped by top-down corporate decisions originating from Silicon Valley. Scholz (2016) says what is needed is a new platform model centered around sharing, aggregation, openness, and cooperation. Scholz (2016) argues that the essence of platform cooperativism isn't about defeating the dominant "death star platforms." Instead, it's about "writing over them in people's minds, incorporating different ownership models, and then inserting them back into the mainstream" (p. 26).

The three design principles of platform cooperativism Scholz (2016) outlines are as follows. The first principle involves emulating the core technology of platforms like Uber, Task Rabbit, Airbnb, or UpWork. Scholz emphasizes using this technology under a different ownership model that adheres to democratic values. This approach aims to rectify the skewed benefits of the sharing or on-demand economy, which typically favor a select few. Scholz (2016, p. 50) asserts, "It is in this sense that platform cooperativism is about structural change, a change of ownership." The second principle revolves around solidarity, which is lacking in the current economy. Scholz envisions platforms that can be owned and operated by various cooperative forms, from inventive unions and cities to multi-stakeholder and worker-owned co-ops. This principle broadens the scope of ownership models, embedding a sense of community and mutual support. The third principle involves rethinking concepts like innovation and efficiency to benefit everyone, not just the few. This principle challenges platform capitalism, and its profit-obsessed model. When put into platform practice, these principles collectively aim to transform the digital platform economy into a more inclusive, fair, and responsive system for workers and users. As Scholz (2016, p. 50) puts it, "Platform

Cooperativism challenges the Silicon Valley frame of reference." He furthermore emphasizes, "You cannot counter economic inequality with the benevolence of owners; together we must redesign the infrastructure with democracy at its core." For others such as James Muldoon (2023), what is needed to go beyond Silicon Valley and digital capitalism is "platform socialism," or "the organisation of the digital economy through the social ownership of digital assets and democratic control over the infrastructure and systems that govern our digital lives" (p. 3).

Worker Social (Media) Movement Activism: "Make Amazon Pay," "#MeToo," "#OscarsSoWhite" and "No Tech for Apartheid"

Throughout capitalism's history, communication media has always played a salient role in making workers' identities, interests, and politics audible and visible. Grohmann et al. (2023) elaborate on this by introducing a tripartite model comprising workers' communication at work, through social media, and in struggle. Communication at work involves verbal and non-verbal interactions among workers that nourish solidarity and build collective capacity despite capital's efforts to control such communicative exchanges. Communication through social media platforms like WhatsApp, Facebook, Instagram, and YouTube entails workers networking and building solidarity. Communication in struggle encompasses all kinds of media tactics, from shaming corporations to streaming and tweeting in support of workers' strikes and protests.

In the DMEI, all three forms of worker communications are at play. Some workers are starting and joining social media movement campaigns that fuse the three when communicating about what happened in the workplace, making tactical uses of social media platforms, and struggling for worker's justice or rights. For example, the "Make Amazon Pay" campaign (https://makeamazonpay.com/), supported by over 80 organizations including labor unions and environmental groups, challenges Amazon's exploitative practices and focuses on labor rights, tax fairness, and environmental responsibility. Workers in Hollywood are also organizing social media campaigns to spotlight injustices within the industry. The #MeToo movement (https://moveme.berkeley.edu/project/metoo/), initiated by Tarana Burke in 2006 and popularized by Alyssa Milano in 2017, has elevated a feminist workers' consciousness in Hollywood and beyond. Triggered by Harvey Weinstein's many crimes, #MeToo led to an outpouring of stories about sexual harassment and assault, shined a light on gender inequality, and prompted reforms in Hollywood. The #OscarsSoWhite campaign, initiated by April Reign in 2015, took on anti-Black racism in Hollywood. Calling out the overwhelming whiteness of all the actors nominated for an Oscar at the 2015 Academy Awards,

Reign's viral hashtag highlighted Hollywood's longstanding underrepresentation of racial and ethnic minorities, women, LGBTQ+ individuals, and people with disabilities. Gaining momentum in 2016 amid similarly white nomination patterns, the campaign drew support from Spike Lee and Jada Pinkett Smith. The No Tech for Apartheid campaign (https://www.notechforapartheid.com/), co-organized by Jewish Voice for Peace and MPower Change, targets the collaborations between Google, Amazon, and the Israeli state. It emerged in response to a $1.22 billion contract signed by Amazon Web Services and Google Cloud to provide cloud technologies to the Israeli government and military, which have been part of the genocidal destruction of Gaza and extensive state surveillance and displacement of Palestinian peoples. The campaign advocates for technology to unite people rather than perpetuate apartheid, and is supported by some brave Google and Amazon workers, who've organized walkouts and protests. These are but four of the many worker social media campaigns that highlight the exploitative and oppressive conditions of work, mobilize public support for workers' interests, shift public opinion, and sometimes even bring about reforms.

Workers' Law: Class Action

Workers in the DMEI are using the law to advance their interests. With class action lawsuits, they are compelling the state to enforce labor laws, bringing to light violations of these and making corporations pay for their crimes. A *class action lawsuit* is a legal proceeding where one or more individuals, known as "class representatives" or "named plaintiffs," bring a case on behalf of a larger group with similar legal claims or grievances, referred to as the "class." This type of lawsuit is commonly used when multiple people suffer similar harm, such as financial losses or rights violations, due to the actions or negligence of a single entity or a group of entities. The process begins with the identification of a potential class with similar legal claims, followed by the filing of the lawsuit by the named plaintiffs. The court then determines if the lawsuit meets the requirements for class certification. Once certified, potential members are notified, allowing them the choice to opt-out and pursue individual claims. The lawsuit progresses through discovery and pretrial proceedings, where both parties exchange evidence and information. Many class action cases, especially in the DMEI, are often settled out of court, but some may proceed to trial. Successful class actions culminate in the court determining the distribution of damages or benefits among class members and the entry of a final judgment, although post-judgment issues like disputes over the distribution of damages may persist.

Significant class action lawsuits in the tech industry, particularly against major corporations, illustrate how workers can take on monopolies and advance workers' rights. A notable case is the "Tech Employee Antitrust Litigation" against Apple Inc., Google Inc., Intel Corp, and Adobe Systems Inc. Initiated in 2011 by the DOJ and led by tech workers, the lawsuit alleged that these companies and their CEOs conspired to prevent employee poaching, restricting job mobility and suppressing salaries. The case, which revealed how CEOs like Steve Jobs and Eric Schmidt agreed behind closed doors not to hire workers employed by each other's corporations, highlighted the adverse impact of such practices on workers' career opportunities and wage growth. In 2015, US District Judge Lucy Koh approved a $415 million settlement, marking a significant victory for tech workers and setting a precedent against monopoly employment practices in Silicon Valley (Lieff Cabraser Heimann & Bernstein, 2015). Another important lawsuit involved Facebook, where in 2020, Oscar Veneszee Jr., Howard Winns Jr., and Jazsmin Smith filed a complaint alleging Facebook's discrimination against Black workers in hiring, evaluations, promotions, and pay. They accused Facebook of violating several civil rights acts, pointing to the low representation of Black employees, which stood at 3.8% despite the company's workforce expanding by 400%. The lawsuit highlighted racial bias in hiring, promotion practices, and the workplace environment, contrasting Facebook's public performance of support for civil rights with its uncivil internal treatment of Black workers.

Working class movements that take on the many corporations that break labor laws with class action suits and aim to reform capitalism through legal action are positive and needed. However, for those seeking a radical change, what's needed is a fundamental rejection of the structural and ideological foundations that the law historically and presently provides to capitalism, corporations and its ruling class (Glasbeek, 2024).

Universal Basic Income (UBI) and Universal Public Goods (UPGs): Left and Right

UBI is supported by some workers as a way to address the precarity of labor and life in the DMEI. According to Wright (2006, p. 5), UBI encompasses the following:

> All citizens are given a monthly stipend sufficiently high to provide them with a standard of living above the poverty line. This monthly income is universal rather than means-tested—it is given automatically to all citizens regardless of their individual economic circumstances. And it is unconditional—receiving the basic income does

not depend upon performing any labor services or satisfying other conditions. In this way basic income is like publicly financed universal health insurance: in a universal health care system, medical care is provided both to citizens who exercise and eat healthy diets and to those who do not. It is not a condition of getting medical care that one be "responsible" with respect to one's health. Unconditional, universal basic income takes the same stance about basic needs: as a matter of basic rights, no one should live in poverty in an affluent society.

The concept of UBI, initially proposed by 16th-century philosophers, has won some support across the political spectrum. On the Left, progressives view UBI as a means to alleviate poverty and precarity. On the Right, some conservatives and libertarians consider it a way to crush what remains of the social welfare state, once and for all. In the US, the Black Panthers and Martin Luther King Jr. supported guaranteed income as a form of economic justice. Neoliberal economist Milton Friedman also proposed it as a form of negative income tax. UBI is sometimes posited as a "post-ideological solution suited to a new era of politics" (Battistoni, 2017). Yet, because UBI is "politically ambiguous, it also has the potential to act as a Trojan horse for the left or right." In the end, the version of UBI we get will depend "on the political forces that shape it," and the movements and parties that make it (Battistoni, 2017).

UBI is currently a subject of intense debate among a wide variety of thinkers (Calnitsky, 2017; Spring Magazine, 2020). Some on the Left view UBI as a transformative strategy capable of mitigating capitalism's numerous harms and paving the way toward a more egalitarian society. Described as a "non-reformist reform," UBI is seen as an achievable goal within capitalism. Influenced by socialist feminist critiques of unwaged reproductive labor and the Civil Rights Movement's push for economic justice, UBI is not just a financial safety net but a material foundation for human fulfillment (Bregman, 2017). Key advocates of UBI include Guy Standing (2011), who sees it as harm reduction for the precariat class, and Erik Olin Wright (2006), who viewed UBI as a means to empower the working class. The endorsement of UBI by the Movement for Black Lives as part of a reparations program and its inclusion in Canada's Leap Manifesto (rejected by the NDP) signify its expansive appeal. For some, UBI is an answer to capitalism's failure to provide a living wage and a security measure against modern workers' greatest threats: precarity and the looming impact of AI-induced joblessness and wagelessness. However, the likelihood of a Left winning a war of position and war of maneuver and using the State to establish UBI is currently slim. Presently, the Right seems to be ascendant in many countries and its acolytes are pushing for a Right-wing variant of UBI.

Much of the excitement around UBI is being driven by right-wing libertarian and capitalist techno-accelerationists. High-profile tech entrepreneurs like Elon Musk, Peter Thiel, Marc Andreessen, and others have promoted UBI. Andrew Yang, during his 2020 presidential campaign, branded UBI as a "freedom dividend," aligning it with free market ideals. However, the right-wing vision of UBI is met with substantial criticism from the democratic socialist and union left. Public Services International's review of 16 UBI trials across various countries found no evidence of sustained long-term benefits or significant improvements in well-being and equality. These trials often offered payments below the poverty line to disadvantaged individuals but failed to demonstrate long-term viability or scalability. Examples like the Alaska Permanent Fund, popular but ineffective in significantly reducing child poverty or income inequalities, and Finland's limited UBI trial, which was not expanded due to political challenges, further highlight the difficulties in implementing and funding UBI at a broader scale. Even if UBI worked and was worth scaling up, it would be extraordinarily costly. The International Labour Office estimates that a sufficient UBI program could consume 20%–30% of most countries' GDP: with an estimated global cost of around 32.7% of GDP, who would pay? UBI would require massively increased taxation on the wealthiest and corporations, the very same entities that have been avoiding taxes in every way they can and lobbying for the dismantling of the social welfare state. Critics also argue that UBI funding could lead to cuts in Universal Public Goods (UPGs) like education and healthcare, which are vital in combating inequality and often benefit the poorest most. The more generous the UBI, the greater the strain on funding for essential public goods and services. Furthermore, UBI is critiqued for potentially solidifying a neoliberal outcome: increasing individuals' dependence on the market, not a democratic state, for goods and service provision. As an alternative to UBI, some call for more robust UPGs, and a remaking of the welfare state, for the digital age (Huws, 2020).

State and Power: Politics, Parties, Policies

Workers are engaging in political action beyond traditional labor unions, cooperatives, and social movement campaigns. Many workers realize that participation in political parties oriented to remaking the state matters. In every country, the state is central in making, upholding, modifying, and enforcing the national laws, policies, and regulations made for the DMEI and other sectors. The laws, policies, and regulations made are not merely about technical problem-solving; they constitute an inherently political process, which is fought over, shaped and steered by political parties, as well as their leaders and constituents, in civil society, and through the institutions of the state and media, where ideas constitute a battleground. While parties frequently formulate their platforms in the name of the broader "national interest," their ideas about law, policy, and regulation align with the specific values, interests, and goals of particular interest groups or coalitions. Furthermore, parties take sides in capital-labor conflicts, influencing labor legislation, policy, and regulation that impacts the conditions of work in the DMEI and structures the economic and political terrain of class politics. Politicians also take sides in battles between capital and labor. While Bernie Sanders may champion workers' rights, conservative Republicans maintain strong anti-union positions, spewing the idea that what's good for capital is good for America, and what's good for American capital is good for the world.

For workers aiming to establish and strengthen their political power, engaging with the state and fighting for and winning pro-worker laws, policies and regulations is vital. For decades, the concept of "changing the world without taking power" guided many emancipatory social movements. But much more than street protests outside the power structures are needed to change them, and the world. Winning state power and also fundamentally democratizing the state itself should be the goal (Panitch, 2020). In this context, distinguishing between "policy from above" and "policy from below" is key (de Peuter & Cohen, 2014). Policy "from above" involves top-down changes in labor policies, often initiated by states on behalf of corporate interests without workers' participation. In contrast, policy "from below" is enacted by the state, but in response to policy decided by workers (de Peuter & Cohen, 2015, p. 310). Proposals for the reform of state policies related to work in the DMEI may not itself bring about a revolution. But the sphere of reform is still a significant domain where positive changes—safeguarding and strengthening existing labor rights and winning new rights for all workers while protecting and promoting the universal provision of public goods and services that meet workers' needs—can be fought for, and sometimes even won by workers. These small but significant victories can increase workers' confidence, and contribute in purposeful ways to the wider rebuilding of the infrastructural resources and capacities that the international labor movement and democratic socialist Left lost. Reform is one way to use policy thinking and action to try to shape a future society where the voice of labor takes center stage, making workers, not capital, the agents of history in the DMEI. In essence, state reformers recognize that meaningful policy change is not merely a hope but a necessity.

Blueprints and Real Utopias

Slogans like "Think Different" (Apple), "Don't Be Evil" (Google), "The Happiest Place on Earth" (Disney), "Empower every person and every organization on the planet to achieve more" (Microsoft), and "Bringing the World Closer Together" (Facebook/Meta) from the DMEI represent dreams of a better society. Yet, these dreams are contradicted by the capitalist system's logics and the business models its leading corporations abide and extend. The false utopianism of the DMEI's branding continuously leads nowhere but to the dystopia of now. More than ever, real utopias are needed. In "Socialism for Realists," Sam Gindin (2018) emphasizes this, stating, "Winning people over to a complex and protracted struggle to introduce profoundly new ways of producing, living, and relating to each other demands a much deeper engagement with socialism's actual possibility." This task necessitates neither proving socialism is an inevitable future nor outlining a detailed blueprint, but in developing a compelling and viable framework for a post-capitalist society that underscores "socialism's plausibility." In a similar vein, Erik Olin Wright's *Envisioning Real Utopias* (2010) introduces an "emancipatory" social science. This involves diagnosing the pitfalls of capitalism, recognizing and examining existing alternatives to the system, and experimenting with social transformation. He conceptualizes "real utopias" as existing formations which prefigure another world. Another world is possible! Just as capitalism emerged from feudalism, post-capitalism has the potential to emerge from within this system. It will be the collective labor power—the knowledge and skills—of millions of workers now harnessed by the DMEI for dystopian ends that power real utopias. "From 'below," "above," and everywhere "in between," the self-emancipation of the working class—its development of the capacities and resources to free itself from the realm of necessity, to exercise democratic self-governance, and to understand and solve some of humanity's greatest social problems—remains essential to "revolution." Its legacy will not be a single glorious event where everything everywhere is transformed all at once, but a "long revolution" in economy, polity, culture and technology, forged from the multitude of present-day collective organizations, practices, and actions that are truly "being creative" when imagining and making a better and different future.

13 Postscript

Not "Being Creative", For a Study of Work in the DMEI, Post-"Creative Exceptionalism"

I opened the introduction to this book by reflecting on my first-gen university student climb into academia, and my refusal to conform to the "creativity dispositif" prevalent in neoliberal states, New Economy firms, and educational institutions as one of my motivations for going to grad school (McRobbie, 2016). Now, as an outro to this book, I wish to leave off with the call for a study of work in the DMEI that poses an alternative to the "creative exceptionalism" that dominates much public discourse about work in the "creative industries" today (and has also characterized some academic theory, research and writing on the topic over the past quarter century or so).

By "creative exceptionalism," I refer to the tendency of government policy-makers, business leaders, and researchers to speak of certain industries, workforces, and products as exceptional solely due to their associations with "creativity." "Creative exceptionalism" is the idea that "creativity" exists in certain industries, distinguishing them from others that are traditionally not considered "creative." It is the idea that the workers employed by these special industries possess uniquely "creative" labor power, and also, that the work they do for these industries depends upon their "creativity." Relatedly, it is the idea that the products of these industries are "creative" because they rely on "creativity" or some kind of uniquely "creative labor" intellectual capacity as a primary input. In the past, I have used phrases like "creative industries," "creative workers" and "creative goods," and even intended to title this book "Work in the Creative Industries: A Critical Introduction." But I now sense the discourse of creative economics has confounded instead of clarified what's going on with work. I expand a multifaceted critique of "creative exceptionalism" below.

Firstly, I part ways with "creative exceptionalism" inherent in creative industries policy frameworks because "creativity" has served the interests of the state and capital while neglecting the actual conditions of workers. Originating from the UK Government Department for Culture, Media and Sport (DCMS) in 1998 using "templates forged in Silicon

DOI: 10.4324/9781003131076-14

Valley and Hollywood where the profitability of intellectual property had been perfected" (Mould, 2018, p. 9), the ideal of the "creative industries" went global and was adapted by states around the world in support of new finance capital-friendly national and urban development plans, post-industrial workplace training and skills regimes, and the higher education sector's role in remaking ways of life and work (Flew & Cunningham, 2010; Florida, 2004; McGuigan, 2010). The United Nations Conference on Trade and Development (UNCTAD) began using an idea of the creative industries to generate data about cross-border trade in creative goods and services and with the United Nations' Development Programme (UNDP), championed them as a "source of structural economic transformation, socio-economic progress, job creation and innovation" that contributes "to social inclusion and sustainable human development" (Palanivel, 2019). From the Global North to the Global South, the creative industries have been promoted by planners as an engine of economic, social, and cultural uplift for all, but all too often, the harsh realities faced by workers in these industries are ignored. The idea that the creative industries can resolve the multiplying crisis caused and worsened by the structures of the political economy they are part of is optimistic, if not naive. Yet, this belief conveniently allows the proprietors of these creative industries to feel virtuous, gives politicians and creative policy-makers a veneer of progressivism, and leads the so-called creative workers within these industries to view themselves as extraordinary. Pronouncements of the "killing of the creative class" (Timburg, 2015) and "the death of the artist" (Deresiewicz, 2020) point to how idealistic "creative solutionism" can be. The COVID-19 pandemic spotlighted the disparity between the ideal of the creative industries and the real condition of its labor force: in 2020, 10 million "creative" jobs were obliterated around the globe, intensifying competition between all those precarious contractors hustling for gigs (Bateman, 2022). Yet, boosted by a Meta Platforms-funded study authored by Richard Florida (2022), the creative industries ideal seems to be revived with the "Creator Economy," a concept that holds out the promise of a "Creator Middle Class" (sans class struggle). There is a need to debunk the myths surrounding the creative industries and get real about the frequently precarious conditions of work (Banks & Hesmondhalgh, 2009; de Peuter, 2011, 2014; de Peuter & Cohen, 2015; Hesmondhalgh & Baker, 2010, 2011; McRobbie, 2016; Mould, 2018; Ross, 2009).

Secondly, the critical research that rightly sheds light on the precarious lives and labor conditions of workers in "creative" industries, often overshadowed by narratives of meritocratic dreams come true, can sometimes exaggerate the uniqueness of these industries, portraying them as fundamentally and exceptionally precarious and their workers as facing a higher level of precarity than those in non-creative industries. Yet, precarity is not a phenomenon exclusive to the creative industries. In *Nice Work If You Can Get It: Life and Labor in Precarious Times*, Andrew Ross (2009, p. 2) avers that precarity is a global condition experienced by workers across numerous industries: "no one, not even those in the traditional professions, can *any longer* expect a fixed pattern of employment in the course of their lifetime, and they are under more and more pressure to anticipate, and prepare for, a future in which they still will be able to compete in a changing marketplace." In many Western countries, the post-war era's Fordist capitalism and social democratic welfare state provided a standard employment regime to many workers, but globally, this arrangement was largely the exception to rule of global capital's exploitation of precarious labor. Today's ubiquitous precarity may only seem novel when viewed against the backdrop of the post-war era' capital-labor regime in some of the world system's imperial societies. "Claims about the precariousness of creative work are commonly highlighted in research focusing on large metropolitan areas in Western Europe, Australia, and North America," say Alacovska and Gill (2019), but "this perspective is not universally applicable to creative work globally and may overlook the broader, more widespread conditions of precarity that exist in many parts of the world." Mahmud (2015, p. 700) avers, stating, "Precarity is an unavoidable historical and structural feature of capitalism" and "a precarious existence for the working class is typical, not an anomaly." Precarity is neither intrinsic to the creative industries, nor the result of its rise in the "neoliberal" fourth quarter of the 21st century, but fundamental to capitalism. Precarity may be intensified or subdued in society by the outcome of class struggles over time and space. At present, in many contexts, capital has the upper hand over labor and in the aftermath of the COVID-19 pandemic, precarious work has increased everywhere, including the "Creator Economy" (Glatt, 2022a, 2022b, 2023). Yet, standard employment has not disappeared from capitalism, nor from the "creative" industries: Walt Disney employs over 223,000 full-time workers; Meta Platforms employs 80,000; the *New York Times* employs over 5000. Labor markets in capitalism continue to be complex and varied, with differing types of employment relations across industries.

Third, I dispute "creative exceptionalism" for implying the "creative industries" have unique logics that are fundamentally different from those which motivate corporate conduct in supposedly "non-creative" other industries of capitalism. Both Ford Motors, a hallmark of the early 20th-century Fordism, and Marvel Studios, a representative of post-Fordism, are influenced by the fundamental logics of the capitalist system. Ford's automobile manufacturing and Marvel's movie production are driven by similar system logics. Each corporation is profit-oriented: Ford sells automobiles at prices exceeding their production costs, while Marvel Studios targets high box office returns for its movies. The manufacture of their products (a tangible automobile or an intangible movie) relies on waged workers in a complex, hierarchical division of labor. At Ford, this includes managers, engineers, and assembly line workers; at Marvel, it entails executive producers, writers, special effects experts, and technicians. Additionally, both companies rely on global supply chains for sourcing product inputs and distribute their finished commodities to a worldwide consumer base. Central to both of their business models is intellectual property (IP) control: Ford holds patents for its automobile designs, and Marvel owns copyrights for its story universe. Furthermore, workers at both Ford and Marvel engage in "manual" and "mental" labor, whether it's engineering at Ford or storytelling at Marvel. In both cases, this labor relies on body and brain and is undertaken through technological interfaces: hands typing ideas on computer keyboards, eyes intently focused on text and images on screens. Ford engineers use digital tools to draft automobile designs, while Marvel's storytellers write scripts. Mind and body converge in all labor processes. While "creative exceptionalism" emphasizes a sharp distinction between Fordism's "blue-collar" proletariat in manufacturing and post-Fordism's "no-collar" creative workers in Hollywood, in reality, the conditions of workers across these two industries have always shared commonalities. The systemic logics of capitalism permeate all corporations, whether in the "creative" industries or those labeled otherwise.

Fourth, I take issue with "creative exceptionalism" for implying that everyone employed by these so-called creative industries is uniquely "creative," that the labor processes of these workers empower "creativity," and that all the copyrighted products sold by these industries count equally as creative expressions. The idea that all the workers toiling at Walt Disney and Google are paid to be creative might be touted by their respective HR departments and job ads but oversimplifies the diversity and complexity of roles within every corporation's division of labor. For a video game, executives secure financing, project managers oversee the entire development process, designers conceptualize the game's structure and rules, programmers write and test the code, artists and animators make the visual elements, writers develop the narrative and dialogue, voice actors perform scripts, audio engineers handle sound effects and music, and testers ensure the game is free of bugs. They are not all equivalently "being creative" in their labor process and contribution to the end product. Also, the idea that the wide range of tasks being done by workers in the creative industries empower their creativity sits uncomfortably with standardized and routinized labor practices which can be just as brutally regimented as the assembly line in any factory. For Marx, all humans are inherently creative, but when they sell their labor power to corporations in exchange for the money they need to live, they "surrender" their "creative power" to the "power of capital." Additionally, far from being a genuine expression of creativity, the IP of the creative industries frequently relies on derivative formulas, templates, and rehashed stories, themes, and tropes. A substantial amount of copyrighted content is more imitative than innovative, an assemblage of copies of copies copied. Even in the "Creator Economy," many popular videos—whether it's a dance to Taylor Swift tune, a mental health tip, a weight loss journey, a prank on Dad, a bathroom renovation guide, an egg cooking technique, a life hack, spiritual advice, or cats being cats—abide by established genre codes and conventions. To suggest they are all equally "creative" stretches the word to the point of meaninglessness. While there is undoubtedly a lot of informative and entertaining content out there on the Internet that is innovative and deserving of recognition and praise, indiscriminately applying the label "creative" to every non-scripted TV format packaged by Endemol Shine Group, every self-published book on Amazon Kindle, and every video posted on TikTok diminishes the concept's significance. Not every worker, process, or product in these industries expresses something "creative."

What, then, does it substantively mean to "be creative"? My critique of the "creative exceptionalism" within much discourse on the creative industries in no way presumes to hold the definitive truth about "creativity." I acknowledge how many shifting definitions of "creative" and "creativity" exist and so my interest is less in nailing down the essence of these words and more in calling attention to the often vague and oversimplified usages of terms like "creative" when applied to "industries," "workers," and "goods." After all, creativity is a complex and inherently contested concept. The oldest word on creative's family tree is "creation" (the divine genesis of the universe). As an adjective, "creative" means "marked by the ability or power to create" (e.g., "the creative impulse") and also, "having the quality of something created rather than imitated" (e.g., a novel *novel*). As a noun, "creative" can refer to "one who is creative" (e.g., a painter or a writer) or "the ability to create" (e.g., a worker's capacity to produce something recognizably "creative"). I've always most valued the idea that "being creative" is rooted in the labor of the imagination—the universal human capacity to envision things not just as they are, but as they could be, or to conceptualize entirely new possibilities that have not yet come into existence, but one day could or should. In this respect, "being creative" is the human labor of imagining something that goes beyond what already is: in feudalism and mercantilism, laissez-faire capitalism, in capitalism, socialism, or Communism, in theocratic monarchies and oligarchies, liberal democracy, in carbon-powered energy regimes, renewables, in terrestrial media systems, the Internet, in mass exploitation, universal emancipation, in oppression, freedom, and in alienating waged labor, self-actualization.

"Being creative" exceeds the industries, labor processes, and products that policy-makers, businesses, and researchers frequently label "creative." Creativity is not confined to Universal Pictures or Apple, a specific segment of the labor force engaged in text and symbol-making and storytelling, nor is it solely evident in media and informational products that communicate cultural meanings. At its core, creativity is a universal potential within everyone, not limited by birthright or biology, not exclusive to any particular "class" or occupational grouping, not constrained to a specific historical period. Creativity spans from pre-modern history to post-modern societies, exists in autocratic and democratic states, and appears in every type of economy, no matter how rich or poor.

While "creativity" is a universally inherent human potential, its meaning is also socially constructed in historical and material conditions that play a role in either suppressing or optimizing it. Not so long ago, creativity was associated with leisure and play, in contrast to work and labor, and ideally, creativity should be driven by the pursuit for freedom rather than necessity. In recent decades, though, the idea of "creativity" has been tied to specific industries, labor processes, and products, with large corporations dominating this sphere. In this society, "being creative" often means a life spent laboring for others, for a corporation, subcontractor or online client. "Being creative" typically involves producing marketable, IP-protected products for sale, rather than dreaming and planning utopia or conceiving radically new visions for our planet's future. It often means investing one's labor into assembling goods and services that contribute to the wealth of copyrights, patents, and trademarks owned by others. Considering this dispossession, "being creative" in our era might not be as genuinely creative as we've been led to believe. For all of these reasons, I part ways with the "creative exceptionalism" of much creative industries and policy discourse. Creativity is real, but to be truly creative vis-à-vis the hegemony of actually existing creativity, now embraced by corporations, states, and educational institutions worldwide as both the means and ends of capital accumulation, might be to think beyond its limited and limiting horizon of the possible and begin to imagine and dream of better and different future societies, where true creativity in and through labor and its product could flourish. Laboring toward that end, within and beyond the DMEI, could be a more inspired way, to "be creative."

Bibliography

Aaker, D. (2009). *Managing brand equity*. Simon & Schuster.
Aaronson, D., & Mazumder, B. (2008). Intergenerational economic mobility in the United States, 1940 to 2000. *Journal of Human Resources*, 43(1), 139–172. https://doi.org/10.3368/jhr.43.1.139
Abidin, C. (2016). Aren't these just young, rich women doing vain things online?: Influencer selfies as subversive frivolity. *Social Media and Society*, 2(2), 1–17. https://doi.org/10.1177/2056305116641342
Abidin, C. (2018). *Internet celebrity: Understanding fame online*. Emerald.
Achor, S., Reece, A., Kellerman, G. R., & Robichaux, A. (2018). 9 out of 10 people are willing to earn less money to do more-meaningful work. *Harvard Business Review*. https://hbr.org/2018/11/9-out-of-10-people-are-willing-to-earn-less-money-to-do-more-meaningful-work
Ajunwa, I. (2023). *The quantified worker: Law and technology in the modern workplace*. Cambridge University Press.
al-Gharbi, M. (2016, March 20). The 1 percent wins again: How entrepreneurship – supposedly the cornerstone of American society – favors the wealthy. *Salon*. https://www.salon.com/2016/03/20/the_1_percent_wins_again_how_the_wealthy_have_all_the_advantages_for_starting_new_businesses/
al-Gharbi, M. (2024). *We have never been woke: The cultural contradictions of a new elite*. Princeton University Press.
Alacovska, A., Bucher, E., & Fieseler, C. (2022). A relational work perspective on the gig economy: Doing creative work on digital labour platforms. *Work, Employment and Society*, 38(1), 161–179. https://doi.org/10.1177/09500170221103146
Alacovska, A., & Gill, R. (2019). De-westernizing creative labour studies: The informality of creative work from an ex-centric perspective. *International Journal of Cultural Studies*, 22(2), 195–212. https://doi.org/10.1177/1367877918821231
Albarran, A. B. (1996). *Media economics: Understanding markets, industries, and concepts*. Iowa State University Press.
Albarran, A. B. (1998). Media economics: Research paradigms, issues, and contributions to mass communication theory. *Mass Communication and Society*, 1(3/4), 117–129.
Albarran, A. B. (2006). Historical trends and patterns in media management research. In A. B. Albarran, S. M. Chan-Olmstead, & M. O. Wirth (Eds.), *Handbook of media management and economics* (pp. 3–23). Routledge.
Albarran, A. B., Chan-Olmstead, S. M., & Wirth, M. O. (2005). *Handbook of media management and economics*. Routledge.
Albo, G., Panitch, L., & Zuege, A. (2021). *Capitalism, technology, labor: A socialist register reader*. Haymarket Books.

Alexander, J. C., Marx, G. T., & Christine L. Williams (Eds.). (2004). *Self, social structure, and beliefs: Explorations in sociology*. University of California Press.
Altenried, M. (2021). *The digital factory: The human labor of automation*. University of Chicago Press.
Altheide, D. L. (1976). *Creating reality: How TV news distorts events*. Sage.
Altheide, D. L., & Elliott, P. (1982). The making of a television series: A case study in the sociology of culture. *Contemporary Sociology, 11*(1), 72. https://doi.org/10.2307/2066649
Alvarado, M., & Stewart, J. (1985). *Made for television: Euston films limited*. BFI Publishing.
Alvesson, M. (2016). Organizational culture and work. In S. Edgell, H. Gottfried, & E. Granter (Eds.), *The SAGE handbook of the sociology of work and employment* (pp. 262–281). Sage. https://doi.org/10.4135/9781473915206.n15
Amrute, S. (2016). *Encoding race, encoding class: Indian IT workers in Berlin*. Duke University Press. https://doi.org/10.1215/9780822374275
Anand, P., & MacBride. (2020, June 16). For Black CEOs in Silicon Valley, humiliation is a part of doing business. *Bloomberg*. https://www.mercurynews.com/2020/06/16/for-black-ceos-in-silicon-valley-humiliation-is-a-part-of-doing-business/
Anderson, E. (2017). *Private government: How employers rule our lives (and why we don't talk about it)*. Yale University Press.
Andrejevic, M. (2002). The work of being watched: Interactive media and the exploitation of self-disclosure. *Critical Studies in Media Communication, 19*(2), 230–248. https://doi.org/10.1080/07393180216561
Andrejevic, M. (2004). *Reality TV: The work of being watched*. Rowman & Littlefield Publishers.
Andrejevic, M. (2007). *iSpy: Surveillance and power in the interactive era*. University Press of Kansas.
Andrejevic, M. (2008). Watching television without pity: The productivity of online fans. *Television & New Media, 9*(1), 24–46. https://doi.org/10.1177/1527476407307241
Andrejevic, M. (2009). Exploiting YouTube: Contradictions of user-generated labor. In P. Snickars & P. Vonderau (Eds.), *The YouTube reader* (pp. 406–423). Wallflower Press.
Andrejevic, M. (2010). Realizing exploitation. In M. Kraidy & K. Sender (Eds.), *The politics of reality television: Global perspectives* (pp. 18–30). Routledge. https://doi.org/10.4324/9780203843567
Andrews, C., & Upadhya, R. K. (2019). Lessons from the Long Sixties for Organizing in Tech. *Science for the People*. https://magazine.scienceforthepeople.org/vol22-1/lessons-from-the-long-sixties-for-organizing-in-tech-today/
Andrijasevic, R., Chen, J. Y., Gregg, M., & Steinberg, M. (2021). *Media and management*. University of Minnesota Press. https://www.upress.umn.edu/book-division/books/media-and-management
Andriole, Steve (2016). 15 Must-Have Technology Capabilities For Digital Transformation (The Final Scream). *Forbes*. https://www.forbes.com/sites/steveandriole/2016/09/20/15-must-have-technology-capabilities-for-digital-transformation-the-final-scream/
Anguiano, D., & Beckett, L. (2023). How Hollywood writers triumphed over AI – and why it matters. *The Guardian*. https://www.theguardian.com/culture/2023/oct/01/hollywood-writers-strike-artificial-intelligence
Anheier, H. K., Gerhards, J., & Romo, F. P. (1995). Forms of capital and social structure in cultural fields: Examining Bourdieu's social topography. *American Journal of Sociology, 100*(4), 859–903. https://doi.org/10.1086/230603

Anna Coote, E. Y. (2019). *Universal basic income a union perspective full report*. World PSI. http://www.world-psi.org/sites/default/files/documents/research/en_ubi_full_report_2019.pdf

Anomaly, J. (2015). Public goods and government action. *Politics, Philosophy and Economics*, 14(2), 109–128. https://doi.org/10.1177/1470594X13505414

Anthony, P. D. (1977). *The ideology of work*. Routledge. https://doi.org/10.4324/9781315824123

Anwar, M. A., & Graham, M. (2020). Hidden transcripts of the gig economy: Labour agency and the new art of resistance among African gig workers. *Environment and Planning A*, 52(7), 1269–1291. https://doi.org/10.1177/0308518X19894584

Arditi, D. (2020). *Getting signed: Record contracts, musicians, and power in society*. Palgrave Macmillan.

Arditi, D. (2023). *Digital feudalism: Creators, credit, consumption and capitalism*. Emerald.

Arditi, D. (2023). Reality TV show contestants are more like unpaid interns than Hollywood stars. *The Conversation*. https://theconversation.com/reality-tv-show-contestants-are-more-like-unpaid-interns-than-hollywood-stars-213437

Arendt, H. (1998). *The human condition*. The University of Chicago Press.

Aronowitz, S. (2004). *How class works: Power and social movement*. Yale University Press. https://doi.org/10.1215/15476715-1-3-160

Aronowitz, S., & Bratsis, P. (Eds.). (2002). *Paradigm lost: State theory reconsidered*. University of Minnesota Press.

Aronowitz, S., & DiFazio, W. (1995). *The jobless future*. University of Minnesota Press.

Arriagada, A., & Ibañez, F. (2019). Communicative value chains: Fashion bloggers and branding agencies as cultural intermediaries. In L. Vodanovic (Ed.), *Lifestyle journalism: Social media, consumption and experience* (pp. 91–101). https://doi.org/10.4324/9781351123389-8

Arriagada, A., & Ibáñez, F. (2020). "You Need At Least One Picture Daily, if Not, You're Dead": Content creators and platform evolution in the social media ecology. *Social Media + Society*, 6(3). https://doi.org/10.1177/2056305120944624

Artists Rights Alliance. (2024, April 1). 200+ Artists Urge Tech Platforms: Stop Devaluing Music. *Medium*. https://artistrightsnow.medium.com/200-artists-urge-tech-platforms-stop-devaluing-music-559fb109bbac

Artz, L. (2006). On the material and the dialectic: Toward a class analysis of communication. In L. Artz, S. Macek, & D. L. Cloud (Eds.), *Marxism and communication studies: The point is to change it* (pp. 5–51). Peter Lang.

Arvidsson, A. (2005). Brands: A critical perspective. *Journal of Consumer Culture*, 5(2), 235–258. https://doi.org/10.1177/1469540505053093

Arvidsson, A. (2008). The ethical economy of customer coproduction. *Journal of Macromarketing*, 28(4), 326–338. https://doi.org/10.1177/0276146708326077

Arvidsson, A. (2009). The ethical economy: Towards a post-capitalist theory of value. *Capital & Class*, 33(1), 13–29. https://doi.org/10.1177/030981680909700102

Arvidsson, A., & Bonini, T. (2015). Valuing audience passions: From Smythe to Tarde. *European Journal of Cultural Studies*, 18(2), 158–173. https://doi.org/10.1177/1367549414563297

Arvidsson, A., & Colleoni, E. (2012). Value in informational capitalism and on the internet. *Information Society*, 28(3), 135–150. https://doi.org/10.1080/01972243.2012.669449

Aschoff, N. (2019). Do managers rule? *Catalyst*, 2(4). https://catalyst-journal.com/vol2/no4/do-managers-rule

Ashforth, B. E., & Humphrey, R. H. (1993). Emotional labor in service roles: The influence of identity. *Academy of Management Review*, 18(1), 88–115. https://doi.org/10.5465/amr.1993.3997508

Attali, J. (1991). *Millennium: Winners and losers in the coming world order*. Random House.

Ayalon, L., & Tesch-Römer, C. (Eds.). (2018). *Contemporary perspectives on ageism*. Springer Open. https://link.springer.com/book/10.1007/978-3-319-73820-8

Ayer, J. (2005). *More than meets the ear: How symphony musicians made labor history*. Syren Book Company.

Aytes, A. (2012). Return of the crowds: Mechanical Turk and neoliberal states of exception. In T. Schotlz (Ed.), *Digital labor: The internet as playground and factory* (pp. 79–97). Routledge. https://doi.org/10.4324/9780203145791

Azzellini, D., Greer, I., & Umney, C. (2022). Why platform capitalism is not the future of work. *Work in the Global Economy*, 2(2), 272–289. https://doi.org/10.1332/273241721x16666858545489

Babe, R. E. (2009). *Cultural studies and political economy: Toward a new integration*. Lexington Books. https://searchworks.stanford.edu/view/7807760

Bader Law. (2023). *Digital platform workers' rights act: An overview*. Employment Law, HR Consulting & Employment Law. https://baderlaw.ca/blogs-news/digital-platform-workers-rights-act-an-overview/

Bacon, David. (2011). Up Against the Open Shop – the Hidden Story of Silicon Valley's High-Tech Workers. *Truthout*. https://truthout.org/articles/up-against-the-open-shop-the-hidden-story-of-silicon-valley-s-high-tech-workers-2/

Baiocco, S., Fernández-Macías, E., Rani, U., & Pesole, A. (2022). *The Algorithmic Management of work and its implications in different contexts*. European Commission. https://joint-research-centre.ec.europa.eu/system/files/2022-06/JRC129749.pdf

Bailey, C., Lips-Wiersma, M., Madden, A., Yeoman, R., Thompson, M., & Chalofsky, N. (2019). The five paradoxes of meaningful work: Introduction to the special issue 'Meaningful Work: Prospects for the 21st Century'. *Journal of Management Studies*, 56(3), 481–499. https://doi.org/10.1111/joms.12422

Bailey, C., & Madden, A. (2017). Time reclaimed: Temporality and the experience of meaningful work. *Work, Employment and Society*, 31(1), 3–18. https://doi.org/10.1177/0950017015604100

Bain, A. (2005). Constructing an artistic identity. *Work, Employment and Society*, 19(1), 25–46.

Bain, P., & Taylor, P. (2000). Entrapped by the "electronic panopticon"? Worker resistance in the call centre. *New Technology, Work and Employment*, 15(1), 2–18. https://doi.org/10.1111/1468-005X.00061

Bain, P., Watson, A., Mulvey, G., Taylor, P., & Gall, G. (2002). Taylorism, targets and the pursuit of quantity and quality by call centre management. *New Technology, Work and Employment*, 17(3), 170–185. https://doi.org/10.1111/1468-005X.00103

Bakker, P. (2012). Aggregation, content farms and huffinization: The rise of low-pay and no-pay journalism. *Journalism Practice*, 6(5–6), 627–637. https://doi.org/10.1080/17512786.2012.667266

Baldonado, A. M. (2015). Workplace fun: Learning from Google, Southwest Airlines, and Facebook. *International Journal of Research in Business Studies and Management*, 2(12), 15–18.

Ballesteros, B., Luján, L., & Pedro, J. (2010). The political economy of communication: Power and resistance, an interview with Vincent Mosco. *Global Media*

Journal, *10*(17). https://www.globalmediajournal.com/open-access/the-political-economy-of-communication-power-andresistancean-interview-with-vincent-mosco.php?aid=35297

Ballo, J. G. (2020). Labour market participation for young people with disabilities: The impact of gender and higher education. *Work, Employment and Society*, *34*(2), 336–355. https://doi.org/10.1177/0950017019868139

Banerjee, A., & Duflo, E. (2022). Forward. *World Inequality Report 2022*. https://doi.org/10.4159/9780674276598

Banet-Weiser, S. (2012). *AuthenticTM: The politics of ambivalence in a brand culture*. New York University Press.

Banks, M. (2007). *The politics of cultural work*. Palgrave MacMillan. https://doi.org/10.1057/9780230288713

Banks, M., Conor, B., & Mayer, V. (Eds.). (2015). *Production studies, the sequel!: Cultural studies of global media industries*. Routledge. https://doi.org/10.4324/9781315736471

Banks, M., & Fortmueller, K. (2023). Unity will determine if the Hollywood writers strike is successful. *The Washington Post*. https://www.washingtonpost.com/made-by-history/2023/06/22/wga-strike-hollywood-unions-solidarity

Banks, M., Gill, R., & Taylor, S. (2013). *Theorizing cultural work: Labour, continuity and change in the cultural and creative industries*. Routledge. https://doi.org/10.4324/9780203519912

Banks, M., & Hesmondhalgh, D. (2009). Looking for work in creative industries policy. *International Journal of Cultural Policy*, *15*(4), 415–430. https://doi.org/10.1080/10286630902923323

Banks, M. J. (2008). Company town: Production communities and the myth of a unified Hollywood. *The Velvet Light Trap*, *62*(1), 62–64. https://doi.org/10.1353/vlt.0.0015

Banks, M. J. (2009). Gender below-the-line: Defining feminist production. In *Production studies* (pp. 95–106). https://doi.org/10.4324/9780203879597-12

Banks, M. J. (2010). Autonomy guaranteed? Cultural work and the "Art-commerce relation". *Journal for Cultural Research*, *14*(3), 251–269. https://doi.org/10.1080/14797581003791487

Banks, M. J. (2010). The picket line online: Creative labor, digital activism, and the 2007–2008 writers guild of America strike. *Popular Communication*, *8*(1), 20–33. https://doi.org/10.1080/15405700903502387

Banks, M. J. (2015). *The writers: A history of American screenwriters and their guild*. University of Michigan.

Barnett, K. (2014). Record men: Talent scouts in the U.S. Recording industry. In D. Johnson, D. Kompare, & A. Santo (Eds.), *Making media work: Cultures of management in the entertainment industries* (pp. 113–141). https://doi.org/10.18574/nyu/9780814764695.003.0006

Barranger, M. S. (2009). *Unfriendly witnesses: Gender, theater, and film in the McCarthy era*. Southern Illinois University Press.

Bärtl, M. (2018). YouTube channels, uploads and views: A statistical analysis of the past 10 years. *Convergence*, *24*(1), 16–32. https://doi.org/10.1177/1354856517736979

Basi, J. K. T. (2009). *Women, identity and India's call centre industry*. Routledge. https://doi.org/10.4324/9780203883792

Bastani, A. (2019). *Fully automated luxury communism*. Verso.

Bateman, K. (2022, February 22). COVID-19 hit the creative industries particularly hard. How can they be supported in future? World Economic Forum, https://www.weforum.org/agenda/2022/02/creatives-job-losses-covid-employment/

Battani, M. (1999). Organizational fields, cultural fields and art worlds: The early effort to make photographs and make photographers in the 19th-century United States of America. *Media, Culture and Society*, 21(5), 601–626. https://doi.org/10.1177/016344399021005002

Battistoni, A. (2017). The false promise of universal basic income. *Dissent*, 64(2), 51–62. https://doi.org/10.1353/dss.2017.0030

Bauer, G. R., Churchill, S. M., Mahendran, M., Walwyn, C., Lizotte, D., & Villa-Rueda, A. A. (2021). Intersectionality in quantitative research: A systematic review of its emergence and applications of theory and methods. *SSM – Population Health*, 14. https://doi.org/10.1016/j.ssmph.2021.100798

Baum, C. (2018). The ugly truth about ageism: It's a prejudice targeting our future selves. *The Guardian*. https://www.theguardian.com/lifeandstyle/2018/sep/14/the-ugly-truth-about-ageism-its-a-prejudice-targeting-our-future-selves

Bauman, Z. (2005). *Work, consumerism and the new poor*. Open University Press.

Bauman, Z. (2017). *Wasted lives: Modernity and its outcasts*. Polity.

Baxter, J., & Tai, T. (2016). Unpaid domestic labor. In S. Edgell, H. Gottfried, & E. Granter (Eds.), *The SAGE handbook of the sociology of work and employment* (pp. 444–464). https://doi.org/10.4135/9781473915206.n24

Baym, N. (2012). *Tune in, log on: Soaps, fandom, and online community*. Sage. https://doi.org/10.4135/9781452204710

Baym, N. K. (2015). Connect with your audience! The relational labor of connection. *Communication Review*, 18(1), 14–22. https://doi.org/10.1080/10714421.2015.996401

Baym, N. K. (2018). *Playing to the crowd: Musicians, audiences, and the intimate work of connection*. New York University Press.

Baym, N. K., & Burnett, R. (2009). Amateur experts: International fan labour in Swedish independent music. *International Journal of Cultural Studies*, 12(5), 433–449. https://doi.org/10.1177/1367877909337857

Beck, A. (Ed.). (2002). *Cultural work: Understanding the cultural industries*. Routledge.

Beck, A. (2002). Introduction: Cultural work, cultural workplace – looking at the cultural industries. In A. Beck (Ed.), *Cultural work: Understanding the cultural industries* (pp. 1–11). Routledge. https://doi.org/10.4324/9780203995020-6

Beck, U. (1992) *Risk society: Towards a new modernity*. Sage.

Beck, U. (2001). *The brave new world of work*. Polity.

Becker, H. S. (1974). Art as collective action. *American Sociological Review*, 39(6), 767–776.

Becker, H. S. (1976). Art worlds and social types. In R. A. Peterson RA (Ed.), *The production of culture* (pp. 41–56). Sage.

Becker, H. S. (1982). *Art worlds*. University of California Press.

Becker, L. B., Fruit, J. W., & Caudill, S. L. (1987). *The training and hiring of journalists*. Ablex.

Becker, L. B., Lauf, E., & Lowrey, W. (1999). Differential employment rates in the journalism and mass communication labor force based on gender, race, and ethnicity: Exploring the impact of affirmative action. *Journalism and Mass Communication Quarterly*, 76(4), 631–645. https://doi.org/10.1177/107769909907600402

Becker, L. B., Vlad, T., Daniels, G. L., & Martin, H. J. (2003). The impact of internal labor markets on newspaper industry diversification. https://esploro.libs.uga.edu/esploro/outputs/9949316208002959

Becker, L. B., Vlad, T., Simpson, H., & Kalpen, K. (2012). *Annual Survey of Journalism and Mass Communication Graduates*. http://www.grady.uga.edu/annualsurveys/Graduate_Survey/Graduate_2012/Graduate_2012_Page.php

Beckett, A. (2019, January 19). Post-work: The radical idea of a world without jobs. *The Guardian.* https://www.theguardian.com/news/2018/jan/19/post-work-the-radical-idea-of-a-world-without-jobs

Beech, N., Gilmore, C., Hibbert, P., & Ybema, S. (2016). Identity-in-the-work and musicians' struggles: The production of self-questioning identity work. *Work, Employment and Society, 30*(3), 506–522. https://doi.org/10.1177/0950017015620767

Bélair-Gagnon, V., Holton, A. E., Deuze, M., & Mellado, C. (Eds.). (2023a). *Happiness in journalism.* Routledge. https://doi.org/10.4324/9781003364597

Bélair-Gagnon, V., Holton, A. E., Deuze, M., & Mellado, C. (2023b). Fostering a culture of well-being in journalism. *Happiness in journalism* (pp. 1–7). Routledge. https://doi.org/10.4324/9781003364597-1

Bell, D. (1999). *The Coming of Post-Industrial Society.* Basic Books.

Benanav, A. (2020). *Automation and the future of work.* Verso.

Benjamin, R. (2019). *Race after technology.* Polity.

Bennett, L. (2014). Tracing textual poachers: Reflections on the development of fan studies and digital fandom. *Journal of Fandom Studies, 2*(1), 5–20. https://doi.org/10.1386/jfs.2.1.5_1

Bennis, W. G. (2009). *On becoming a leader.* Basic Books.

Berg, H. (2021). *Porn work: Sex, labor, and late capitalism.* University of North Carolina Press.

Berardi, F. (2009). *The soul at work: from alienation to autonomy.* Semiotext.

Berger, E. (2021). *Ageism at work: Deconstructing age and gender in the discriminating labour market.* University of Toronto Press. https://doi.org/10.1177/00943061221129662c

Berger, S. (2019). Top reason CEOs were ousted in 2018 was because of scandal. *CNBC.* https://www.cnbc.com/2019/05/15/pwc-strategy-report-top-reason-ceos-were-ousted-in-2018-was-scandals.html

Berger, S. D., & Bell, D. (1974). The coming of post-industrial society: A venture in social forecasting. *Contemporary Sociology, 3*(2), 101. https://doi.org/10.2307/2062869

Bergmann, W. (1992). The problem of time in sociology: An overview of the literature on the state of theory and research on the 'Sociology of Time', 1900-82. *Time & Society, 1*(1), 81–134. https://doi.org/10.1177/0961463X92001001007

Bergvall-Kåreborn, B., & Howcroft, D. (2013). "The future's bright, the future's mobile": A study of Apple and Google mobile application developers. *Work, Employment and Society, 27*(6), 964–981. https://doi.org/10.1177/0950017012474709

Berle, Adolf A., & Means, Gardiner C. (1933). *The modern corporation and private property.* The Macmillan Company.

Bernstein, M. (2000). *Controlling Hollywood: Censorship and regulation in the studio era.* Rutgers University Press.

Bevan, R. (2022). Bernie Sanders says that Microsoft's Activision Blizzard acquisition could undermine worker's rights. *The Gamer.* https://www.thegamer.com/activision-blizzard-microsoft-bernie-sanders-elizabeth-warren-ftc-union/

Bhalla, N. (2023). Mental trauma: African content moderators push Big Tech on rights. *Reuters.* https://www.reuters.com/article/idUSL4N3BB27W/

Bhatt, A. (2018). *High-tech housewives: Indian IT workers, gendered labor, and transmigration.* University of Washington Press.

Bhattacharya, T. (Ed.). (2017). *Social reproduction theory: Remapping class, recentering oppression.* Pluto.

Bhuiyan, J. (2021, October 8). 'Welcome to the party': Five past tech whistleblowers on the pitfalls of speaking out. *The Guardian.* https://www.theguardian.

com/technology/2021/oct/08/tech-whistleblowers-facebook-frances-haugen-amazon-google-pinterest

Bielby, D. D. (2009). Gender inequality in culture industries: Women and men writers in film and television. *Sociologie Du Travail, 51*(2), 237–252. https://doi.org/10.4000/sdt.16462

Bielby, D. D., & Bielby, W. T. (1996). Women and men in film gender inequality among writers in a culture industry. *Gender and Society, 10*(3), 248–270. https://doi.org/10.1177/089124396010003004

Bielby, D. D., & Bielby, W. T. (2002). Hollywood dreams, harsh realities: Writing for film and television. *Contexts, 1*(4), 21–27. https://doi.org/10.1525/ctx.2002.1.4.21

Bielby, W. T., & Bielby, D. D. (1994). "All Hits Are Flukes": Institutionalized decision making and the rhetoric of network prime-time program development. *American Journal of Sociology, 99*(5), 1287–1313. https://doi.org/10.1086/230412

Bielby, W. T., & Bielby, D. D. (1999). Organizational mediation of project-based labor markets: Talent agencies and the careers of screenwriters. *American Sociological Review, 64*(1), 64–85. https://doi.org/10.2307/2657278

Billig, M. (1999). Commodity fetishism and repression – reflections on Marx, Freud and the psychology of consumer capitalism. *Theory & Psychology, 9*(3), 313–329.

Bilton, N. (2014). *Hatching twitter*. Portfolio.

Birkinbine, B., Gomez, Rodrigo, & Wasko, J. (Eds.). (2017). *Global media giants*. Routledge.

Bishop, S. (2019). Managing visibility on YouTube through algorithmic gossip. *New Media and Society, 21*(11–12), 2589–2606. https://doi.org/10.1177/1461444819854731

Bishop, S. (2021). Influencer management tools: Algorithmic cultures, brand safety, and bias. *Social Media and Society, 7*(1). https://doi.org/10.1177/20563051211003066

Bishop, S. (2018a). #YouTuberAnxiety: Anxiety as emotional labour and masquerade in beauty vlogs. *Youth Mediations and Affective Relations*, 89–105. https://doi.org/10.1007/978-3-319-98971-6_6

Bishop, S. (2018b). Anxiety, panic and self-optimization: Inequalities and the YouTube algorithm. *Convergence, 24*(1), 69–84. https://doi.org/10.1177/1354856517736978

Bishop, S. (2022, June 9). Influencer creep. *Real Life*. https://reallifemag.com/influencer-creep/

Bivens, J., & Kandra, J. (2023, September 21). CEO pay slightly declined in 2022. Economic Policy Institute. https://www.epi.org/publication/ceo-pay-in-2022/

Black, B. (1986). The Abolition of Work. https://theanarchistlibrary.org/library/bob-black-the-abolition-of-work

Blackburn, I. (2024). The Creator Union: A Voice for Creators & Influencers. *The Media Moment*. https://www.themediamoment.com/analysis/the-creator-union-voice-for-creators-influencers

Blair, H. (2001). 'You're Only as Good as Your Last Job': The labour process and labour market in the British film industry. *Work, Employment & Society, 15*(1), 149–169. https://doi.org/10.1017/s0950017001000071

Blair, J. L. (2010). Surviving reality TV: The ultimate challenge for reality show contestants. *Loyola of Los Angeles Entertainment Law Review, 31*(1), 1–26.

Blaising, A., Kotturi, Y., Kulkarni, C., & Dabbish, L. (2020). Making it work, or not : A longitudinal study of career trajectories among online freelancers. *ACM Human-Computer Interaction 4, CSCW3*, 4(December), 29.

Blauner, R. (1965). *Alienation and freedom: The factory worker and his industry*. The John Hopkins University Press.

Bojczuk, I. (2019). The Kariakoo Market: Mobile phone repair workers and the shrinking planet. *Global Media Technologies & Cultures Lab*. https://globalmedia.mit.edu/2019/02/03/the-kariakoo-market-mobile-phone-repair-workers-and-the-shrinking-planet/

Bolden-Barrett, V. (2018). Tech workers at Tesla, Intel say NDAs have 'silenced' them. *HR Drive*. https://www.hrdive.com/news/tech-workers-at-tesla-intel-say-ndas-have-silenced-them/532024/

Bolin, G. (2005). Notes from inside the factory. The production and consumption of signs and sign value in media industries. *Social Semiotics, 15*(3), 289–306.

Bolin, G. (2009). Symbolic production and value in media industries. *Journal of Cultural Economy, 2*(3), 345–361.

Boltanski, L., & Chiapello, E. (2005). *The new spirit of capitalism*. Verso.

Bolton, S. (2009). Getting to the heart of the emotional labour process: A reply to Brook. *Work, Employment and Society, 23*(3), 549–560.

Bolton, S. C. (2003). Trolley dolly or skilled emotion manager? Moving on from Hochschild's managed heart. *Work, Employment and Society, 17*(2), 289–308.

Bolton, S. C. (2004). *Emotion management in the workplace*. Palgrave Macmillan. https://doi.org/10.5040/9781350390751

Bolton, S. C. (2007). Dignity in and at work: Why it matters. In S. C. Bolton (Ed.), *Dimensions of dignity at work*. Butterworth-Heinemann.

Bonini, T., & Gandini, A. (2020). The field as a black box: Ethnographic research in the age of platforms. *Social Media + Society, 6*(4). https://doi.org/10.1177/2056305120984477

Bourdieu, P. (1984). *Distinction: A social critique of the judgement of taste*. Harvard University Press.

Bourdieu, P. (1986). The forms of capital. In J. Richardson (Ed.), *Handbook of theory and research for the sociology of education* (pp. 241–258). Greenwood. https://www.marxists.org/reference/subject/philosophy/works/fr/bourdieu-forms-capital.htm

Boussebaa, M. (2016). Offshore call centre work is breeding a new colonialism. *The Conversation*. https://theconversation.com/offshore-call-centre-work-is-breeding-a-new-colonialism-32999

Boussebaa, M., Sinha, S., & Gabriel, Y. (2014). Englishization in offshore call centers: A postcolonial perspective. *Journal of International Business Studies, 45*(9), 1152–1169. https://doi.org/10.1057/jibs.2014.25

Bowe, M., Bowe, J., & Streeter, S. (2000). *Gig: Americans talk about their jobs at the turn of the millennium*. Crown.

Boyd-Barrett, O., & Mirrlees, T. (2019). *Media imperialism: Continuity and change*. Rowman & Littlefield.

Boyle, D., & Oakley, K. (2018). *Co-operatives in the creative industries*. Co-operatives UK. https://culturalworkersorganize.org/wp-content/uploads/2018/10/Cooperatives-and-Creative-Industries-Boyle-and-Oakley.pdf

Boyle, M., & Green, J. (2023). *Work shift: Women CEOs (Finally) outnumber those named John*. Bloomberg. https://www.bloomberg.com/news/newsletters/2023-04-25/women-ceos-at-big-companies-finally-outnumber-those-named-john

Brabham, D. C. (2012). The myth of amateur crowds. *Information, Communication & Society*, *15*(3), 394–410. https://doi.org/10.1080/1369118x.2011.641991

Brabham, D. C. (2013). *Crowdsourcing*. MIT Press.

Brabham, D. C. (2017). How crowdfunding discourse threatens public arts. *New Media and Society*, *19*(7), 983–999. https://doi.org/10.1177/1461444815625946

Bradley, H. (2016). Gender and work. In S. Edgell, H. Gottfried, & E. Granter (Eds.), *The SAGE handbook of the sociology of work and employment* (pp. 73–92). Sage.

Branch, T. (2011). *The cartel: Inside the rise and imminent fall of the NCAA*. Byliner.

Bratt, C. (2021). *How game publishers buy crunch overseas*. https://www.youtube.com/watch?v=bm7KUE1Kwts

Braverman, H. (1974/1998). *Labor and monopoly capital: The degradation of work in the twentieth century*. Monthly Review Press.

Bregman, R. (2017). *Utopia for realists: The case for a universal basic income, open borders, and a 15-hour workweek*. Brown & Company.

Brenner, J., & M. Ramas. (1984). Rethinking women's opression. *New Left Review*, *1*(144). https://newleftreview.org/issues/i144/articles/johanna-brenner-maria-ramas-rethinking-women-s-oppression.pdf

Breslow, J. (2018). Moderating the 'worst of humanity': Sexuality, witnessing, and the digital life of coloniality. *Porn Studies*, *5*(3), 225–240. https://doi.org/10.1080/23268743.2018.1472034

Brimeyer, T. M., Eaker, A. V., & Clair, R. P. (2004). Rhetorical strategies in union organizing: A case of labor versus management. *Management Communication Quarterly*, *18*(1), 45–75. https://doi.org/10.1177/0893318904265128

Bristol Creative Industries. (2021). *Creative industries must act on urgent need for diversity and equality, says parliamentary report*. https://bristolcreativeindustries.com/creative-industries-diversity-and-equality/

British Academy. (2024). *Media, Screen, Journalism and Communication Studies: Provision in UK Higher Education*. https://www.thebritishacademy.ac.uk/publications/media-screen-journalism-and-communication-studies-provision-in-uk-higher-education/

Briziarelli, M. (2014). The ideological reproduction: (Free) Labouring and (social) working within digital landscapes. *TripleC: Communication, Capitalism & Critique*, *12*(2), 620–631. https://doi.org/10.31269/triplec.v12i2.537

Bröckling, U. (2015). *The entrepreneurial self: Fabricating a new type of subject*. Sage.

Brodmerkel, S., & Barker, R. (2019). Hitting the 'glass wall': Investigating everyday ageism in the advertising industry. *Sociological Review*, *67*(6), 1383–1399. https://doi.org/10.1177/0038026119837147

Brogan, R. (2021). The digital sweatshop: Why heightened labor protections must be implemented before crunch causes the backbone of the video game industry to collapse. *Texas Review of Entertainment & Sports Law*. https://doi.org/10.2139/ssrn.3777466

Bronowicka, J., & Ivanova, M. (2020). Resisting the algorithmic boss: Guessing, gaming, reframing and contesting rules in app-based management. *SSRN Electronic Journal*. https://doi.org/10.2139/ssrn.3624087

Brook, O., Miles, A., O'Brien, D., & Taylor, M. (2020). *Culture is bad for you: Inequality in the cultural and creative industries*. Manchester University Press.

Brook, O., Miles, A., O'Brien, D., & Taylor, M. (2023). Social mobility and 'Openness' in creative occupations since the 1970s. *Sociology*, *57*(4), 789–810. https://doi.org/10.1177/00380385221129953

Brook, P. (2009a). In critical defence of "emotional labour": Refuting Bolton's critique of Hochschild's concept. *Work, Employment and Society, 23*(3), 531–548. https://doi.org/10.1177/0950017009337071

Brook, P. (2009b). The Alienated Heart: Hochschild's 'emotional labour' thesis and the anticapitalist politics of alienation. *Capital & Class, 33*(2), 7–31. https://doi.org/10.1177/030981680909800101

Brophy, E. (2006). System error: Labour precarity and collective organizing at Microsoft. *Canadian Journal of Communication, 31*(3), 619–638. https://doi.org/10.22230/cjc.2006v31n3a1767

Brophy, E. (2017). *Language put to work: The making of the global call centre work force*. Palgrave Macmillan.

Brophy, E., Cohen, N. S., & De Peuter, G. (2015). Labor messaging: Practices of autonomous communication. In R. Maxwell (Ed.), *The Routledge companion to labor and media* (pp. 315–326). Routledge.

Brophy, E., & De Peuter, G. (2014). Labours of mobility: Communicative capitalism and the smartphone cybertariat. In A. Herman, J. Hadlaw, and T. Swiss (Eds.), *Theories of the mobile internet: Materialities and imaginaries* (pp. 60–84). Routledge.

Brouillette, S. (2009). Creative labor. *Mediations, 24*(2), 140–149.

Browne, I., & Misra, J. (2003). The intersection of gender and race in the labor market. *Annual Review of Sociology, 29*, 487–513. https://doi.org/10.1146/annurev.soc.29.010202.100016

Browne, P., & Schram, B. R. (2021). Intermediating the everyday: Indie game development and the labour of co-working spaces. In O. Sotamma & J. Švelch (Eds.), *Game production studies* (pp. 83–101). https://doi.org/10.5117/9789463725439_ch04

Browning, K. (2021). The Labor Department is investigating Apple's treatment of employees. *The New York Times*. https://www.nytimes.com/2021/12/13/technology/apple-labor-investigation-employees.html

Bruce, G. (2021). Doctor, vet, esports star, influencer: Dream jobs among US teens. *YouGovAmerica*. https://today.yougov.com/topics/technology/articles-reports/2021/12/14/influencer-dream-jobs-among-us-teens

Bruns, A. (2008). *Blogs, Wikipedia, second life, and beyond: From production to produsage*. Peter Lang.

Bruun, H. (2016). The qualitative interview in media production studies. In C. Paterson, D. Lee, A. Saha, & A. Zoellner (Eds.), *Advancing media production research* (pp. 121–146). Palgrave Macmillan. https://doi.org/10.1057/9781137541949_9

Brynjolfsson, E., & McAfee, A. (2011). *Race against the machine – How the digital revolution is accelerating innovation, driving productivity, and irreversibly transforming employment and the economy*. Digital Frontier Press.

Bucher, E., & Fieseler, C. (2015). The flow of digital labor. *Academy of Management Proceedings*, (1), 11525. https://doi.org/10.5465/ambpp.2015.11525abstract

Bucher, T. (2012). Want to be on the top? Algorithmic power and the threat of invisibility on Facebook. *New Media and Society, 14*(7), 1164–1180. https://doi.org/10.1177/1461444812440159

Bucher, T. (2017). The algorithmic imaginary: Exploring the ordinary affects of Facebook algorithms. *Information Communication and Society, 20*(1), 30–44. https://doi.org/10.1080/1369118X.2016.1154086

Buhle, P., & Wagner, D. (2002). *Radical Hollywood: The untold story behind America's favorite movies*. New Press.

Buhle, P., & Wagner, D. (2003). *Hide in plain sight: The Hollywood blacklistees in film and television, 1950–2002*. Palgrave Macmillan.

Bulut, E. (2015). Playboring in the tester pit: The convergence of precarity and the degradation of fun in video game testing. *Television and New Media*, 16(3), 240–258. https://doi.org/10.1177/1527476414525241

Bulut, E. (2018). One-dimensional creativity: A marcusean critique of work and play in the video game industry. *TripleC: Communication, Capitalism & Critique*, 16(2), 757–771. https://doi.org/10.31269/triplec.v16i2.930

Bulut, E. (2020). *A precarious game: The illusion of dream jobs in the video game industry*. Cornell University Press.

Burawoy, M. (1979). *Manufacturing consent*. University of Chicago Press.

Burawoy, M., & Wright, E. O. (1990). Coercion and consent in contested exchange. *Politics & Society*, 18(2), 251–266. https://doi.org/10.1177/003232929001800206

Burgard, S. A., & Lin, K. Y. (2013). Bad jobs, bad health? How work and working conditions contribute to health disparities. *American Behavioral Scientist*, 57(8), 1105–1127. https://doi.org/10.1177/0002764213487347

Burgmann, V. (2016). *Globalization and labour in the twenty-first century*. Routledge. https://doi.org/10.4324/9781315624044

Burnham, J. (1941). *The managerial revolution: What is happening in the world*. Day.

Burns, J. M. (2010). *Leadership*. Harper Perennial Modern Classics

Burnside, S. (2014). Investing in a brilliant new YOU™: the rise and tyranny of the 'personal brand'. *The Guardian*. https://www.theguardian.com/commentisfree/2014/apr/15/investing-in-a-brilliant-new-youtm-the-rise-and-tyranny-of-the-personal-brand

Burrell, J., & Fourcade, M. (2021). The society of algorithms. *Annual Review of Sociology*, 47, 213–237. https://doi.org/10.1146/annurev-soc-090820-020800

Burrows, R., & Curran, J. (2021). Not such a small business: Reflections on the rhetoric, the reality and the future of the enterprise culture. In M. Cross & G. Payne (Eds.), *Work and the enterprise culture*. Falmer.

Burton, D., Lee, M. J., Fine, B., & Leopold, E. (1995). Consumer culture reborn: The cultural politics of consumption. *The British Journal of Sociology*, 46(1), 156. https://doi.org/10.2307/591641

Caffentzis, G. (1999). The end of work or the rennaissance of slavery? *Journal of the Edinburgh Conference of Socialist Economists*, 24, 20–38.

Caldwell, J. T. (2008). *Production culture: Industrial reflexivity and critical practice in film and television*. Duke University Press. https://doi.org/10.1215/9780822388968

Caliandro, A. (2018). Digital methods for ethnography: Analytical concepts for ethnographers exploring social media environments. *Journal of Contemporary Ethnography*, 47(5), 551–578. https://doi.org/10.1177/0891241617702960

Calnitsky, D. (2017). Debating basic income. *Catalyst*, 1(3), 1–23. https://catalyst-journal.com/2017/12/debating-basic-income

Campbell, A. K. (2001). Inciting legal fictions: "Disability's" date with ontology and the ableist body of the law. *Griffith Law Review*, 10(1), 42.

Campbell, F. K. (2009). *Contours of ableism: The production of disability and abledness*. Springer. https://doi.org/10.1057/9780230245181

Campbell, M. (2021). *Reimagining the creative industries*. Routledge. https://doi.org/10.4324/9781003031338

Campos Rabadán, M. (2022). Understanding media production. *Revista Latina de Comunicación Social*, 81, 1–3. https://doi.org/10.4185/rlcs-2023-1843

Canadian Press. (2022). Ontario law allowing employees to disconnect from technology after hours kicks in. *Toronto Star*. https://www.thestar.com/business/ontario-law-allowing-employees-to-disconnect-from-technology-after-hours-kicks-in/article_dc1e1a9f-d5ed-5c70-b392-351c0dd55c3c.html

Bibliography

Cannizzo, F., & Strong, C. (2020). 'Put some balls on that woman': Gendered repertoires of inequality in screen composers' careers. *Gender, Work and Organization*, 27(6), 1346–1360. https://doi.org/10.1111/gwao.12496

Caraway, B. (2011). Audience labor in the new media environment: A Marxian revisiting of the audience commodity. *Media, Culture and Society*, 33(5), 693–708. https://doi.org/10.1177/0163443711404463

Carey, H., O'Brien, D., & Gable, O. (2021). *Social mobility in the Creative Economy*. Policy Review Series: Class in the Creative Industries. https://pec.ac.uk/assets/publications/PEC-report-Social-mobility-in-the-Creative-Economy-Sept-2021.pdf

Carey, J. W. (1965). The communications revolution and the professional communicator. *The Sociological Review*, 13(1 S), 23–38. https://doi.org/10.1111/j.1467-954X.1965.tb03107.x

Carlyle, T. (1841). *On heroes, hero-worship, & the heroic in history*. James Fraser Publishers.

Carman, A. (2020, July 14). Black influencers are underpaid, and a new Instagram account is proving it. *The Verge*. https://www.theverge.com/21324116/instagram-influencer-pay-gapaccount-expose

Carneiro, B., & Costa, H. A. (2022). Digital unionism as a renewal strategy? Social media use by trade union confederations. *Journal of Industrial Relations*, 64(1), 26–51. https://doi.org/10.1177/00221856209793 37

Carpenter, N. (2023, November 21). Video game company layoffs are creating an industry crisis. *Polygon*. https://www.polygon.com/23964448/video-game-industry-layoffs-crisis-2023

Carpenter, S., & Lertpratchya, A. P. (2016). A qualitative and quantitative study of social media communicators: An extension of role theory to digital media workers. *Journal of Broadcasting and Electronic Media*, 60(3), 448–464. https://doi.org/10.1080/08838151.2016.1203317

Carr, N. (2015). *The glass cage: Automation and us*. Norton & Company.

Carrigan, J. R. (2012, October 26). Hollywood intern lawsuits: Overworked, underpaid and illegal? *Hollywood Reporter*. http://www.hollywoodreporter.com/thr-esq/hollywood-interns-overworked-underpaid-illegal-382190

Catmull, E. (2023). *Creativity, Inc*. Random House.

Corrigan, T. (2018). Making implicit methods explicit: Trade press analysis in the political economy of communication. *International Journal of Communication*, 12(1), 2751–2772.

Casilli, A. A. (2017). Digital labor studies go global: Toward a digital decolonial turn. *International Journal of Communication*, 11, 3934–3954.

Caves, R. (2002). *Creative industries: Contracts between art and commerce*. Harvard University Press.

Cech, E. A. (2021). *The trouble with passion: How searching for fulfillment at work fosters inequality*. University of California Press.

Chan, B., & Gray, K. (2020). Microstreaming, microcelebrity, and marginalized masculinity: Pathways to visibility and self-definition for Black men in Gaming. *Women's Studies in Communication*, 43(4), 354–362. https://doi.org/10.1080/07491409.2020.1833634

Chan, J. (2021). The Foxconn suicide express. *Proletarian China: A Century of Chinese Labour*, 625–634. https://madeinchinajournal.com/2021/12/01/proletarian-china/

Chan, J., & Pun, N. (2010). Suicide as protest for the new generation of Chinese migrant. *The Asia-Pacific Journal*, 18(37), 1–50.

Chan, J., Selden, M., & Ngai, P. (2020). *Dying for an iPhone: Apple, Foxconn, and the lives of China's workers*. Pluto Press. https://doi.org/10.1111/bjir.12568

Chan, R. (2020). Meet the developer group trying to break the mental health stigma in tech, where moving fast and breaking things leads developers to burnout and health issues. *Business Insider*. https://www.businessinsider.com/open-sourcing-mental-illness-stigma-tech-2019-12

Chanan, M. (1976). *Labour power in the British film industry*. British Film Institute.

Chanan, M. (1980). Labour power and aesthetic labour in film and television in Britain. *Media, Culture & Society*, 2(2), 117–137. https://doi.org/10.1177/016344378000200202

Chang, H.-J. (2010). *23 things they don't tell you about capitalism*. Penguin.

Chayka, K. (2017). Time is money. But that doesn't mean you need to work non-stop. *Pacific Standard*. 2017–2019. https://psmag.com/economics/time-money-doesnt-mean-need-work-non-stop-81438

Chayka, K. (2021). What the "Creator Economy" promises—and what it actually does. *The New Yorker*. https://www.newyorker.com/culture/infinite-scroll/what-the-creator-economy-promises-and-what-it-actually-does

Chen, A. (2014). The laborers who keep Dick pics and beheadings out of your Facebook feed. *Wired*. https://www.wired.com/2014/10/content-moderation/

Chen, J. Y. (2018). Thrown under the bus and outrunning it! The logic of didi and taxi drivers' labour and activism in the on-demand economy. *New Media & Society*, 20(8), 2691–2711.

Chen, J. Y., Delfanti, A., & Phan, M. (2023). Worker resistance in digital capitalism. *International Journal of Communication*, 17(2023), 3891–3898.

Chen, M. A. (2016). Informal employment: Theory and reality. In S. Edgell, H. Gottfried, & E. Granter (Eds.), *The SAGE handbook of the sociology of work and employment* (pp. 407–427). Sage. https://doi.org/10.4135/9781473915206.n22

Chen, Z. (2023). Ethics and discrimination in artificial intelligence-enabled recruitment practices. *Humanities and Social Sciences Communications*, 10(1). https://doi.org/10.1057/s41599-023-02079-x

Cherney, J. L. (2011). The rhetoric of ableism. *Disability Studies Quarterly*, 31(3). https://doi.org/10.18061/dsq.v31i3.1665

Chia, A. (2021). Self-making and game making in the future of work. *Game Production Studies*. https://doi.org/10.5117/9789463725439_ch02

Chia, A. (2022). The artist and the automaton in digital game production. *Convergence: The International Journal of Research into New Media Technologies*, 28(2): 389–412.

Cho, W. (2024). A Ban on Noncompetes Could Raise Pay — and Complicate Contracts — in Hollywood. *Hollywood Reporter*. https://www.hollywoodreporter.com/business/business-news/ban-noncompetes-could-raise-pay-complicate-contracts-hollywood-1235879986

Cho, W. (2024, May 21). Scarlett Johansson's AI Legal Threat Sets Stage for Actors' Battle With Tech Giants. *The Hollywood Reporter*. https://www.hollywoodreporter.com/business/business-news/scarlett-johansson-ai-legal-threat-1235905899/

Chotiner, I. (2019). The underworld of online content moderation. *The New Yorker*. https://www.newyorker.com/news/q-and-a/the-underworld-of-online-content-moderation

Christin, A., & Lu, Y. (2023). The influencer pay gap: Platform labor meets racial capitalism. *New Media and Society*, 0/0. https://doi.org/10.1177/14614448231164995

Christopherson, S. (2004). The divergent worlds of new media: How policy shapes work in the creative economy. *Review of Policy Research*, 21(4), 543–558. https://doi.org/10.1111/j.1541-1338.2004.00093.x

Christopherson, S. (2006). Behind the scenes: How transnational firms are constructing a new international division of labor in media work. *Geoforum*, 37(5), 739–751. https://doi.org/10.1016/j.geoforum.2006.01.003

Christopherson. S. (2008). Beyond the self-expressive creative worker: An industry perspective on entertainment media. *Theory, Culture & Society*, 25(7–8).
Christopherson, S. (2009). Working in the creative economy: Risk, adaptation, and the persistence of exclusionary networks. *Creative Labour*, 72–90.
Christopherson, S., Garretsen, H., & Martin, R. (2008). The world is not flat: Putting globalization in its place. *Cambridge Journal of Regions, Economy and Society*, 1(3), 343–349. https://doi.org/10.1093/cjres/rsn023
Chun, J. J., & Agarwala, R. (2016). Global labour politics in informal and precarious jobs. In S. Edgell, H. Gottfried, & E. Granter (Eds.), *The SAGE handbook of the sociology of work and employment* (pp. 634–650). Sage. https://doi.org/10.4135/9781473915206.n34
Chung, H. J. (2018). *Media heterotopias: Digital effects and material labor in global film production*. Duke University Press. https://doi.org/10.1215/9780822372158
Cianci, C. C. (2009). Entertainment or exploitation?: Reality television and the inadequate protection of child participants under the law. *Southern California Interdisciplinary Law Journal*, 18(1), 363–94.
Cicero, M. T. (1933). *De natura deorum: Academica*. https://archive.org/details/denaturadeorumac00ciceuoft/mode/2up
Clark, D. (1995). *Negotiating Hollywood: The cultural politics of actors' labor*. University of Minnesota Press.
Clark, S. (2020). *The making of the American creative class: New York's culture workers and twentieth-century consumer capitalism*. Oxford University Press. https://doi.org/10.1093/oso/9780199731626.001.0001
Cleaver, H. (1989). Work, value and domination: On the continuing relevance of the Marxian labour theory of value in the crisis of the Keynesian planner state. *The Commoner*, 10. https://thecommoner.org/wp-content/uploads/2020/06/Harry-Cleaver-Work-Value-and-Domination-1.pdf
Cliff, T. (1999). *Trotskyism after Trotsky: The origins of the international socialists*. Bookmarks.
CLJE (Center for Labor and Just Economy at Harvard Law School). (2024) Worker power and voice in the AI response. https://clje.law.harvard.edu/app/uploads/2024/01/Worker-Power-and-the-Voice-in-the-AI-Response-Report.pdf
Cloud, D. L. (2005). Fighting words: Labor and the limits of communication at Staley, 1993 to 1996. *Management Communication Quarterly*, 18(4), 509–542. https://doi.org/10.1177/0893318904273688
Cohen, N., & de Peuter, G. (2013). The politics of precarity: Can the urban worker strategy address precarious employment for all? *Cultural Workers Organization*. https://culturalworkersorganize.org/politics-of-precarity/
Cohen, N. S. (2004, 2008). The valorization of surveillance: Towards a political economy of Facebook. *Democratic Communiqué*, 22, 5–22. http://udc.igc.org/communique/issues/Spring2008/cohen.pdf
Cohen, N. S. (2011). Negotiating writers' rights: Freelance cultural labour and the challenge of organizing. *Just Labour*. https://doi.org/10.25071/1705-1436.36
Cohen, N. S. (2012). Cultural work as a site of struggle: Freelancers and exploitation. *TripleC: Communication, Capitalism & Critique*, 10(2), 141–155. https://doi.org/10.31269/triplec.v10i2.384
Cohen, N. S. (2013). Commodifying free labor online: Social media, audiences, and advertising. In E. West & M. McAllister (Eds.), *The Routledge companion to advertising and promotional culture* (pp. 177–191).
Cohen, N. S. (2015a). Entrepreneurial journalism and the precarious state of media work. *South Atlantic Quarterly*, 114(3), 513–533. https://doi.org/10.1215/00382876-3130723

Cohen, N. S. (2015b). From pink slips to pink slime: Transforming media labor in a digital age. *Communication Review*, 18(2), 98–122. https://doi.org/10.1080/10714421.2015.1031996

Cohen, N. S. (2016). *Writers' rights: Freelance journalism in a digital age*. McGill-Queen's University Press.

Cohen, N. S. (2019). At work in the digital newsroom. *Digital Journalism*, 7(5), 571–591. https://doi.org/10.1080/21670811.2017.1419821

Cohen, N. S., & de Peuter, G. (2018). Interns talk back: Disrupting media narratives about unpaid work. *The Political Economy of Communication*, 6(2), 3–24. https://www.polecom.org/index.php/polecom/article/view/96

Cohen, N. S., & de Peuter, G. (2020). *New media unions: Organizing digital journalists*. Routledge. https://doi.org/10.4324/9780429449451

Coleman, A. (2016). Is Google's model of the creative workplace the future of the office? *The Guardian*. http://www.theguardian.com/careers/2016/feb/11/isgoogles-model-of-the-creative-workplace-the-future-of-the-office

Coleman, K., James, D., & Sharma, J. (2018). Photography and work. *Radical History Review*, 1(132), 1–22. doi: https://doi.org/10.1215/01636545-6942345

Coles, A. (2006). Acting in the name of culture? Organized labour campaigns for Canadian dramatic programming. *Canadian Journal of Communication*, 31(3), 519–540. https://doi.org/10.22230/cjc.2006v31n3a1765

Coles, A. (2010). Unintended consequences: Examining the impact of tax credit programmes on work in the Canadian independent film and television production sector. *Cultural Trends*, 19(1–2), 109–124. https://doi.org/10.1080/09548961003696120

Coles, A. (2016). Creative class politics: Unions and the creative economy. *International Journal of Cultural Policy*, 22(3), 456–472. https://doi.org/10.1080/10286632.2014.994612

Coles, A. (2023). Collective action! Unions in the Canadian film and television industry. Deakin University. https://hdl.handle.net/10779/DRO/DU:20580759.v1

Coles, A., Ferrer, J., Zemaityte, V., & Banks, M. (2022). *A wider lens: Australian camera workforce development and diversity – Executive summary*. Deakin University.

Collins, P., & Power, D. (2019). A co-evolving cultural cluster in the periphery: Film and TV production in Galway, Ireland. *City, Culture and Society*, 18. https://doi.org/10.1016/j.ccs.2019.05.003

Collins, S. (2008). Making the most out of 15 minutes: Reality TV's dispensable celebrity. *Television & New Media*, 9(2), 87–110. https://doi.org/10.1177/1527476407313814

Columbia Law School. (2017). Kimberlé Crenshaw on Intersectionality, More than Two Decades Later. https://www.law.columbia.edu/news/archive/kimberle-crenshaw-intersectionality-more-two-decades-later

Comitta, T. (2023). Death of an Author Prophesies the Future of AI Novels. *Wired*. https://www.wired.com/story/death-of-an-author-ai-book-review/

Comor, E. (2010). Digital prosumption and alienation. *Ephemera: Theory & Politics in Organization*, 10(3/4), 439–454.

Comtois, J. (2020). Sony pictures unveils details of new racial equity and inclusion initiative. *Syfy*. https://www.syfy.com/syfy-wire/sony-pictures-racial-equity-and-inclusion-initiative

Cong, L., & Li, S. (2023). A model of influencer economy. *SSRN Electronic Journal*. https://doi.org/10.2139/ssrn.3975727

Connell, R. (2006). Glass ceilings or gendered institutions? Mapping the gender regimes of public sector worksites. *Public Administration Review*, 66(6), 837–849. https://doi.org/10.1111/j.1540-6210.2006.00652.x

Connell, R. W. (2002). Gender regimes and the general order. In *The polity reader in gender studies* (pp. 29–40). Polity.

Conor, B. (2010). Everybody's a writer theorizing screenwriting as creative labour. *Journal of Screenwriting*, 1(1), 27–43. https://doi.org/10.1386/josc.1.1.27/1

Conor, B. (2014). Gurus and Oscar winners: How-to screenwriting manuals in the new cultural economy. *Television and New Media*, 15(2), 121–138. https://doi.org/10.1177/1527476412452798

Conor, B., Gill, R., & Taylor, S. (2015). Gender and creative labour. *Sociological Review*, 63(S1), 1–22. https://doi.org/10.1111/1467-954X.12237

Consalvo, M. (2008). Crunched by passion: Women game developers and workplace challenges. In Y. B. Kafai, C. Heeter, J. Denner, & J. Y. Sun (Eds.), *Beyond Barbie and Mortal Kombat* (pp. 177–192). https://doi.org/10.7551/mitpress/7477.003.0017

Cooper, P. (2023). New Study Investigates Why Elite Colleges Favor Rich Kids. *Forbes*. https://www.forbes.com/sites/prestoncooper2/2023/08/22/new-study-investigates-why-elite-colleges-favor-rich-kids/

Coote, A. and Yazici, Edanur (2019). Universal basic income doesn't work. Let's boost the public realm instead. *The Guardian*. https://www.theguardian.com/commentisfree/2019/may/06/universal-basic-income-public-realm-poverty-inequality

Corbin, T., & Deranty, J. (2020). *Foucault on the centrality of work*. OnWork Newsletter. https://onwork.substack.com/p/foucault-on-the-centrality-of-work

Cornwall, G. (2023). How Rich (or Not) Do You Have to Be to Get Into the Ivy League? *New York Magazine*. https://nymag.com/intelligencer/article/college-acceptance-rates-ivy-league-schools-wealth.html

Coser, L. A. (1978). The production of culture. *Social Research*, 48(2), 225–224.

Cosin, B. R., Bowles, S., & Gintis, H. (1979). Schooling in capitalist America. *The British Journal of Sociology*, 30(2), 256. https://doi.org/10.2307/589546

Cote, A. C., & Harris, B. C. (2021). 'Weekends became something other people did': Understanding and intervening in the habitus of video game crunch. *Convergence*, 27(1), 161–176. https://doi.org/10.1177/1354856520913865

Cote, A. C., & Harris, B. C. (2023a). The cruel optimism of "good crunch": How game industry discourses perpetuate unsustainable labor practices. *New Media & Society*, 25(3), 609–627. https://doi.org/10.1177/14614448211014213

Cote, A. C., & Harris, B. C. (2023b). Inevitable or exploitative? A case study of consumers' divergent attitudes towards video game crunch. *Media Industries (Austin, Tex.)*, 10(1). https://doi.org/10.3998/mij.2357

Cotter, K. (2019). Playing the visibility game: How digital influencers and algorithms negotiate influence on Instagram. *New Media and Society*, 21(4), 895–913. https://doi.org/10.1177/1461444818815684

Cottle, S. (2007). Ethnography and news production: New(s) developments in the field. *Sociology Compass*, 1(1), 1–16. https://doi.org/10.1111/j.1751-9020.2007.00002.x

Cowan, R. S. (1984). *More work for mother: The ironies of household technology from the open hearth to the microwave*. Basic Books.

Cox, J. (1998). An introduction to Marx's theory of alienation. *International Socialism Journal*, 79(July), 41–62. https://www.marxists.org/history/etol/newspape/isj2/1998/isj2-079/cox.htm

Coyle, J. (2020). *Hollywood says Black Lives Matter, but more diversity needed*. Associated Press. https://apnews.com/73d0b84a5fce32e97af8f7b0bb9b9261

Coyle, J. (2023). *In Hollywood writers' battle against AI, humans win (for now)*. Associated Press. https://apnews.com/article/hollywood-ai-strike-wga-artificial-intelligence-39ab72582c3a15f77510c9c30a45ffc8

Crabapple, M. (2022, December 21). Op-Ed: Beware a world where artists are replaced by robots. It's starting now. *Los Angeles Times*. https://www.latimes.com/opinion/story/2022-12-21/artificial-intelligence-artists-stability-ai-digital-images

Crabapple, M. (2023, May 3). Artists, writers and activists open petition against the use of AI artwork. *Hypebeast*. https://hypebeast.com/2023/5/molly-crabapple-artificial-intelligence-art-petition

Craig, D. (2020). Creator management in the social media entertainment industry. In M. Deuze & M. Prenger (Eds.), *Making media* (pp. 363–374). https://doi.org/10.1017/9789048540150.027

Craig, D., & Cunningham, S. (2023). With the end of the Hollywood writers and actors strikes, the creator economy is the next frontier for organized labor. *The Conversation*. https://theconversation.com/with-the-end-of-the-hollywood-writers-and-actors-strikes-the-creator-economy-is-the-next-frontier-for-organized-labor-217657

Crain, M. (2021). *Profit over privacy: How surveillance advertising conquered the internet*. University of Minnesota Press.

Crane, D. (1992). *The production of culture*. Sage.

Crane, D. (1997). Globalization, organizational size, and innovation in the French luxury fashion industry: Production of culture theory revisited. *Poetics*, *24*(6), 393–414. https://doi.org/10.1016/S0304-422X(97)00004-1

Crary, J. (2013). *24/7*. Verso.

Crenshaw, K. (1989). Demarginalizing the intersection of race and sex: A Black feminist critique of antidiscrimination doctrine, feminist theory and antiracist politics. *University of Chicago Legal Forum*, *1*(8), 139–167. http://chicagounbound.uchicago.edu/uclf/vol1989/iss1/8

Crenshaw, K. (2006). Race, reform, and retrenchment: Transformation and legitimation in antidiscrimination law. In *Law and social movements* (pp. 475–531). https://doi.org/10.4324/9781315091983-19

Crenshaw, L. (1991). Mapping the margins: Intersectionality, identity politics, and violence against women of color. *Stanford Law Review*, *43*(6), 1241–1299.

Criscitiello, R. (2018). There is platform-power in a union. In T. Scholz & N. Schneider (Eds.), *Ours to hack and to own: The rise of platform cooperativism, a new vision for the future of work and a fairer internet* (pp. 145–148). OR Books. https://doi.org/10.2307/j.ctv62hfq7.27

Cullins, A., Pener, D., & Ritman, A. (2020). Hollywood's mental health reckoning has arrived. *The Hollywood Reporter*. https://www.hollywoodreporter.com/movies/movie-features/hollywoods-mental-health-reckoning-has-arrived-1269807/

Cunningham, S., & Craig, D. (Eds.). (2021). *Creator culture*. New York University Press.

Cunningham, S., & Craig, D. (2016). Online entertainment: A new wave of media globalization? *International Journal of Communication*, *10*, 5409–5425.

Cunningham, S., & Craig, D. (2017). Being 'really real' on YouTube: Authenticity, community and brand culture in social media entertainment. *Media International Australia*, *164*(1), 71–81. https://doi.org/10.1177/1329878X17709098

Cunningham, S., & Craig, D. R. (2019). *Social media entertainment: The new intersection of Hollywood and Silicon Valley*. New York University Press.

Cunningham, S., Flew, T., & Swift, A. (2015). *Media economics*. Palgrave.

Curl, A. (2022). Turning the channel: Why online content creators can and should unionize under the NLRA. *ABA Journal of Labor & Employment Law*, *3*(1), 517–542.

Curran, J. (2002). *The media and power*. Routledge. https://www.routledge.com/Media-and-Power/Curran/p/book/9780415077408

Curtin, M. (2016). Regulating the global infrastructure of film labor exploitation. *International Journal of Cultural Policy*, 22(5), 673–685. https://doi.org/10.1080/10286632.2016.1223636

Curtin, M., & Sanson, K. (Eds.). (2016). *Voices of labor: Creativity, craft, and conflict in global Hollywood*. University of California Press. https://doi.org/10.1353/book.63436

Curtin, M., & Sanson, K. (2017). *Precarious creativity: Global media, local labor*. University of California Press.

Cushing, E. (2012, August 1). Dawn of the digital sweatshop. *EastBay Express*, https://eastbayexpress.com/dawn-of-the-digital-sweatshop-1

Cushion, S. (2007). Rich media, poor journalists: Journalists' salaries. *Journalism Practice*, 1(1), 120–129. https://doi.org/10.1080/17512780601078910

The DAIR Institute, Collective Action School, and Collective Action in Tech (2024). *Bits in the Machine: A Time Capsule of Worker's Stories in the Age of Generative AI. Collective Action in Tech*. https://collectiveaction.tech/2024/bits-in-the-machine/

D'Cruz, P., & Noronha, E. (2016). Positives outweighing negatives: The experiences of Indian crowdsourced workers. *Work Organisation, Labour and Globalisation*, 10(1), 44–63. https://doi.org/10.13169/workorgalaboglob.10.1.0044

Dalla Costa, M., & James. S. (1975). *The power of women and the subversion of the community*. Falling Wall Press. https://files.libcom.org/files/Dalla%20Costa%20and%20James%20-%20Women%20and%20the%20Subversion%20of%20the%20Community.pdf

Danaher, J. (2019). *Automation and utopia : Human flourishing in a world without work*. Harvard University Press.

Darbinyan, R. (2023). Council post: The growing role of AI in content moderation. *Forbes*. https://www.forbes.com/sites/forbestechcouncil/2022/06/14/the-growing-role-of-ai-in-content-moderation/

Daub, A. (2020). *What tech calls thinking*. FSG Originals

Davis, C. (2023, May 19). Attention, Hollywood: De-Aging Isn't Working, So Please Stop Using It. *Variety*. https://variety.com/2023/film/awards/indiana-jones-5-harrison-ford-de-aging-not-working-1235618698/

Davis, M. (2020). *Prisoners of the American dream: Politics and economy in the history of the US working class*. Verso.

DCMS(Department of Culture Media and Sport UK). (2001). *Creative industries mapping documents*. https://www.gov.uk/government/publications/creative-industries-mapping-documents-2001

Dean, M. (1999). *Governmentality: Power and rule in modern society*. Sage.

de Castell, S., & Skardzius, K. (2019). Speaking in public: What women say about working in the video game industry. *Television and New Media*, 20(8), 836–847. https://doi.org/10.1177/1527476419851078

de los Reyes, P. (2017). Working life inequalities: Do we need intersectionality? *Society, Health & Vulnerability*, 8(1). https://doi.org/10.1080/20021518.2017.1332858

de Peuter, G. (2011). Creative economy and labor precarity: A contested convergence. *Journal of Communication Inquiry*, 35(4), 417–425. https://doi.org/10.1177/0196859911416362

de Peuter, G. (2012). Modelling workers' rights. *Shameless*. https://shamelessmag.com/blog/entry/modelling-workers-rights

de Peuter, G. (2014). Beyond the model worker: Surveying a creative precariat. *Culture Unbound*, 6(1), 263–284. https://doi.org/10.3384/cu.2000.1525.146263

de Peuter, G. (2017). Coworking and co-operation: A union in the making. *Stir: The Magazine for the New Economy*. https://culturalworkersorganize.org/wp-content/uploads/2017/10/coworking-and-co-operatives-a-union-in-the-making.pdf

de Peuter, G., & Cohen, N. S. (2015). Emerging labour politics in creative industries. In K. Oakley & J. O'Connor (Eds.), *The Routledge companion to the cultural industries* (pp. 305–318). https://doi.org/10.4324/9781315725437-36

de Peuter, G., Cohen, N., & Brophy, E. (2012). Interns Unite! (you have nothing to lose—Literally). *Briarpatch*. https://culturalworkersorganize.org/interns-unite-you-have-nothing-to-lose-literally/

de Peuter, G., Cohen, N. S., & Brophy, E. (2015). Interrogating internships: Unpaid work, creative industries, and higher education. *TripleC: Communication, Capitalism & Critique, 13*(2), 329–335. https://doi.org/10.31269/triplec.v13i2.717

de Peuter, G., Cohen, N. S., & Saraco, F. (2017). The ambivalence of coworking: On the politics of an emerging work practice. *European Journal of Cultural Studies, 20*(6), 687–706. https://doi.org/10.1177/1367549417732997

de Peuter, G., de Verteuil, G., & Machaka, S. (2022). *Co-operatives, work, and the digital economy: A knowledge synthesis report*. Social Sciences and Humanities Research Council of Canada, Knowledge Synthesis Program, Skills and Work in the Digital Economy. https://culturalworkersorganize.org/wp-content/uploads/2022/05/Cooperatives-Work-and-the-Digital-Economy-KSG-Report.pdf

de Peuter, G., Dreyer, B., Sandoval, M., & Szaflarska, A. (2020). *Sharing like we mean it working co-operatively in the cultural and tech sectors*. https://culturalworkersorganize.org/wp-content/uploads/2021/01/Sharing-Like-We-Mean-It-Web.pdf

de Waal, M., Poell, T., & van Dijck, J. (2018). *The platform society*. Oxford University Press. https://doi.org/10.1093/oso/9780190889760.001.0001

de Castell, S., & Skardzius, K. (2019). Speaking in public: What women say about working in the video game industry. *Television & New Media, 20*(8), 836–847. https://doi.org/10.1177/1527476419851078

Dean, J. (2018). Communicative capitalism: Circulation and the foreclosure of politics. *Digital Media and Democracy*, 101–122. https://doi.org/10.7551/mitpress/7687.003.0006

Delfanti, A. (2021a). Machinic dispossession and augmented despotism: Digital work in an Amazon warehouse. *New Media and Society, 23*(1), 39–55. https://doi.org/10.1177/1461444819891613

Delfanti, A. (2021b). *The warehouse: Workers and robots at Amazon*. Pluto.

Delfanti, A., & Arvidsson, A. (2019a). *Introduction to digital media*. John Wiley & Sons.

Delfanti, A., & Phan, M. (2024). Rip it up and start again: Creative labor and the industrialization of remix. *Television & New Media*, https://doi.org/10.1177/15274764241227613

Delfanti, A., Radovac, L. and Walker, T. (2021). *The Amazon panopticon: A guide for workes, organizers & policymakers*. UNI Global Union. https://uniglobalunion.org/wp-content/uploads/amazon_panopticon_en_final.pdf

Delfanti, A., & Sharma, S. (2019). Log Out! The Platform Economy and Worker Resistance. *Notes from Below*. https://notesfrombelow.org/article/log-out-platform-economy-and-worker-resistance

Delmar Sentíes, D. (2023). *What we build with power: The fight for economic justice in tech*. Beacon Press.

Denby, C. (1989). *Indignant heart: A black worker's journal*. Wayne State University Press.

Dencik, L., & Wilkin, P. (2015). Worker resistance and media: Challenging global corporate power in the 21st century. *European Journal of Communication*, *31*(6), 715–717. https://doi.org/10.1177/0267323116677489

Deneroff, H. (1987). "We Can't Get Much Spinach"! The organization and implementation of the Fleischer animation strike. *Film History*, *1*(1), 1–14.

Denning, M. (1996). *The cultural front: The laboring of American culture in the twentieth century*. Verso.

Denning, M. (2016). Wageless life. *Global Histories of Work*, 273–290. https://doi.org/10.1515/9783110437201-011

Department of Justice (DOJ). (2010). Justice Department Requires Six High Tech Companies to Stop Entering into Anticompetitive Employee Solicitation Agreements. http://www.justice.gov/opa/pr/2010/September/10-at-1076.html

Deresiewicz, W. (2020). *The death of the artist: How creators are struggling to survive in the age of billionaires and big tech*. Macmillan Publishers.

Deuze, M. (2007). *Media work*. Polity Press.

Deuze, M. (2009). The people formerly known as the employers. *Journalism*, *10*(3), 315–318. https://doi.org/10.1177/1464884909102574

Deuze, M., Chase Bowen, M. and Allen, C. (2007). The professional identity of gameworkers. *Convergence: The International Journal of Research into New Media Technologies*, *13*(4), 335–353.

Deuze, M., & Prenger, M. (Eds.). (2020). *Making media: Production, practices, and professions*. Amsterdam University Press. https://doi.org/10.1017/9789048540150.001

Deuze, M., & Steward, B. (Eds.). (2010). *Managing media work*. Sage.

Deuze, M. (contracted). *Well-Being in Creative Careers: What Makes You Happy Can Also Make You Sick*. Intellect.

Dibbell, J. (2003). Black snow interactive and the world's first virtual sweat shop. *Wired*. http://www.juliandibbell.com/texts/blacksnow.html

Dillan, P. (2018). Hold the line: Interview with Enda Brophy. *Rabble*. https://www.rabble.ie/2018/01/18/hold-the-line

DiMaggio, P. (1977). Market structure, the creative process, and popular culture: Toward an organizational reinterpretation of mass-culture theory. *The Journal of Popular Culture*, *11*(2), 436–452. https://doi.org/10.1111/j.0022-3840.1977.00436.x

DiMaggio, P. (2004). Cultural entrepreneurship in nineteenth-century Boston: The creation of an organizational base for high culture in America. *Sociology of Art: A Reader*, 178–193. https://doi.org/10.1525/9780520354647-014

Dockterman, E. (2019).The True Story Behind Bombshell and the Fox News Sexual Harassment Scandal. *TIME*. https://time.com/5748267/bombshell-true-story-fox-news/

Dockterman, E. (2023). A major Hollywood diversity report shows little change—Except for one promising stat. *Time*. https://time.com/6305012/hollywood-diversity-report-asian-representation/

Doherty, M. (2009). When the working day is through: The end of work as identity? *Work, Employment and Society*, *23*(1), 84–101. https://doi.org/10.1177/0950017008099779

Dolber, B. (2016a). Blindspots and blurred lines: Dallas Smythe, the audience commodity, and the transformation of labor in the digital age. *Sociology Compass*, *10*(9), 747–755. https://doi.org/10.1111/soc4.12387

Dolber, B. (2016b). Commodifying alternative media audiences: A historical case study of the Jewish Daily Forward. *Communication, Culture and Critique*, *9*(2), 175–192. https://doi.org/10.1111/cccr.12101

Donoghue, C. D. (2017). *Localising Hollywood*. Bloomsbury.
Donovan, P. (2020). *Profit and prejudice : The luddites of the fourth industrial revolution*. Routledge.
Dorschel, R. (2022). Reconsidering digital labour: Bringing tech workers into the debate. *New Technology, Work and Employment, 37*(2), 288–307. https://doi.org/10.1111/ntwe.12225
Dowd, T. J., & Blyler, M. (2002). Charting race: The success of Black performers in the mainstream recording market, 1940 to 1990. *Poetics, 30*(1–2), 87–110. https://doi.org/10.1016/S0304-422X(02)00008-6
Downey, G. J. (2014). Making media work: Time, space, identity, and labor in the analysis of information and communication infrastructures. In T, Gillespie, P. J. Boczkowski, & K. A. Foot (Eds.), *Media technologies: Essays on communication, materiality, and society*. MIT Press. https://doi.org/10.7551/mitpress/9780262525374.003.0008
Downie, J. (2023). Watch this multi-millionaire CEO say the quiet part out loud about class warfare. *MSNBC*. https://www.msnbc.com/opinion/msnbc-opinion/tim-gurner-australian-ceo-unemployment-video-rcna104957
Doyle, G. (2014). *Understanding media economics*. Sage. https://doi.org/10.4135/9781446279960
Dreyer, B. C., de Peuter, G., Sandoval, M. Szaflarska (2020). The co-operative alternative and the creative industries: A technical report on a survey of co-operatives in the cultural and technology sectors in Canada, the United Kingdom, and the United States. *Cultural Workers Organize*. https://culturalworkersorganize.org/wp-content/uploads/2020/12/The-Cooperative-Alternative-Technical-Report-Web.pdf
Drucker, P. (1996). *Landmarks of tomorrow: A report on the new "Post-Modern" world*. Routledge.
Drucker, P. (2006). *The practice of management*. Harper Business.
Duda, J. (2016). Beyond luxury cooperativism. In T. Scholz & N. Schneider (Eds.), *Ours to hack and to own* (pp. 182–186). OR Books.
du Gay, P. (Ed.). (1997). *Production of culture/cultures of production*. Sage.
du Gay, P., Hall, S., Janes, L., Mackay, H., & Negus, K. (1997). *Doing cultural studies: The story of the Sony Walkman*. Sage.
Dubal, V. (2020). Digital piecework. *Dissent, 67*(4), 37–44. https://doi.org/10.1353/dss.2020.0089
Dubois, L. E., & Weststar, J. (2022). Games-as-a-service: Conflicted identities on the new front-line of video game development. *New Media and Society, 24*(10), 2332–2353. https://doi.org/10.1177/1461444821995815
Duffy, B. E. (2015). Gendering the labor of social media production. *Feminist Media Studies, 15*(4), 710–714. https://doi.org/10.1080/14680777.2015.1053715
Duffy, B. E. (2016). The romance of work: Gender and aspirational labour in the digital culture industries. *International Journal of Cultural Studies, 19*(4), 441–457. https://doi.org/10.1177/1367877915572186
Duffy, B. E. (2017). *(Not) getting paid to do what you love: Gender, social media, and aspirational work*. Yale University Press.
Duffy, B. E. (2020). Social media influencers. In *The international encyclopedia of gender, media, and communication* (pp. 1–4). https://doi.org/10.1002/9781119429128.iegmc219
Duffy, B. E. (contracted). *The Visibility Bind: Creators and the Perils of Platform Labor*. University of Chicago Press.
Duffy, B. E., & Hund, E. (2015). "Having it All" on social media: Entrepreneurial femininity and self-branding among fashion bloggers. *Social Media + Society, 1*(2). https://doi.org/10.1177/2056305115604337

Duffy, B. E., & Meisner, C. (2023). Platform governance at the margins: Social media creators' experiences with algorithmic (in)visibility. *Media, Culture and Society, 45*(2), 285–304. https://doi.org/10.1177/01634437221111923

Duffy, B. E., Pinch, A., Sannon, S., & Sawey, M. (2021). The nested precarities of creative labor on social media. *Social Media and Society, 7*(2). https://doi.org/10.1177/20563051211021368

Duffy, B. E., Poell, T., & Nieborg, D. B. (2019). Platform practices in the cultural industries: Creativity, labor, and citizenship. *Social Media + Society, 5*(4). https://doi.org/10.1177/2056305119879672

Duffy, B. E., & Schwartz, B. (2018). Digital "women's work?": Job recruitment ads and the feminization of social media employment. *New Media and Society, 20*(8), 2972–2989. https://doi.org/10.1177/1461444817738237

Duffy, B. E., & Wissinger, E. (2017). Mythologies of creative work in the social media age: Fun, free, and "just being me". *International Journal of Communication, 11*, 4652–4671.

Duggan, J., Sherman, U., Carbery, R., & McDonnell, A. (2020). Algorithmic management and app-work in the gig economy: A research agenda for employment relations and HRM. *Human Resource Management Journal, 30*(1), 114–132. https://doi.org/10.1111/1748-8583.12258

Duguay, S. (2019). "Running the Numbers": Modes of microcelebrity labor in Queer Women's self-representation on Instagram and Vine. *Social Media + Society, 5*(4). https://doi.org/10.1177/2056305119894002

Duin, A. H., & Pedersen, I. (2023). *Augmentation technologies and artificial intelligence in technical communication: Designing ethical futures*. Routledge.

Dukes, R., & Streeck, W. (2022). *Democracy at work: Contract, status and post-industrial justice*. Wiley.

Dumas, T. L., & Sanchez-Burks, J. (2015). The professional, the personal, and the ideal worker: Pressures and objectives shaping the boundary between life domains. *Academy of Management Annals, 9*(1), 803–843. https://doi.org/10.5465/19416520.2015.1028810

Duménil, G., & Lévy, D. (2018). *Managerial capitalism : Ownership, management and the coming new mode of production*. Pluto.

Dworkin, D. (2007). *Class struggles*. Pearson.

Dyer-Witheford, N. (1999). *Cyber-Marx: Cycles and circuits of struggle in high technology capitalism*. University of Illinois Press.

Dyer-Witheford, N. (2015). *Cyber-proletariat: Global labour in the digital vortex*. Pluto Press.

Dyer-Witheford, N., & de Peuter, G. (2006). "EA Spouse" and the crisis of video game labour: Enjoyment, exclusion, exploitation, exodus. *Canadian Journal of Communication, 31*(3), 599–617. https://doi.org/10.22230/cjc.2006v31n3a1771

Dyer-Witheford, N., & de Peuter, G. (2009). *Games of empire*. University of Minnesota Press.

Dyer-Witheford, N., & de Peuter, G. (2020). Postscript: Gaming while empire burns. *Games and Culture, 16*(3), 371–380. https://doi.org/10.1177/1555412020954998

Dyer-Witheford, N., Mikkola Kjosen, A., & Steinhoff, J. (2019). *Inhuman power: Artificial intelligence and the future of capitalism*. Pluto.

Edgell, S. (1993). *Class*. Routledge. https://doi.org/10.4324/9780203137024

Edgell, S., Gottfried, H., & Granter, E. (2016a). Introduction: Studies of work and employment at the global frontier. In *The SAGE handbook of the sociology of work and employment* (pp. 1–13). https://doi.org/10.4135/9781473915206.n1

Edgell, S., Gottfried, H., & Granter, E. (Eds.). (2016b). *The SAGE handbook of the sociology of work and employment*. https://doi.org/10.4135/9781473915206

Edwards, R. (1979). Contested terrain: The transformation of the workplace in the twentieth century. *Capital & Class*, 5(2), 151–155. https://doi.org/10.1177/030981688101400116

Edwards, S. (2022). Branded dreams, boss babes: influencer retreats and the cultural logics of the influencer para-industry. *Social Media + Society*, 8(3). https://doi.org/10.1177/20563051221116846

Ehrenreich, B., & Ehrenreich, J. (1977). The professional-managerial class. *Radical America*, 11(2), 7–31.

Ehrenreich, B., & Ehrenreich, J. (2013). Death of a yuppie dream: The rise and fall of the professional-managerial class. *Rosa Luxemburg Stiftung*, 2–11. https://rosalux.nyc/wp-content/uploads/2021/09/ehrenreich_death_of_a_yuppie_dream90.pdf

Eidlin, B. (2016). Class and work. In S. Edgell, H. Gottfried, & G. Granter (Eds.), *The SAGE handbook of the sociology of work and employment* (pp. 52–72). Sage. https://doi.org/10.4135/9781473915206.n4

El Khachab, C. (2021). *Making film in Egypt: How labor, technology, and meditation shape the industry*. American University in Cairo Press.

Elber, L. (2018). Hollywood's diversity push snubs actors with disabilities. *Associated Press*. https://apnews.com/article/910abfe1b02c416eb60c76cbb897bdc1

Elefante, P. H., & Deuze, M. (2012). Media work, career management, and professional identity: Living labour precarity. *Northern Lights*, 10(1), 9–24. https://doi.org/10.1386/nl.10.1.9_1

Elias, J. (2020). U.S. Labor Board accuses Google of spying on employees, discouraging worker organization, and retaliation. *CNBC*. https://www.cnbc.com/2020/12/02/google-spied-on-employees-illegally-terminated-them-nlrb-alleges.html

Elliot, V. (2022). Tech's offshore hiring has gone into overdrive. *Wired*. https://www.wired.com/story/techs-offshore-hiring-has-gone-into-overdrive/

Ellis, K. (2016). *Disability media work: Opportunities and obstacles*. Springer. https://doi.org/10.1057/978-1-137-52871-1

Elmer, G. & Gasher, M. (2005). *Contracting out Hollywood: Runaway production and foreign location shooting*. Rowman & Littlefield.

Ember, S. (2018). HuffPost, breaking from its roots, ends unpaid contributions. *New York Times*. https://www.nytimes.com/2018/01/18/business/media/huffpost-unpaid-contributors.html

Engels, F. (1958). *The condition of the working class in England*. Stanford University Press.

Engels, F. (1972). *The origin of the family, private property and the state*. International Publishers.

Englert, S., Woodcock, J., & Cant, C. (2020). Digital workerism: Technology, platforms, and the circulation of workers' struggles. *TripleC: Communication, Capitalism & Critique*, 18(1), 132–145. https://doi.org/10.31269/triplec.v18i1.1133

Entertainment Partners. (2023). *Production Incentives Update: July 2023*. https://www.ep.com/industry-news/production-incentives-update-july-2023/

Entman, R. M., & Rojecki, A. (2013). *The black image in the white mind*. University of Chicago Press. https://doi.org/10.7208/chicago/9780226210773.001.0001

Epstein, C. F. (2018). The cultural perspective and the study of work. In K. Erikson & S. P. Vailas (Eds.), *The nature of work* (pp. 88–98). Yale University Press. https://doi.org/10.2307/j.ctt1xp3v27.8

Erkan, E. (2018). Media heterotopias: Digital effects and material labor in global film production. *New Review of Film and Television Studies*, 17(4), 496–500. https://doi.org/10.1080/17400309.2019.1663603

Evans, P., & Tilly, C. (2016). The future of work: Escaping the current dystopian trajectory and building better alternatives. In S. Edgell, H. Gottfried, & E. Granter (Eds.), *The SAGE handbook of the sociology of work and employment* (pp. 651–668). https://doi.org/10.4135/9781473915206.n35

Ezzy, D. (1997). Subjectivity and the labour process: Conceptualising "good work". *Sociology*, 31(3), 427–444. https://doi.org/10.1177/0038038597031003004

Fantasia, R. (1989). *Cultures of solidarity*. University of California Press. https://doi.org/10.1525/9780520909670

Farrow, R. (2019). *Catch and kill. Lies, spies, and a conspiracy to protect predators*. Little Brown and Company.

Fast, K., Örnebring, H., & Karlsson, M. (2016). Metaphors of free labor: A typology of unpaid work in the media sector. *Media, Culture and Society*, 38(7), 963–978. https://doi.org/10.1177/0163443716635861

Fayol, H. (2013). *General and industrial management*. Martino Fine Books.

Federici, S. (2014). The reproduction of labour power in the global economy and the unfinished feminist revolution. In M. Atzeni (Ed.), *Workers and labour in a globalised capitalism* (pp. 85–107). https://doi.org/10.1007/978-1-137-36134-9_5

Filimowicz, M (Ed.). (2023). *AI and the future of creative work*. Routledge.

Fine, G. (1992). The culture of production. *American Journal of Sociology*, 97(1), 1268–1294.

Fineman, S. (2012). *Work: A very short introduction*. Oxford University Press.

Fischer, A. (2018). *valley of genius: The uncensored history of Silicon Valley (As told by the hackers, founders, and freaks who made it boom)*. Twelve.

Fish, A., & Srinivasan, R. (2012). Digital labor is the new killer app. *New Media and Society*, 14(1), 137–152. https://doi.org/10.1177/1461444811412159

Fisher, E. (2015a). Class struggles in the digital frontier: Audience labour theory and social media users. *Information Communication and Society*, 18(9), 1108–1122. https://doi.org/10.1080/1369118X.2015.1018300

Fisher, E. (2015b). 'You Media': Audiencing as marketing in social media. *Media, Culture and Society*, 37(1), 50–67. https://doi.org/10.1177/0163443714549088

Fisher, M. (2009). *Capitalist realism: Is there no alternative?* Zero Books.

Fisk, C. (2016). *Writing for hire: Unions, Hollywood, and Madison Avenue*. Harvard University Press.

Fisk, C., & Szalay, M. (2017). Story work: Non-proprietary autonomy and contemporary television writing. *Television & New Media*, 18 (7): 605–620.

Fleming, M. (2008). Labor strikes in the entertainment industry: Essential to preserving the collective bargaining process. *Southern Law Journal*, 18, 99–116.

Fleming, P. (2009). *Authenticity and the cultural politics of work: New forms of informal control*. Routledge. https://doi.org/10.1093/acprof:oso/9780199547159.001.0001

Fleming, P. (2015). *The mythology of work*. Pluto. https://doi.org/10.2307/j.ctt183p83x

Fleming, P. (2017a). *The death of homo economicus*. Pluto. https://doi.org/10.2307/j.ctt1v2xw07

Fleming, P., & Spicer, A. (2003). Working at a cynical distance. *Oral History Review*, 10(1), 157–179. http://hjb.sagepub.com.proxy.lib.umich.edu/content/9/2/183.full.pdf+html

Fleming, P., & Sturdy, A. (2011). "Being yourself" in the electronic sweatshop: New forms of normative control. *Human Relations*, 64(2), 177–200. https://doi.org/10.1177/0018726710375481

Flew, T. (2023). *Creative AI: The death of the author?* University of Sydney. https://sbi.sydney.edu.au/creative-ai-the-death-of-the-author/

Flew, T., & Cunningham, S. (2010). Creative industries after the first decade of debate. *Information Society*, 26(2), 113–123. https://doi.org/10.1080/01972240903562753

Flisfeder, M. (2022). Severance, Alienation, and the Futility of Reintegration. *The Philosophical Salon*. https://thephilosophicalsalon.com/severance-alienation-and-the-futility-of-reintegration/

Flisfeder, M., & Fuchs, C. (2015). Digital labour and the internet prosumer commodity: In conversation with Christian Fuchs. *Alternate Routes*, 1(January), 267–278. http://www.alternateroutes.ca/index.php/ar/article/download/22403/18185

Flores, E. T., & Cleaver, H. (1981). Reading capital politically. *Contemporary Sociology*, 10(2), 275. https://doi.org/10.2307/2066926

Florida, R. (2004). *The rise of the creative class*. Basic Books.

Florida, R. (2022). *The rise of the creator economy*. Creativeclass.com Reports: https://creativeclass.com/reports/The_Rise_of_the_Creator_Economy.pdf

Forberg, P., & Schilt, K. (2023). What is ethnographic about digital ethnography? A sociological perspective. *Frontiers in Sociology*. https://doi.org/10.3389/fsoc.2023.1156776

Ford, M. (2015). *The rise of the robots: Technology and the threat of mass unemployment*. OneWorld Publications.

Forde, S. (2024). Shifting Neoliberalism in US Telecommunications Policy: A Critical Reading of Chicago School Roads. tripleC, 22(1): 434–453.

Fortmueller, K. (2021). *Below the stars: How the labor of working actors and extras shapes media production*. University of Texas Press.

Fortmueller, K. (2023). The writers strike opens old wounds. *Los Angeles Review of Books*. https://lareviewofbooks.org/article/the-writers-strike-opens-old-wounds/

Fortmueller, K., & Marzola, L. (Eds.). (2024). *Hollywood unions*. Rutger University Press.

Fortunati, L. (2018). Immaterial labor. In *The Blackwell encyclopedia of sociology* (pp. 1–2). https://doi.org/10.1002/9781405165518.wbeos1128

Foucault, M. (1977). *Discipline and punish: The birth of the prison*. Vintage Books.

Foucault, M. (1982). The subject and power. Critical Inquiry, 8(4), 777–795.

Foucault, M. (1991). Governmentality. In G. Burchell, C. Gordon and P. Miller (Eds.), *The foucault effect: Studies in governmentality* (pp. 87–104). University of Chicago Press.

Frankl, V. E. (1959). *Man's search for meaning: An introduction to logotherapy*. Beacon Press.

Fraser, N., & Monticelli, L. (2021). Progressive neoliberalism isn't the solution. We need a radical, counter-hegemonic and anti-capitalist alliance. *Emancipations: A Journal of Critical Social Analysis*, 1(1). https://scholarsjunction.msstate.edu/emancipations/vol1/iss1/2

Fraser, S. (2018). *Class matters: The strange career of an American delusion*. Yale University Press.

Frayne, D. (2015). *The refusal of work: The theory and practice of resistance to work*. Zed Books.

Freedman, D. (2004). *Television policies of the labour party 1951–2001*. Routledge. https://doi.org/10.4324/9780203501061

Freeman, C. (2000). *High tech and high heels in the global economy: Women, work, and pink-collar identities in the Caribbean*. Duke University Press.

Freeman, M. (2016). *Industrial approaches to media: A methodological gateway to industry studies*. Palgrave Macmillan.

Friedman, J. S. (2022). *The Disney Revolt: The great labor war of Animation's golden age*. Chicago Review Press.
Frith, S. (2017). Are workers musicians? *Popular Music*, 36 (1), 111–115.
Fritsch, K., O'Connor, C., & Thompson, A. K. (Eds.). (2016). *Keywords for radicals: The contested vocabulary of late-capitalist struggle*. AK Press.
Fuchs, C. (2010). Labor in informational capitalism and on the internet. *Information Society*, 26(3), 179–196. https://doi.org/10.1080/01972241003712215
Fuchs, C. (2014). *Digital labor and Karl Marx*. Routledge. https://doi.org/10.4324/9781315880075
Fuchs, C. (2011). Web 2.0, prosumption, and surveillance. *Surveillance and Society*, 8(3), 288–308. https://doi.org/10.24908/ss.v8i3.4165
Fuchs, C. (2012a). Dallas Smythe today-the audience commodity, the digital labour debate. *TripleC: Communication, Capitalism & Critique*, 10(2), 692–740. http://www.triplec.at/index.php/tripleC/article/view/443/414
Fuchs, C. (2012b). The political economy of privacy on Facebook. *Television and New Media*, 13(2), 139–159. https://doi.org/10.1177/1527476411415699
Fuchs, C. (2012c). Towards Marxian internet studies. *TripleC: Communication, Capitalism & Critique*, 10(2), 392–412. https://doi.org/10.31269/triplec.v10i2.277
Fuchs, C. (2012d). With or without Marx? With or without capitalism? A rejoinder to Adam Arvidsson and Eleanor Colleoni. *TripleC: Communication, Capitalism & Critique*, 10(2), 633–645. https://doi.org/10.31269/triplec.v10i2.434
Fuchs, C., & Mosco, V. (2015a). *Marx and the political economy of the media*. Brill. https://doi.org/10.1163/9789004291416
Fuchs, C., & Mosco, V. (2015b). *Marx in the age of digital capitalism*. Brill. https://doi.org/10.1163/9789004291393
Fuchs, C., & Sevignani, S. (2013). What is digital labour? What is digital work? What's their difference? And why do these questions matter for understanding social media? *TripleC: Communication, Capitalism & Critique*, 11(2), 237–293. https://doi.org/10.31269/triplec.v11i2.461
Funk, A. G., & Bradley, H. (1990). Men's work, Women's work: A sociological history of the sexual division of labour in employment. *Contemporary Sociology*, 19(6), 807. https://doi.org/10.2307/2073176
Gajjala, R. (2018). Feminism, labour and digital media: The digital housewife. *Australian Feminist Studies*, 33(96), 275–277. https://doi.org/10.1080/08164649.2018.1517251
Galbraith, K. (1958). *The affluent society*. Houghton Mifflin.
Galbraith, K. (1967). *The new industrial state*. Princeton University Press.
Galer, D. (2012). "Disabled capitalists: Exploring the intersections of disability and identity formation in the world of work." *Disability Studies Quarterly*, 32 (3). http://dsq-sds.org/article/view/3277/3122.
Gallie, D. (2017). The quality of work in a changing labour market. *Social Policy and Administration*, 51(2), 226–243. https://doi.org/10.1111/spol.12285
Gamble, M. (2018). *Classism: America's overlooked problem*. Rutgers Review. https://www.therutgersreview.com/2018/02/10/classism-americas-overlooked-problem/
Gandini, A. (2015). Digital work: Self-branding and social capital in the freelance knowledge economy. *Marketing Theory*, 16(1), 123–141.
Gandini, A. (2016). *The reputation economy. Understanding knowledge work in digital society*. Palgrave Macmillan.
Gandini, A. (2020). Digital labour: An empty signifier? *Media, Culture & Society*, 43(2), 369–380.

Gandini, A., Bandinelli, C., & Cossu, A. (2017). Collaborating, competing, co-working, coalescing: Artists, freelancers and social entrepreneurs as the 'New Subjects' of the creative economy. *Collaborative Production in the Creative Industries*. https://doi.org/10.16997/book4.b

Gandini, A., & Cossu, A. (2021). The third wave of coworking: 'Neo-corporate' model versus 'resilient' practice. *European Journal of Cultural Studies*, 24(2), 430–447. https://doi.org/10.1177/1367549419886060

Gandini, A., Pais, I., & Beraldo, D. (2016). Reputation and trust on online labour markets: The reputation economy of Elance. *Work Organisation, Labour and Globalisation*, 10(1), 27–43. https://doi.org/10.13169/workorgalaboglob.10.1.0027

Gandy, O. H. (1993). *The panoptic sort: A political economy of personal information*. Westview Press.

Gandy, O. H. (2003). Privatization and identity: The formation of a racial class. In G. Murdock & J. Wasko (Eds.), *Media in the age of marketization* (pp. 1–25). Hampton Press.

Gandy, O. H. (2004). Audiences on demand. In A. Calabrese & C. Sparks (Eds.), *Toward a political economy of culture: Capitalism and communication in the twenty-first century* (pp. 327–341). Rowman & Littlefield.

Gans, H. (2012). Deciding what's news. *Key Readings in Journalism*, 95–104. https://doi.org/10.4135/9781412953993.n140

Gardiner, J. (1975). Women's domestic labour. *New Left Review*. 1(89), https://newleftreview.org/issues/i89/articles/jean-gardiner-women-s-domestic-labour

Garner, D. (2023). A Human Wrote This Book Review. A.I. Wrote the Book. *The New York Times*. https://www.nytimes.com/2023/05/01/books/aidan-marchine-death-of-an-author.html

Garnham, N. (1979). Contribution to a political economy of mass-communication. *Media, Culture & Society*, 1(2), 123–146. https://doi.org/10.1177/016344377900100202

Garnham, N. (1987). Concepts of culture: Public policy and the cultural industries. *Cultural Studies*, 1(1), 23–37. https://doi.org/10.1080/09502388700490021

Gerber, C., & Krzywdzinski, M. (2019). Brave new digital work? new forms of performance control in crowdwork. In P. S. Vallas & A. Kovalainen (Eds.) *Work and labor in the digital age* (pp. 121–143). Emerald.

Gibbons, S. (2023). 2023 Business Predictions As AI and Automation Rise in Popularity. *Forbes*. https://www.forbes.com/sites/serenitygibbons/2023/02/02/2023-business-predictions-as-ai-and-automation-rise-in-popularity/

Giblin, R., & Doctorow, C. (2023). *Chokepoint capitalism: How big tech and big content captured creative labor markets and how well win them back*. Beacon Press.

Giddens, A. (1991). *The consequences of modernity*. Polity Press.

Gilbreth, L. (1914). *The psychology of management: The function of the mind in determining, teaching, and installing methods of least waste*. Sturgis & Walton Company.

Gill, R. (2011). "Life is a pitch": Managing the self in new media work. In *Managing media work* (pp. 249–262).

Gill, R. (2014). Academics, cultural workers and critical labour studies. *Journal of Cultural Economy*, 7(1), 12–30. https://doi.org/10.1080/17530350.2013.861763

Gillespie, M. (1998). Cassette culture: Popular music and technology in North India. *American Ethnologist*, 25(1), 85–87. https://doi.org/10.1525/ae.1998.25.1.85

Gillespie, T. (2013). The politics of "Platforms." *A Companion to New Media Dynamics*, 407–416. https://doi.org/10.1002/9781118321607.ch28

Gillespie, T. (2017). Regulation of and by platforms. In *The SAGE handbook of social media* (pp. 254–278). https://doi.org/10.4135/9781473984066.n15

Gillespie, T. (2018). *Custodians of the internet: Platforms, content moderation, and the hidden decisions that shape social media*. Yale University Press.

Gill, R., & Pratt, A. (2008). In the social factory?: Immaterial labour, precariousness and cultural work. *Theory, Culture & Society*, 25(8), 1–30. https://doi.org/10.1177/0263276408097794

Gin Choi, Y., Kwon, J., & Kim, W. (2013). Effects of attitudes vs experience of workplace fun on employee behaviors. *International Journal of Contemporary Hospitality Management*, 25(3), 410–427. https://doi.org/10.1108/09596111311311044

Gindin, S. (2018). Socialism for realists. *Catalyst*, 2(3). https://catalyst-journal.com/2018/12/socialism-for-realists

Gindin, S. (2021). Why workers don't revolt. *Jacobin*. https://jacobin.com/2021/06/working-class-revolt-competition-capitalism-exploitation

Gitlin, T. (2005). *Inside Prime Time*. https://doi.org/10.4324/9780203977293

Glasbeeck, H. (2024). *Law at work: The coercion and co-option of the working class*. Between the Lines.

Glatt, Z. (2022a). Precarity, discrimination and (in)visibility: An ethnography of "The Algorithm" in the YouTube influencer industry. In *The Routledge companion to media anthropology* (pp. 544–556). https://doi.org/10.4324/9781003175605-53

Glatt, Z. (2022b). "We're All Told Not to Put Our Eggs in One Basket": Uncertainty, precarity and cross-platform labor in the online video influencer industry. *International Journal of Communication*, 16, 3853–3871.

Glatt, Z. (2023). The intimacy triple bind: Structural inequalities and relational labour in the influencer industry. *European Journal of Cultural Studies*. https://doi.org/10.1177/13675494231194156

Glatt, Z. (2024, February 1). Influencer Industries and Creator Culture Collaborative Reading List. https://zoeglatt.com/wp-content/uploads/2024/01/INFLUENCER-INDUSTRIES-CREATOR-CULTURE-Collective-Reading-List-February-2024-1.pdf

Glatt, Z., & Banet-Weiser, S. (2022). Productive ambivalence, economies of visibility, and the political potential of feminist YouTubers. In S. Cunningham & D. Craig (Eds.), *Creator culture* (pp. 39–56). https://doi.org/10.18574/nyu/9781479890118.003.0006

Gleick, J. (1999). *Faster: The acceleration of just about everything*. Vintage.

Glover, E. (2022). *Behind the rise in abuse towards call centre workers*. Huck. https://www.huckmag.com/article/how-the-abuse-of-call-centre-workers-spiralled-amid-covid

Goffman, E. (2023). The presentation of self in everyday life. *Social theory rewired* (pp. 450–459). https://doi.org/10.4324/9781003320609-59

Goggin, G., & Newell, C. (2002). *Digital disability: The social construction of disability in new media*. Rowman & Littlefield.

Goldman Sachs. (2023, April 5). Generative AI Could Increase GPP by 7%. https://www.goldmansachs.com/intelligence/pages/generative-ai-could-raise-global-gdp-by-7-percent.html

Goldsmith, B., & O'Regan, T. (2008). International film production: Interests and motivations. *Cross-border cultural production* (pp. 13–44).

Goldstein, M. N., & Dahl, R. A. (1962). Who governs? Democracy and power in an American City. *American Sociological Review*, 27(6), 860. https://doi.org/10.2307/2090423

Gollmitzer, M. (2014). Precariously employed watchdogs? *Journalism Practice*, 8(6), 826–841. https://doi.org/10.1080/17512786.2014.882061

Goodey, S., & Davies, R. (2018). Martin Sorrell's WPP exit came amid bullying and sex worker allegations. *The Guardian*. https://www.theguardian.com/media/2018/jun/11/martin-sorrells-wpp-exit-came-amid-bullying-and-sex-worker-allegations

Goodley, D., Lawthom, R., Liddiard, K., & Runswick-Cole, K. (2019). Provocations for critical disability studies. *Disability and Society*, 34(6), 972–997. https://doi.org/10.1080/09687599.2019.1566889

Gordon, L., Berg, I., & Gorelick, S. (1971). Education and jobs: The great training robbery. *American Sociological Review*, 36(2), 378. https://doi.org/10.2307/2094111

Gorz, A. (1982). *Farewell to the working class*. Pluto.

Gorz, A. (1985). *Paths to paradise: On the liberation from work*. Routledge.

Gould, E., & Bivens, J. (2024, January 17). Opinion: Why a new study gives a misleading view of inequality. CNN. https://www.msn.com/en-us/money/markets/opinion-why-a-new-study-gives-a-misleading-view-of-inequality-in-america

Goyanes, M., & Rodriguez-Gomez, E. F. (2018). Beyond journalism: Theorizing the transformation of journalism. *Journalism*, 19(2), 165–181. https://doi.org/10.1177/1464884916688550

Graeber, D. (2018). *Bullshit jobs*. Penguin.

Graham, P. (2006). Issues in political economy. In *Handbook of media management and economics*. Lawrence Erlbaum Associates. https://doi.org/10.1007/978-1-349-16232-1

Graham, M., & Anwar, M. (2018). Digital labour. In *Digital geographies* (pp. 177–188). Sage.

Graham, M., Cant, C., & Muldoon, J. (2024). *Feeding the Machine: The Hidden Human Labor Powering A. I.* Bloomsbury.

Graham, M., & Woodcock, J. (2018). Towards a fairer platform economy: Introducing the Fairwork Foundation. *Alternate Routes*, 29, 242–253. http://oro.open.ac.uk/68721/

Graham, P., & Luke, A. (2011). Critical discourse analysis and political economy of communication: Understanding the new corporate order. *Cultural Politics*, 7(1), 103–132. https://doi.org/10.2752/175174311x12861940861824

Granberg, M. (2015). The ideal worker as real abstraction: Labour conflict and subjectivity in nursing. *Work, Employment and Society*, 29(5), 792–807. https://doi.org/10.1177/0950017014563102

Granter, E., & Tischer, D. (2014). Teaching the crisis: A primer. *Sociology*, 48(5), 904–920. https://doi.org/10.1177/0038038514539062

Gray, L. S., & Seeber, R. L. (Eds.). (1996). *Under the stars: Essays on labor relations in arts and entertainment*. Cornell University Press.

Gray, M. L., & Suri, S. (2019). *Ghost work: How to stop Silicon Valley from building a new global underclass*. Harper Business.

Grayer, S., & Brophy, E. (2019). Platform organizing. *Notes from Below*. https://notesfrombelow.org/article/platform-organizing

Green, D. (2010). *The American worker on film: A critical history*. McFarland & Company.

Gregg, M. (2011). *Work's intimacy*. Polity.

Gregg, M. (2018). *Counterproductive: Time management in the knowledge economy*. Duke University Press.

Gregg, M., & Andrijasevic, R. (2019). Virtually absent: The gendered histories and economies of digital labour. *Feminist Review*, *123*(1), 1–7. https://doi.org/10.1177/0141778919878929

Gregory, M. (2015). *Stuntwomen: The untold Hollywood story*. The University Press of Kentucky.

Grimes, S., & Sun, Y. (2016). China's evolving role in Apple's global value chain. *Area Development and Policy*, *1*(1), 94–112. https://doi.org/10.1080/23792949.2016.1149434

Grindstaff, L. (2002). *The money shot: Trash, class, and the making of TV talk shows*. University of Chicago Press.

Grint, K., & Woolgar, S. (2013). *The machine at work: Technology, work and organization*. Polity.

Grohmann, R. (2018). History of struggle: Pioneering studies on social class in communication studies. *MATRIZes*, *12*(3), 215–235. https://doi.org/10.11606/issn.1982-8160.v12i3p215-235

Grohmann, R. (2021). Rider platforms? Building worker-owned experiences in Spain, France, and Brazil. *South Atlantic Quarterly*, *120*(4), 839–852. https://doi.org/10.1215/00382876-9443392

Grohmann, R. (2022). Beyond platform cooperativism: Worker-owned platforms in Brazil. *Interactions*, *29*(4), 87–89. https://doi.org/10.1145/3540251

Grohmann, R. (2023). Not just platform, nor cooperatives: Worker-owned technologies from below. *Communication, Culture and Critique*, 274–282. https://doi.org/10.1093/ccc/tcad036/10.1145/3540251

Grohmann, R., & Araújo, W. F. (2021). Beyond mechanical Turk: The work of Brazilians on global AI platforms. In *AI for everyone? critical perspectives* (pp. 247–266). https://doi.org/10.16997/book55.n

Grohmann, R., Menonca, M., & Woodcock, J. (2023). Communication and work from below: The role of communication organizing delivery platform workers. *International Journal of Communication*, *17*, 3919–3937.

Grusky, D. B., & Sørensen, J. B. (1998). Can class analysis be salvaged? *American Journal of Sociology*, *103*(5), 1187–1234. https://doi.org/10.1086/231351

Gulka, H. J., Macleod, H., & Gewurtz, R. (2022). Acting the part: A thematic analysis of the experiences of actors with disabilities. *Canadian Journal of Disability Studies*, *11*(1), 119–149. https://doi.org/10.15353/cjds.v11i1.856

Guo, E. (2021). Universal basic income is here—It just looks different from what you expected. *MIT Technology Review*. https://www.technologyreview.com/2021/05/07/1024674/ubi-guaranteed-income-pandemic/

Guschwan, M. (2012). Fandom, brandom and the limits of participatory culture. *Journal of Consumer Culture*, *12*(1), 19–40. https://doi.org/10.1177/1469540512438154

Gustin, S. (2016). Systemic racial discrimination worsens the US digital divide, study says. *Vice*. https://www.vice.com/en_us/article/aek85p/systemic-racial-discrimination-worsens-the-us-digital-divide-study-says

Guynn, J. (2020). #SiliconValleySoWhite: Black Facebook and Google employees speak out on big tech racism. *USA Today*. https://www.usatoday.com/story/tech/2020/02/10/racial-discrimination-persists-facebook-google-employees-say/4307591002/

Guynn, J., & Fraser, J. (2023). Who has power in corporate America? Men do. *Men Today*. https://www.usatoday.com/in-depth/money/2023/03/16/men-run-corporate-america/11173762002/

Gynnild, A. (2005). Winner takes it all: Freelance journalism on the global communication market. *Nordicom Review*, *26*(1), 111–120. http://search.ebscohost.com/login.aspx?direct=true&db=ufh&AN=17497380&site=ehost-live

Hahnel, R., & Wright, E. O. (2016). *Alternatives to capitalism: Proposals for a democratic economy.* Verso.
Haider, A., & Mohandesi, S. (2013). Workers' inquiry : A genealogy. *ViewPoint Magazine.* https://www.viewpointmag.com/2013/09/27/workers-inquiry-a-genealogy/
Halford, S., & Strangleman, T. (2009). In search of the sociology of work: Past, present and future. *Sociology*, 43(5), 811–828. https://doi.org/10.1177/0038038509341307
Hall, S., & O'Shea, A. (2015). Common-sense neoliberalism. In *After neoliberalism?: The Kilburn Manifesto* (pp. 52–68). https://doi.org/10.3898/136266213809450194
Hambleton, J. (2018). Collective values in an entrepreneurial world: Imagining craft labour in cultural work. *Work Organisation, Labour and Globalisation*, 12(1), 43–61. https://doi.org/10.13169/workorgalaboglob.12.1.0043
Hamilton, J. F. (2014). Historical forms of user production. *Media, Culture and Society*, 36(4), 491–507. https://doi.org/10.1177/0163443714523812
Hammar, E. (2020). Imperialism and fascism intertwined. A materialist analysis of the games industry and reactionary gamers. *Gamevironments, 13*, 317–357.
Hammar, E. L. (2015). Manufacturing consent in video games—The hegemonic memory politics of *metal gear solid V: The phantom pain. Nordlit*, (42). https://doi.org/10.7557/13.5016
Hammar, E. L. (2022). International Solidarity between Game Workers in the Global North and Global South: Reflections on the Challenges Posed by Labor Aristocracy. https://journals.suub.uni-bremen.de/.
Hammar, E. L., de Wildt, L., Mukherjee, S., & Pelletier, C. (2021). Politics of production: Videogames 10 years after games of empire. *Games and Culture*, 16(3), 287–293. https://doi.org/10.1177/1555412020954996
Handel, J. (2011). *Hollywood on strike! : An industry at war in the internet age.* CreateSpace.
Handel, J. (2013). *Entertainment labor: An interdisciplinary bibliography.* CreateSpace.
Handel, J. (2023). *Hollywood Reporter entertainment labor articles.* https://www.hollywoodreporter.com/results/#?q=Jonathan Handel
Handel, M. J. (Ed.). (2003). *The sociology of organizations: Classic, contemporary and critical readings.* Sage.
Handy, J., & Rowlands, L. (2014). Gendered inequality regimes and female labour market disadvantage within the New Zealand film industry. *Women's Studies Journal*, 28(2), 24–38.
Hardimon, M. O., & Honneth, A. (1997). The struggle for recognition: The moral grammar of social conflicts. *The Journal of Philosophy*, 94(1), 46. https://doi.org/10.2307/2941013
Hardt, H. (1990). Newsworkers, technology, and journalism history. *Critical Studies in Mass Communication*, 7(4), 346–365. https://doi.org/10.1080/15295039009360184
Hardt, H., & Brennen, B. (1995). *Newsworkers: Toward a history of the rank and file.* University of Minnesota Press.
Hardt, M., & Negri, A. (2000). *Empire.* Harvard University Press.
Hardy, J. (2014). Critical political economy of communications: A mid-term review. *International Journal of Media and Cultural Politics*, 10(2), 189–202. https://doi.org/10.1386/macp.10.2.189_1
Haring, B. (2023). SAG-AFTRA Making Moves To Enlist More Online Content Creators – Report. *Deadline.* https://deadline.com/2023/07/sag-aftra-making-moves-to-enlist-more-online-content-creators-wapo-report-1235445921/

Harpur, P. D. (2022). *Ableism at work: Disablement and hierarchies of impairment*. Cambridge University Press.

Harris, M. (2017). *Kids these days: Human capital and the making of millennials*. Little, Brown and Company.

Harrison, S. (2019). Five years of tech diversity reports—and little progress. *Wired*, 1–7. https://www.wired.com/story/five-years-tech-diversity-reports-little-progress/

Hart-Landsberg, M. (2024). AI Chatbots: Hype Meets Reality. *The Bullet*. https://socialistproject.ca/2024/04/ai-chatbots-hype-meets-reality/

Hartley, J. (2005). *Creative industries*. Blackwell.

Hartmann, H. I. (1976). Capitalism, patriarchy, and job segregation by sex. *Signs: Journal of Women in Culture and Society*, 1(3), 137–169. https://doi.org/10.1086/493283

Hartmann, H. I. (1981). The family as the locus of gender, class, and political struggle: The example of housework. *Signs: Journal of Women in Culture and Society*, 6(3), 366–394.

Harvey, A. (2019). Becoming gamesworkers: Diversity, higher education, and the future of the game industry. *Television & New Media*, 20(8), 756–766. https://doi.org/10.1177/1527476419851080

Harvey, A. (2019). *Feminist Media Studies*. Polity.

Harvey, A., & Shepherd, T. (2017). When passion isn't enough: Gender, affect and credibility in digital games design. *International Journal of Cultural Studies*, 20(5), 492–508. https://doi.org/10.1177/1367877916636140

Harvey, B. (2023). Thousands of performing artists went on strike over automation nearly a century ago. What's different this time? *The Toronto Star*. https://www.thestar.com/opinion/contributors/thousands-of-performing-artists-went-on-strike-over-automation-nearly-a-century-ago-what-s/article_21cf8a7a-8e63-5b2b-8442-b1d245cdaf0e.html

Harvey, D. (1989). *The condition of postmodernity: An enquiry into the origins of cultural change*. Blackwell. https://doi.org/10.2307/2072256

Harvey, D. (2005). *A brief history of neoliberalism*. Oxford University Press.

Harvey, D. (2006). Neoliberalism as creative destruction. *Geografiska Annaler, Series B: Human Geography*, 88(2), 145–158. https://doi.org/10.1111/j.0435-3684.2006.00211.x

Haskins, C. (2024). The Low-Paid Humans Behind AI's Smarts Ask Biden to Free Them From 'Modern Day Slavery'. *Wired*. https://www.wired.com/story/low-paid-humans-ai-biden-modern-day-slavery/

Haug, W. (1986). *Critique of commodity aesthetics: Appearance, sexuality and advertising in capitalist society*. Blackwell.

Havens, T. (2013). *Black Television Travels: African American media around the globe*. https://doi.org/10.1080/01439685.2014.942967

Healy, M. (2020). *Marx and the machines: Alienation, technology, capitalism*. University of Westminster Press.

Hearn, A. (2008a). "Meat, mask, burden": Probing the contours of the branded "self". *Journal of Consumer Culture*, 8(2), 197–217.

Hearn, A. (2008b). Variations on the branded self: Theme, invention, improvisation and inventory. In *The media and social theory* (pp. 194–210).

Hearn, A. (2010a). Reality television, the hills, and the limits of the immaterial labour thesis. *TripleC: Communication, Capitalism & Critique*, 8(1), 60–76. https://doi.org/10.31269/vol8iss1pp60-76

Hearn, A. (2010b). Structuring feeling: Web 2.0, online ranking and rating, and the digital "reputation" economy. *Ephemera: Theory & Politics in Organization*, 10(3/4), 421–438.

Hearn, A. (2014). Producing "Reality" branded content, branded selves, precarious futures. In *Companion to reality television* (pp. 437–455).
Hearn, A., & Schoenhoff, S. (2015). From celebrity to influencer: Tracing the diffusion of celebrity value across the data stream. In *A companion to celebrity* (pp. 194–212). https://doi.org/10.1002/9781118475089.ch11
Heeks, R. (2009). Understanding "Gold Farming" and real-money trading as the intersection of real and virtual economies. *Journal for Virtual Worlds Research*, 2(4). https://jvwr-ojs-utexas.tdl.org/jvwr/article/view/868
Heimann, L. C., & Bernstein. (2015). *High tech employee class action lawsuit*. https://www.lieffcabraser.com/antitrust/high-tech-employees/
Helppie, S. (2013). *15 minutes of fame: Reality TV contracts*. Dallas Bar Association; Headnotes. http://www.dallasbar.org/content/15-minutes-fame-reality-tv-contracts
Hendershot, H. (2009). Belabored reality: Making it work on the simple life and project runway. In S. Murray & L. Ouellette (Eds.), *Reality TV: Remaking television culture* (pp. 243–259). New York University Press.
Hendrix, J. (2023). Checking on the progress of content moderators in Africa. *TechPolicyPress*. https://www.techpolicy.press/checking-on-the-progress-of-content-moderators-in-africa/
Hennebert, M., Pasquier, V., & Lévesque, C. (2021). What do unions do … with digital technologies? An affordance approach. *New Technology, Work and Employment*, 36(2), 177–200.
Herbert, D. (2015). *Videoland: Movie culture at the American video store*. University of California Press.
Herbert, D., Lotz, A., & Punathambekar, A. (2020). *Media industry studies*. Polity.
Herbert, G. (1975). *Popular culture and high culture*. Basic Books.
Herman, A. (2020). Amid the Black lives matter movement, Hollywood examines its own history of racism. *The Ringer*. https://www.theringer.com/tv/2020/7/10/21319242/hollywood-racism-blackface-tv-episodes-song-of-the-south
Hermann, C. (2014). *Capitalism and the political economy of work time*. Routledge. https://doi.org/10.4324/9781315745770
Hern, A. (2019). Google whistleblower launches project to keep tech ethical. *The Guardian*. https://www.theguardian.com/world/2019/jul/13/google-whistleblower-launches-project-to-keep-tech-ethical
Herod, A. (2017). *Labor*. Polity.
Herren, P. (2023). What primetime TV ads cost in Fall 2023. *AdAge*. https://adage.com/article/media/tv-commercial-prices-advertising-costs-fall-2023/2520931
Hesmondhalgh, D. (2000). Alternative media, alternative texts? Rethinking democratization in the cultural industries. In J. Curran (Ed.), *Media organizations in society*. Arnold.
Hesmondhalgh, D. (2006). *Media production*. Open University Press.
Hesmondhalgh, D. (2008). Cultural and creative industries. In *The SAGE handbook of cultural analysis* (pp. 552–569). https://doi.org/10.4135/9781848608443.n26
Hesmondhalgh, D. (2009). Politics, theory and method in media industies research. In J. Holt & A. Perren (Eds.), *Media industries: History, theory, method* (pp. 245–255). Blackwell publishing.
Hesmondhalgh, D. (2018). The media's failure to represent the working class: Explanations from media production and beyond. In J. Deery & A. Press (Eds.), *The media and class* (pp. 21–37). Routledge. https://doi.org/10.4324/9781315387987-2

Hesmondhalgh, D. (2010a). Media industry studies, media production studies. In J. Curran (Ed.), *Media and society* (pp. 145–163). Sage.

Hesmondhalgh, D. (2010b). Normativity and social justice in the analysis of creative labour. *Journal for Cultural Research*, *14*(3), 231–249. https://doi.org/10.1080/14797581003791461

Hesmondhalgh, D. (2010c). User-generated content, free labor and the cultural industries. *Ephemera: Theory & Politics in Organization*, *10*(3/4), 267–284.

Hesmondhalgh, D. (2016). Exploitation and media labor. In R. Maxwell (Ed.), *The Routledge companion to labor and media*. Routledge. https://www.taylorfrancis.com/chapters/edit/10.4324/9780203404119-4/exploitation-media-labor-david-hesmondhalgh

Hesmondhalgh, D. (2019). *The cultural industries*. Sage.

Hesmondhalgh, D., & Baker, S. (2008). Creative work and emotional labour in the television industry. *Theory, Culture & Society*, *25*(8), 97–118. https://doi.org/10.1177/0263276408097798

Hesmondhalgh, D., & Baker, S. (2011). Toward a political economy of labor in the media industries. In J. Wasko, G. Murdock, & H. Sousa (Eds.), *The handbook of political economy of communications* (pp. 381–400). https://doi.org/10.1002/9781444395402.ch17

Hesmondhalgh, D., & Baker, S. (2013). *Creative labour: Media work in three cultural industries*. Routledge. https://doi.org/10.4324/9780203855881

Hesmondhalgh, D., & Baker, S. (2015). Sex, gender and work segregation in the cultural industries. *Sociological Review*, *63*(S1), 23–36. https://doi.org/10.1111/1467-954X.12238

Hesmondhalgh, D., & Pratt, A. C. (2005). Cultural industries and cultural policy. *International Journal of Cultural Policy*, *11*(1), 1–13. https://doi.org/10.1080/10286630500067598

Hester, H., & Srnicek, N. (2023). *After work: A history of the home and the fight for free time*. Verso.

Hill, E. (2014a). Re-casting the casting director: Managed change, gendered labor from making media work: Cultures of management in the entertainment industries. In D. Johnson, D. Kompare, & A. Santo (Eds.), *Making media work: Cultures of management in the entertainment industries*. New York University Press.

Hill, E. (2014b). *Never done: A history of Women's work in media production*. Rutgers University Press.

Hill, E. (2022). Organizing 'Women's Work': Logics of feminization and unionization. In K. Fortmueller & L. Marzola (Eds.), *Hollywood unions anthology*. Rutgers University Press.

Hill, L. (2020). Adam Smith on political corruption. In *Adam Smith's pragmatic liberalism* (pp. 119–141). https://doi.org/10.1007/978-3-030-19337-9_5

Himmelweit, S., & Mohun, S. (1977). Domestic labour and capital. *Cambridge Journal of Economics*, *1*(1), 15–31. https://doi.org/10.1093/oxfordjournals.cje.a035348

Hirsch, P. M. (1978). Production and distribution roles among cultural organizations: On the division of labor across intellectual disciplines. *Social Research*, *45*, 315–330. https://www.jstor.org/stable/40970335

Hobsbawm, E. (1952). *The machine-breakers, past and present*. http://libcom.org/history/machine-breakers-eric-hobsbawm

Hochschild, A. (2000[1983]). *The managed heart: Commercialization of human feeling*. University of California Press.

Hochschild, A. R. (1997). The time bind: When work becomes home and home becomes work. *Political Science Quarterly*, *113*(1), 169–170. https://doi.org/10.2307/2657684

Hochschild, A. R. (2012). *The outsourced self: Intimate life in market times*. Metropolitan Books.

Hodson, R. (2009). *Dignity at work*. Cambridge University Press.

Holt, D. B., & du Gay, P. (1997). Consumption and identity at work. *Contemporary Sociology*, *26*(2), 228. https://doi.org/10.2307/2076801

Holt, J., & Perren, A. (Eds.). (2009). *Media industries: History, theory, and method*. Blackwell.

Holt, J., & Perren, A. (2019). Media industries: A decade in review. In M. Prenger & M. Deuze (Eds.), *Making media* (pp. 31–44). https://doi.org/10.1017/9789048540150.002

Horgan, A. (2021). *Lost in work: Escaping capitalism*. Pluto.

Horkheimer, M., & Adorno, T. (1995). The culture industry: Enlightenment as mass deception. In *The dialectic of the enlightenment*. Continuum.

Horne, G. (2001). *Class struggle in Hollywood, 1930–1950: Moguls, mobsters, stars, reds, & trade unionists*. University of Texas Press.

Horowitz, D., & Levine, L. W. (1989). Highbrow/Lowbrow: The emergence of cultural hierarchy in America. *Journal of Interdisciplinary History*, *20*(2), 329. https://doi.org/10.2307/204869

House, J., & Rashid, A. (2022). *Solidarity beyond bars: Unionizing prison labour*. Fernwood Publishing.

Howcroft, D., & Bergvall-Kåreborn, B. (2014). Amazon mechanical turk and the commodification of labour. *New Technology, Work and Employment*, *29*(3), 213–223.

Howe, J. (2008). *Crowdsourcing: Why the power of the crowd is driving the future of business*. Crown Business.

Howe, J. (2006). The rise of crowdsourcing. *Wired*. http://www.wired.com/2006/06/crowds/

HRDQ Staff. (2023). *Essential elements of Lewin's leadership theory: A breakdown*. https://hrdqstore.com/blogs/hrdq-blog/lewins-leadership-theory-breakdown

Huber, M. (2022). *Climate change as class war*. Verso.

Hudders, L., & Lou, C. (2023). The rosy world of influencer marketing? Its bright and dark sides, and future research recommendations. *International Journal of Advertising*, *42*(1), 151–161. https://doi.org/10.1080/02650487.2022.2137318

Hughes, E. V. (1958). *Men and their work*. The Free Press of Glencoe.

Hughes, L., & Woodcock, J. (2023). *Troublemaking: Why you should organize your workplace*. Verso.

Hund, E. (2023). *The influencer industry: The quest for authenticity on social media*. Princeton University Press.

Hung, C.-L. (2011). Labor, class formation, and China's informationized policy of economic development. *Journal of Information Policy*, *1*(1), 174–178. https://doi.org/10.5325/jinfopoli.1.2011.174

Hunt, D. (2017). Writers' room: How Hollywood whitewashes the stories that shape America. *Color of Change Hollywood*, October, 1–83. https://hollywood.colorofchange.org/wp-content/uploads/2019/03/COC_Hollywood_Race_Report.pdf

Hunt, D., & Ramón, A. (2020). *Hollywood Diversity Report 2020: A Tale of Two Hollywoods*. UCL Institute for Research on Labor & Employment. https://socialsciences.ucla.edu/wp-content/uploads/2020/02/UCLA-Hollywood-Diversity-Report-2020-Film-2-6-2020.pdf

Huntemann, N. B. (2013). Women in video games: The case of hardware production and promotion. In *Gaming globally* (pp. 41–57). https://doi.org/10.1057/9781137006332_3

Hunter, A., & Shearer, M. (2023). *Women and new Hollywood: Gender, creative labor, and 1970s American cinema*. Rutgers University Press.

Hutchinson, J. (2017). Cultural intermediaries. In *Encyclopedia of consumer culture*. https://doi.org/10.4135/9781412994248.n147

Huws, U. (2003). *The making of a cybertariat? Virtual work in a real world*. Monthly Review Press.

Huws, U. (2007a). Defragmenting: Towards a critical understanding of the new global division of labour. *Work Organisation, Labour and Globalisation*, 1(2), 1–4.

Huws, U. (2007b). The spark in the engine: Creative workers in a global economy. *Work Organisation, Labour and Globalisation*, 1(1). https://doi.org/10.13169/workorgalaboglob.1.1.0001

Huws, U. (2010). Expression and expropriation: The dialectics of autonomy and control in creative labour. *Ephemera: Theory and Politics in Organization*, 10(3/4), 504–521.

Huws, U. (2013). The underpinnings of class in the digital age: Living, labour and value. In L. Panitch, G. Albo, & V. Chibber (Eds.), *Registering class: Socialist register 2014* (pp. 80–107). Merlin Press.

Huws, U. (2014). *Labour in the digital economy*. Monthly Review Press.

Huws, U. (2015). When Adam blogs: Cultural work and the gender division of labour in Utopia. *Sociological Review*, 63(S1), 158–173. https://doi.org/10.1111/1467-954X.12247

Huws, U. (2019). *Labour in contemporary capitalism*. Palgrave Macmillan. https://doi.org/10.1057/978-1-137-52042-5

Huws, U. (2020). *Reinventing the welfare state : Digital platforms and public policies*. Pluto.

Huws, U., Spencer, N. H., Coates, M., & Holts, K. (2019). The platformisation of work in Europe, highlights from research in 13 European countries. *Foundation for European Progressive Studies – FEPS*. https://feps-europe.eu/wp-content/uploads/2019/07/The-platformisation-of-work-in-Europe.pdf

Hwang, S., Zhang, S., Liu, X., & Srinivasan, K. (2024). Should your brand hire a virtual influencer? *Harvard Business Review*, May-June, https://hbr.org/2024/05/should-your-brand-hire-a-virtual-influencer

Iger, R. (2019). *The ride of a lifetime*. Random House.

International Labour Organization (ILO). (2023). What are forced labor, modern slavery and international trafficking. https://www.ilo.org/global/topics/forced-labour/definition/lang--en/index.htm

Im, Y. H. (1997). Towards a labour-process history of newsworkers. *Javnost*, 4(1), 31–48. https://doi.org/10.1080/13183222.1997.11008639

Incorporated Society of Musicians. (20178). Dignity at work : A survey of discrimination in the music sector. *Incorporated Society of Musicians*.

Ingold, T. (2021). Work, time and industry. In *The perception of the environment* (pp. 406–425). Routledge. https://doi.org/10.4324/9781003196662-21

International, U. S., & Trade Administration. (2023). Media and entertainment. https://www.trade.gov/media-entertainment

Irani, L. (2015). The cultural work of microwork. *New Media and Society*, 17(5), 720–739. https://doi.org/10.1177/1461444813511926

Irani, L. (2019). *Chasing innovation: Making entrepreneurial citizens in modern India*. Princeton University Press.

Isaacson, W. (2011). *Steve Jobs*. Simon & Schuster.
Jackson, M. C. (2021). Artificial intelligence & algorithmic bias: The issues with technology reflecting history & humans. *Journal of Business & Technology Law, 16*(2), 299–316. https://search.ebscohost.com/login.aspx?direct=true&db=bth&AN=152595734&site=ehost-live
Jaeger, J. (2021). Embattled Activision Blizzard confirms SEC subpoenas. *Compliance Weekly*. https://www.complianceweek.com/regulatory-enforcement/embattled-activision-blizzard-confirms-sec-subpoenas/30821.article
Jaffe, S. (2021). *Work won't love you back: How devotion to our jobs keeps us exploited, exhausted, and alone*. Bold Type Books.
Jamal, A., & Lavie, N. (2020). Subaltern agency in the cultural industries: Palestinian Creative labor in the Israeli series Fauda. *International Journal of Communication, 14*(1), 2403–2421.
James, N. (1989). Emotional labour: Skill and work in the social regulation of feelings. *The Sociological Review, 37*(1), 15–42. https://doi.org/10.1111/j.1467-954X.1989.tb00019.x
Jarrett, J. (2022). *Digital Labor*. Wiley.
Jarrett, K. (2016). *Feminism, labour and digital media: The digital housewife*. Routledge.
Jenkins, H. (1993). Textual poachers: Television fans and participatory culture. *Public Relations Review, 19*(3), 307–308. https://doi.org/10.1016/0363-8111(93)90051-d
Jenkins, H. (2006a). *Convergence culture: Where old and new media collide*. New York University Press.
Jenkins, H. (2006b). *Fans, bloggers and gamers: Media consumers in a digital age*. New York University Press.
Jereza, R. (2022). "I'm not this Person": Racism, content moderators, and protecting and denying voice online. *New Media and Society*. https://doi.org/10.1177/14614448221122224
Jhally, S. (1982). Probing the blindspot: The audience commodity. *Canadian Journal of Political and Social Theory, 6*(1–2), 204–210.
Jhally, S. (1987). *The codes of advertising: Fetishism and the political economy of meaning in the consumer society*. Routledge.
Jhally, S., & Livant, B. (1986). Watching as working: The valorization of audience consciousness. *Journal of Communication, 36*(3), 124–143. https://doi.org/10.1111/j.1460-2466.1986.tb01442.x
Jhally, S., & Lewis, J. (2019). *Enlightened racism: The Cosby show, audiences, and the myth of the American dream*. Routledge. https://doi.org/10.4324/9780429034343
Jia, Y. (2021). The construction of identity and digital labor of playbour: Case on mobile game Arena of Valor. *Radio & TV Journal, 9*, 178–179.
Jin, D. Y. (2015). *Digital platforms, imperialism and political culture*. Routledge.
Jin, L., Shroff, L., & Duke Kominers, S. (2021). A labor movement for the platform economy. *Harvard Business Review*. https://hbr.org/2021/09/a-labor-movement-for-the-platform-economy
Johnson, C. (2020). Don't let blackwashing save the investor class. *Jacobin*. https://jacobinmag.com/2020/06/blackwashing-corporations-woke-capitalism-protests
Johnson, D., Kompare, D., & Santo, A. (Eds.). (2014). *Making media work: Cultures of management in the entertainment industries*. New York University Press.
Johnson, M. R., & Woodcock, J. (2017). 'It's like the gold rush': The lives and careers of professional video game streamers on Twitch.tv. *Information Communication and Society, 22*(3), 336–351. https://doi.org/10.1080/1369118X.2017.1386229

Johnson, M. R., & Woodcock, J. (2018). The impacts of live streaming and Twitch.tv on the video game industry. *Media, Culture and Society*, 41(5), 670–688. https://doi.org/10.1177/0163443718818363

Johnson, M. R., & Woodcock, J. (2019). "And Today's Top Donator is": How live streamers on *Twitch.tv* monetize and gamify their broadcasts. *Social Media + Society*, 5(4), 205630511988169. https://doi.org/10.1177/2056305119881694

Johnson, R. (2019). Major Study Finds Diverse Members of the Tech Sector Experience Discrimination and Stress. BIMA. https://bima.co.uk/major-study-finds-diverse-members-of-the-tech-sector-experience-discrimination-and-stress-2/

Johnson-Yale, C. (2008). "So-called runaway film production": Countering Hollywood's outsourcing narrative in the Canadian press. *Critical Studies in Media Communication*, 25(2), 113–134. https://doi.org/10.1080/15295030802032259

Johnson-Yale, C. (2017). *A history of Hollywood's outsourcing debate: Runaway production*. Lexington Books.

Johnstone, J. W. C., Slawski, E. J., & Bowman, W. W. (1976). *The news people: A sociological portrait of American journalists and their work*. University of Illinois Press.

Jones, D., & Pringle, J. K. (2015). Unmanageable inequalities: Sexism in the film industry. *Sociological Review*, 63(S1), 37–49. https://doi.org/10.1111/1467-954X.12239

Jones, P. (2021). *Work without the worker: Labour in the age of platform capitalism*. Verso.

Jones, S. (2006). *Against technology: From the luddites to neo-luddism*. Routledge.

Jones, S. G. (2018). *Workers at play: A social and economic history of leisure, 1918–1939*. Routledge. https://doi.org/10.4324/9780429449512

Joseph, D. (2022, July 25). Delivering people: Media make audiences, not content. *Real Life*, https://reallifemag.com/delivering-people/

Joyce, S., Umney, C., Whittaker, X., & Stuart, M. (2023). New social relations of digital technology and the future of work: Beyond technological determinism. *New Technology, Work and Employment*, 38(2), 145–161. https://doi.org/10.1111/ntwe.12276

Jung, E. A. (2014). Wages for Facebook. *Dissent*, 61(2), 47–50. https://www.dissentmagazine.org/article/wages-for-facebook/

Kalleberg, A. L., & Leicht, K. (2021). Eight key themes in sociology of work. *La Nouvelle revue du travail* 19(19). https://journals.openedition.org/nrt/10168

Kantor, J., & Twohey, M. (2019). *She said: Breaking the sexual harassment story that helped ignite a movement*. Penguin Press.

Kapit, S. P. (2018). Oscars 2018: The shape of disability representation. *NOS Magazine*. http://nosmag.org/oscars-2018-the-shape-of-disability-representation/

Kara, S. (2023). *Cobalt red: How the blood of the Congo powers our lives*. MacMillan Publishers.

Kashani, T., & Nocella, A. J. (2010). Hollywood's cinema of ableism: A disability studies perspective on the Hollywood industrial complex. In R. Van Heertum (Ed.), *Hollywood's exploited* (pp. 105–114). https://doi.org/10.1057/9780230117426_7

Kasperkevic, J. (2016). Verizon strike ends as tentative deal promises "big gains" for workers. *The Guardian*. https://www.theguardian.com/business/2016/may/27/verizon-strike-ends-tentative-deal-union

Kaul, A. J. (1986). The proletarian journalist: A critique of professionalism. *Journal of Mass Media Ethics*, 1(2), 47–55. https://doi.org/10.1080/08900528609358266

Kaur, P. (2020). "If Globalization Is Happening, It Should Work Both Ways": Race, labor, and resistance among Bollywood's stunt workers. *Media Industries Journal*, 7(1). https://doi.org/10.3998/mij.15031809.0007.107

Kealey, G. S. (2023). Work control, the labour process, and nineteenth-century Canadian printers. In *Workers and Canadian history* (pp. 209–237). https://doi.org/10.1515/9780773565678-010

Keating, G. (2012). *Netflixed*. Portfolio.

Kelley, L. (2020). I am the portrait of downward mobility. *New York Times*. https://www.nytimes.com/interactive/2020/04/17/opinion/inequality-economy-1980.html

Kelley, P. (2023, November 16). AI is coming for our jobs! Could universal basic income be the solution? *The Guardian*. https://www.theguardian.com/global-development/2023/nov/16/ai-is-coming-for-our-jobs-could-universal-basic-income-be-the-solution

Kelley, T. (2006). Reality show participants: Employees or independent contractors? *Employee Relations Law Journal*, 32(1), 15–38.

Kellogg, K., Valentine, M., & Christin, A. (2019). Algorithms at work: The new contested terrain of control. *Academy of Management Annals*, 14 (1). https://doi.org/10.5465/annals.2018.0174

Kelly, S., Klézl, V., Israilidis, J., Malone, N., & Butler, S. (2021). Digital supply chain management in the videogames industry: A systematic literature review. *The Computer Games Journal*, 10(1–4), 19–40. https://doi.org/10.1007/s40869-020-00118-0

Kemper, T. (2009). Hidden talent: The emergence of Hollywood agents. *Hidden Talent: The Emergence of Hollywood Agents*. https://doi.org/10.5860/choice.47-6148

Kempton, B. (2023). *Gig economy statistics and key takeaways for 2024*. Upwork. https://www.upwork.com/resources/gig-economy-statistics

Kendall, D. (2005). *Framing class: Media representations of wealth and poverty in America*. Rowman & Littlefield.

Keogh, B. (2023). *The videogame industry does not exist : Why we should think beyond commercial game production*. MIT Press. https://doi.org/10.7551/mitpress/14513.001.0001

Keogh, B. (2021a). Hobbyist game making between self-exploitation and self-emancipation. *Game Production Studies*. https://doi.org/10.5117/9789463725439_ch01

Keogh, B. (2021b). The cultural field of video game production in Australia. *Games and Culture*, 16(1), 116–135. https://doi.org/10.1177/1555412019873746

Keogh, B., & Abraham, B. (2022). Challenges and opportunities for collective action and unionization in local games industries. *Organization*. https://doi.org/10.1177/13505084221082269

Kerr, A. (2017). *Global games: Production, circulation and policy in the networked era*. https://doi.org/10.4324/9780203704028

Kessler-Harris, A. (2003). *Out to work: A history of wage-earning women in the United States*. Oxford University Press.

Keynes, J. M. (2010). Economic possibilities for our grandchildren. In *Essays in persuasion* (321–333). https://link.springer.com/chapter/10.1007/978-1-349-59072-8_25

Kilkenny, K., & Cho, W. (2023). Hollywood's high stakes strike: Actors and writers make history with bid to reshape industry. *The Hollywood Reporter*. https://www.hollywoodreporter.com/business/business-news/sag-aftra-wga-actors-writers-strike-hollywood-1235533651/

Kim, C. (2014). Labor and the limits of seduction in Korea's creative economy. *Television and New Media*, *15*(6), 562–576. https://doi.org/10.1177/1527476413485644

Kim, C., & Lee, S. (2023). Putting creative labour in its place in the shadow of the Korean Wave. *International Journal of Cultural Policy*, *29*(5), 603–617. https://doi.org/10.1080/10286632.2022.2087643

Kinane, S. (2023). Companies are using automation to proactively identify—and automatically solve—potential IT incidents before they occur. Kyndryl. https://www.kyndryl.com/ca/en/about-us/news/2023/07/why-business-leaders-are-investing-in-automation

Kindelan, K. (2023). Illinois becomes 1st state to regulate kid influencers: What to know about the law. *ABC*. https://abcnews.go.com/GMA/Family/illinois-1st-state-regulate-kid-influencers-law/story?id=102259218#

King, A. D. K. (2021). The strike that could halt Hollywood. *The Maple*. https://www.readthemaple.com/the-strike-that-could-halt-hollywood/

King, B. (1987). The star and the commodity: Notes towards a performance theory of stardom. *Cultural Studies*, 17–34. https://doi.org/10.4324/9780203989692-2

Kirkpatrick, D. (2011). *The Facebook effect: The inside story of the company that is connecting the world*. Simon & Schuster.

Kirshner, L. (2024). *Sex work in popular culture*. University of Toronto Press.

Klein, N. (2000). *No logo*. Vintage.

Klein, N. (2023, May 8). AI machines aren't 'Hallucinating,' but their makers are. *The Guardian*. https://www.theguardian.com/commentisfree/2023/may/08/ai-machines-hallucinating-naomi-klein

Kline, S., Dyer-Witheford, N., & de Peuter, G. (2003). *Digital play: The interaction of technology, culture, and marketing*. McGill-Queen's University Press.

Knight, P. (2018). *Shoe dog*. Scribner.

Kokas, A. (2017). Precarious creativity: Global media, local labor. *Chinese Journal of Communication*, *10*(3), 328–329. https://doi.org/10.1080/17544750.2017.1358933

Kolb, B. M. (2015). *Entrepreneurship for the creative and cultural industries*. Routledge. https://doi.org/10.4324/9781315778907

Komenda, E. (2023). Corporate Amazon workers protest company's climate impact and return-to-office mandate in walkout. *AP*. https://apnews.com/article/amazon-seattle-walkout-ebfade076bd529e39b83e2c9edcea9ae

Kouzes, J., & Posner, B. (2002). *The leadership challenge*. Jossey-Bass.

Krauss, S., & Orth, U. (2022). Work experiences and self-esteem development: A meta-analysis of longitudinal studies. *European Journal of Personality*, *36*(6), 849–869. https://doi.org/10.1177/08902070211027142

Kruppa, M. (2020). Racism in the Valley: Why tech investing has not changed. *Financial Times*. https://www.ft.com/content/d3e0d448-ab88-4270-8ecd-a9fd908d915d

Kryszczuk, M. D. (2010). New capitalism? The transformation of work. *Polish Sociological Review*, *1*, 120–122.

Kücklich, J. (2005). Precarious playbour : Modders and the digital games. *Fibreculture*, *5*, 1–8. http://five.fibreculturejournal.org/fcj-025-precarious-playbour-modders-and-the-digital-games-industry/

Kuehn, K., & Corrigan, T. F. (2013). Hope Labor: The role of employment prospects in online social production. *The Political Economy of Communication*, *1*(1), 9–25. http://www.polecom.org/index.php/polecom/article/view/9/64

Kulwin, N. (2017). Facebook will hire 3,000 people to watch videos of murder, suicides, and mayhem. *Vice*. https://www.vice.com/en/article/4xkyzp/facebook-will-hire-3000-people-to-watch-videos-of-murder-suicide-and-mayhem

Kumar, D. (2007). *Outside the box*. University of Illinois Press.

Küng, L. (2023). *Strategic management in the media: Theory to practice*. Sage.
Lafargue, P., (1883). The right to be lazy. https://www.marxists.org/archive/lafargue/1883/lazy/
Lall, C. (2020). Tech's elephant in the room: Digital ableism. Medium. https://medium.com/access-bridge/techs-elephant-in-the-room-digital-ableism-fd989db30b45
Lane, M. (2020). *Regulating platform work in the digital age*. Going Digital Toolkit Policy Note. https://goingdigital.oecd.org/toolkitnotes/regulating-platform-work-in-thedigital-age.pdf.
Lang, B. (2023). Media Mogul Paydays: How the biggest CEOs in Hollywood made bank in 2021. *Variety*. https://variety.com/2022/film/news/media-ceo-paydays-bob-chapek-reed-hastings-rupert-murdoch-reed-hastings-david-zaslav-1235253667/
Laslett, B. & Brenner, J. (1989). Gender and social reproduction: historical perspectives. *Annual Review Sociology*, *15*(1), 381–404. doi: 10.1146/annurev.so.15.080189.002121.
Lavie, N., & Jamal, A. (2019). Constructing ethno-national differentiation on the set of the TV series, Fauda. *Ethnicities*, *19*(6), 1038–1061. https://doi.org/10.1177/1468796819857180
Lazar, T., Ribak, R., & Davidson, R. (2020). Mobile social media as platforms in workers' unionization. *Information, Communication & Society*, *23*(3), 437–453. https://doi.org/10.1080/1369118X.2018.1510536
Lazzarato, M. (1996). *Immaterial labor*. In M. Hardt & P. Virno (Eds.), *Radical thought in Italy: A potential politics* (pp. 133–147). University of Minnesota Press.
Lazzarato, M. (2004). From Capital-Labour to Capital-Life. *Ephemera: Theory & Politics in Organization*, *4*(3), 187–208.
Leab, D. J., Hardt, H., & Brennen, B. (1996). Newsworkers: Toward a history of the rank and file. *The Journal of American History*, *83*(2), 645. https://doi.org/10.2307/2945025
Leadbeater, C., & Oakley, K. (1999). *The independents: Britain's new cultural entrepreneur*. Demos.
Leadbeater, C., & Oakley, K. (2005). Why cultural entrepreneurs matter. In *Creative industries* (pp. 299–311). Blackwell.
Lebovits, H. (2019). Automating inequality: How high-tech tools profile, police, and punish the poor. *Public Integrity*, *21*(4), 448–452. https://doi.org/10.1080/10999922.2018.1511671
Lebowitz, M. A. (1986). Too many blindspots on the media. *Studies in Political Economy*, *21*(1), 165–173. https://doi.org/10.1080/19187033.1986.11675585
Lebowitz, M. A. (2003). *Beyond capital: Marx's political economy of the working class*. Palgrave Macmillan.
Lee, D., & Zoellner, A. (2020). Media production research and the challenge of normativity. In *Making media* (pp. 45–60). https://doi.org/10.1017/9789048540150.003
Lee, M. (2011). Google ads and the blindspot debate. *Media, Culture and Society*, *33*(3), 433–447. https://doi.org/10.1177/0163443710394902
Lee, M. S. (2023, September 19). Artificial intelligence and the right of publicity: The undiscovered country. *Rimon*. https://www.rimonlaw.com/artificial-intelligence-and-the-right-of-publicity-the-undiscovered-country/
Lefebvre, H. (1991). *The production of space*. Blackwell.
Lena, J. C., & Schmutz, V. (2020). *Cultural production and circulation*. Oxford Bibliographies. https://www.oxfordbibliographies.com/display/document/obo-9780199756384/obo-9780199756384-0195.xml
Lent, J. A. (1998). The animation industry and its offshore factories. In G. Sussman & J. A. Lent (Eds.), *Global productions: Labor in the making of the 'Information society'* (pp. 239–254). Hampton Press.

Lent, J. A. (2010). The global cartooning labour force, its problems and coping mechanisms: The travails of the marginalised cartoonist. *Work Organisation, Labour and Globalisation*, 4(2). https://doi.org/10.13169/workorgalaboglob.4.2.0160

Leonard, M. (2016). 'Girls at work: Gendered identities, sex segregation, and employment experiences in the music industries. In J. Warwick & A. Adrian (Eds.), *Voicing girlhood in popular music: Performance, authority, authenticity* (pp. 37–55). Routledge.

Leonardi, P. (2013). Theoretical foundations for the study of sociomateriality. *Information and Organization*, 23, 59–76.

Leonhardt, D., & Scheiber, N. (2023). Labor's very good year. *New York Times*. https://www.nytimes.com/2023/12/06/briefing/labors-very-good-year.html

Lester, M., & Fishman, M. (1981). Manufacturing the news. *Contemporary Sociology*, 10(6), 807. https://doi.org/10.2307/2067233

Levine, E. (2001). Toward AI realism: Opening notes on machine learning and our collective future. *Critical Studies in Media Communication*, 18(1), 66–82. https://doi.org/10.1080/15295030109367124

Lewis, H. (2024). Toward AI Realism: Opening Notes on Machine Learning and Our Collective Future. *Spectre*. https://spectrejournal.com/toward-ai-realism/

Liddy, S., & O'Brien, A. (Eds.). (2021). *Media work, mothers and motherhood: Negotiating the international audio-visual industry*. Routledge. https://doi.org/10.4324/9781003082552

Liederman, E. (2024). The creators are unionizing. Here's what it could mean for marginalized creators. *Banknotes*. https://hashtagpaid.com/banknotes/creators-are-unionizing-what-sag-aftras-influencer-agreement-means-for-marginalized-creators

Likert, R. (1961). *New patterns of management*. McGraw-Hill.

Lin, J. (2023). *Chinese creator economies: Labor and bilateral creative workers*. New York University Press.

Lincoln, A. E., Allen, M. P., Forum, S., & Dec, N. (2004). Double jeopardy in Hollywood : Age and gender in the careers of film actors. *Film*, 19(4), 611–631.

Lindström, S. (2017). Be creative: Making a living in the new culture industries. *International Journal of Cultural Policy*, 23(5), 652–654. https://doi.org/10.1080/10286632.2017.1330334

Lipscombe, P. (2023). Report: Telecoms industry workforce slims down post-covid. https://www.datacenterdynamics.com/en/news/report-telecoms-industry-workforce-slims-down-post-covid/

Littler, J. (2017). *Against meritocracy: Culture, power and myths of mobility*. Routledge. https://doi.org/10.4324/9781315712802

Littleton, C. (2013). *TV on strike: Why Hollywood went to war over the internet*. Syracuse University Press.

Liu, C. (2021). *Virtue hoarders: The case against the professional managerial class*. Minnesota University Press.

Livant, B. (1979). The audience commodity: On the "Blindspot Debate". *CTheory*, 3(1), 91–106.

Livingstone, S. (2019). Audiences in an age of datafication: Critical questions for media research. *Television & New Media*, 20(2), 170–183. https://doi.org/10.1177/1527476418811118

Logic Magazine. (2019). Game workers of the World Unite: An interview with an anonymous game worker. *Logic Magazine*. https://logicmag.io/play/interview-with-an-anonymous-game-worker/

Lorenz, T. (2021). TikTok stars and social media creators can now join Hollywood's top union. *The New York Times*. https://www.nytimes.com/2021/02/12/style/influencer-union-hollywood-SAG-AFTRA.html

Lotz, A., & Havens, T. (2011). *Understanding media industries*. Oxford University Press.
Lotz, C. (2022). The brave new world of Amazon Turk – breaking the logic of alienation. Real Democracy Movement. https://realdemocracymovement.org/the-brave-new-world-of-amazon-turk-breaking-the-logic-of-alienation/
Low, E., & Jackson, A. (2020). The reckoning over representation: Black Hollywood speaks out, but is the industry listening? *Variety*. https://variety.com/2020/biz/features/black-representation-hollywood-inclusion-diversity-entertainment-1234693219/
Low, E., & Yap, A. C. (2020). Netflix, Hulu, Amazon, HBO and other Hollywood players take a stand in support of Black lives matter movement amid George Floyd protests. *Variety*. https://variety.com/2020/tv/news/netflix-hulu-amazon-hbo-black-lives-matter-george-floyd-protests-1234621292/
Lowrey, A. (2023, January 20) How ChatGPT will destabilize white-collar work. *The Atlantic*. https://www.theatlantic.com/ideas/archive/2023/01/chatgpt-ai-economy-automation-jobs/672767/
Lu, M. (2020). Is the American dream over? Here's what the data says. World Economic Forum. https://www.weforum.org/agenda/2020/09/social-mobility-upwards-decline-usa-us-america-economics
Lucas, K., Manikas, A. S., Mattingly, E. S., & Crider, C. J. (2017). Engaging and misbehaving: How dignity affects employee work behaviors. *Organization Studies*, 38(11), 1505–1527. https://doi.org/10.1177/0170840616677634
Lüthje, B., & Butollo, F. (2017). Why the Foxconn model does not die: Production networks and labour relations in the IT industry in South China. *Globalizations*, 14(2), 216–231. https://doi.org/10.1080/14747731.2016.1203132
Luxton, M. (2009). *More than a labour of love: Three generations of women's work in the home*. Women's Press.
Lyon, D. (1994). *The Electronic Eye: The Rise of Surveillance Society*. University of Minnesota Press.
Macdonald, B. (2022). 54% of young people want to be influencers – is it a bad thing? *1News*. https://www.1news.co.nz/2022/09/29/54-of-young-people-want-to-be-influencers-is-it-a-bad-thing/
Macdonald, M. (2023, November 9). The double exploitation of Deepfake Porn. *The Walrus*. https://thewalrus.ca/the-double-exploitation-of-deepfake-porn/
Machlup, F. (1962). *The production and distribution of knowledge in the United States*. Princeton University Press.
MacKenzie, D. A., & Wajcman, J. (1999). *The social shaping of technology*. Open University Press.
Mackenzie, E., & McKinlay, A. (2021). Hope labour and the psychic life of cultural work. *Human Relations*, 74(11), 1841–1863. https://doi.org/10.1177/0018726720940777
Maddox, J. (2023). Why aren't there any legal protections for the children of influencers? *The Conversation*. https://theconversation.com/why-arent-there-any-legal-protections-for-the-children-of-influencers-196463
Madison, E. (2014). Training digital age journalists: Blurring the distinction between students and professionals. *Journalism and Mass Communication Educator*, 69(3), 314–324. https://doi.org/10.1177/1077695814532926
Madowo, L. (2023). Laid-off Twitter Africa team 'ghosted' without severance pay or benefits, former employees say. CNN Business. https://www.cnn.com/2023/07/17/tech/ghana-twitter-layoffs-severance-intl-hnk/index.html
Maffie, D. (2020). The role of digital communities in organizing gig workers. *Industrial Relations*, 59(1), 123–149. https://doi.org/10.1111/irel.12251

Maglio, T. (2013a). Has Hollywood ignited and intern uprising? Examining the brewing revolution. *The Wrap*. http://www.thewrap.com/media/article/has-hollywood-ignited-intern-uprising-examining-coffee-brewing-revolution-99136/

Maglio, T. (2013b). Hollywood intern lawsuit panic: Who's really paying the price? *The Wrap*. http://www.thewrap.com/media/article/interns-and-employers-face-brave-new-world-amid-lawsuits-102556/

Mahmud, T. (2015). Precarious existence and capitalism : A permanent state of exception. *Southwestern Law Review, 40*, 699–726.

Malkin, M., & Miano, J. (2015). *Sold out: How high-tech billionaires & bipartisan beltway crapweasels are screwing America's Best & brightest workers*. Mercury Inc.

Malm, A. (2016). *Fossil capital: The rise of steam power and the roots of global warming*. Verso.

Manins, R. (2023, December 29). Transgender woman sues AT&T for $3M after being fired, alleges discrimination. *The Atlanta Journal-Constitution*. https://www.ajc.com/news/atlanta-news/transgender-woman-sues-att-for-3m-after-being-fired-alleges-discrimination/

Manuel P. (1993). *Cassette culture: popular music and technology in North India*. University of Chicago Press.

Manzerolle, V. (2010). Mobilizing the audience commodity: Digital labour in a wireless world. *Ephemera: Theory and Politics in Organization, 10*(3/4), 455–469. http://www.ephemerajournal.org/sites/default/files/10-3manzerolle.pdf

Mari, W. (2018). Unionization in the American newsroom, 1930 to 1960. *Journal of Historical Sociology, 31*(3), 265–281. https://doi.org/10.1111/johs.12177

Marjoribanks, T. (2002). News corporation, technology and the workplace: Global strategies, local change. *Capital & Class, 26*(3), 180–182. https://doi.org/10.1177/030981680207800118

Markovits, D. (2016). *The meritocracy trap: How America's foundational myth feeds inequality, dismantles the middle class, and devours the elite*. Penguin Press.

Marks, A., & Baldry, C. (2009). Stuck in the middle with who? The class identity of knowledge workers. *Work, Employment and Society, 23*(1), 49–65. https://doi.org/10.1177/0950017008099777

Marks, A., & Scholarios, D. (2007). Revisiting technical workers: Professional and organisational identities in the software industry. *New Technology, Work and Employment, 22*(2), 98–117. https://doi.org/10.1111/j.1468-005X.2007.00193.x

Marr, B. (2022). The 5 biggest media and entertainment technology trends in 2022. *Forbes*. https://www.forbes.com/sites/bernardmarr/2022/03/02/the-5-biggest-media-and-entertainment-technology-trends-in-2022/?sh=4926c8453277

Marszal, A. (2020). #OscarsSoWhite: The Hollywood "hashtag" activists demanding diversity | Channel. *News24*. https://www.news24.com/channel/Movies/News/oscarssowhite-the-hollywood-hashtag-activists-demanding-diversity-20200202

Martin, A. (2018). The Queer Business of Casting Gay Characters on U.S. Television. *Communication, Culture & Critique, 11* (2), 282–297. https://doi.org/10.1093/ccc/tcy005

Martin, A. (2021). *The generic closet: Black gayness and the black-cast Sitcom*. Indiana University Press.

Martin, A. L. (2015). Scripting Black Gayness: Television Authorship in Black-Cast Sitcoms. *Television and New Media, 16* (7), 648–663. http://journals.sagepub.com.libproxy.uoregon.edu/doi/pdf/10.1177/1527476414560443

Martin, C. R. (2003). *Framed!: Labor and the corporate media*. ILR Press.

Martin, C. R. (2019). *No longer newsworthy: How the mainstream media abandoned the working class*. Cornell University Press.

Marwick, A. E. (2013). *Status update: Celebrity, publicity, and branding in the social media age*. Yale University Press.
Marwick, A. E. (2015). You may know me from YouTube: (Micro-)Celebrity in social media. In *A companion to celebrity* (pp. 333–350). https://doi.org/10.1002/9781118475089.ch18
Marx, K. (1845). The German ideology. In *Nineteenth-century philosophy: Philosophic classics, volume IV*. https://doi.org/10.4324/9781003320609-16
Marx, K. (1852). The eighteenth Brumaire of Louis Bonaparte. https://doi.org/10.2307/j.ctt18fs6hn.5
Marx, K. (1880). A workers' inquiry. In *La Revue Socialiste*. Marxist Internet Archive. https://www.marxists.org/archive/marx/works/1880/04/20.htm
Marx, K. (1888[1978]). Theses on Feuerbach. In *The Marx-Engels reader*. W.W. Norton & Company.
Marx, K. (1867[1990]). *Capital, a critique of political economy, Volume I*. Vintage Books.
Marx, K. (1992). Economic and philosophical manuscripts [1844]. In *Karl Marx: Early writings* (pp. 334–400). Penguin Classics.
Marx, K., & Engels, F. (2012). *The communist manifesto: A modern edition*. Verso.
Maslow, A. (1943). A Theory of Human Motivation. *Psychological Review* 50(4): 370–396.
Matthews, D. (2023). Spotify cuts 1,500 jobs in latest round of layoffs. *Daily News*. https://www.nydailynews.com/2023/12/04/spotify-layoffs-1500-jobs/
Maxwell, R. (1991). The image is gold: Value, the audience commodity, and fetishism. *Journal of Film and Video*, 43(1/2), 29–45.
Maxwell, R. (Ed.). (2001). *Culture works: The political economy of culture*. New York University Press.
Maxwell, R. (Ed.). (2015). *The Routledge companion to labor and media*. Routledge. https://doi.org/10.4324/9780203404119
Maxwell, R., & Miller, T. (2006). The cultural labor issue. *Social Semiotics*, 15(3), 261–266.
Maxwell, R., & Miller, T. (2014). *Greening the media*. Oxford University Press.
Maxwell, R., & Miller, T. (2023). Who makes our smartphones? Four moments in their lifecycle. In *The Routledge handbook of ecomedia studies* (pp. 220–228). https://doi.org/10.4324/9781003176497-27
May, C. (2002). The political economy of proximity: Intellectual property and the global division of information labour. *New Political Economy*, 7(3), 317–342. https://doi.org/10.1080/1356346022000018711
Mayer, V. (2009). Bringing the social back in: Studies of production cultures and social theory. In *Production studies: Cultural studies of media industries* (pp. 15–24). https://doi.org/10.4324/9780203879597
Mayer, V. (2011). *Below the line: Producers and production studies in the new television economy*. Duke University Press.
Mayer, V. (2013). To communicate is human; to chat is female: The feminization of US media work. In *The Routledge companion to media & gender* (pp. 51–60).
Mayer, V. (2017). *Almost Hollywood, nearly new Orleans: The lure of the local film economy*. University of California Press. https://doi.org/10.1525/luminos.25
Mayer, V., Banks, M., & Caldwell, J. (2009a). *Production studies: Cultural studies of Media industries*. Routledge. https://doi.org/10.4324/9780203879597
Mayo, E. (2010). *The human problems of an industrial civilization*. Routledge.
McAlevey, J. (2020). *A collective bargain: Unions, organizing, and the fight for democracy*. Harper Collins.

McAllister, M. P., & West, E. (Eds.). (2015). *The Routledge companion to advertising and promotional culture*. Routledge. https://doi.org/10.4324/9780203071434

McCallum, J. K. (2020). *Worked over: How round-the-clock work is killing the American dream*. Basic Books.

McCann, D., & Yazici, E. (2018). Disrupting together: the challenges (and opportunities) for platform cooperatives. *New Economic Foundation*. https://neweconomics.org/uploads/files/Disrupting-Together.pdf

McChesney, R. W. (2004). *The problem with the U.S. Media: Communication politics in the 21st century*. Monthly Review Press.

McChesney, R. W. (2008). *The political economy of media: Enduring issues, emerging dilemmas*. Monthly Review Press.

McChesney, R. W. (2014). *Digital disconnect: How capitalism is turning the internet against democracy*. The New Press.

McChesney, R. W., & Nichols, J. (2016). *People get ready: The fight against a jobless economy and a citizenless democracy*. Nation Books.

McChesney, R. W., & Pickard, V. (Eds.). (2011). *Will The last reporter please turn out the lights: The collapse of journalism and what can be done to fix it*. The New Press.

McCluskey, M. (2023). Study: Wealthy kids are more likely to attend elite schools. *Mercury News*. https://www.mercurynews.com/2023/07/24/study-wealthy-families-more-likely-to-send-kids-to-elite-schools/

McCreadie, M. (2005). *Women screenwriters today: Their lives and words*. Praeger.

McGee, P., & Temple-West, P. (2021). Apple faces probe over whether it retaliated against whistleblower. *Financial Times*. https://www.ft.com/content/973aae8d-21d9-4e84-8912-ead071c7935d

McGuigan, J. (2009). Doing a Florida thing: The creative class thesis and cultural policy. *International Journal of Cultural Policy*, *15*(3), 291–300. https://doi.org/10.1080/10286630902763281

McGuigan, J. (2010). Creative labour, cultural work and individualization. *International Journal of Cultural Policy*, *16*(3), 323–335. https://doi.org/10.1080/10286630903029658

McGuigan, L. (2012). Consumers: The commodity product of interactive commercial television, or, is Dallas Smythe's thesis more Germane than ever? *Journal of Communication Inquiry*, *36*(4), 288–304. https://doi.org/10.1177/0196859912459756

McGuigan, J. (2016). Cool capitalism. In *The Blackwell encyclopedia of sociology*, 1–2. https://doi.org/10.1002/9781405165518.wbeos0702

McGuigan, L. (2023). *Selling the American people: Advertising, optimization, and the origins of Adtech*. MIT Press. https://doi.org/10.7551/mitpress/13562.001.0001

McGuigan, L., & Manzerolle, V. (Eds.). (2014). *The audience commodity in a digital age: Revisiting a critical theory of commercial media*. Peter Lang.

McIlwain, C. D. (2019). *Black software: The internet & racial justice, from the AfroNet to Black lives matter*. Oxford University Press.

McIlwain, C. D. (2020). Silicon Valley's cocaine problem shaped our racist tech. *The Guardian*. https://www.theguardian.com/commentisfree/2020/jan/30/silicon-valleys-cocaine-problem-shaped-our-racist-tech

McKay, S. C. (2007). Satanic mills or silicon islands? The politics of high-tech production in the Philippines. *Contemporary Sociology: A Journal of Reviews*, *36*(3), 246–248. https://doi.org/10.1177/009430610703600323

McKercher, C. (2002). *Newsworkers unite*. Rowman & Littlefield.

McKercher, C. (2006). Editorial: The labouring of communication. *Canadian Journal of Communication*, *31*(3), 493–497. https://doi.org/10.22230/cjc.2006v31n3a1841

McKercher, C. (2009). Writing on the margins: Precarity and the freelance journalist. *Feminist Media Studies*, 9(3), 370–374. https://doi.org/10.1080/14680770903068332

McKercher, C. (2013). Precarious times, precarious work: A feminist political economy of freelance journalists in Canada and the United States. In *Critique, social media and the information society* (pp. 219–230). https://doi.org/10.4324/9780203764077

McKercher, C., & Mosco, V. (Eds.). (2007a). *Knowledge workers in the information society*. Rowman & Littlefield.

McKercher, C., & Mosco, V. (2007b). Introduction. Theorizing knowledge labor and the information society. In *Knowledge workers in the information society: Introduction* (pp. vii–xxiv). Rowman & Littlefield.

McMahon, J. (2020). The political economy of cultural production. In *Handbook of cultural sociology* (pp. 593–600). https://doi.org/10.4324/9780203891377-70

McMahon, L. (2024). Billie Eilish and Nicki Minaj want stop to 'predatory' music AI. *BBC*. https://www.bbc.com/news/technology-68717863

McMenamin, L. (2021). Lost in work: Escaping capitalism' proposes that we put workers first. *Teen Vogue*. https://www.teenvogue.com/story/escaping-capitalism-workers-rights

McNally, D. (2020). *Blood and money: War, slavery, finance and empire*. Haymarket.

McRobbie, A. (1998). *British fashion design: Rag trade or image industry?* Routledge.

McRobbie, A. (2002). Clubs to companies: Notes on the decline of political culture in speeded up creative worlds. *Cultural Studies*, 16(4), 516–531. https://doi.org/10.1080/09502380210139098

McRobbie, A. (2011). 'Everyone is creative': Artists as pioneers of the new economy? In *Culture and contestation in the new century* (pp. 77–92). Intellect.

McRobbie, A. (2012). From Holloway to Hollywood: Happiness at work in the new cultural economy? In *Cultural economy: cultural analysis and commercial life* (pp. 97–114). https://doi.org/10.4135/9781446218440.n6

McRobbie, A. (2016). *Be creative. Making a living in the new culture industries*. Polity Press.

Meehan, E. (1990). Why we don't count: The commodity audience. In *Logics of television* (pp. 117–137). Indiana University Press.

Meehan, E. (2005). *Why TV is not our fault: Television programming, viewers, and who's really in control*. Rowman & Littlefield.

Meehan, E. R. (1984). Ratings and the institutional approach: A third answer to the commodity question. *Critical Studies in Mass Communication*, 1(2), 216–225. https://doi.org/10.1080/15295038409360032

Meehan, E. R. (1999). Commodity, culture, common sense: Media research and paradigm dialogue. *Journal of Media Economics*, 12(2), 149–163. https://doi.org/10.1207/s15327736me1202_6.

Meehan, E. R. (2000). Leisure or labor?: Fan ethnography and political economy. In *Consuming audiences?: Production and reception in media research* (pp. 71–92). Hampton Press.

Meehan, E. R. (2007). Understanding how the popular becomes popular: The role of political economy in the study of popular communication. *Popular Communication*, 5(3), 161–170. https://doi.org/10.1080/15405700701384830

Meehan, E. R. (2018). A history of the commodity audience. In *A companion to the history of American broadcasting* (pp. 347–369). https://doi.org/10.1002/9781118646151.ch16

Meehan, E. R. (2019). Watching television: A political economic approach. In *A companion to television* (pp. 345–360). https://doi.org/10.1002/9781119269465.ch17

Meehan, E. R., & Wasko, J. (2013). Defence of a political economy of the media. *Javnost - The Public*, 20(1), 39–53. https://doi.org/10.1080/13183222.2013.11009107

Meehan, E. R., & Wyatt, J. (2002). Gendering the commodity audience: Critical media research, feminism, and political economy. In *Sex & money: Feminism and political economy in the media* (pp. 209–222). University of Minnesota Press.

Menger, P. M. (1999). Artistic labor markets and careers. *Annual Review of Sociology*, 25, 541–574. https://doi.org/10.1146/annurev.soc.25.1.541

Mentortribes. (2022). Mental health – A major concern in the tech industry. *LinkedIn*. https://www.linkedin.com/pulse/mental-health-major-concern-tech-industry-mentortribes/

Menzies, H. (2005). *No time: Stress and the crisis of modern life*. Douglas and McIntyre.

Merchant, B. (2023a). *Blood in the machine: The origins of the rebellion against big tech*. Hachette Book Group.

Merchant, B. (2023b, May 11). Your boss wants AI to replace you. The writers' strike shows how to fight back. *Los Angeles Times*. https://www.latimes.com/business/technology/story/2023-05-11/column-the-writers-strike-is-only-the-beginning-a-rebellion-against-ai-is-underway

Microsoft NZ News Centre. (2019). Using Gamified performance and learning to drive call center agents. *Microsoft*. https://news.microsoft.com/en-nz/2019/05/16/using-gamified-performance-learning-to-drive-call-center-agents/

Miège, B. (1989). *The capitalisation of cultural production*. International General.

Mierzjewska, B. I., & Hollifield, A. C. (2006). Theoretical approaches in media management research. In *Historical trends and patterns in media management research* (pp. 37–66). Routledge.

Mignon, D. (2007). Doing the dirty work: Gender, race, and reproductive labor in historical perspective. *Gender and Society*, 21(3), 313–336.

Milberry, K. (2006). Gatewatching: Collaborative online news production. *Canadian Journal of Communication*, 31(3), 771–772. https://doi.org/10.22230/cjc.2006v31n3a1740

Milburn, K. (2019). *Generation left*. Polity.

Milestone, K. (2015). Gender and the cultural industries. In *The Routledge companion to the cultural industries* (pp. 501–511). https://doi.org/10.4324/9781315725437-55

Miliband, R. (2009). *The state in capitalist society*. Fernwood Press.

Milkman, R. (2016). *On gender, labor, and inequality*. University of Illinois Press.

Miller, T. (2004). A view from a fossil: The new economy, creativity and consumption – two or three things I don't believe in. *International Journal of Cultural Studies*, 7(1), 55–65.

Miller, T. (2009). Can natural luddites make things explode or travel faster? The new humanities, cultural policy studies, and creative industries. In *Media industries: History, theory, and method* (pp. 184–198). Wiley.

Miller, T. (2010). Culture + Labour = Precariat. *Communication and Critical/Cultural Studies*, 7(10), 99–102.

Miller, T. (2015). Hollywood cognitarians. In K. Oakley and J. Lewis (Eds.), *The Routledge companion to the cultural industries* (pp. 319–329). Routledge.

Miller, T. (2016). The new international division of cultural labor revisited. *Revista ICONO14. Revista Científica de Comunicación y Tecnologías Emergentes*, 14(2), 97. https://doi.org/10.7195/ri14.v14i2.992

Miller, T., Govil, N., McMurria, J., Maxwell, R., & Wang, T. (2004). *Global Hollywood, 2*. British Film Institute.

Miller, T., & Maxwell, R. (Eds.). (2005). The cultural labor issue. *Social Semiotics*, 15(3), 261–360.

Mills, C. W. (1954). *White collar: The American middle classes*. Oxford University Press.

Mills, C. W. (1956). *The Power Elite*. Oxford University Press.

Mills, C. W. (2006). The cultural apparatus. In *Power, politics and people* (pp. 43–96). Oxford University Press. https://doi.org/10.1075/pbns.144.04reh

Milner, R. M. (2009). Working for the text: Fan labor and the new organization. *International Journal of Cultural Studies*, 12(5), 491–508. https://doi.org/10.1177/1367877909337861

Min, S. (2019). 86% of young Americans want to become a social media influencer. CBS. https://www.cbsnews.com/news/social-media-influencers-86-of-young-americans-want-to-become-one/

Minardi, S. (2024). Unions, technology and social class inequalities in the US, 1984–2019. *Work, Employment and Society*, https://doi.org/10.1177/09500170241229277

Mirrlees, T. (2013). *Global entertainment media: Between cultural imperialism and cultural globalization*. Routledge.

Mirrlees, T. (2015). Reality TV's embrace of the intern. *TripleC: Communication, Capitalism & Critique*, 13(2), 404–422. https://doi.org/10.31269/triplec.v13i2.605

Mirrlees, T. (2016a). *Hearts and mines: The US empire's culture industry*. UBC Press.

Mirrlees, T. (2016b). Global Hollywood's suicide squad: Made in Canada, for Warner Bros. *Oshawa This Week/Metrolandmedia*. http://www.durhamregion.com/opinion-story/6841950-global-hollywood-s-suicide-squad-made-in-canada-for-warner-bros/C

Mirrlees, T. (2016c). Pokemon Go's precarious "Playlabour": Real work, augmenting the economy. *Oshawa This Week/Metrolandmedia*. http://www.durhamregion.com/opinion-story/6787664-pok-mon-go-s-precarious-play-bour-real-work-augmenting-the-economy/

Mirrlees, T. (2016d). Reality TV's low-wage and no-wage work. *Alternate Routes: A Journal of Critical Social Research*, 27. https://alternateroutes.ca/index.php/ar/article/view/22398

Mirrlees, T. (2016e). Writers' rights: Freelance journalism in a digital age. *Journal of Labor and Society*. https://onlinelibrary.wiley.com/doi/abs/10.1111/wusa.12292

Mirrlees, T. (2018). Global Hollywood: An entertainment imperium, by integration. *Cineaction*. http://cineaction.ca/CURRENT/GLOBAL-HOLLYWOODAN-ENTERTAINMENT-IMPERIUM-BY-INTEGRATION/

Mirrlees, T. (2020). Socialists on social media platforms: Communicating within and against digital capitalism. In L. Panitch & G. Albo (Eds.), *Beyond digital capitalism: Socialist register*. Monthly Review Press.

Mirrlees, T. (2021a). Getting at Gafam's "Power" in society: A structural-relational framework. *Heliotrope*. https://heliotropejournal.net/helio/gafams-power-in-society

Mirrlees, T (2021b). GAFAM and hate content moderation: Deplatforming and deleting the alt-right. In Mathieu Deflem and Derek M. D. Silva (Eds.), *Media and law: Between free speech and censorship* (pp. 81–97). Emerald Publishing.

Mirrlees, T. (2023a). The socialist project on social media platforms. *South Atlantic Quarterly (Special Issue: Beyond the Echo Chamber: The Tactical Use of Social Media in Social Movements)*, 122(4), 697–712.

Mirrlees, T. (2023b). Ten postulates of a media imperialism framework: For critical research on China's media power and influence in the global south. *Global Media and China*. Online First.

Mirrlees, T. (2023c). A new cultural imperialist rivalry? A political economy of communication, for neither Washington nor Beijing. In Lee Artz (Ed.), *Global media dialogues: Industry, politics and culture* (pp. 193–233). Routledge.

Mirrlees, T. (2024). The US and China's digital tech war: A new rivalry within and beyond the US empire? In Greg Albo (Ed.), *A New global geometry? Socialist register 2024* (pp. 105–140). Merlin Press.

Mirrlees, T., & Alvi, S. (2019). *EdTech inc.: Selling, automating and globalizing higher education in the digital age*. Routledge. https://doi.org/10.4324/9780429343940

Mittal, N., Saif, I., & Ammanath, B. (2022). Fueling the AI transformation: Four key actions powering widespread value from AI, right now. *Deloitte's State of AI in the Enterprise*. https://www2.deloitte.com/content/dam/Deloitte/us/Documents/deloitte-analytics/us-ai-institute-state-of-ai-fifth-edition.pdf

Molotch, H., & Lester, M. (1974). News as purposive behavior. *American Sociological Review*, 39(1), 101–112. http://www.jstor.org/stable/2094279?origin=crossref

Moreschi, B., Pereira, G., & Cozman, F. G. (2020). The Brazilian workers in amazon mechanical Turk: Dreams and realities of ghost workers. *Revista Contracampo*, 39(1). https://doi.org/10.22409/contracampo.v39i1.38252

Morris, L., & Lips-Wiersma, M. (2009). Discriminating between 'Meaningful Work' and the 'Management of meaning. *Journal of Business Ethics*, 88(3), 491–511.

Morris, W. (1885). Useful work versus useless toil. Marxist Internet Archive. https://www.marxists.org/archive/morris/works/1884/useful.htm

Mosco, V. (2008). Trade unions and worker movements in the North American communications industries. *Work Organisation, Labour and Globalisation*, 2(1). https://doi.org/10.13169/workorgalaboglob.2.1.0024

Mosco, V. (2009). *The political economy of communication*. Sage.

Mosco, V. (2011). The political economy of labor. In *The Handbook of political economy of communications* (pp. 358–380). https://doi.org/10.1002/9781444395402.ch16

Mosco, V., & Kaye, L. (2000). Questioning the concept of the audience. In *Consuming audiences?: Production and reception in media research* (pp. 31–46). Hampton Press.

Mosco, V., & McKercher, C. (2008). *The laboring of communication: Will knowledge workers of the world unite?* Lexington Books.

Mosco, V., & Wasko, J. (1983). *Critical communications review: Volume I: Labor, the working class and the media*. Ablex Publishing Corporation.

Moss, S. (2023). Microsoft data center contractor fired workers for protesting wage theft, union claims. DCD. https://www.datacenterdynamics.com/en/news/microsoft-data-center-contractor-fired-workers-for-protesting-wage-theft-union-claims/

Moulaï, K., Islam, G., Manning, S., & Terlinden, L. (2022). "All too human" or the emergence of a techno-induced feeling of being less-able: Identity work, ableism and new service technologies. *International Journal of Human Resource Management*, 33(22), 4499–4531. https://doi.org/10.1080/09585192.2022.2066982

Mould, O. (2018). *Against creativity*. Verso.

Morgan, G., & Nelligan, P. (2018). *The creativity hoax: Precarious work in the gig economy*. Anthem.

Mueller, G. (2012). Reality TV and the flexible future. *Jacobin*. https://www.jacobinmag.com/2012/10/reality-t-v-and-flexible-future/
Mueller, G. (2021). *Breaking things at work: The luddites were right about why you hate your job*. Verso.
Muirhead, R. (2007). *Just Work*. https://doi.org/10.4159/9780674041271
Muldoon, J. (2020). *The Co-operativist Challenge to the Platform Economy The Rise of Platform Co-operativism*. https://autonomy.work/wp-content/uploads/2020/09/Muldoon.pdf
Muldoon, J. (2023). *Platform socialism: How to reclaim our digital future from big tech*. Pluto.
Muldoon, J., Graham, M., & Cant, C. (2024, July 12). Opinion: What's behind the AI boom? Exploited humans. Los Angeles Times. https://www.latimes.com/opinion/story/2024-07-12/artificial-intelligence-workers-labor-feeding-the-machine
Murdock, G. (1978). Blindspots about Western Marxism: A reply to Dallas Smythe. *CTheory*, 2(2), 109–115.
Murdock, G. (2000). Peculiar commodities: Audiences at large in the world of goods. In *Consuming audiences?: Production and reception in media research* (pp. 46–47). Hampton Press.
Murdock, G. (2002). Back to work: Cultural labor in altered times. In *Cultural work: Understanding the cultural industries* (pp. 15–36). https://doi.org/10.4324/9780203995020-8
Murray, C. (2015). A framework for cultural labour: Shoring up the good jobs, well done. In *The Routledge companion to the cultural industries* (pp. 427–441). https://doi.org/10.4324/9781315725437-48
Murray, S., & Ouellette, L. (2009). *Reality TV: Remaking television culture*. New York University Press.
Nadella, S. (2019). *Hit refresh: The quest to rediscover Microsoft's soul and imagine a better future for everyone*. Harper Business.
Nagele-Piazza, L. (2021, February 5). *Google settles pay and hiring bias case for $3.8 million*. Society of Human Resources Management. https://www.shrm.org/topics-tools/employment-law-compliance/google-settles-pay-hiring-bias-case-3-8-million
Nakamura, L. (2009). Don't hate the player, hate the game: The racialization of labor in World of Warcraft. *Critical Studies in Media Communication*, 26(2), 128–144. https://doi.org/10.1080/15295030902860252
Napoli, P. M. (2010). Revisiting 'Mass Communication' and the "work" of the audience in the new media environment. *Media, Culture and Society*, 32(3), 505–516. https://doi.org/10.1177/0163443710361658
Napoli, P. M. (2014). On automation in media industries: Integrating algorithmic media production into media industries scholarship. *Media Industries Journal*, 1(1), 33–38. https://doi.org/10.3998/mij.15031809.0001.107
Nario-Redmond, M. R. (2019). *Ableism: The causes and consequences of disability prejudice*. Wiley-Blackwell.
Naudin, A. (2019). *Cultural entrepreneurship: The cultural Worker's experience of entrepreneurship*. Routledge.
Neff, G. (2012). *Venture labor: Work and the burden of risk in innovative industries*. MIT Press.
Neff, G., Wissinger, E., & Zukin, S. (2005). Entrepreneurial labor among cultural producers: 'Cool' jobs in 'Hot' industries. *Social Semiotics*, 15(3), 307–334.
Negus, K. (1992). *Producing pop: Culture and conflict in the popular music industry*. Routledge.

Neilsen, M., & Mailes, G. (1995). *Hollywood's other blacklist: Union struggles in the studio system*. British Film Institute.

Neilson, B., & Rossiter, N. (2008). Precarity as a political concept, or, Fordism as exception. *Theory, Culture and Society, 25*(7–8), 51–72. https://doi.org/10.1177/0263276408097796

Nelson, C. (2023, January 4). Big-name companies where workers are fighting to unionize. *Cheapism*. https://blog.cheapism.com/companies-that-are-unionizing/

Nelson, T. D. (Ed.). (2002). *Ageism: Stereotyping and prejudice against older persons*. MIT Press.

Nemkova, E., Demirel, P., & Baines, L. (2019). In search of meaningful work on digital freelancing platforms: The case of design professionals. *New Technology, Work and Employment, 34*(3), 226–243. https://doi.org/10.1111/ntwe.12148

Newcomb, H. M., & Alley, R. S. (1982). The producer as artist: Commercial television. In J. S. Ettema & D. C. Whitney (Eds.), *Individuals in mass media organizations: Creativity and constraint* (pp. 69–89). SAGE.

Newton, C. (2019, February 25). The trauma floor. *The Verge*. https://www.theverge.com/2019/2/25/18229714/cognizant-facebook-content-moderator-interviews-trauma-working-conditions-arizona

Newton, C. (2020, May 12). Facebook will pay $52 million in settlement with moderators who developed PTSD on the job. *The Verge*. https://www.theverge.com/2020/5/12/21255870/facebook-content-moderator-settlement-scola-ptsd-mental-health

Ngai, P., & Chan, J. (2012). Global capital, the state, and Chinese workers: The Foxconn experience. *Modern China, 38*(4), 383–410. https://doi.org/10.1177/0097700412447164

Nguyen, J. (2023a, June 8). How much less are screenwriters getting paid compared to what they used to? *NPR Marketplace*. https://www.marketplace.org/2023/06/08/how-much-less-are-screenwriters-getting-paid-compared-to-what-they-used-to/

Nguyen, M. (2023b). Virtual influencers: meet the AI-generated figures posing as your new online friends – as they try to sell you stuff. *The Conversation*. https://theconversation.com/virtual-influencers-meet-the-ai-generated-figures-posing-as-your-new-online-friends-as-they-try-to-sell-you-stuff-212001

Nguyen, T. (2022, April 22). Gen Z does not dream of labor. *Vox*. https://www.vox.com/the-highlight/22977663/gen-z-antiwork-capitalism

Nichols, L. D. (2021). Gnarly freelancers: Professional Skateboarders' labor and social-media use in the neoliberal economy. *Journal of Sport and Social Issues, 45*(5), 426–446.

Nichols, L. D. (2024). alternative media in alternative sport: Platforming working conditions in professional skateboarding. *Communication & Sport, 0*(0). https://doi.org/10.1177/21674795231223396

Nicoli, M., & Paltrinieri, L. (2019). Platform cooperativism: Some. *South Atlantic Quarterly, 118*(4), 801–819. https://doi.org/10.1215/00382876-7825624

Nieborg, D. B., & Poell, T. (2018). The platformization of cultural production: Theorizing the contingent cultural commodity. *New Media and Society, 20*(11), 4275–4292. https://doi.org/10.1177/1461444818769694

Nieborg, D. B., & van der Graaf, S. (2008). The mod industries? The industrial logic of non-market game production. *European Journal of Cultural Studies, 11*(2), 177–195. https://doi.org/10.1177/1367549407088331

Nielsen, M. (1983). 'Toward a workers' history of the U.S. Film industry. In V. Mosco & J. Wasko (Eds.), *The critical communications review, 1: Labor, the working class, and the media* (pp. 47–84). Ablex.

Nielsen, M., & Mailes, G. (1995). *Hollywood's other blacklist: Union struggles in the studio system*. British Film Institute.
Nixon, H. L. (2014). *The athletic trap: How college sports corrupted the academy*. Johns Hopkins University Press.
Noam, E. (2009). *Media ownership concentration in America*. Oxford University Press.
Noble, D. (1979). *America by design: Science, technology and the rise of corporate capitalism*. Oxford University Press.
Noble, D. (1984). *Forces of production: A social history of industrial automation*. Alfred A. Knopf.
Noble, S. U. (2018). *Algorithms of oppression: How search engines reinforce racism*. New York University Press.
Noble, S. U., & Tynes, B. M. (2016). *The intersectional internet: Race, sex, class and culture online*. Peter Lang Publishing.
Nocera, J., & Strauss, B. (2016). *Indentured: The inside story of the rebellion against the NCAA*. Penguin Random House.
Nolan, H. (2024). The era of abundant labor reporting is coming to an end. *In These Times*. https://inthesetimes.com/article/labor-unions-journalism-media-layoffs
Nondo, N. (2023). Facing disturbing content daily, online moderators in Africa want better protections and a fair wage. *CBC*. https://www.cbc.ca/radio/thecurrent/content-moderators-union-social-media-ai-1.6848949
Noonan, C. (2015). Constructing creativities: Higher education and the cultural industries workforce. In K. Oakley & J. O'Connor (Eds.), *The Routledge companion to the cultural industries*. Routledge.
Oakley, A. (2019). *The sociology of housework*. Policy Press.
O'Brien, A. (2015). Producing television and reproducing gender. *Television and New Media*, 16(3), 259–274. https://doi.org/10.1177/1527476414557952
O'Brien, A. (2019). *Women, inequality and media work*. Routledge.
O'Brien, N. (2010). Blogging the writers strike: Identity, interaction and engagement for collective action. *Work Organisation, Labour and Globalisation*, 4(2), 126–141. https://doi.org/10.13169/workorgalaboglob.4.2.0126
O'Brien, D., Laurison, D., Miles, A., & Friedman, S. (2016). Are the creative industries meritocratic? An analysis of the 2014 British labour force survey. *Cultural Trends*, 25(2), 116–131. https://doi.org/10.1080/09548963.2016.1170943
O'Brien, D., & Oakley, K. (2015). *Cultural value and inequality: A literature review*. Arts and Humanities Research Council.
O'Carroll, A. (2015). *Working time, knowledge work and post-industrial society*. Palgrave Macmillan.
O'Doherty, D., & Willmott, H. (2009). The decline of labour process analysis and the future sociology of work. *Sociology*, 43(5), 931–951. https://doi.org/10.1177/0038038509340742
O'Donnell, C. (2014). *Developer's dilemma: The secret world of video game developers*. MIT Press.
O'Meara, V. (2019). Weapons of the chic: Instagram influencer engagement pods as practices of resistance to Instagram platform labor. *Social Media + Society*, 5(4), 2056305119879671.
O'Neill, E. E. (2019). Influencing the future: Compensating children in the age of social-media influencer marketing. *Stan. Law Review*, 72, 42.
O'Reilly, A., & Garrett, P. M. (2019). 'Playing the Game?': The sexual harassment of female social workers across professional workspaces. *International Social Work*, 62(1), 105–118. https://doi.org/10.1177/0020872817706410

Oakley, K., & O'Connor, J. (Eds.). (2015). *The Routledge companion to the cultural industries*. Routledge. https://doi.org/10.4324/9781315725437

Oppenheimer, A. (2019). *The robots are coming! The future of jobs in the age of automation*. Vintage.

Oppenheimer, M. (2001). "We all did voluntary work of some kind": Voluntary work and labour history. *Labour History*, 74(81), 1–11. https://doi.org/10.2307/27516549

Oremus, W. (June 13, 2020). Silicon Valley is playing defense on racism. OneZero. https://onezero.medium.com/silicon-valley-is-playing-defense-on-racism-74151860b0c9

Orlikowski, W. J., & Scott, S. V. (2008). Sociomateriality: Challenging the separation of technology, work and organization. *Academy of Management Annals*, 2(1), 433–474. https://doi.org/10.5465/19416520802211644

Örnebring, H. (2010). Technology and journalism-as-labor: Historical perspectives. *Journalism*, 11(1), 58–74.

Oscar, H. (2000). Audience construction: Race, ethnicity and segmentation in popular media. *Popular Communication Divison*, 15(May), 1–29.

Ouellette, L., & Hay, J. (2008). *Better living through reality TV*. Blackwell Publishing.

Ovetz, R. (2023). AI and the future of work. *Dollars & Sense* (November/12), 2, 9–16.

Owolade, T. (2022, December 18). A rich life in the UK's creative industries is a long shot if you are born poor. *The Guardian*. https://www.theguardian.com/commentisfree/2022/dec/18/uk-creative-industries-low-pay-job-insecurity-diverse-poor

Ozimek, A. (2023, July 5). The simple mistake that almost triggered a recession. *Atlantic*. https://www.theatlantic.com/ideas/archive/2023/07/inflation-jobs-unemployment-recession/674593/.

Ozimek, A. M. (2019a). Outsourcing digital game production: The case of Polish testers. *Television and New Media*, 20(8), 824–835. https://doi.org/10.1177/1527476419851088

Ozimek, A. M. (2019b). The "grey area" of employment relations in the Polish videogame industry. *International Journal of Cultural Studies*, 22(2), 298–314. https://doi.org/10.1177/1367877918821238

Palanivel, T. (2019, January 23) *How cultural and creative industries can power human development in the 21st century*. United Nations Human Development Programme. https://hdr.undp.org/content/how-cultural-and-creative-industries-can-power-human-development-21st-century

Palm, M. (2017). *Technologies of consumer labor: A history of self-service*. Routledge.

Palmer, B. D. (2013). Reconsiderations of class: Precariousness as proletarianization. In L. Panitch, G. Albo, & V. Chibber (Eds.), *Registering class: Socialist register 2014* (pp. 40–62). Merlin Press.

Panagiotopoulos, P. (2021). Digital audiences of union organizing: A social media analysis. *New Technology, Work and Employment*, 36(2), 201–218.

Pang, L. (2015). Art and cultural industries: Autonomy and community. In K. Oakley & J. Lewis (Eds.), *The Routledge companion to the cultural industries* (pp. 45–55). Routledge.

Panitch, L. (2020). Class theory for our time. *Catalyst*, 4(1). https://catalyst-journal.com/2020/06/class-theory-for-our-time.

Panitch, L., & Albo, G. (2016). *Rethinking revolution: Socialist register 2017*. Merlin Press.

Panitch, L., Albo, G., & Chibber, V. (Eds.). *Registering class: Socialist register 2014*. Merlin Press.
Panitch, L., Gindin, S., & Maher, S. (2020). *The socialist challenge today: Syriza, Corbyn, and Sanders*. Haymarket Books.
Papadimitropoulos, E. (2021). Platform capitalism, platform cooperativism, and the commons. *Rethinking Marxism*, *33*(2), 246–262.
Papper, R., & Gerhard, M. (2000). Women and minorities: In radio and TV news. *Communicator*, *54*(7), 36–38.
Pardes, A. (2020, February 24). Silicon Valley ruined work culture. *Wired*. https://www.wired.com/story/how-silicon-valley-ruined-work-culture/
Parent-Rocheleau, X., & Parker, S. K. (2022). Algorithms as work designers: How algorithmic management influences the design of jobs. *Human Resource Management Review*, *32*(3), 1–17. https://doi.org/10.1016/j.hrmr.2021.100838
Parker, M. (2000). The sociology of organizations and the organization of sociology: Some reflections on the making of a division of labour. *Sociological Review*, *48*(1), 124–146. https://doi.org/10.1111/1467-954X.00206
Parkes, T. (2000). Race against the machine: How the digital revolution is accelerating innovation, driving productivity, and irreversibly transforming employment and the economy. *Journal of Psychiatric and Mental Health Nursing*, *7*(2), 185–187.
Pasquale, F. (2015). *The black box society: The secret algorithms that control money and information*. Harvard University Press.
Pasquale, F. (2016). Two narratives of platform capitalism. *Yale Law & Policy Review*, *35*, 309–319.
Paterson, C., Lee, D., Saha, A., & Zoellner, A. (Eds.). (2015). *Advancing media production research*. Palgrave Macmillan.
Paterson, R. (2001). Work histories in television. *Media, Culture and Society*, *23*(4), 495–520. https://doi.org/10.1177/016344301023004005
Patten, D. (2023, September 15). Entertainment partners layoffs: Dozens cut at residuals distributing company. *Deadline*. https://deadline.com/2023/09/layoffs-entertainment-partners-residuals-1235548140/
Paulsen, R. (2014). *Empty labor: Idleness and workplace resistance*. Cambridge University Press.
Peck, J. (2005). Struggling with the creative class. *International Journal of Urban and Regional Research*, *29*(4), 740–770. https://doi.org/10.1111/j.1468-2427.2005.00620.x
Peck, J. (2006). Why we shouldn't be bored with the political economy versus cultural studies debate. *Cultural Critique*, *64*(1), 92–125. https://doi.org/10.1353/cul.2006.0029
Pedersen, M. A., Albris, K., & Seaver, N. (2021). The political economy of attention. *Annual Review of Anthropology*, *50*(1), 309–325. https://doi.org/10.1146/annurev-anthro-101819-110356
Pedro-Carañana, J., Gómez, R., Corrigan, C., & Caballero, F. S. (2024). *Political economy of media and communication: Methodological approaches*. Routledge.
Pellow, D., & Sun-Hee, L. (2002). *The Silicon Valley of dreams: Environmental injustice, immigrant workers, and the high-tech global economy*. New York University Press.
Pendakur, M. (1998). Hollywood north: Film and TV production in Canada. In G. Sussman & J. A. Lent (Eds.), *Global productions: Labor in the making of the "information society"* (pp. 213–238). Hampton Press.
Penix-Tadsen, P., & Frasca, G. (Eds.). (2019). *Video games and the global south*. Carnegie Mellon University.

Bibliography

Percival, N., & Lee, D. (2022). Get up, stand up? Theorizing mobilization in creative work. *Television and New Media*, 23(2), 202–218. https://doi.org/10.1177/1527476420969909

Perlin, R. (2012). *Intern nation: How to earn nothing and earn little in the brave new economy*. Verso.

Perrigo, B. (2022, February 17). Inside Facebook's African sweatshop. *Time*. https://time.com/6147458/facebook-africa-content-moderation-employee-treatment/

Perrigo, B. (2023a, January 10). Under fire, Facebook's "ethical" outsourcing partner quits content moderation work. *Time*. https://time.com/6246018/facebook-sama-quits-content-moderation/

Perrigo, B. (2023b, January 18). Exclusive: OpenAI used Kenyan workers on less than $2 per hour to make ChatGPT less toxic. *Time*. https://time.com/6247678/openai-chatgpt-kenya-workers/

Perrigo, B. (2023c). 150 African Workers for ChatGPT, TikTok and Facebook Vote to Unionize at Landmark Nairobi Meeting. *TIME*. https://time.com/6275995/chatgpt-facebook-african-workers-union/

Perry, L. B., & Perry, R. S. (1963). *A history of the Los Angeles labor movement, 1911–1941*. University of California Press.

Peters, J. (2021, September 8). Google settles with worker allegedly fired for his workplace activism. *The Verge*. https://www.theverge.com/2021/9/8/22663354/google-laurence-berland-workplace-activism-nlrb

Peters, T. (1997). The brand called you. https://www.fastcompany.com/28905/brand-called-you

Peterson, R. A. (1976). The production of culture: A prolegomenon. In R. A. Peterson (Ed.), *The production of culture* (pp. 7–22). SAGE.

Peterson, R. A. (1997). *Creating country music: Fabricating authenticity*. University of Chicago Press.

Peterson, R. A., & Anand, N. (2002). How chaotic careers create orderly fields. In M. A. Peiperl, M. Arthur, & N. Anand (Eds.), *Career creativity: Explorations in the remaking of work* (pp. 257–279). Oxford University Press.

Peterson, R. A., & Anand, N. (2004). The production of culture perspective. *Annual Review of Sociology*, 30(1), 311–334. https://doi.org/10.1146/annurev.soc.30.012703.110557

Peterson, R. A., Kingston, P. W., & Cole, J. R. (1988). The wages of writing: per word, per piece, or perhaps. *Social Forces*, 66(4), 1155. https://doi.org/10.2307/2579464

Peticca-Harris, A., Weststar, J., & McKenna, S. (2015). The perils of project-based work: Attempting resistance to extreme work practices in video game development. *Organization*, 22(4), 570–587. https://doi.org/10.1177/1350508415572509

Phelan, S. (2021). Media critique in a very online world. OpenDemocracy. https://www.opendemocracy.net/en/can-europe-make-it/media-critique-very-online-world/

Phelan, S., & Maeseele, P. (2023). Critiquing "mainstream media" on Twitter: Between moralized suspicion and democratic possibility. *International Journal of Communications*, 17, 4304–4325.

Phelps, O. (1957). A structural model of the U.S. Labor market. *Industrial and Labor Relations Review*, 10, 402–423.

Picard, R. (1989). *Media economics: Concepts and issues*. SAGE.

Pickard, V. (2019). *Democracy without journalism? Confronting the misinformation society*. Oxford University Press.

Pickerill, J., Pottinger, L., & Eghartner, U. (2021). Participatory Activist Research. http://aspect.ac.uk/wp-content/uploads/2021/03/Jenny-Pickerill-A4-Guide.pdf

Pickering, M. (2013). Chavs: The demonization of the working class. *European Journal of Communication*, 28(5), 584–587. https://doi.org/10.1177/0267323113494045

Pietrykowski, B. (2019). *Work*. Polity.

Piketty, T. (2014). *Capital in the twenty-first century*. Harvard University Press.

Pillar, C. (1980, April 24). Silicon valley plant electronic workers win on health and safety issue. *Synapse: The UCSF Student Newspaper*, 24(24).

Pincus, F. L., & Sokoloff, N. (2008). Does "classism" help us to understand class oppression? Race, *Gender and Class*, 15(1/2), 9–23.

Plant, L. (2023). EXCLUSIVE: New survey reveals that many game developers consider their career unsustainable. *IGN*. https://www.ign.com/articles/the-iatse-is-shining-a-light-on-the-video-game-industrys-lack-of-unions-with-a-new-survey

Poell, T., Nieborg, D. N., & Duffy, B. E. (2021). *Platforms and cultural production*. Polity Press.

Policy Research Group of Canada. (2013). The creative economy: Key concepts and literature review highlights. *Canadian Heritage*. https://cch.novascotia.ca/sites/default/files/inline/documents/creative-economy-synthesis_201305.pdf

Pollard, G. (1995). Job satisfaction among news workers: The influence of professionalism, perceptions of organizational structure, and social attributes. *Journalism and Mass Communication Quarterly*, 72(3), 682–697. https://doi.org/10.1177/107769909507200317

Polson, E., Schofield Clark, L., & Gajjala, R. (Eds.). (2021). *The Routledge companion to media and class*. Routledge.

Popiel, P. (2017). 'Boundaryless' in the creative economy: Assessing freelancing on upwork. *Critical Studies in Media Communication*, 34(3), 220–233. https://doi.org/10.1080/15295036.2017.1282618

Posada, J. (2019). From the computer to the streets. *Notes from Below*. https://notesfrombelow.org/article/computer-streets

Posada, J. (2020). *The future of work is here: Toward a comprehensive approach to artificial intelligence and labour*. Ethics of AI in Context.

Posada, J., & Shade, L. (2020). Platform labour discourse: How Hyr targets the "Bucket List Generation". *Democratic Communiqué*, 29(1), 78–96.

Postigo, H. (2016). The socio-technical architecture of digital labor: Converting play into YouTube money. *New Media and Society*, 18(2), 332–349. https://doi.org/10.1177/1461444814541527

Poulantzas, N. (2014). *State, power, socialism*. Verso.

Powdermaker, H. (1950). *Hollywood, the dream factory*. Little, Brown.

Powell, A., & Sang, K. (2015). Everyday experiences of sexism in male-dominated professions: A Bourdieusian perspective. *Sociology*, 49(5), 919–936.

Powell, W. W. (1985). *Getting into print*. University of Chicago Press.

Power, D., & Scott, A. J. (Eds.). (2004). *Cultural industries and the production of culture*. Routledge.

Prahalad, C. K., & Ramaswamy, V. (2000). Co-opting customer competence. *Harvard Business Review*, 78(1), 79–90.

Praslova, L. N. (2022, June 21). An intersectional approach to inclusion at work. *Harvard Business Review*. https://hbr.org/2022/06/an-intersectional-approach-to-inclusion-at-work.

Pratt, A. C. (2005). Cultural industries and public policy. *International Journal of Cultural Policy*, *11*(1), 31–44. https://doi.org/10.1080/10286630500067739

Pratt, A. C. (2009). The creative and cultural economy and the recession. *Geoforum*, *40*(4), 495–496. https://doi.org/10.1016/j.geoforum.2009.05.002

Press, A. (2018). Code Red: Organizing the tech sector. *N+1*, 31. Spring. https://www.nplusonemag.com/issue-31/politics/code-red/.

Press, A. (2019). On the origins of the professional managerial class: An interview with Barbara Ehrenreich. *Dissent*. https://www.dissentmagazine.org/online_articles/on-the-origins-of-the-professional-managerial-class-an-interview-with-barbara-ehrenreich/.

Press, A. N. (202, November 22). Microworkers are "disempowered to a degree previously unseen in capitalist history: an interview with Phil Jones." *Jacobin*. https://jacobin.com/2021/11/microwork-amazon-mechanical-turk-machine-learning

Press, A. N. (2021). The labor beat is dead—Long live the labor beat. *Jacobin*. https://jacobin.com/2021/11/labor-beat-reporting-newspapers-journalism-unions

Preston, J. (2016). *The fantasy of disability: Images of loss in popular culture*. Routledge.

Prince, A. E., & Schwarcz, D. (2019). Proxy discrimination in the age of artificial intelligence and big data. *Iowa Law Review*, *105*, 1257.

Prindle, D. F. (1988). *The politics of glamour: Ideology and democracy in the Screen Actors Guild*. University of Wisconsin Press.

Prins, S. J., McKetta, S., Platt, J., Muntaner, C., Keyes, K. M., & Bates, L. M. (2021). The serpent of their agonies: Exploitation as structural determinant of mental illness. *Epidemiology*, *32*(2), 303–309. https://doi.org/10.1097/EDE.0000000000001304.

Psarras, E., Stein, K., & Shah, P. (2023). You're not here for the right reasons! *Feminist Media Studies*, *23*(2), 571–587. https://doi.org/10.1080/14680777.2021.1984276

Puette, W. (1992). *Through jaundiced eyes: How the media view organized labor*. Cornell University Press.

Pullin, G. (2009). *Design meets disability*. MIT Press.

Pulver, A. (2017). Rogue One VFX head: 'We didn't do anything Peter Cushing would've objected to'. *The Guardian*. https://www.theguardian.com/film/2017/jan/16/rogue-one-vfx-jon-knoll-peter-cushing-ethics-of-digital-resurrections

PWC (PricewaterhouseCooper). (2023). Global entertainment and media outlook, 2023–2027. https://www.pwc.com/gx/en/industries/tmt/media/outlook.html

Qiu, J. (2016a). *Goodbye iSlave: A manifesto for digital abolition*. University of Illinois Press.

Qiu, J. (2016b). Social media on the picket line. *Media, Culture & Society*, *38*(4), 619–633.

Qiu, J. L., Gregg, M., & Crawford, K. (2014). Circuits of labour: A labour theory of the iPhone era. *TripleC: Communication, Capitalism & Critique*, *12*(2), 564–581.

Quinn, E. (2012). Closing doors: Hollywood, affirmative action, and the revitalization of conservative racial politics. *Journal of American History*, *99*(2), 466–491. https://doi.org/10.1093/jahist/jas302

Quinn, E. (2013). Black talent and conglomerate Hollywood: Will Smith, Tyler Perry, and the continuing significance of race. *Popular Communication*, *11*(3), 196–210. https://doi.org/10.1080/15405702.2013.810070

Rabinow, P. (Ed.). (1984). *Foucault reader*. Pantheon.

Rabinow, P., & Rose, N. (Eds.). (1994). *The essential foucault*. The New Press.

Racker, M. (2022, November 1). How democrats are using social media influencers to get out the vote. *Time*. https://time.com/6227149/democrats-tiktok-influencers-midterms-2022/

Raddats, C., Kowalkowski, C., Benedettini, O., Burton, J., & Gebauer, H. (2019). Servitization: A contemporary thematic review of four major research streams, *Industrial Marketing Management*, 83, 207–223. https://doi.org/10.1016/j.indmarman.2019.03.015

Raghavan, M., Barocas, S., Kleinberg, J., & Levy, K. (2020). Mitigating Bias in Algorithmic Hiring: Evaluating Claims and Practices. FAACT Proceedings. https://dl.acm.org/doi/10.1145/3351095.3372828

Randle, K., Forson, C., & Calveley, M. (2015). Towards a Bourdieusian analysis of the social composition of the UK film and television workforce. *Work, Employment and Society*, 29(4), 590–606. https://doi.org/10.1177/0950017014542498

Rangarajan, S. (2018, June 25). Here's the clearest picture of Silicon Valley's diversity yet: It's bad. But some companies are doing less bad. *Reveal news*. https://www.revealnews.org/article/heres-the-clearest-picture-of-silicon-valleys-diversity-yet/

Ransome, P. (2020). *Sociology and the future of work: Contemporary discourses and debates*. Routledge.

Raphael, C. (1997). The political economic origins of Reali-TV. *Jump Cut*, 41(2), 102–109.

Rapuano, D. (2009). Working at fun: Conceptualizing leisurework. *Current Sociology*, 57(5), 617–636. https://doi.org/10.1177/0011392109337648

Rauchberg, J. S. (2022). #Shadowbanned: Queer, trans, and disabled creator responses to algorithmic oppression on TikTok. In P. Pain (Ed.), *LGBTQ digital cultures: A global perspective* (pp. 196–209). Routledge.

Ravindran, M. (2020, February 12). U.K. film and TV industry faces mental health crisis: "seismic shifts need to happen". *Variety*. https://variety.com/2020/film/directors/uk-film-tv-mental-health-crisis-film-and-tv-charity-1203502271/.

Rawick, G. (1969). Working class self-activity. *Radical America*, 3(2), 23–31.

Rawls, J. (1985). Justice as fairness: Political not metaphysical. *Philosophy and Public Affairs*, 14(3), 223–251.

Rawlins, J. O. (2024). *Imagining the method*. University of Texas Press.

Read, M. (2019, February 28). Who pays for Silicon Valley's hidden costs? *New York Magazine Intelligencer*. https://nymag.com/intelligencer/2019/02/the-shadow-workforce-of-facebooks-content-moderation.html

Reagan, M. B. (2021). *Intersectional class struggle: Theory and practice*. AK Press.

Reckwitz, A. (2017). *The invention of creativity: Modern society and the culture of the new*. Polity Press.

Redman, T., & Mathews, B. P. (2002). Managing services: Should we be having fun? *Service Industries Journal*, 22(3), 51–62. https://doi.org/10.1080/714005085

Regev, R. (2018). *Working in Hollywood: How the studio system turned creativity into labor*. University of North Carolina Press.

Reich, R. B. (2021). *The system: Who rigged it, how we fix it*. Penguin Random House Canada.

Reichenberger, I. (2018). Digital nomads–a quest for holistic freedom in work and leisure. *Annals of Leisure Research*, 21(3), 364–380. https://doi.org/10.1080/11745398.2017.1358098

Reid, E. (2015). Embracing, passing, revealing, and the ideal worker image: How people navigate expected and experienced professional identities. *Organization Science*, 26(4), 997–1017. https://doi.org/10.1287/orsc.2015.0975

Reilly, P. (2017). Disney's $3.8 million labor violation: Costumes push paychecks below minimum wage. *The Christian Science Monitor.* https://www.csmonitor.com/Business/2017/0318/Disney-s-3.8-million-labor-violation-Costumes-push-paychecks-below-minimum-wage

Reuters. (2022, June 13). Microsoft union enter into labor neutrality agreement. https://www.reuters.com/technology/microsoft-union-enter-into-labor-neutrality-agreement-2022-06-13/.

Rhee, J. (2018). *The robotic imaginary: The human and the price of dehumanized labor.* University of Minnesota Press.

Rice, L., Hayes, Dade, & Andreeva, N. (2023, April 19). Bracing for the bloodbath: Disney layoffs to resume Monday. *Deadline.* https://deadline.com/2023/04/disney-layoffs-coming-tv-film-departments-1235329916/

Richman, L. S., & Zucker, A. N. (2019). Quantifying intersectionality: An important advancement for health inequality research. *Social Science and Medicine, 226,* 246–248. https://doi.org/10.1016/j.socscimed.2019.01.036

Riedl, M. J., Lukito, J., & Woolley, S. C. (2023). Political influencers on social media: An introduction. *Social Media + Society, 9*(2). https://doi.org/10.1177/20563051231177938

Rifkin, J. (1995). *The end of work: The decline of the global labor force and the dawn of the post-market era.* Putnam Publishing Group.

Rinehart, J. W. (2006). *The tyranny of work: Alienation and the labour process.* Nelson Canada.

Ritzer, G. (2009). *The McDonaldization of society.* Pine Forge Press. https://doi.org/10.4135/9781446279007

Ritzer, G. (1983). The "McDonaldization" of society. *Journal of American Culture, 6*(1), 100–107. https://doi.org/10.1111/j.1542-734X.1983.0601_100.x

Ritzer, G., & Jurgenson, N. (2010). Production, consumption, prosumption: The nature of capitalism in the age of the digital "prosumer". *Journal of Consumer Culture, 10*(1), 13–36. https://doi.org/10.1177/1469540509354673

Ritzer, G., & Lair, C. (2007). Outsourcing: Globalization and beyond. In G. Ritzer (Ed.), *Blackwell companion to globalization* (pp. 307–329). Blackwell.

Ritzer, G., & Leidner, R. (1994). fast food, fast talk: Service work and the routinization of everyday life. *Contemporary Sociology, 23*(3), 430. https://doi.org/10.2307/2075368

Roberts, M. J. (2022). Television at work: Industrial media and American labor. *Contemporary Sociology: A Journal of Reviews, 51*(1), 51–53. https://doi.org/10.1177/00943061211062906m

Roberts, S. T. (2016). Commercial content moderation: Digital laborers' dirty work. http://ir.lib.uwo.ca/commpub/12.

Roberts, S. T. (2019). *Behind the screen: Content moderation in the shadows of social media.* Yale University Press.

Robertson, R. (1992). *Globalization: Social theory and global culture.* Sage.

Rodgers, J. (2015). Jobs for creatives outside the creative industries: A study of creatives working in the Australian manufacturing industry. *Creative Industries Journal, 8*(1), 3–23. https://doi.org/10.1080/17510694.2015.1034572

Rodino-Colocino, M. (2012, November 9). Participant activism: Exploring a methodology for scholar-activists through lessons learned as a precarious labor organizer. *Communication, Culture and Critique, 5*(4), 541–562. https://doi.org/10.1111/j.1753-9137.2012.01140.x

Rodino-Colocino, M., Wolfson, T., Dolber, B., & Kumanyika, C. (Eds.). (2021). *The gig economy: Workers and media in the age of convergence.* Routledge. https://doi.org/10.4324/9781003140054

Rodnitzky, J. L., & Leab, D. J. (1971). A union of individuals: The formation of the American newspaper Guild, 1933–1936. *American Quarterly, 23*(3), 315. https://doi.org/10.2307/2711780

Romano, P., & Stone, R. (1946). *The American worker.* Facing Reality Publishing Company.

Roose, K. (2022). An A.I.-generated picture won an art prize. Artists aren't happy. *New York Times.* https://www.nytimes.com/2022/09/02/technology/ai-artificial-intelligence-artists.html

Rosales, A., & Fernández-Ardèvol, M. (2020). Ageism in the era of digital platforms. *Convergence, 26*(5–6), 1074–1087. https://doi.org/10.1177/1354856520930905

Rosales, A., & Svensson, J. (2021). Perceptions of age in contemporary tech. *Nordicom Review, 42*(1), 79–91. https://doi.org/10.2478/nor-2021-0021

Rosalind, G. (2002). Cool, creative and egalitarian? Exploring gender in project-based new media work in Euro. *Information, Communication & Society, 5*(1), 70–89.

Rosalsky, G. (2023). Affirmative action for rich kids: It's more than just legacy admissions. *NPR.* https://www.npr.org/sections/money/2023/07/24/1189443223/affirmative-action-for-rich-kids-its-more-than-just-legacy-admissions

Rosenfeld, J. (2021). *You're paid what you're worth: And other myths of the modern economy.* Belknap Press.

Ross, A. (2000). The mental labor problem. *Social Text, 18*(2), 1–31. https://doi.org/10.1215/01642472-18-2_63-1

Ross, A. (2001). No-collar labor in America's "new economy". *Socialist Register, 37,* 76–87.

Ross, A. (2003). *No collar: The human workplace and its hidden costs.* Temple University Press.

Ross, A. (2007). *Fast boat to China: High-tech outsourcing and the consequences of free trade: Lessons from Shanghai.* Vintage Book Company.

Ross, A. (2008). The new geography of work. *Theory, Culture and Society, 25*(7–8), 31–49. https://doi.org/10.1177/0263276408097795

Ross, A. (2009). *Nice work if you can get it: Life and labor in precarious times.* New York University Press.

Ross, A. (2013). In search of the lost paycheck. In T. Scholz (Ed.), *Digital labor: The internet as playground and factory* (pp. 13–32). Routledge.

Ross, A. (2014). Reality television and the political economy of amateurism. In L. Ouellette (Ed.), *A companion to reality television* (pp. 29–39). Blackwell.

Ross, A. (2015). *The gulf: High culture/hard labour.* OR Books.

Ross, M. (1941). *Stars and strikes: Unionization of Hollywood.* Columbia University Press.

Ross, S., & Savage, L. (2018). *Labor under attack: Anti-unionism in Canada.* Fernwood.

Ross, S., & Savage, L. (2023). *Building a better world: An introduction to the labour movement in Canada.* Fernwood.

Rosten, L. (1941). *Hollywood, the movie colony, the movie makers.* Harcourt Publishers, Brace & Co.

Rowbotham, S. (1977). *Hidden from history: 300 years of women's oppression and the fight against it.* Pluto Press.

Ruberg, B. (2019). The precarious labor of queer indie game-making: Who benefits from making video games "better"? *Television and New Media*, 20(8), 778–788. https://doi.org/10.1177/1527476419851090

Ruffino, P. (2021). Workers' visibility and union organizing in the UK videogames industry. *Critical Studies in Media Communication*, 1–14. https://doi.org/10.1080/15295036.2021.1985157

Ruffino, P., & Woodcock, J. (2021). Game workers and the Empire: Unionisation in the UK video game industry. *Games and Culture*, 16(3), 317–328. https://doi.org/10.1177/1555412020947096

Russell, B. (1932) In Praise of Idleness. *Harper's Magazine.* https://harpers.org/archive/1932/10/in-praise-of-idleness/

Russell, S., & Williams, R. (2002). Social shaping of technology: Frameworks, findings and implications for policy with glossary of social shaping concepts. In K. H. Sørensen & R. Williams (Eds.), *Shaping technology, guiding policy: Concepts, spaces and tools* (pp. 37–132). Edward Elgar Publishing.

Ruthizer, J. (2022). *Labor pains: A tale of kicking, discomfort, and joy on the broadcasting delivery table.* Archway Publishing.

Ryan, B. (1992). *Making capital from culture: The corporate form of capitalist cultural production.* Walter de Gruyter.

Ryan, M. (2023). *Burn it down: Power, complicity, and a call for change in Hollywood.* Mariner Books.

Ryan, J., & Wentworth, W. M. (1998). *Media and society: The production of culture in the mass media.* Prentice Hall.

Ryan, W. (1992). *Blaming the victim.* Vintage Book Company.

Saad, L. (2023, August 30). More in U.S. See Unions Strengthening and Want it That Way. https://news.gallup.com/poll/510281/unions-strengthening.aspx.

Saha, A. (2018). *Race and the cultural industries.* Polity Press.

Sainato, M. (2023, February 17). Tesla fires more than 30 workers after union drive announcement. *The Guardian.* https://www.theguardian.com/technology/2023/feb/17/tesla-fires-workers-union-buffalo

Salamon, E. (2015). (De)valuing intern labour: Journalism internship pay rates and collective representation in Canada. *TripleC: Communication, Capitalism & Critique*, 13(2), 438–458. https://doi.org/10.31269/triplec.v13i2.573

Salamon, E. (2016). E-lancer resistance: Precarious freelance journalists use digital communications to refuse rights-grabbing contracts. *Digital Journalism*, 4(8), 980–1000. https://doi.org/10.1080/21670811.2015.1116953

Salamon, E. (2020). Digitizing freelance media labor: A class of workers negotiates entrepreneurialism and activism. *New Media and Society*, 22(1), 105–122. https://doi.org/10.1177/1461444819861958

Salamon, E. (2023a). Converging media unions: A labor history of newsworkers in a predigital age. *International Journal of Communications*, 17, 5574–5586.

Salamon, E. (2023b). Communicative labor resistance practices: Organizing digital news media unions and precarious work. *Communication Theory* [Advance online publication], 33(4), 186–196. https://doi.org/10.1093/ct/qtac023

Salamon, E. (2023c). Happiness in newsroom contracts: Communicative resistance for digital work and life satisfaction. *Media, Culture and Society.* https://doi.org/10.1177/01634437231191353

Salamon, E. (2023d). Media unions' online resistance rhetoric: Reproducing social movement genres of organizational communication. *Management Communication Quarterly*, 37(2), 368–395. https://doi.org/10.1177/08933189221097067

Salamon, E. (2018a). Freelance journalists' rights, contracts, labor organizing, and digital resistance. In S. A. Eldridge II & B. Franklin (Eds.), *The*

Routledge handbook of developments in digital journalism studies (pp. 186–197). Routledge.
Salamon, E. (2018b). The "free press" of unionized journalists and students: An alternative journalistic collaboration. *Journalism Practice*, *12*(5), 565–584. https://doi.org/10.1080/17512786.2017.1335607
Salem, M. (2018, August 2). Hollywood is as white, straight and male as ever. *The New York Times*. https://www.nytimes.com/2018/08/02/arts/hollywood-movies-diversity.html
Sallaz, J. J. (2018). Working the phones: Control and resistance in call centres. *Contemporary Sociology: A Journal of Reviews*, *47*(2), 241–243. https://doi.org/10.1177/0094306118755396vv
Sandoval, M. (2013). Foxconned labour as the dark side of the information age: Working conditions at Apple's contract manufacturers in China. *TripleC: Communication, Capitalism & Critique*, *11*(2), 318–347. https://doi.org/10.31269/triplec.v11i2.481
Sandoval, M. (2016). Fighting precarity with co-operation? Worker co-operatives in the cultural sector. *New Formations*, *88*(88), 51–68. https://doi.org/10.3898/NEWF.88.04.2016
Sandoval, M. (2018). From passionate labour to compassionate work: Cultural co-ops, do what you love and social change. *European Journal of Cultural Studies*, *21*(2), 113–129. https://doi.org/10.1177/1367549417719011
Sandoval, M. (2020). Entrepreneurial activism? Platform cooperativism between subversion and co-optation. *Critical Sociology*, *46*(6), 801–817. https://doi.org/10.1177/0896920519870577
Sandoval, M., Fuchs, C., Prodnik, J. A., Sevignani, S., & Allmer, T. (2014). Philosophers of the world unite! Theorising digital labour and virtual work – Definitions, dimensions and forms. *Triple C: Communication, Capitalism and Critique*, *12*(2), 464–801.
Saraiya, S. (2021, September 30). These Hollywood horror stories could Inspire the biggest industry strike since World War II. *Vanity Fair*. https://www.vanityfair.com/hollywood/2021/09/iatse-stories-instagram-strike-amptp
Savage, C. (2023, May 14). Child social media stars have few protections. Illinois aims to fix that. *AP*. https://apnews.com/article/tiktok-influencer-child-social-media-illinois-law-65a837e2ba7151c91c17f69b08862022.
Saval, N. (2014). *Cubed: A secret history of the workplace*. Doubleday.
Savaş, Ö, Greenwood, R. M., Blankenship, B. T., Stewart, A. J., & Deaux, K. (2021). All immigrants are not alike: Intersectionality matters in views of immigrant groups. *Journal of Social and Political Psychology*, *9*(1), 86–104. https://doi.org/10.5964/jspp.5575
Sayer, A. (2009). Contributive justice and meaningful work. *Res Publica*, *15*(1), 1–16. https://doi.org/10.1007/s11158-008-9077-8
Schaffer, E. (2023, October 26). Ageism in tech: A history, what we can do to help, and more. Educative. https://www.educative.io/blog/ageism-in-tech
Schiffer, Z. (2021, January 21). Instacart is firing every employee who voted to unionize. *The Verge*. https://www.theverge.com/2021/1/21/22242676/instacart-firing-every-union-employee-coronavirus-pandemic
Schiller, D. (2000). *Digital capitalism*. MIT Press.
Schiller, D. (2014). *Digital depression*. University of Illinois Press.
Schlender, B., & Tezeli, R. (2016). *Becoming Steve Jobs*. Crown Currency.
Scholz, T. (Ed.). (2012). *Digital labor: The internet as playground and factory*. Routledge.

Scholz, T. (2017). *Uberworked and underpaid: How workers are disrupting the digital economy.* John Wiley & Sons.
Scholz, T. (2016a). Platform cooperativism: Challenging the corporate sharing economy. Rosa Luxemburg Stiftung. https://rosalux.nyc/wp-content/uploads/2020/11/RLS-NYC_platformcoop.pdf. New York Office.
Scholz, T., & Schneider, N. (Eds.). (2016). *Ours to hack and to own.* OR Books.
Schomer, A. (2023, December 1). Generative AI in film and TV: A special report. *Variety.* https://variety.com/vip-special-reports/generative-ai-in-film-tv-1235792168/
Schomer, A. (2023, April 28). Avatars as Actors: Will AI Unleash Celebrity 'Simulation Rights'? *Variety.* https://variety.com/2023/digital/news/avatars-as-actors-will-ai-unleash-celeb-simulation-rights-1235583875/
Schöpke-Gonzalez, A. M., Atreja, S., Shin, H. N., Ahmed, N., & Hemphill, L. (2022). Why do volunteer content moderators quit? Burnout, conflict, and harmful behaviors. *New Media & Society.* https://doi.org/10.1177/14614448221138529
Schor, J. (1992). *The overworked American: The unexpected decline of leisure.* Basic Books.
Schor, J. B. (2020). Gig worker employment fights like those in California pit flexibility against livable wage – But "platform cooperatives" could ensure workers get both. *The conversation,* https://theconversation.com/gig-worker-employment-fights-like-those-in-california-pit-flexibility-against-a-livable-wage-but-platform-cooperatives-could-ensure-workers-get-both-145609
Schradie, J. (2019). *The revolution that wasn't: How digital activism favors conservatives.* Harvard University Press.
Schradie, J. (2021). Context, class, and community: A methodological framework for studying labor organizing and digital unionizing. *Information, Communication & Society, 24*(5), 700–716.
Schreier, J. (2017). *Blood, sweat, and pixels: The triumphant, turbulent stories behind how video games are made.* HarperCollins.
Schreier, J. (2021). *Press reset: Ruin and recovery in the video game industry.* Grand Central Publishing.
Schudson, M. (1988). The profession of journalism in the United States. In N. O. Hatch (Ed.), *The professions in American history, 1988* (pp. 145–161). University of Notre Dame Press.
Schudson, M. (1989). The sociology of news production. *Media, Culture and Society, 11*(3), 263–282. https://doi.org/10.1177/016344389011003002
Schudson, M. (2003). *The sociology of news.* W. W. Norton.
Schuessler, K., & Becker, G. S. (1958). The economics of discrimination. *American Sociological Review, 23*(1), 108. https://doi.org/10.2307/2088646
Schwartz, A. (1982). Meaningful work. *Ethics, 92*(4), 634–646. https://doi.org/10.1086/292380
Schwartz, T. P., Deal, T. E., & Kennedy, A. A. (1983). corporate cultures: The rites and rituals of corporate life. *Contemporary Sociology, 12*(5), 566. https://doi.org/10.2307/2068737
Scolere, L., Pruchniewska, U., & Duffy, B. E. (2018). Constructing the platform-specific self-brand: The labor of social media promotion. *Social Media + Society, 4*(3). https://doi.org/10.1177/2056305118784768
Scott, A. (1988). *Metropolis: From the division of labor to urban form.* University of California Press.
Scott, A. (2005). *On Hollywood: The place, the industry.* Princeton University Press.
Scott, S. V., & Orlikowski, W. J. (2013). Sociomateriality—Taking the wrong turning? A response to mutch. *Information and Organization, 23*(2), 77–80. https://doi.org/10.1016/j.infoandorg.2013.02.003

Scott-Campbell, C., & Williams, M. (2020). Validating the workplace dignity scale. *Collabra: Psychology*, 6(1), 31. https://doi.org/10.1525/collabra.337

Sears, A. (2014). *The next new left: A history of the future*. Fernwood Publishing.

Seaver, N. (2017). Algorithms as culture: Some tactics for the ethnography of algorithmic systems. *Big Data and Society*, 4(2), 1–12. https://doi.org/10.1177/2053951717738104

Seaver, N. (2018a). *Computing taste algorithms and the makers of music recommendation*. University of Chicago Press.

Seaver, N. (2018b). What should an anthropology of algorithms do? *Cultural Anthropology*, 33(3), 375–385. https://doi.org/10.14506/ca33.3.04

Seccombe, W. (1974). The housewife and her labour under capitalism. *New Left Review*, 83, 3–24.

Segrave, K. (2007). *Actors organize: A history of union formation efforts in America, 1880–1919*. McFarland & Company.

Segrave, K. (2009). *Film actors organize: Union formation efforts in America, 1912–1937*. McFarland & Company.

Selling, N., & Strimling, P. (2023). Liberal and anti-establishment: An exploration of the political ideologies of American tech workers. *Sociological Review*, 71(6), 1467–1497. https://doi.org/10.1177/00380261231182522

Semuels, A. (2018, January 23). The Internet is enabling a new kind of poorly paid hell. *The Atlantic*, https://www.theatlantic.com/business/archive/2018/01/amazon-mechanical-turk/551192/

Sennett, R. (1998). *The corrosion of character: The personal consequences of work in the new capitalism*. W. W. Norton.

Sennett, R. (2007). *The culture of the new capitalism*. Yale University Press.

Sennett, R., & Cobb, J. (2023). *The hidden injuries of class*. Verso.

Seyferth, P. (2019). Anti-work: A stab in the heart of capitalism. In *Routledge handbook of radical politics* (pp. 374–390). Routledge.

Shakespeare, T. (2013). The social model of disability. In L. J. Davis (Ed.), *The disability studies reader* (pp. 214–221). Routledge.

Shang, R. A., Chen, Y. C., & Liao, H. J. (2006). The value of participation in virtual consumer communities on brand loyalty. *Internet Research*, 16(4), 398–418. https://doi.org/10.1108/10662240610690025

Sharma, S. (2014). *In the meantime: Temporality and cultural politics*. Duke University Press.

Sheldrake, J. (2003). *Management theory*. Thompson.

Shestack, M. (2021, October 12). The ghost workers in the machine. *Jacobin*. https://jacobin.com/2021/10/ghost-work-review-mechanical-turk-gig-workers-amazon

Shi, A. (2020, November 19). *Mind your business: Ableism is rooted in capitalism*. The Daily Free Press.

Shimpach, S. (2005). Working watching: The creative and cultural labor of the media audience. *Social Semiotics*, 15(3), 343–360. https://doi.org/10.1080/10350330500310145

Siciliano, M. L. (2021). *Creative control: The ambivalence of work in the culture industries*. Columbia University Press.

Simkins, M. (2019, June 5). Only 2% of actors make a living. How do You Become One of Them? *The Guardian*. https://www.theguardian.com/film/shortcuts/2019/jun/05/only-2-per-cent-of-actors-make-a-living-how-do-you-become-one-of-them

Sito, T. (2006). *Drawing the line: The untold story of the animation unions from Bosko to Bart Simpson*. University Press of Kentucky.

Skeggs, B., & Wood, H. (2011). *Reality television and class*. BFI Publishing.

Slater, D. (1997). *Consumer culture & modernity*. Polity.

Slee, T. (2015). *What's yours is mine*. OR Books.
Smith, J. (2013). Between colorblind and colorconscious: Contemporary Hollywood films and struggles over racial representation. *Journal of Black Studies*, 44(8), 779–797. https://doi.org/10.1177/0021934713516860
Smith, C., & McKinlay, A. (2009). Creative industries and labour process analysis. In A. McKinlay & C. Smith (Eds.), *Creative labour: Working in the creative industries* (pp. 3–28). Palgrave Macmillan.
Smith, E., Gelrud Shiro, A., Pulliam, C., & Reeves, R. V. (2022, June 29). Stuck on the ladder: Wealth mobility is low and decreases with age. Brookings Institute. https://www.brookings.edu/articles/stuck-on-the-ladder-wealth-mobility-is-low-and-decreases-with-age/.
Smith, J. E. (2020). *Smart machines and service work: Automation in an age of stagnation*. Reaktion Books.
Smith, L. (2023). Ableism. https://cdrnys.org/blog/uncategorized/ableism/
Smythe, D. (1981). *Dependency road: Communication, capitalism, consciousness, and Canada*. Ablex.
Smythe, D. W. (1977). Communications: Blind spot of western Marxism. *Canadian Journal of Political and Social Theory*, 1(3), 1–27.
Smythe, D. W. (1978). Rejoinder to Graham Murdock. *Canadian Journal of Political and Social Theory*, 2(2), 120–127.
Smythe, D. W. (1981). On the audience commodity and its work. *Media and Cultural Studies: Keyworks*, 230, 256.
Smythe, T. C. (1980). 1880–1900: Working conditions and their influence on the news. *Journalism History*, 7(1), 1–10. https://doi.org/10.1080/00947679.1980.12066933
Snider, M. (2016). Nearly 40,000 Verizon workers go on strike. *USA Today*. https://www.usatoday.com/story/tech/news/2016/04/13/nearly-40000-verizon-workers-go-strike/82972508
Soper, K. (1995). *What is nature? Culture, politics and the nonhuman*. Routledge.
Sørensen, B. M. (2008). 'Behold, I am Making all Things New': The entrepreneur as savior in the age of creativity. *Scandinavian Journal of Management*, 24(2), 85–93. https://doi.org/10.1016/j.scaman.2008.03.002
Sotamaa, O. (2007). On modder labour, commodification of play, and mod competitions. *First Monday*, 12(9), n.p. https://doi.org/10.5210/fm.v12i9.2006
Sotamma, O., & Švelch, J. (Eds.). (2021). *Game production studies*. Amsterdam University Press.
Spangler, T. (2018, June 18). HuffPost shuts down unpaid contributor blogger program. *Variety*. https://variety.com/2018/digital/news/huffington-post-ends-unpaid-contributor-blogger-program-1202668053/.
Spangler, T. (2021). *Activision blizzard sued by California over sexual harassment, unequal pay in 'Pervasive Frat Boy' culture*. Variety. https://variety.com/2021/digital/news/activision-blizzard-sued-sexual-harassment-unequal-pay-1235025376/
Spangler, T. (2023). Activision Blizzard to Pay Nearly $55 Million to Settle Lawsuit Alleging Pay Discrimination Against Women. *Variety*. https://variety.com/2023/biz/news/activision-blizzard-settlement-lawsuit-california-sexual-harassment-pay-discrimination-1235841843/
Speth, J. G., & Courrier, K. (Eds.). (2021). *The new systems reader: Alternatives to a failed economy*. Routledge.
Spivak, G. C. (1988). Subaltern studies: Deconstructing historiography. In R. Guha (Ed.), *Selected subaltern studies*. Oxford University Press.

Spivak, G. C. (1996). Can the subaltern speak? In D. Landry & G. Maclean (Eds.), *The Spivak reader*. Routledge.

Spring magazine. (2020, May 5). Basic income: A critical reader. *Spring: A Magazine of Socialist Ideas in Action*. https://springmag.ca/basic-income-a-critical-reader.

Srnicek, N. (2017a). *Platform capitalism*. Polity Press.

Srnicek, N. (2017b). The challenges of platform capitalism: Understanding the logic of a new business model. *Juncture*, 23(4), 254–257. https://doi.org/10.1111/newe.12023

Srnicek, N., & Williams, A. (2015). *Inventing the future: Postcapitalism and a world without work*. Verso.

Stacy, L., Pieper, K., & Wheeler, S. (2023). Inequality in 1,600 Popular Films: Examining Portrayals of Gender, Race/Ethnicity, LGBTQ+ & Disability from 2007 to 2022. Annenberg, U. S. C. Inclusion initiative. https://assets.uscannenberg.org/docs/aii-inequality-in-1600-popular-films-20230811.pdf

Stahl, M. (2009). Privilege and distinction in production worlds: Copyright, collective bargaining, and working conditions in media making. In V. Mayer, M. Banks, Caldwell, & J. (Eds.), *Production studies: Cultural studies of media industries*. Routledge.

Stahl, M. (2010a). Cultural Labor's "democratic deficits": Employment, autonomy and alienation in US film animation. *Journal for Cultural Research*, 14(3), 271–293. https://doi.org/10.1080/14797581003791495

Stahl, M. (2010b). Primitive accumulation, the social common, and the contractual lockdown of recording artists at the threshold of digitalization'. *Ephemera: Theory & Politics in Organization*, 10(3–4), 337–355.

Stahl, M. (2013). *Unfree masters: Recording artists and the politics of work*. Duke University Press.

Stahl, M. (2021). Are workers musicians? Kesha Sebert, Johanna Wagner and the gendered commodification of star singers, 1853–2014. *Popular Music*, 40(2), 191–209.

Standing, G. (2011). *The precariat: The new dangerous class*. Bloomsbury Publishing Academic.

Stanford, J. (2015). *Economics for everyone: A short guide to the economics of capitalism*. Fernwood Publishing.

Stanley, G. (2024, January 30). Even the top 4% of creators want a union. *PassionFruit*, https://passionfru.it/newsletter/archive/even-the-top-4-of-creators-want-a-union/

Stanton, E. (2023). James Dean reportedly appearing in new film with AI, experts weigh in on benefits for stars after death. *Fox News*. https://www.foxnews.com/entertainment/james-dean-reportedly-appearing-new-film-ai-experts-weigh-benefits-stars-after-death

Steedman, R., & Brydges, T. (2023). Hustling in the creative industries: Narratives and work practices of female filmmakers and fashion designers. *Gender, Work and Organization*, 30(3), 793–809. https://doi.org/10.1111/gwao.12916

Steimer, L. (2019). Never done: A history of Women's work in media production by Erin Hill. *JCMS: Journal of Cinema and Media Studies*, 58(3), 194–198. https://doi.org/10.1353/cj.2019.0038

Steinberg, M. (2003). Capitalist development, the labor process, and the law. *American Journal of Sociology*, 109(2), 445–495.

Steinberg, R., & Figart, D. (1999). Emotional labor since the managed heart. *Annals–AAPSS*, 561, 8–26.

Steiner, C. (2012). *Automate this: How algorithms came to rule our world*. Penguin.

Steinhoff, J. (2021). *Automation and autonomy: Labour, capital and machines in the artificial intelligence industry*. Palgrave Macmillan.

Stevens, W. E. (2022). Black influencers: Interrogating the racialization and commodification of digital labor. Temple University. https://scholarshare.temple.edu/handle/20.500.12613/7743

Stewart, J. (2006). *DisneyWar*. Simon & Schuster.

Stewart, J. (2013, March 15). Looking for a lesson in Google's perks. *New York Times*. https://www.nytimes.com/2013/03/16/business/at-google-a-place-to-work-and-play.html

Stokes, S. (2021). *Art and copyright*. London.

Stoldt, R., Wellman, M., Ekdale, B., & Tully, M. (2019). Professionalizing and profiting: The rise of intermediaries in the social media influencer industry. *Social Media + Society*, 5(1). https://doi.org/10.1177/2056305119832587

Stone, B. (2013). *The everything store*. Little, Brown & Company.

Stone, V. A. (1987). Changing profiles of news directors of radio and TV stations, 1972–1986. *Journalism Quarterly*, 64(4), 745–749. https://doi.org/10.1177/107769908706400409

Stone, V. A. (1988). Trends in the status of minorities and women in broadcast news. *Journalism Quarterly*, 65(2), 288–293. https://doi.org/10.1177/107769908806500204

Stoner, R., & Dutra, J. (2022). *Copyright industries in the U. S. Economy* [2022 report]. https://www.wipo.int/export/sites/www/copyright/en/docs/performance/report_2022_us.pdf International Intellectual Property Alliance.

Stowell, O. (2024). You better work, Ben: On labor and Ben Stiller. *ASAP Journal*. https://asapjournal.com/feature/you-better-work-ben-on-labor-and-ben-stiller/

Storey, J. (1985). The means of management control. *Sociology*, 19(2), 193–211. https://doi.org/10.1177/0038038585019002004

Streeck, W. (2014a). *Buying time: The delayed crisis of democratic capitalism*. Verso.

Streeck, W. (2014b). How will capitalism end? *New Left Review*, 87, 35–64.

Stringer, A. (2023, December 4). A comprehensive list of 2023 tech layoffs. *Tech Crunch*. https://techcrunch.com/2023/12/4/tech-layoffs-2023-list/

Strong, C., & Raine, S. (2018). Gender politics in the music industry. *IASPM Journal*, 8(1), 2–8.

Strong, L. S. (2020, February 27). A dirty secret: You can only be a writer if you can afford it. *The Guardian*. https://www.theguardian.com/us-news/2020/feb/27/a-dirty-secret-you-can-only-be-a-writer-if-you-can-afford-it

Stronge, W., & Lewis, K. (2021). *Overtime: Why we need a shorter working week*. Verso.

Stuart Hall. (1996). Introduction: Who needs 'Identity'? In *Questions of identity* (pp. 1–17). Sage.

Su, C. (2023). Contingency, precarity and short-video creativity: Platformization based analysis of Chinese online screen industry. *Television and New Media*, 24(2), 173–189. https://doi.org/10.1177/15274764221087994

Sufit, A. (2023, June 14). Ageism in tech: Too old to code? Poppulo. https://www.poppulo.com/blog/ageism-in-tech-too-old-to-code

Sunkara, B. (2019). *The socialist manifesto: The case for radical politics in an era of extreme inequality*. Basic Books.

Susskind, D. (2020). *A world without work: Technology, automation, and how we should respond*. Allen Lane.

Sussman, G., & Lent, J. (Eds.). (1998). *Global productions: Labor in the making of the "Information Society"*. Hampton.

The Sutton Trust. (2019). *Elitist Britain?* https://www.suttontrust.com/our-research/elitist-britain-2019/

Svec, H. A. (2015). On Dallas Smythe's "audience commodity": An interview with Lee McGuigan and Vincent Manzerolle. *TripleC: Communication, Capitalism, and Critique, 13*(2), 270–273. https://doi.org/10.31269/triplec.v13i2.691

Swyngedouw, E. (2022). 'Don't They jump on The seats?' The underrepresentation of migrant and minority artists in the cultural labour market of Brussels. *Ethnic and Racial Studies, 45*(15), 2934–2955. https://doi.org/10.1080/01419870.2022.2058883

Szeman, I. (2015). Entrepreneurship as the new common sense. *South Atlantic Quarterly, 114*(3), 471–490. https://doi.org/10.1215/00382876-3130701

Táíwò, O. O. (2022). *Elite capture: How the powerful took over identity politics (And Everything Else).* Pluto Press.

Tapscott, D., & Williams, A. D. (2006). *Wikinomics: How mass collaboration changes everything.* Portfolio.

Tarnoff, B. (2020). The making of the tech worker movement. *Logic.* https://logicmag.io/the-making-of-the-tech-worker-movement/full-text/

Tarnoff, B., & Weigel, M. (2020). *Voices from the valley. Tech workers talk about what they do – And how they do it.* Farrar, Straus and Giroux.

Taylor, C. (1994). The politics of recognition. In A. Gutmann (Ed.), *Multiculturalism: Examining the politics of recognition* (pp. 25–73). Princeton University Press.

Taylor, F. F. (1911). *Principles of scientific management.* Harper & Brothers.

Taylor, P., & Bain, P. (2005). 'India calling to the far away towns': The call centre labour process and globalization. *Work, Employment and Society, 19*(2), 261–282. https://doi.org/10.1177/0950017005053170

Taylor, R. F. (2004). Extending conceptual boundaries: Work, voluntary work and employment. *Work, Employment and Society, 18*(1), 29–49. https://doi.org/10.1177/0950017004040761

Taylor, S. (2001). Emotional labour and the new workplace. In P. Thompson & C. Warhurst (Eds.), *Workplaces of the future* (pp. 84–103). Palgrave Macmillan.

Ter Minassian, H., & Zabban, V. (2021). Should I stay or should I go? The circulations and biographies of French game workers in a 'Global Games' era. *Game Production Studies.* https://doi.org/10.5117/9789463725439_ch03

Terkel, S. (1997). *Working: People talk about what they do all day and how they feel about what they do.* The New Press.

Terranova, T. (2000). Free labour: Producing culture for the digital economy. *Social Text, 18*(2), 33–58. https://doi.org/10.1215/01642472-18-2_63-33

Terranova, T. (2004). *Network culture: Politics for the information age.* Pluto Press.

Terrasi, E. (2018). *Global study on youth cooperative entrepreneurship: With a focus on worker, social and independent producers/workers cooperatives.* https://www.cicopa.coop/wp-content/uploads/2018/06/CICOPA_YouthReport_2018.pdf. CICOPA.

The British Interactive Media Association. (2019). Major study finds diverse members of the tech sector experience discrimination and stress | BIMA. https://bima.co.uk/major-study-finds-diverse-members-of-the-tech-sector-experience-discrimination-and-stress-2/

Theorell, T., Hammarström, A., Aronsson, G., Träskman Bendz, L., Grape, T., Hogstedt, C., Marteinsdottir, I., Skoog, I., & Hall, C. (2015). A systematic review including meta-analysis of work environment and depressive symptoms. *BMC Public Health, 15,* 738. https://doi.org/10.1186/s12889-015-1954-4

Thier, H. (2020). *A People's guide to capitalism.* Haymarket Books.

Thom, M. (2019). Do state corporate tax incentives create jobs? Quasi-experimental evidence from the entertainment industry. *State and Local Government Review*, *51*(2), 92–103. https://doi.org/10.1177/0160323X19877232

Thomas, K. (Ed.). (1999). *The Oxford book of work*. Oxford University Press.

Thomas, M. P., & Vosko, L. (2019). Canadian political economy in the new millennium. In M. P. Thomas, L. F. Vosko, C. Fanelli, & O. Lyubchenko (Eds.), *Change and Continuity: Canadian political economy in the new millennium* (pp. 3–24). McGill-Queen's University Press.

Thompson, D. (Ed.). (2001). *The essential E. P. Thompson*. New Press.

Thompson, E. P. (1966). *The making of the English working class*. Vintage Book Company.

Thompson, E. P. (1967). Time, work-discipline, and industrial capitalism. *Past & Present*, *38*(1), 56–97. https://academic.oup.com/past/article-abstract/38/1/56/1454624

Thompson, P. (1997). *The nature of work: An introduction to debates on the labour process*. Palgrave Macmillan.

Thompson, P., & Laaser, K. (2021). Beyond technological determinism: Revitalising labour process analyses of technology, capital and labour. *Work in the Global Economy*, *1*(1–2), 139–159. https://doi.org/10.1332/273241721X16276384832119

Thompson, P., Parker, R., & Cox, S. (2016). Interrogating creative theory and creative work: Inside the games studio. *Sociology*, *50*(2), 316–332. https://doi.org/10.1177/0038038514565836

Thompson, P., & Smith, C. (Eds.). (2010). *Working life: Renewing labour process analysis*. Palgrave Macmillan.

Thompson, P., & Smith, C. (2009). Labour power and labour process: Contesting the marginality of the sociology of work. *Sociology*, *43*(5), 913–930. https://doi.org/10.1177/0038038509340728

Thomsen, M. (2018, February 6). The Universe has been outsourced: The unseen labor behind the video game industry's biggest titles. *The Outline*. https://theoutline.com/post/3087/outsourcing-blockbuster-video-games-made-in-china-horizon-zero-dawn

Thomsen, M. (2021). Why is the games industry so burdened with crunch? It starts with labor laws. *The Washington Post*. https://www.washingtonpost.com/video-games/2021/03/24/crunch-laws/

Tichenor, P. J. (1978). The news people: A sociological portrait of American journalists and their work. *American Journal of Sociology*, *83*(6), 1559–1560. https://doi.org/10.1086/226730

Tillmann, L. M., Norsworthy, K., & Schoen, S. (Eds.). (2022). *Mindful activism*. Routledge.

Timburg, S. (2015). *Culture crash: The killing of the creative class*. Yale University Press.

Toffler, A. (1980). *The third wave*. William Morrow.

Tokumitsu, M. (2014). In the Name of Love. *Jacobin*. https://jacobin.com/2014/01/in-the-name-of-love

Tomlinson, J. (1999). *Globalization and culture*. University of Chicago Press.

Toupin, L. (2018). *Wages for housework: A history of an international feminist movement*. Pluto.

Towse, R. (1992). The earnings of singers: an economic analysis. In R. Towse and A. Khakee (Eds.), *Cultural economics* (pp. 209–217). Springer.

Towse, R. (2003). Cultural policy and support for artists. In W. J. Gordon & R. Watt (Eds.), *The economics of copyright* (pp. 66–80). Edward Elgar Publishing.

Towse, R. (2006). Human capital and artists' labour markets. In V. Ginsburgh & D. Throsby (Eds.), *Handbook of the economics of art and culture* (pp. 865–894). https://doi.org/10.1016/S1574-0676(06)01024-6

Tran, C. H. (2022). Never battle alone. *Television and New Media*, 23(5), 509–520. https://doi.org/10.1177/15274764221080930

Troncoso, S., & Utratel, A. M. (2019). If I only had a heart: A DisCO manifesto: Value sovereignty, care work, commons, and distributed cooperative organizations. *DisCO.coop, the transnational institute, and guerilla media collective*. https://www.tni.org/files/profiles-downloads/disco_manifesto_v.1.pdf

Tronti, M. (2019). *Workers and capital*. Verso.

Trueman, C. (2023, November 21). Tech layoffs in 2023: A timeline. *Computerworld*. https://www.computerworld.com/article/3685936/tech-layoffs-in-2023-a-timeline.html.

Trujillo, T. (2016). *Intern insider: Getting the most out of your internship in the entertainment field*. Routledge.

Trusolino, M. (2022). Laughter from the sidelines: Precarious work in the Canadian comedy industry. In M. Campbell & C. Thompson (Eds.), *Creative industries in Canada*. Canadian Scholars' Press.

Trusolino, M. (2022, April 8). No Joke. *Maisonneuve*. https://maisonneuve.org/article/2022/04/8/no-joke/

Tuchman, G. (1973). Making news by doing work: Routinizing the unexpected. *American Journal of Sociology*, 79(1), 110–131. https://doi.org/10.1086/225510

Tuchman, G. (1978). *Making news*. Free Press.

Tuchman, G. (1989). *Edging women out: Victorian novelists, publishers, and social change*. Yale University Press.

Tucker, B. (2017, April 26). Technocapitalist disability rhetoric: When technology is confused with social justice. *Enculturation: A Journal of Rhetoric, Writing and Culture*. https://www.enculturation.net/technocapitalist-disability-rhetoric

Turow, J. (1997). *Breaking up America: Advertisers in the new media world*. University of Chicago Press.

Tygiel, J., & Horne, G. (2002). Class struggle in Hollywood, 1930–1950: Moguls, mobsters, stars, reds & trade unionists. *The Western Historical Quarterly*, 33(1), 98. https://doi.org/10.2307/4144755

UCLA. (2020). *Hollywood diversity report 2002*. https://socialsciences.ucla.edu/wp-content/uploads/2019/02/UCLA-Hollywood-Diversity-Report-2019-2-21-2019.pdf

Ugwu, R. (2020, February 6). The hashtag that changed the Oscars: An oral history. *The New York Times*. https://www.nytimes.com/2020/02/06/movies/oscarssowhite-history.html

United Nations Committee on Trade, Aid and Development. (2008). *Creative economy report 2008*. UNCTAD.

United Nations Conference on Trade and Development (UNCTAD). (2022). *Creative economy outlook 2022*. https://unctad.org/publication/creative-economy-outlook-2022

United Nations Educational, Scientific and Cultural Organization (UNESCO) (2007). *The 2009 UNESCO framework for cultural statistics*. UNESCO Institute for Statistics.

United States Census. (2023). National Volunteer Week: April 16–22, 2023. https://www.census.gov/newsroom/stories/volunteer-week.html

United States Department of the Treasury. (2023, August 28). *Fact sheet: Treasury department releases first-Of-Its-kind report on benefits of unions to the U. S. Economy*. https://home.treasury.gov/news/press-releases/jy1706

United States International Trade Administration. (2021). Media & Entertainment Global Team. https://www.trade.gov/sites/default/files/2021-11/M%26E_Resource%20Guides_2021_0.pdf

Ursell, G. (2000). Television production: Issues of exploitation, commodification and subjectivity in UK television labour markets. *Media, Culture and Society*, 22(6), 805–825. https://doi.org/10.1177/016344300022006006

Ursell, G. (2006). Working in the media. In D. Hesmondhalgh (Ed.), *Media production* (pp. 133–172). Open University Press/the Open University.

Vallance, C. (2022). "Art is dead Dude" – the rise of the AI artists stirs debate. *BBC*. https://www.bbc.com/news/technology-62788725

Vallas, S. (1990). The concept of skill: A critical review. *Work and Occupations*, 17(4), 379–398. https://doi.org/10.1177/0730888490017004001

Vallas, S. (2011). *Work: A critique*. Wiley.

Vallas, S., & Hill, A. L. (2018). Reconfiguring worker subjectivity: Career advice literature and the "branding" of the Worker's self. *Sociological Forum*, 33(2), 287–309. http://www.jstor.org/stable/26625976. https://doi.org/10.1111/socf.12418 https://doi.org/10.1111/socf.12418

Vallas, S., & Schor, J. B. (2020). What do platforms do? Understanding the Gig Economy. *Annual Review of Sociology*, 46(1), 273–294. https://doi.org/10.1146/annurev-soc-121919-054857

Vance, A. (2017). *Elon Musk: Tesla, SpaceX, and the quest for a fantastic future*. Ecco.

van Dijck, J., Poell, T., & de Waal, M. (2018). *The platform society*. Oxford University Press. https://doi.org/10.1093/oso/9780190889760.001.0001

van Dijck, J. (2009). Users like you? Theorizing agency in user-generated content. *Media, Culture and Society*, 31(1), 41–58. https://doi.org/10.1177/0163443708098245

van Dijck, J., & Nieborg, D. (2009). Wikinomics and its discontents: A critical analysis of Web 2.0 business manifestos. *New Media and Society*, 11(5), 855–874. https://doi.org/10.1177/1461444809105356

van Dijck, J., & Poell, T. (2013). Understanding social media logic. *Media and Communication*, 1(1), 2–14. https://doi.org/10.17645/mac.v1i1.70

van Dijk, T. A. (2006). Ideology and discourse analysis. *Journal of Political Ideologies*, 11(2), 115–140. https://doi.org/10.1080/13569310600687908

van Doorn, N. (2017a). Platform labor: On the gendered and racialized exploitation of low-income service work in the "on-demand" economy. *Information, Communication and Society*, 20(6), 898–914. https://doi.org/10.1080/1369118X.2017.1294194

van Doorn, N. (2017b). Platform cooperativism and the problem of the outside. *Culture digitally*. https://culturedigitally.org/2017/02/platform-cooperativism-and-the-problem-of-the-outside/

Vaughn, H. (2019). *Hollywood's dirtiest secret: The hidden environmental costs of the movies*. Columbia University Press.

Verhoeven, D., Musial, K., Palmer, S., Taylor, S., Abidi, S., Zemaityte, V., & Simpson, L. (2020). Controlling for openness in the male-dominated collaborative networks of the global film industry. *PLOS ONE*, 15(6), e0234460. https://doi.org/10.1371/journal.pone.0234460

Verrier, R. (2010). Hollywood writers' age-discrimination case settled. *Los Angeles Times*. https://www.latimes.com/archives/la-xpm-2010-jan-23-la-fi-ct-writers23-2010jan23-story.html

Vernace, M. (2020, November). Loots of their labor: Analyzing wage and hour challenges in gaming's "crunch culture". *CardozoAELJ*. https://cardozoaelj.com/2020/11/02/loots-of-their-labor-analyzing-wage-hour-challenges-in-gamings-crunch-culture/

Vicks, A. (2021, November 30). The neoliberal view of inflation is convenient for capitalists—But it's wrong. *Jacobin*. https://jacobin.com/2021/11/inflation-solutions-neoliberalism-biden-manchin-volcker-shock-economy

Vlachou, A. (2007). Beyond capital: Marx's political economy of the working class. *Rethinking Marxism*, 19(2), 282–288. https://doi.org/10.2307/25143718

Wachter-Boettcher, S. (2017). *Technically wrong: Sexist apps, biased algorithms, and other threats of toxictech*. W. W. Norton and Company.

Wagner, K. B. (2014). Historicizing labor cinema: Recovering class and lost work on screen. *Labor History*, 55(3), 309–325. https://doi.org/10.1080/0023656X.2014.909989

Wajcman, J. (1991). *Feminism confronts technology*. Polity Press.

Wajcman, J. (2002). Addressing technological change: The challenge to social theory. *Current Sociology*, 50(3), 347–363. https://doi.org/10.1177/0011392102050003004

Wajcman, J. (2016). *Pressed for time: The acceleration of life in digital capitalism*. The University of Chicago Press.

Wajcman, J. (2019a). How Silicon Valley sets time. *New Media and Society*, 21(6), 1272–1289. https://doi.org/10.1177/1461444818820073

Wajcman, J. (2019b). The digital architecture of time management. *Science, Technology, and Human Values*, 44(2), 315–337. https://doi.org/10.1177/0162243918795041

Wasko, J. (1983). Trade unions and broadcasting: A case study of the national association of broadcast employees and technicians. In V. Mosco & J. Wasko (Eds.), *The critical communications review*, 1: Labor, the working class and the media (pp. 85–114). Ablex.

Wasko, J. (1998). Challenges to Hollywood's labor force in the 1990s. In G. Sussman & J. A. Lent (Eds.), *Global productions: Labor in the making of the "information society"* (pp. 173–190). Hampton Press.

Wasko, J. (2003). *How Hollywood works*. SAGE.

Wasko, J. (2014). The study of the political economy of the media in the twenty-first century. *International Journal of Media and Cultural Politics*, 10(3), 259–271. https://doi.org/10.1386/macp.10.3.259_1

Wasko, J. (2015). Learning from the history of the field. *Media Industries Journal*, 1(3), 67–70. https://doi.org/10.3998/mij.15031809.0001.312

Wasko, J., & Erikson, M. (Eds.). (2009). *Cross border cultural production: Economy runaway or globalization?* Cambria Press.

Wasko, J., Murdock, G., & Sousa, H. (2011). Introduction: The political economy of communications–core concerns and issues. In J. Wasko, G. Murdock, & H. Sousa (Eds.), *The handbook of political economy of communications* (pp. 1–10). Blackwell Publishing.

Watson, T. (2017). *Sociology, work and organisation*. Routledge.

Wayne, M. (2003). *Marxism and media studies: Key concepts and contemporary trends*. Pluto Press.

Weale, S. (2024). Media studies are popular, dynamic and have 'profound impact', report says. *The Guardian*. https://www.theguardian.com/education/article/2024/jun/11/media-studies-popular-dynamic-profound-impact-report

Weaver, D., Beam, R., Brownlee, B., Voakes, P., & Wilhoit, G. C. (2006). *The American journalist in the 21st century*. Routledge.

Weaver, D. H., & Wilhoit, G. C. (1996). *The American journalist in the 1990s: U.S. news people at the end of an era*. Lawrence Erlbaum Associates.

Weber, M. (1993). Power, domination, and legitiamcy. In M. E. Olsen, M. N., Marger, & V. Fonseca (Eds.), *Power in the modern societies*. Routledge. https://doi.org/10.4324/9780429302824

Weber, M. (2019). *Economy and society*. Princeton University Press.

Webber, V., MacDonald, M., Duguay, S., & McKelvey, F. (2023). Pornhub and policy: Examining the erasure of pornography workers in Canadian platform governance. *Canadian Journal of Communication*, 48(2), 381–404.

Weeks, K. (2005). The refusal of work as demand and perspective. In T. S. Murphy & A.-K. Mustapha (Eds.), *The philosophy of Antonio Negri: Resistance in practice* (pp. 109–135). Pluto Press.

Weeks, K. (2011). *The problem with work: Feminism, Marxism, antiwork politics, and postwork imaginaries*. Duke University Press.

Wellman, M. L. (2021). Trans-mediated parasocial relationships: Private Facebook groups foster influencer–follower connection. *New Media and Society*, 23(12), 3557–3573. https://doi.org/10.1177/1461444820958719

Wellman, M. L. (2020). What it means to be a bodybuilder: Social media influencer labor and the construction of identity in the bodybuilding subculture. *Communication Review*, 23(4), 273–289. https://doi.org/10.1080/10714421.2020.1829303

Wells, R. (2015). The labor of reality TV: The case of "The Deadliest Catch". *Labor*, 12(4), 33–49. https://doi.org/10.1215/15476715-3155143

West, E. (2017). *Affect theory and advertising: A new look at IMC, spreadability, and engagement. Explorations in critical studies of advertising*. Routledge.

Weststar, J. (2015). Understanding video game developers as an occupational community. *Information, Communication and Society*, 18(10), 1238–1252. https://doi.org/10.1080/1369118X.2015.1036094

Weststar, J., & Dubois, L.-É. (2022). From crunch to grind: Adopting servitization in project-based creative work. *Work, Employment and Society*. https://doi-org.uproxy.library.dc-uoit.ca/10.1177/09500170211061228.

Weststar, J., & Legault, M.-J. (2017). Why might a videogame developer join a union? *Labor Studies Journal*, 42(4), 295–321. https://doi.org/10.1177/0160449X17731878

Weststar, J., & Legault, M.-J. (2019). Building momentum for collectivity in the digital game community. *Television and New Media*, 20(8), 848–861. https://doi.org/10.1177/1527476419851087

Weststar, J., O'Meara, V., & Legault, M.-J. (2018). Developer satisfaction survey 2017 – Summary report [Online]. International Game Developer Association. Retrieved November 9, 2022, from https://s3-us-east-2.amazonaws.com/igda-website/wp-content/uploads/2019/04/11143720/IGDA_DSS_2017_SummaryReport.pdf.

Wharry, M. (2023, September 12). EEOC: Verizon violated Ada, civil right act with unlawful employment practice. *Law.com*. https://www.law.com/2023/09/12/eeoc-verizon-violated-ada-civil-rights-act-with-unlawful-employment-practices/

White, H., & White, C. A. (1965). *Canvases and careers: Institutional change in the French painting world*. Wiley.

Williams, A. (2016, July 23). Fun and work as effective management strategy: The example of google. LinkedIn. https://www.linkedin.com/pulse/fun-work-effective-management-strategy-example-google-williams-alfred/
Williams, K., & Bain, V. (2022). Dignity at Work 2: Discrimination in the music sector. Independent society of musicians (ISM). https://www.ism.org/wp-content/uploads/2023/08/02-ISM-Dignity-2-report.pdf
Williams, R. (1976). *Keywords: A vocabulary of culture and society.* Fontana.
Williams, R. (1981). *Culture.* Fontana Press.
Williams, R. (1992). *Television: Technology and cultural form.* University Press of New England and Wesleyan University Press.
Williams, R. (2005). *Culture and materialism.* Verso.
Williams, R. (2019). The social shaping of technology (SST). In T. Pittinsky (Ed.), *Science, technology, and society: New perspectives and directions* (pp. 138–162). Cambridge University Press. https://doi.org/10.1017/9781316691489.006
Willis, P. (1977). *Learning to labour: How working class kids get working class jobs.* Gower.
Willnat, L., Weaver, D. H., & Wilhoit, C. (2022). *The American journalist under attack: Key findings 2022.* S.I. Newhouse School of Public Communications, Syracuse University. https://www.theamericanjournalist.org/_files/ugd/46a507_4fe1c4d6ec6d4c229895282965258a7a.pdf
Winseck, D. (2011). Introductory essay: The political economies of media and the transformation of the global media industries. In D. Winseck & D. Y. Jin (Eds.), *The political economies of media: The transformation of the global media industries* (pp. 3–48). Bloomsbury Publishing Academic.
Winseck, D. (2023a). Media and internet concentration in Canada, 1984–2022. In *Global media and internet concentration project.* Carleton University. https://doi.org/10.22215/gmicp/2023.2.
Winseck, D. (2023b). Growth and upheaval in the network media economy, 1984–2022 (Canada). In *Global media and internet concentration project.* Carleton University. https://doi.org/10.22215/gmicp/2023.1.
Winseck, D. (2024, January 26). Media concentration and the conditions of work and labor. Personal Correspondence.
Wirth, M. O., & Bloch, H. (1995). Industrial organization theory and media industry analysis. *Journal of Media Economics, 8*(2), 15–26. https://doi.org/10.1207/s15327736me0802_3
Wirtz, B. W. (2016). *Media management: Strategy, business models and case studies.* SpringerLink.
Wiscomb, A. (2016, May 12). The entrepreneurship racket. *Jacobin.* https://jacobin.com/2016/05/entrepreneurship-innovation-toyotism-college-startups/
Wolff, R. (2012). *Democracy at work: A cure for capitalism.* Haymarket Books.
Wolff, R. D. (2017). Start with worker self-directed enterprises. The Next System Project: https://thenextsystem.org/sites/default/files/2017-08/RickWolff.pdf
Women Business Collaborative. (2022, September 22). 8.8% Fortune 500 CEOs are women - the highest of all indices - according to the Women CEOs in America Report 2022. *PR News Wire.* https://www.prnewswire.com/news-releases/8-8-fortune-500-ceos-are-women---the-highest-of-all-indices--according-to-the-women-ceos-in-america-report-2022--301630455.html
Woodburn, D., & Kopić, K. (2016). The Ruderman white paper: On employment of actors with disabilities in television. Ruderman Family Foundation. https://rudermanfoundation.org/wp-content/uploads/2016/07/TV-White-Paper_7-1-003.pdf.

Woodcock, J. (2014). The Workers' inquiry from Trotskyism to Operaismo: A political methodology for investigating the workplace. *Ephemera, 14*(3), 493–513.

Woodcock, J. (2016). *Working the phones: Control and resistance in call centres*. Pluto Press.

Woodcock, J. (2019). *Marx at the arcade: Consoles, controllers, and class struggle*. Haymarket Books.

Woodcock, J. (2020). Game workers unite: Unionization among independent developers. In P. Ruffino (Ed.), *Independent videogames: Cultures, networks, techniques and politics* (pp. 163–174). Routledge.

Woodcock, J. (2021). *The fight against platform capitalism: An inquiry into the global struggles of the gig economy*. University of Westminster Press. https://library.oapen.org/bitstream/id/ec7fb7dd-01be-4bfc-bbab-b12132393bc5/the-fight-against-platform-capitalism.pdf

Woodcock, J., & Graham, M. (2019). *The gig economy: A critical introduction*. Polity.

Woodcock, J., & Johnson, M. R. (2018). Gamification: What it is, and how to fight it. *The Sociological Review, 66*(3), 542–558. https://doi.org/10.1177/0038026117728620

Wreyford, N. (2015). Birds of a feather: Informal recruitment practices and gendered outcomes for screenwriting work in the UK film industry. *Sociological Review, 63*(1_suppl), 84–96. https://doi.org/10.1111/1467-954X.12242

Wreyford, N., O'Brien, D., & Dent, T. (2021). *Creative Majority: An APPG for Creative Diversity report on "What Works" to support, encourage and improve diversity, equity and inclusion in the creative sector. A report for the All Party Parliamentary Group for Creative Diversity*. Accessed here. http://www.kcl.ac.uk/cultural/projects/creative-majority

Wright, A. (2024). ChatGPT 'racially discriminates' against job seekers by filtering out 'black names' in recruitment searches. *DailyMail*. https://www.dailymail.co.uk/news/article-13173589/ChatGPT-racially-discriminates-against-job-seekers-filtering-black-names-recruitment-searches.html

Wright, E. O. (1976). Class boundaries in advanced capitalist societies. *New Left Review, I*(98 (July–August)), 3–41.

Wright, E. O. (1978). Intellectuals and the class structure of capitalist society. In P. Walker (Ed.), *Between labor and capital* (pp. 191–211). Black Rose Books.

Wright, E. O. (1997). *Class counts: Comparative studies in class analysis*. Cambridge University Press.

Wright, E. O. (2006). Two redistributive proposals—Universal basic income and stakeholder grants. *Focus, 24*(2), 5–7.

Wright, E. O. (2010). *Envisioning real utopias*. Verso.

Wright, I. (2023, October 20). The brands with the most product placements in movies and TV shows. https://merchantmachine.co.uk/brands-movies-tv/

Wright, R. E. (2018). Making IT work: A history of the computer services industry. *Journal of American History, 105*(3), 770–771. https://doi.org/10.1093/jahist/jay434

Wright, S. (2002). *Storming heaven: Class composition and struggle in Italian autonomist Marxism*. Pluto Press.

Wu, T. (2014). *The attention merchants: The epic scramble to get inside our heads*. Knopf.

Wu, T. (2020). The labour of fun: Masculinities and the organisation of labour games in a modern workplace. *New Technology, Work and Employment, 35*(3), 336–356. https://doi.org/10.1111/ntwe.12180

Yan, R. (2023). Wanghong as social media entertainment in China. *Information, Communication & Society*, 26(3), 658–661. https://doi.org/10.1080/1369118x.2022.2032263

Yates, M. D. (2021). *Work work work: Labor, alienation, and class struggle*. Monthly Review Press.

Yeo, S. (2023). *Behind the search box: Google and the global internet industry*. University of Illinois Press.

Yeoman, R. (2014). *Meaningful work and workplace democracy: A philosophy of work and a politics of meaningfulness*. https://doi.org/10.1057/9781137370587

Yost, J. R. (2017). *Making IT work: A history of the computer services industry*. The MIT Press.

Yuan, Y., & Constine, J. (2020). SignalFire's creator economy market map. *SignalFire*. https://signalfire.com/blog/creator-economy/

Zeiler, X., & Mukherjee, S. (2022). Video game development in India: A cultural and creative industry embracing regional cultural heritage(s). *Games and Culture*, 17(4), 509–527. https://doi.org/10.1177/15554120211045143

Ziegler, A. (2022). The tech company: On the neglected second nature of platforms. *Weizenbaum Series*, 22. https://doi.org/10.34669/wi.ws/22

Zinkula, J., & Mok, A. (2024, January 15). ChatGPT may be coming for our jobs. Here are the 10 roles that AI is most likely to replace. *Business Insider*, https://www.businessinsider.com/chatgpt-jobs-at-risk-replacement-artificial-intelligence-ai-labor-trends-2023-02

Zuboff, S. (2018). *The age of surveillance capitalism: The fight for a human future at the new frontier of power*. Profile Books.

Zuboff, S. (2019). Surveillance capitalism and the challenge of collective action. *New Labor Forum*, 28(1), 10–29. https://doi.org/10.1177/1095796018819461

Zuboff, S. (2020). The age of surveillance capitalism: The fight for a human future at the new frontier of power. *Yale Law Journal*, 129(5), 1460–1515. https://doi.org/10.26522/brocked.v29i2.849

Zyskowski, K., & Milland, K. (2018). A crowded future: Working against abstraction on turker. *Catalyst: Feminism, Theory, Technoscience*, 4(2), 1–30. https://catalystjournal.org/index.php/catalyst/article/view/29581/23436

Index

AAMAM (Alphabet-Google, Apple, Meta Platforms, Amazon, Microsoft) 62, 182, 197, 228, 239
ableism 11–12, 179–181
activism 13, 20, 32, 81, 88, 130, 165, 232, 276, 283, 287–288
activist auto-ethnography 93–94
advertising 258–260
African Content Moderators Union 209–210
age / ageism 11, 92, 136, 179–180
agenda setting 40–41, 239
AI art 236, 256
AI ethics 138, 254–255
algorithmic bias 190, 222
algorithmic management 11, 92
alienation 40, 96, 100, 161, 245–246
amateur 218, 219, 270
Amazon Mechanical Turk (AMT) 107, 210, 211
American Dream 169, 281
amusement parks 64, 66, 67
analog to digital transition 68–69
apprenticeships 272
artificial intelligence 11, 161, 211, 236–239, 249–257
artist 55, 79, 105–106, 237–238, 256, 295
ascription biases 190
aspirational labor 2, 49–50, 170–171
audience commodity 259, 261–262, 275
audience engagement 229, 230, 263
automation 5, 11, 44, 51, 236–242; and, deskilling, dependency, displacement, depression and development 242–243; 248, 253

autonomy 31, 47, 87, 88, 95, 96, 116, 131, 153, 156, 159, 161, 205, 220, 224

barriers to collective action 279–282
Black Lives Matter (BLM) 181
blacklisting 164–165
blue-collar work 37, 99, 102, 240, 253, 297
board of directors 114, 147, 151, 254
boom and bust cycles 122, 231
brands 37, 78, 105, 106, 118, 119, 152, 156, 157, 161, 165, 189, 209, 267–270
bullying 134, 160, 164, 276
bureaucracy 155–156
burnout 93, 204, 208, 222, 223, 233

call centers 8, 107, 204, 205, 213
canceling 164–165
capital (cultural, economic, social) 183–184
capitalism 110–124
care work 32
case studies 93, 222
CEOs 6, 21, 31, 38, 60, 72, 73, 101, 111–113, 115, 121, 123, 147–150, 151–152, 229, 231
celebrity culture 6, 170, 221, 232, 251–252
censorship 39, 140, 274–276
charismatic authority 147
ChatGPT 76, 190, 236–239, 251–252
circuit of culture 80
class: classism 11, 40, 177–178, 191, 192, conflict 124–125; division, 115, 145, 177, 178, 274;

mobility, 171, 172, 176; struggle, 21, 116, 232, 279, 296
class action lawsuits 133, 135–136, 137, 163, 214, 273, 288–289
class politics of AI 241, 251, 255
climate change 35, 36, 117, 165, 213
coercion in management 134, 155, 160–165
collective action 13, 14, 15, 16, 20, 101, 124, 152, 157, 178, 208, 211, 232, 241, 244, 251, 255, 274, 277–293
collective action in tech 15, 256, 282
collective bargaining 19, 93, 94, 130, 151, 167, 280, 282
colonialism / imperialism / neo-colonialism 81, 100, 171, 178, 193–194, 197, 204, 207–208, 214
commercial content moderation (CCM) 207–209
commodity audience 262–264
communication policies and regulations 5, 14, 17, 77, 82, 83, 138–139
consumerism 47, 258–259
content creators 31, 49, 131, 218–235
content moderators 8, 17, 31, 107, 108, 137–138, 168, 207–209
convergence (technological and economic) 64, 69–70, 119, 139
Coogan Act 131–132
cooperatives 13, 91, 166, 212, 257, 284–287, 291
corporations 99, 110, 111, 114–124
creative class 2, 191–192, 219, 249, 195
creative destruction 122–123
creative exceptionalism 294–299
creative industries 2, 7, 20, 61, 95, 191, 219, 294–298
creative worker 106–107, 110, 142, 249, 253
creativity 299
creator capitalism 228–232
crisis 18, 51, 122, 129, 231, 278, 295
crowdsourcing 211, 270–271
crunch time 39, 132–134
cultural capital 3, 183–186, 187–192, 269
cultural distinction 3, 185, 186

cultural industries 7, 47, 53–56, 60–67, 70, 79, 81–83, 93, 96, 105, 106–107, 127
"cultural Marxism" conspiracy theory 22, 281
cultural production 5, 6, 217, 218, 221
cultural worker 106–107, 110, 144, 250, 282
cultural workers organize 15, 282
culture 38–40
cyber-tariat 107

DALL-E 27, 237–239
data: data analytics 38, 62, 73; data centers 35, 65, 67; data commodification 32, 65, 108, 197, 218, 263, 265; data discrimination 183; data entry clerk 50, 107, 212, 240, 241; data profile 266; data scientist 27, 104, 116, 117, 140, 143; data-veillance 17, 161, 239, 254
decision-making power 151
deepfake 250, 252
deskilling 86, 87, 241, 242, 243, 244, 253, 255, 256
digital capitalism 7, 107, 139, 221
digital divide 56, 183
digital labor 108, 264, 265
digital literacy 139
digital media and entertainment industries (DMEI) 5, 53; classified 60–67, 67; relationship to work 70–74
digital society 50, 56–60, 63, 64, 70–74, 145, 186, 196, 253, 279
digitization 67–68
disability 11, 81, 136, 174, 180–181, 190
discrimination 11, 77, 93, 96, 134, 135, 136, 138, 149, 165, 171, 174, 176–193, 187, 188, 190, 196, 289
diversity 11, 18, 61, 77, 79, 84–85, 88, 90, 102, 107, 150, 176, 181, 182, 218
division between owners and workers 115, 229
division of labor 12, 32, 37, 50, 76, 79, 110, 115, 117, 200, 203, 229, 280, 297

emotional labor 103–104
employee 224–225
employment contracts 116, 121, 129–131, 156, 163
entertainment news platforms 270
entrepreneurialism 2, 9, 41, 79, 214, 218, 222, 224, 225, 278, 281, 291
Equal Employment Opportunity Commission (EEOC) 135
equity, diversity and inclusion (EDI) 11, 61, 77, 176
exploitation 49, 88, 95, 121–122, 129, 174, 230–231

Fair Labor Standards Act (FLSA) 44, 132
fairness in factual TV campaign 284
family 46, 54, 69, 135, 151, 171, 172, 174, 175, 184–186, 188, 189
fandom / fan labor 267–270
Federal Communications Commission (FCC) 138–140
federal labor laws 131–137
Federal Trade Commission (FTC) 141–142, 163, 220
firing 119, 135, 152, 164, 168, 243
forced labor 30–32, 115
Fordism and post–Fordism 37, 100, 296, 297
framing 41, 83
franchise 30, 117, 202, 250, 269–270
Frederick Winslow Taylor 153
free labor 262, 264–266, 270–274
freedom of expression 39, 207, 274–276
freelancers 19, 31, 42, 91, 121, 206, 207, 226–227, 283
Freelancers Union 283
fun 29, 51, 71, 158–159
future of work 5, 95, 248, 253–254, 257, 277–279

Gamergate 276
games industry / games workers 12, 29, 34, 40, 45, 65–66, 67, 71, 76, 80, 91, 132–133, 204, 213, 251, 285
gamification 159
gender 12, 32, 33, 79, 101, 136, 149, 150, 179, 246
Ghost Work 9, 210–211
gig economy 19, 37, 41, 109, 116

global Hollywood 7, 198–201
global labor arbitrage 213
Global Media and Internet Concentration Project (GMICP) / Canadian Media Concentration Research Project (CMCRP) 120–121
globalization 5, 12, 123, 193–212, 278
governmentality 2, 155
Great Leader Theory (GLT) 147–151
Great Resignation 50–51

hard and soft power tactics 154–155
hard power at work 160–164
health and safety in the workplace 46, 98, 137–138, 143, 168, 185, 187, 273, 282, 284
health and wellness 12, 17, 36–37, 88, 179, 208
higher education industries 3, 15, 55, 66, 73–74, 76, 116, 144, 171, 187, 247, 295
Hollywood Diversity Report 90, 182
Hollywood Writer's Strike 93, 250–251, 256
hope labor 49–50
housework 12, 32, 101, 267
human relations engineering 153–154
human-machine hybrid work 242, 253
humane workplace 159

identity and work 26, 36–37, 106, 113, 243
identity politics 150, 176, 180, 281
ideology 40, 49, 81, 128, 164, 171, 192, 275, 281
immaterial labor 88, 104–105
industrial working class 99–101
inequality 123–124
influencers 5, 9, 15, 27, 34, 49, 59, 66, 76, 92, 93, 131, 203, 216–224
intellectual property (IP) 2, 63, 130, 297
International Labor Organization (ILO) 31, 257
internationalism 210, 212, 215
interns and internships 9, 30, 49, 144, 187–188, 272–273
intersectionality 83, 169, 176–177, 180
Ivy League schools 185

kid influencers 131–132
knowledge workers 7, 13, 104, 253

labor 28; paid labor 29; unpaid forced labor 30; unpaid reproductive labor 32; unpaid volunteer labor 33
labor force research 84–85, 90
labor laws 129–137
labor process engineering 153, 154
labor process theory (LPT) 85–87
labor turn 6–13, 83
labor-saving technologies (LSTs) 236, 239–244, 254
leadership 147
likeness licensing 251–252
lobbies, lobbying 17, 82, 119, 128–129, 140, 201, 291
Luddism 244, 255–256

#Make Amazon Pay 287
management 146–166
market competition and control 230
McDonaldization 201–203
media industries 6, 7, 15, 61, 84, 120
media labor literacy 1, 14, 16
media management 84–85
media ownership 120, 139
methods 90–94
meritocracy 171; assumptions 172–176
#MeToo 287
micro, meso, and macro scale research 76
micro-tasking 9, 210; and, piecework 207, 210
middle class/professional managerial class (PMC) 2, 85, 100, 111, 113, 281, 295
misinformation and disinformation 17, 207, 221
mode of Production 37, 110–111, 194
mutual aid 20, 134, 234, 244, 284

NAICS codes 64–67, 227
National Labor Relations Act (NLRA) 130, 134, 135, 234
National Labor Relations Board (NLRB) 134–135
nation-state, nation, nationalism 40, 193–195, 213, 220, 221, 280

needs 26, 42, 44, 46, 47, 115, 117–118, 175, 245, 278
neo-colonialism 204, 207–208, 214
neoliberalism 2, 15, 67, 73, 93, 127–129, 159, 191, 194, 220, 246–247, 275, 278, 290–291, 296
networks 79, 81, 184, 186, 188–189, 204, 212, 214, 257
network effects 108, 229, 230, 266, 271
No-Cold-Call Agreements (NCCA) 162
Non-Compete Clauses (NCC) 163
Non-Disclosure Agreements (NDA) 93, 131, 138, 161, 276
normativity in research 94–98

Occupational Safety and Health Administration (OSHA) 137–138
occupational segregation 190
Office of Federal Contract Compliance Programs (OFCCP) 136
online campaigns 256–257
online creators 10, 19, 39, 56, 63, 66, 68, 103, 120, 216–232, 274
Open AI 251–252
Operaismo 87
organizational culture 39–40, 118, 149
organizational sociology 78–80
#OscarsSoWhite 287
outsourcing 12, 41, 144, 193–214, 270
ownership 69, 70, 82, 111, 112, 114

participation 156–157
participatory action research 94
patriarchy 12, 32, 33, 101, 179
perks 157–158
platform capitalism 71, 108, 217
platform cooperativism 93
platform cultural producers / production 9, 56, 59, 62, 66, 68, 92, 107, 131, 216–234
platform dependency 31
platform imperialism 198
platform labor market 116, 188, 206–207, 210–212
platform management 72, 161, 166
platform policies and regulations 207, 220
platform society 58, 216–217

382 *Index*

platform worker 108, 10, 41, 42, 91, 108–109, 110, 120, 206–207
platforms 22, 58, 217
playbour 29
political economy of communication 81–84
political parties 18, 83, 88, 100, 130, 144, 145, 213, 215, 221, 243, 244, 278, 290, 291–292
post-work 50–52
precarity 89, 91, 98, 111, 121, 128, 131, 139, 142, 173, 179, 189, 199, 204, 211, 213, 219, 231, 233, 234, 247, 278, 295, 296
privilege 48, 56, 89, 101, 113, 118, 171, 172, 176, 179, 180, 182, 183–188, 191, 222, 232, 274
production of culture approach 78–79, 80–81
professional managerial class (PMC) 113
professional networks 81, 188
project-based labor 42, 43, 72, 103, 111, 117, 118, 152, 202, 206, 226, 227
prosumer 10, 264–267, 270
public goods 128, 278, 291, 292
public relations 65, 144, 259

race to the bottom 199, 214
racial capitalism 178, 182–183
racism 12, 40, 101, 177, 178, 181–183, 213, 276
ratings 22, 65, 83, 262–264
real utopias 14, 293
remote work 33, 45, 157, 206–207, 225
reproductive labor 12, 32–33, 187, 189, 290
reputation 106, 118, 119, 152, 158, 189, 207, 252, 268
reskilling and upskilling 170, 243, 244
risk 2, 20, 137, 170, 225
ruling class 111–112

SAG-AFTRA 19, 163, 250
scientific management 153
self-branding 186, 189, 226
self-exploitation 49, 51, 72, 92, 158
self-realization 245, 47, 92, 95, 96, 245, 254

sexism 12, 40, 101, 171, 177, 179, 276
sexual Harassment 141, 149, 162, 276, 287
shareholders 31, 35, 111–113, 114–115, 117, 121, 123, 151
skills 73, 84, 243
slavery 31, 115, 171, 198
small business owner-entrepreneur 225–227
social capital 49, 184–190
social media entertainment (SME) 12, 218
social mobility 171, 175–176, 191
social reproduction 12, 32–33, 187, 189, 290
soft power at work 146, 154
space and work 41, 44–46, 57, 72, 116, 206, 215, 225, 266, 285
state 126; labor law maker, investigator and enforcer 129–138; neoliberal superintendent 127; politics and parties 144; tacit labor law 138–144
strikes 7, 41, 93, 124, 130, 151, 168, 208, 241, 250–251, 281, 283
structural and relational power 228
subsidies 127, 142–143, 199
surveillance and surveillance technologies 42, 86, 134, 161, 205, 217, 265, 266
surveys 38, 91, 133, 191, 219

Taylorism 153, 154, 159, 202
technological determinism 21–22, 57
technological unemployment 243, 246–249
terms of service agreements 225
texts 8, 39, 40–41, 62, 68, 79, 105, 106, 236, 238
theory 77–85
time and work 41–43

unemployment 122, 170, 246–249
union busting 163–164
unions 18, 19, 43, 78, 82, 88, 93, 100, 124, 128, 130, 134, 135, 141, 151–152, 157, 163–164, 166–167, 198, 204, 205, 215, 233–234, 241, 257, 273, 276, 278, 281, 282–283, 287

Universal Basic Income (UBI) 289–290
upwork 27, 42, 73, 109, 116, 206–207
user-generated content (UGC) 266, 270

virtual influencers 223–224
volunteerism 30, 33–34, 270, 271

wage and hour division 132–133
waged labor 30, 42, 46, 51, 115–116, 229–231, 247, 253
wages for Facebook 267
wants 26, 47, 84, 110, 111, 117

white-collar work 37, 102–103, 113, 253, 257
whiteness 22, 57, 90, 91, 100, 101, 102, 148,–150, 174, 181–183, 196, 209, 276, 287
work 28–34; motivations for work 46–49; why work matters 34–37; work and culture 38–40; work, time and space 41–44
working class 5, 15, 18, 30, 51, 82–83, 88, 89, 99–102, 99–108, 113–114, 177–178, 185, 278–283, 293; in-itself, for-itself 214, 279

For Product Safety Concerns and Information please contact our EU
representative GPSR@taylorandfrancis.com
Taylor & Francis Verlag GmbH, Kaufingerstraße 2≤, 80331 München, Germany

www.ingramcontent.com/pod-product-compliance
Lightning Source LLC
LaVergne TN
LVHW020248020825
817679LV00004B/210